American Prisoners of War

Held at

Barbados, New Providence and Newfoundland

During the War of 1812

Transcribed by
Harrison Scott Baker II

Society of the War of 1812
in the
State of Ohio

HERITAGE BOOKS
2007

HERITAGE BOOKS
AN IMPRINT OF HERITAGE BOOKS, INC.

Books, CDs, and more—Worldwide

For our listing of thousands of titles see our website
at
www.HeritageBooks.com

Published 2007 by
HERITAGE BOOKS, INC.
Publishing Division
65 East Main Street
Westminster, Maryland 21157-5026

Copyright © 2007 Society of the War of 1812 in the State of Ohio

Other Heritage Books by Harrison Scott Baker II:
American Prisoners of War Held at Halifax During the War of 1812, Volumes I and II
American Prisoners of War Held at Bermuda, Cape of Good Hope and Jamaica During the War of 1812

All rights reserved. No part of this book may be reproduced or transmitted in any form or by any means, electronic or mechanical, including photocopying, recording or by any information storage and retrieval system without written permission from the author, except for the inclusion of brief quotations in a review.

International Standard Book Number: 978-0-7884-4498-2

- Table of Contents -

Introduction	ii
The Dead	v
Barbados -	
Alphabetical listing of names	1
Numeric listing by prison number	77
Crew listing by ship	88
Americans on British ships	99
Service affiliation not known	100
New Providence -	
Alphabetical listing of names	101
Numeric listing by prison number	151
Crew listing by ship	158
United States Marines	167
Americans on British ships	168
Newfoundland -	
Alphabetical listing of names	169
Numeric listing by prison number	192
Crew listing by ship	195
Americans on British ships	198
Service affiliation not known	199

Introduction

This is a transcription of prisoner of war records of American marines, merchantmen and sailors held at the internment facilities at Barbados, West Indies; New Providence, Bahamas and Newfoundland, Canada during the War of 1812 by the British Empire.

The list was compiled from microfilm copies of the original roster books of the British Admiralty made by the Public Record Office in London (ADM 103 / 13; ADM 103 / 246 and ADM 103 / 248).

The *General Entry Book* records are composed of bound volumes that were printed with lines for the recording of names of those incarcerated. The record of each prisoner is comprised of two facing pages. The clerk making the entries wrote page numbers on the upper right corner on each right side page of the book.

<u>The columns across the top on the left side:</u>
Current Number
By what Ship, or how Taken
Time when - Day, Month, Year
Place where
Name of prize
Whither Man of War, Privateer, or Merchant Vessel
Prisoners' Names

<u>The columns across the top on the right side:</u>
Quality - Navy, Army
Time when received into Custody - Day, Month, Year
From what Ship, or whence received
Exchanged, Discharged, Died, or Escaped
Time when - Day, Month, Year
Whither, and by what order, or Number of Re-entry

The volume for Barbados has prisoner numbers 1 through 1453 with a total of 61 pages, with no index of captured ships. It was in operation from August 1812 to March 1815.

The volume for New Providence has prisoner numbers 1 through 836 with a total of 36 pages, with an index of captured ships. It was in operation from August 1812 to March 1815.

The volume for Newfoundland has prisoner numbers 1 through 364 with a total of 15 pages, with no index of captured ships. It was in operation from July 1812 to November 1812.

Barbados has 1454 entries, with one name crossed out and the number reissued; the facility has 45 duplicate records, most being recaptures of escapees who were issued new prison numbers. New Providence has three entries with no name. There are no blank lines for Barbados or Newfoundland.

The photocopy and the handwriting varies from good to very good, except for Barbados where the penmanship is poor. It appears that the spelling of non-familiar names was done phonically and the entries were copied from another source.

One clerk for New Providence made an error in the entries for the *USS Frolic*. There is a diagonal line across lines 609 through 630 on page ' 25-26 ' and he wrote:

> "begin overleaf with No 609
> These Names having been misplaced
> these Names recommence No 644"

Those that were crossed out, as well as additional names, are from the same ship. It appears the clerk was putting them in the same order as the original and the sheets he was copying from were out of sequence.

The volume for New Providence has several entries where the dates or places of capture are blank. The phrase 'not mentioned' is used where the clerk had no data.

The last column has the means of leaving the facility. The column width is not adequate and at times the writing is compressed, which makes for difficult reading.

Fifty seven men escaped from Barbados, with most being recaptured. Some departed in groups: on April 24, 1814 - ten; January 13, 1815 - seven; July 8, 1814 - six and on July 10, 1814 - five left without permission. A few were caught in the act or were 'recaptured immediately'.

The roster for New Providence shows that one man escaped. Seven from the *Castor* that escaped from Newfoundland were captured three days later on September 1, 1812.

One problem is the use of the ditto mark (both the symbol ' " ' and the letter '*d* '); it is used on practically every page. Some records have information that over runs from the previous entries.

During the operation of the New Providence prison camp: a total of 95 went to Bermuda, 19 to England, 17 to Jamaica and 121 to Halifax. With few exceptions, the transfers from Barbados do not show where they were being sent. From the records, all those incarcerated at Newfoundland were either exchanged or sent on parole to the United States.

Ninety were incarcerated for being Americans at Barbados; ten at New Providence and thirteen at Newfoundland. Apparently they were American citizens serving on British merchantmen and warships.

The rosters for New Providence and Newfoundland refer to unnamed prison ships. Several of the escapes for Barbados say the prisoner 'cut through the ship', so the prisoners were housed on prison ships there as well.

The roster for Barbados indicate three died as prisoners of war, nine at New Providence, while no deaths were recorded at Newfoundland.

Any errors or omissions are regretted and are the fault of the transcriber.

Harrison Scott Baker II

President (1996 - 1999)
Society of the War of 1812 in the State of Ohio

- In memory of those who did not return -

- The Dead -

Anderson, Oliver
Chester, Samuel
Cheve, Daniel
Coglan, William
Cross, John
Doyle, James
Edmunds, William
Joseph, James
Norbao, Peter
Ringold, Henry
Ross, Robert
Sanders, George

- Those who die in service to the United States should not be forgotten -

American Prisoners of War Held at Barbados During the War of 1812

---, Alfonso   Prisoner 1236. Rank: Seaman, from: Fox, Privateer.
    Cap: 26 Dec 1814 off St Bartholomew by HM Brig Barbados Int: 14 Jan 1815 Dis: 08 Feb 1815.
    Received from HM Brig Barbados. HM Ship Swiftsure. (Last name not recorded.)

---, Alias   Prisoner 1257. Rank: Seaman, from: Fox, Privateer.
    Cap: 26 Dec 1814 off St Bartholomew by HM Brig Barbados Int: 14 Jan 1815 Dis: 31 Mar 1815.
    Received from HM Brig Barbados. Rear Adl Durham. (Last name not recorded.)

---, Antonio   Prisoner 649. Rank: Seaman, from: Comet, Privateer.
    Cap: 08 Mar 1813 at Sea by HM Ship Lightning Int: 20 May 1813 Dis: 11 Aug 1813.
    Received from HM Sloop Crane. Malmore American Cartel. (Last name not recorded.)

---, Blondell   Prisoner 1241. Rank: Seaman, from: Fox, Privateer.
    Cap: 26 Dec 1814 off St Bartholomew by HM Brig Barbados Int: 14 Jan 1815 Dis: 08 Feb 1815.
    Received from HM Brig Barbados. HM Ship Swiftsure. (Last name not recorded.)

---, Cassimine   Prisoner 1252. Rank: Seaman, from: Fox, Privateer.
    Cap: 26 Dec 1814 off St Bartholomew by HM Brig Barbados Int: 14 Jan 1815 Dis: 08 Feb 1815.
    Received from HM Brig Barbados. HM Ship Swiftsure. (Last name not recorded.)

---, Celesbin   Prisoner 1221. Rank: Seaman, from: Fox, Privateer.
    Cap: 26 Dec 1814 off St Bartholomew by HM Brig Barbados Int: 14 Jan 1815 Dis: 08 Feb 1815.
    Received from HM Brig Barbados. HM Ship Swiftsure. (Last name not recorded.)

---, Domingo   Prisoner 1290. Rank: Seaman, from: Mary, Merchant Schooner.
    Cap: 15 Jan 1815 Lat 22.40, Long 66 by HM Ship Pique Int: 29 Jan 1815 Dis: 14 Feb 1815.
    Received from HMS Pique. HM Ship Piqua. (Last name not recorded.)

---, Fanhassie   Prisoner 1223. Rank: Seaman, from: Fox, Privateer.
    Cap: 26 Dec 1814 off St Bartholomew by HM Brig Barbados Int: 14 Jan 1815 Dis: 08 Feb 1815.
    Received from HM Brig Barbados. HM Ship Swiftsure. (Last name not recorded.)

---, Forsette   Prisoner 1245. Rank: Seaman, from: Fox, Privateer.
    Cap: 26 Dec 1814 off St Bartholomew by HM Brig Barbados Int: 14 Jan 1815 Dis: 08 Feb 1815.
    Received from HM Brig Barbados. HM Ship Swiftsure. (Last name not recorded.)

---, Philadelphia   Prisoner 283. Rank: Seaman, from: Rea, Privateer.
    Cap: 29 Nov 1812 off Barbados by HM Ship Lightning Int: 29 Nov 1812 Dis: 11 Aug 1813.
    Received from HM Ship Lightning. Ship having been captured by the Bona American. Malmore
    American Cartel. (Last name recorded.)

Abbot, Daniel   Prisoner 1440. Rank: Seaman, from: Avon, Privateer.
    Cap: 08 Mar 1815 off Nevis by HM Sloop Barbados Int: 13 Mar 1815 Dis: 15 Mar 1815.
    Received from HM Sloop Barbados. HMS Numen Rear Admiral Durham.

Acker, Jose   Prisoner 949. Rank: Seaman, from: President, Privateer.
    Cap: 07 May 1814 off Porto Rico by HM Ship Piqua Int: 20 Jun 1814 Dis: 22 Jul 1814.
    Received from HM Ship Vestal. HM Ship Gloucester Rear Admiral Durham.

Acomplado, August   Prisoner 948. Rank: Seaman, from: President, Privateer.
    Cap: 07 May 1814 off Porto Rico by HM Ship Piqua Int: 20 Jun 1814 Dis: 22 Jul 1814.
    Received from HM Ship Vestal. HM Ship Gloucester Rear Admiral Durham.

Adams, ---   Prisoner 829. Rank: 2 Mate, from: Rattle Snake, Letter of Marque.
    Cap: 11 Mar 1814 Lat 24.07 N, Long 66.47 W by HM Ship Rhin Int: 25 Mar 1814 Dis: 22 Jul 1814.
    Received from HM Ship Rhin. HM Ship Gloucester Rear Admiral Durham. (First name not legible.)

Adams, James   Prisoner 1030. Rank: Seaman, from: Grey Hound, Merchant Schooner.
    Cap: 05 Jun 1814 off Bermuda by HM Brig Crane Int: 11 Jul 1814 Dis: 22 Jul 1814.
    Received from HM Schooner Flying Fish. HM Ship Gloucester Rear Admiral Durham.

Adams, John B   Prisoner 1207. Rank: Seaman, from: Fox, Privateer.
    Cap: 26 Dec 1814 off St Bartholomew by HM Brig Barbados Int: 14 Jan 1815 Dis: 08 Feb 1815.
    Received from HM Brig Barbados. HM Ship Swiftsure.

Adams, Theophilus B   Prisoner 146. Rank: Seaman, from: Yankee, Privateer.
    Cap: 25 Oct 1812 off Sombero by HM Sloop Peruvian Int: 13 Nov 1812 Dis: 10 Jul 1813.
    Received from HM Ship Mercury. Perseverance American Cartel.

Adams, William   Prisoner 547. Rank: Seaman, from: John, Privateer.
    Cap: 06 Feb 1813 Lat 10.0 N, Long 61.0 W by HM Sloop Peruvian Int: 20 Feb 1813 Dis: 11 Aug
    1813. Received from HM Ship Cumberland. American Cartel Malmore.

Adams, William   Prisoner 914. Rank: Seaman, from: Hawk, Privateer.
    Cap: 26 Apr 1814 Near the Mona Passage by HM Ship Piqua Int: 20 Jun 1814 Dis: 20 Jul 1814.
    Received from HM Ship Vestal. HM Sloop Hazard Rear Adml Durham.

Adians, Jose   Prisoner 941. Rank: Seaman, from: President, Privateer.
    Cap: 07 May 1814 off Porto Rico by HM Ship Piqua Int: 20 Jun 1814 Dis: 22 Jul 1814.
    Received from HM Ship Vestal. HM Ship Gloucester Rear Admiral Durham.

American Prisoners of War Held at Barbados During the War of 1812

Albantio, Augustin   Prisoner 1234. Rank: Seaman, from: Fox, Privateer.
    Cap: 26 Dec 1814 off St Bartholomew by HM Brig Barbados Int: 14 Jan 1815 Dis: 08 Feb 1815.
    Received from HM Brig Barbados. HM Ship Swiftsure.

Albenans, Jose   Prisoner 958. Rank: Seaman, from: President, Privateer.
    Cap: 07 May 1814 off Porto Rico by HM Ship Piqua Int: 20 Jun 1814 Dis: 22 Jul 1814.
    Received from HM Ship Vestal. HM Ship Gloucester Rear Admiral Durham.

Albery, Martine   Prisoner 959. Rank: Seaman, from: President, Privateer.
    Cap: 07 May 1814 off Porto Rico by HM Ship Piqua Int: 20 Jun 1814 Dis: 22 Jul 1814.
    Received from HM Ship Vestal. HM Ship Gloucester Rear Admiral Durham.

Aldoe, William   Prisoner 1175. Rank: Mate, from: Sophia, Merchant.
    Cap: 02 Dec 1814 Lat 30.30N, Long 79.30 W by HM Ship Ister Int: 27 Dec 1814 Dis: 08 Feb 1815.
    Received from HMS Ister. HM Ship Swiftsure.

Alexander, Phillippe   Prisoner 1246. Rank: Seaman, from: Fox, Privateer.
    Cap: 26 Dec 1814 off St Bartholomew by HM Brig Barbados Int: 14 Jan 1815 Dis: 08 Feb 1815.
    Received from HM Brig Barbados. HM Ship Swiftsure.

Allan, Elisha   Prisoner 863. Rank: Seaman, from: Geneal Hamilton, Merchant.
    Cap: 27 Jul 1812 Surinam by HMS Surinam Int: 26 Mar 1814 Dis: 25 Apr 1814.
    Received from HM Ship Palama. HM Ship Vestal.

Allen, John   Prisoner 1293. Rank: Mate & Passenger, from: Mary, Merchant Schooner.
    Cap: 15 Jan 1815 Lat 22.40, Long 66 by HM Ship Pique Int: 29 Jan 1815 Dis: 31 Mar 1815.
    Received from HMS Pique. Rear Adl Durham.

Allen, Richard   Prisoner 311. Rank: Seaman, from: Venus, Merchant Ship.
    Cap: 15 Dec 1812 Lat 32 N, Long 54 W by HM Ship Herald Int: 31 Dec 1812 Dis: 06 Jun 1813.
    Received from HM Ship Herald. America on Parole Sir F. Laforey.

Alleyn, John   Prisoner 55. Rank: Seaman, from: Providence, Privateer.
    Cap: 11 Sep 1812 off St. Barthlomew by HM Sloop Dominica Int: 13 Nov 1812 Dis: 10 Apr 1813.
    Received from HM Ship Mercury. America on Parole being very ill.

Allman, Samuel   Prisoner 364. Rank: Seaman, from: Decatur, Privateer.
    Cap: 16 Jan 1813 Lat 13.00 N, Long 41.00 N by HM Ship Surprise Int: 26 Jan 1813 Dis: 10 Jul 1813.
    Received from HM Ship Surprise. Perseverance American Cartel.

Ames, Sears   Prisoner 732. Rank: Seaman, from: Greyhound, Merchant Schooner.
    Cap: 13 Jan 1814 off the Virginia (not legible) by HM Schooner Elizabeth Int: 02 Feb 1814 Dis: 02
    Feb 1814. Received from HM Brig Liberty. Rising States American Cartel. Rear Adml Sir F. Laforey.

Anden, Peter   Prisoner 1291. Rank: Seaman, from: Mary, Merchant Schooner.
    Cap: 15 Jan 1815 Lat 22.40, Long 66 by HM Ship Pique Int: 29 Jan 1815 Dis: 14 Feb 1815.
    Received from HMS Pique. HM Ship Piqua.

Anderson, George   Prisoner 1183. Rank: Prize Master, from: Hope, Merchant.
    Cap: 28 Dec 1814 off St Bartholomew by HMS Fairy Int: 10 Jan 1815 Dis: 31 Mar 1815.
    Received from Brig Hope. Recaptured Brig. Rear Adl Durham.

Anderson, Hugh   Prisoner 286. Rank: Seaman, from: Rea, Privateer.
    Cap: 29 Nov 1812 off Barbados by HM Ship Lightning Int: 03 Dec 1812 Dis: 10 Jul 1813.
    Received from HM Ship Lightning. Ship having been captured by the Bona American. Perseverance
    American Cartel.

Anderson, Jacob   Prisoner 416. Rank: Seaman, from: Apollo, Merchant Ship.
    Cap: 22 Dec 1812 off Tenioff by HM Ship Grampus Int: 30 Jan 1813 Dis: 10 Jul 1813.
    Received from HM Sloop Demerary. Perseverance American Cartel.

Anderson, James   Prisoner 518. Rank: Seaman, from: John, Privateer.
    Cap: 06 Feb 1813 Lat 10.0 N, Long 61.0 W by HM Sloop Peruvian Int: 20 Feb 1813 Dis: 11 Aug
    1813. Received from HM Ship Cumberland. Malmore American Cartel.

Anderson, John   Prisoner 883. Rank: Lieutenant, from: Hawk, Privateer.
    Cap: 26 Apr 1814 Near the Mona Passage by HM Ship Piqua Int: 13 Jun 1814 Dis: 22 Jul 1814.
    Received from HM Ship Vestal. HM Ship Gloucester Rear Admiral Durham.

Andrew, Peter   Prisoner 610. Rank: Seaman, from: Thomas Penrose, Privateer.
    Cap: 23 Mar 1813 Lat 20.14 W, Long 61.20 W by HM Ship Tribune Int: 28 Mar 1813 Dis: 26 Apr
    1813. Received from HM Ship Tribune. America on Parole Sir F. Laforey.

Andrews, Amos   Prisoner 1070. Rank: Master, from: Engineer, Letter of Marque.
    Cap: 21 Sep 1814 of Porto Rico by HM Ship Barossa Int: 29 Sep 1814 Dis: 21 Nov 1814.
    Received from HM Ship Barossa. Exchanged.

Andrews, Eben   Prisoner 1438. Rank: Seaman, from: Avon, Privateer.
    Cap: 08 Mar 1815 off Nevis by HM Sloop Barbados Int: 13 Mar 1815 Dis: 15 Mar 1815.
    Received from HM Sloop Barbados. HMS Numen Rear Admiral Durham.

American Prisoners of War Held at Barbados During the War of 1812

Andrews, L   Prisoner 1085. Rank: Seaman, from: Engineer, Letter of Marque.
    Cap: 21 Sep 1814 of Porto Rico by HM Ship Barossa Int: 29 Sep 1814 Dis: 31 Mar 1815.
    Received from HM Ship Barossa. Rear Adl Durham.

Andrews, Nathaniel   Prisoner 761. Rank: Seaman, from: Frolic, Privateer.
    Cap: 25 Jan 1814 off St Thomas by HM Sloop Heron Int: 06 Feb 1814 Dis: 25 Apr 1814.
    Received from HM Sloop Heron. HM Ship Vestal.

Ansley, John   Prisoner 590. Rank: Captain, from: Thomas Penrose, Privateer.
    Cap: 23 Mar 1813 Lat 20.14 W, Long 61.20 W by HM Ship Tribune Int: 28 Mar 1813 Dis: 26 Apr 1813. Received from HM Ship Tribune. America on Parole Sir F. Laforey.

Antonio, John   Prisoner 885. Rank: Seaman, from: Hawk, Privateer.
    Cap: 26 Apr 1814 Near the Mona Passage by HM Ship Piqua Int: 20 Jun 1814 Dis: 20 Jul 1814.
    Received from HM Ship Vestal. HM Sloop Hazard Rear Adml Durham.

Archer, Nathaniel   Prisoner 1444. Rank: Prize Master, from: Ivan Francisco, Not Recorded.
    Cap: 08 Mar 1815 off Nevis by HM Brig Muros Int: 26 Mar 1815 Dis: 31 Mar 1815.
    Received from HM Brig Maria. Recaptured from the Grand Turk Privateer. Out of Custody Rear Adl Durham.

Arnold, Charles   Prisoner 1286. Rank: Seaman, from: Josephus, Merchant Schooner.
    Cap: 14 Dec 1814 Lat 19.13, Long 64 by HMS Pique Int: 29 Jan 1814 Dis: 31 Mar 1815.
    Received from HMS Pique. Rear Adl Durham.

Arnold, Isaac   Prisoner 33. Rank: Lieutenant, from: Providence, Privateer.
    Cap: 11 Sep 1812 off St. Bartholomew by HM Sloop Dominica Int: 24 Oct 1812 Dis: 10 Jul 1813.
    Received from HM Sloop Vestal. Perseverance American Cartel.

Arnold, James   Prisoner 846. Rank: Seaman, from: Rattle Snake, Letter of Marque.
    Cap: 11 Mar 1814 Lat 24.07 N, Long 66.47 W by HM Ship Rhin Int: 25 Mar 1814 Dis: 25 Apr 1814.
    Received from HM Ship Rhin. HM Ship Vestal.

Ashton, William   Prisoner 806. Rank: Mate, from: Blanch, Merchant Schooner.
    Cap: 24 Jan 1814 off Saint Bartholomew by HM Brig Barbados Int: 12 Feb 1814 Dis: 22 Jul 1814.
    Received from HM Schooner Ballahou. HM Ship Gloucester Rear Admiral Durham.

Ausourd, John C   Prisoner 460. Rank: Seaman, from: Bowrey, Privateer.
    Cap: 02 Feb 1813 off Barbados by HM Sloop Opossum Int: 18 Feb 1813 Dis: 11 Aug 1813.
    Received from HM Sloop Opossum. English Brig Captured by the Comet. Malmore American Cartel.

Austin, David   Prisoner 1363. Rank: Seaman, from: Spencer, Merchant.
    Cap: 15 Feb 1815 off St Bartholomew by HMS Dasher Int: 03 Mar 1815 Dis: 31 Mar 1815.
    Received from HM Ship Dasher. Out of Custody Rear Adl Durham.

Austin, Purnel   Prisoner 1137. Rank: Master, from: High Flyer, Letter of Marque.
    Cap: 14 Nov 1814 off Anguilla by HM Ship Barossa Int: 18 Nov 1814 Dis: 31 Mar 1815.
    Received from HM Ship Barossa. Rear Adl Durham.

Averell, Samuel   Prisoner 539. Rank: Seaman, from: John, Privateer.
    Cap: 06 Feb 1813 Lat 10.0 N, Long 61.0 W by HM Sloop Peruvian Int: 20 Feb 1813 Dis: 11 Aug 1813. Received from HM Ship Cumberland. American Cartel Malmore.

Avis, John   Prisoner 1400. Rank: Purser, from: Avon, Privateer.
    Cap: 08 Mar 1815 off Nevis by HM Sloop Barbados Int: 13 Mar 1815 Dis: 15 Mar 1815.
    Received from HM Sloop Barbados. HMS Numen Rear Admiral Durham.

Azunes, Jerune   Prisoner 952. Rank: Seaman, from: President, Privateer.
    Cap: 07 May 1814 off Porto Rico by HM Ship Piqua Int: 20 Jun 1814 Dis: 22 Jul 1814.
    Received from HM Ship Vestal. HM Ship Gloucester Rear Admiral Durham.

Babbit, Erasmus   Prisoner 469. Rank: Surgeon, from: John, Privateer.
    Cap: 06 Feb 1813 Lat 10.0 N, Long 61.0 W by HM Sloop Peruvian Int: 20 Feb 1813 Dis: 13 Mar 1813. Received from HM Ship Cumberland. Being a non Combatant.

Babcock, William   Prisoner 112. Rank: Seaman, from: William Rathbone, Brig.
    Cap: 09 Oct 1812 at Sea by HM Sloop Charybdis Int: 13 Nov 1812 Dis: 10 Jul 1813.
    Received from HM Ship Mercury. Retaken Brig Part of Crew of Savory Jack Privateer. Perseverance American Cartel.

Babut, Peter   Prisoner 638. Rank: Seaman, from: Active, Merchant Ship.
    Cap: 23 Feb 1813 off St Bartholomew by HM Ship Surprise Int: 11 Apr 1813 Dis: 11 Aug 1813.
    Received from HM Schooner Elizabeth. Malmore American Cartel.

Backman, John   Prisoner 768. Rank: Seaman, from: Frolic, Privateer.
    Cap: 25 Jan 1814 off St Thomas by HM Sloop Heron Int: 06 Feb 1814 Escaped: 26 Mar 1814.
    Received from HM Sloop Heron. Escaped. Naval Hospital. Reentry (869).

Backman, John   Prisoner 869. Rank: Seaman, from: Frolic, Privateer.
    Cap: 27 Jan 1814 off St Thomas by HM Sloop Heron Int: 04 Apr 1814 Dis: 16 Apr 1814.
    Retaken by the Constables. Out of Custody Rear Adml Durham having given information of (not legible).

American Prisoners of War Held at Barbados During the War of 1812

Backman, John   Prisoner 981. Rank: Seaman, from: Frolic, Privateer.
    Cap: 20 Mar 1814 off Saba by HM Ship Ister Int: 20 Jun 1814 Escaped: 28 Jun 1814.
    Received from HM Ship Vestal. Escaped.

Backman, John   Prisoner 1039. Rank: Seaman, from: North Star, Merchant Schooner.
    Cap: 10 Jun 1814 off St Bartholomew by HM Brig Crane Int: 29 Jul 1814 Dis: 21 Nov 1814.
    Retaken former No 981. Out of Custody in consequence of having given information of a conspiracy among the Prisoners to impair the guard. Rear A Durham.

Bacomon, Joseph   Prisoner 473. Rank: Prize Master, from: John, Privateer.
    Cap: 06 Feb 1813 Lat 10.0 N, Long 61.0 W by HM Sloop Peruvian Int: 20 Feb 1813 Dis: 11 Aug 1813. Received from HM Ship Cumberland. Malmore American Cartel.

Bagman, Jacob   Prisoner 8. Rank: Lieutenant, from: Providence, Privateer.
    Cap: 11 Sep 1812 off St. Bartholomew by HM Sloop Dominica Int: 05 Oct 1812 Dis: 10 Jul 1813.
    Received from HM Ship Vestal. Perseverance American Cartel.

Bailey, Ransfor   Prisoner 729. Rank: Mate, from: Burnt, Merchant Schooner.
    Cap: 13 Jan 1814 Lat 19.35 N, Long 62.32 W by HMS Piqua Int: 02 Feb 1814 Dis: 02 Feb 1814.
    Received from HM Brig Liberty. Rising States American Cartel. Rear Adml Sir F. Laforey.

Bailey, Thomas   Prisoner 805. Rank: Seaman, from: Blanch, Merchant Schooner.
    Cap: 24 Jan 1814 off Saint Bartholomew by HM Brig Barbados Int: 12 Feb 1814 Dis: 25 Apr 1814.
    Received from HM Schooner Ballahou. HM Ship Vestal.

Bailoci, Thomas   Prisoner 76. Rank: Seaman, from: Providence, Privateer.
    Cap: 11 Sep 1812 off St. Barthlomew by HM Sloop Dominica Int: 13 Nov 1812 Dis: 10 Jul 1813.
    Received from HM Ship Mercury. Perseverance American Cartel.

Bakagen, John   Prisoner 73. Rank: Seaman, from: Neptune, Merchant Brig.
    Cap: 29 Aug 1812 at Sea by HM Brig Maria Int: 13 Nov 1812 Dis: 19 Nov 1812.
    Received from HM Ship Mercury. Out of Custody per order of Rear Adml Sir F. Laforey being crew of a licensed vessel.

Baker, Daniel   Prisoner 1078. Rank: Steward, from: Engineer, Letter of Marque.
    Cap: 21 Sep 1814 of Porto Rico by HM Ship Barossa Int: 29 Sep 1814 Dis: 08 Feb 1815.
    Received from HM Ship Barossa. HM Ship Swiftsure.

Baker, Joseph   Prisoner 1258. Rank: Seaman, from: Fox, Privateer.
    Cap: 26 Dec 1814 off St Bartholomew by HM Brig Barbados Int: 14 Jan 1815 Dis: 08 Feb 1815.
    Received from HM Brig Barbados. HM Ship Swiftsure.

Ballen, Elle   Prisoner 623. Rank: Seaman, from: Fly, Privateer.
    Cap: 19 Jan 1813 Lat 15.00 N, Long 45.00 W by HMS Venus Int: 02 Apr 1813 Dis: 11 Aug 1813.
    Received from HMS Venus. Recaptured from the Yankee. Malmore American Cartel.

Ballentine, Samuel   Prisoner 822. Rank: Seaman, from: HM Ship Piqua, Not Recorded.
    Cap: Not Recorded by Not Recorded Int: 07 Mar 1814 Dis: 25 Apr 1814.
    Received from HM Ship Piqua. Part of Crew of HM Ship Piqua. HMS Vestal. (Date of capture not recorded.)

Banchi, Louis   Prisoner 1248. Rank: Seaman, from: Fox, Privateer.
    Cap: 26 Dec 1814 off St Bartholomew by HM Brig Barbados Int: 14 Jan 1815 Dis: 08 Feb 1815.
    Received from HM Brig Barbados. HM Ship Swiftsure.

Bangs, William   Prisoner 770. Rank: Seaman, from: Frolic, Privateer.
    Cap: 25 Jan 1814 off St Thomas by HM Sloop Heron Int: 06 Feb 1814 Dis: 16 Feb 1814.
    Received from HM Sloop Heron. HM Ship Dromedary on suspicion of being a British subject.

Bangs, William   Prisoner 825. Rank: Seaman, from: Frolic, Privateer.
    Cap: 25 Jan 1814 off St Thomas by HM Sloop Heron Int: 15 Mar 1814 Dis: 25 Apr 1814.
    Received from HM Ship Venerable. HM Ship Vestal. (Apparent duplicate of # 770.)

Baptist, John   Prisoner 496. Rank: Seaman, from: John, Privateer.
    Cap: 06 Feb 1813 Lat 10.0 N, Long 61.0 W by HM Sloop Peruvian Int: 20 Feb 1813 Dis: 11 Aug 1813. Received from HM Ship Cumberland. Malmore American Cartel. John Baptist (1st).

Baptist, John   Prisoner 516. Rank: Seaman, from: John, Privateer.
    Cap: 06 Feb 1813 Lat 10.0 N, Long 61.0 W by HM Sloop Peruvian Int: 20 Feb 1813 Dis: 11 Aug 1813. Received from HM Ship Cumberland. Malmore American Cartel. John Baptist (2nd).

Baptist, Joseph S   Prisoner 1131. Rank: Mate, from: Clio, Merchant Schooner.
    Cap: 13 Nov 1814 off Anguilla by HM Ship Barossa Int: 18 Nov 1814 Dis: 31 Mar 1815.
    Received from HM Ship Barossa. Rear Adl Durham.

Baptiste, Jean   Prisoner 1216. Rank: Seaman, from: Fox, Privateer.
    Cap: 26 Dec 1814 off St Bartholomew by HM Brig Barbados Int: 14 Jan 1815 Dis: 08 Feb 1815.
    Received from HM Brig Barbados. HM Ship Swiftsure.

Barbados, Joseph   Prisoner 1173. Rank: Seaman, from: Dolphin, Letter of Marque.
    Cap: 04 Dec 1814 Lat 18.00 N, Long 60.00 W by HM Brig Columbia Int: 08 Dec 1814 Dis: 14 Feb 1815. Received from HM Brig Columbia. HM Ship Piqua.

American Prisoners of War Held at Barbados During the War of 1812

Barer, Jacob   Prisoner 1311. Rank: Mate & Passenger, from: Mary, Merchant Schooner.
    Cap: 15 Jan 1815 Lat 22.40, Long 66 by HM Ship Pique Int: 30 Jan 1815 Dis: 31 Mar 1815.
    Received from HMS Pique. Rear Adl Durham.

Barnard, Adonijah   Prisoner 132. Rank: Seaman, from: Providence, Privateer.
    Cap: 12 Sep 1812 off St. Bartholomew by HM Sloop Dominica Int: 13 Nov 1812 Dis: 21 Apr 1813.
    Received from HM Ship Mercury. America on Parole.

Barne, Donny   Prisoner 197. Rank: Seaman, from: Blockade, Privateer.
    Cap: 31 Oct 1812 off Saba by HM Sloop Charybdis Int: 19 Nov 1812 Dis: 10 Jul 1813.
    Received from HM Sloop Charybdis. Perseverance American Cartel.

Barrett, Tobias   Prisoner 933. Rank: Seaman, from: President, Privateer.
    Cap: 07 May 1814 off Porto Rico by HM Ship Piqua Int: 20 Jun 1814 Dis: 22 Jul 1814.
    Received from HM Ship Vestal. HM Ship Gloucester Rear Admiral Durham.

Barron, John   Prisoner 870. Rank: Seaman, from: Martin, Merchant.
    Cap: 13 Mar 1814 off St Thomas by HM Brig Swaggerer Int: 15 Apr 1814 Dis: 25 Apr 1814.
    Received from HM Ship Ister. HM Ship Vestal.

Barron, John   Prisoner 970. Rank: Seaman, from: Martin, Letter of Marque.
    Cap: 13 Mar 1814 off Saint Thomas by HM Brig Swaggerer Int: 20 Jun 1814 Dis: 22 Jul 1814.
    Received from HM Ship Vestal. HM Ship Gloucester Rear Admiral Durham. (Apparent duplicate of # 870.)

Barry, John   Prisoner 1339. Rank: Seaman, from: Vidett, Letter of Marque.
    Cap: 14 Feb 1815 off St Bartholomew by HM Ship Dasher Int: 03 Mar 1815 Dis: 31 Mar 1815.
    Received from HM Ship Dasher. Out of Custody Rear Adl Durham.

Bartlett, Gibbon   Prisoner 140. Rank: Prize Master, from: Yankee, Privateer.
    Cap: 25 Oct 1812 off Sombero by HM Sloop Peruvian Int: 13 Nov 1812 Dis: 10 Jul 1813.
    Received from HM Ship Mercury. Perseverance American Cartel.

Bartlett, William   Prisoner 651. Rank: Prize Master, from: Adelphia, Privateer.
    Cap: 24 Feb 1813 Surinam by Not Recorded Int: 20 May 1813 Dis: 10 Jul 1813.
    Received from HM Sloop Crane. Part of Crew of Comet having charge of the Ship, which floundered at Sea. Surrendering themselves at Main's Point Surinam. Perseverance American Cartel.

Bartlin, Thomas   Prisoner 605. Rank: Seaman, from: Thomas Penrose, Privateer.
    Cap: 23 Mar 1813 Lat 20.14 W, Long 61.20 W by HM Ship Tribune Int: 28 Mar 1813 Dis: 26 Apr 1813. Received from HM Ship Tribune. America on Parole Sir F. Laforey.

Bartridge, Henry   Prisoner 1028. Rank: Seaman, from: Grey Hound, Merchant Schooner.
    Cap: 05 Jun 1814 off Bermuda by HM Brig Crane Int: 11 Jul 1814 Dis: 22 Jul 1814.
    Received from HM Schooner Flying Fish. HM Ship Gloucester Rear Admiral Durham.

Bassett, Nathaniel   Prisoner 523. Rank: Seaman, from: John, Privateer.
    Cap: 06 Feb 1813 Lat 10.0 N, Long 61.0 W by HM Sloop Peruvian Int: 20 Feb 1813 Dis: 11 Aug 1813. Received from HM Ship Cumberland. Malmore American Cartel.

Batchelder, Jeremiah   Prisoner 142. Rank: Prize Master, from: Yankee, Privateer.
    Cap: 25 Oct 1812 off Sombero by HM Sloop Peruvian Int: 13 Nov 1812 Dis: 10 Jul 1813.
    Received from HM Ship Mercury. Detected cutting through the Ship. Perseverance American Cartel.

Bateman, Xenus   Prisoner 1159. Rank: Seaman, from: High Flyer, Letter of Marque.
    Cap: 14 Nov 1814 off Anguilla by HM Ship Barossa Int: 18 Nov 1814 Dis: 08 Feb 1815.
    Received from HM Ship Barossa. HM Ship Swiftsure.

Bates, Oran   Prisoner 718. Rank: Seaman, from: Olive Branch, Merchant Brig.
    Cap: 12 Apr 1813 Lat 17.00 N, Long 59.30 W by HM Sloop Eclipse Int: 07 Jul 1813 Dis: 24 Jul 1813.
    Received from HM Sloop Eclipse. Out of Custody the Vessel being liberated.

Baxter, Charles   Prisoner 1439. Rank: Seaman, from: Avon, Privateer.
    Cap: 08 Mar 1815 off Nevis by HM Sloop Barbados Int: 13 Mar 1815 Dis: 15 Mar 1815.
    Received from HM Sloop Barbados. HMS Numen Rear Admiral Durham.

Bayley, Joshua K   Prisoner 298. Rank: Seaman, from: Tigra, Not Recorded.
    Cap: Not Recorded by Not Recorded Int: 28 Dec 1812 Dis: 23 Apr 1813.
    Received from Ship Tigra. Part of Crew of Ship Tigra. HM Ship Tribune. Not to be exchanged during the War having behaved in a wanton riotous (not legible). (Date of capture not recorded.)

Baynard, Henry   Prisoner 457. Rank: Seaman, from: Bowrey, Privateer.
    Cap: 02 Feb 1813 off Barbados by HM Sloop Opossum Int: 18 Feb 1813 Dis: 11 Aug 1813.
    Received from HM Sloop Opossum. English Brig Captured by the Comet. Malmore American Cartel.

Beadle, Maning   Prisoner 190. Rank: Prize Master, from: Blockade, Privateer.
    Cap: 31 Oct 1812 off Saba by HM Sloop Charybdis Int: 19 Nov 1812 Dis: 10 Jul 1813.
    Received from HM Sloop Charybdis. Perseverance American Cartel.

Belding, Clifford   Prisoner 186. Rank: Carpenter, from: Blockade, Privateer.
    Cap: 31 Oct 1812 off Saba by HM Sloop Charybdis Int: 19 Nov 1812 Dis: 10 Jul 1813.
    Received from HM Sloop Charybdis. Perseverance American Cartel.

American Prisoners of War Held at Barbados During the War of 1812

Belding, James Prisoner 220. Rank: Seaman, from: Blockade, Privateer.
  Cap: 31 Oct 1812 off Saba by HM Sloop Charybdis Int: 19 Nov 1812 Dis: 11 Aug 1813.
  Received from HM Sloop Charybdis. Malmore American Cartel.
Bell, Jacob Prisoner 794. Rank: Seaman, from: Atalante, Merchant Schooner.
  Cap: 19 Jan 1814 off Saint Bartholomew by HM Brig Barbados Int: 12 Feb 1814 Dis: 25 Apr 1814.
  Received from HM Schooner Ballahou. HM Ship Vestal.
Bell, Zachariah Prisoner 994. Rank: Seaman, from: Hawk, Privateer.
  Cap: 26 Apr 1814 Near the Mona Passage by HM Ship Piqua Int: 20 Jun 1814 Dis: 22 Jul 1814.
  Received from HM Ship Vestal. HM Ship Gloucester Rear Admiral Durham.
Benner, Thomas Prisoner 13. Rank: Seaman, from: Shepherdess, Merchant Schooner.
  Cap: 12 Oct 1812 Lat 20.00 N, Long 56.00 W by HM Sloop Lightning Int: 22 Oct 1812 Dis: 24 Oct 1812. Received from HM Sloop Lightning. America on Parole per order of Captain Reynolds Tribune.
Bennett, Peter Prisoner 258. Rank: Seaman, from: Brandy Wine, Merchant Brig.
  Cap: 17 Nov 1812 Lat 19.30, Long 57.00 W by HM Ship Lightning Int: 23 Nov 1812 Dis: 02 Dec 1812. Received from HM Ship Lightning. America on Parole Sir F. Laforey.
Benson, William B Prisoner 63. Rank: Seaman, from: Providence, Privateer.
  Cap: 11 Sep 1812 off St. Bartholomew by HM Sloop Dominica Int: 13 Nov 1812 Escaped: 24 Apr 1813. Received from HM Ship Mercury. Escaped 4/24/13. Retaken April 30th 1813. Note of reentry (646). Perseverance American Cartel.
Benson, William B Prisoner 646. Rank: Seaman, from: Not Recorded, Not Recorded.
  Cap: Not Recorded by Retaken Int: 30 Apr 1813 Dis: 10 Jul 1813.
  Received from The Constibles. Retaken former N 63. Perseverance American Cartel. (Date of capture not recorded.)
Berg, Daniel Prisoner 741. Rank: Prize Master, from: Frolic, Privateer.
  Cap: 25 Jan 1814 off St Thomas by HM Sloop Heron Int: 06 Feb 1814 Dis: 22 Jul 1814.
  Received from HM Sloop Heron. HM Ship Gloucester Rear Admiral Durham.
Berham, John Prisoner 1297. Rank: Seaman, from: Mary, Merchant Schooner.
  Cap: 15 Jan 1815 Lat 22.40, Long 66 by HM Ship Pique Int: 29 Jan 1815 Dis: 14 Feb 1815.
  Received from HMS Pique. HM Ship Piqua.
Berry, Owen Prisoner 986. Rank: Seaman, from: Providence, Privateer.
  Cap: 11 Sep 1812 off Saint Bartholomew by HM Sloop Dominica Int: 20 Jun 1814 Escaped: 28 Jun 1814. Received from HM Ship Vestal. Escaped.
Berry, Owen Prisoner 1020. Rank: Seaman, from: Not Recorded, Privateer.
  Cap: Not Recorded by Not Recorded Int: 01 Jul 1814 Dis: 22 Jul 1814.
  Retaken former number 986. HM Ship Gloucester Rear Adml Durham. (Date of capture not recorded.)
Beven, Lelah Prisoner 210. Rank: Seaman, from: Blockade, Privateer.
  Cap: 31 Oct 1812 off Saba by HM Sloop Charybdis Int: 19 Nov 1812 Dis: 10 Jul 1813.
  Received from HM Sloop Charybdis. Perseverance American Cartel.
Bevin, John Prisoner 41. Rank: Seaman, from: William Rathbone, Not Recorded.
  Cap: 09 Oct 1812 Lat 22.00 N, Long 60.00 W by HM Sloop Chandler Int: 01 Nov 1812 Dis: 10 Jul 1813. Received from HM Brig Swaggerer. Having been taken by the Savory Jack American privateer. Perseverance American Cartel.
Bevin, Thomas Prisoner 36. Rank: Prize Master, from: William Rathbone, Not Recorded.
  Cap: 09 Oct 1812 Lat 22.00 N, Long 60.00 W by HM Sloop Chandler Int: 01 Nov 1812 Dis: 10 Jul 1813. Received from HM Brig Swaggerer. Having been taken by the Savory Jack American privateer. Perseverance American Cartel.
Bickford, Paul Prisoner 342. Rank: Prize Master, from: Decatur, Privateer.
  Cap: 16 Jan 1813 Lat 13.00 N, Long 41.00 N by HM Ship Surprise Int: 26 Jan 1813 Dis: 10 Jul 1813.
  Received from HM Ship Surprise. Perseverance American Cartel.
Biddle, John Prisoner 128. Rank: Seaman, from: Providence, Privateer.
  Cap: 11 Sep 1812 off St. Bartholomew by HM Sloop Dominica Int: 13 Nov 1812 Dis: 10 Jul 1813.
  Received from HM Ship Mercury. Perseverance American Cartel.
Bigelow, Thomas C Prisoner 211. Rank: Seaman, from: Blockade, Privateer.
  Cap: 31 Oct 1812 off Saba by HM Sloop Charybdis Int: 19 Nov 1812 Dis: 10 Jul 1813.
  Received from HM Sloop Charybdis. Perseverance American Cartel.
Bird, Robert Prisoner 582. Rank: Seaman, from: HM Ship Vestal, Not Recorded.
  Cap: Not Recorded by Not Recorded Int: 16 Mar 1813 Dis: 10 Jul 1813.
  Received from HM Ship Vestal. Part of Crew of HM Ship Vestal. Perseverance American Cartel. (Date of capture not recorded.)
Birhau, Jacque Prisoner 1281. Rank: Seaman, from: Hero, Merchant Schooner.
  Cap: 14 Dec 1814 Lat 19.13, Long 64 by HMS Pique Int: 29 Jan 1815 Dis: 14 Feb 1815.
  Received from HMS Pique. HM Ship Piqua.

American Prisoners of War Held at Barbados During the War of 1812

Bisbee, Elijah   Prisoner 668. Rank: Seaman, from: William, Merchant Brig.
    Cap: 16 Apr 1813 Lat 35.00 N, Long 57.00 W by Heron Int: 22 May 1813 Dis: 11 Aug 1813.
    Received from HM Sloop Heron. Malmore American Cartel.

Bisbee, John   Prisoner 665. Rank: Seaman, from: William, Merchant Brig.
    Cap: 16 Apr 1813 Lat 35.00 N, Long 57.00 W by Heron Int: 22 May 1813 Dis: 11 Aug 1813.
    Received from HM Sloop Heron. Malmore American Cartel.

Bissell, Charles   Prisoner 1177. Rank: Master & Passenger, from: San Francisco, Merchant.
    Cap: 07 Dec 1814 Lat 32.30 N, Long 65.00 W by HM Ship Ister Int: 28 Dec 1814 Dis: 31 Mar 1815.
    Received from HMS Ister. Rear Adl Durham.

Bissit, John   Prisoner 1180. Rank: Seaman, from: Gallant Hull, Merchant.
    Cap: 28 Dec 1814 off St Bartholomew by HM Ship Barossa Int: 10 Jan 1815 Dis: 15 Mar 1815.
    Received from HMS Barossa. HMS Numen.

Bixby, James   Prisoner 1178. Rank: Merchant, from: San Francisco, Merchant.
    Cap: 07 Dec 1814 Lat 32.30 N, Long 65.00 W by HM Ship Ister Int: 28 Dec 1814 Dis: 31 Mar 1815.
    Received from HMS Ister. Rear Adl Durham.

Blagze, John   Prisoner 1140. Rank: Passenger, from: High Flyer, Letter of Marque.
    Cap: 14 Nov 1814 off Anguilla by HM Ship Barossa Int: 18 Nov 1814 Dis: 21 Nov 1814.
    Received from HM Ship Barossa. Out of Custody noncombatant.

Blair, Harvey   Prisoner 558. Rank: Seaman, from: Rebecca, Merchant Brig.
    Cap: 15 Jan 1813 off Demuary by Detained by Custom House Int: 02 Mar 1813 Dis: 27 May 1813.
    Received from Army Schooner Maria. America on Parole Sir Francis Laforey.

Blair, Hosea   Prisoner 553. Rank: Passenger, from: Rebecca, Merchant Brig.
    Cap: 15 Jan 1813 off Demuary by Detained by Custom House Int: 02 Mar 1813 Dis: 13 Mar 1813.
    Received from Army Schooner Maria. America on Parole Sir Francis Laforey.

Blair, Robert   Prisoner 548. Rank: Seaman, from: John, Privateer.
    Cap: 06 Feb 1813 Lat 10.0 N, Long 61.0 W by HM Sloop Peruvian Int: 20 Feb 1813 Dis: 11 Aug
    1813. Received from HM Ship Cumberland. American Cartel Malmore.

Blake, Daniel   Prisoner 1272. Rank: Seaman, from: Weasel, Brig.
    Cap: Not Recorded by Not Recorded Int: 15 Jan 1815 Dis: 14 Feb 1815.
    Received from HMS Crescent. (Not legible) from Brig Weasel by HMS Crescent. HM Ship Piqua.
    (Date of capture not recorded.)

Blanchard, Louis   Prisoner 1253. Rank: Seaman, from: Fox, Privateer.
    Cap: 26 Dec 1814 off St Bartholomew by HM Brig Barbados Int: 14 Jan 1815 Dis: 08 Feb 1815.
    Received from HM Brig Barbados. HM Ship Swiftsure.

Blardile, Jacob   Prisoner 697. Rank: Seaman, from: HM Ship Bedford, Not Recorded.
    Cap: Not Recorded by Not Recorded Int: 12 Jun 1813 Dis: 11 Aug 1813.
    Received from HMS Vestal. Gave himself up as a Prisoner of War on Board HM Ship Bedford.
    Malmore American Cartel. (Date of capture not recorded.)

Blish, Samuel   Prisoner 904. Rank: Seaman, from: Hawk, Privateer.
    Cap: 26 Apr 1814 Near the Mona Passage by HM Ship Piqua Int: 20 Jun 1814 Escaped: 08 Jul 1814.
    Received from HM Ship Vestal. Escaped.

Blish, Samuel   Prisoner 1023. Rank: Seaman, from: Hawk, Privateer.
    Cap: 26 Apr 1814 Near the Mona Passage by HM Ship Piqua Int: 10 Jul 1814 Dis: 22 Jul 1814.
    Retaken former No 904. HM Ship Gloucester Rear Admiral Durham.

Bliss, Moses   Prisoner 223. Rank: Seaman, from: Blockade, Privateer.
    Cap: 31 Oct 1812 off Saba by HM Sloop Charybdis Int: 19 Nov 1812 Dis: 10 Jul 1813.
    Received from HM Sloop Charybdis. Perseverance American Cartel. Cut through the hull Retaken
    Immediately.

Blumore, Benjamin   Prisoner 1370. Rank: Seaman, from: Isabella, Merchant.
    Cap: 23 Feb 1815 off Berbrida by HMS Dasher Int: 03 Mar 1815 Dis: 31 Mar 1815.
    Received from HM Ship Dasher. Out of Custody Rear Adl Durham.

Board, John P   Prisoner 920. Rank: Seaman, from: President, Privateer.
    Cap: 07 May 1814 off Porto Rico by HM Ship Piqua Int: 20 Jun 1814 Dis: 20 Jul 1814.
    Received from HM Ship Vestal. HM Sloop Hazard Rear Adml Durham.

Boddety, John   Prisoner 1171. Rank: Seaman, from: Dolphin, Letter of Marque.
    Cap: 04 Dec 1814 Lat 18.00 N, Long 60.00 W by HM Brig Columbia Int: 08 Dec 1814 Dis: 31 Mar
    1815. Received from HM Brig Columbia. Rear Adl Durham.

Boggs, Francis   Prisoner 1110. Rank: Prize Master, from: Mars, Privateer.
    Cap: 01 Sep 1814 Lat 41 N, Long 52 W by HM Ship Piqua Int: 21 Oct 1814 Dis: 31 Mar 1815.
    Received from HMS Piqua. Taken by the David Porter Privateer. Rear Adl Durham.

Bogman, James   Prisoner 471. Rank: Prize Master, from: John, Privateer.
    Cap: 06 Feb 1813 Lat 10.0 N, Long 61.0 W by HM Sloop Peruvian Int: 20 Feb 1813 Dis: 25 Feb
    1813. Received from HM Ship Cumberland. Merchant Ship for England.

American Prisoners of War Held at Barbados During the War of 1812

Bogs, James   Prisoner 16. Rank: Seaman, from: Shepherdess, Merchant Schooner.
    Cap: 12 Oct 1812 Lat 20.00 N, Long 56.00 W by HM Sloop Lightning Int: 22 Oct 1812 Dis: 24 Oct 1812. Received from HM Sloop Lightning. America on Parole per order of Captain Reynolds Tribune.

Bolding, Garrat   Prisoner 898. Rank: Seaman, from: Hawk, Privateer.
    Cap: 26 Apr 1814 Near the Mona Passage by HM Ship Piqua Int: 20 Jun 1814 Dis: 20 Jul 1814. Received from HM Ship Vestal. HM Sloop Hazard Rear Adml Durham.

Bond, Oliver C   Prisoner 27. Rank: Seaman, from: Hope, Merchant Ship.
    Cap: 27 Sep 1812 Lat 22.30 N, Long 40.45 by HM Sloop Tribune Int: 22 Oct 1812 Dis: 24 Oct 1812. Received from HM Sloop Tribune. America on Parole per order of Captain Reynolds Tribune.

Bond, Thomas   Prisoner 1392. Rank: Seaman, from: Avon, Privateer.
    Cap: 08 Mar 1815 off Nevis by HM Sloop Barbados Int: 13 Mar 1815 Dis: 31 Mar 1815. Received from HM Sloop Barbados. Out of Custody Rear Adl Durham.

Bonne, Jean Jack   Prisoner 1190. Rank: Captain, from: Fox, Privateer.
    Cap: 11 Jan 1815 off St Bartholomew by HM Brig Barbados Int: 14 Jan 1815 Dis: 08 Feb 1815. Received from HM Brig Barbados. HM Ship Swiftsure. (Capture date is Dec 26, 1814 for all entries for Fox except records 1190 - 1198.)

Bosson, John James   Prisoner 1388. Rank: Assistant Surgeon, from: Avon, Privateer.
    Cap: 08 Mar 1815 off Nevis by HM Sloop Barbados Int: 05 Mar 1815 Dis: 31 Mar 1815. Received from HM Ship Dasher. Out of Custody Rear Adl Durham. (Date of Interment before Capture.)

Boudy, William   Prisoner 797. Rank: Mate, from: Kirran, Merchant Brig.
    Cap: 25 Jan 1814 off Saint Bartholomew by HM Brig Barbados Int: 12 Feb 1814 Dis: 22 Jul 1814. Received from HM Schooner Ballahou. HM Ship Gloucester Rear Admiral Durham.

Bouldin, Nathan L   Prisoner 260. Rank: Surgeon, from: Rea, Privateer.
    Cap: 29 Nov 1812 off Barbados by HM Ship Lightning Int: 29 Nov 1812 Dis: 02 Dec 1812. Received from HM Ship Lightning. Ship having been captured by the Bona American. Sir F. Laforey being a non Combatant.

Bowden, Samuel   Prisoner 403. Rank: Seaman, from: Decatur, Privateer.
    Cap: 16 Jan 1813 Lat 13.00 N, Long 41.00 N by HM Ship Surprise Int: 26 Jan 1813 Dis: 10 Jul 1813. Received from HM Ship Surprise. Perseverance American Cartel.

Bowdwish, John   Prisoner 88. Rank: Seaman, from: Providence, Privateer.
    Cap: 11 Sep 1812 off St. Barthlomew by HM Sloop Dominica Int: 13 Nov 1812 Dis: 10 Jul 1813. Received from HM Ship Mercury. Perseverance American Cartel.

Bowen, John   Prisoner 248. Rank: Seaman, from: Maxwell, Not Recorded.
    Cap: Not Recorded by Not Recorded Int: 22 Nov 1812 Dis: 25 Apr 1813. Received from HM Ship Dragon. Part of Crew of Ship Maxwell taken out in consequence of being mutinous. Merchant Ship for England. (Date of capture not recorded.)

Bowman, John   Prisoner 1314. Rank: 2 Mate, from: Whalebone, Merchant Schooner.
    Cap: 25 Jan 1815 off St Bartholomew by HMB Espringle Int: 09 Feb 1815 Dis: 09 Mar 1815. Received from HMB Satellite. Being a Prussian.

Boy, Jolly   Prisoner 1233. Rank: Seaman, from: Fox, Privateer.
    Cap: 26 Dec 1814 off St Bartholomew by HM Brig Barbados Int: 14 Jan 1815 Dis: 08 Feb 1815. Received from HM Brig Barbados. HM Ship Swiftsure.

Boyd, James   Prisoner 1247. Rank: Seaman, from: Fox, Privateer.
    Cap: 26 Dec 1814 off St Bartholomew by HM Brig Barbados Int: 14 Jan 1815 Dis: 08 Feb 1815. Received from HM Brig Barbados. HM Ship Swiftsure.

Boyle, George   Prisoner 696. Rank: Seaman, from: HM Ship Bedford, Not Recorded.
    Cap: Not Recorded by Not Recorded Int: 12 Jun 1813 Dis: 11 Aug 1813. Received from HMS Vestal. Gave himself up as a Prisoner of War on Board HM Ship Bedford. Malmore American Cartel. (Date of capture not recorded.)

Bradie, Thomas   Prisoner 983. Rank: Seaman, from: Hart, Letter of Marque.
    Cap: 01 Feb 1814 off Sandy Hook by HM Ship Castor Int: 20 Jun 1814 Dis: 22 Jul 1814. Received from HM Ship Vestal. HM Ship Gloucester Rear Admiral Durham.

Bray, Isaac   Prisoner 333. Rank: 2 Lieutenant, from: Decatur, Privateer.
    Cap: 16 Jan 1813 Lat 13.00 N, Long 41.00 N by HM Ship Surprise Int: 25 Jan 1813 Dis: 10 Jul 1813. Received from HM Ship Surprise. Perseverance American Cartel.

Brewer, Nathaniel   Prisoner 1129. Rank: Seaman, from: Nancy, Privateer.
    Cap: 06 Sep 1814 Lat 32 N, Long 47 W by HM Ship Piqua Int: 23 Oct 1814 Dis: 08 Feb 1815. Received from HMS Piqua. Taken by the Amelia Privateer. Formerly Master of a Merchantman. Left on shore (not legible) the American Cartel Perseverance. This man chartered the American Cartel. Perseverance. HM Ship Swiftsure.

American Prisoners of War Held at Barbados During the War of 1812

Brian, Richard   Prisoner 354. Rank: Seaman, from: Decatur, Privateer.
    Cap: 16 Jan 1813 Lat 13.00 N, Long 41.00 N by HM Ship Surprise Int: 26 Jan 1813 Dis: 10 Jul 1813.
    Received from HM Ship Surprise. Perseverance American Cartel.

Brigam, Charles   Prisoner 466. Rank: Seaman, from: John, Privateer.
    Cap: 06 Feb 1813 Lat 10.0 N, Long 61.0 W by HM Sloop Peruvian Int: 18 Feb 1813 Dis: 11 Aug
    1813. Received from HM Ship Cumberland. Malmore American Cartel.

Briggs, William   Prisoner 1068. Rank: Seaman, from: Harmony, Merchant Brig.
    Cap: Not Recorded by Not Recorded Int: 12 Sep 1814 Escaped: 07 Jan 1815.
    Received from Merchant Brig Harmony. Part of Crew of Merchant Brig Harmony. Riotous Character.
    Escaped. (Date of capture not recorded.)

Briggs, William   Prisoner 1274. Rank: Seaman, from: Susannah, Schooner.
    Cap: Not Recorded by Not Recorded Int: 18 Jan 1815 Dis: 14 Feb 1815.
    Received from HMS Crescent. (Not legible) from Schooner Susannah by HMS Crescent. Retaken
    former No (1068). HM Ship Piqua. (Date of capture not recorded.)

Britade, E F   Prisoner 916. Rank: Seaman, from: President, Privateer.
    Cap: 07 May 1814 off Porto Rico by HM Ship Piqua Int: 20 Jun 1814 Dis: 20 Jul 1814.
    Received from HM Ship Vestal. HM Sloop Hazard Rear Adml Durham.

Brockings, Samuel   Prisoner 376. Rank: Seaman, from: Decatur, Privateer.
    Cap: 16 Jan 1813 Lat 13.00 N, Long 41.00 N by HM Ship Surprise Int: 29 Jan 1815 Dis: 10 Jul 1813.
    Received from HM Ship Surprise. Perseverance American Cartel.

Brodie, John   Prisoner 1092. Rank: Seaman, from: Engineer, Letter of Marque.
    Cap: 21 Sep 1814 of Porto Rico by HM Ship Barossa Int: 29 Sep 1814 Dis: 31 Mar 1815.
    Received from HM Ship Barossa. Rear Adl Durham.

Brook, David   Prisoner 906. Rank: Seaman, from: Hawk, Privateer.
    Cap: 26 Apr 1814 Near the Mona Passage by HM Ship Piqua Int: 20 Jun 1814 Dis: 22 Jul 1814.
    Received from HM Ship Vestal. HM Ship Gloucester Rear Admiral Durham.

Brook, John E   Prisoner 1146. Rank: Seaman, from: High Flyer, Letter of Marque.
    Cap: 14 Nov 1814 off Anguilla by HM Ship Barossa Int: 18 Nov 1814 Dis: 14 Feb 1815.
    Received from HM Ship Barossa. HM Ship Piqua Rear Admiral Durham.

Brooks, Edward   Prisoner 489. Rank: Seaman, from: John, Privateer.
    Cap: 06 Feb 1813 Lat 10.0 N, Long 61.0 W by HM Sloop Peruvian Int: 20 Feb 1813 Dis: 11 Aug
    1813. Received from HM Ship Cumberland. Malmore American Cartel.

Brown, Benjamin   Prisoner 744. Rank: Clerk, from: Frolic, Privateer.
    Cap: 25 Jan 1814 off St Thomas by HM Sloop Heron Int: 06 Feb 1814 Dis: 22 Jul 1814.
    Received from HM Sloop Heron. HM Ship Gloucester Rear Adml Durham.

Brown, Benjamin   Prisoner 1232. Rank: Seaman, from: Fox, Privateer.
    Cap: 26 Dec 1814 off St Bartholomew by HM Brig Barbados Int: 14 Jan 1815 Dis: 08 Feb 1815.
    Received from HM Brig Barbados. HM Ship Swiftsure.

Brown, Ezekiah   Prisoner 93. Rank: Seaman, from: Providence, Privateer.
    Cap: 11 Sep 1812 off St. Barthlomew by HM Sloop Dominica Int: 13 Nov 1812 Dis: 10 Jul 1813.
    Received from HM Ship Mercury. Perseverance American Cartel.

Brown, Henry   Prisoner 1309. Rank: Master, from: Mary, Merchant Schooner.
    Cap: 15 Jan 1815 Lat 22.40, Long 66 by HM Ship Pique Int: 29 Jan 1815 Dis: 31 Mar 1815.
    Received from HMS Pique. Rear Adl Durham.

Brown, James   Prisoner 601. Rank: Seaman, from: Thomas Penrose, Privateer.
    Cap: 23 Mar 1813 Lat 20.14 W, Long 61.20 W by HM Ship Tribune Int: 28 Mar 1813 Dis: 26 Apr
    1813. Received from HM Ship Tribune. America on Parole Sir F. Laforey.

Brown, James   Prisoner 1182. Rank: Seaman, from: Gallant Hull, Merchant.
    Cap: 28 Dec 1814 off St Bartholomew by HM Ship Barossa Int: 10 Jan 1815 Dis: 14 Feb 1815.
    Received from HMS Barossa. HM Ship Piqua.

Brown, Jesse   Prisoner 384. Rank: Seaman, from: Decatur, Privateer.
    Cap: 16 Jan 1813 Lat 13.00 N, Long 41.00 N by HM Ship Surprise Int: 26 Jan 1813 Dis: 10 Jul 1813.
    Received from HM Ship Surprise. Perseverance American Cartel.

Brown, John   Prisoner 337. Rank: Seaman, from: Decatur, Privateer.
    Cap: 16 Jan 1813 Lat 13.00 N, Long 41.00 N by HM Ship Surprise Int: 26 Jan 1813 Dis: 10 Jul 1813.
    Received from HM Ship Surprise. Perseverance American Cartel.

Brown, John   Prisoner 470. Rank: Prize Master, from: John, Privateer.
    Cap: 06 Feb 1813 Lat 10.0 N, Long 61.0 W by HM Sloop Peruvian Int: 20 Feb 1813 Dis: 26 Apr
    1813. Received from HM Ship Cumberland. America on Parole.

Brown, John   Prisoner 790. Rank: Seaman, from: Princess Royal, Not Recorded.
    Cap: Not Recorded by Not Recorded Int: 11 Feb 1814 Dis: 25 Apr 1814.
    Received from HM Brig Liberty. Part of Crew of Ship Princess Royal. HM Ship Vestal. (Date of
    capture not recorded.)

American Prisoners of War Held at Barbados During the War of 1812

Brown, John   Prisoner 1185. Rank: Seaman, from: Not Recorded, Not Recorded.
    Cap: Barbados by Not Recorded Int: 12 Jan 1815 Dis: 14 Feb 1815.
    Received from HM Brig Watsisin. (Not legible) at Barbados. HM Ship Piqua. (Date of capture not recorded.)

Brown, John   Prisoner 1279. Rank: Seaman, from: Hero, Merchant Schooner.
    Cap: 14 Dec 1814 Lat 19.13, Long 64 by HMS Pique Int: 29 Jan 1815 Dis: 14 Feb 1815.
    Received from HMS Pique. HM Ship Piqua.

Brown, Joseph   Prisoner 739. Rank: Surgeon, from: Frolic, Privateer.
    Cap: 25 Jan 1814 off St Thomas by HM Sloop Heron Int: 06 Feb 1814 Dis: 08 Apr 1814.
    Received from HM Sloop Heron. Out of Custody being a noncombatant.

Brown, Robert   Prisoner 15. Rank: Seaman, from: Shepherdess, Merchant Schooner.
    Cap: 12 Oct 1812 Lat 20.00 N, Long 56.00 W by HM Sloop Lightning Int: 22 Oct 1812 Dis: 24 Oct 1812. Received from HM Sloop Lightning. America on Parole per order of Captain Reynolds Tribune.

Brown, Robert   Prisoner 1095. Rank: Seaman, from: Engineer, Letter of Marque.
    Cap: 21 Sep 1814 of Porto Rico by HM Ship Barossa Int: 29 Sep 1814 Escaped: 13 Jan 1815.
    Received from HM Ship Barossa. Escaped. Reentry 1268.

Brown, Robert   Prisoner 1268. Rank: Seaman, from: Fox, Privateer.
    Cap: 26 Dec 1814 off St Bartholomew by HM Brig Barbados Int: 15 Jan 1815 Dis: 14 Feb 1815.
    Received from HM Brig Barbados. Retaken former No 1095. HM Ship Piqua.

Brown, Thomas   Prisoner 844. Rank: Seaman, from: Rattle Snake, Letter of Marque.
    Cap: 11 Mar 1814 Lat 24.07 N, Long 66.47 W by HM Ship Rhin Int: 25 Mar 1814 Dis: 25 Apr 1814.
    Received from HM Ship Rhin. HM Ship Vestal.

Brown, William   Prisoner 273. Rank: Seaman, from: Rea, Privateer.
    Cap: 29 Nov 1812 off Barbados by HM Ship Lightning Int: 29 Nov 1812 Dis: 20 Dec 1812.
    Received from HM Ship Lightning. Ship having been captured by the Bona American. HM Sloop Demerara having given himself up as a British Subject.

Brown, William   Prisoner 512. Rank: Seaman, from: John, Privateer.
    Cap: 06 Feb 1813 Lat 10.0 N, Long 61.0 W by HM Sloop Peruvian Int: 20 Feb 1813 Dis: 11 Aug 1813. Received from HM Ship Cumberland. Malmore American Cartel.

Brown, William   Prisoner 1288. Rank: Seaman, from: Mary, Merchant Schooner.
    Cap: 15 Jan 1815 Lat 22.40, Long 66 by HM Ship Pique Int: 29 Jan 1815 Dis: 14 Feb 1815.
    Received from HMS Pique. HM Ship Piqua.

Bruce, Jeremiah   Prisoner 59. Rank: Seaman, from: Providence, Privateer.
    Cap: 11 Sep 1812 off St. Barthlomew by HM Sloop Dominica Int: 13 Nov 1812 Dis: 10 Jul 1813.
    Received from HM Ship Mercury. Perseverance American Cartel.

Brumbloom, Merit   Prisoner 521. Rank: Seaman, from: John, Privateer.
    Cap: 06 Feb 1813 Lat 10.0 N, Long 61.0 W by HM Sloop Peruvian Int: 20 Feb 1813 Dis: 11 Aug 1813. Received from HM Ship Cumberland. Malmore American Cartel.

Brush, Samuel   Prisoner 851. Rank: Seaman, from: Rattle Snake, Letter of Marque.
    Cap: 11 Mar 1814 Lat 24.07 N, Long 66.47 W by HM Ship Rhin Int: 25 Mar 1814 Dis: 25 Apr 1814.
    Received from HM Ship Rhin. HM Ship Vestal.

Bryant, Lewis   Prisoner 899. Rank: Seaman, from: Hawk, Privateer.
    Cap: 26 Apr 1814 Near the Mona Passage by HM Ship Piqua Int: 20 Jun 1814 Dis: 20 Jul 1814.
    Received from HM Ship Vestal. HM Sloop Hazard Rear Adml Durham.

Buchannon, Robert   Prisoner 756. Rank: Seaman, from: Frolic, Privateer.
    Cap: 25 Jan 1814 off St Thomas by HM Sloop Heron Int: 06 Feb 1814 Dis: 25 Apr 1814.
    Received from HM Sloop Heron. HM Ship Vestal.

Buck, Edward   Prisoner 613. Rank: Seaman, from: Thomas Penrose, Privateer.
    Cap: 23 Mar 1813 Lat 20.14 W, Long 61.20 W by HM Ship Tribune Int: 28 Mar 1813 Dis: 26 Apr 1813. Received from HM Ship Tribune. America on Parole Sir F. Laforey.

Buckall, William   Prisoner 838. Rank: Seaman, from: Rattle Snake, Letter of Marque.
    Cap: 11 Mar 1814 Lat 24.07 N, Long 66.47 W by HM Ship Rhin Int: 25 Mar 1814 Dis: 25 Apr 1814.
    Received from HM Ship Rhin. HM Ship Vestal.

Buckley, William   Prisoner 988. Rank: Seaman, from: Hawk, Privateer.
    Cap: 26 Apr 1814 Near the Mona Passage by HM Ship Piqua Int: 20 Jun 1814 Dis: 22 Jul 1814.
    Received from HM Ship Vestal. HM Ship Gloucester Rear Admiral Durham.

Bunker, Nathaniel   Prisoner 20. Rank: Seaman, from: Hope, Merchant Ship.
    Cap: 27 Sep 1812 Lat 22.30 N, Long 40.45 W by HM Ship Tribune Int: 22 Oct 1812 Dis: 24 Oct 1812. Received from Ship Hope. America on Parole per order of Captain Reynolds Tribune.

Burchak, James   Prisoner 1338. Rank: Seaman, from: Vidett, Letter of Marque.
    Cap: 14 Feb 1815 off St Bartholomew by HM Ship Dasher Int: 03 Mar 1815 Dis: 31 Mar 1815.
    Received from HM Ship Dasher. Out of Custody Rear Adl Durham.

American Prisoners of War Held at Barbados During the War of 1812

Burgess, Francis   Prisoner 486. Rank: Seaman, from: John, Privateer.
    Cap: 06 Feb 1813 Lat 10.0 N, Long 61.0 W by HM Sloop Peruvian Int: 20 Feb 1813 Dis: 11 Aug 1813. Received from HM Ship Cumberland. Malmore American Cartel.

Buridge, Robert   Prisoner 480. Rank: Gunner, from: John, Privateer.
    Cap: 06 Feb 1813 Lat 10.0 N, Long 61.0 W by HM Sloop Peruvian Int: 20 Feb 1813 Dis: 11 Aug 1813. Received from HM Ship Cumberland. Malmore American Cartel.

Buriman, Herman   Prisoner 382. Rank: Seaman, from: Decatur, Privateer.
    Cap: 16 Jan 1813 Lat 13.00 N, Long 41.00 N by HM Ship Surprise Int: 26 Jan 1813 Dis: 10 Jul 1813. Received from HM Ship Surprise. Perseverance American Cartel.

Burk, Henry   Prisoner 731. Rank: Mate, from: Greyhound, Merchant Schooner.
    Cap: 13 Jan 1814 off the Virginia (not legible) by HM Schooner Elizabeth Int: 02 Feb 1814 Dis: 02 Feb 1814. Received from HM Brig Liberty. Rising States American Cartel. Rear Adml Sir F. Laforey.

Burk, Thomas   Prisoner 1115. Rank: Seaman, from: Aquila, Privateer.
    Cap: 04 Sep 1814 Lat 22 N, Long 36 W by HM Ship Piqua Int: 21 Oct 1814 Escaped: 14 Dec 1814. Received from HMS Piqua. Taken by the Whig Privateer. Escaped.

Burke, John C   Prisoner 491. Rank: Seaman, from: John, Privateer.
    Cap: 06 Feb 1813 Lat 10.0 N, Long 61.0 W by HM Sloop Peruvian Int: 20 Feb 1813 Dis: 25 Apr 1813. Received from HM Ship Cumberland. Merchant Ship for England.

Burns, John   Prisoner 1152. Rank: Seaman, from: High Flyer, Letter of Marque.
    Cap: 14 Nov 1814 off Anguilla by HM Ship Barossa Int: 18 Nov 1814 Dis: 08 Feb 1815. Received from HM Ship Barossa. HM Ship Swiftsure.

Burns, Peter   Prisoner 730. Rank: Seaman, from: Burnt, Merchant Schooner.
    Cap: 13 Jan 1814 Lat 19.35 N, Long 62.32 W by HMS Piqua Int: 02 Feb 1814 Dis: 02 Feb 1814. Received from HM Brig Liberty. Rising States American Cartel. Rear Adml Sir F. Laforey.

Burrell, Charles   Prisoner 74. Rank: Seaman, from: Providence, Privateer.
    Cap: 11 Sep 1812 off St. Barthlomew by HM Sloop Dominica Int: 13 Nov 1812 Dis: 10 Jul 1813. Received from HM Ship Mercury. Perseverance American Cartel.

Burrows, William   Prisoner 593. Rank: 1 Mate, from: Thomas Penrose, Privateer.
    Cap: 23 Mar 1813 Lat 20.14 W, Long 61.20 W by HM Ship Tribune Int: 28 Mar 1813 Dis: 26 Apr 1813. Received from HM Ship Tribune. America on Parole Sir F. Laforey.

Burt, William   Prisoner 833. Rank: Seaman, from: Rattle Snake, Letter of Marque.
    Cap: 11 Mar 1814 Lat 24.07 N, Long 66.47 W by HM Ship Rhin Int: 25 Mar 1814 Dis: 25 Apr 1814. Received from HM Ship Rhin. HM Ship Vestal.

Burton, William   Prisoner 599. Rank: Seaman, from: Thomas Penrose, Privateer.
    Cap: 23 Mar 1813 Lat 20.14 W, Long 61.20 W by HM Ship Tribune Int: 28 Mar 1813 Dis: 26 Apr 1813. Received from HM Ship Tribune. America on Parole Sir F. Laforey.

Butcher, Benjamin   Prisoner 414. Rank: Seaman, from: Apollo, Merchant Ship.
    Cap: 22 Dec 1812 off Tenioff by HM Ship Grampus Int: 30 Jan 1813 Dis: 10 Jul 1813. Received from HM Sloop Demerary. Perseverance American Cartel.

Butheir, William   Prisoner 661. Rank: Seaman, from: Adelphia, Privateer.
    Cap: 24 Feb 1813 Surinam by Not Recorded Int: 20 May 1813 Dis: 11 Aug 1813. Received from HM Sloop Crane. Part of Crew of Comet having charge of the Ship, which floundered at Sea. Surrendering themselves at Main's Point Surinam. Malmore American Cartel.

Butler, Andrew   Prisoner 782. Rank: Seaman, from: Old Friend, Not Recorded.
    Cap: 01 Jan 1814 off St. Bartholomew by Viper Privateer Int: 11 Feb 1814 Dis: 25 Apr 1814. Received from HM Brig Liberty. Retaken from the Globe Privateer. HM Ship Vestal.

Butler, Daniel   Prisoner 184. Rank: Master, from: Blockade, Privateer.
    Cap: 31 Oct 1812 off Saba by HM Sloop Charybdis Int: 19 Nov 1812 Dis: 10 Jul 1813. Received from HM Sloop Charybdis. Perseverance American Cartel.

Butler, George   Prisoner 106. Rank: Seaman, from: Diana, Merchant Brig.
    Cap: 25 Sep 1812 at Sea by HM Sloop Spider Int: 13 Nov 1812 Dis: 02 Dec 1812. Received from HM Ship Mercury. Per Order Sir F. Laforey being part of crew of a Licensed Vessel.

Butler, Levi   Prisoner 214. Rank: Seaman, from: Blockade, Privateer.
    Cap: 31 Oct 1812 off Saba by HM Sloop Charybdis Int: 19 Nov 1812 Dis: 10 Jul 1813. Received from HM Sloop Charybdis. Perseverance American Cartel.

Butman, Thomas   Prisoner 1093. Rank: Seaman, from: Engineer, Letter of Marque.
    Cap: 21 Sep 1814 of Porto Rico by HM Ship Barossa Int: 29 Sep 1814 Dis: 31 Mar 1815. Received from HM Ship Barossa. Rear Adl Durham.

Cain, James   Prisoner 309. Rank: Seaman, from: Venus, Merchant Ship.
    Cap: 15 Dec 1812 Lat 32 N, Long 54 W by HM Ship Herald Int: 31 Dec 1812 Dis: 06 Jun 1813. Received from HM Ship Herald. America on Parole Sir F. Laforey.

American Prisoners of War Held at Barbados During the War of 1812

Calder, William   Prisoner 1071. Rank: Mate, from: Engineer, Letter of Marque.
> Cap: 21 Sep 1814 of Porto Rico by HM Ship Barossa Int: 29 Sep 1814 Dis: 31 Mar 1815.
> Received from HM Ship Barossa. Rear Adl Durham.

Call, Henry P   Prisoner 542. Rank: Seaman, from: John, Privateer.
> Cap: 06 Feb 1813 Lat 10.0 N, Long 61.0 W by HM Sloop Peruvian Int: 20 Feb 1813 Dis: 11 Aug 1813. Received from HM Ship Cumberland. American Cartel Malmore.

Cameron, Archibald   Prisoner 1058. Rank: Seaman, from: Mary, Letter of Marque.
> Cap: 07 Jun 1814 La Quisa by HM Ship Heron Int: 31 Jul 1814 Dis: 31 Mar 1815.
> Received from HM Sloop Mosquito. Rear Adl Durham.

Cameron, Daniel   Prisoner 1313. Rank: Mate, from: Whalebone, Merchant Schooner.
> Cap: 25 Jan 1815 off St Bartholomew by HMB Espringle Int: 09 Feb 1815 Dis: 31 Mar 1815.
> Received from HMB Satellite. Rear Adl Durham.

Card, James   Prisoner 1025. Rank: Mate, from: North Star, Merchant Schooner.
> Cap: 10 Jun 1814 off St Bartholomew by HM Brig Crane Int: 11 Jul 1814 Dis: 22 Jul 1814.
> Received from HM Schooner Flying Fish. HM Ship Gloucester Rear Admiral Durham.

Carli, William   Prisoner 1201. Rank: Seaman, from: Fox, Privateer.
> Cap: 26 Dec 1814 off St Bartholomew by HM Brig Barbados Int: 14 Jan 1815 Dis: 08 Feb 1815.
> Received from HM Brig Barbados. HM Ship Swiftsure.

Carnes, William   Prisoner 472. Rank: Prize Master, from: John, Privateer.
> Cap: 06 Feb 1813 Lat 10.0 N, Long 61.0 W by HM Sloop Peruvian Int: 20 Feb 1813 Dis: 11 Aug 1813. Received from HM Ship Cumberland. Malmore American Cartel.

Carning, William   Prisoner 1380. Rank: Seaman, from: Laurence, Merchant.
> Cap: 14 Feb 1815 off Porto Rico by HMS Dasher Int: 04 Mar 1815 Dis: 31 Mar 1815.
> Received from HM Ship Dasher. Out of Custody Rear Adl Durham.

Carny, John   Prisoner 1227. Rank: Seaman, from: Fox, Privateer.
> Cap: 26 Dec 1814 off St Bartholomew by HM Brig Barbados Int: 14 Jan 1815 Dis: 08 Feb 1815.
> Received from HM Brig Barbados. HM Ship Swiftsure.

Carpenter, William   Prisoner 1045. Rank: Seaman, from: Mary, Letter of Marque.
> Cap: 07 Jun 1814 La Quisa by HM Ship Heron Int: 31 Jul 1814 Dis: 31 Mar 1815.
> Received from HM Sloop Mosquito. Rear Adl Durham.

Carroll, James   Prisoner 270. Rank: Seaman, from: Rea, Privateer.
> Cap: 29 Nov 1812 off Barbados by HM Ship Lightning Int: 29 Nov 1812 Dis: 10 Jul 1813.
> Received from HM Ship Lightning. Ship having been captured by the Bona American. Perseverance American Cartel.

Carter, John   Prisoner 317. Rank: Seaman, from: Dolphin, Merchant Brig.
> Cap: 15 Dec 1812 near Bermuda by HM Sloop Nimrod Int: 11 Jan 1813 Dis: 06 Jun 1813.
> Received from HM Sloop Nimrod. America on Parole Sir F. Laforey.

Carter, John   Prisoner 893. Rank: Seaman, from: Hawk, Privateer.
> Cap: 26 Apr 1814 Near the Mona Passage by HM Ship Piqua Int: 20 Jun 1814 Dis: 20 Jul 1814.
> Received from HM Ship Vestal. HM Sloop Hazard Rear Adml Durham.

Carter, John   Prisoner 1435. Rank: Seaman, from: Avon, Privateer.
> Cap: 08 Mar 1815 off Nevis by HM Sloop Barbados Int: 13 Mar 1815 Dis: 15 Mar 1815.
> Received from HM Sloop Barbados. HMS Numen Rear Admiral Durham.

Carthers, Richard   Prisoner 1331. Rank: Seaman, from: Vidett, Letter of Marque.
> Cap: 14 Feb 1815 off St Bartholomew by HM Ship Dasher Int: 03 Mar 1815 Dis: 31 Mar 1815.
> Received from HM Ship Dasher. Out of Custody Rear Adl Durham.

Cartwright, Samuel   Prisoner 713. Rank: Seaman, from: HM Sloop Grampus, Not Recorded.
> Cap: Not Recorded by Not Recorded Int: 05 Jul 1813 Dis: 11 Aug 1813.
> Received from HM Sloop Grampus. Part of Crew of HM Sloop Grampus. Malmore American Cartel.
> (Date of capture not recorded.)

Caruthers, John   Prisoner 997. Rank: Seaman, from: Hawk, Privateer.
> Cap: 26 Apr 1814 Near the Mona Passage by HM Ship Piqua Int: 20 Jun 1814 Dis: 22 Jul 1814.
> Received from HM Ship Vestal. HM Ship Gloucester Rear Admiral Durham.

Caryle, Lawson   Prisoner 1412. Rank: Seaman, from: Avon, Privateer.
> Cap: 08 Mar 1815 off Nevis by HM Sloop Barbados Int: 13 Mar 1815 Dis: 15 Mar 1815.
> Received from HM Sloop Barbados. HMS Numen Rear Admiral Durham.

Cassiday, John   Prisoner 1411. Rank: Seaman, from: Avon, Privateer.
> Cap: 08 Mar 1815 off Nevis by HM Sloop Barbados Int: 13 Mar 1815 Dis: 15 Mar 1815.
> Received from HM Sloop Barbados. HMS Numen Rear Admiral Durham.

Cassise, James   Prisoner 1333. Rank: Seaman, from: Vidett, Letter of Marque.
> Cap: 14 Feb 1815 off St Bartholomew by HM Ship Dasher Int: 03 Mar 1815 Dis: 31 Mar 1815.
> Received from HM Ship Dasher. Out of Custody Rear Adl Durham.

American Prisoners of War Held at Barbados During the War of 1812

Caswell, John R   Prisoner 4. Rank: Mate, from: Orpha, Merchant Sloop.
    Cap: 02 Sep 1812 off Porto Rico by HM Sloop Ringdove Int: 25 Sep 1812 Dis: 24 Oct 1812.
    Received from HM Sloop Ringdove. America on Parole per order of Captain Reynolds Tribune.

Caswell, Richard B   Prisoner 504. Rank: Seaman, from: John, Privateer.
    Cap: 06 Feb 1813 Lat 10.0 N, Long 61.0 W by HM Sloop Peruvian Int: 20 Feb 1813 Dis: 11 Aug 1813. Received from HM Ship Cumberland. Malmore American Cartel.

Cathell, William   Prisoner 454. Rank: Prize Master, from: Bowrey, Privateer.
    Cap: 02 Feb 1813 off Barbados by HM Sloop Opossum Int: 18 Feb 1813 Dis: 10 Jul 1813.
    Received from HM Sloop Opossum. English Brig Captured by the American Comet. Perseverance American Cartel.

Catlage, William   Prisoner 1001. Rank: Seaman, from: Hawk, Privateer.
    Cap: 26 Apr 1814 Near the Mona Passage by HM Ship Piqua Int: 20 Jun 1814 Dis: 22 Jul 1814.
    Received from HM Ship Vestal. HM Ship Gloucester Rear Admiral Durham.

Cave, Matthew   Prisoner 1263. Rank: Seaman, from: Fox, Privateer.
    Cap: 26 Dec 1814 off St Bartholomew by HM Brig Barbados Int: 14 Jan 1815 Dis: 08 Feb 1815.
    Received from HM Brig Barbados. HM Ship Swiftsure.

Cegg, Phillip   Prisoner 249. Rank: Seaman, from: Maxwell, Not Recorded.
    Cap: Not Recorded by Not Recorded Int: 22 Nov 1812 Dis: 25 Jun 1813.
    Received from HM Ship Dragon. Part of Crew of Ship Maxwell taken out in consequence of being mutinous. Merchant Ship for England. (Date of capture not recorded.)

Chabeau, Point   Prisoner 1222. Rank: Seaman, from: Fox, Privateer.
    Cap: 26 Dec 1814 off St Bartholomew by HM Brig Barbados Int: 14 Jan 1815 Dis: 08 Feb 1815.
    Received from HM Brig Barbados. HM Ship Swiftsure.

Chadwick, Seth   Prisoner 674. Rank: Mate, from: Sterling, Merchant Ship.
    Cap: 19 May 1813 Lat 22.00 N, Long 53.00 W by HM Ship Grampus Int: 26 May 1813 Dis: 05 Jun 1813. Received from HM Ship Grampus. America on Parole Sir F. Laforey.

Chanders, Dublin   Prisoner 686. Rank: Seaman, from: Sterling, Merchant Ship.
    Cap: 19 May 1813 Lat 22.00 N, Long 53.00 W by HM Ship Grampus Int: 26 May 1813 Dis: 11 Aug 1813. Received from HM Ship Grampus. Malmore American Cartel.

Chapman, James   Prisoner 864. Rank: Seaman, from: Perseverance, Mechant.
    Cap: 15 Feb 1814 St Thomas by HM Ship Amaranthe Int: 26 Mar 1814 Dis: 25 Apr 1814.
    HM Ship Vestal.

Chapman, James   Prisoner 966. Rank: Seaman, from: Maria, Merchant.
    Cap: 20 Mar 1814 off St Bartholomew by HM Sloop Charybdis Int: 20 Jun 1814 Dis: 22 Jul 1814.
    Received from HM Ship Vestal. HM Ship Gloucester Rear Admiral Durham.

Chapman, John   Prisoner 527. Rank: Seaman, from: John, Privateer.
    Cap: 06 Feb 1813 Lat 10.0 N, Long 61.0 W by HM Sloop Peruvian Int: 20 Feb 1813 Dis: 11 Aug 1813. Received from HM Ship Cumberland. Malmore American Cartel.

Chapman, Stephen   Prisoner 479. Rank: Mate, from: John, Privateer.
    Cap: 06 Feb 1813 Lat 10.0 N, Long 61.0 W by HM Sloop Peruvian Int: 20 Feb 1813 Dis: 11 Aug 1813. Received from HM Ship Cumberland. Malmore American Cartel.

Chase, A   Prisoner 1427. Rank: Seaman, from: Avon, Privateer.
    Cap: 08 Mar 1815 off Nevis by HM Sloop Barbados Int: 13 Mar 1815 Dis: 15 Mar 1815.
    Received from HM Sloop Barbados. HMS Numen Rear Admiral Durham.

Chase, Benjamin   Prisoner 475. Rank: Prize Master, from: John, Privateer.
    Cap: 06 Feb 1813 Lat 10.0 N, Long 61.0 W by HM Sloop Peruvian Int: 20 Feb 1813 Dis: 10 Apr 1813. Received from HM Ship Cumberland. America on Parole being very ill.

Chaviens, Sidney   Prisoner 203. Rank: Seaman, from: Blockade, Privateer.
    Cap: 31 Oct 1812 off Saba by HM Sloop Charybdis Int: 19 Nov 1812 Dis: 10 Jul 1813.
    Received from HM Sloop Charybdis. Perseverance American Cartel.

Cheve, Daniel   Prisoner 464. Rank: Prize Master, from: John, Privateer.
    Cap: 06 Feb 1813 Lat 10.0 N, Long 61.0 W by HM Sloop Peruvian Int: 18 Feb 1813 Died: 20 Feb 1813. Received from HM Ship Cumberland. Died at the Naval Hospital.

Cinnan, Joseph   Prisoner 616. Rank: Seaman, from: Sudfrost, Not Recorded.
    Cap: Not Recorded by Not Recorded Int: 30 Mar 1813 Dis: 11 Aug 1813.
    Received from HM Ship Frolic. Part of Crew of Ship Sudfrost. Malmore American Cartel. (Date of capture not recorded.)

Clallow, William   Prisoner 1013. Rank: Seaman, from: William, Merchant.
    Cap: 18 May 1814 off Charleston by HM Ship Ister Int: 21 Jun 1814 Dis: 22 Jul 1814.
    Received from HM Ship Vestal. HM Ship Gloucester Rear Adml Durham.

Clark, Benjamin   Prisoner 406. Rank: Seaman, from: Decatur, Privateer.
    Cap: 16 Jan 1813 Lat 13.00 N, Long 41.00 N by HM Ship Surprise Int: 26 Jan 1813 Dis: 10 Jul 1813.
    Received from HM Ship Surprise. Perseverance American Cartel.

American Prisoners of War Held at Barbados During the War of 1812

Clark, George   Prisoner 199. Rank: Seaman, from: Blockade, Privateer.
    Cap: 31 Oct 1812 off Saba by HM Sloop Charybdis Int: 19 Nov 1812 Dis: 10 Jul 1813.
    Received from HM Sloop Charybdis. Perseverance American Cartel.

Clark, John   Prisoner 137. Rank: Prize Master, from: Yankee, Privateer.
    Cap: 25 Oct 1812 off Sombero by HM Sloop Peruvian Int: 13 Nov 1812 Dis: 10 Jul 1813.
    Received from HM Ship Mercury. Perseverance American Cartel.

Clarke, Barney   Prisoner 1305. Rank: Seaman, from: Mary, Merchant Schooner.
    Cap: 15 Jan 1815 Lat 22.40, Long 66 by HM Ship Pique Int: 29 Jan 1815 Dis: 14 Feb 1815.
    Received from HMS Pique. HM Ship Piqua.

Clarke, David   Prisoner 1048. Rank: Seaman, from: Mary, Letter of Marque.
    Cap: 07 Jun 1814 La Quisa by HM Ship Heron Int: 31 Jul 1814 Dis: 31 Mar 1815.
    Received from HM Sloop Mosquito. Rear Adl Durham.

Clarke, James   Prisoner 235. Rank: Seaman, from: Blockade, Privateer.
    Cap: 31 Oct 1812 off Saba by HM Sloop Charybdis Int: 19 Nov 1812 Dis: 10 Jul 1813.
    Received from HM Sloop Charybdis. Perseverance American Cartel.

Clarke, James   Prisoner 1302. Rank: Seaman, from: Mary, Merchant Schooner.
    Cap: 15 Jan 1815 Lat 22.40, Long 66 by HM Ship Pique Int: 29 Jan 1815 Dis: 14 Feb 1815.
    Received from HMS Pique. HM Ship Piqua.

Clarke, Rubin   Prisoner 1296. Rank: Seaman, from: Mary, Merchant Schooner.
    Cap: 15 Jan 1815 Lat 22.40, Long 66 by HM Ship Pique Int: 29 Jan 1815 Dis: 14 Feb 1815.
    Received from HMS Pique. HM Ship Piqua.

Clarke, Thomas   Prisoner 620. Rank: Seaman, from: HM Ship Venus, Not Recorded.
    Cap: Not Recorded by Not Recorded Int: 02 Apr 1813 Dis: 11 Aug 1813.
    Received from HM Ship Venus. Part of Crew of HMS Venus. Malmore American Cartel. Malmore American Cartel. (Date of capture not recorded.)

Clarke, William   Prisoner 650. Rank: Seaman, from: William, Merchant Ship.
    Cap: Trinidad by HM Brig Liberty Int: 20 May 1813 Dis: 11 Aug 1813.
    Received from HM Sloop Crane. Taken from the English Ship William. Malmore American Cartel. (Date of capture not recorded.)

Class, Peter   Prisoner 308. Rank: Seaman, from: Venus, Merchant Ship.
    Cap: 15 Dec 1812 Lat 32 N, Long 54 W by HM Ship Herald Int: 31 Dec 1812 Dis: 06 Jun 1813.
    Received from HM Ship Herald. America on Parole Sir F. Laforey.

Claxton, Robert   Prisoner 758. Rank: Seaman, from: Frolic, Privateer.
    Cap: 25 Jan 1814 off St Thomas by HM Sloop Heron Int: 06 Feb 1814 Dis: 25 Apr 1814.
    Received from HM Sloop Heron. HM Ship Vestal.

Cleaves, Nathaniel   Prisoner 569. Rank: Prize Master, from: John, Privateer.
    Cap: 06 Feb 1813 Lat 10 N, Long 61 W by HM Sloop Peruvian Int: 08 Mar 1813 Dis: 11 Aug 1813.
    Received from HM Sloop Arachne. Malmore American Cartel.

Clemons, Samuuel   Prisoner 748. Rank: Seaman, from: Frolic, Privateer.
    Cap: 25 Jan 1814 off St Thomas by HM Sloop Heron Int: 06 Feb 1814 Dis: 25 Apr 1814.
    Received from HM Sloop Heron. HM Ship Vestal Rear Admiral Durham.

Clerge, Nicholas   Prisoner 1212. Rank: Seaman, from: Fox, Privateer.
    Cap: 26 Dec 1814 off St Bartholomew by HM Brig Barbados Int: 14 Jan 1815 Dis: 08 Feb 1815.
    Received from HM Brig Barbados. HM Ship Swiftsure.

Cleveland, David   Prisoner 253. Rank: Mate, from: Brandy Wine, Merchant Brig.
    Cap: 17 Nov 1812 Lat 19.30, Long 57.00 W by HM Ship Lightning Int: 23 Nov 1812 Dis: 02 Dec 1812. Received from HM Ship Lightning. America on Parole Sir F. Laforey.

Cliff, Thomas   Prisoner 537. Rank: Seaman, from: John, Privateer.
    Cap: 06 Feb 1813 Lat 10.0 N, Long 61.0 W by HM Sloop Peruvian Int: 20 Feb 1813 Dis: 11 Aug 1813. Received from HM Ship Cumberland. American Cartel Malmore.

Clinton, Ebenezer   Prisoner 427. Rank: Mate, from: Ocean, Merchant Schooner.
    Cap: 15 Aug 1812 Martinique by Detained at Martinique Int: 05 Feb 1813 Dis:
    Received from HM Ship Vestal. Carried to Sea in HM Ship Vestal through mistake the 12th Instant (not legible) up to. Reentry (549). (Date of discharge not recorded.)

Clinton, Ebenezer   Prisoner 549. Rank: Mate, from: Ocean, Merchant Brig.
    Cap: 15 Aug 1812 Martinique by Detained at Martinique Int: 05 Feb 1813 Dis: 10 Apr 1813.
    Received from HM Ship Vestal. America on Parole Sir F. Laforey.

Clossmann, P   Prisoner 1073. Rank: Supercargo, from: Engineer, Letter of Marque.
    Cap: 21 Sep 1814 of Porto Rico by HM Ship Barossa Int: 29 Sep 1814 Dis: 14 Oct 1814.
    Received from HM Ship Barossa. Out of Custody being a noncombatant.

Clough, Samuel   Prisoner 476. Rank: Prize Master, from: John, Privateer.
    Cap: 06 Feb 1813 Lat 10.0 N, Long 61.0 W by HM Sloop Peruvian Int: 20 Feb 1813 Dis: 11 Aug 1813. Received from HM Ship Cumberland. Malmore American Cartel.

American Prisoners of War Held at Barbados During the War of 1812

Coale, James   Prisoner 154. Rank: Seaman, from: Yankee, Privateer.
    Cap: 25 Oct 1812 off Sombero by HM Sloop Peruvian Int: 13 Nov 1812 Dis: 10 Jul 1813.
    Received from HM Ship Mercury. Perseverance American Cartel.

Coburne, Miles   Prisoner 705. Rank: Seaman, from: Saturn, Merchant Brig.
    Cap: 10 May 1813 off Martinique by HM Ship Mercury Int: 17 Jun 1813 Dis: 11 Aug 1813.
    Received from HM Ship Mercury. Malmore American Cartel.

Coffin, Able   Prisoner 343. Rank: Prize Master, from: Decatur, Privateer.
    Cap: 16 Jan 1813 Lat 13.00 N, Long 41.00 N by HM Ship Surprise Int: 26 Jan 1813 Dis: 10 Jul 1813.
    Received from HM Ship Surprise. Perseverance American Cartel.

Coffin, Benjamin   Prisoner 28. Rank: Seaman, from: Hope, Merchant Ship.
    Cap: 27 Sep 1812 Lat 22.30 N, Long 40.45 by HM Sloop Tribune Int: 22 Oct 1812 Dis: 24 Oct 1812.
    Received from HM Sloop Tribune. America on Parole per order of Captain Reynolds Tribune.

Coffin, Robert S   Prisoner 1174. Rank: Seaman, from: Dolphin, Letter of Marque.
    Cap: 04 Dec 1814 Lat 18.00 N, Long 60.00 W by HM Brig Columbia Int: 08 Dec 1814 Dis: 14 Feb 1815. Received from HM Brig Columbia. HM Ship Piqua.

Cohoon, Isaiah   Prisoner 571. Rank: Master, from: St Bartholomew, Merchant Brig.
    Cap: 05 Mar 1813 Carlisle Bay by HM Ship Cumberland Int: 10 Mar 1813 Dis: 13 Mar 1813.
    Received from HM Ship Cumberland. America on Parole Sir Francis Laforey.

Cole, James   Prisoner 363. Rank: Seaman, from: Decatur, Privateer.
    Cap: 16 Jan 1813 Lat 13.00 N, Long 41.00 N by HM Ship Surprise Int: 26 Jan 1813 Dis: 10 Jul 1813.
    Received from HM Ship Surprise. Perseverance American Cartel.

Cole, Nathaniel   Prisoner 1340. Rank: Seaman, from: Vidett, Letter of Marque.
    Cap: 14 Feb 1815 off St Bartholomew by HM Ship Dasher Int: 03 Mar 1815 Dis: 31 Mar 1815.
    Received from HM Ship Dasher. Out of Custody Rear Adl Durham.

Cole, Stephen   Prisoner 115. Rank: Seaman, from: William Rathbone, Brig.
    Cap: 09 Oct 1812 at Sea by HM Sloop Charybdis Int: 13 Nov 1812 Dis: 23 Apr 1813.
    Received from HM Ship Mercury. Retaken Brig Part of Crew of Savory Jack Privateer. HM Ship Tribune. Not to be exchanged during the War having behaved in a wanton riotous and infamous manner.

Cole, Thomas   Prisoner 113. Rank: Seaman, from: William Rathbone, Brig.
    Cap: 09 Oct 1812 at Sea by HM Sloop Charybdis Int: 13 Nov 1812 Escaped: 24 Apr 1813.
    Received from HM Ship Mercury. Retaken Brig Part of Crew of Savory Jack Privateer. Escaped. (Not legible) upon the guard.

Coleman, Charles   Prisoner 1357. Rank: Seaman, from: Spencer, Merchant.
    Cap: 15 Feb 1815 off St Bartholomew by HMS Dasher Int: 03 Mar 1815 Dis: 31 Mar 1815.
    Received from HM Ship Dasher. Out of Custody Rear Adl Durham.

Coleman, Christopher   Prisoner 1138. Rank: Mate, from: High Flyer, Letter of Marque.
    Cap: 14 Nov 1814 off Anguilla by HM Ship Barossa Int: 18 Nov 1814 Dis: 31 Mar 1815.
    Received from HM Ship Barossa. Rear Adl Durham.

Coleman, William   Prisoner 897. Rank: Seaman, from: Hawk, Privateer.
    Cap: 26 Apr 1814 Near the Mona Passage by HM Ship Piqua Int: 20 Jun 1814 Dis: 20 Jul 1814.
    Received from HM Ship Vestal. HM Sloop Hazard Rear Adml Durham.

Collins, John   Prisoner 1432. Rank: Seaman, from: Avon, Privateer.
    Cap: 08 Mar 1815 off Nevis by HM Sloop Barbados Int: 13 Mar 1815 Dis: 15 Mar 1815.
    Received from HM Sloop Barbados. HMS Numen Rear Admiral Durham.

Collins, Stephen   Prisoner 823. Rank: Seaman, from: HMS Mydus, Not Recorded.
    Cap: Not Recorded by Not Recorded Int: 07 Mar 1814 Escaped: 26 Mar 1814.
    Received from HM Ship Piqua. Part of Crew of HMS Mydus. Escaped from Naval Hospital. (Date of capture not recorded.)

Combs, William   Prisoner 17. Rank: Seaman, from: Shepherdess, Merchant Schooner.
    Cap: 12 Oct 1812 Lat 20.00 N, Long 56.00 W by HM Sloop Lightning Int: 22 Oct 1812 Dis: 24 Oct 1812. Received from HM Sloop Lightning. America on Parole per order of Captain Reynolds Tribune.

Compeche, S Yaga   Prisoner 953. Rank: Seaman, from: President, Privateer.
    Cap: 07 May 1814 off Porto Rico by HM Ship Piqua Int: 20 Jun 1814 Dis: 22 Jul 1814.
    Received from HM Ship Vestal. HM Ship Gloucester Rear Admiral Durham.

Compstock, Stephen   Prisoner 1053. Rank: Seaman, from: Mary, Letter of Marque.
    Cap: 07 Jun 1814 La Quisa by HM Ship Heron Int: 31 Jul 1814 Dis: 31 Mar 1815.
    Received from HM Sloop Mosquito. Rear Adl Durham.

Condon, Joseph   Prisoner 105. Rank: Seaman, from: Diana, Merchant Brig.
    Cap: 25 Sep 1812 at Sea by HM Sloop Spider Int: 13 Nov 1812 Dis: 02 Dec 1812.
    Received from HM Ship Mercury. Per Order Sir F. Laforey being part of crew of a Licensed Vessel.

American Prisoners of War Held at Barbados During the War of 1812

Connor, Galen   Prisoner 878. Rank: Mate, from: Not Recorded, Merchant.
    Cap: 31 Jan 1814 Lat 18.04 N, Long 59.00 W by HM Brig Barbados Int: 18 Apr 1814 Dis: 22 Jul 1814. Received from HM Ship Vestal. HM Ship Gloucester Rear Admiral Durham.

Connor, Peter   Prisoner 1147. Rank: Seaman, from: High Flyer, Letter of Marque.
    Cap: 14 Nov 1814 off Anguilla by HM Ship Barossa Int: 18 Nov 1814 Dis: 14 Feb 1815. Received from HM Ship Barossa. HM Ship Piqua Rear Admiral Durham.

Cony, Hudson   Prisoner 1447. Rank: Seaman, from: Ivan Francisco, Not Recorded.
    Cap: 08 Mar 1815 off Nevis by HM Brig Muros Int: 26 Mar 1815 Dis: 31 Mar 1815. Received from HM Brig Maria. Recaptured from the Grand Turk Privateer. Out of Custody Rear Adl Durham.

Cook, Aaron   Prisoner 233. Rank: Seaman, from: Blockade, Privateer.
    Cap: 31 Oct 1812 off Saba by HM Sloop Charybdis Int: 19 Nov 1812 Dis: 10 Jul 1813. Received from HM Sloop Charybdis. Perseverance American Cartel.

Cook, Aaron   Prisoner 868. Rank: Seaman, from: Not Recorded, Not Recorded.
    Cap: Not Recorded by Not Recorded Int: 04 Apr 1814 Dis: 15 Apr 1814. Received from HM Ship Rhin, Escaped from Prison at Halifax. HM Ship Hydra having volunteered for the British Navy Rear Adml Durham. (Date of capture not recorded.)

Cook, Benjamin   Prisoner 134. Rank: Master, from: Yankee, Privateer.
    Cap: 25 Oct 1812 off Sombero by HM Sloop Peruvian Int: 13 Nov 1812 Dis: 10 Jul 1813. Received from HM Ship Mercury. Perseverance American Cartel.

Cook, C   Prisoner 1402. Rank: Masters Mate, from: Avon, Privateer.
    Cap: 08 Mar 1815 off Nevis by HM Sloop Barbados Int: 13 Mar 1815 Dis: 15 Mar 1815. Received from HM Sloop Barbados. HMS Numen Rear Admiral Durham.

Cook, Francis   Prisoner 1306. Rank: Seaman, from: Mary, Merchant Schooner.
    Cap: 15 Jan 1815 Lat 22.40, Long 66 by HM Ship Pique Int: 29 Jan 1815 Dis: 14 Feb 1815. Received from HMS Pique. HM Ship Piqua.

Cook, John   Prisoner 678. Rank: Seaman, from: Sterling, Merchant Ship.
    Cap: 19 May 1813 Lat 22.00 N, Long 53.00 W by HM Ship Grampus Int: 26 May 1813 Dis: 11 Aug 1813. Received from HM Ship Grampus. Malmore American Cartel.

Cooley, William   Prisoner 183. Rank: Surgeon, from: Blockade, Privateer.
    Cap: 31 Oct 1812 off Saba by HM Sloop Charybdis Int: 19 Nov 1812 Dis: 02 Dec 1812. Received from HM Sloop Charybdis. Per Order Sr. F. Laforey being a non Combatant.

Coomais, Henry   Prisoner 1054. Rank: Seaman, from: Mary, Letter of Marque.
    Cap: 07 Jun 1814 La Quisa by HM Ship Heron Int: 31 Jul 1814 Dis: 08 Feb 1815. Received from HM Sloop Mosquito. HM Ship Swiftsure.

Coon, Caesar   Prisoner 371. Rank: Seaman, from: Decatur, Privateer.
    Cap: 16 Jan 1813 Lat 13.00 N, Long 41.00 N by HM Ship Surprise Int: 26 Jan 1813 Dis: 10 Jul 1813. Received from HM Ship Surprise. Perseverance American Cartel.

Copper, William   Prisoner 985. Rank: Seaman, from: John, Merchant Schooner.
    Cap: Not Recorded by Not Recorded Int: 20 Jun 1814 Dis: 22 Jul 1814. Received from HM Ship Vestal. Part of Crew of English Merchant Schooner John. HM Ship Gloucester Rear Admiral Durham. (Date of capture not recorded.)

Copps, Darius   Prisoner 160. Rank: Seaman, from: Yankee, Privateer.
    Cap: 25 Oct 1812 off Sombero by HM Sloop Peruvian Int: 13 Nov 1812 Dis: 10 Jul 1813. Received from HM Ship Mercury. Perseverance American Cartel. Cut through the Ship escaped. Retaken immediately.

Corinth, Henry   Prisoner 385. Rank: Seaman, from: Decatur, Privateer.
    Cap: 16 Jan 1813 Lat 13.00 N, Long 41.00 N by HM Ship Surprise Int: 26 Jan 1813 Dis: 10 Jul 1813. Received from HM Ship Surprise. Perseverance American Cartel.

Corwin, Thomas   Prisoner 998. Rank: Seaman, from: Hawk, Privateer.
    Cap: 26 Apr 1814 Near the Mona Passage by HM Ship Piqua Int: 20 Jun 1814 Dis: 22 Jul 1814. Received from HM Ship Vestal. HM Ship Gloucester Rear Admiral Durham.

Cottle, John   Prisoner 634. Rank: Mate, from: Active, Merchant Ship.
    Cap: 23 Feb 1813 off St Bartholomew by HM Ship Surprise Int: 11 Apr 1813 Dis: 18 Apr 1813. Received from HM Schooner Elizabeth. America on Parole Sir F. Laforey.

Coulfrey, Robert   Prisoner 682. Rank: Seaman, from: Sterling, Merchant Ship.
    Cap: 19 May 1813 Lat 22.00 N, Long 53.00 W by HM Ship Grampus Int: 26 May 1813 Dis: 11 Aug 1813. Received from HM Ship Grampus. Malmore American Cartel.

Courroix, Jean   Prisoner 1441. Rank: Seaman, from: Avon, Privateer.
    Cap: 08 Mar 1815 off Nevis by HM Sloop Barbados Int: 13 Mar 1815 Dis: 15 Mar 1815. Received from HM Sloop Barbados. HMS Numen Rear Admiral Durham.

American Prisoners of War Held at Barbados During the War of 1812

Cousins, John   Prisoner 412. Rank: Seaman, from: Apollo, Merchant Ship.
    Cap: 22 Dec 1812 off Tenioff by HM Ship Grampus Int: 30 Jan 1813 Dis: 10 Jul 1813.
    Received from HM Sloop Demerary. Perseverance American Cartel.

Cowslip, Charles   Prisoner 709. Rank: Seaman, from: Emma, Not Recorded.
    Cap: Not Recorded by Not Recorded Int: 01 Jul 1813 Dis: 11 Aug 1813.
    Received from Emma Army Ship. Part of Crew of Army Ship Emma. Malmore American Cartel. (Date of capture not recorded.)

Craft, Thomas   Prisoner 488. Rank: Seaman, from: John, Privateer.
    Cap: 06 Feb 1813 Lat 10.0 N, Long 61.0 W by HM Sloop Peruvian Int: 20 Feb 1813 Dis: 11 Aug 1813. Received from HM Ship Cumberland. Malmore American Cartel.

Craig, Alexander   Prisoner 117. Rank: Seaman, from: William Rathbone, Brig.
    Cap: 09 Oct 1812 at Sea by HM Sloop Charybdis Int: 13 Nov 1812 Dis: 10 Jul 1813.
    Received from HM Ship Mercury. Retaken Brig Part of Crew of Savory Jack Privateer. Perseverance American Cartel.

Craiss, John E   Prisoner 965. Rank: Surgeon, from: President, Privateer.
    Cap: 07 May 1814 off Porto Rico by HM Ship Piqua Int: 20 Jun 1814 Dis: 22 Jul 1814.
    Received from HM Ship Piqua. HM Ship Gloucester Rear Admiral Durham.

Craps, James   Prisoner 456. Rank: Seaman, from: Bowrey, Privateer.
    Cap: 02 Feb 1813 off Barbados by HM Sloop Opossum Int: 18 Feb 1813 Dis: 23 Apr 1813.
    Received from HM Sloop Opossum. English Brig Captured by the American Comet. Escaped. (not legible). This man escaped from (not legible). Tribune for passage to England.

Crawford, John   Prisoner 1261. Rank: Seaman, from: Fox, Privateer.
    Cap: 26 Dec 1814 off St Bartholomew by HM Brig Barbados Int: 14 Jan 1815 Dis: 08 Feb 1815.
    Received from HM Brig Barbados. HM Ship Swiftsure.

Cricall, South   Prisoner 832. Rank: Seaman, from: Rattle Snake, Letter of Marque.
    Cap: 11 Mar 1814 Lat 24.07 N, Long 66.47 W by HM Ship Rhin Int: 25 Mar 1814 Dis: 25 Apr 1814.
    Received from HM Ship Rhin. HM Ship Vestal.

Croaker, Edward   Prisoner 1205. Rank: Seaman, from: Fox, Privateer.
    Cap: 26 Dec 1814 off St Bartholomew by HM Brig Barbados Int: 14 Jan 1815 Dis: 08 Feb 1815.
    Received from HM Brig Barbados. HM Ship Swiftsure.

Crofton, Henry   Prisoner 67. Rank: Seaman, from: Providence, Privateer.
    Cap: 11 Sep 1812 off St. Barthlomew by HM Sloop Dominica Int: 13 Nov 1812 Dis: 10 Jul 1813.
    Received from HM Ship Mercury. Perseverance American Cartel.

Cross, John   Prisoner 1278. Rank: Seaman, from: Hero, Merchant Schooner.
    Cap: 14 Dec 1814 Lat 19.13, Long 64 by HMS Pique Int: 29 Jan 1815 Died: 25 Mar 1815.
    Received from HMS Pique. Died.

Crow, Robert   Prisoner 1315. Rank: Seaman, from: Whalebone, Merchant Schooner.
    Cap: 25 Jan 1815 off St Bartholomew by HMB Espringle Int: 09 Feb 1815 Dis: 31 Mar 1815.
    Received from HMB Satellite. Rear Adl Durham.

Crowder, John   Prisoner 96. Rank: Seaman, from: Dragon, Not Recorded.
    Cap: Not Recorded by Not Recorded Int: 13 Nov 1812 Dis: 10 Jul 1813.
    Received from HM Ship Mercury. Part of the crew of the Ship Dragon. Perseverance American Cartel. (Date of capture not recorded.)

Crowell, Prentiss   Prisoner 1133. Rank: Mate, from: Clio, Merchant Schooner.
    Cap: 13 Nov 1814 off Anguilla by HM Ship Barossa Int: 18 Nov 1814 Dis: 31 Mar 1815.
    Received from HM Ship Barossa. Rear Adl Durham.

Cruff, Tobias   Prisoner 492. Rank: Seaman, from: John, Privateer.
    Cap: 06 Feb 1813 Lat 10.0 N, Long 61.0 W by HM Sloop Peruvian Int: 20 Feb 1813 Dis: 11 Aug 1813. Received from HM Ship Cumberland. Malmore American Cartel.

Crumbley, Benjamin   Prisoner 1445. Rank: Seaman, from: Ivan Francisco, Not Recorded.
    Cap: 08 Mar 1815 off Nevis by HM Brig Muros Int: 26 Mar 1815 Dis: 31 Mar 1815.
    Received from HM Brig Maria. Recaptured from the Grand Turk Privateer. Out of Custody Rear Adl Durham.

Cullin, Thomas   Prisoner 1052. Rank: Seaman, from: Mary, Letter of Marque.
    Cap: 07 Jun 1814 La Quisa by HM Ship Heron Int: 31 Jul 1814 Dis: 08 Feb 1814.
    Received from HM Sloop Mosquito. Riotous Character HM Ship Swiftsure.

Cunie, Horace   Prisoner 1086. Rank: Seaman, from: Engineer, Letter of Marque.
    Cap: 21 Sep 1814 of Porto Rico by HM Ship Barossa Int: 29 Sep 1814 Dis: 08 Feb 1815.
    Received from HM Ship Barossa. HM Ship Swiftsure.

Curriel, Henry   Prisoner 1429. Rank: Seaman, from: Avon, Privateer.
    Cap: 08 Mar 1815 off Nevis by HM Sloop Barbados Int: 13 Mar 1815 Dis: 15 Mar 1815.
    Received from HM Sloop Barbados. HMS Numen Rear Admiral Durham.

American Prisoners of War Held at Barbados During the War of 1812

Curtis, John   Prisoner 102. Rank: Seaman, from: Jane, Merchant Brig.
    Cap: 25 Sep 1812 at Sea by HM Sloop Spider Int: 13 Nov 1812 Dis: 17 Nov 1812.
    Received from HM Ship Mercury. Out of Custody per order of Sir F. Laforey being crew of a licensed vessel.

Cushing, Chance   Prisoner 80. Rank: Seaman, from: Providence, Privateer.
    Cap: 11 Sep 1812 off St. Barthlomew by HM Sloop Dominica Int: 13 Nov 1812 Dis: 10 Jul 1813.
    Received from HM Ship Mercury. Perseverance American Cartel.

Cushion, Nathaniel   Prisoner 344. Rank: Seaman, from: Decatur, Privateer.
    Cap: 16 Jan 1813 Lat 13.00 N, Long 41.00 N by HM Ship Surprise Int: 26 Jan 1813 Dis: 10 Jul 1813.
    Received from HM Ship Surprise. Perseverance American Cartel.

Dale, Arthur   Prisoner 1353. Rank: Seaman, from: Vidett, Letter of Marque.
    Cap: 14 Feb 1815 off St Bartholomew by HMS Dasher Int: 03 Mar 1815 Dis: 31 Mar 1815.
    Received from HM Ship Dasher. Out of Custody Rear Adl Durham.

Dale, John   Prisoner 873. Rank: Seaman, from: Camilla, Not Recorded.
    Cap: 29 Mar 1814 Sombrero Passage by HM Ship Ister Int: 15 Apr 1814 Dis: 25 Apr 1814.
    Received from HM Ship Ister. Recaptured from Fairy Privateer. HM Ship Vestal.

Dale, John   Prisoner 973. Rank: Seaman, from: Fairy, Privateer.
    Cap: 20 Mar 1814 off Saba by HM Ship Ister Int: 20 Jun 1814 Dis: 22 Jul 1814.
    Received from HM Ship Vestal. HM Ship Gloucester Rear Admiral Durham. (Apparent duplicate of # 873.)

Dame, John   Prisoner 894. Rank: Seaman, from: Hawk, Privateer.
    Cap: 26 Apr 1814 Near the Mona Passage by HM Ship Piqua Int: 20 Jun 1814 Dis: 22 Jul 1814.
    Received from HM Ship Vestal. HM Ship Gloucester Rear Admiral Durham.

Daniels, Nathaniel   Prisoner 799. Rank: Seaman, from: Kirran, Merchant Brig.
    Cap: 25 Jan 1814 off Saint Bartholomew by HM Brig Barbados Int: 12 Feb 1814 Dis: 25 Apr 1814.
    Received from HM Schooner Ballahou. HM Ship Vestal.

Dau, George   Prisoner 1125. Rank: Seaman, from: Nancy, Privateer.
    Cap: 06 Sep 1814 Lat 32 N, Long 47 W by HM Ship Piqua Int: 21 Oct 1814 Dis: 31 Mar 1815.
    Received from HMS Piqua. Taken by the Amelia Privateer. Rear Adl Durham.

Davis, Benjamin   Prisoner 1398. Rank: Prize Master, from: Avon, Privateer.
    Cap: 08 Mar 1815 off Nevis by HM Sloop Barbados Int: 13 Mar 1815 Dis: 15 Mar 1815.
    Received from HM Sloop Barbados. HMS Numen Rear Admiral Durham.

Davis, Francis   Prisoner 1114. Rank: Prize Master, from: Aquila, Privateer.
    Cap: 04 Sep 1814 Lat 22 N, Long 36 W by HM Ship Piqua Int: 21 Oct 1814 Dis: 08 Feb 1815.
    Received from HMS Piqua. Taken by the Whig Privateer. HMS Swiftsure escaped and Retaken immediately on the 24th January 1815.

Davis, George   Prisoner 926. Rank: Seaman, from: President, Privateer.
    Cap: 07 May 1814 off Porto Rico by HM Ship Piqua Int: 20 Jun 1814 Dis: 20 Jul 1814.
    Received from HM Ship Vestal. HM Sloop Hazard Rear Adml Durham.

Davis, John   Prisoner 123. Rank: Seaman, from: William Rathbone, Brig.
    Cap: 09 Oct 1812 at Sea by HM Sloop Charybdis Int: 13 Nov 1812 Dis: 10 Jul 1813.
    Received from HM Ship Mercury. Retaken Brig Part of Crew of Savory Jack Privateer. Perseverance American Cartel.

Davis, John   Prisoner 250. Rank: Seaman, from: Emma, Not Recorded.
    Cap: Not Recorded by Not Recorded Int: 22 Nov 1812 Escaped: 29 Mar 1813.
    Received from Emma. Part of Crew of Army Ship Emma, a riotous character. Escaped. A most riotous character. (Date of capture not recorded.)

Davis, John   Prisoner 789. Rank: Seaman, from: HM Ship Vestal, Not Recorded.
    Cap: Not Recorded by Not Recorded Int: 11 Feb 1814 Dis: 25 Apr 1814.
    Received from HM Brig Liberty. Part of Crew of HM Ship Vestal. HM Ship Vestal. (Date of capture not recorded.)

Davis, John   Prisoner 932. Rank: Seaman, from: President, Privateer.
    Cap: 07 May 1814 off Porto Rico by HM Ship Piqua Int: 20 Jun 1814 Dis: 22 Jul 1814.
    Received from HM Ship Vestal. HM Ship Gloucester Rear Admiral Durham. John Davis (1st).

Davis, John   Prisoner 1383. Rank: Master, from: Spencer, Merchant.
    Cap: 15 Feb 1815 off St Bartholomew by HMS Dasher Int: 05 Mar 1815 Dis: 31 Mar 1815.
    Received from HM Ship Dasher. Out of Custody Rear Adl Durham.

Davis, Joseph   Prisoner 788. Rank: Seaman, from: Esperanza, Mechant Schooner.
    Cap: 30 Oct 1813 off Caracas by HM Schooner Elizabeth Int: 11 Feb 1814 Dis: 25 Apr 1814.
    Received from HM Brig Liberty. HM Ship Vestal.

American Prisoners of War Held at Barbados During the War of 1812

Davis, William   Prisoner 654. Rank: Seaman, from: Adelphia, Privateer.
>Cap: 24 Feb 1813 Surinam by Not Recorded Int: 20 May 1813 Dis: 10 Jul 1813.
>Received from HM Sloop Crane. Part of Crew of Comet having charge of the Ship, which floundered at Sea. Surrendering themselves at Main's Point Surinam. Perseverance American Cartel.

Davis, Wyatt B   Prisoner 1091. Rank: Seaman, from: Engineer, Letter of Marque.
>Cap: 21 Sep 1814 of Porto Rico by HM Ship Barossa Int: 29 Sep 1814 Escaped: 15 Jan 1815.
>Received from HM Ship Barossa. Escaped. Reentry 1271.

Davis, Wyatt B   Prisoner 1271. Rank: Seaman, from: Fox, Privateer.
>Cap: 26 Dec 1814 off St Bartholomew by HM Brig Barbados Int: 15 Jan 1815 Dis: 14 Feb 1815.
>Received from HM Brig Barbados. Retaken former No 1091. HM Ship Piqua.

Day, Grove   Prisoner 204. Rank: Seaman, from: Blockade, Privateer.
>Cap: 31 Oct 1812 off Saba by HM Sloop Charybdis Int: 19 Nov 1812 Dis: 10 Jul 1813.
>Received from HM Sloop Charybdis. Perseverance American Cartel.

Days, Thomas   Prisoner 1008. Rank: Seaman, from: Hawk, Privateer.
>Cap: 26 Apr 1814 Near the Mona Passage by HM Ship Piqua Int: 20 Jun 1814 Dis: 22 Jul 1814.
>Received from HM Ship Vestal. HM Ship Gloucester Rear Adml Durham.

De Brais, Henry   Prisoner 1194. Rank: Prize Master, from: Fox, Privateer.
>Cap: 11 Jan 1815 off St Bartholomew by HM Brig Barbados Int: 14 Jan 1815 Dis: 08 Feb 1815.
>Received from HM Brig Barbados. HM Ship Swiftsure. (Capture date is Dec 26, 1814 for all entries for Fox except records 1190 - 1198.)

De Forer, Victor   Prisoner 1239. Rank: Seaman, from: Fox, Privateer.
>Cap: 26 Dec 1814 off St Bartholomew by HM Brig Barbados Int: 14 Jan 1815 Dis: 08 Feb 1815.
>Received from HM Brig Barbados. HM Ship Swiftsure.

De la Ench Parker, Jose   Prisoner 951. Rank: Seaman, from: President, Privateer.
>Cap: 07 May 1814 off Porto Rico by HM Ship Piqua Int: 20 Jun 1814 Dis: 22 Jul 1814.
>Received from HM Ship Vestal. HM Ship Gloucester Rear Admiral Durham.

De la Lantos Lepos, Jose   Prisoner 956. Rank: Seaman, from: President, Privateer.
>Cap: 07 May 1814 off Porto Rico by HM Ship Piqua Int: 20 Jun 1814 Dis: 22 Jul 1814.
>Received from HM Ship Vestal. HM Ship Gloucester Rear Admiral Durham.

de la Statius, Levein   Prisoner 95. Rank: Seaman, from: Providence, Privateer.
>Cap: 11 Sep 1812 off St. Barthlomew by HM Sloop Dominica Int: 13 Nov 1812 Dis: 10 Jul 1813.
>Received from HM Ship Mercury. Perseverance American Cartel.

de Leon, Daniel   Prisoner 336. Rank: Seaman, from: Decatur, Privateer.
>Cap: 16 Jan 1813 Lat 13.00 N, Long 41.00 N by HM Ship Surprise Int: 26 Jan 1813 Dis: 10 Jul 1813.
>Received from HM Ship Surprise. Perseverance American Cartel.

De Loze, Jean   Prisoner 1237. Rank: Seaman, from: Fox, Privateer.
>Cap: 26 Dec 1814 off St Bartholomew by HM Brig Barbados Int: 14 Jan 1815 Dis: 08 Feb 1815.
>Received from HM Brig Barbados. HM Ship Swiftsure.

Dean, W C   Prisoner 474. Rank: Prize Master, from: John, Privateer.
>Cap: 06 Feb 1813 Lat 10.0 N, Long 61.0 W by HM Sloop Peruvian Int: 20 Feb 1813 Dis: 10 Jul 1813.
>Received from HM Ship Cumberland. Perseverance American Cartel.

Deans, Penja   Prisoner 1319. Rank: Seaman, from: Whalebone, Merchant Schooner.
>Cap: 25 Jan 1815 off St Bartholomew by HMB Espringle Int: 09 Feb 1815 Dis: 31 Mar 1815.
>Received from HMB Satellite. Rear Adl Durham.

Debot, Henry   Prisoner 612. Rank: Seaman, from: Thomas Penrose, Privateer.
>Cap: 23 Mar 1813 Lat 20.14 W, Long 61.20 W by HM Ship Tribune Int: 28 Mar 1813 Dis: 26 Apr 1813. Received from HM Ship Tribune. America on Parole Sir F. Laforey.

Delile, Francis   Prisoner 338. Rank: Prize Master, from: Decatur, Privateer.
>Cap: 16 Jan 1813 Lat 13.00 N, Long 41.00 N by HM Ship Surprise Int: 26 Jan 1813 Dis: 10 Jul 1813.
>Received from HM Ship Surprise. Perseverance American Cartel.

Delling, Lewis   Prisoner 202. Rank: Seaman, from: Blockade, Privateer.
>Cap: 31 Oct 1812 off Saba by HM Sloop Charybdis Int: 19 Nov 1812 Dis: 10 Jul 1813.
>Received from HM Sloop Charybdis. Perseverance American Cartel.

Deming, Henry   Prisoner 12. Rank: Mate, from: Shepherdess, Merchant Schooner.
>Cap: 12 Oct 1812 Lat 20.00 N, Long 56.00 W by HM Sloop Lightning Int: 21 Oct 1812 Dis: 24 Oct 1812. Received from HM Sloop Lightning. America on Parole per order of Captain Reynolds Tribune.

Deming, Isaac   Prisoner 246. Rank: Seaman, from: Blockade, Privateer.
>Cap: 31 Oct 1812 off Saba by HM Sloop Charybdis Int: 19 Nov 1812 Dis: 10 Jul 1813.
>Received from HM Sloop Charybdis. Perseverance American Cartel.

Deming, Maning   Prisoner 234. Rank: Seaman, from: Blockade, Privateer.
>Cap: 31 Oct 1812 off Saba by HM Sloop Charybdis Int: 19 Nov 1812 Dis: 10 Jul 1813.
>Received from HM Sloop Charybdis. Perseverance American Cartel.

American Prisoners of War Held at Barbados During the War of 1812

Dempson, John   Prisoner 1344. Rank: Seaman, from: Vidett, Letter of Marque.
    Cap: 14 Feb 1815 off St Bartholomew by HMS Dasher Int: 03 Mar 1815 Dis: 31 Mar 1815.
    Received from HM Ship Dasher. Out of Custody Rear Adl Durham.

Denison, Charles W   Prisoner 1. Rank: Master, from: Hannibal, Merchant Brig.
    Cap: 14 Aug 1812 at sea by HM Sloop Ringdove Int: 24 Aug 1812 Dis: 08 Sep 1812.
    Received from HM Ship Vestal. By Application from Sir George Beckwith it being stated that they landed under a License. Confirmed by Sir F. Laforey.

Dennis, James   Prisoner 545. Rank: Seaman, from: John, Privateer.
    Cap: 06 Feb 1813 Lat 10.0 N, Long 61.0 W by HM Sloop Peruvian Int: 20 Feb 1813 Dis: 11 Aug 1813. Received from HM Ship Cumberland. American Cartel Malmore.

Dennis, William   Prisoner 813. Rank: Lieutenant, from: Frolic, Privateer.
    Cap: 25 Jan 1814 off St Thomas by HM Sloop Heron Int: 22 Feb 1814 Dis: 22 Jul 1814.
    Received from HM Brig Liberty. HM Ship Gloucester Rear Admiral Durham.

Dennison, John   Prisoner 1365. Rank: Seaman, from: Spencer, Merchant.
    Cap: 15 Feb 1815 off St Bartholomew by HMS Dasher Int: 03 Mar 1815 Dis: 31 Mar 1815.
    Received from HM Ship Dasher. Out of Custody Rear Adl Durham.

Denny, John   Prisoner 711. Rank: Seaman, from: Betsey, Merchant Brig.
    Cap: Not Recorded by Not Recorded Int: 03 Jul 1813 Dis: 11 Aug 1813.
    Received from HM Schooner Elizabeth. Part of Crew of Merchant Brig Betsey. Gave himself up as a Prisoner of War. Malmore American Cartel. (Date of capture not recorded.)

Denny, Thomas   Prisoner 1349. Rank: Seaman, from: Vidett, Letter of Marque.
    Cap: 14 Feb 1815 off St Bartholomew by HMS Dasher Int: 03 Mar 1815 Dis: 31 Mar 1815.
    Received from HM Ship Dasher. Out of Custody Rear Adl Durham.

Devins, Charles   Prisoner 252. Rank: Master, from: Brandy Wine, Merchant Brig.
    Cap: 17 Nov 1812 Lat 19.30, Long 57.00 W by HM Ship Lightning Int: 23 Nov 1812 Dis: 02 Dec 1812. Received from HM Ship Lightning. America on Parole Sir F. Laforey.

Dickson, Henry   Prisoner 1088. Rank: Seaman, from: Engineer, Letter of Marque.
    Cap: 21 Sep 1814 of Porto Rico by HM Ship Barossa Int: 29 Sep 1814 Dis: 31 Mar 1815.
    Received from HM Ship Barossa. Rear Adl Durham.

Dill, David   Prisoner 1409. Rank: Seaman, from: Avon, Privateer.
    Cap: 08 Mar 1815 off Nevis by HM Sloop Barbados Int: 13 Mar 1815 Dis: 15 Mar 1815.
    Received from HM Sloop Barbados. HMS Numen Rear Admiral Durham.

Dipplac, Domike   Prisoner 458. Rank: Seaman, from: Bowrey, Privateer.
    Cap: 02 Feb 1813 off Barbados by HM Sloop Opossum Int: 18 Feb 1813 Dis: 11 Aug 1813.
    Received from HM Sloop Opossum. English Brig Captured by the Comet. Malmore American Cartel.

Disney, George   Prisoner 551. Rank: Mate, from: Mary, Merchant Brig.
    Cap: 11 Aug 1812 Surinam by HM Sloop Surinam Int: 02 Mar 1813 Dis: 13 Mar 1813.
    Received from Schooner Jack. America on Parole Sir Francis Laforey.

Doane, Henry   Prisoner 405. Rank: Seaman, from: Decatur, Privateer.
    Cap: 16 Jan 1813 Lat 13.00 N, Long 41.00 N by HM Ship Surprise Int: 26 Jan 1813 Dis: 10 Jul 1813.
    Received from HM Ship Surprise. Perseverance American Cartel.

Dodd, Edward   Prisoner 180. Rank: 1 Lieutenant, from: Blockade, Privateer.
    Cap: 31 Oct 1812 off Saba by HM Sloop Charybdis Int: 19 Nov 1812 Dis: 10 Jul 1813.
    Received from HM Sloop Charybdis. Perseverance American Cartel.

Dodd, Joseph   Prisoner 901. Rank: Seaman, from: Hawk, Privateer.
    Cap: 26 Apr 1814 Near the Mona Passage by HM Ship Piqua Int: 20 Jun 1814 Escaped: 08 Jul 1814.
    Received from HM Ship Vestal. Escaped.

Dodd, Joseph   Prisoner 1022. Rank: Seaman, from: Hawk, Privateer.
    Cap: 26 Apr 1814 Near the Mona Passage by HM Ship Piqua Int: 10 Jul 1814 Dis: 22 Jul 1814.
    Retaken former No 901. HM Ship Gloucester Rear Admiral Durham.

Dods, George   Prisoner 1074. Rank: Boatswain, from: Engineer, Letter of Marque.
    Cap: 21 Sep 1814 of Porto Rico by HM Ship Barossa Int: 29 Sep 1814 Dis: 31 Mar 1815.
    Received from HM Ship Barossa. Rear Adl Durham.

Doliver, William   Prisoner 495. Rank: Seaman, from: John, Privateer.
    Cap: 06 Feb 1813 Lat 10.0 N, Long 61.0 W by HM Sloop Peruvian Int: 20 Feb 1813 Dis: 11 Aug 1813. Received from HM Ship Cumberland. Malmore American Cartel. William Doliver (1st).

Doliver, William   Prisoner 544. Rank: Seaman, from: John, Privateer.
    Cap: 06 Feb 1813 Lat 10.0 N, Long 61.0 W by HM Sloop Peruvian Int: 20 Feb 1813 Dis: 11 Aug 1813. Received from HM Ship Cumberland. American Cartel Malmore. William Doliver (2nd).

Donald, Joseph   Prisoner 1087. Rank: Seaman, from: Engineer, Letter of Marque.
    Cap: 21 Sep 1814 of Porto Rico by HM Ship Barossa Int: 29 Sep 1814 Escaped: 13 Jan 1815.
    Received from HM Ship Barossa. Escaped. Reentry 1267.

American Prisoners of War Held at Barbados During the War of 1812

Donald, Joseph   Prisoner 1267. Rank: Seaman, from: Fox, Privateer.
    Cap: 26 Dec 1814 off St Bartholomew by HM Brig Barbados Int: 15 Jan 1815 Dis: 14 Feb 1815.
    Received from HM Brig Barbados. Retaken former No 1087. HM Ship Piqua.

Doughty, Jacob   Prisoner 445. Rank: Seaman, from: Isaac, Merchant Brig.
    Cap: 01 Jan 1813 off Porto Rico by HM Sloop Charybdis Int: 12 Feb 1813 Dis: 11 Aug 1813.
    Received from HM Brig Liberty. Malmore American Cartel.

Douglass, George   Prisoner 422. Rank: Seaman, from: Anna, Not Recorded.
    Cap: 03 Jan 1813 off Maderia by HM Ship Cumberland Int: 30 Jan 1813 Dis: 10 Jul 1813.
    Received from HM Sloop Demerary. Recaptured from the Mars Privateer. Perseverance American Cartel.

Douglass, James   Prisoner 1103. Rank: Seaman, from: Engineer, Letter of Marque.
    Cap: 21 Sep 1814 of Porto Rico by HM Ship Barossa Int: 29 Sep 1814 Dis: 31 Mar 1815.
    Received from HM Ship Barossa. Rear Adl Durham.

Downes, John   Prisoner 1154. Rank: Seaman, from: High Flyer, Letter of Marque.
    Cap: 14 Nov 1814 off Anguilla by HM Ship Barossa Int: 18 Nov 1814 Dis: 08 Feb 1815.
    Received from HM Ship Barossa. HM Ship Swiftsure.

Duett, Thomas   Prisoner 1417. Rank: Seaman, from: Avon, Privateer.
    Cap: 08 Mar 1815 off Nevis by HM Sloop Barbados Int: 13 Mar 1815 Dis: 15 Mar 1815.
    Received from HM Sloop Barbados. HMS Numen Rear Admiral Durham.

Dufroint, Julien   Prisoner 1243. Rank: Seaman, from: Fox, Privateer.
    Cap: 26 Dec 1814 off St Bartholomew by HM Brig Barbados Int: 14 Jan 1815 Dis: 08 Feb 1815.
    Received from HM Brig Barbados. HM Ship Swiftsure.

Dufrus, Simon   Prisoner 1195. Rank: Prize Master, from: Fox, Privateer.
    Cap: 11 Jan 1815 off St Bartholomew by HM Brig Barbados Int: 14 Jan 1815 Dis: 08 Feb 1815.
    Received from HM Brig Barbados. HM Ship Swiftsure. (Capture date is Dec 26, 1814 for all entries for Fox except records 1190 - 1198.)

Dugan, Able S   Prisoner 259. Rank: Lieutenant, from: Rea, Privateer.
    Cap: 29 Nov 1812 off Barbados by HM Ship Lightning Int: 29 Nov 1812 Dis: 09 May 1813.
    Received from HM Ship Lightning. Ship having been captured by the Bona American. America on Parole very ill. (Remarks not legible.)

Duncan, Charles   Prisoner 617. Rank: Seaman, from: HM Ship Venus, Not Recorded.
    Cap: Not Recorded by Not Recorded Int: 02 Apr 1813 Dis: 11 Aug 1813.
    Received from HM Ship Venus. Part of Crew of HMS Venus. Malmore American Cartel. Malmore American Cartel. (Date of capture not recorded.)

Duncan, Jesse   Prisoner 810. Rank: Seaman, from: Goutlan, Merchant Schooner.
    Cap: 31 Jan 1814 off Saint Bartholomew by HM Brig Barbados Int: 12 Feb 1814 Dis: 25 Apr 1814.
    Received from HM Schooner Ballahou. HM Ship Vestal.

Duncan, William   Prisoner 777. Rank: Seaman, from: HM Ship Cleopatra, Not Recorded.
    Cap: Not Recorded by Not Recorded Int: 11 Feb 1814 Dis: 25 Apr 1814.
    Received from HM Brig Liberty. Part of Crew of HM Ship Cleopatra. HM Ship Vestal. (Date of capture not recorded.)

Durham, Thomas   Prisoner 1369. Rank: Seaman, from: Spencer, Merchant.
    Cap: 15 Feb 1815 off St Bartholomew by HMS Dasher Int: 03 Mar 1815 Dis: 31 Mar 1815.
    Received from HM Ship Dasher. Out of Custody Rear Adl Durham.

Durive, Antoun   Prisoner 1198. Rank: Apprentice, from: Fox, Privateer.
    Cap: 11 Jan 1815 off St Bartholomew by HM Brig Barbados Int: 14 Jan 1815 Dis: 08 Feb 1815.
    Received from HM Brig Barbados. HM Ship Swiftsure. (Capture date is Dec 26, 1814 for all entries for Fox except records 1190 - 1198.)

Dutch, Edward   Prisoner 490. Rank: Seaman, from: John, Privateer.
    Cap: 06 Feb 1813 Lat 10.0 N, Long 61.0 W by HM Sloop Peruvian Int: 20 Feb 1813 Dis: 11 Aug 1813. Received from HM Ship Cumberland. Malmore American Cartel.

Dutilth, John A   Prisoner 591. Rank: Supercargo, from: Thomas Penrose, Privateer.
    Cap: 23 Mar 1813 Lat 20.14 W, Long 61.20 W by HM Ship Tribune Int: 28 Mar 1813 Dis: 26 Apr 1813. Received from HM Ship Tribune. America on Parole Sir F. Laforey.

Eainis, Ebenezer   Prisoner 82. Rank: Seaman, from: Providence, Privateer.
    Cap: 11 Sep 1812 off St. Barthlomew by HM Sloop Dominica Int: 13 Nov 1812 Dis: 10 Jul 1813.
    Received from HM Ship Mercury. Perseverance American Cartel.

Ebein, Joseph   Prisoner 942. Rank: Seaman, from: President, Privateer.
    Cap: 07 May 1814 off Porto Rico by HM Ship Piqua Int: 20 Jun 1814 Dis: 22 Jul 1814.
    Received from HM Ship Vestal. HM Ship Gloucester Rear Admiral Durham.

Eblin, Aaron   Prisoner 992. Rank: Seaman, from: Hawk, Privateer.
    Cap: 26 Apr 1814 Near the Mona Passage by HM Ship Piqua Int: 20 Jun 1814 Dis: 22 Jul 1814.
    Received from HM Ship Vestal. HM Ship Gloucester Rear Admiral Durham.

American Prisoners of War Held at Barbados During the War of 1812

Ebnoles, Wimlon   Prisoner 1437. Rank: Seaman, from: Avon, Privateer.
>Cap: 08 Mar 1815 off Nevis by HM Sloop Barbados Int: 13 Mar 1815 Dis: 15 Mar 1815.
>Received from HM Sloop Barbados. HMS Numen Rear Admiral Durham.

Eden, John   Prisoner 97. Rank: Seaman, from: Dragon, Not Recorded.
>Cap: Not Recorded by Not Recorded Int: 13 Nov 1812 Dis: 10 Jul 1813.
>Received from HM Ship Mercury. Part of the crew of the Ship Dragon. Perseverance American Cartel. (Date of capture not recorded.)

Edgar, Thomas   Prisoner 1211. Rank: Seaman, from: Fox, Privateer.
>Cap: 26 Dec 1814 off St Bartholomew by HM Brig Barbados Int: 14 Jan 1815 Dis: 08 Feb 1815.
>Received from HM Brig Barbados. HM Ship Swiftsure.

Edwards, Jean   Prisoner 793. Rank: Seaman, from: Atalante, Merchant Schooner.
>Cap: 19 Jan 1814 off Saint Bartholomew by HM Brig Barbados Int: 12 Feb 1814 Dis: 25 Apr 1814.
>Received from HM Schooner Ballahou. HM Ship Vestal.

Edwards, Thomas   Prisoner 116. Rank: Seaman, from: William Rathbone, Brig.
>Cap: 09 Oct 1812 at Sea by HM Sloop Charybdis Int: 13 Nov 1812 Dis: 10 Jul 1813.
>Received from HM Ship Mercury. Retaken Brig Part of Crew of Savory Jack Privateer. Perseverance American Cartel.

Edwards, Timothy R   Prisoner 189. Rank: Prize Master, from: Blockade, Privateer.
>Cap: 31 Oct 1812 off Saba by HM Sloop Charybdis Int: 19 Nov 1812 Dis: 10 Jul 1813.
>Received from HM Sloop Charybdis. Perseverance American Cartel.

Effords, John   Prisoner 1064. Rank: 2 Mate, from: Mary, Letter of Marque.
>Cap: 07 Jun 1814 La Quisa by HM Ship Heron Int: 31 Jul 1814 Escaped: 13 Jan 1815.
>Received from HM Sloop Mosquito. Escaped. (Not legible) preparation of opium to administer to the guard. Reentry 1265.

Effords, John   Prisoner 1265. Rank: 2 Mate, from: Fox, Privateer.
>Cap: 26 Dec 1814 off St Bartholomew by HM Brig Barbados Int: 15 Jan 1815 Dis: 14 Feb 1815.
>Received from HM Brig Barbados. Retaken former No 1064. HM Ship Piqua.

Egart, Jacob   Prisoner 122. Rank: Seaman, from: William Rathbone, Brig.
>Cap: 09 Oct 1812 at Sea by HM Sloop Charybdis Int: 13 Nov 1812 Dis: 10 Jul 1813.
>Received from HM Ship Mercury. Retaken Brig Part of Crew of Savory Jack Privateer. Perseverance American Cartel.

Eldon, James S   Prisoner 991. Rank: Seaman, from: Hawk, Privateer.
>Cap: 26 Apr 1814 Near the Mona Passage by HM Ship Piqua Int: 20 Jun 1814 Dis: 22 Jul 1814.
>Received from HM Ship Vestal. HM Ship Gloucester Rear Admiral Durham.

Eldridge, Edmund   Prisoner 505. Rank: Seaman, from: John, Privateer.
>Cap: 06 Feb 1813 Lat 10.0 N, Long 61.0 W by HM Sloop Peruvian Int: 20 Feb 1813 Dis: 11 Aug 1813. Received from HM Ship Cumberland. Malmore American Cartel.

Eldridge, Henry   Prisoner 213. Rank: Seaman, from: Blockade, Privateer.
>Cap: 31 Oct 1812 off Saba by HM Sloop Charybdis Int: 19 Nov 1812 Dis: 10 Jul 1813.
>Received from HM Sloop Charybdis. Perseverance American Cartel.

Elliott, Nathaniel   Prisoner 449. Rank: Seaman, from: Mary Caroline, Merchant Brig.
>Cap: 02 Jan 1813 off Porto Rico by HM Sloop Charybdis Int: 12 Feb 1813 Dis: 11 Aug 1813.
>Received from HM Brig Liberty. Malmore American Cartel.

Ellis, Cornelius   Prisoner 855. Rank: Seaman, from: Rattle Snake, Letter of Marque.
>Cap: 11 Mar 1814 Lat 24.07 N, Long 66.47 W by HM Ship Rhin Int: 25 Mar 1814 Dis: 25 Apr 1814.
>Received from HM Ship Rhin. HM Ship Vestal.

Ellis, Joseph   Prisoner 1060. Rank: Seaman, from: Mary, Letter of Marque.
>Cap: 07 Jun 1814 La Quisa by HM Ship Heron Int: 31 Jul 1814 Dis: 31 Mar 1815.
>Received from HM Sloop Mosquito. Rear Adl Durham.

Ellwell, Samuel   Prisoner 884. Rank: Seaman, from: Hawk, Privateer.
>Cap: 26 Apr 1814 Near the Mona Passage by HM Ship Piqua Int: 20 Jun 1814 Dis: 20 Jul 1814.
>Received from HM Ship Vestal. HM Sloop Hazard Rear Adml Durham.

Endley, James   Prisoner 1080. Rank: Seaman, from: Engineer, Letter of Marque.
>Cap: 21 Sep 1814 of Porto Rico by HM Ship Barossa Int: 29 Sep 1814 Dis: 08 Feb 1815.
>Received from HM Ship Barossa. HM Ship Swiftsure Rear A Durham.

English, John   Prisoner 318. Rank: Seaman, from: Dolphin, Merchant Brig.
>Cap: 15 Dec 1812 near Bermuda by HM Sloop Nimrod Int: 11 Jan 1813 Escaped: 24 Apr 1813.
>Received from HM Sloop Nimrod. Escaped.

Ennick, William   Prisoner 647. Rank: Seaman, from: Delirious, Merchant Schooner.
>Cap: 25 Apr 1813 off the River Orinoco by HM Brig Liberty Int: 20 May 1813 Dis: 11 Aug 1813.
>Received from HM Sloop Crane. Malmore American Cartel.

American Prisoners of War Held at Barbados During the War of 1812

Ennis, John   Prisoner 1394. Rank: Boy, from: Avon, Privateer.
    Cap: 08 Mar 1815 off Nevis by HM Sloop Barbados Int: 13 Mar 1815 Dis: 31 Mar 1815.
    Received from HM Sloop Barbados. Out of Custody Rear Adl Durham.

Estes, John   Prisoner 444. Rank: Seaman, from: Isaac, Merchant Brig.
    Cap: 01 Jan 1813 off Porto Rico by HM Sloop Charybdis Int: 12 Feb 1813 Dis: 11 Aug 1813.
    Received from HM Brig Liberty. Malmore American Cartel.

Evans, Edward   Prisoner 1031. Rank: Seaman, from: North Star, Merchant Schooner.
    Cap: 10 Jun 1814 off St Bartholomew by HM Brig Crane Int: 11 Jul 1814 Dis: 22 Jul 1814.
    Received from HM Schooner Flying Fish. HM Ship Gloucester Rear Admiral Durham.

Evans, John   Prisoner 161. Rank: Seaman, from: Yankee, Privateer.
    Cap: 25 Oct 1812 off Sombero by HM Sloop Peruvian Int: 13 Nov 1812 Dis: 10 Jul 1813.
    Received from HM Ship Mercury. Perseverance American Cartel.

Evarell, Samuel   Prisoner 849. Rank: Seaman, from: Rattle Snake, Letter of Marque.
    Cap: 11 Mar 1814 Lat 24.07 N, Long 66.47 W by HM Ship Rhin Int: 25 Mar 1814 Dis: 25 Apr 1814.
    Received from HM Ship Rhin. HM Ship Vestal.

Everson, James   Prisoner 1368. Rank: Seaman, from: Spencer, Merchant.
    Cap: 15 Feb 1815 off St Bartholomew by HMS Dasher Int: 03 Mar 1815 Dis: 31 Mar 1815.
    Received from HM Ship Dasher. Out of Custody Rear Adl Durham.

Every, William   Prisoner 1056. Rank: Seaman, from: Mary, Letter of Marque.
    Cap: 07 Jun 1814 La Quisa by HM Ship Heron Int: 31 Jul 1814 Dis: 31 Mar 1815.
    Received from HM Sloop Mosquito. Rear Adl Durham.

Fairfield, James M   Prisoner 566. Rank: Captain, from: John, Privateer.
    Cap: 06 Feb 1813 Lat 10 N, Long 61 W by HM Sloop Peruvian Int: 08 Mar 1813 Dis: 10 Jul 1813.
    Received from HM Sloop Arachne. Perseverance American Cartel.

Faleon, Jose B   Prisoner 946. Rank: Seaman, from: President, Privateer.
    Cap: 07 May 1814 off Porto Rico by HM Ship Piqua Int: 20 Jun 1814 Dis: 22 Jul 1914.
    Received from HM Ship Vestal. HM Ship Gloucester Rear Admiral Durham.

Farebrook, George   Prisoner 100. Rank: Seaman, from: Jane, Merchant Brig.
    Cap: 25 Sep 1812 at Sea by HM Sloop Spider Int: 13 Nov 1812 Dis: 17 Nov 1812.
    Received from HM Ship Mercury. Out of Custody per order of Sir F. Laforey being crew of a licensed vessel.

Farnham, John   Prisoner 145. Rank: Seaman, from: Yankee, Privateer.
    Cap: 25 Oct 1812 off Sombero by HM Sloop Peruvian Int: 13 Nov 1812 Dis: 10 Jul 1813.
    Received from HM Ship Mercury. Perseverance American Cartel.

Farra, Vincent   Prisoner 1217. Rank: Seaman, from: Fox, Privateer.
    Cap: 26 Dec 1814 off St Bartholomew by HM Brig Barbados Int: 14 Jan 1815 Dis: 08 Feb 1815.
    Received from HM Brig Barbados. HM Ship Swiftsure.

Farris, James   Prisoner 693. Rank: Seaman, from: HM Ship Bedford, Not Recorded.
    Cap: Not Recorded by Not Recorded Int: 12 Jun 1813 Dis: 11 Aug 1813.
    Received from HM Ship Vestal. Gave himself up as a Prisoner of War on Board HM Ship Bedford. Malmore American Cartel. (Date of capture not recorded.)

Felix, John   Prisoner 1450. Rank: Seaman, from: Ivan Francisco, Not Recorded.
    Cap: 08 Mar 1815 off Nevis by HM Brig Muros Int: 26 Mar 1815 Dis: 31 Mar 1815.
    Received from HM Brig Maria. Recaptured from the Grand Turk Privateer. Out of Custody Rear Adl Durham.

Fenderson, Nathaniel   Prisoner 266. Rank: Seaman, from: Rea, Privateer.
    Cap: 29 Nov 1812 off Barbados by HM Ship Lightning Int: 29 Nov 1812 Dis: 10 Jul 1813.
    Received from HM Ship Lightning. Ship having been captured by the Bona American. Perseverance American Cartel.

Fenhorn, Morris   Prisoner 714. Rank: Seaman, from: Belfast, Merchant Ship.
    Cap: 30 May 1813 at Sea by HM Ship Heron Int: 07 Jul 1813 Dis: 11 Aug 1813.
    Received from HM Ship Heron. Malmore American Cartel.

Fenner, Charles   Prisoner 77. Rank: Seaman, from: Providence, Privateer.
    Cap: 11 Sep 1812 off St. Barthlomew by HM Sloop Dominica Int: 13 Nov 1812 Dis: 10 Jul 1813.
    Received from HM Ship Mercury. Perseverance American Cartel.

Fernado, Manuel   Prisoner 367. Rank: Seaman, from: Decatur, Privateer.
    Cap: 16 Jan 1813 Lat 13.00 N, Long 41.00 N by HM Ship Surprise Int: 26 Jan 1813 Dis: 10 Jul 1813.
    Received from HM Ship Surprise. Perseverance American Cartel.

Ferring, Isaiah   Prisoner 1401. Rank: Captains Clerk, from: Avon, Privateer.
    Cap: 08 Mar 1815 off Nevis by HM Sloop Barbados Int: 13 Mar 1815 Dis: 15 Mar 1815.
    Received from HM Sloop Barbados. HMS Numen Rear Admiral Durham.

American Prisoners of War Held at Barbados During the War of 1812

Fetch, Elias   Prisoner 662. Rank: Seaman, from: Pocahontas, Merchant Schooner.
  Cap: 10 Aug 1812 Surinman by HM Sloop Surinam Int: 20 May 1813 Dis: 11 Aug 1813.
  Received from HM Ship Crane. Malmore American Cartel.

Fielding, William   Prisoner 107. Rank: Seaman, from: Diana, Merchant Brig.
  Cap: 25 Sep 1812 at Sea by HM Sloop Spider Int: 13 Nov 1812 Dis: 02 Dec 1812.
  Received from HM Ship Mercury. Per Order Sir F. Laforey being part of crew of a Licensed Vessel.

Fields, William   Prisoner 289. Rank: Seaman, from: Rea, Not Recorded.
  Cap: Not Recorded by Not Recorded Int: 09 Dec 1812 Dis: 10 Jul 1813.
  Received from HM Brig Swaggerer. Part of Crew of Ship Rea. Perseverance American Cartel. (Date of capture not recorded.)

Fillerson, Thomas   Prisoner 603. Rank: Seaman, from: Thomas Penrose, Privateer.
  Cap: 23 Mar 1813 Lat 20.14 W, Long 61.20 W by HM Ship Tribune Int: 28 Mar 1813 Dis: 26 Apr 1813. Received from HM Ship Tribune. America on Parole Sir F. Laforey.

Fisher, John   Prisoner 483. Rank: Seaman, from: John, Privateer.
  Cap: 06 Feb 1813 Lat 10.0 N, Long 61.0 W by HM Sloop Peruvian Int: 20 Feb 1813 Dis: 11 Aug 1813. Received from HM Ship Cumberland. Malmore American Cartel.

Fisher, Lewis P   Prisoner 50. Rank: Seaman, from: Providence, Privateer.
  Cap: 11 Sep 1812 off St. Barthlomew by HM Sloop Dominica Int: 13 Nov 1812 Dis: 10 Jul 1813.
  Received from HM Ship Mercury. Perseverance American Cartel.

Fitzgerald, John   Prisoner 818. Rank: Mate, from: Hero, Merchant Schooner.
  Cap: 27 Sep 1813 off Bermuda by HM Sloop Rattler Int: 24 Feb 1814 Dis: 25 Apr 1814.
  Received from HM Ship Galatea. N. B. This man escaped from HM Brig Liberty and was retaken on shore. HMS Vestal.

Flanders, Daniel   Prisoner 152. Rank: Seaman, from: Yankee, Privateer.
  Cap: 25 Oct 1812 off Sombero by HM Sloop Peruvian Int: 13 Nov 1812 Dis: 10 Jul 1813.
  Received from HM Ship Mercury. Perseverance American Cartel.

Fletcher, Benjamin   Prisoner 798. Rank: Seaman, from: Kirran, Merchant Brig.
  Cap: 25 Jan 1814 off Saint Bartholomew by HM Brig Barbados Int: 12 Feb 1814 Dis: 25 Apr 1814.
  Received from HM Schooner Ballahou. HM Ship Vestal.

Fletcher, Samuel   Prisoner 351. Rank: Seaman, from: Decatur, Privateer.
  Cap: 16 Jan 1813 Lat 13.00 N, Long 41.00 N by HM Ship Surprise Int: 26 Jan 1813 Dis: 10 Jul 1813.
  Received from HM Ship Surprise. Perseverance American Cartel.

Flinn, John F   Prisoner 963. Rank: Lieutenant, from: President, Privateer.
  Cap: 07 May 1814 off Porto Rico by HM Ship Piqua Int: 20 Jun 1814 Dis: 22 Jul 1814.
  Received from HM Ship Piqua. HM Ship Gloucester Rear Admiral Durham.

Flint, William   Prisoner 238. Rank: Seaman, from: Blockade, Privateer.
  Cap: 31 Oct 1812 off Saba by HM Sloop Charybdis Int: 19 Nov 1812 Dis: 10 Apr 1813.
  Received from HM Sloop Charybdis. America on Parole being very ill.

Flood, William   Prisoner 370. Rank: Seaman, from: Decatur, Privateer.
  Cap: 16 Jan 1813 Lat 13.00 N, Long 41.00 N by HM Ship Surprise Int: 26 Jan 1813 Dis: 10 Jul 1813.
  Received from HM Ship Surprise. Perseverance American Cartel.

Flood, William   Prisoner 550. Rank: Master, from: Mary, Merchant Brig.
  Cap: 11 Aug 1812 Surinam by HM Sloop Surinam Int: 02 Mar 1813 Dis: 13 Mar 1813.
  Received from Schooner Jack. America on Parole Sir Francis Laforey.

Florintino, Andre   Prisoner 377. Rank: Seaman, from: Decatur, Privateer.
  Cap: 16 Jan 1813 Lat 13.00 N, Long 41.00 N by HM Ship Surprise Int: 26 Jan 1813 Dis: 10 Jul 1813.
  Received from HM Ship Surprise. Perseverance American Cartel.

Fogg, John   Prisoner 928. Rank: Seaman, from: President, Privateer.
  Cap: 07 May 1814 off Porto Rico by HM Ship Piqua Int: 20 Jun 1814 Dis: 20 Jul 1814.
  Received from HM Ship Vestal. HM Sloop Hazard Rear Adml Durham.

Foot, James   Prisoner 643. Rank: Seaman, from: Decatur, Privateer.
  Cap: 16 Jan 1813 Lat 13.00 N, Long 41.00 W by HM Ship Surprise Int: 13 Apr 1813 Dis: 18 Apr 1813. Received from Naval Hospital. America on Parole being very ill having lost his leg.

Foot, Thomas   Prisoner 149. Rank: Seaman, from: Yankee, Privateer.
  Cap: 25 Oct 1812 off Sombero by HM Sloop Peruvian Int: 13 Nov 1812 Dis: 10 Jul 1813.
  Received from HM Ship Mercury. Perseverance American Cartel.

Forbes, Bracket   Prisoner 1300. Rank: Seaman, from: Mary, Merchant Schooner.
  Cap: 15 Jan 1815 Lat 22.40, Long 66 by HM Ship Pique Int: 29 Jan 1815 Dis: 31 Mar 1815.
  Received from HMS Pique. Rear Adl Durham.

Forbes, William   Prisoner 1287. Rank: Mate, from: Mary, Merchant Schooner.
  Cap: 15 Jan 1815 Lat 22.40, Long 66 by HM Ship Pique Int: 29 Jan 1815 Dis: 31 Mar 1815.
  Received from HMS Pique. Rear Adl Durham.

American Prisoners of War Held at Barbados During the War of 1812

Forbes, William   Prisoner 1442. Rank: Seaman, from: Avon, Privateer.
    Cap: 08 Mar 1815 off Nevis by HM Sloop Barbados Int: 14 Mar 1815 Dis: 15 Mar 1815.
    Received from HM Sloop Barbados. HMS Numen Rear Admiral Durham.

Fordick, Joseph   Prisoner 843. Rank: Seaman, from: Rattle Snake, Letter of Marque.
    Cap: 11 Mar 1814 Lat 24.07 N, Long 66.47 W by HM Ship Rhin Int: 25 Mar 1814 Dis: 25 Apr 1814.
    Received from HM Ship Rhin. HM Ship Vestal.

Forster, John   Prisoner 22. Rank: Seaman, from: HM Sloop Dominica, Not Recorded.
    Cap: 22 Oct 1812 Not Recorded by Not Recorded Int: 22 Oct 1812 Dis: 24 Oct 1812.
    Received from HM Sloop Dominica. Gave themselves up on Reason of war being part of the crew of HM Sloop Dominica. America on Parole per order of Captain Reynolds Tribune.

Fort, Benjamin   Prisoner 428. Rank: Seaman, from: Ocean, Merchant Schooner.
    Cap: 15 Aug 1812 Martinique by Detained at Martinique Int: 05 Feb 1813 Dis: 10 Jul 1813.
    Received from HM Ship Vestal. Perseverance American Cartel.

Fortney, William   Prisoner 284. Rank: Seaman, from: Rea, Privateer.
    Cap: 29 Nov 1812 off Barbados by HM Ship Lightning Int: 29 Nov 1812 Dis: 10 Jul 1813.
    Received from HM Ship Lightning. Ship having been captured by the Bona American. Perseverance American Cartel.

Fortune, Thomas   Prisoner 780. Rank: Seaman, from: Old Friend, Not Recorded.
    Cap: 01 Jan 1814 off St. Bartholomew by Viper Privateer Int: 11 Feb 1814 Dis: 25 Apr 1814.
    Received from HM Brig Liberty. Retaken from the Globe Privateer. HM Ship Vestal.

Foster, James   Prisoner 374. Rank: Seaman, from: Decatur, Privateer.
    Cap: 16 Jan 1813 Lat 13.00 N, Long 41.00 N by HM Ship Surprise Int: 26 Jan 1813 Dis: 10 Jul 1813.
    Received from HM Ship Surprise. Perseverance American Cartel.

Foster, Major   Prisoner 1136. Rank: Seaman, from: Clio, Merchant Schooner.
    Cap: 13 Nov 1814 off Anguilla by HM Ship Barossa Int: 18 Nov 1814 Dis: 31 Mar 1815.
    Received from HM Ship Barossa. Rear Adl Durham.

Fouche, Jean   Prisoner 1209. Rank: Seaman, from: Fox, Privateer.
    Cap: 26 Dec 1814 off St Bartholomew by HM Brig Barbados Int: 14 Jan 1815 Dis: 08 Feb 1815.
    Received from HM Brig Barbados. HM Ship Swiftsure.

Foxtrum, Samuel   Prisoner 628. Rank: Seaman, from: Fly, Privateer.
    Cap: 19 Jan 1813 Lat 15.00 N, Long 45.00 W by HMS Venus Int: 02 Apr 1813 Dis: 11 Aug 1813.
    Received from HMS Venus. Recaptured from the Yankee. Malmore American Cartel.

Foy, Daniel   Prisoner 784. Rank: Seaman, from: Old Friend, Not Recorded.
    Cap: 01 Jan 1814 off St. Bartholomew by Viper Privateer Int: 11 Feb 1814 Dis: 25 Apr 1814.
    Received from HM Brig Liberty. Retaken from the Globe Privateer. HM Ship Vestal.

Francis, John   Prisoner 150. Rank: Seaman, from: Yankee, Privateer.
    Cap: 25 Oct 1812 off Sombero by HM Sloop Peruvian Int: 13 Nov 1812 Dis: 10 Jul 1813.
    Received from HM Ship Mercury. Perseverance American Cartel.

Francis, Oliver William   Prisoner 536. Rank: Seaman, from: John, Privateer.
    Cap: 06 Feb 1813 Lat 10.0 N, Long 61.0 W by HM Sloop Peruvian Int: 20 Feb 1813 Dis: 11 Aug 1813. Received from HM Ship Cumberland. American Cartel Malmore.

Francis, Richard   Prisoner 404. Rank: Seaman, from: Decatur, Privateer.
    Cap: 16 Jan 1813 Lat 13.00 N, Long 41.00 N by HM Ship Surprise Int: 26 Jan 1813 Dis: 10 Jul 1813.
    Received from HM Ship Surprise. Perseverance American Cartel.

Frankland, William H   Prisoner 1002. Rank: Seaman, from: Hawk, Privateer.
    Cap: 26 Apr 1814 Near the Mona Passage by HM Ship Piqua Int: 20 Jun 1814 Escaped: 08 Jul 1814.
    Received from HM Ship Vestal. Escaped.

Frankland, William H   Prisoner 1034. Rank: Seaman, from: North Star, Merchant Schooner.
    Cap: 10 Jun 1814 off St Bartholomew by HM Brig Crane Int: 21 Jul 1814 Dis: 22 Jul 1814.
    Retaken former No 1002. HM Ship Gloucester Rear Adml Durham. (Entry has line drawn through it.)

Frankland, William H   Prisoner 1035. Rank: Seaman, from: North Star, Merchant Schooner.
    Cap: 10 Jun 1814 off St Bartholomew by HM Brig Crane Int: 21 Jul 1814 Dis: 22 Jul 1814.
    Retaken former No 1002. HM Ship Gloucester Rear Adml Durham.

Franklin, Moses   Prisoner 187. Rank: Boatswain, from: Blockade, Privateer.
    Cap: 31 Oct 1812 off Saba by HM Sloop Charybdis Int: 19 Nov 1812 Dis: 10 Jul 1813.
    Received from HM Sloop Charybdis. Bad character acting (not legible). Perseverance American Cartel.

Frasier, John   Prisoner 1122. Rank: Seaman, from: Nancy, Privateer.
    Cap: 06 Sep 1814 Lat 32 N, Long 47 W by HM Ship Piqua Int: 21 Oct 1814 Dis: 10 Nov 1814.
    Received from HMS Piqua. Taken by the Amelia Privateer. (Not legible) Riotous Character HM Ship Venerable having declared himself to be a British Subject.

American Prisoners of War Held at Barbados During the War of 1812

Freeman, Joseph S   Prisoner 66. Rank: Seaman, from: Providence, Privateer.
    Cap: 11 Sep 1812 off St. Barthlomew by HM Sloop Dominica Int: 13 Nov 1812 Dis: 10 Jul 1813.
    Received from HM Ship Mercury. Perseverance American Cartel.

Freeman, Peter   Prisoner 372. Rank: Seaman, from: Decatur, Privateer.
    Cap: 16 Jan 1813 Lat 13.00 N, Long 41.00 N by HM Ship Surprise Int: 26 Jan 1813 Dis: 10 Jul 1813.
    Received from HM Ship Surprise. Perseverance American Cartel.

Freeman, Philemon   Prisoner 1097. Rank: Seaman, from: Engineer, Letter of Marque.
    Cap: 21 Sep 1814 of Porto Rico by HM Ship Barossa Int: 29 Sep 1814 Dis: 31 Mar 1815.
    Received from HM Ship Barossa. Rear Adl Durham.

Freeman, Pline   Prisoner 450. Rank: Seaman, from: Mary Caroline, Merchant Brig.
    Cap: 02 Jan 1813 off Porto Rico by HM Sloop Charybdis Int: 12 Feb 1813 Dis: 11 Aug 1813.
    Received from HM Brig Liberty. Malmore American Cartel.

Freeman, Samuel   Prisoner 552. Rank: Master, from: Gustava, Merchant Brig.
    Cap: 20 Feb 1813 off Demuary by HM Sloop Bacock Int: 02 Mar 1813 Dis: 13 Mar 1813.
    Received from Army Schooner Maria. America on Parole Sir Francis Laforey.

Fry, A Julius   Prisoner 939. Rank: Seaman, from: President, Privateer.
    Cap: 07 May 1814 off Porto Rico by HM Ship Piqua Int: 20 Jun 1814 Dis: 22 Jul 1814.
    Received from HM Ship Vestal. HM Ship Gloucester Rear Admiral Durham.

Fuller, Andrew   Prisoner 430. Rank: Seaman, from: Ocean, Merchant Schooner.
    Cap: 15 Aug 1812 Martinique by Detained at Martinique Int: 05 Feb 1813 Dis: 10 Jul 1813.
    Received from HM Ship Vestal. Perseverance American Cartel.

Fuller, Benjamin   Prisoner 181. Rank: 2 Lieutenant, from: Blockade, Privateer.
    Cap: 31 Oct 1812 off Saba by HM Sloop Charybdis Int: 19 Nov 1812 Escaped: 24 Apr 1813.
    Received from HM Sloop Charybdis. Escaped Retaken Reentry No (687). Came forward in a handsome manner Deported being involved in a plot to run from the guard.

Fuller, Benjamin   Prisoner 687. Rank: 2 Lieutenant, from: Blockade, Privateer.
    Cap: 31 Oct 1812 off Saba by HM Sloop Charybdis Int: 26 May 1813 Escaped: 08 Jun 1813.
    Received from HM Sloop Peruvian, having escaped & been retaken. Escaped.

Fuller, William   Prisoner 781. Rank: Seaman, from: Old Friend, Not Recorded.
    Cap: 01 Jan 1814 off St. Bartholomew by Viper Privateer Int: 11 Feb 1814 Dis: 25 Apr 1814.
    Received from HM Brig Liberty. Retaken from the Globe Privateer. HM Ship Vestal.

Fullerton, Thomas   Prisoner 692. Rank: Seaman, from: Not Recorded, Merchant.
    Cap: 29 May 1813 at Barbados by HM Ship Rhin Int: 04 Jun 1813 Dis: 11 Aug 1813.
    Received from HM Ship Rhine. Malmore American Cartel.

Furdge, Henry   Prisoner 1124. Rank: Seaman, from: Nancy, Privateer.
    Cap: 06 Sep 1814 Lat 32 N, Long 47 W by HM Ship Piqua Int: 21 Oct 1814 Dis: 08 Feb 1815.
    Received from HMS Piqua. Taken by the Amelia Privateer. HM Ship Swiftsure.

Gair, Thomas   Prisoner 856. Rank: Lieutenant, from: Rattle Snake, Letter of Marque.
    Cap: 11 Mar 1814 Lat 24.07 N, Long 66.47 W by HM Ship Rhin Int: 25 Mar 1814 Dis: 22 Jul 1814.
    Received from HM Ship Rhin. Lieutenant of a Privateer and Passenger on the Rattle Snake. HM Ship Gloucester Rear Admiral Durham.

Gale, Benjamin   Prisoner 498. Rank: Seaman, from: John, Privateer.
    Cap: 06 Feb 1813 Lat 10.0 N, Long 61.0 W by HM Sloop Peruvian Int: 20 Feb 1813 Dis: 11 Aug 1813. Received from HM Ship Cumberland. Malmore American Cartel.

Galley, Henry   Prisoner 608. Rank: Seaman, from: Thomas Penrose, Privateer.
    Cap: 23 Mar 1813 Lat 20.14 W, Long 61.20 W by HM Ship Tribune Int: 28 Mar 1813 Dis: 26 Apr 1813. Received from HM Ship Tribune. America on Parole Sir F. Laforey.

Gallin, Samuel   Prisoner 1420. Rank: Seaman, from: Avon, Privateer.
    Cap: 08 Mar 1815 off Nevis by HM Sloop Barbados Int: 13 Mar 1815 Dis: 15 Mar 1815.
    Received from HM Sloop Barbados. HMS Numen Rear Admiral Durham.

Gardiner, Samuel   Prisoner 564. Rank: Seaman, from: Isabella, Merchant Brig.
    Cap: 08 Dec 1812 off Demuary by Detained by the Custom House Int: 02 Mar 1813 Dis: 11 Aug 1813. Received from Army Schooner Moushe. Malmore American Cartel.

Gardner, Francis   Prisoner 824. Rank: Seaman, from: John, English Merchant.
    Cap: Not Recorded by Not Recorded Int: 11 Mar 1814 Dis: 25 Apr 1814.
    Received from Schooner John. Part of Crew of Schooner John. HM Ship Vestal. (Date of capture not recorded.)

Gardner, Willet C   Prisoner 86. Rank: Seaman, from: Providence, Privateer.
    Cap: 11 Sep 1812 off St. Barthlomew by HM Sloop Dominica Int: 13 Nov 1812 Dis: 10 Jul 1813.
    Received from HM Ship Mercury. Perseverance American Cartel.

American Prisoners of War Held at Barbados During the War of 1812

Gardner, William   Prisoner 1366. Rank: Seaman, from: Spencer, Merchant.
    Cap: 15 Feb 1815 off St Bartholomew by HMS Dasher Int: 03 Mar 1815 Dis: 31 Mar 1815.
    Received from HM Ship Dasher. Out of Custody Rear Adl Durham.

Garner, William   Prisoner 598. Rank: Seaman, from: Thomas Penrose, Privateer.
    Cap: 23 Mar 1813 Lat 20.14 W, Long 61.20 W by HM Ship Tribune Int: 28 Mar 1813 Dis: 26 Apr 1813. Received from HM Ship Tribune. America on Parole Sir F. Laforey.

Garry, Alexander   Prisoner 580. Rank: Seaman, from: HM Ship Vestal, Not Recorded.
    Cap: Not Recorded by Not Recorded Int: 16 Mar 1813 Dis: 11 Aug 1813.
    Received from HM Ship Vestal. Part of Crew of HM Ship Vestal. Malmore American Cartel. (Date of capture not recorded.)

George, John   Prisoner 925. Rank: Seaman, from: President, Privateer.
    Cap: 07 May 1814 off Porto Rico by HM Ship Piqua Int: 20 Jun 1814 Dis: 20 Jul 1814.
    Received from HM Ship Vestal. HM Sloop Hazard Rear Adml Durham.

Germon, Pierre   Prisoner 1214. Rank: Seaman, from: Fox, Privateer.
    Cap: 26 Dec 1814 off St Bartholomew by HM Brig Barbados Int: 14 Jan 1815 Dis: 31 Mar 1815.
    Received from HM Brig Barbados. Rear Adl Durham.

Gerris, Jeremiah   Prisoner 389. Rank: Seaman, from: Decatur, Privateer.
    Cap: 16 Jan 1813 Lat 13.00 N, Long 41.00 N by HM Ship Surprise Int: 26 Jan 1813 Dis: 10 Jul 1813.
    Received from HM Ship Surprise. Perseverance American Cartel.

Gevine, William   Prisoner 570. Rank: Seaman, from: John, Privateer.
    Cap: 06 Feb 1813 Lat 10 N, Long 61 W by HM Sloop Peruvian Int: 08 Mar 1813 Dis: 11 Aug 1813.
    Received from HM Sloop Arachne. Malmore American Cartel.

Gibb, Thomas   Prisoner 53. Rank: Seaman, from: Providence, Privateer.
    Cap: 11 Sep 1812 off St. Barthlomew by HM Sloop Dominica Int: 13 Nov 1812 Dis: 10 Jul 1813.
    Received from HM Ship Mercury. Perseverance American Cartel.

Gibbs, Moses   Prisoner 1396. Rank: Prize Master, from: Avon, Privateer.
    Cap: 08 Mar 1815 off Nevis by HM Sloop Barbados Int: 13 Mar 1815 Dis: 15 Mar 1815.
    Received from HM Sloop Barbados. HMS Numen Rear Admiral Durham.

Giddings, Joseph   Prisoner 335. Rank: Lieutenant, from: Decatur, Privateer.
    Cap: 16 Jan 1813 Lat 13.00 N, Long 41.00 N by HM Ship Surprise Int: 26 Jan 1813 Dis: 10 Jul 1813.
    Received from HM Ship Surprise. Perseverance American Cartel.

Gifford, John   Prisoner 1377. Rank: Seaman, from: Laurence, Merchant.
    Cap: 14 Feb 1815 off Porto Rico by HMS Dasher Int: 04 Mar 1815 Dis: 31 Mar 1815.
    Received from HM Ship Dasher. Out of Custody Rear Adl Durham.

Gilbert, John   Prisoner 1259. Rank: Seaman, from: Fox, Privateer.
    Cap: 26 Dec 1814 off St Bartholomew by HM Brig Barbados Int: 14 Jan 1815 Dis: 31 Mar 1815.
    Received from HM Brig Barbados. Rear Adl Durham.

Gilbert, Timothy   Prisoner 888. Rank: Seaman, from: Hawk, Privateer.
    Cap: 26 Apr 1814 Near the Mona Passage by HM Ship Piqua Int: 20 Jun 1814 Dis: 20 Jul 1814.
    Received from HM Ship Vestal. HM Sloop Hazard Rear Adml Durham.

Gildchrist, Simon   Prisoner 796. Rank: Seaman, from: Atalante, Merchant Schooner.
    Cap: 19 Jan 1814 off Saint Bartholomew by HM Brig Barbados Int: 12 Feb 1814 Dis: 25 Apr 1814.
    Received from HM Schooner Ballahou. HM Ship Vestal.

Gill, James   Prisoner 37. Rank: Mate, from: William Rathbone, Not Recorded.
    Cap: 09 Oct 1812 Lat 22.00 N, Long 60.00 W by HM Sloop Chandler Int: 01 Nov 1812 Dis: 10 Jul 1813. Received from HM Brig Swaggerer. Having been taken by the Savory Jack American privateer. Perseverance American Cartel.

Gilldon, John   Prisoner 1316. Rank: Seaman, from: Whalebone, Merchant Schooner.
    Cap: 25 Jan 1815 off St Bartholomew by HMB Espringle Int: 09 Feb 1815 Dis: 31 Mar 1815.
    Received from HMB Satellite. Rear Adl Durham.

Glading, Joseph   Prisoner 853. Rank: Seaman, from: Rattle Snake, Letter of Marque.
    Cap: 11 Mar 1814 Lat 24.07 N, Long 66.47 W by HM Ship Rhin Int: 25 Mar 1814 Dis: 25 Apr 1814.
    Received from HM Ship Rhin. HM Ship Vestal.

Glover, Benjamin   Prisoner 820. Rank: Seaman, from: Sally & Betsey, Merchant Schooner.
    Cap: 27 Sep 1813 off Porto Rico by HM Sloop Piqua Int: 07 Mar 1814 Dis: 25 Apr 1814.
    Received from HM Ship Piqua. HMS Vestal.

Glover, John   Prisoner 534. Rank: Seaman, from: John, Privateer.
    Cap: 06 Feb 1813 Lat 10.0 N, Long 61.0 W by HM Sloop Peruvian Int: 20 Feb 1813 Dis: 11 Aug 1813. Received from HM Ship Cumberland. American Cartel Malmore.

Glover, Samuel   Prisoner 361. Rank: Seaman, from: Decatur, Privateer.
    Cap: 16 Jan 1813 Lat 13.00 N, Long 41.00 N by HM Ship Surprise Int: 26 Jan 1813 Dis: 10 Jul 1813.
    Received from HM Ship Surprise. Perseverance American Cartel.

American Prisoners of War Held at Barbados During the War of 1812

Godard, William   Prisoner 280. Rank: Seaman, from: Rea, Privateer.
    Cap: 29 Nov 1812 off Barbados by HM Ship Lightning Int: 29 Nov 1812 Dis: 10 Jul 1813.
    Received from HM Ship Lightning. Ship having been captured by the Bona American. Perseverance American Cartel.

Godfrey, John   Prisoner 735. Rank: Prize Master, from: Old Friend, Privateer.
    Cap: 01 Jan 1814 off St Barthlomew by Viper Privateer Int: 02 Feb 1814 Dis: 22 Jul 1814.
    Received from HM Brig Liberty. HM Ship Gloucester Rear Admiral Durham.

Goldthwait, C   Prisoner 1326. Rank: Mate, from: Vidett, Letter of Marque.
    Cap: 14 Feb 1815 off St Bartholomew by HM Ship Dasher Int: 03 Mar 1815 Dis: 31 Mar 1815.
    Received from HM Ship Dasher. Out of Custody Rear Adl Durham.

Goodman, John   Prisoner 373. Rank: Seaman, from: Decatur, Privateer.
    Cap: 16 Jan 1813 Lat 13.00 N, Long 41.00 N by HM Ship Surprise Int: 26 Jan 1813 Dis: 10 Jul 1813.
    Received from HM Ship Surprise. Perseverance American Cartel.

Goodrich, Edward   Prisoner 345. Rank: Seaman, from: Decatur, Privateer.
    Cap: 16 Jan 1813 Lat 13.00 N, Long 41.00 N by HM Ship Surprise Int: 26 Jan 1813 Dis: 10 Jul 1813.
    Received from HM Ship Surprise. Perseverance American Cartel.

Goodwin, E   Prisoner 1426. Rank: Seaman, from: Avon, Privateer.
    Cap: 08 Mar 1815 off Nevis by HM Sloop Barbados Int: 13 Mar 1815 Dis: 15 Mar 1815.
    Received from HM Sloop Barbados. HMS Numen Rear Admiral Durham.

Gordon, Sherwood H   Prisoner 19. Rank: 3 Mate, from: Hope, Merchant Ship.
    Cap: 27 Sep 1812 Lat 22.30 N, Long 40.45 W by HM Ship Tribune Int: 22 Oct 1812 Dis: 24 Oct 1812. Received from Ship Hope. America on Parole per order of Captain Reynolds Tribune.

Goss, John   Prisoner 379. Rank: Seaman, from: Decatur, Privateer.
    Cap: 16 Jan 1813 Lat 13.00 N, Long 41.00 N by HM Ship Surprise Int: 26 Jan 1813 Dis: 10 Jul 1813.
    Received from HM Ship Surprise. Perseverance American Cartel.

Goss, John   Prisoner 840. Rank: Seaman, from: Rattle Snake, Letter of Marque.
    Cap: 11 Mar 1814 Lat 24.07 N, Long 66.47 W by HM Ship Rhin Int: 25 Mar 1814 Dis: 25 Apr 1814.
    Received from HM Ship Rhin. HM Ship Vestal.

Grace, John   Prisoner 887. Rank: Seaman, from: Hawk, Privateer.
    Cap: 26 Apr 1814 Near the Mona Passage by HM Ship Piqua Int: 20 Jun 1814 Dis: 20 Jul 1814.
    Received from HM Ship Vestal. HM Sloop Hazard Rear Adml Durham.

Gracey, Archibald   Prisoner 1443. Rank: Seaman, from: Not Recorded, Not Recorded.
    Cap: Not Recorded by Not Recorded Int: 15 Mar 1815 Dis: 31 Mar 1915.
    Received from Sprighty Mail Boat. Sent from St Vincent by His Excellency Sir C. Brisbane. Out of Custody Rear Adl   Durham. (Date of capture not recorded.)

Grall, Charles   Prisoner 841. Rank: Seaman, from: Rattle Snake, Letter of Marque.
    Cap: 11 Mar 1814 Lat 24.07 N, Long 66.47 W by HM Ship Rhin Int: 25 Mar 1814 Dis: 25 Apr 1814.
    Received from HM Ship Rhin. HM Ship Vestal.

Grambery, Samuel   Prisoner 1317. Rank: Seaman, from: Whalebone, Merchant Schooner.
    Cap: 25 Jan 1815 off St Bartholomew by HMB Espringle Int: 09 Feb 1815 Dis: 31 Mar 1815.
    Received from HMB Satellite. Rear Adl Durham.

Graner, Christopher   Prisoner 1375. Rank: Seaman, from: Laurence, Merchant.
    Cap: 14 Feb 1815 off Porto Rico by HMS Dasher Int: 04 Mar 1815 Dis: 31 Mar 1815.
    Received from HM Ship Dasher. Out of Custody Rear Adl Durham.

Graves, Moses   Prisoner 1418. Rank: Seaman, from: Avon, Privateer.
    Cap: 08 Mar 1815 off Nevis by HM Sloop Barbados Int: 13 Mar 1815 Dis: 15 Mar 1815.
    Received from HM Sloop Barbados. HMS Numen Rear Admiral Durham.

Gravier, Gubviel   Prisoner 1254. Rank: Seaman, from: Fox, Privateer.
    Cap: 26 Dec 1814 off St Bartholomew by HM Brig Barbados Int: 14 Jan 1815 Dis: 08 Feb 1815.
    Received from HM Brig Barbados. HM Ship Swiftsure.

Green, James   Prisoner 119. Rank: Seaman, from: William Rathbone, Brig.
    Cap: 09 Oct 1812 at Sea by HM Sloop Charybdis Int: 13 Nov 1812 Dis: 10 Apr 1813.
    Received from HM Ship Mercury. Retaken Brig Part of Crew of Savory Jack Privateer. America on Parole being very ill.

Green, John   Prisoner 657. Rank: Seaman, from: Adelphia, Privateer.
    Cap: 24 Feb 1813 Surinam by Not Recorded Int: 20 May 1813 Dis: 11 Aug 1813.
    Received from HM Sloop Crane. Part of Crew of Comet having charge of the Ship, which floundered at Sea. Surrendering themselves at Main's Point Surinam. Malmore American Cartel.

Green, John   Prisoner 1219. Rank: Seaman, from: Fox, Privateer.
    Cap: 26 Dec 1814 off St Bartholomew by HM Brig Barbados Int: 14 Jan 1815 Dis: 15 Mar 1815.
    Received from HM Brig Barbados. HMS Numen.

American Prisoners of War Held at Barbados During the War of 1812

Green, Rathbourn   Prisoner 733. Rank: Seaman, from: Greyhound, Merchant Schooner.
    Cap: 13 Jan 1814 off the Virginia (not legible) by HM Schooner Elizabeth Int: 02 Feb 1814 Dis: 02 Feb 1814. Received from HM Brig Liberty. Rising States American Cartel. Rear Adml Sir F. Laforey.

Green, William   Prisoner 648. Rank: Seaman, from: HM Brig Liberty, Not Recorded.
    Cap: Not Recorded by Not Recorded Int: 20 May 1813 Escaped: 30 Jun 1813.
    Received from HM Sloop Crane. Part of Crew of the Brig Liberty. Escaped. (Date of capture not recorded.)

Greene, Samuel   Prisoner 256. Rank: Seaman, from: Brandy Wine, Merchant Brig.
    Cap: 17 Nov 1812 Lat 19.30, Long 57.00 W by HM Ship Lightning Int: 23 Nov 1812 Dis: 02 Dec 1812. Received from HM Ship Lightning. America on Parole Sir F. Laforey.

Greenwood, Maurice   Prisoner 40. Rank: Seaman, from: William Rathbone, Not Recorded.
    Cap: 09 Oct 1812 Lat 22.00 N, Long 60.00 W by HM Sloop Chandler Int: 01 Nov 1812 Dis: 10 Jul 1813. Received from HM Brig Swaggerer. Having been taken by the Savory Jack American privateer. Perseverance American Cartel.

Greer, John   Prisoner 917. Rank: Seaman, from: President, Privateer.
    Cap: 07 May 1814 off Porto Rico by HM Ship Piqua Int: 20 Jun 1814 Dis: 20 Jul 1814.
    Received from HM Ship Vestal. HM Sloop Hazard Rear Adml Durham.

Gregory, Cornelius   Prisoner 1157. Rank: Seaman, from: High Flyer, Letter of Marque.
    Cap: 14 Nov 1814 off Anguilla by HM Ship Barossa Int: 18 Nov 1814 Dis: 08 Feb 1815.
    Received from HM Ship Barossa. HM Ship Swiftsure.

Grey, Francis   Prisoner 766. Rank: Seaman, from: Frolic, Privateer.
    Cap: 25 Jan 1814 off St Thomas by HM Sloop Heron Int: 06 Feb 1814 Dis: 25 Apr 1814.
    Received from HM Sloop Heron. HM Ship Vestal.

Grey, William   Prisoner 1163. Rank: Seaman, from: High Flyer, Letter of Marque.
    Cap: 14 Nov 1814 off Anguilla by HM Ship Barossa Int: 18 Nov 1814 Dis: 08 Feb 1815.
    Received from HM Ship Barossa. Rear Adl Durham.

Gribble, James   Prisoner 546. Rank: Seaman, from: John, Privateer.
    Cap: 06 Feb 1813 Lat 10.0 N, Long 61.0 W by HM Sloop Peruvian Int: 20 Feb 1813 Dis: 11 Aug 1813. Received from HM Ship Cumberland. American Cartel Malmore.

Griest, William   Prisoner 905. Rank: Seaman, from: Hawk, Privateer.
    Cap: 26 Apr 1814 Near the Mona Passage by HM Ship Piqua Int: 20 Jun 1814 Dis: 20 Jul 1814.
    Received from HM Ship Vestal. HM Sloop Hazard Rear Adml Durham.

Griffen, Ebenezer   Prisoner 494. Rank: Seaman, from: John, Privateer.
    Cap: 06 Feb 1813 Lat 10.0 N, Long 61.0 W by HM Sloop Peruvian Int: 20 Feb 1813 Dis: 11 Aug 1813. Received from HM Ship Cumberland. Malmore American Cartel.

Griffen, William   Prisoner 725. Rank: Mate, from: Ellen, Merchant Schooner.
    Cap: 07 Jan 1814 Lat 21.15 N, Long 65.00 W by HMS Piqua Int: 02 Feb 1814 Dis: 02 Feb 1814.
    Received from HM Brig Liberty. Rising States American Cartel. Rear Adml Sir F. Laforey.

Grimes, Richard   Prisoner 195. Rank: Prize Master, from: Blockade, Privateer.
    Cap: 31 Oct 1812 off Saba by HM Sloop Charybdis Int: 19 Nov 1812 Dis: 10 Jul 1813.
    Received from HM Sloop Charybdis. Perseverance American Cartel.

Griswald, Jerard   Prisoner 230. Rank: Seaman, from: Blockade, Privateer.
    Cap: 31 Oct 1812 off Saba by HM Sloop Charybdis Int: 19 Nov 1812 Dis: 10 Apr 1813.
    Received from HM Sloop Charybdis. America on Parole being very ill.

Griswald, Josiah   Prisoner 182. Rank: 3 Lieutenant, from: Blockade, Privateer.
    Cap: 31 Oct 1812 off Saba by HM Sloop Charybdis Int: 19 Nov 1812 Escaped: 24 Apr 1813.
    Received from HM Sloop Charybdis. Escaped Retaken Reentry No (688).

Griswald, Josiah   Prisoner 688. Rank: 3 Lieutenant, from: Blockade, Privateer.
    Cap: 31 Oct 1812 off Saba by HM Sloop Charybdis Int: 26 May 1813 Dis: 14 Jun 1813.
    Received from HM Sloop Peruvian, having escaped & been retaken. HMS Cufay for passage to England. Sir F. Laforey.

Griswald, Truman   Prisoner 237. Rank: Seaman, from: Blockade, Privateer.
    Cap: 31 Oct 1812 off Saba by HM Sloop Charybdis Int: 19 Nov 1812 Dis: 10 Jul 1813.
    Received from HM Sloop Charybdis. Perseverance American Cartel.

Grove, George W   Prisoner 1026. Rank: Seaman, from: HM Brig Spider, Not Recorded.
    Cap: Not Recorded by Not Recorded Int: 11 Jul 1814 Dis: 22 Jul 1814.
    Received from HM Schooner Flying Fish. Part of Crew of HM Brig Spider. HM Ship Gloucester Rear Admiral Durham. (Date of capture not recorded.)

Groves, Thomas   Prisoner 839. Rank: Seaman, from: Rattle Snake, Letter of Marque.
    Cap: 11 Mar 1814 Lat 24.07 N, Long 66.47 W by HM Ship Rhin Int: 25 Mar 1814 Dis: 25 Apr 1814.
    Received from HM Ship Rhin. HM Ship Vestal.

American Prisoners of War Held at Barbados During the War of 1812

Grush, Thomas   Prisoner 339. Rank: Prize Master, from: Decatur, Privateer.
    Cap: 16 Jan 1813 Lat 13.00 N, Long 41.00 N by HM Ship Surprise Int: 26 Jan 1813 Dis: 10 Jul 1813.
    Received from HM Ship Surprise. Perseverance American Cartel.

Grush, Thomas   Prisoner 543. Rank: Seaman, from: John, Privateer.
    Cap: 06 Feb 1813 Lat 10.0 N, Long 61.0 W by HM Sloop Peruvian Int: 20 Feb 1813 Dis: 11 Aug 1813. Received from HM Ship Cumberland. American Cartel Malmore.

Guanough, William   Prisoner 1108. Rank: Seaman, from: Mars, Privateer.
    Cap: 01 Sep 1814 Lat 41 N, Long 52 W by HM Ship Piqua Int: 21 Oct 1814 Dis: 08 Feb 1815.
    Received from HMS Piqua. Taken by the David Porter Privateer. Riotous Character. HM Ship Swiftsure.

Guisar, Nicholas   Prisoner 1049. Rank: Seaman, from: Mary, Letter of Marque.
    Cap: 07 Jun 1814 La Quisa by HM Ship Heron Int: 31 Jul 1814 Dis: 31 Mar 1815.
    Received from HM Sloop Mosquito. Rear Adl Durham.

Gunney, Thomas   Prisoner 375. Rank: Seaman, from: Decatur, Privateer.
    Cap: 16 Jan 1813 Lat 13.00 N, Long 41.00 N by HM Ship Surprise Int: 26 Jan 1813 Dis: 10 Jul 1813.
    Received from HM Ship Surprise. Perseverance American Cartel.

Gyles, William   Prisoner 254. Rank: 2 Mate, from: Brandy Wine, Merchant Brig.
    Cap: 17 Nov 1812 Lat 19.30, Long 57.00 W by HM Ship Lightning Int: 23 Nov 1812 Dis: 02 Dec 1812. Received from HM Ship Lightning. America on Parole Sir F. Laforey.

Hacker, Isaac   Prisoner 484. Rank: Seaman, from: John, Privateer.
    Cap: 06 Feb 1813 Lat 10.0 N, Long 61.0 W by HM Sloop Peruvian Int: 20 Feb 1813 Dis: 10 Jul 1813.
    Received from HM Ship Cumberland. Perseverance American Cartel.

Hackett, John   Prisoner 922. Rank: Seaman, from: President, Privateer.
    Cap: 07 May 1814 off Porto Rico by HM Ship Piqua Int: 20 Jun 1814 Dis: 20 Jul 1814.
    Received from HM Ship Vestal. HM Sloop Hazard Rear Adml Durham.

Hackleton, John   Prisoner 533. Rank: Seaman, from: John, Privateer.
    Cap: 06 Feb 1813 Lat 10.0 N, Long 61.0 W by HM Sloop Peruvian Int: 20 Feb 1813 Dis: 11 Aug 1813. Received from HM Ship Cumberland. American Cartel Malmore.

Halbrut, Henry   Prisoner 830. Rank: Seaman, from: Rattle Snake, Letter of Marque.
    Cap: 11 Mar 1814 Lat 24.07 N, Long 66.47 W by HM Ship Rhin Int: 25 Mar 1814 Dis: 22 Jul 1814.
    Received from HM Ship Rhin. HM Ship Vestal.

Hale, Christopher   Prisoner 1111. Rank: Seaman, from: Mars, Privateer.
    Cap: 01 Sep 1814 Lat 41 N, Long 52 W by HM Ship Piqua Int: 21 Oct 1814 Dis: 31 Mar 1815.
    Received from HMS Piqua. Taken by the David Porter Privateer. Rear Adl Durham.

Hale, James   Prisoner 1327. Rank: 2 Mate, from: Vidett, Letter of Marque.
    Cap: 14 Feb 1815 off St Bartholomew by HM Ship Dasher Int: 03 Mar 1815 Dis: 31 Mar 1815.
    Received from HM Ship Dasher. Out of Custody Rear Adl Durham.

Hall, John   Prisoner 779. Rank: Seaman, from: Old Friend, Not Recorded.
    Cap: 01 Jan 1814 off St. Bartholomew by Viper Privateer Int: 11 Feb 1814 Dis: 25 Apr 1814.
    Received from HM Brig Liberty. Retaken from the Globe Privateer. HM Ship Vestal.

Hall, Samuel   Prisoner 418. Rank: Seaman, from: Apollo, Merchant Ship.
    Cap: 22 Dec 1812 off Tenioff by HM Ship Grampus Int: 30 Jan 1813 Dis: 10 Jul 1813.
    Received from HM Sloop Demerary. Perseverance American Cartel.

Hall, William   Prisoner 584. Rank: Seaman, from: HM Ship Vestal, Not Recorded.
    Cap: Not Recorded by Not Recorded Int: 16 Mar 1813 Dis: 11 Aug 1813.
    Received from HM Ship Vestal. Part of Crew of HM Ship Vestal. Malmore American Cartel. (Date of capture not recorded.)

Hallcock, Edward   Prisoner 1149. Rank: Seaman, from: High Flyer, Letter of Marque.
    Cap: 14 Nov 1814 off Anguilla by HM Ship Barossa Int: 18 Nov 1814 Dis: 14 Feb 1815.
    Received from HM Ship Barossa. HM Ship Piqua Rear Admiral Durham.

Hambert, William   Prisoner 1431. Rank: Seaman, from: Avon, Privateer.
    Cap: 08 Mar 1815 off Nevis by HM Sloop Barbados Int: 13 Mar 1815 Dis: 15 Mar 1815.
    Received from HM Sloop Barbados. HMS Numen Rear Admiral Durham.

Hamilton, Benjamin   Prisoner 359. Rank: Seaman, from: Decatur, Privateer.
    Cap: 16 Jan 1813 Lat 13.00 N, Long 41.00 N by HM Ship Surprise Int: 26 Jan 1813 Dis: 10 Jul 1813.
    Received from HM Ship Surprise. Perseverance American Cartel.

Hamilton, Charles   Prisoner 323. Rank: Seaman, from: James Murdock, Merchant Brig.
    Cap: 05 Jan 1813 Lat 21 N, Long 57 W by HM Sloop Nimrod Int: 11 Jan 1813 Dis: 25 Jan 1813.
    Received from HM Sloop Nimrod. Being Married in England.

Handcock, James   Prisoner 982. Rank: Seaman, from: Atlas, Merchant.
    Cap: 20 Mar 1814 off Saba by HM Ship Ister Int: 20 Jun 1814 Dis: 22 Jul 1814.
    Received from HM Ship Vestal. HM Ship Gloucester Rear Admiral Durham.

American Prisoners of War Held at Barbados During the War of 1812

Hansford, Stephen   Prisoner 125. Rank: Seaman, from: William Rathbone, Brig.
  Cap: 09 Oct 1812 at Sea by HM Sloop Charybdis Int: 13 Nov 1812 Dis: 10 Jul 1813.
  Received from HM Ship Mercury. Retaken Brig Part of Crew of Savory Jack Privateer. Perseverance American Cartel.

Hanton, William   Prisoner 1118. Rank: Seaman, from: Aquila, Privateer.
  Cap: 04 Sep 1814 Lat 22 N, Long 36 W by HM Ship Piqua Int: 21 Oct 1814 Dis: 08 Feb 1815.
  Received from HMS Piqua. Taken by the Whig Privateer. HM Ship Swiftsure.

Harby, Levy   Prisoner 60. Rank: Seaman, from: Providence, Privateer.
  Cap: 11 Sep 1812 off St. Barthlomew by HM Sloop Dominica Int: 13 Nov 1812 Dis: 10 Jul 1813.
  Received from HM Ship Mercury. Perseverance American Cartel.

Hardy, James   Prisoner 247. Rank: Seaman, from: HM Sloop Arachne, Not Recorded.
  Cap: Not Recorded by Not Recorded Int: 22 Nov 1812 Dis: 10 Jul 1813.
  Received from HM Sloop Arachne. Part of Crew of HM Sloop Arachne. Perseverance American Cartel. (Date of capture not recorded.)

Hargood, Richard   Prisoner 1328. Rank: Pilot, from: Vidett, Letter of Marque.
  Cap: 14 Feb 1815 off St Bartholomew by HM Ship Dasher Int: 03 Mar 1815 Dis: 31 Mar 1815.
  Received from HM Ship Dasher. Out of Custody Rear Adl Durham.

Harlow, Lewis   Prisoner 664. Rank: Seaman, from: William, Merchant Brig.
  Cap: 16 Apr 1813 Lat 35.00 N, Long 57.00 W by Heron Int: 22 May 1813 Dis: 10 Jul 1813.
  Received from HM Sloop Heron. Perseverance American Cartel.

Harman, John   Prisoner 924. Rank: Seaman, from: President, Privateer.
  Cap: 07 May 1814 off Porto Rico by HM Ship Piqua Int: 20 Jun 1814 Dis: 20 Jul 1814.
  Received from HM Ship Vestal. HM Sloop Hazard Rear Adml Durham.

Harris, Benjamin   Prisoner 801. Rank: Seaman, from: Reassurance, Merchant Schooner.
  Cap: 25 Jan 1814 off Saint Bartholomew by HM Brig Barbados Int: 12 Feb 1814 Dis: 25 Apr 1814.
  Received from HM Schooner Ballahou. HM Ship Vestal.

Harris, Benjamin   Prisoner 1330. Rank: Seaman, from: Vidett, Letter of Marque.
  Cap: 14 Feb 1815 off St Bartholomew by HM Ship Dasher Int: 03 Mar 1815 Dis: 31 Mar 1815.
  Received from HM Ship Dasher. Out of Custody Rear Adl Durham.

Harris, James   Prisoner 814. Rank: Seaman, from: Frolic, Privateer.
  Cap: 25 Jan 1814 off St Thomas by HM Sloop Heron Int: 22 Feb 1814 Dis: 25 Apr 1814.
  Received from HM Brig Liberty. HM Ship Vestal.

Harris, William   Prisoner 271. Rank: Seaman, from: Rea, Privateer.
  Cap: 29 Nov 1812 off Barbados by HM Ship Lightning Int: 29 Nov 1812 Dis: 10 Jul 1813.
  Received from HM Ship Lightning. Ship having been captured by the Bona American. Perseverance American Cartel.

Harris, William   Prisoner 522. Rank: Seaman, from: John, Privateer.
  Cap: 06 Feb 1813 Lat 10.0 N, Long 61.0 W by HM Sloop Peruvian Int: 20 Feb 1813 Dis: 11 Aug 1813. Received from HM Ship Cumberland. Malmore American Cartel.

Harrison, John   Prisoner 728. Rank: Seaman, from: Ellen, Merchant Schooner.
  Cap: 07 Jan 1814 Lat 21.15 N, Long 65.00 W by HMS Piqua Int: 02 Feb 1814 Dis: 02 Feb 1814.
  Received from HM Brig Liberty. Rising States American Cartel. Rear Adml Sir F. Laforey.

Harrison, Silus   Prisoner 1004. Rank: Seaman, from: Hawk, Privateer.
  Cap: 26 Apr 1814 Near the Mona Passage by HM Ship Piqua Int: 20 Jun 1814 Dis: 22 Jul 1814.
  Received from HM Ship Vestal. HM Ship Gloucester Rear Admiral Durham.

Harthorn, John   Prisoner 765. Rank: Seaman, from: Frolic, Privateer.
  Cap: 25 Jan 1814 off St Thomas by HM Sloop Heron Int: 06 Feb 1814 Dis: 25 Apr 1814.
  Received from HM Sloop Heron. HM Ship Vestal.

Harvey, Francis   Prisoner 1196. Rank: Prize Master, from: Fox, Privateer.
  Cap: 11 Jan 1815 off St Bartholomew by HM Brig Barbados Int: 14 Jan 1815 Dis: 08 Feb 1815.
  Received from HM Brig Barbados. HM Ship Swiftsure. (Capture date is Dec 26, 1814 for all entries for Fox except records 1190 - 1198.)

Harvey, John   Prisoner 1102. Rank: Seaman, from: Engineer, Letter of Marque.
  Cap: 21 Sep 1814 of Porto Rico by HM Ship Barossa Int: 29 Sep 1814 Dis: 31 Mar 1815.
  Received from HM Ship Barossa. Rear Adl Durham.

Harvey, Samuel   Prisoner 1083. Rank: Seaman, from: Engineer, Letter of Marque.
  Cap: 21 Sep 1814 of Porto Rico by HM Ship Barossa Int: 29 Sep 1814 Dis: 31 Mar 1815.
  Received from HM Ship Barossa. Rear Adl Durham.

Hassard, Jason   Prisoner 215. Rank: Seaman, from: Blockade, Privateer.
  Cap: 31 Oct 1812 off Saba by HM Sloop Charybdis Int: 19 Nov 1812 Dis: 10 Jul 1813.
  Received from HM Sloop Charybdis. Perseverance American Cartel.

American Prisoners of War Held at Barbados During the War of 1812

Hastings, John   Prisoner 815. Rank: Seaman, from: Globe, Privateer.
    Cap: 01 Jan 1814 off St Bartholomew by Viper Privateer Int: 22 Feb 1814 Dis: 25 Apr 1814.
    Received from HM Brig Liberty. HM Ship Vestal.

Hatchet, John   Prisoner 1027. Rank: Seaman, from: North Star, Merchant Schooner.
    Cap: 10 Jun 1814 off St Bartholomew by HM Brig Crane Int: 11 Jul 1814 Dis: 22 Jul 1814.
    Received from HM Schooner Flying Fish. HM Ship Gloucester Rear Admiral Durham.

Hathaway, William   Prisoner 1067. Rank: 1 Mate, from: Mary, Letter of Marque.
    Cap: 07 Jun 1814 La Quisa by HM Ship Heron Int: 31 Jul 1814 Dis: 21 Nov 1814.
    Received from HM Sloop Mosquito. Exchanged.

Haulbut, Nathanial   Prisoner 5. Rank: Master, from: Neptune, Merchant Brig.
    Cap: 29 Aug 1812 Lat 29 N, Lon 59.30 W by HM Brig Maria Int: 04 Oct 1812 Dis: 04 Nov 1812.
    Received from HM Ship Vestal. America on Parole per order of Captain Reynolds Tribune.

Hausford, Stephen   Prisoner 1231. Rank: Seaman, from: Fox, Privateer.
    Cap: 26 Dec 1814 off St Bartholomew by HM Brig Barbados Int: 14 Jan 1815 Dis: 08 Feb 1815.
    Received from HM Brig Barbados. HM Ship Swiftsure.

Hawkes, M   Prisoner 1387. Rank: Surgeon, from: Avon, Privateer.
    Cap: 08 Mar 1815 off Nevis by HM Sloop Barbados Int: 05 Mar 1815 Dis: 31 Mar 1815.
    Received from HM Ship Dasher. Out of Custody Rear Adl Durham. (Date of Interment before Capture.)

Hawkins, Henry   Prisoner 295. Rank: Passenger, from: Phoenix, Merchant Brig.
    Cap: 24 Nov 1812 Lat 37.03 N, Long 60.00 W by HM Sloop Morgiana Int: 16 Dec 1812 Dis: 17 Jan 1813.
    Received from HM Sloop Morgiana. America being a non Combatant.

Hawkins, Samuel   Prisoner 481. Rank: Carpenter, from: John, Privateer.
    Cap: 06 Feb 1813 Lat 10.0 N, Long 61.0 W by HM Sloop Peruvian Int: 20 Feb 1813 Dis: 11 Aug 1813.
    Received from HM Ship Cumberland. Malmore American Cartel.

Hawse, Hance Thomas   Prisoner 704. Rank: Seaman, from: Saturn, Merchant Brig.
    Cap: 10 May 1813 off Martinique by HM Ship Mercury Int: 17 Jun 1813 Dis: 11 Aug 1813.
    Received from HM Ship Mercury. Malmore American Cartel.

Hawthorn, Stephen   Prisoner 48. Rank: Seaman, from: Providence, Privateer.
    Cap: 11 Sep 1812 off St. Bartholomew by HM Sloop Dominica Int: 13 Nov 1812 Dis: 10 Jul 1813.
    Received from HM Ship Mercury. Perseverance American Cartel.

Hayden, Uriah   Prisoner 1355. Rank: Mate, from: Spencer, Merchant.
    Cap: 15 Feb 1815 off St Bartholomew by HMS Dasher Int: 03 Mar 1815 Dis: 31 Mar 1815.
    Received from HM Ship Dasher. Out of Custody Rear Adl Durham.

Hayford, Gardner   Prisoner 47. Rank: Seaman, from: Providence, Privateer.
    Cap: 11 Sep 1812 off St. Barthlemew by HM Sloop Dominica Int: 13 Nov 1812 Dis: 10 Jul 1813.
    Received from HM Ship Mercury. Perseverance American Cartel.

Hayward, Abraham   Prisoner 1130. Rank: Seaman, from: Nancy, Privateer.
    Cap: 06 Sep 1814 Lat 32 N, Long 47 W by HM Ship Piqua Int: 23 Oct 1814 Dis: 08 Feb 1815.
    Received from HMS Piqua. Taken by the Amelia Privateer. Formerly Master of a Merchantman. HM Ship Swiftsure.

Hazler, Henry   Prisoner 1256. Rank: Clerk, from: Fox, Privateer.
    Cap: 26 Dec 1814 off St Bartholomew by HM Brig Barbados Int: 14 Jan 1815 Dis: 08 Feb 1815.
    Received from HM Brig Barbados. HM Ship Swiftsure.

Headings, Isaac   Prisoner 787. Rank: Seaman, from: Fox, Privateer.
    Cap: Not Recorded by Not Recorded Int: 11 Feb 1814 Dis: 25 Apr 1814.
    Received from HM Brig Liberty. Picked up in a boat at Sea part of Crew of Fox. HM Ship Vestal. (Date of capture not recorded.)

Hedrick, Samuel   Prisoner 1176. Rank: Mate & Passenger, from: San Francisco, Merchant.
    Cap: 07 Dec 1814 Lat 32.30 N, Long 65.00 W by HM Ship Ister Int: 28 Dec 1814 Dis: 08 Feb 1815.
    Received from HMS Ister. HM Ship Swiftsure.

Heislop, Matthew   Prisoner 1230. Rank: Seaman, from: Fox, Privateer.
    Cap: 26 Dec 1814 off St Bartholomew by HM Brig Barbados Int: 14 Jan 1815 Dis: 08 Feb 1815.
    Received from HM Brig Barbados. HM Ship Swiftsure.

Helah, Timothy   Prisoner 778. Rank: 2 Mate, from: Georgianna, Merchant Schooner.
    Cap: 01 Oct 1813 off St. Michaels by HM Ship Lacedaemonian Int: 11 Feb 1814 Dis: 14 May 1814.
    Received from HM Brig Liberty. HM Ship Vestal.

Henion, John   Prisoner 362. Rank: Seaman, from: Decatur, Privateer.
    Cap: 16 Jan 1813 Lat 13.00 N, Long 41.00 N by HM Ship Surprise Int: 26 Jan 1813 Escaped: 06 Jun 1813. Received from HM Ship Surprise. Escaped.

Henry, David   Prisoner 409. Rank: Seaman, from: Washington, Merchant Ship.
    Cap: 25 Dec 1812 off Cadiz by HM Ship Grampus Int: 30 Jan 1813 Dis: 26 Apr 1813.
    Received from HM Sloop Demerary. Out of Custody the Vessel being liberated.

American Prisoners of War Held at Barbados During the War of 1812

Henry, John B   Prisoner 1208. Rank: Seaman, from: Fox, Privateer.
 Cap: 26 Dec 1814 off St Bartholomew by HM Brig Barbados Int: 14 Jan 1815 Dis: 08 Feb 1815.
 Received from HM Brig Barbados. HM Ship Swiftsure.

Henry, William   Prisoner 424. Rank: Seaman, from: Anna, Not Recorded.
 Cap: 03 Jan 1813 off Maderia by HM Ship Cumberland Int: 30 Jan 1813 Dis: 10 Jul 1813.
 Received from HM Sloop Demerary. Recaptured from the Mars Privateer. Perseverance American Cartel.

Herbert, Peter   Prisoner 268. Rank: Seaman, from: Rea, Privateer.
 Cap: 29 Nov 1812 off Barbados by HM Ship Lightning Int: 29 Nov 1812 Dis: 10 Jul 1813.
 Received from HM Ship Lightning. Ship having been captured by the Bona American. Perseverance American Cartel.

Hercules, David   Prisoner 561. Rank: Seaman, from: Isabella, Merchant Brig.
 Cap: 08 Dec 1812 off Demuary by Detained by the Custom House Int: 02 Mar 1813 Dis: 11 Aug 1813. Received from Army Schooner Moushe. Malmore American Cartel.

Hermines, Hoasa   Prisoner 1244. Rank: Seaman, from: Fox, Privateer.
 Cap: 26 Dec 1814 off St Bartholomew by HM Brig Barbados Int: 14 Jan 1815 Dis: 08 Feb 1815.
 Received from HM Brig Barbados. HM Ship Swiftsure.

Hester, Stephen   Prisoner 1179. Rank: Seaman, from: Gallant Hull, Merchant.
 Cap: 28 Dec 1814 off St Bartholomew by HM Ship Barossa Int: 10 Jan 1815 Dis: 14 Feb 1815.
 Received from HMS Barossa. HM Ship Piqua.

Hewet, Robert   Prisoner 451. Rank: Seaman, from: HM Brig Scorpion, Not Recorded.
 Cap: Not Recorded by Not Recorded Int: 12 Feb 1812 Dis: 11 Aug 1813.
 Received from HM Brig Liberty. Part of Crew of HM Brig Scorpion given up as a Prisoner of War. Malmore American Cartel. (Date of capture not recorded.)

Hickey, William   Prisoner 274. Rank: Seaman, from: Rea, Privateer.
 Cap: 29 Nov 1812 off Barbados by HM Ship Lightning Int: 29 Nov 1812 Dis: 10 Jul 1813.
 Received from HM Ship Lightning. Ship having been captured by the Bona American. Perseverance American Cartel.

Hicks, John C   Prisoner 1193. Rank: Master, from: Fox, Privateer.
 Cap: 11 Jan 1815 off St Bartholomew by HM Brig Barbados Int: 14 Jan 1815 Dis: 08 Feb 1815.
 Received from HM Brig Barbados. HM Ship Swiftsure. (Capture date is Dec 26, 1814 for all entries for Fox except records 1190 - 1198.)

Hidalgo, Balace   Prisoner 919. Rank: Seaman, from: President, Privateer.
 Cap: 07 May 1814 off Porto Rico by HM Ship Piqua Int: 20 Jun 1814 Dis: 20 Jul 1814.
 Received from HM Ship Vestal. HM Sloop Hazard Rear Adml Durham.

Hidalgo, Vincent   Prisoner 947. Rank: Seaman, from: President, Privateer.
 Cap: 07 May 1814 off Porto Rico by HM Ship Piqua Int: 20 Jun 1814 Dis: 22 Jul 1814.
 Received from HM Ship Vestal. HM Ship Gloucester Rear Admiral Durham.

Hidge, Josiah   Prisoner 1390. Rank: Sergeant Marines, from: Avon, Privateer.
 Cap: 08 Mar 1815 off Nevis by HM Sloop Barbados Int: 05 Mar 1815 Dis: 31 Mar 1815.
 Received from HM Ship Dasher. Out of Custody Rear Adl Durham. (Date of Interment before Capture.)

Higgins, Freeman   Prisoner 1012. Rank: Seaman, from: William, Merchant.
 Cap: 18 May 1814 off Charleston by HM Ship Ister Int: 21 Jun 1814 Dis: 22 Jul 1814.
 Received from HM Ship Vestal. HM Ship Gloucester Rear Adml Durham.

Higgins, William H   Prisoner 221. Rank: Seaman, from: Blockade, Privateer.
 Cap: 31 Oct 1812 off Saba by HM Sloop Charybdis Int: 19 Nov 1812 Dis: 10 Jul 1813.
 Received from HM Sloop Charybdis. Perseverance American Cartel.

Hill, Daniel   Prisoner 294. Rank: Seaman, from: Phoenix, Merchant Brig.
 Cap: 24 Nov 1812 Lat 37.03 N, Long 60.00 W by HM Sloop Morgiana Int: 16 Dec 1812 Dis: 17 Jan 1813. Received from HM Sloop Morgiana. Exchanged.

Hill, Shadrock   Prisoner 1312. Rank: Master, from: Whalebone, Merchant Schooner.
 Cap: 25 Jan 1815 off St Bartholomew by HMB Espringle Int: 30 Jan 1815 Dis: 31 Mar 1815.
 Received from HMB Espringle. Rear Adl Durham.

Hillman, Benjamin   Prisoner 1389. Rank: Boy, from: Avon, Privateer.
 Cap: 08 Mar 1815 off Nevis by HM Sloop Barbados Int: 05 Mar 1815 Dis: 31 Mar 1815.
 Received from HM Ship Dasher. Out of Custody Rear Adl Durham. (Date of Interment before Capture.)

Hilton, Samuel   Prisoner 399. Rank: Seaman, from: Decatur, Privateer.
 Cap: 16 Jan 1813 Lat 13.00 N, Long 41.00 N by HM Ship Surprise Int: 26 Jan 1813 Dis: 10 Jul 1813.
 Received from HM Ship Surprise. Perseverance American Cartel.

American Prisoners of War Held at Barbados During the War of 1812

Hine, Henry   Prisoner 201. Rank: Seaman, from: Blockade, Privateer.
    Cap: 31 Oct 1812 off Saba by HM Sloop Charybdis Int: 19 Nov 1812 Dis: 10 Jul 1813.
    Received from HM Sloop Charybdis. Perseverance American Cartel.

Hine, Isaiah   Prisoner 1041. Rank: Seaman, from: Mary, Letter of Marque.
    Cap: 07 Jun 1814 La Quisa by HM Ship Heron Int: 31 Jul 1814 Dis: 31 Mar 1815.
    Received from HM Sloop Mosquito. Rear Adl Durham.

Hobbeston, Thomas A   Prisoner 508. Rank: Seaman, from: John, Privateer.
    Cap: 06 Feb 1813 Lat 10.0 N, Long 61.0 W by HM Sloop Peruvian Int: 20 Feb 1813 Dis: 11 Aug 1813. Received from HM Ship Cumberland. Malmore American Cartel.

Hodetron, John   Prisoner 394. Rank: Seaman, from: Decatur, Privateer.
    Cap: 16 Jan 1813 Lat 13.00 N, Long 41.00 N by HM Ship Surprise Int: 26 Jan 1813 Dis: 10 Jul 1813.
    Received from HM Ship Surprise. Perseverance American Cartel.

Hodgskins, Phillip   Prisoner 1164. Rank: Seaman, from: Not Recorded, Not Recorded.
    Cap: 03 Dec 1814 Barbados by Not Recorded Int: 03 Dec 1814 Dis: 31 Mar 1815.
    Received from HMS Espingle. (Not legible) on Shore at Barbados. Rear Adl Durham.

Holbrook, Gideon   Prisoner 663. Rank: Mate, from: William, Merchant Brig.
    Cap: 16 Apr 1813 Lat 35.00 N, Long 57.00 W by Heron Int: 22 May 1813 Dis: 05 Jun 1813.
    Received from HM Sloop Heron. America on Parole Sir F. Laforey.

Holden, Arnold   Prisoner 205. Rank: Seaman, from: Blockade, Privateer.
    Cap: 31 Oct 1812 off Saba by HM Sloop Charybdis Int: 19 Nov 1812 Dis: 10 Jul 1813.
    Received from HM Sloop Charybdis. Perseverance American Cartel.

Holden, Charles   Prisoner 746. Rank: Boatswain, from: Frolic, Privateer.
    Cap: 25 Jan 1814 off St Thomas by HM Sloop Heron Int: 06 Feb 1814 Dis: 25 Apr 1814.
    Received from HM Sloop Heron. HM Ship Vestal Rear Admiral Durham.

Holden, Horace   Prisoner 14. Rank: Seaman, from: Shepherdess, Merchant Schooner.
    Cap: 12 Oct 1812 Lat 20.00 N, Long 56.00 W by HM Sloop Lightning Int: 22 Oct 1812 Dis: 24 Oct 1812. Received from HM Sloop Lightning. America on Parole per order of Captain Reynolds Tribune.

Holden, John   Prisoner 482. Rank: Boatswain, from: John, Privateer.
    Cap: 06 Feb 1813 Lat 10.0 N, Long 61.0 W by HM Sloop Peruvian Int: 20 Feb 1813 Dis: 11 Aug 1813. Received from HM Ship Cumberland. Malmore American Cartel.

Holmes, George   Prisoner 990. Rank: Seaman, from: Hawk, Privateer.
    Cap: 26 Apr 1814 Near the Mona Passage by HM Ship Piqua Int: 20 Jun 1814 Dis: 22 Jul 1814.
    Received from HM Ship Vestal. HM Ship Gloucester Rear Admiral Durham.

Holmes, William   Prisoner 1425. Rank: Seaman, from: Avon, Privateer.
    Cap: 08 Mar 1815 off Nevis by HM Sloop Barbados Int: 13 Mar 1815 Dis: 15 Mar 1815.
    Received from HM Sloop Barbados. HMS Numen Rear Admiral Durham.

Homes, Barblett   Prisoner 1386. Rank: 2 Lieutenant, from: Avon, Privateer.
    Cap: 08 Mar 1815 off Nevis by HM Sloop Barbados Int: 05 Mar 1815 Dis: 31 Mar 1815.
    Received from HM Ship Dasher. Out of Custody Rear Adl Durham. (Date of Interment before Capture.)

Hooram, William   Prisoner 1354. Rank: Seaman, from: Vidett, Letter of Marque.
    Cap: 14 Feb 1815 off St Bartholomew by HMS Dasher Int: 03 Mar 1815 Dis: 31 Mar 1815.
    Received from HM Ship Dasher. Out of Custody Rear Adl Durham.

Hooters, John   Prisoner 653. Rank: Seaman, from: Adelphia, Privateer.
    Cap: 24 Feb 1813 Surinam by Not Recorded Int: 20 May 1813 Dis: 11 Aug 1813.
    Received from HM Sloop Crane. Part of Crew of Comet having charge of the Ship, which floundered at Sea. Surrendering themselves at Main's Point Surinam. Malmore American Cartel.

Hopkins, Nicholas   Prisoner 6. Rank: Captain, from: Providence, Privateer.
    Cap: 11 Sep 1812 off St. Bartholomew by HM Sloop Dominica Int: 04 Oct 1812 Dis: 10 Jul 1813.
    Received from HM Ship Vestal. Perseverance American Cartel.

Hopkins, Richard L D   Prisoner 1121. Rank: Prize Master, from: Nancy, Privateer.
    Cap: 06 Sep 1814 Lat 32 N, Long 47 W by HM Ship Piqua Int: 21 Oct 1814 Dis: 08 Mar 1815.
    Received from HMS Piqua. Taken by the Amelia Privateer. Rear Adl Durham.

Horace, Kemble   Prisoner 263. Rank: Prize Master, from: Rea, Privateer.
    Cap: 29 Nov 1812 off Barbados by HM Ship Lightning Int: 29 Nov 1812 Dis: 10 Apr 1813.
    Received from HM Ship Lightning. Ship having been captured by the Bona American. America on Parole being very ill.

Hordoffer, John   Prisoner 1057. Rank: Seaman, from: Mary, Letter of Marque.
    Cap: 07 Jun 1814 La Quisa by HM Ship Heron Int: 31 Jul 1814 Dis: 31 Mar 1815.
    Received from HM Sloop Mosquito. Rear Adl Durham.

American Prisoners of War Held at Barbados During the War of 1812

Horner, James   Prisoner 579. Rank: Seaman, from: HM Ship Vestal, Not Recorded.
    Cap: Not Recorded by Not Recorded Int: 16 Mar 1813 Dis: 11 Aug 1813.
    Received from HM Ship Vestal. Part of Crew of HM Ship Vestal. Malmore American Cartel. (Date of capture not recorded.)

Horton, Henry   Prisoner 583. Rank: Seaman, from: HM Ship Vestal, Not Recorded.
    Cap: Not Recorded by Not Recorded Int: 16 Mar 1813 Dis: 11 Aug 1813.
    Received from HM Ship Vestal. Part of Crew of HM Ship Vestal. Malmore American Cartel. (Date of capture not recorded.)

Hosmer, George   Prisoner 226. Rank: Seaman, from: Blockade, Privateer.
    Cap: 31 Oct 1812 off Saba by HM Sloop Charybdis Int: 19 Nov 1812 Dis: 10 Jul 1813.
    Received from HM Sloop Charybdis. Perseverance American Cartel.

Hosse, Fourier   Prisoner 1213. Rank: Seaman, from: Fox, Privateer.
    Cap: 26 Dec 1814 off St Bartholomew by HM Brig Barbados Int: 14 Jan 1815 Dis: 08 Feb 1815.
    Received from HM Brig Barbados. HM Ship Swiftsure.

Hossnogle, John   Prisoner 455. Rank: Seaman, from: Bowrey, Privateer.
    Cap: 02 Feb 1813 off Barbados by HM Sloop Opossum Int: 18 Feb 1813 Dis: 11 Aug 1813.
    Received from HM Sloop Opossum. English Brig Captured by the American Comet. Malmore American Cartel.

Hotchess, John   Prisoner 703. Rank: Seaman, from: Saturn, Merchant Brig.
    Cap: 10 May 1813 off Martinique by HM Ship Mercury Int: 17 Jun 1813 Dis: 11 Aug 1813.
    Received from HM Ship Mercury. Malmore American Cartel.

Housan, Thomas   Prisoner 386. Rank: Seaman, from: Decatur, Privateer.
    Cap: 16 Jan 1813 Lat 13.00 N, Long 41.00 N by HM Ship Surprise Int: 26 Jan 1813 Dis: 10 Jul 1813.
    Received from HM Ship Surprise. Perseverance American Cartel.

Houstaon, John   Prisoner 175. Rank: Seaman, from: HM Ship Hyperion, Not Recorded.
    Cap: Not Recorded by Not Recorded Int: 14 Nov 1812 Dis: 10 Jul 1813.
    Received from HM Ship Hyperion. Gave up as Prisoners of War Part of the Crew of HM Ship Hyperion. Perseverance American Cartel. (Date of capture not recorded.)

Howard, Hyman   Prisoner 85. Rank: Seaman, from: Providence, Privateer.
    Cap: 11 Sep 1812 off St. Barthlomew by HM Sloop Dominica Int: 13 Nov 1812 Dis: 10 Jul 1813.
    Received from HM Ship Mercury. Perseverance American Cartel.

Howber, Serrin   Prisoner 1424. Rank: Seaman, from: Avon, Privateer.
    Cap: 08 Mar 1815 off Nevis by HM Sloop Barbados Int: 13 Mar 1815 Dis: 15 Mar 1815.
    Received from HM Sloop Barbados. HMS Numen Rear Admiral Durham.

Howes, Samuel   Prisoner 1090. Rank: Seaman, from: Engineer, Letter of Marque.
    Cap: 21 Sep 1814 of Porto Rico by HM Ship Barossa Int: 29 Sep 1814 Dis: 08 Feb 1815.
    Received from HM Ship Barossa. HM Ship Swiftsure.

Howland, Robert   Prisoner 431. Rank: Seaman, from: Ocean, Merchant Schooner.
    Cap: 15 Aug 1812 Martinique by Detained at Martinique Int: 05 Feb 1813 Dis: 10 Jul 1813.
    Received from HM Ship Vestal. Perseverance American Cartel.

Hoyt, Charles   Prisoner 1191. Rank: 2 Lieutenant, from: Fox, Privateer.
    Cap: 11 Jan 1815 off St Bartholomew by HM Brig Barbados Int: 14 Jan 1815 Dis: 08 Feb 1815.
    Received from HM Brig Barbados. HM Ship Swiftsure. (Capture date is Dec 26, 1814 for all entries for Fox except records 1190 - 1198.)

Hoyt, Hapthtum   Prisoner 1187. Rank: Seaman, from: Not Recorded, Not Recorded.
    Cap: Barbados by Not Recorded Int: 14 Jan 1815 Dis: 14 Jan 1815.
    Received from HM Brig Watsisin. (Not legible) at Barbados. (Not legible) from the Merchant Ship Mary. Out of Custody per order Rear Admiral Durham. (Date of capture not recorded.)

Hughes, Thomas   Prisoner 775. Rank: Seaman, from: Not Recorded, Not Recorded.
    Cap: 29 Dec 1813 Not Recorded by Not Recorded Int: 09 Feb 1814 Dis: 25 Apr 1814.
    Received from HM Ship Crane. Taken up at Caracas. HM Ship Vestal.

Hulen, Abraham   Prisoner 478. Rank: Mate, from: John, Privateer.
    Cap: 06 Feb 1813 Lat 10.0 N, Long 61.0 W by HM Sloop Peruvian Int: 20 Feb 1813 Dis: 11 Aug 1813. Received from HM Ship Cumberland. Malmore American Cartel.

Hulon, Henry   Prisoner 497. Rank: Seaman, from: John, Privateer.
    Cap: 06 Feb 1813 Lat 10.0 N, Long 61.0 W by HM Sloop Peruvian Int: 20 Feb 1813 Dis: 11 Aug 1813. Received from HM Ship Cumberland. Malmore American Cartel.

Humphreys, A Y   Prisoner 1453. Rank: Chaplin, from: HM Ship Levant, Not Recorded.
    Cap: 08 Mar 1815 Not Recorded by HM Ship Leander Int: 27 Mar 1815 Dis: 31 Mar 1815.
    Received from HM Brig Maria. Recaptured from the Constitution frigate. Out of Custody Rear Adl Durham.

American Prisoners of War Held at Barbados During the War of 1812

Humphreys, Edward   Prisoner 515. Rank: Seaman, from: John, Privateer.
    Cap: 06 Feb 1813 Lat 10.0 N, Long 61.0 W by HM Sloop Peruvian Int: 20 Feb 1813 Dis: 11 Aug 1813. Received from HM Ship Cumberland. Malmore American Cartel.

Humphreys, William   Prisoner 500. Rank: Seaman, from: John, Privateer.
    Cap: 06 Feb 1813 Lat 10.0 N, Long 61.0 W by HM Sloop Peruvian Int: 20 Feb 1813 Dis: 11 Aug 1813. Received from HM Ship Cumberland. Malmore American Cartel.

Hunt, Job   Prisoner 487. Rank: Seaman, from: John, Privateer.
    Cap: 06 Feb 1813 Lat 10.0 N, Long 61.0 W by HM Sloop Peruvian Int: 20 Feb 1813 Dis: 11 Aug 1813. Received from HM Ship Cumberland. Malmore American Cartel.

Hunt, Walter R   Prisoner 216. Rank: Seaman, from: Blockade, Privateer.
    Cap: 31 Oct 1812 off Saba by HM Sloop Charybdis Int: 19 Nov 1812 Dis: 10 Jul 1813. Received from HM Sloop Charybdis. (Not legible.) Perseverance American Cartel.

Hunter, Alexander   Prisoner 861. Rank: Seaman, from: Chapman, Privateer.
    Cap: 28 Feb 1814 off St Bartholomew by Thistle Privateer Int: 26 Mar 1814 Dis: 25 Apr 1814. Received from HM Ship Palama. HM Ship Vestal.

Hunter, John   Prisoner 857. Rank: Seaman, from: Rattle Snake, Letter of Marque.
    Cap: 11 Mar 1814 Lat 24.07 N, Long 66.47 W by HM Ship Rhin Int: 25 Mar 1814 Dis: 05 Apr 1814. Received from HM Ship Rhin. Out of Custody in consequence of having saved the life of a British Seaman at the (not legible) of his own.

Huntington, E   Prisoner 1072. Rank: 2 Mate, from: Engineer, Letter of Marque.
    Cap: 21 Sep 1814 of Porto Rico by HM Ship Barossa Int: 29 Sep 1814 Dis: 08 Feb 1815. Received from HM Ship Barossa. HM Ship Swiftsure Concerned in a conspiracy to impair the guard.

Hurbert, James   Prisoner 557. Rank: Seaman, from: Rebecca, Merchant Brig.
    Cap: 15 Jan 1813 off Demuary by Detained by Custom House Int: 02 Mar 1813 Dis: 27 May 1813. Received from Army Schooner Maria. America on Parole Sir Francis Laforey.

Hushall, Stephen   Prisoner 191. Rank: Prize Master, from: Blockade, Privateer.
    Cap: 31 Oct 1812 off Saba by HM Sloop Charybdis Int: 19 Nov 1812 Dis: 10 Jul 1813. Received from HM Sloop Charybdis. Perseverance American Cartel.

Hussey, Samuel S   Prisoner 3. Rank: Master, from: Orpha, Merchant Sloop.
    Cap: 02 Sep 1812 off Porto Rico by HM Sloop Ringdove Int: 25 Sep 1812 Dis: 24 Oct 1812. Received from HM Sloop Ringdove. America on Parole per order of Captain Reynolds Tribune.

Hussy, Abraham   Prisoner 313. Rank: Seaman, from: Venus, Merchant Ship.
    Cap: 15 Dec 1812 Lat 32 N, Long 54 W by HM Ship Herald Int: 31 Dec 1812 Dis: 06 Jun 1813. Received from HM Ship Herald. America on Parole Sir F. Laforey.

Hutchings, William   Prisoner 69. Rank: Seaman, from: Neptune, Merchant Brig.
    Cap: 29 Aug 1812 at Sea by HM Brig Maria Int: 13 Nov 1812 Dis: 19 Nov 1812. Received from HM Ship Mercury. Out of Custody per order of Rear Adml Sir F. Laforey being crew of a licensed vessel.

Hutchinson, Joseph   Prisoner 287. Rank: Seaman, from: HM Sloop Surinam, Not Recorded.
    Cap: Not Recorded by Not Recorded Int: 04 Dec 1812 Dis: 10 Jul 1813. Received from HM Sloop Surinam. Part of Crew of HM Sloop Surinam. Perseverance American Cartel. (Date of capture not recorded.)

Ingless, John   Prisoner 355. Rank: Seaman, from: Decatur, Privateer.
    Cap: 16 Jan 1813 Lat 13.00 N, Long 41.00 N by HM Ship Surprise Int: 26 Jan 1813 Dis: 10 Jul 1813. Received from HM Ship Surprise. Perseverance American Cartel.

Ingraham, Josiah   Prisoner 1350. Rank: Seaman, from: Vidett, Letter of Marque.
    Cap: 14 Feb 1815 off St Bartholomew by HMS Dasher Int: 03 Mar 1815 Dis: 31 Mar 1815. Received from HM Ship Dasher. Out of Custody Rear Adl Durham.

Ives, William   Prisoner 155. Rank: Seaman, from: Yankee, Privateer.
    Cap: 25 Oct 1812 off Sombero by HM Sloop Peruvian Int: 13 Nov 1812 Dis: 10 Jul 1813. Received from HM Ship Mercury. Perseverance American Cartel.

Jack, John   Prisoner 1413. Rank: Seaman, from: Avon, Privateer.
    Cap: 08 Mar 1815 off Nevis by HM Sloop Barbados Int: 13 Mar 1815 Dis: 15 Mar 1815. Received from HM Sloop Barbados. HMS Numen Rear Admiral Durham.

Jackman, David   Prisoner 772. Rank: Seaman, from: Frolic, Privateer.
    Cap: 25 Jan 1814 off St Thomas by HM Sloop Heron Int: 06 Feb 1814 Dis: 22 Jul 1814. Received from HM Sloop Heron. HM Ship Gloucester Rear Admiral Durham.

Jackson, Caleb   Prisoner 164. Rank: Seaman, from: Yankee, Privateer.
    Cap: 25 Oct 1812 off Sombero by HM Sloop Peruvian Int: 13 Nov 1812 Dis: 10 Jul 1813. Received from HM Ship Mercury. Perseverance American Cartel.

Jackson, Frederick   Prisoner 676. Rank: Seaman, from: Sterling, Merchant Ship.
    Cap: 19 May 1813 Lat 22.00 N, Long 53.00 W by HM Ship Grampus Int: 26 May 1813 Dis: 11 Aug 1813. Received from HM Ship Grampus. Malmore American Cartel.

American Prisoners of War Held at Barbados During the War of 1812

Jackson, George   Prisoner 745. Rank: Gunner, from: Frolic, Privateer.
    Cap: 25 Jan 1814 off St Thomas by HM Sloop Heron Int: 06 Feb 1814 Dis: 25 Apr 1814.
    Received from HM Sloop Heron. HM Ship Vestal Rear Admiral Durham.

Jackson, George   Prisoner 821. Rank: Seaman, from: Sally & Betsey, Merchant Schooner.
    Cap: 27 Sep 1813 off Porto Rico by HM Sloop Piqua Int: 07 Mar 1814 Dis: 25 Apr 1814.
    Received from HM Ship Piqua. HMS Vestal.

Jackson, Gowan   Prisoner 708. Rank: Seaman, from: HM Ship Grampus, Not Recorded.
    Cap: Not Recorded by Not Recorded Int: 29 Jun 1813 Dis: 11 Aug 1813.
    Received from HM Ship Grampus. Part of Crew of HM Ship Grampus. Malmore American Cartel. (Date of capture not recorded.)

Jackson, Harden   Prisoner 441. Rank: Seaman, from: Blockade, Privateer.
    Cap: 31 Oct 1812 off Saba by HM Sloop Charybdis Int: 12 Feb 1813 Dis: 11 Aug 1813.
    Received from HM Brig Liberty. Malmore American Cartel.

Jackson, James   Prisoner 606. Rank: Seaman, from: Thomas Penrose, Privateer.
    Cap: 23 Mar 1813 Lat 20.14 W, Long 61.20 W by HM Ship Tribune Int: 28 Mar 1813 Dis: 11 Aug 1813. Received from HM Ship Tribune. Malmore American Cartel.

Jackson, James   Prisoner 880. Rank: Seaman, from: Not Recorded, Not Recorded.
    Cap: Martinique by Not Recorded Int: 18 Apr 1814 Dis: 25 Apr 1814.
    Received from HM Ship Vestal. Taken at Martinique. HM Ship Vestal. (Date of capture not recorded.)

Jackson, James   Prisoner 979. Rank: Seaman, from: Polly, Merchant.
    Cap: 20 Mar 1814 off Saba by HM Ship Ister Int: 20 Jun 1814 Dis: 22 Jul 1814.
    Received from HM Ship Vestal. HM Ship Gloucester Rear Admiral Durham. (Apparent duplicate of # 880.)

Jackson, John   Prisoner 1077. Rank: Cook, from: Engineer, Letter of Marque.
    Cap: 21 Sep 1814 of Porto Rico by HM Ship Barossa Int: 29 Sep 1814 Dis: 31 Mar 1815.
    Received from HM Ship Barossa. Rear Adl Durham.

Jacobs, Henry   Prisoner 153. Rank: Seaman, from: Yankee, Privateer.
    Cap: 25 Oct 1812 off Sombero by HM Sloop Peruvian Int: 13 Nov 1812 Dis: 23 Jan 1813.
    Received from HM Ship Mercury. Being a native of Sweden.

Jacobs, John   Prisoner 79. Rank: Seaman, from: Providence, Privateer.
    Cap: 11 Sep 1812 off St. Barthlomew by HM Sloop Dominica Int: 13 Nov 1812 Dis: 10 Jul 1813.
    Received from HM Ship Mercury. Perseverance American Cartel.

James, John   Prisoner 304. Rank: Seaman, from: Nancy, Merchant Brig.
    Cap: 08 Dec 1812 off Tortilla by HM Brig Liberty Int: 31 Dec 1812 Dis: 10 Jul 1813.
    Received from HM Brig Liberty. Perseverance American Cartel.

James, John   Prisoner 783. Rank: Seaman, from: Old Friend, Not Recorded.
    Cap: 01 Jan 1814 off St. Bartholomew by Viper Privateer Int: 11 Feb 1814 Dis: 25 Apr 1814.
    Received from HM Brig Liberty. Retaken from the Globe Privateer. HM Ship Vestal.

James, Paul   Prisoner 257. Rank: Seaman, from: Brandy Wine, Merchant Brig.
    Cap: 17 Nov 1812 Lat 19.30, Long 57.00 W by HM Ship Lightning Int: 23 Nov 1812 Dis: 02 Dec 1812. Received from HM Ship Lightning. America on Parole Sir F. Laforey.

James, Simon   Prisoner 58. Rank: Seaman, from: Providence, Privateer.
    Cap: 11 Sep 1812 off St. Barthlomew by HM Sloop Dominica Int: 13 Nov 1812 Dis: 10 Jul 1813.
    Received from HM Ship Mercury. Perseverance American Cartel.

James, William   Prisoner 44. Rank: Seaman, from: HM Ship Lightning, Not Recorded.
    Cap: Not Recorded by Not Recorded Int: 08 Nov 1812 Dis: 10 Jul 1813.
    Part of Crew of HM Ship Lightning; gave themselves up as Prisoners of War. Perseverance American Cartel. (Date of capture not recorded.)

Jarvis, Francis   Prisoner 365. Rank: Seaman, from: Decatur, Privateer.
    Cap: 16 Jan 1813 Lat 13.00 N, Long 41.00 N by HM Ship Surprise Int: 26 Jan 1813 Dis: 10 Jul 1813.
    Received from HM Ship Surprise. Perseverance American Cartel.

Jarvis, Isaac   Prisoner 909. Rank: Seaman, from: Hawk, Privateer.
    Cap: 26 Apr 1814 Near the Mona Passage by HM Ship Piqua Int: 20 Jun 1814 Dis: 20 Jul 1814.
    Received from HM Ship Vestal. HM Sloop Hazard Rear Adml Durham.

Jeffery, Thomas   Prisoner 560. Rank: Seaman, from: Isabella, Merchant Brig.
    Cap: 08 Dec 1812 off Demuary by Detained by the Custom House Int: 02 Mar 1813 Dis: 11 Aug 1813. Received from Army Schooner Moushe. Malmore American Cartel.

Jenkins, Walter   Prisoner 1188. Rank: Seaman, from: Gallant Hull, Merchant.
    Cap: 26 Dec 1814 off St Bartholomew by HM Ship Barossa Int: 14 Jan 1815 Dis: 14 Feb 1815.
    Received from HMS Barossa. HM Ship Piqua.

Jennings, John   Prisoner 912. Rank: Seaman, from: Hawk, Privateer.
    Cap: 26 Apr 1814 Near the Mona Passage by HM Ship Piqua Int: 20 Jun 1814 Dis: 20 Jul 1814.
    Received from HM Ship Vestal. HM Sloop Hazard Rear Adml Durham.

American Prisoners of War Held at Barbados During the War of 1812

Jeppets, Benjamin   Prisoner 624. Rank: Seaman, from: Fly, Privateer.
    Cap: 19 Jan 1813 Lat 15.00 N, Long 45.00 W by HMS Venus Int: 02 Apr 1813 Dis: 11 Aug 1813.
    Received from HMS Venus. Recaptured from the Yankee. Malmore American Cartel.

Jerome, John   Prisoner 1061. Rank: Seaman, from: Mary, Letter of Marque.
    Cap: 07 Jun 1814 La Quisa by HM Ship Heron Int: 31 Jul 1814 Dis: 31 Mar 1815.
    Received from HM Sloop Mosquito. Rear Adl Durham.

Jerratt, Abraham   Prisoner 1226. Rank: Seaman, from: Fox, Privateer.
    Cap: 26 Dec 1814 off St Bartholomew by HM Brig Barbados Int: 14 Jan 1815 Dis: 08 Feb 1815.
    Received from HM Brig Barbados. HM Ship Swiftsure.

Jerrett, Jasper   Prisoner 837. Rank: Seaman, from: Rattle Snake, Letter of Marque.
    Cap: 11 Mar 1814 Lat 24.07 N, Long 66.47 W by HM Ship Rhin Int: 25 Mar 1814 Dis: 25 Apr 1814.
    Received from HM Ship Rhin. HM Ship Vestal.

Jervett, Richard   Prisoner 347. Rank: Seaman, from: Decatur, Privateer.
    Cap: 16 Jan 1813 Lat 13.00 N, Long 41.00 N by HM Ship Surprise Int: 26 Jan 1813 Dis: 10 Jul 1813.
    Received from HM Ship Surprise. Perseverance American Cartel.

Johannes, Joseph   Prisoner 921. Rank: Seaman, from: President, Privateer.
    Cap: 07 May 1814 off Porto Rico by HM Ship Piqua Int: 20 Jun 1814 Dis: 20 Jul 1814.
    Received from HM Ship Vestal. HM Sloop Hazard Rear Adml Durham.

John, Davis   Prisoner 993. Rank: Seaman, from: Hawk, Privateer.
    Cap: 26 Apr 1814 Near the Mona Passage by HM Ship Piqua Int: 20 Jun 1814 Dis: 22 Jul 1814.
    Received from HM Ship Vestal. HM Ship Gloucester Rear Admiral Durham. John Davis 2nd.

Johnson, Abel   Prisoner 1165. Rank: Master, from: Dolphin, Letter of Marque.
    Cap: 04 Dec 1814 Lat 18.00 N, Long 60.00 W by HM Brig Columbia Int: 08 Dec 1814 Dis: 31 Mar 1815. Received from HM Brig Columbia. Rear Adl Durham.

Johnson, Artemas   Prisoner 1452. Rank: Surgeons Mate, from: HM Ship Levant, Not Recorded.
    Cap: 08 Mar 1815 Not Recorded by HM Ship Leander Int: 27 Mar 1815 Dis: 31 Mar 1815.
    Received from HM Brig Maria. Recaptured from the Constitution frigate. Out of Custody Rear Adl Durham.

Johnson, Frederick   Prisoner 1098. Rank: Seaman, from: Engineer, Letter of Marque.
    Cap: 21 Sep 1814 of Porto Rico by HM Ship Barossa Int: 29 Sep 1814 Dis: 08 Feb 1815.
    Received from HM Ship Barossa. HM Ship Swiftsure.

Johnson, George   Prisoner 1089. Rank: Seaman, from: Engineer, Letter of Marque.
    Cap: 21 Sep 1814 of Porto Rico by HM Ship Barossa Int: 29 Sep 1814 Dis: 08 Feb 1815.
    Received from HM Ship Barossa. HM Ship Swiftsure.

Johnson, James   Prisoner 819. Rank: Seaman, from: Sally & Betsey, Merchant Schooner.
    Cap: 27 Sep 1813 off Porto Rico by HM Sloop Piqua Int: 07 Mar 1814 Dis: 25 Apr 1814.
    Received from HM Ship Piqua. HMS Vestal.

Johnson, John   Prisoner 23. Rank: Seaman, from: HM Sloop Dominica, Not Recorded.
    Cap: 22 Oct 1812 Not Recorded by Not Recorded Int: 22 Oct 1812 Dis: 24 Oct 1812.
    Received from HM Sloop Dominica. Gave themselves up on Reason of war being part of the crew of HM Sloop Dominica. America on Parole per order of Captain Reynolds Tribune.

Johnson, John   Prisoner 251. Rank: Seaman, from: Emma, Not Recorded.
    Cap: Not Recorded by Not Recorded Int: 22 Nov 1812 Dis: 02 Dec 1812.
    Received from Emma. Part of Crew of Army Ship Emma, but of good character. America on Parole Sir F. Laforey. (Date of capture not recorded.)

Johnson, John   Prisoner 940. Rank: Seaman, from: President, Privateer.
    Cap: 07 May 1814 off Porto Rico by HM Ship Piqua Int: 20 Jun 1814 Dis: 22 Jul 1814.
    Received from HM Ship Vestal. HM Ship Gloucester Rear Admiral Durham.

Johnson, Joseph   Prisoner 1181. Rank: Seaman, from: Gallant Hull, Merchant.
    Cap: 28 Dec 1814 off St Bartholomew by HM Ship Barossa Int: 10 Jan 1815 Dis: 14 Feb 1815.
    Received from HMS Barossa. HM Ship Piqua.

Johnson, Kelly   Prisoner 316. Rank: Seaman, from: Dolphin, Merchant Brig.
    Cap: 15 Dec 1812 near Bermuda by HM Sloop Nimrod Int: 11 Jan 1813 Dis: 06 Jun 1813.
    Received from HM Sloop Nimrod. America on Parole Sir F. Laforey.

Johnson, Luke   Prisoner 1029. Rank: Seaman, from: North Star, Merchant Schooner.
    Cap: 10 Jun 1814 off St Bartholomew by HM Brig Crane Int: 11 Jul 1814 Dis: 22 Jul 1814.
    Received from HM Schooner Flying Fish. HM Ship Gloucester Rear Admiral Durham.

Johnson, Thomas   Prisoner 755. Rank: Seaman, from: Frolic, Privateer.
    Cap: 25 Jan 1814 off St Thomas by HM Sloop Heron Int: 06 Feb 1814 Dis: 25 Apr 1814.
    Received from HM Sloop Heron. HM Ship Vestal.

Johnston, John   Prisoner 1336. Rank: Seaman, from: Vidett, Letter of Marque.
    Cap: 14 Feb 1815 off St Bartholomew by HM Ship Dasher Int: 03 Mar 1815 Dis: 31 Mar 1815.
    Received from HM Ship Dasher. Out of Custody Rear Adl Durham.

American Prisoners of War Held at Barbados During the War of 1812

Johnstone, William   Prisoner 1011. Rank: Seaman, from: William, Merchant.
    Cap: 18 May 1814 off Charleston by HM Ship Ister Int: 21 Jun 1814 Dis: 22 Jul 1814.
    Received from HM Ship Vestal. HM Ship Gloucester Rear Adml Durham.

Jones, David   Prisoner 1014. Rank: Seaman, from: William, Merchant.
    Cap: 18 May 1814 off Charleston by HM Ship Ister Int: 21 Jun 1814 Dis: 22 Jul 1814.
    Received from HM Ship Vestal. HM Ship Gloucester Rear Adml Durham.

Jones, John   Prisoner 776. Rank: Seaman, from: HM Ship Venus, Not Recorded.
    Cap: Not Recorded by Not Recorded Int: 11 Feb 1814 Dis: 25 Apr 1814.
    Received from HM Brig Liberty. Part of Crew of HM Ship Vensus. HM Ship Vestal. (Date of capture not recorded.)

Jones, John   Prisoner 913. Rank: Seaman, from: Hawk, Privateer.
    Cap: 26 Apr 1814 Near the Mona Passage by HM Ship Piqua Int: 20 Jun 1814 Dis: 20 Jul 1814.
    Received from HM Ship Vestal. HM Sloop Hazard Rear Adml Durham.

Jones, John   Prisoner 1096. Rank: Seaman, from: Engineer, Letter of Marque.
    Cap: 21 Sep 1814 of Porto Rico by HM Ship Barossa Int: 29 Sep 1814 Dis: 31 Mar 1815.
    Received from HM Ship Barossa. Rear Adl Durham.

Jones, John   Prisoner 1303. Rank: Seaman, from: Mary, Merchant Schooner.
    Cap: 15 Jan 1815 Lat 22.40, Long 66 by HM Ship Pique Int: 29 Jan 1815 Dis: 14 Feb 1815.
    Received from HMS Pique. HM Ship Piqua. John Jones (2nd).

Jones, Paul   Prisoner 1009. Rank: Seaman, from: Hawk, Privateer.
    Cap: 26 Apr 1814 Near the Mona Passage by HM Ship Piqua Int: 20 Jun 1814 Dis: 22 Jul 1814.
    Received from HM Ship Vestal. HM Ship Gloucester Rear Adml Durham.

Jones, Richard   Prisoner 143. Rank: Prize Master, from: Yankee, Privateer.
    Cap: 25 Oct 1812 off Sombero by HM Sloop Peruvian Int: 13 Nov 1812 Dis: 10 Jul 1813.
    Received from HM Ship Mercury. Perseverance American Cartel.

Jones, Thomas   Prisoner 945. Rank: Seaman, from: President, Privateer.
    Cap: 07 May 1814 off Porto Rico by HM Ship Piqua Int: 20 Jun 1814 Dis: 22 Jul 1814.
    Received from HM Ship Vestal. HM Ship Gloucester Rear Admiral Durham.

Jones, William   Prisoner 314. Rank: Seaman, from: HM Sloop Opossum, Not Recorded.
    Cap: Not Recorded by Not Recorded Int: 01 Jan 1813 Dis: 10 Jul 1813.
    Received from HM Sloop Opossum. Part of Crew of HM Sloop Opossum. Perseverance American Cartel. (Date of capture not recorded.)

Jones, William   Prisoner 602. Rank: Seaman, from: Thomas Penrose, Privateer.
    Cap: 23 Mar 1813 Lat 20.14 W, Long 61.20 W by HM Ship Tribune Int: 28 Mar 1813 Dis: 26 Apr 1813. Received from HM Ship Tribune. America on Parole Sir F. Laforey.

Jordon, Ralph   Prisoner 282. Rank: Seaman, from: Rea, Privateer.
    Cap: 29 Nov 1812 off Barbados by HM Ship Lightning Int: 29 Nov 1812 Dis: 10 Jul 1813.
    Received from HM Ship Lightning. Ship having been captured by the Bona American. Perseverance American Cartel.

Jordon, Simon   Prisoner 989. Rank: Seaman, from: Hawk, Privateer.
    Cap: 26 Apr 1814 Near the Mona Passage by HM Ship Piqua Int: 20 Jun 1814 Dis: 22 Jul 1814.
    Received from HM Ship Vestal. HM Ship Gloucester Rear Admiral Durham.

Joseph, Nathaniel   Prisoner 769. Rank: Seaman, from: Frolic, Privateer.
    Cap: 25 Jan 1814 off St Thomas by HM Sloop Heron Int: 06 Feb 1814 Dis: 25 Apr 1814.
    Received from HM Sloop Heron. HM Ship Vestal.

Joseph, Pedro   Prisoner 943. Rank: Seaman, from: President, Privateer.
    Cap: 07 May 1814 off Porto Rico by HM Ship Piqua Int: 20 Jun 1814 Dis: 22 Jul 1814.
    Received from HM Ship Vestal. HM Ship Gloucester Rear Admiral Durham.

Joshua, John   Prisoner 771. Rank: Seaman, from: Frolic, Privateer.
    Cap: 25 Jan 1814 off St Thomas by HM Sloop Heron Int: 06 Feb 1814 Dis: 25 Apr 1814.
    Received from HM Sloop Heron. HM Ship Vestal.

Jouanin, John B   Prisoner 1145. Rank: Passenger, from: High Flyer, Letter of Marque.
    Cap: 14 Nov 1814 off Anguilla by HM Ship Barossa Int: 18 Nov 1814 Dis: 18 Nov 1814.
    Received from HM Ship Barossa. Out of Custody being a passenger.

Joy, Robert M   Prisoner 18. Rank: Mate, from: Hope, Merchant Ship.
    Cap: 27 Sep 1812 Lat 22.30 N, Long 40.45 W by HM Ship Tribune Int: 22 Oct 1812 Dis: 24 Oct 1812.
    Received from Ship Hope. America on Parole per order of Captain Reynolds Tribune.

Julius, John   Prisoner 243. Rank: Seaman, from: HM Sloop Charybdis, Not Recorded.
    Cap: Not Recorded by Not Recorded Int: 19 Nov 1812 Dis: 10 Jul 1813.
    Received from HM Sloop Charybdis. Part of Crew of HM Sloop Charybdis. Perseverance American Cartel. (Date of capture not recorded.)

American Prisoners of War Held at Barbados During the War of 1812

Justice, John   Prisoner 607. Rank: Seaman, from: Thomas Penrose, Privateer.
   Cap: 23 Mar 1813 Lat 20.14 W, Long 61.20 W by HM Ship Tribune Int: 28 Mar 1813 Dis: 26 Apr 1813. Received from HM Ship Tribune. America on Parole Sir F. Laforey.

Keasoner, Samuel   Prisoner 1148. Rank: Seaman, from: High Flyer, Letter of Marque.
   Cap: 14 Nov 1814 off Anguilla by HM Ship Barossa Int: 18 Nov 1814 Dis: 14 Feb 1815. Received from HM Ship Barossa. HM Ship Piqua Rear Admiral Durham.

Keen, Tilden   Prisoner 669. Rank: Seaman, from: William, Merchant Brig.
   Cap: 16 Apr 1813 Lat 35.00 N, Long 57.00 W by Heron Int: 22 May 1813 Dis: 11 Aug 1813. Received from HM Sloop Heron. Malmore American Cartel.

Kelley, James   Prisoner 1150. Rank: Seaman, from: High Flyer, Letter of Marque.
   Cap: 14 Nov 1814 off Anguilla by HM Ship Barossa Int: 18 Nov 1814 Dis: 08 Feb 1815. Received from HM Ship Barossa. HM Ship Swiftsure.

Kelley, Joseph   Prisoner 672. Rank: Mate, from: Sterling, Merchant Ship.
   Cap: 19 May 1813 Lat 22.00 N, Long 53.00 W by HM Ship Grampus Int: 26 May 1813 Dis: 05 Jun 1813. Received from HM Ship Grampus. America on Parole Sir F. Laforey.

Kelly, Jarret   Prisoner 630. Rank: Seaman, from: Jane, Privateer.
   Cap: 06 Mar 1813 Lat 14.22 N, Long 65.35 W by HM Brig Swaggerer Int: 02 Apr 1813 Dis: 11 Aug 1813. Received from Army Schooner Maria. Recaptured from the Comet. Malmore American Cartel.

Kelly, John   Prisoner 224. Rank: Seaman, from: Blockade, Privateer.
   Cap: 31 Oct 1812 off Saba by HM Sloop Charybdis Int: 19 Nov 1812 Dis: 10 Jul 1813. Received from HM Sloop Charybdis. Perseverance American Cartel.

Kemble, Nathaniel   Prisoner 573. Rank: Seaman, from: St Bartholomew, Merchant Brig.
   Cap: 05 Mar 1813 Carlisle Bay by HM Ship Cumberland Int: 10 Mar 1813 Dis: 06 Jun 1813. Received from HM Ship Cumberland. America on Parole Sir Francis Laforey.

Kemp, Nathaniel   Prisoner 1397. Rank: Prize Master, from: Avon, Privateer.
   Cap: 08 Mar 1815 off Nevis by HM Sloop Barbados Int: 13 Mar 1815 Dis: 15 Mar 1815. Received from HM Sloop Barbados. HMS Numen Rear Admiral Durham.

Kendall, David   Prisoner 1282. Rank: Seaman, from: Hero, Merchant Schooner.
   Cap: 14 Dec 1814 Lat 19.13, Long 64 by HMS Pique Int: 29 Jan 1815 Dis: 14 Feb 1815. Received from HMS Pique. HM Ship Piqua.

Kennedy, Henry   Prisoner 1285. Rank: 2 Mate, from: Hero, Merchant Schooner.
   Cap: 14 Dec 1814 Lat 19.13, Long 64 by HMS Pique Int: 29 Jan 1815 Dis: 14 Feb 1815. Received from HMS Pique. HM Ship Piqua.

Kennedy, Thomas D   Prisoner 1310. Rank: Mate & Passenger, from: Mary, Merchant Schooner.
   Cap: 15 Jan 1815 Lat 22.40, Long 66 by HM Ship Pique Int: 30 Jan 1815 Dis: 31 Mar 1815. Received from HMS Pique. Rear Adl Durham.

Kenniston, Daniel   Prisoner 147. Rank: Seaman, from: Yankee, Privateer.
   Cap: 25 Oct 1812 off Sombero by HM Sloop Peruvian Int: 13 Nov 1812 Dis: 10 Jul 1813. Received from HM Ship Mercury. Perseverance American Cartel.

Kent, Jacob Henry   Prisoner 43. Rank: Seaman, from: William Rathbone, Not Recorded.
   Cap: 09 Oct 1812 Lat 22.00 N, Long 60.00 W by HM Sloop Chandler Int: 01 Nov 1812 Dis: 10 Jul 1813. Received from HM Brig Swaggerer. Having been taken by the Savory Jack American privateer. Perseverance American Cartel.

Kentfield, Eliza   Prisoner 244. Rank: Seaman, from: HM Sloop Charybdis, Not Recorded.
   Cap: Not Recorded by Not Recorded Int: 19 Nov 1812 Dis: 10 Jul 1813. Received from HM Sloop Charybdis. Part of Crew of HM Sloop Charybdis. Perseverance American Cartel. (Date of capture not recorded.)

Keyser, John   Prisoner 462. Rank: Seaman, from: Bowrey, Privateer.
   Cap: 02 Feb 1813 off Barbados by HM Sloop Opossum Int: 18 Feb 1813 Dis: 11 Aug 1813. Received from HM Sloop Opossum. English Brig Captured by the Comet. Malmore American Cartel.

Kimball, Ezekiah   Prisoner 138. Rank: Prize Master, from: Yankee, Privateer.
   Cap: 25 Oct 1812 off Sombero by HM Sloop Peruvian Int: 13 Nov 1812 Dis: 10 Jul 1813. Received from HM Ship Mercury. Perseverance American Cartel.

Kimball, John   Prisoner 144. Rank: Prize Master, from: Yankee, Privateer.
   Cap: 25 Oct 1812 off Sombero by HM Sloop Peruvian Int: 13 Nov 1812 Dis: 10 Jul 1813. Received from HM Ship Mercury. Perseverance American Cartel.

Kimball, John W   Prisoner 395. Rank: Seaman, from: Decatur, Privateer.
   Cap: 16 Jan 1813 Lat 13.00 N, Long 41.00 N by HM Ship Surprise Int: 26 Jan 1813 Dis: 10 Jul 1813. Received from HM Ship Surprise. Perseverance American Cartel.

King, Joseph   Prisoner 910. Rank: Seaman, from: Hawk, Privateer.
   Cap: 26 Apr 1814 Near the Mona Passage by HM Ship Piqua Int: 20 Jun 1814 Dis: 20 Jul 1814. Received from HM Ship Vestal. HM Sloop Hazard Rear Adml Durham.

American Prisoners of War Held at Barbados During the War of 1812

King, Samuel W   Prisoner 7. Rank: Surgeon, from: Providence, Privateer.
    Cap: 11 Sep 1812 off St. Bartholomew by HM Sloop Dominica Int: 04 Oct 1812 Dis: 24 Oct 1812.
    Received from HM Ship Vestal. America on Parole per order of Captain Reynolds Tribune.

Kingsberry, Sandford   Prisoner 218. Rank: Seaman, from: Blockade, Privateer.
    Cap: 31 Oct 1812 off Saba by HM Sloop Charybdis Int: 19 Nov 1812 Dis: 10 Jul 1813.
    Received from HM Sloop Charybdis. Perseverance American Cartel. Concerned in a conspiracy to run from the Guard.

Kingsbury, Joseph   Prisoner 1346. Rank: Seaman, from: Vidett, Letter of Marque.
    Cap: 14 Feb 1815 off St Bartholomew by HMS Dasher Int: 03 Mar 1815 Dis: 31 Mar 1815.
    Received from HM Ship Dasher. Out of Custody Rear Adl Durham.

Kinwright, John   Prisoner 1199. Rank: Seaman, from: Fox, Privateer.
    Cap: 26 Dec 1814 off St Bartholomew by HM Brig Barbados Int: 14 Jan 1815 Dis: 08 Feb 1815.
    Received from HM Brig Barbados. HM Ship Swiftsure.

Kirby, Abel   Prisoner 1101. Rank: Seaman, from: Engineer, Letter of Marque.
    Cap: 21 Sep 1814 of Porto Rico by HM Ship Barossa Int: 29 Sep 1814 Escaped: 13 Jan 1815.
    Received from HM Ship Barossa. Escaped. Reentry 1269.

Kirby, Able   Prisoner 1269. Rank: Seaman, from: Fox, Privateer.
    Cap: 26 Dec 1814 off St Bartholomew by HM Brig Barbados Int: 15 Jan 1815 Dis: 14 Feb 1815.
    Received from HM Brig Barbados. Retaken former No 1101. HM Ship Piqua. (Abel Kirby)

Kirby, Benjamin   Prisoner 278. Rank: Seaman, from: Rea, Privateer.
    Cap: 29 Nov 1812 off Barbados by HM Ship Lightning Int: 29 Nov 1812 Dis: 10 Jul 1813.
    Received from HM Ship Lightning. Ship having been captured by the Bona American. Perseverance American Cartel.

Knabbs, James   Prisoner 930. Rank: Seaman, from: President, Privateer.
    Cap: 07 May 1814 off Porto Rico by HM Ship Piqua Int: 20 Jun 1814 Dis: 22 Jul 1814.
    Received from HM Ship Vestal. HM Ship Gloucester Rear Admiral Durham.

Knight, John   Prisoner 506. Rank: Seaman, from: John, Privateer.
    Cap: 06 Feb 1813 Lat 10.0 N, Long 61.0 W by HM Sloop Peruvian Int: 20 Feb 1813 Dis: 11 Aug 1813. Received from HM Ship Cumberland. Malmore American Cartel.

Knight, Solomon   Prisoner 360. Rank: Seaman, from: Decatur, Privateer.
    Cap: 16 Jan 1813 Lat 13.00 N, Long 41.00 N by HM Ship Surprise Int: 26 Jan 1813 Dis: 10 Jul 1813.
    Received from HM Ship Surprise. Perseverance American Cartel.

Knoulton, Asahal Joseph   Prisoner 881. Rank: Surgeon, from: Hawk, Privateer.
    Cap: 26 Apr 1814 Near the Mona Passage by HM Ship Piqua Int: 19 May 1814 Dis: 20 Jun 1814.
    Received from Hawk Privateer. Out of Custody being a noncombatant.

Knowles, Daniel   Prisoner 1405. Rank: Seaman, from: Avon, Privateer.
    Cap: 08 Mar 1815 off Nevis by HM Sloop Barbados Int: 13 Mar 1815 Dis: 15 Mar 1815.
    Received from HM Sloop Barbados. HMS Numen Rear Admiral Durham.

Knowls, Morton   Prisoner 615. Rank: Seaman, from: HM Sloop Tribune, Not Recorded.
    Cap: Not Recorded by Not Recorded Int: 28 Mar 1813 Dis: 26 Apr 1813.
    Received from HM Ship Tribune. Part of Crew of HM Sloop Tribune. America on Parole Sir F. Laforey. (Date of capture not recorded.)

La Crouse, Jean   Prisoner 1235. Rank: Seaman, from: Fox, Privateer.
    Cap: 26 Dec 1814 off St Bartholomew by HM Brig Barbados Int: 14 Jan 1815 Dis: 08 Feb 1815.
    Received from HM Brig Barbados. HM Ship Swiftsure.

Labbi, Constant   Prisoner 585. Rank: Seaman, from: Alexis, Privateer.
    Cap: 09 Mar 1813 Not Recorded by HM Ship Lightning Int: 22 Mar 1813 Dis: 11 Aug 1813.
    Received from HM Ship Lightning. English Retaken by Comet. Malmore American Cartel.

Labolt, Adam   Prisoner 463. Rank: Seaman, from: Bowrey, Privateer.
    Cap: 02 Feb 1813 off Barbados by HM Sloop Opossum Int: 18 Feb 1813 Dis: 11 Aug 1813.
    Received from HM Sloop Opossum. English Brig Captured by the Comet. Malmore American Cartel.

Lacerf, Henry   Prisoner 960. Rank: Seaman, from: President, Privateer.
    Cap: 07 May 1814 off Porto Rico by HM Ship Piqua Int: 20 Jun 1814 Dis: 22 Jul 1814.
    Received from HM Ship Vestal. HM Ship Gloucester Rear Admiral Durham.

Laes, Domingo   Prisoner 950. Rank: Seaman, from: President, Privateer.
    Cap: 07 May 1814 off Porto Rico by HM Ship Piqua Int: 20 Jun 1814 Dis: 22 Jul 1814.
    Received from HM Ship Vestal. HM Ship Gloucester Rear Admiral Durham.

Lahy, George   Prisoner 1112. Rank: Seaman, from: Mars, Privateer.
    Cap: 01 Sep 1814 Lat 41 N, Long 52 W by HM Ship Piqua Int: 21 Oct 1814 Dis: 14 Feb 1815.
    Received from HMS Piqua. Taken by the David Porter Privateer. HM Ship Piqua.

Lain, Samuel   Prisoner 369. Rank: Seaman, from: Decatur, Privateer.
    Cap: 16 Jan 1813 Lat 13.00 N, Long 41.00 N by HM Ship Surprise Int: 26 Jan 1813 Dis: 10 Jul 1813.
    Received from HM Ship Surprise. Perseverance American Cartel.

American Prisoners of War Held at Barbados During the War of 1812

Landon, George   Prisoner 625. Rank: Seaman, from: Fly, Privateer.
    Cap: 19 Jan 1813 Lat 15.00 N, Long 45.00 W by HMS Venus Int: 02 Apr 1813 Dis: 11 Aug 1813.
    Received from HMS Venus. Recaptured from the Yankee. Malmore American Cartel.

Lane, James   Prisoner 509. Rank: Seaman, from: John, Privateer.
    Cap: 06 Feb 1813 Lat 10.0 N, Long 61.0 W by HM Sloop Peruvian Int: 20 Feb 1813 Dis: 11 Aug 1813. Received from HM Ship Cumberland. Malmore American Cartel.

Lane, John   Prisoner 609. Rank: Seaman, from: Thomas Penrose, Privateer.
    Cap: 23 Mar 1813 Lat 20.14 W, Long 61.20 W by HM Ship Tribune Int: 28 Mar 1813 Dis: 11 Aug 1813. Received from HM Ship Tribune. Malmore American Cartel.

Lang, William   Prisoner 173. Rank: Clerk, from: Yankee, Privateer.
    Cap: 25 Oct 1812 off Sombero by HM Sloop Peruvian Int: 13 Nov 1812 Dis: 10 Jul 1813.
    Received from HM Ship Mercury. Perseverance American Cartel.

Lange, James   Prisoner 792. Rank: Mate, from: Atalante, Merchant Schooner.
    Cap: 19 Jan 1814 off Saint Bartholomew by HM Brig Barbados Int: 12 Feb 1814 Dis: 22 Jul 1814.
    Received from HM Schooner Ballahou. HM Ship Gloucester Rear Adml Durham.

Larabee, Samuel   Prisoner 1066. Rank: Passenger, from: Mary, Letter of Marque.
    Cap: 07 Jun 1814 La Quisa by HM Ship Heron Int: 31 Jul 1814 Dis: 31 Mar 1815.
    Received from HM Sloop Mosquito. Formally mate. Rear Adl Durham.

Larcom, Robert   Prisoner 206. Rank: Seaman, from: Blockade, Privateer.
    Cap: 31 Oct 1812 off Saba by HM Sloop Charybdis Int: 19 Nov 1812 Dis: 10 Jul 1813.
    Received from HM Sloop Charybdis. Perseverance American Cartel.

Larkin, Lewis   Prisoner 562. Rank: Seaman, from: Isabella, Merchant Brig.
    Cap: 08 Dec 1812 off Demuary by Detained by the Custom House Int: 02 Mar 1813 Dis: 11 Aug 1813. Received from Army Schooner Moushe. Malmore American Cartel.

Lathrop, Acahel   Prisoner 716. Rank: Seaman, from: Olive Branch, Merchant Brig.
    Cap: 12 Apr 1813 Lat 17.00 N, Long 59.30 W by HM Sloop Eclipse Int: 07 Jul 1813 Dis: 24 Jul 1813.
    Received from HM Sloop Eclipse. Out of Custody the Vessel being liberated.

Latimore, Samuel   Prisoner 554. Rank: Mate, from: Rebecca, Merchant Brig.
    Cap: 15 Jan 1813 off Demuary by Detained by Custom House Int: 02 Mar 1813 Dis: 13 Mar 1813.
    Received from Army Schooner Maria. America on Parole Sir Francis Laforey.

Latimore, Titus   Prisoner 642. Rank: Seaman, from: Active, Merchant Ship.
    Cap: 23 Feb 1813 off St Bartholomew by HM Ship Surprise Int: 11 Apr 1813 Dis: 11 Aug 1813.
    Received from HM Schooner Elizabeth. Malmore American Cartel.

Laurence, Elisha   Prisoner 680. Rank: Seaman, from: Sterling, Merchant Ship.
    Cap: 19 May 1813 Lat 22.00 N, Long 53.00 W by HM Ship Grampus Int: 26 May 1813 Dis: 11 Aug 1813. Received from HM Ship Grampus. Malmore American Cartel.

Lavis, Lewis   Prisoner 1107. Rank: Seaman, from: Mars, Privateer.
    Cap: 01 Sep 1814 Lat 41 N, Long 52 W by HM Ship Piqua Int: 21 Oct 1814 Dis: 08 Feb 1815.
    Received from HMS Piqua. Taken by the David Porter Privateer. HM Ship Swiftsure.

Lawton, Thomas   Prisoner 126. Rank: Seaman, from: Providence, Privateer.
    Cap: 11 Sep 1812 off St. Bartholomew by HM Sloop Dominica Int: 13 Nov 1812 Dis: 10 Jul 1813.
    Received from HM Ship Mercury. Perseverance American Cartel.

Le Compte, Phillippe   Prisoner 1255. Rank: Surgeon, from: Fox, Privateer.
    Cap: 26 Dec 1814 off St Bartholomew by HM Brig Barbados Int: 14 Jan 1815 Dis: 31 Mar 1815.
    Received from HM Brig Barbados. Rear Adl Durham.

Le Foque, Gabriel   Prisoner 453. Rank: Mate, from: Hamilton, Merchant Ship.
    Cap: 11 Aug 1812 Surinam by HM Ship Surinam Int: 14 Feb 1813 Dis: 13 Mar 1813.
    Received from HM Brig Liberty. America on Parole Sir Francis Laforey.

Le Hoy, Jean B   Prisoner 1242. Rank: Seaman, from: Fox, Privateer.
    Cap: 26 Dec 1814 off St Bartholomew by HM Brig Barbados Int: 14 Jan 1815 Dis: 08 Feb 1815.
    Received from HM Brig Barbados. HM Ship Swiftsure.

Leaburn, Thomas   Prisoner 114. Rank: Seaman, from: William Rathbone, Brig.
    Cap: 09 Oct 1812 at Sea by HM Sloop Charybdis Int: 13 Nov 1812 Dis: 10 Jul 1813.
    Received from HM Ship Mercury. Retaken Brig Part of Crew of Savory Jack Privateer. Perseverance American Cartel.

Leach, George   Prisoner 749. Rank: Seaman, from: Frolic, Privateer.
    Cap: 25 Jan 1814 off St Thomas by HM Sloop Heron Int: 06 Feb 1814 Dis: 25 Apr 1814.
    Received from HM Sloop Heron. HM Ship Vestal Rear Admiral Durham.

Leany, Pierre L   Prisoner 1192. Rank: 1 Lieutenant, from: Fox, Privateer.
    Cap: 11 Jan 1815 off St Bartholomew by HM Brig Barbados Int: 14 Jan 1815 Escaped: 19 Jan 1815.
    Received from HM Brig Barbados. Escaped. (Capture date is Dec 26, 1814 for all entries for Fox except records 1190 - 1198.)

American Prisoners of War Held at Barbados During the War of 1812

Lee, Abraham   Prisoner 1126. Rank: Seaman, from: Nancy, Privateer.
    Cap: 06 Sep 1814 Lat 32 N, Long 47 W by HM Ship Piqua Int: 21 Oct 1814 Dis: 31 Mar 1815.
    Received from HMS Piqua. Taken by the Amelia Privateer. Rear Adl Durham.

Lee, John   Prisoner 1275. Rank: Pilot, from: Meatbone, Merchant Schooner.
    Cap: 25 Jan 1815 off St Bartholomew by HM Sloop Espringle Int: 28 Jan 1815 Dis: 14 Feb 1815.
    Received from HM Sloop Espringle. HM Ship Piqua.

Lee, Washington   Prisoner 631. Rank: Seaman, from: Jane, Privateer.
    Cap: 06 Mar 1813 Lat 14.22 N, Long 65.35 W by HM Brig Swaggerer Int: 02 Apr 1813 Dis: 10 Jul 1813. Received from Army Schooner Maria. Recaptured from the Comet. Perseverance American Cartel.

Lefort, John   Prisoner 11. Rank: Master, from: Shepherdess, Merchant Schooner.
    Cap: 12 Oct 1812 Lat 20.00 N, Long 56.00 W by HM Sloop Lightning Int: 21 Oct 1812 Dis: 26 Oct 1812. Received from HM Sloop Lightning. America on Parole per order of Captain Reynolds Tribune.

Leman, Ambrose   Prisoner 957. Rank: Seaman, from: President, Privateer.
    Cap: 07 May 1814 off Porto Rico by HM Ship Piqua Int: 20 Jun 1814 Dis: 22 Jul 1814.
    Received from HM Ship Vestal. HM Ship Gloucester Rear Admiral Durham.

Lemon, Niel C   Prisoner 568. Rank: Lieutenant, from: John, Privateer.
    Cap: 06 Feb 1813 Lat 10 N, Long 61 W by HM Sloop Peruvian Int: 08 Mar 1813 Escaped: 24 Apr 1813. Received from HM Sloop Arachne. Escaped. Retaken Reentry (690).

Lemon, Niel C   Prisoner 690. Rank: 2 Lieutenant, from: John, Privateer.
    Cap: 06 Feb 1813 Lat 10.00 N, Long 61.00 W by HM Sloop Peruvian Int: 26 May 1813 Dis: 14 Jun 1813. Received from HM Sloop Peruvian. HMS Cufay for passage to England. Sir F. Laforey.

Leon, Acy   Prisoner 1415. Rank: Seaman, from: Avon, Privateer.
    Cap: 08 Mar 1815 off Nevis by HM Sloop Barbados Int: 13 Mar 1815 Dis: 15 Mar 1815.
    Received from HM Sloop Barbados. HMS Numen Rear Admiral Durham.

Lepierre, Francis   Prisoner 1249. Rank: Seaman, from: Fox, Privateer.
    Cap: 26 Dec 1814 off St Bartholomew by HM Brig Barbados Int: 14 Jan 1815 Dis: 31 Mar 1815.
    Received from HM Brig Barbados. Rear Adl Durham.

Lester, James   Prisoner 872. Rank: Prize Master, from: Camilla, Not Recorded.
    Cap: 29 Mar 1814 Sombrero Passage by HM Ship Ister Int: 15 Apr 1814 Dis: 25 Apr 1814.
    Received from HM Ship Ister. Recaptured from Fairy Privateer. HM Ship Vestal.

Lester, James   Prisoner 972. Rank: Seaman, from: Fairy, Privateer.
    Cap: 20 Mar 1814 off Saba by HM Ship Ister Int: 20 Jun 1814 Dis: 22 Jul 1814.
    Received from HM Ship Vestal. HM Ship Gloucester Rear Admiral Durham. (Apparent duplicate of # 872.)

Lewis, Daniel   Prisoner 411. Rank: Seaman, from: Apollo, Merchant Ship.
    Cap: 22 Dec 1812 off Tenioff by HM Ship Grampus Int: 30 Jan 1813 Dis: 10 Jul 1813.
    Received from HM Sloop Demerary. Perseverance American Cartel.

Lewis, John   Prisoner 417. Rank: Seaman, from: Apollo, Merchant Ship.
    Cap: 22 Dec 1812 off Tenioff by HM Ship Grampus Int: 30 Jan 1813 Dis: 10 Jul 1813.
    Received from HM Sloop Demerary. Perseverance American Cartel.

Lewis, John   Prisoner 627. Rank: Seaman, from: Fly, Privateer.
    Cap: 19 Jan 1813 Lat 15.00 N, Long 45.00 W by HMS Venus Int: 02 Apr 1813 Dis: 11 Aug 1813.
    Received from HMS Venus. Recaptured from the Yankee. Malmore American Cartel.

Lewis, John   Prisoner 636. Rank: Seaman, from: Active, Merchant Ship.
    Cap: 23 Feb 1813 off St Bartholomew by HM Ship Surprise Int: 11 Apr 1813 Dis: 11 Aug 1813.
    Received from HM Schooner Elizabeth. Malmore American Cartel.

Lewis, Thomas   Prisoner 1017. Rank: Seaman, from: HM Ship Ister, Not Recorded.
    Cap: Not Recorded by Not Recorded Int: 21 Jun 1814 Dis: 22 Jul 1814.
    Received from HM Ship Ister. Part of Crew of HM Ship Ister. HM Ship Gloucester Rear Adml Durham. (Date of capture not recorded.)

Lewis, William   Prisoner 632. Rank: Seaman, from: Jane, Privateer.
    Cap: 06 Mar 1813 Lat 14.22 N, Long 65.35 W by HM Brig Swaggerer Int: 02 Apr 1813 Dis: 11 Aug 1813. Received from Army Schooner Maria. Recaptured from the Comet. Malmore American Cartel.

Linch, William   Prisoner 875. Rank: Seaman, from: Camilla, Not Recorded.
    Cap: 29 Mar 1814 Sombrero Passage by HM Ship Ister Int: 15 Apr 1814 Dis: 25 Apr 1814.
    Received from HM Ship Ister. Recaptured from Fairy Privateer. HM Ship Vestal.

Lincon, Nathaniel   Prisoner 726. Rank: 2 Mate, from: Ellen, Merchant Schooner.
    Cap: 07 Jan 1814 Lat 21.15 N, Long 65.00 W by HMS Piqua Int: 02 Feb 1814 Dis: 02 Feb 1814.
    Received from HM Brig Liberty. Rising States American Cartel. Rear Adml Sir F. Laforey.

Lines, William   Prisoner 699. Rank: Master, from: Saturn, Merchant Brig.
    Cap: 10 May 1813 off Martinique by HM Ship Mercury Int: 17 Jun 1813 Dis: 10 Jul 1813.
    Received from HM Ship Mercury. Exchanged.

American Prisoners of War Held at Barbados During the War of 1812

Lipid, Caesar   Prisoner 683. Rank: Seaman, from: Sterling, Merchant Ship.
  Cap: 19 May 1813 Lat 22.00 N, Long 53.00 W by HM Ship Grampus Int: 26 May 1813 Dis: 11 Aug 1813.
  Received from HM Ship Grampus. Malmore American Cartel.
Little, John   Prisoner 1218. Rank: Seaman, from: Fox, Privateer.
  Cap: 26 Dec 1814 off St Bartholomew by HM Brig Barbados Int: 14 Jan 1815 Dis: 08 Feb 1815.
  Received from HM Brig Barbados. HM Ship Swiftsure.
Little, William   Prisoner 70. Rank: Seaman, from: Neptune, Merchant Brig.
  Cap: 29 Aug 1812 at Sea by HM Brig Maria Int: 13 Nov 1812 Dis: 19 Nov 1812.
  Received from HM Ship Mercury. Out of Custody per order of Rear Adml Sir F. Laforey being crew of a licensed vessel.
Littlefield, Samuel   Prisoner 848. Rank: Seaman, from: Rattle Snake, Letter of Marque.
  Cap: 11 Mar 1814 Lat 24.07 N, Long 66.47 W by HM Ship Rhin Int: 25 Mar 1814 Dis: 25 Apr 1814.
  Received from HM Ship Rhin. HM Ship Vestal.
Lloyd, John   Prisoner 383. Rank: Seaman, from: Decatur, Privateer.
  Cap: 16 Jan 1813 Lat 13.00 N, Long 41.00 N by HM Ship Surprise Int: 26 Jan 1813 Dis: 10 Jul 1813.
  Received from HM Ship Surprise. Perseverance American Cartel.
Lockwood, William   Prisoner 640. Rank: Seaman, from: Active, Merchant Ship.
  Cap: 23 Feb 1813 off St Bartholomew by HM Ship Surprise Int: 11 Apr 1813 Dis: 11 Aug 1813.
  Received from HM Schooner Elizabeth. Malmore American Cartel.
Long, Joseph   Prisoner 1273. Rank: Seaman, from: Susannah, Schooner.
  Cap: Not Recorded by Not Recorded Int: 15 Jan 1815 Dis: 14 Feb 1815.
  Received from HMS Crescent. (Not legible) from Schooner Susannah by HMS Crescent. HM Ship Piqua. (Date of capture not recorded.)
Long, William   Prisoner 807. Rank: Seaman, from: Goutlan, Merchant Schooner.
  Cap: 31 Jan 1814 off Saint Bartholomew by HM Brig Barbados Int: 12 Feb 1814 Dis: 25 Apr 1814.
  Received from HM Schooner Ballahou. HM Ship Vestal.
Looke, Jacob   Prisoner 836. Rank: Seaman, from: Rattle Snake, Letter of Marque.
  Cap: 11 Mar 1814 Lat 24.07 N, Long 66.47 W by HM Ship Rhin Int: 25 Mar 1814 Dis: 25 Apr 1814.
  Received from HM Ship Rhin. HM Ship Vestal.
Lookey, Joseph   Prisoner 587. Rank: Seaman, from: Alexis, Privateer.
  Cap: 09 Mar 1813 Not Recorded by HM Ship Lightning Int: 22 Mar 1813 Dis: 25 Apr 1813.
  Received from HM Ship Lightning. English Retaken by Comet. Merchant Ship for England.
Loper, Lyon   Prisoner 448. Rank: Seaman, from: Mary Caroline, Merchant Brig.
  Cap: 02 Jan 1813 off Porto Rico by HM Sloop Charybdis Int: 12 Feb 1813 Dis: 11 Aug 1813.
  Received from HM Brig Liberty. Malmore American Cartel.
Lorang, Monroe   Prisoner 937. Rank: Seaman, from: President, Privateer.
  Cap: 07 May 1814 off Porto Rico by HM Ship Piqua Int: 20 Jun 1814 Dis: 22 Jul 1814.
  Received from HM Ship Vestal. HM Ship Gloucester Rear Admiral Durham.
Lorant, John   Prisoner 1010. Rank: Seaman, from: Hawk, Privateer.
  Cap: 26 Apr 1814 Near the Mona Passage by HM Ship Piqua Int: 20 Jun 1814 Dis: 22 Jul 1814.
  Received from HM Ship Vestal. HM Ship Gloucester Rear Adml Durham.
Lovell, William   Prisoner 1419. Rank: Seaman, from: Avon, Privateer.
  Cap: 08 Mar 1815 off Nevis by HM Sloop Barbados Int: 13 Mar 1815 Dis: 15 Mar 1815.
  Received from HM Sloop Barbados. HMS Numen Rear Admiral Durham.
Lovely, Pasley   Prisoner 892. Rank: Seaman, from: Hawk, Privateer.
  Cap: 26 Apr 1814 Near the Mona Passage by HM Ship Piqua Int: 20 Jun 1814 Dis: 20 Jul 1814.
  Received from HM Ship Vestal. HM Sloop Hazard Rear Adml Durham.
Lowder, Samuel   Prisoner 176. Rank: Seaman, from: HM Ship Hyperion, Not Recorded.
  Cap: Not Recorded by Not Recorded Int: 14 Nov 1812 Dis: 23 Apr 1813.
  Received from HM Ship Hyperion. Gave up as Prisoners of War Part of the Crew of HM Ship Hyperion. HM Ship Tribune a Riotous Character. (Date of capture not recorded.)
Lukies, Thomas M   Prisoner 156. Rank: Seaman, from: Yankee, Privateer.
  Cap: 25 Oct 1812 off Sombero by HM Sloop Peruvian Int: 13 Nov 1812 Dis: 10 Jul 1813.
  Received from HM Ship Mercury. Perseverance American Cartel.
Lukin, ---   Prisoner 1408. Rank: Seaman, from: Avon, Privateer.
  Cap: 08 Mar 1815 off Nevis by HM Sloop Barbados Int: 13 Mar 1815 Dis: 15 Mar 1815.
  Received from HM Sloop Barbados. HMS Numen Rear Admiral Durham. (First name not legible.)
Lumsden, Stephen   Prisoner 621. Rank: Seaman, from: HM Ship Venus, Not Recorded.
  Cap: Not Recorded by Not Recorded Int: 02 Apr 1813 Dis: 11 Aug 1813.
  Received from HM Ship Venus. Part of Crew of HMS Venus. Malmore American Cartel. Malmore American Cartel. (Date of capture not recorded.)

American Prisoners of War Held at Barbados During the War of 1812

Lumtich, Laurance   Prisoner 310. Rank: Seaman, from: Venus, Merchant Ship.
    Cap: 15 Dec 1812 Lat 32 N, Long 54 W by HM Ship Herald Int: 31 Dec 1812 Dis: 06 Jun 1813.
    Received from HM Ship Herald. America on Parole Sir F. Laforey.

Luther, Alexander   Prisoner 178. Rank: Seaman, from: HM Ship Hyperion, Not Recorded.
    Cap: Not Recorded by Not Recorded Int: 14 Nov 1812 Dis: 10 Jul 1813.
    Received from HM Ship Hyperion. Gave up as Prisoners of War Part of the Crew of HM Ship
    Hyperion. Perseverance American Cartel.(Date of capture not recorded.)

Lynch, William   Prisoner 975. Rank: Seaman, from: Fairy, Privateer.
    Cap: 20 Mar 1814 off Saba by HM Ship Ister Int: 20 Jun 1814 Dis: 22 Jul 1814.
    Received from HM Ship Vestal. HM Ship Gloucester Rear Admiral Durham. (Apparent duplicate of #
    875. William Linch.)

Lynn, Herman   Prisoner 326. Rank: Seaman, from: James Murdock, Merchant Brig.
    Cap: 05 Jan 1813 Lat 21 N, Long 57 W by HM Sloop Nimrod Int: 11 Jan 1813 Dis: 20 Jan 1813.
    Received from HM Sloop Nimrod. Being Native of Sweden.

Lyons, William   Prisoner 1100. Rank: Seaman, from: Engineer, Letter of Marque.
    Cap: 21 Sep 1814 of Porto Rico by HM Ship Barossa Int: 29 Sep 1814 Dis: 31 Mar 1815.
    Received from HM Ship Barossa. Rear Adl Durham.

Mabread, Thomas   Prisoner 357. Rank: Seaman, from: Decatur, Privateer.
    Cap: 16 Jan 1813 Lat 13.00 N, Long 41.00 N by HM Ship Surprise Int: 26 Jan 1813 Dis: 10 Jul 1813.
    Received from HM Ship Surprise. Perseverance American Cartel.

Mackey, John   Prisoner 108. Rank: Seaman, from: HM Brig Morne Fortunee, Not Recorded.
    Cap: Not Recorded by Not Recorded Int: 13 Nov 1812 Dis: 10 Jul 1813.
    Received from HM Ship Mercury. Part of Crew of HM Brig Morne Fortunee. Per Order Sir F. Laforey
    being part of crew of a Licensed Vessel. (Date of capture not recorded.)

Macomber, Anson   Prisoner 721. Rank: Seaman, from: Susannah, Merchant Schooner.
    Cap: 19 Jul 1813 Barbados by By the Constables on Shore Int: 19 Jul 1813 Dis: 11 Aug 1813.
    Malmore American Cartel.

Madison, Alexander   Prisoner 767. Rank: Seaman, from: Frolic, Privateer.
    Cap: 25 Jan 1814 off St Thomas by HM Sloop Heron Int: 06 Feb 1814 Dis: 22 Jul 1814.
    Received from HM Sloop Heron. HM Ship Gloucester Rear Admiral Durham.

Maffet, John   Prisoner 261. Rank: Prize Master, from: Rea, Privateer.
    Cap: 29 Nov 1812 off Barbados by HM Ship Lightning Int: 29 Nov 1812 Dis: 10 Jul 1813.
    Received from HM Ship Lightning. Ship having been captured by the Bona American. Perseverance
    American Cartel.

Mann, Samuel   Prisoner 791. Rank: Seaman, from: Old Friend, Not Recorded.
    Cap: 01 Jan 1814 off Saint Bartholomew by Viper Privateer Int: 11 Feb 1814 Dis: 25 Apr 1814.
    Received from HM Brig Liberty. Retaken from the Globe Privateer. HM Ship Vestal.

Manning, Joseph   Prisoner 1372. Rank: Seaman, from: Isabella, Merchant.
    Cap: 23 Feb 1815 off Berbrida by HMS Dasher Int: 03 Mar 1815 Dis: 31 Mar 1815.
    Received from HM Ship Dasher. Out of Custody Rear Adl Durham.

Mansfield, Thomas   Prisoner 217. Rank: Seaman, from: Blockade, Privateer.
    Cap: 31 Oct 1812 off Saba by HM Sloop Charybdis Int: 19 Nov 1812 Dis: 10 Jul 1813.
    Received from HM Sloop Charybdis. Perseverance American Cartel.

Manson, Stephen   Prisoner 51. Rank: Seaman, from: Providence, Privateer.
    Cap: 11 Sep 1812 off St. Barthlomew by HM Sloop Dominica Int: 13 Nov 1812 Dis: 10 Jul 1813.
    Received from HM Ship Mercury. Perseverance American Cartel.

Mapaba, Pierre   Prisoner 1197. Rank: Prize Master, from: Fox, Privateer.
    Cap: 11 Jan 1815 off St Bartholomew by HM Brig Barbados Int: 14 Jan 1815 Dis: 08 Feb 1815.
    Received from HM Brig Barbados. HM Ship Swiftsure. (Capture date is Dec 26, 1814 for all entries for
    Fox except records 1190 - 1198.)

Mapano, Pedro   Prisoner 1251. Rank: Seaman, from: Fox, Privateer.
    Cap: 26 Dec 1814 off St Bartholomew by HM Brig Barbados Int: 14 Jan 1815 Dis: 31 Mar 1815.
    Received from HM Brig Barbados. Rear Adl Durham.

March, William   Prisoner 655. Rank: Seaman, from: Adelphia, Privateer.
    Cap: 24 Feb 1813 Surinam by Not Recorded Int: 20 May 1813 Dis: 11 Aug 1813.
    Received from HM Sloop Crane. Part of Crew of Comet having charge of the Ship, which floundered
    at Sea. Surrendering themselves at Main's Point Surinam. Malmore American Cartel.

Maria, John   Prisoner 936. Rank: Seaman, from: President, Privateer.
    Cap: 07 May 1814 off Porto Rico by HM Ship Piqua Int: 20 Jun 1814 Dis: 22 Jul 1814.
    Received from HM Ship Vestal. HM Ship Gloucester Rear Admiral Durham.

American Prisoners of War Held at Barbados During the War of 1812

Maria, Joseph   Prisoner 660. Rank: Seaman, from: Adelphia, Privateer.
    Cap: 24 Feb 1813 Surinam by Not Recorded Int: 20 May 1813 Dis: 11 Aug 1813.
    Received from HM Sloop Crane. Part of Crew of Comet having charge of the Ship, which floundered at Sea. Surrendering themselves at Main's Point Surinam. Malmore American Cartel.
Marshall, Ellet   Prisoner 89. Rank: Seaman, from: Providence, Privateer.
    Cap: 11 Sep 1812 off St. Barthlomew by HM Sloop Dominica Int: 13 Nov 1812 Dis: 10 Jul 1813.
    Received from HM Ship Mercury. Perseverance American Cartel.
Marshall, Leway   Prisoner 896. Rank: Seaman, from: Hawk, Privateer.
    Cap: 26 Apr 1814 Near the Mona Passage by HM Ship Piqua Int: 20 Jun 1814 Dis: 20 Jul 1814.
    Received from HM Ship Vestal. HM Sloop Hazard Rear Adml Durham.
Marshall, Phillip   Prisoner 327. Rank: Seaman, from: James Murdock, Merchant Brig.
    Cap: 05 Jan 1813 Lat 21 N, Long 57 W by HM Sloop Nimrod Int: 11 Jan 1813 Dis: 04 Feb 1813.
    Received from HM Sloop Nimrod. Out of Custody the Vessel being liberated having a License.
Martin, Isaac   Prisoner 68. Rank: Seaman, from: Providence, Privateer.
    Cap: 11 Sep 1812 off St. Barthlomew by HM Sloop Dominica Int: 13 Nov 1812 Dis: 10 Jul 1813.
    Received from HM Ship Mercury. Perseverance American Cartel.
Martin, Silvenis P   Prisoner 130. Rank: Seaman, from: Providence, Privateer.
    Cap: 11 Sep 1812 off St. Bartholomew by HM Sloop Dominica Int: 13 Nov 1812 Dis: 10 Jul 1813.
    Received from HM Ship Mercury. Perseverance American Cartel.
Martin, William   Prisoner 57. Rank: Seaman, from: Providence, Privateer.
    Cap: 11 Sep 1812 off St. Barthlomew by HM Sloop Dominica Int: 13 Nov 1812 Dis: 10 Jul 1813.
    Received from HM Ship Mercury. Perseverance American Cartel.
Marwich, Atwood   Prisoner 452. Rank: Master, from: Hamilton, Merchant Ship.
    Cap: 11 Aug 1812 Surinam by HM Ship Surinam Int: 14 Feb 1813 Dis: 13 Mar 1813.
    Received from HM Brig Liberty. America on Parole Sir Francis Laforey.
Mason, Charles   Prisoner 1322. Rank: Seaman, from: Whalebone, Merchant Schooner.
    Cap: 25 Jan 1815 off St Bartholomew by HMB Espringle Int: 09 Feb 1815 Dis: 10 Feb 1815.
    Received from HMB Satellite. Out of Custody being a Swede, Rear Adml Durham.
Mason, James   Prisoner 540. Rank: Seaman, from: John, Privateer.
    Cap: 06 Feb 1813 Lat 10.0 N, Long 61.0 W by HM Sloop Peruvian Int: 20 Feb 1813 Dis: 11 Aug 1813. Received from HM Ship Cumberland. American Cartel Malmore.
Mason, Joseph J   Prisoner 468. Rank: Master, from: John, Privateer.
    Cap: 06 Feb 1813 Lat 10.0 N, Long 61.0 W by HM Sloop Peruvian Int: 20 Feb 1813 Escaped: 24 Apr 1813. Received from HM Ship Cumberland. Escaped. Retaken Reentry (691).
Mason, Joseph J   Prisoner 691. Rank: Mate, from: John, Privateer.
    Cap: 06 Feb 1813 Lat 10.00 N, Long 61.00 W by HM Sloop Peruvian Int: 26 May 1813 Dis: 14 Jun 1813. Received from HM Sloop Peruvian. HMS Cufay for passage to England. Sir F. Laforey.
Mason, May D   Prisoner 127. Rank: Seaman, from: Providence, Privateer.
    Cap: 11 Sep 1812 off St. Barthlomew by HM Sloop Dominica Int: 13 Nov 1812 Dis: 10 Jul 1813.
    Received from HM Ship Mercury. Perseverance American Cartel.
Mason, Simon   Prisoner 292. Rank: Mate, from: Phoenix, Merchant Brig.
    Cap: 24 Nov 1812 Lat 37.03 N, Long 60.00 W by HM Sloop Morgiana Int: 16 Dec 1812 Dis: 17 Jan 1813. Received from HM Sloop Morgiana. Exchanged.
Masters, Coons   Prisoner 862. Rank: Seaman, from: Chapman, Privateer.
    Cap: 28 Feb 1814 off St Bartholomew by Thistle Privateer Int: 26 Mar 1814 Dis: 25 Apr 1814.
    Received from HM Ship Palama. HM Ship Vestal.
Mathews, Edward   Prisoner 1155. Rank: Seaman, from: High Flyer, Letter of Marque.
    Cap: 14 Nov 1814 off Anguilla by HM Ship Barossa Int: 18 Nov 1814 Dis: 31 Mar 1815.
    Received from HM Ship Barossa. Rear Adl Durham.
Mathey, James   Prisoner 915. Rank: Captain, from: President, Privateer.
    Cap: 07 May 1814 off Porto Rico by HM Ship Piqua Int: 20 Jun 1814 Dis: 20 Jul 1814.
    Received from HM Ship Vestal. HM Sloop Hazard Rear Adml Durham.
Maulton, Joseph   Prisoner 151. Rank: Seaman, from: Yankee, Privateer.
    Cap: 25 Oct 1812 off Sombero by HM Sloop Peruvian Int: 13 Nov 1812 Dis: 10 Jul 1813.
    Received from HM Ship Mercury. Perseverance American Cartel. Detected cutting through the ship.
Maulton, Nathaniel   Prisoner 159. Rank: Seaman, from: Yankee, Privateer.
    Cap: 25 Oct 1812 off Sombero by HM Sloop Peruvian Int: 13 Nov 1812 Dis: 02 May 1813.
    Received from HM Ship Mercury. Merchant Ship.
Maxan, Darville   Prisoner 1215. Rank: Seaman, from: Fox, Privateer.
    Cap: 26 Dec 1814 off St Bartholomew by HM Brig Barbados Int: 14 Jan 1815 Dis: 08 Feb 1815.
    Received from HM Brig Barbados. HM Ship Swiftsure.

American Prisoners of War Held at Barbados During the War of 1812

May, William   Prisoner 724. Rank: Master, from: Lucretia, Merchant Schooner.
    Cap: 30 Jun 1813 off St Bartholomew by HM Brig Maria Int: 02 Feb 1814 Dis: 02 Feb 1814.
    Received from HM Brig Liberty. Rising States American Cartel. Rear Adml Sir F. Laforey.

May, William   Prisoner 1318. Rank: Seaman, from: Whalebone, Merchant Schooner.
    Cap: 25 Jan 1815 off St Bartholomew by HMB Espringle Int: 09 Feb 1815 Dis: 31 Mar 1815.
    Received from HMB Satellite. Rear Adl Durham.

McCall, James   Prisoner 715. Rank: Mate, from: Olive Branch, Merchant Brig.
    Cap: 12 Apr 1813 Lat 17.00 N, Long 59.30 W by HM Sloop Eclipse Int: 07 Jul 1813 Dis: 24 Jul 1813.
    Received from HM Sloop Eclipse. Out of Custody the Vessel being liberated.

McCarthy, James   Prisoner 528. Rank: Seaman, from: John, Privateer.
    Cap: 06 Feb 1813 Lat 10.0 N, Long 61.0 W by HM Sloop Peruvian Int: 20 Feb 1813 Dis: 11 Aug 1813. Received from HM Ship Cumberland. Malmore American Cartel.

McCastin, James   Prisoner 1158. Rank: Seaman, from: High Flyer, Letter of Marque.
    Cap: 14 Nov 1814 off Anguilla by HM Ship Barossa Int: 18 Nov 1814 Dis: 08 Feb 1815.
    Received from HM Ship Barossa. HM Ship Swiftsure.

McCeaver, Peter   Prisoner 174. Rank: Seaman, from: HM Ship Hyperion, Not Recorded.
    Cap: Not Recorded by Not Recorded Int: 14 Nov 1812 Dis: 26 Apr 1813.
    Received from HM Ship Hyperion. Gave up as Prisoners of War Part of the Crew of HM Ship Hyperion. America on Parole Sir F. Laforey. (Date of capture not recorded.)

McDaniel, John   Prisoner 61. Rank: Seaman, from: Providence, Privateer.
    Cap: 11 Sep 1812 off St. Barthlomew by HM Sloop Dominica Int: 13 Nov 1812 Dis: 10 Jul 1813.
    Received from HM Ship Mercury. Perseverance American Cartel.

McDermott, Andrew   Prisoner 1284. Rank: Seaman, from: Hero, Merchant Schooner.
    Cap: 14 Dec 1814 Lat 19.13, Long 64 by HMS Pique Int: 29 Jan 1815 Dis: 14 Feb 1815.
    Received from HMS Pique. HM Ship Piqua.

McDonald, John   Prisoner 1084. Rank: Seaman, from: Engineer, Letter of Marque.
    Cap: 21 Sep 1814 of Porto Rico by HM Ship Barossa Int: 29 Sep 1814 Dis: 31 Mar 1815.
    Received from HM Ship Barossa. Rear Adl Durham.

McDuff, Daniel   Prisoner 209. Rank: Seaman, from: Blockade, Privateer.
    Cap: 31 Oct 1812 off Saba by HM Sloop Charybdis Int: 19 Nov 1812 Dis: 10 Jul 1813.
    Received from HM Sloop Charybdis. Perseverance American Cartel.

McDuff, Phillp S   Prisoner 229. Rank: Seaman, from: Blockade, Privateer.
    Cap: 31 Oct 1812 off Saba by HM Sloop Charybdis Int: 19 Nov 1812 Dis: 10 Jul 1813.
    Received from HM Sloop Charybdis. Perseverance American Cartel.

McFoy, Daniel   Prisoner 32. Rank: Master, from: Providence, Privateer.
    Cap: 11 Sep 1812 off St. Bartholomew by HM Sloop Dominica Int: 24 Oct 1812 Dis: 10 Jul 1813.
    Received from HM Sloop Vestal. Perseverance American Cartel.

McGill, James   Prisoner 262. Rank: Prize Master, from: Rea, Privateer.
    Cap: 29 Nov 1812 off Barbados by HM Ship Lightning Int: 29 Nov 1812 Dis: 10 Jul 1813.
    Received from HM Ship Lightning. Ship having been captured by the Bona American. Perseverance American Cartel.

McHam, Daniel   Prisoner 1139. Rank: 2 Mate, from: High Flyer, Letter of Marque.
    Cap: 14 Nov 1814 off Anguilla by HM Ship Barossa Int: 18 Nov 1814 Dis: 08 Feb 1815.
    Received from HM Ship Barossa. HM Ship Swiftsure.

McLean, Ferdin   Prisoner 1250. Rank: Seaman, from: Fox, Privateer.
    Cap: 26 Dec 1814 off St Bartholomew by HM Brig Barbados Int: 14 Jan 1815 Dis: 08 Feb 1815.
    Received from HM Brig Barbados. HM Ship Swiftsure.

McQueen, Caleb   Prisoner 1006. Rank: Seaman, from: Hawk, Privateer.
    Cap: 26 Apr 1814 Near the Mona Passage by HM Ship Piqua Int: 20 Jun 1814 Dis: 22 Jul 1814.
    Received from HM Ship Vestal. HM Ship Gloucester Rear Admiral Durham.

Meadows, George   Prisoner 38. Rank: Seaman, from: William Rathbone, Not Recorded.
    Cap: 09 Oct 1812 Lat 22.00 N, Long 60.00 W by HM Sloop Chandler Int: 01 Nov 1812 Dis: 10 Jul 1813. Received from HM Brig Swaggerer. Having been taken by the Savory Jack American privateer. Perseverance American Cartel.

Melbourne, William   Prisoner 165. Rank: Seaman, from: Yankee, Privateer.
    Cap: 25 Oct 1812 off Sombero by HM Sloop Peruvian Int: 13 Nov 1812 Dis: 10 Jul 1813.
    Received from HM Ship Mercury. Perseverance American Cartel.

Melbourne, William   Prisoner 923. Rank: Seaman, from: President, Privateer.
    Cap: 07 May 1814 off Porto Rico by HM Ship Piqua Int: 20 Jun 1814 Dis: 20 Jul 1814.
    Received from HM Ship Vestal. HM Sloop Hazard Rear Adml Durham.

Mendoza, Nicholas   Prisoner 944. Rank: Seaman, from: President, Privateer.
    Cap: 07 May 1814 off Porto Rico by HM Ship Piqua Int: 20 Jun 1814 Dis: 22 Jul 1814.
    Received from HM Ship Vestal. HM Ship Gloucester Rear Admiral Durham.

American Prisoners of War Held at Barbados During the War of 1812

Mennedy, Bennet   Prisoner 265. Rank: Seaman, from: Rea, Privateer.
    Cap: 29 Nov 1812 off Barbados by HM Ship Lightning Int: 29 Nov 1812 Escaped: 02 Jun 1813.
    Received from HM Ship Lightning. Ship having been captured by the Bona American. Escaped. Bad Character (not legible).

Merchant, James   Prisoner 1434. Rank: Seaman, from: Avon, Privateer.
    Cap: 08 Mar 1815 off Nevis by HM Sloop Barbados Int: 13 Mar 1815 Dis: 15 Mar 1815.
    Received from HM Sloop Barbados. HMS Numen Rear Admiral Durham.

Merill, Charles   Prisoner 232. Rank: Seaman, from: Blockade, Privateer.
    Cap: 31 Oct 1812 off Saba by HM Sloop Charybdis Int: 19 Nov 1812 Dis: 27 May 1813.
    Received from HM Sloop Charybdis. American on Parole ill health.

Merrit, Silvanus   Prisoner 302. Rank: Seaman, from: Carl Frederick, Privateer.
    Cap: 11 Oct 1812 at Sea by HM Sloop Ringdove Int: 29 Dec 1812 Dis: 10 Jul 1813.
    Received from HM Brig Liberty. Captured by the Odyssey in (not legible). Perseverance American Cartel.

Metz, Joseph   Prisoner 1373. Rank: Seaman, from: Isabella, Merchant.
    Cap: 23 Feb 1815 off Berbrida by HMS Dasher Int: 03 Mar 1815 Dis: 31 Mar 1815.
    Received from HM Ship Dasher. Out of Custody Rear Adl Durham.

Meyer, John   Prisoner 42. Rank: Seaman, from: William Rathbone, Not Recorded.
    Cap: 09 Oct 1812 Lat 22.00 N, Long 60.00 W by HM Sloop Chandler Int: 01 Nov 1812 Dis: 10 Jul 1813. Received from HM Brig Swaggerer. Having been taken by the Savory Jack American privateer. Perseverance American Cartel.

Michael, Ed   Prisoner 1352. Rank: Seaman, from: Vidett, Letter of Marque.
    Cap: 14 Feb 1815 off St Bartholomew by HMS Dasher Int: 03 Mar 1815 Dis: 31 Mar 1815.
    Received from HM Ship Dasher. Out of Custody Rear Adl Durham.

Michell, John   Prisoner 1378. Rank: Seaman, from: Laurence, Merchant.
    Cap: 14 Feb 1815 off Porto Rico by HMS Dasher Int: 04 Mar 1815 Dis: 31 Mar 1815.
    Received from HM Ship Dasher. Out of Custody Rear Adl Durham.

Michell, Phillip   Prisoner 437. Rank: Seaman, from: James Murdock, Merchant Brig.
    Cap: 05 Jan 1813 Lat 21N, Long 57 W by HM Ship Nimrod Int: 05 Feb 1813 Dis: 10 Apr 1813.
    Received from Brig James Murdock. Out of Custody the Vessel being liberated.

Micons, John   Prisoner 1024. Rank: Seaman, from: Snake Packet, Not Recorded.
    Cap: Not Recorded by Not Recorded Int: 10 Jul 1814 Dis: 22 Jul 1814.
    Received from Snake Packet. Part of Crew of Snake Packet. HM Ship Gloucester Rear Admiral Durham. (Date of capture not recorded.)

Midler, John   Prisoner 1276. Rank: Seaman, from: Hero, Merchant Schooner.
    Cap: 14 Dec 1814 Lat 19.13, Long 64 by HMS Pique Int: 29 Jan 1815 Dis: 14 Feb 1815.
    Received from HMS Pique. HM Ship Piqua.

Mie, Elisha   Prisoner 179. Rank: Captain, from: Blockade, Privateer.
    Cap: 31 Oct 1812 off Saba by HM Sloop Charybdis Int: 19 Nov 1812 Dis: 10 Jul 1813.
    Received from HM Sloop Charybdis. Perseverance American Cartel.

Miller, Isaac   Prisoner 328. Rank: Master, from: Mercator, Merchant Brig.
    Cap: 25 Aug 1812 off Cayman by HM Sloop Surinam Int: 12 Jan 1813 Dis: 15 Jan 1813.
    Received from Schooner Peggy. Exchanged America.

Miller, James   Prisoner 1391. Rank: Seaman, from: Avon, Privateer.
    Cap: 08 Mar 1815 off Nevis by HM Sloop Barbados Int: 13 Mar 1815 Dis: 31 Mar 1815.
    Received from HM Sloop Barbados. Out of Custody Rear Adl Durham.

Miller, John   Prisoner 1360. Rank: Seaman, from: Spencer, Merchant.
    Cap: 15 Feb 1815 off St Bartholomew by HMS Dasher Int: 03 Mar 1815 Dis: 31 Mar 1815.
    Received from HM Ship Dasher. Out of Custody Rear Adl Durham.

Miller, Nicholas   Prisoner 340. Rank: Prize Master, from: Decatur, Privateer.
    Cap: 16 Jan 1813 Lat 13.00 N, Long 41.00 N by HM Ship Surprise Int: 26 Jan 1813 Dis: 10 Jul 1813.
    Received from HM Ship Surprise. Perseverance American Cartel.

Miller, Peter   Prisoner 388. Rank: Seaman, from: Decatur, Privateer.
    Cap: 16 Jan 1813 Lat 13.00 N, Long 41.00 N by HM Ship Surprise Int: 26 Jan 1813 Escaped: 25 Feb 1813. Received from HM Ship Surprise. Perseverance American Cartel.

Miller, Peter   Prisoner 565. Rank: Seaman, from: Decatur, Privateer.
    Cap: 16 Jan 1813 Lat 13 N, Long 41 W by HM Ship Surprise Int: 03 Mar 1813 Dis: 11 Aug 1813.
    Retaken having escaped. Malmore American Cartel.

Millet, Joseph   Prisoner 493. Rank: Seaman, from: John, Privateer.
    Cap: 06 Feb 1813 Lat 10.0 N, Long 61.0 W by HM Sloop Peruvian Int: 20 Feb 1813 Dis: 11 Aug 1813. Received from HM Ship Cumberland. Malmore American Cartel.

American Prisoners of War Held at Barbados During the War of 1812

Milton, Thomas   Prisoner 622. Rank: Prize Master, from: Fly, Privateer.
    Cap: 19 Jan 1813 Lat 15.00 N, Long 45.00 W by HMS Venus Int: 02 Apr 1813 Dis: 10 Jul 1813.
    Received from HMS Venus. Recaptured from the Yankee. Perseverance American Cartel.

Mincer, Joseph   Prisoner 1075. Rank: Gunner, from: Engineer, Letter of Marque.
    Cap: 21 Sep 1814 of Porto Rico by HM Ship Barossa Int: 29 Sep 1814 Dis: 08 Feb 1815.
    Received from HM Ship Barossa. Out of Custody being a Dutchman, Rear Adml Durham.

Mister, William   Prisoner 804. Rank: Seaman, from: Atalante, Merchant Schooner.
    Cap: 19 Jan 1814 off Saint Bartholomew by HM Brig Barbados Int: 12 Feb 1814 Dis: 25 Apr 1814.
    Received from HM Schooner Ballahou. HM Ship Vestal.

Mitchmore, John   Prisoner 71. Rank: Seaman, from: Neptune, Merchant Brig.
    Cap: 29 Aug 1812 at Sea by HM Brig Maria Int: 13 Nov 1812 Dis: 19 Nov 1812.
    Received from HM Ship Mercury. Out of Custody per order of Rear Adml Sir F. Laforey being crew of a licensed vessel.

Moasee, Abraham   Prisoner 1451. Rank: Seaman, from: Ivan Francisco, Not Recorded.
    Cap: 08 Mar 1815 off Nevis by HM Brig Muros Int: 26 Mar 1815 Dis: 31 Mar 1815.
    Received from HM Brig Maria. Recaptured from the Grand Turk Privateer. Out of Custody Rear Adl Durham.

Monger, Bella   Prisoner 222. Rank: Seaman, from: Blockade, Privateer.
    Cap: 31 Oct 1812 off Saba by HM Sloop Charybdis Int: 19 Nov 1812 Dis: 10 Jul 1813.
    Received from HM Sloop Charybdis. Perseverance American Cartel. (Not legible) Retaken Immediately.

Montgomery, John   Prisoner 1325. Rank: Seaman, from: Spencer, Merchant Schooner.
    Cap: 15 Feb 1815 off St Bartholomew by HM Ship Dasher Int: 25 Feb 1815 Dis: 31 Mar 1815.
    Received from Schooner Spencer. Out of Custody Rear Adl Durham.

Montgomery, W P   Prisoner 962. Rank: Prize Master, from: President, Privateer.
    Cap: 07 May 1814 off Porto Rico by HM Ship Piqua Int: 20 Jun 1814 Escaped: 08 Jul 1814.
    Received from HM Ship Piqua. Escaped.

Montgomery, W P   Prisoner 1037. Rank: Prize Master, from: North Star, Merchant Schooner.
    Cap: 10 Jun 1814 off St Bartholomew by HM Brig Crane Int: 22 Jul 1814 Dis: 22 Jul 1814.
    Retaken former No (962). HM Ship Gloucester Rear Adml Durham.

Moody, David   Prisoner 467. Rank: Seaman, from: John, Privateer.
    Cap: 06 Feb 1813 Lat 10.0 N, Long 61.0 W by HM Sloop Peruvian Int: 20 Feb 1813 Dis: 11 Aug 1813. Received from HM Ship Cumberland. Malmore American Cartel.

Moore, Dennis   Prisoner 514. Rank: Seaman, from: John, Privateer.
    Cap: 06 Feb 1813 Lat 10.0 N, Long 61.0 W by HM Sloop Peruvian Int: 20 Feb 1813 Dis: 11 Aug 1813. Received from HM Ship Cumberland. Malmore American Cartel.

Moore, Robert   Prisoner 208. Rank: Seaman, from: Blockade, Privateer.
    Cap: 31 Oct 1812 off Saba by HM Sloop Charybdis Int: 19 Nov 1812 Dis: 10 Jul 1813.
    Received from HM Sloop Charybdis. Perseverance American Cartel.

Mooring, Thomas   Prisoner 1062. Rank: Seaman, from: Mary, Letter of Marque.
    Cap: 07 Jun 1814 La Quisa by HM Ship Heron Int: 31 Jul 1814 Dis: 31 Mar 1815.
    Received from HM Sloop Mosquito. Rear Adl Durham.

Morgan, Richard   Prisoner 555. Rank: Seaman, from: Rebecca, Merchant Brig.
    Cap: 15 Jan 1813 off Demuary by Detained by Custom House Int: 02 Mar 1813 Dis: 27 May 1813.
    Received from Army Schooner Maria. America on Parole Sir Francis Laforey.

Morrell, Richard   Prisoner 356. Rank: Seaman, from: Decatur, Privateer.
    Cap: 16 Jan 1813 Lat 13.00 N, Long 41.00 N by HM Ship Surprise Int: 26 Jan 1813 Dis: 10 Jul 1813.
    Received from HM Ship Surprise. Perseverance American Cartel.

Morris, Peter   Prisoner 633. Rank: Seaman, from: Jane, Privateer.
    Cap: 06 Mar 1813 Lat 14.22 N, Long 65.35 W by HM Brig Swaggerer Int: 02 Apr 1813 Dis: 11 Aug 1813. Received from Army Schooner Maria. Recaptured from the Comet. Malmore American Cartel.

Morris, Thomas   Prisoner 1364. Rank: Seaman, from: Spencer, Merchant.
    Cap: 15 Feb 1815 off St Bartholomew by HMS Dasher Int: 03 Mar 1815 Dis: 31 Mar 1815.
    Received from HM Ship Dasher. Out of Custody Rear Adl Durham.

Moss, Alfred   Prisoner 1295. Rank: Seaman, from: Mary, Merchant Schooner.
    Cap: 15 Jan 1815 Lat 22.40, Long 66 by HM Ship Pique Int: 29 Jan 1815 Dis: 31 Mar 1815.
    Received from HMS Pique. Rear Adl Durham.

Moutrie, Henry W   Prisoner 592. Rank: Surgeon, from: Thomas Penrose, Privateer.
    Cap: 23 Mar 1813 Lat 20.14 W, Long 61.20 W by HM Ship Tribune Int: 28 Mar 1813 Dis: 26 Apr 1813. Received from HM Ship Tribune. America on Parole Sir F. Laforey.

Mullin, John   Prisoner 387. Rank: Seaman, from: Decatur, Privateer.
    Cap: 16 Jan 1813 Lat 13.00 N, Long 41.00 N by HM Ship Surprise Int: 26 Jan 1813 Dis: 10 Jul 1813.
    Received from HM Ship Surprise. Perseverance American Cartel.

American Prisoners of War Held at Barbados During the War of 1812

Murray, James   Prisoner 1038. Rank: Seaman, from: North Star, Merchant Schooner.
    Cap: 10 Jun 1814 off St Bartholomew by HM Brig Crane Int: 22 Jul 1814 Dis: 22 Jul 1814.
    (Not legible) on shore. Received from HM Ship Orntes.
    HM Ship Gloucester Rear Adml Durham.

Murray, John   Prisoner 763. Rank: Seaman, from: Frolic, Privateer.
    Cap: 25 Jan 1814 off St Thomas by HM Sloop Heron Int: 06 Feb 1814 Dis: 25 Apr 1814.
    Received from HM Sloop Heron. HM Ship Vestal.

Murray, Richard   Prisoner 228. Rank: Seaman, from: Blockade, Privateer.
    Cap: 31 Oct 1812 off Saba by HM Sloop Charybdis Int: 19 Nov 1812 Dis: 10 Jul 1813.
    Received from HM Sloop Charybdis. Perseverance American Cartel.

Murray, William   Prisoner 303. Rank: Seaman, from: Carl Frederick, Privateer.
    Cap: 11 Oct 1812 at Sea by HM Sloop Ringdove Int: 29 Dec 1812 Dis: 10 Jul 1813.
    Received from HM Brig Liberty. Captured by the Odyssey in (not legible). Perseverance American Cartel. Cut through the Ship Escaped Retaken Immediately.

Murrell, William   Prisoner 670. Rank: Seaman, from: William, Merchant Ship.
    Cap: 09 Apr 1813 off Santa Crews by HM Ship Spider Int: 23 May 1813 Dis: 11 Aug 1813.
    Received from HM Ship Vestal. Malmore American Cartel.

Myer, William F   Prisoner 827. Rank: Master, from: Rattle Snake, Letter of Marque.
    Cap: 11 Mar 1814 Lat 24.07 N, Long 66.47 W by HM Ship Rhin Int: 25 Mar 1814 Dis: 05 Apr 1814.
    Received from HM Ship Rhin. Out of Custody in consequence of having saved the life of a British Seaman at the (not legible) of his own.

Myers, Charles   Prisoner 94. Rank: Seaman, from: Providence, Privateer.
    Cap: 11 Sep 1812 off St. Barthlomew by HM Sloop Dominica Int: 13 Nov 1812 Dis: 10 Jul 1813.
    Received from HM Ship Mercury. Perseverance American Cartel.

Myers, Henry   Prisoner 306. Rank: 2 Mate, from: Venus, Merchant Ship.
    Cap: 15 Dec 1812 Lat 32 N, Long 54 W by HM Ship Herald Int: 31 Dec 1812 Dis: 07 Feb 1813.
    Received from HM Ship Herald. Being a German.

Nay, John R   Prisoner 288. Rank: Seaman, from: HM Sloop Surinam, Not Recorded.
    Cap: Not Recorded by Not Recorded Int: 04 Dec 1812 Dis: 10 Jul 1813.
    Received from HM Sloop Surinam. Part of Crew of HM Sloop Surinam. Perseverance American Cartel. (Date of capture not recorded.)

Newberry, John   Prisoner 754. Rank: Seaman, from: Frolic, Privateer.
    Cap: 25 Jan 1814 off St Thomas by HM Sloop Heron Int: 06 Feb 1814 Dis: 22 Jul 1814.
    Received from HM Sloop Heron. HM Ship Gloucester Rear Admiral Durham.

Newell, Charles   Prisoner 1032. Rank: Seaman, from: North Star, Merchant Schooner.
    Cap: 10 Jun 1814 off St Bartholomew by HM Brig Crane Int: 11 Jul 1814 Dis: 22 Jul 1814.
    Received from HM Schooner Flying Fish. HM Ship Gloucester Rear Adml Durham.

Newell, Samuel Swift   Prisoner 1021. Rank: Prize Master, from: Comet, Privateer.
    Cap: Not Recorded by Not Recorded Int: 05 Jul 1814 Dis: 22 Jul 1814.
    Sent from Guadeloupe by Genl (not legible). Out of Custody having the Oath of Allegiance to His Britannic Majesty. (Date of capture not recorded.)

Newell, Samuel S   Prisoner 1105. Rank: Prize Master, from: Engineer, Letter of Marque.
    Cap: 21 Sep 1814 of Porto Rico by HM Ship Barossa Int: 10 Oct 1814 Dis: 31 Mar 1815.
    Received from HM Ship Barossa. Rear Adl Durham.

Newell, Thomas   Prisoner 1399. Rank: Captain Marines, from: Avon, Privateer.
    Cap: 08 Mar 1815 off Nevis by HM Sloop Barbados Int: 13 Mar 1815 Dis: 15 Mar 1815.
    Received from HM Sloop Barbados. HMS Numen Rear Admiral Durham.

Nicholls, William   Prisoner 976. Rank: Seaman, from: Fairy, Privateer.
    Cap: 20 Mar 1814 off Saba by HM Ship Ister Int: 20 Jun 1814 Dis: 22 Jul 1814.
    Received from HM Ship Vestal. HM Ship Gloucester Rear Admiral Durham. (Apparent duplicate of # 876. William Nichols.)

Nichols, William   Prisoner 331. Rank: Captain, from: Decatur, Privateer.
    Cap: 16 Jan 1813 Lat 13.00 N, Long 41.00 N by HM Ship Surprise Int: 25 Jan 1813 Dis: 23 Apr 1813.
    Received from HM Ship Surprise. Out of Custody the Vessel being liberated by Admiralty (not legible).

Nichols, William   Prisoner 876. Rank: Seaman, from: Camilla, Not Recorded.
    Cap: 29 Mar 1814 Sombrero Passage by HM Ship Ister Int: 15 Apr 1814 Dis: 25 Apr 1814.
    Received from HM Ship Ister. Recaptured from Fairy Privateer. HM Ship Vestal.

Noah, Nathaniel   Prisoner 507. Rank: Seaman, from: John, Privateer.
    Cap: 06 Feb 1813 Lat 10.0 N, Long 61.0 W by HM Sloop Peruvian Int: 20 Feb 1813 Dis: 11 Aug 1813. Received from HM Ship Cumberland. Malmore American Cartel.

American Prisoners of War Held at Barbados During the War of 1812

Noble, D Prisoner 867. Rank: Seaman, from: Martha, Merchant Schooner.
    Cap: Not Recorded by Not Recorded Int: 01 Apr 1814 Dis: 25 Apr 1814.
    Received from Sloop Martha. Gave himself up as a Prisoner of War from Merchant Schooner Martha. HM Ship Vestal. (Date of capture not recorded.)

Noble, D Prisoner 969. Rank: Seaman, from: Martha, Merchant Sloop.
    Cap: Not Recorded by Not Recorded Int: 20 Jun 1814 Dis: 22 Jul 1814.
    Received from HM Ship Vestal. Part of Crew of English Merchant Sloop Martha. HM Ship Gloucester Rear Admiral Durham. (Date of capture not recorded. Apparent duplicate of # 867.)

Norris, Samuel Prisoner 439. Rank: Seaman, from: HM Sloop Arab, Not Recorded.
    Cap: Not Recorded by Not Recorded Int: 10 Apr 1813 Dis: 11 Aug 1813.
    Received from HM Sloop Arab. Part of Crew of HM Sloop Arab given up as Prisoner of War. Malmore American Cartel. (Date of capture not recorded.)

Norris, William Prisoner 1332. Rank: Seaman, from: Vidett, Letter of Marque.
    Cap: 14 Feb 1815 off St Bartholomew by HM Ship Dasher Int: 03 Mar 1815 Dis: 31 Mar 1815.
    Received from HM Ship Dasher. Out of Custody Rear Adl Durham.

Noyes, Jeremiah Prisoner 172. Rank: Seaman, from: Yankee, Privateer.
    Cap: 25 Oct 1812 off Sombero by HM Sloop Peruvian Int: 13 Nov 1812 Dis: 10 Jul 1813.
    Received from HM Ship Mercury. Perseverance American Cartel.

Nye, David Prisoner 1384. Rank: Captain, from: Avon, Privateer.
    Cap: 08 Mar 1815 off Nevis by HM Sloop Barbados Int: 05 Mar 1815 Dis: 31 Mar 1815.
    Received from HM Ship Dasher. Out of Custody Rear Adl Durham. (Date of Interment before Capture.)

Nye, Stephen Prisoner 575. Rank: Seaman, from: St Bartholomew, Merchant Brig.
    Cap: 05 Mar 1813 Carlisle Bay by HM Ship Cumberland Int: 10 Mar 1813 Dis: 06 Jun 1813.
    Received from HM Ship Cumberland. America on Parole Sir Francis Laforey.

Oackum, John Prisoner 1225. Rank: Seaman, from: Fox, Privateer.
    Cap: 26 Dec 1814 off St Bartholomew by HM Brig Barbados Int: 14 Jan 1815 Dis: 08 Feb 1815.
    Received from HM Brig Barbados. HM Ship Swiftsure.

Oakam, Archibald Prisoner 877. Rank: Seaman, from: Camilla, Not Recorded.
    Cap: 29 Mar 1814 Sombrero Passage by HM Ship Ister Int: 15 Apr 1814 Dis: 25 Apr 1814.
    Received from HM Ship Ister. Recaptured from Fairy Privateer. HM Ship Vestal.

Oakes, Jacob Prisoner 1446. Rank: Seaman, from: Ivan Francisco, Not Recorded.
    Cap: 08 Mar 1815 off Nevis by HM Brig Muros Int: 26 Mar 1815 Dis: 31 Mar 1815.
    Received from HM Brig Maria. Recaptured from the Grand Turk Privateer. Out of Custody Rear Adl Durham.

Oakum, Archibald Prisoner 977. Rank: Seaman, from: Fairy, Privateer.
    Cap: 20 Mar 1814 off Saba by HM Ship Ister Int: 20 Jun 1814 Dis: 22 Jul 1814.
    Received from HM Ship Vestal. HM Ship Gloucester Rear Admiral Durham. (Apparent duplicate of # 877. William Oakam.)

Odiorne, John Prisoner 737. Rank: Captain, from: Frolic, Privateer.
    Cap: 25 Jan 1814 off St Thomas by HM Sloop Heron Int: 06 Feb 1814 Dis: 22 Jul 1814.
    Received from HM Sloop Heron. HM Ship Gloucester Rear Admiral Durham.

Olmstead, Jesse Prisoner 185. Rank: Clerk, from: Blockade, Privateer.
    Cap: 31 Oct 1812 off Saba by HM Sloop Charybdis Int: 19 Nov 1812 Dis: 10 Jul 1813.
    Received from HM Sloop Charybdis. Perseverance American Cartel.

Osborne, Ambrose Prisoner 400. Rank: Seaman, from: Decatur, Privateer.
    Cap: 16 Jan 1813 Lat 13.00 N, Long 41.00 N by HM Ship Surprise Int: 26 Jan 1813 Dis: 10 Jul 1813.
    Received from HM Ship Surprise. Perseverance American Cartel.

Osborne, John Prisoner 1005. Rank: Seaman, from: Hawk, Privateer.
    Cap: 26 Apr 1814 Near the Mona Passage by HM Ship Piqua Int: 20 Jun 1814 Dis: 22 Jul 1814.
    Received from HM Ship Vestal. HM Ship Gloucester Rear Admiral Durham.

Osburn, Able Prisoner 1449. Rank: Seaman, from: Ivan Francisco, Not Recorded.
    Cap: 08 Mar 1815 off Nevis by HM Brig Muros Int: 26 Mar 1815 Dis: 31 Mar 1815.
    Received from HM Brig Maria. Recaptured from the Grand Turk Privateer. Out of Custody Rear Adl Durham.

Oscott, Stephen Prisoner 903. Rank: Seaman, from: Hawk, Privateer.
    Cap: 26 Apr 1814 Near the Mona Passage by HM Ship Piqua Int: 20 Jun 1814 Escaped: 08 Jul 1814.
    Received from HM Ship Vestal. Escaped.

Oscott, Stephen Prisoner 1033. Rank: Seaman, from: North Star, Merchant Schooner.
    Cap: 10 Jun 1814 off St Bartholomew by HM Brig Crane Int: 13 Jul 1814 Escaped: 21 Jul 1814.
    Retaken former No 903. Escaped.

American Prisoners of War Held at Barbados During the War of 1812

Ouveire, Joseph   Prisoner 658. Rank: Seaman, from: Adelphia, Privateer.
    Cap: 24 Feb 1813 Surinam by Not Recorded Int: 20 May 1813 Dis: 11 Aug 1813.
    Received from HM Sloop Crane. Part of Crew of Comet having charge of the Ship, which floundered at Sea. Surrendering themselves at Main's Point Surinam. Malmore American Cartel.

Paddock, Aaron   Prisoner 10. Rank: Mate, from: Hope, Merchant Ship.
    Cap: 27 Sep 1812 Lat 22.30 N, (Long) 40.45 W by HM Ship Tribune Int: 07 Oct 1812 Dis: 24 Oct 1812. Received from Ship Hope. America on Parole per order of Captain Reynolds Tribune.

Page, Cato   Prisoner 786. Rank: Seaman, from: Fox, Privateer.
    Cap: Not Recorded by Not Recorded Int: 11 Feb 1814 Dis: 25 Apr 1814.
    Received from HM Brig Liberty. Picked up in a boat at Sea part of Crew of Fox. HM Ship Vestal. (Date of capture not recorded.)

Page, George   Prisoner 443. Rank: Seaman, from: Isaac, Merchant Brig.
    Cap: 01 Jan 1813 off Porto Rico by HM Sloop Charybdis Int: 12 Feb 1813 Dis: 06 Jun 1813.
    Received from HM Brig Liberty. America on Parole Sir F. Laforey.

Paget, Levi   Prisoner 1371. Rank: Seaman, from: Isabella, Merchant.
    Cap: 23 Feb 1815 off Berbrida by HMS Dasher Int: 03 Mar 1815 Dis: 31 Mar 1815.
    Received from HM Ship Dasher. Out of Custody Rear Adl Durham.

Paine, Francis   Prisoner 503. Rank: Seaman, from: John, Privateer.
    Cap: 06 Feb 1813 Lat 10.0 N, Long 61.0 W by HM Sloop Peruvian Int: 20 Feb 1813 Dis: 23 Jun 1813. Received from HM Ship Cumberland. To assist in navigating merchant ship to England.

Pairse, John   Prisoner 39. Rank: Seaman, from: William Rathbone, Not Recorded.
    Cap: 09 Oct 1812 Lat 22.00 N, Long 60.00 W by HM Sloop Chandler Int: 01 Nov 1812 Dis: 10 Jul 1813. Received from HM Brig Swaggerer. Having been taken by the Savory Jack American privateer. Perseverance American Cartel.

Palfrey, Jonathan   Prisoner 530. Rank: Seaman, from: John, Privateer.
    Cap: 06 Feb 1813 Lat 10.0 N, Long 61.0 W by HM Sloop Peruvian Int: 20 Feb 1813 Dis: 11 Aug 1813. Received from HM Ship Cumberland. Malmore American Cartel.

Palmer, Isaac   Prisoner 231. Rank: Seaman, from: Blockade, Privateer.
    Cap: 31 Oct 1812 off Saba by HM Sloop Charybdis Int: 19 Nov 1812 Dis: 10 Jul 1813.
    Received from HM Sloop Charybdis. Perseverance American Cartel.

Pardy, Daniel   Prisoner 196. Rank: Seaman, from: Blockade, Privateer.
    Cap: 31 Oct 1812 off Saba by HM Sloop Charybdis Int: 19 Nov 1812 Dis: 10 Jul 1813.
    Received from HM Sloop Charybdis. Perseverance American Cartel.

Parker, Charles   Prisoner 785. Rank: Seaman, from: Atalante, Merchant Schooner.
    Cap: 19 Jan 1814 off Saint Bartholomew by HM Brig Barbados Int: 12 Feb 1814 Dis: 25 Apr 1814.
    Received from HM Schooner Ballahou. HM Ship Vestal.

Parker, Henry   Prisoner 141. Rank: Prize Master, from: Yankee, Privateer.
    Cap: 25 Oct 1812 off Sombero by HM Sloop Peruvian Int: 13 Nov 1812 Dis: 10 Jul 1813.
    Received from HM Ship Mercury. Not to be exchanged during the War having acted in a wanton riotous and infamous manner. Perseverance American Cartel.

Parker, John   Prisoner 421. Rank: Prize Master, from: Anna, Not Recorded.
    Cap: 03 Jan 1813 off Maderia by HM Ship Cumberland Int: 30 Jan 1813 Dis: 10 Jul 1813.
    Received from HM Sloop Demerary. Recaptured from the Mars Privateer. Perseverance American Cartel.

Parker, Samuel   Prisoner 1433. Rank: Seaman, from: Avon, Privateer.
    Cap: 08 Mar 1815 off Nevis by HM Sloop Barbados Int: 13 Mar 1815 Dis: 15 Mar 1815.
    Received from HM Sloop Barbados. HMS Numen Rear Admiral Durham.

Parker, Thomas   Prisoner 81. Rank: Seaman, from: Providence, Privateer.
    Cap: 11 Sep 1812 off St. Barthlomew by HM Sloop Dominica Int: 13 Nov 1812 Dis: 10 Jul 1813.
    Received from HM Ship Mercury. Perseverance American Cartel.

Parker, William   Prisoner 1343. Rank: Seaman, from: Vidett, Letter of Marque.
    Cap: 14 Feb 1815 off St Bartholomew by HMS Dasher Int: 03 Mar 1815 Dis: 31 Mar 1815.
    Received from HM Ship Dasher. Out of Custody Rear Adl Durham.

Parron, Henry   Prisoner 1000. Rank: Seaman, from: Hawk, Privateer.
    Cap: 26 Apr 1814 Near the Mona Passage by HM Ship Piqua Int: 20 Jun 1814 Dis: 22 Jul 1814.
    Received from HM Ship Vestal. HM Ship Gloucester Rear Admiral Durham.

Parsons, Charles   Prisoner 118. Rank: Seaman, from: William Rathbone, Brig.
    Cap: 09 Oct 1812 at Sea by HM Sloop Charybdis Int: 13 Nov 1812 Dis: 10 Jul 1813.
    Received from HM Ship Mercury. Retaken Brig Part of Crew of Savory Jack Privateer. Perseverance American Cartel.

American Prisoners of War Held at Barbados During the War of 1812

Pass, Benjamin   Prisoner 826. Rank: Seaman, from: Not Recorded, Not Recorded.
    Cap: Not Recorded by Not Recorded Int: 23 Mar 1814 Dis: 25 Apr 1814.
    Received from HM Ship Dromedary. (Not legible) by HM Ship Ister. HM Ship Vestal. (Date of capture not recorded.)

Patch, Joseph   Prisoner 168. Rank: Seaman, from: Yankee, Privateer.
    Cap: 25 Oct 1812 off Sombero by HM Sloop Peruvian Int: 13 Nov 1812 Dis: 10 Jul 1813.
    Received from HM Ship Mercury. Perseverance American Cartel.

Pate, James   Prisoner 269. Rank: Seaman, from: Rea, Privateer.
    Cap: 29 Nov 1812 off Barbados by HM Ship Lightning Int: 29 Nov 1812 Dis: 10 Jul 1813.
    Received from HM Ship Lightning. Ship having been captured by the Bona American. Perseverance American Cartel.

Patens, Vincent   Prisoner 954. Rank: Seaman, from: President, Privateer.
    Cap: 07 May 1814 off Porto Rico by HM Ship Piqua Int: 20 Jun 1814 Dis: 22 Jul 1814.
    Received from HM Ship Vestal. HM Ship Gloucester Rear Admiral Durham.

Patman, Samuel   Prisoner 773. Rank: Seaman, from: Frolic, Privateer.
    Cap: 25 Jan 1814 off St Thomas by HM Sloop Heron Int: 06 Feb 1814 Dis: 25 Apr 1814.
    Received from HM Sloop Heron. HM Ship Vestal.

Pattee, John   Prisoner 526. Rank: Seaman, from: John, Privateer.
    Cap: 06 Feb 1813 Lat 10.0 N, Long 61.0 W by HM Sloop Peruvian Int: 20 Feb 1813 Dis: 11 Aug 1813. Received from HM Ship Cumberland. Malmore American Cartel.

Patterson, David   Prisoner 293. Rank: Seaman, from: Phoenix, Merchant Brig.
    Cap: 24 Nov 1812 Lat 37.03 N, Long 60.00 W by HM Sloop Morgiana Int: 16 Dec 1812 Dis: 17 Jan 1813. Received from HM Sloop Morgiana. Exchanged.

Paul, Daniel   Prisoner 907. Rank: Seaman, from: Hawk, Privateer.
    Cap: 26 Apr 1814 Near the Mona Passage by HM Ship Piqua Int: 20 Jun 1814 Dis: 20 Jul 1814.
    Received from HM Ship Vestal. HM Sloop Hazard Rear Adml Durham.

Paulin, Louis   Prisoner 1210. Rank: Seaman, from: Fox, Privateer.
    Cap: 26 Dec 1814 off St Bartholomew by HM Brig Barbados Int: 14 Jan 1815 Dis: 08 Feb 1815.
    Received from HM Brig Barbados. HM Ship Swiftsure.

Peabody, George W   Prisoner 1448. Rank: Seaman, from: Ivan Francisco, Not Recorded.
    Cap: 08 Mar 1815 off Nevis by HM Brig Muros Int: 26 Mar 1815 Dis: 31 Mar 1815.
    Received from HM Brig Maria. Recaptured from the Grand Turk Privateer. Out of Custody Rear Adl Durham.

Peas, Joseph   Prisoner 595. Rank: 3 Mate, from: Thomas Penrose, Privateer.
    Cap: 23 Mar 1813 Lat 20.14 W, Long 61.20 W by HM Ship Tribune Int: 28 Mar 1813 Dis: 26 Apr 1813. Received from HM Ship Tribune. America on Parole Sir F. Laforey.

Pease, James   Prisoner 529. Rank: Seaman, from: John, Privateer.
    Cap: 06 Feb 1813 Lat 10.0 N, Long 61.0 W by HM Sloop Peruvian Int: 20 Feb 1813 Dis: 11 Aug 1813. Received from HM Ship Cumberland. Malmore American Cartel.

Pelot, Samuel G   Prisoner 817. Rank: Mate, from: Sarah Ann, Brig.
    Cap: Not Recorded by Not Recorded Int: 23 Feb 1814 Dis: 22 Jul 1814.
    Received from HM Sloop Dasher. Part of Crew (Chief Mate) of English Brig Sarah Ann. HM Ship Gloucester Rear Admiral Durham. (Date of capture not recorded.)

Pemperton, Samuel   Prisoner 626. Rank: Seaman, from: Fly, Privateer.
    Cap: 19 Jan 1813 Lat 15.00 N, Long 45.00 W by HMS Venus Int: 02 Apr 1813 Dis: 11 Aug 1813.
    Received from HMS Venus. Recaptured from the Yankee. Malmore American Cartel.

Pendal, James   Prisoner 1081. Rank: Seaman, from: Engineer, Letter of Marque.
    Cap: 21 Sep 1814 of Porto Rico by HM Ship Barossa Int: 29 Sep 1814 Dis: 08 Feb 1815.
    Received from HM Ship Barossa. HM Ship Swiftsure Rear A Durham.

Penyan, Antoine   Prisoner 276. Rank: Seaman, from: Rea, Privateer.
    Cap: 29 Nov 1812 off Barbados by HM Ship Lightning Int: 29 Nov 1812 Dis: 10 Jul 1813.
    Received from HM Ship Lightning. Ship having been captured by the Bona American. Perseverance American Cartel.

Percival, John   Prisoner 911. Rank: Seaman, from: Hawk, Privateer.
    Cap: 26 Apr 1814 Near the Mona Passage by HM Ship Piqua Int: 20 Jun 1814 Dis: 20 Jul 1814.
    Received from HM Ship Vestal. HM Sloop Hazard Rear Adml Durham.

Perkins, Jonathan   Prisoner 743. Rank: Prize Master, from: Frolic, Privateer.
    Cap: 25 Jan 1814 off St Thomas by HM Sloop Heron Int: 06 Feb 1814 Dis: 22 Jul 1814.
    Received from HM Sloop Heron. HM Ship Gloucester Rear Adml Durham.

Perkins, Michael   Prisoner 245. Rank: Seaman, from: Blockade, Privateer.
    Cap: 31 Oct 1812 off Saba by HM Sloop Charybdis Int: 19 Nov 1812 Dis: 10 Jul 1813.
    Received from HM Sloop Charybdis. Perseverance American Cartel.

American Prisoners of War Held at Barbados During the War of 1812

Perry, Ebenezer   Prisoner 727. Rank: Seaman, from: Ellen, Merchant Schooner.
    Cap: 07 Jan 1814 Lat 21.15 N, Long 65.00 W by HMS Piqua Int: 02 Feb 1814 Dis: 02 Feb 1814.
    Received from HM Brig Liberty. Rising States American Cartel. Rear Adml Sir F. Laforey.

Perry, John   Prisoner 535. Rank: Seaman, from: John, Privateer.
    Cap: 06 Feb 1813 Lat 10.0 N, Long 61.0 W by HM Sloop Peruvian Int: 20 Feb 1813 Dis: 11 Aug 1813. Received from HM Ship Cumberland. American Cartel Malmore.

Perry, Onan   Prisoner 170. Rank: Seaman, from: Yankee, Privateer.
    Cap: 25 Oct 1812 off Sombero by HM Sloop Peruvian Int: 13 Nov 1812 Dis: 12 May 1813.
    Received from HM Ship Mercury. HM Treasury Schooner with (not legible) per request of Sir R Banks.

Petengill, James   Prisoner 752. Rank: Seaman, from: Frolic, Privateer.
    Cap: 25 Jan 1814 off St Thomas by HM Sloop Heron Int: 06 Feb 1814 Dis: 25 Apr 1814.
    Received from HM Sloop Heron. HM Ship Vestal Rear Admiral Durham.

Peters, John   Prisoner 419. Rank: Seaman, from: HM Ship Grampus, Not Recorded.
    Cap: Not Recorded by Not Recorded Int: 30 Jan 1813 Dis: 17 Mar 1813.
    Received from HM Sloop Demerary. Part of Crew of HMS Grampus gave up as a Prisoner of War. Into Merchant Ship being a Spaniard. (Date of capture not recorded.)

Peterson, Jacob   Prisoner 984. Rank: Seaman, from: John, Merchant Schooner.
    Cap: Not Recorded by Not Recorded Int: 20 Jun 1814 Dis: 22 Jul 1814.
    Received from HM Ship Vestal. Part of Crew of English Merchant Schooner John. HM Ship Gloucester Rear Admiral Durham. (Date of capture not recorded.)

Peterson, Peter   Prisoner 92. Rank: Seaman, from: Providence, Privateer.
    Cap: 11 Sep 1812 off St. Barthlomew by HM Sloop Dominica Int: 13 Nov 1812 Dis: 06 Feb 1813.
    Received from HM Ship Mercury. Out of custody being a Russian.

Pettingale, William   Prisoner 391. Rank: Seaman, from: Decatur, Privateer.
    Cap: 16 Jan 1813 Lat 13.00 N, Long 41.00 N by HM Ship Surprise Int: 26 Jan 1813 Dis: 10 Jul 1813.
    Received from HM Ship Surprise. Perseverance American Cartel.

Phillips, John   Prisoner 307. Rank: Seaman, from: Venus, Merchant Ship.
    Cap: 15 Dec 1812 Lat 32 N, Long 54 W by HM Ship Herald Int: 31 Dec 1812 Dis: 27 May 1813.
    Received from HM Ship Herald. America on Parole Sir F. Laforey.

Phippin, William   Prisoner 72. Rank: Seaman, from: Neptune, Merchant Brig.
    Cap: 29 Aug 1812 at Sea by HM Brig Maria Int: 13 Nov 1812 Dis: 19 Nov 1812.
    Received from HM Ship Mercury. Out of Custody per order of Rear Adml Sir F. Laforey being crew of a licensed vessel.

Picken, John   Prisoner 101. Rank: Seaman, from: Jane, Merchant Brig.
    Cap: 25 Sep 1812 at Sea by HM Sloop Spider Int: 13 Nov 1812 Dis: 17 Nov 1812.
    Received from HM Ship Mercury. Out of Custody per order of Sir F. Laforey being crew of a licensed vessel.

Pickering, William   Prisoner 1277. Rank: Seaman, from: Hero, Merchant Schooner.
    Cap: 14 Dec 1814 Lat 19.13, Long 64 by HMS Pique Int: 29 Jan 1815 Dis: 14 Feb 1815.
    Received from HMS Pique. HM Ship Piqua.

Picket, John   Prisoner 378. Rank: Seaman, from: Decatur, Privateer.
    Cap: 16 Jan 1813 Lat 13.00 N, Long 41.00 N by HM Ship Surprise Int: 26 Jan 1813 Dis: 10 Jul 1813.
    Received from HM Ship Surprise. Perseverance American Cartel.

Pierce, John   Prisoner 510. Rank: Seaman, from: John, Privateer.
    Cap: 06 Feb 1813 Lat 10.0 N, Long 61.0 W by HM Sloop Peruvian Int: 20 Feb 1813 Dis: 11 Aug 1813. Received from HM Ship Cumberland. Malmore American Cartel.

Pierre, John   Prisoner 1220. Rank: Seaman, from: Fox, Privateer.
    Cap: 26 Dec 1814 off St Bartholomew by HM Brig Barbados Int: 14 Jan 1815 Dis: 31 Mar 1815.
    Received from HM Brig Barbados. Rear Adl Durham.

Pike, Jeremiah   Prisoner 348. Rank: Seaman, from: Decatur, Privateer.
    Cap: 16 Jan 1813 Lat 13.00 N, Long 41.00 N by HM Ship Surprise Int: 26 Jan 1813 Dis: 10 Jul 1813.
    Received from HM Ship Surprise. Perseverance American Cartel.

Pilsbury, Timothy   Prisoner 240. Rank: Captain, from: Yankee, Privateer.
    Cap: 25 Oct 1812 off Sombrero by HM Sloop Peruvian Int: 19 Nov 1812 Dis: 13 Mar 1813.
    Received from HM Sloop Peruvian. America on Parole Sir Francis Laforey on account of ill health.

Pique, Ville   Prisoner 120. Rank: Seaman, from: William Rathbone, Brig.
    Cap: 09 Oct 1812 at Sea by HM Sloop Charybdis Int: 13 Nov 1812 Dis: 10 Jul 1813.
    Received from HM Ship Mercury. Retaken Brig Part of Crew of Savory Jack Privateer. Perseverance American Cartel.

Place, John   Prisoner 408. Rank: Seaman, from: Washington, Merchant Ship.
    Cap: 25 Dec 1812 off Cadiz by HM Ship Grampus Int: 30 Jan 1813 Dis: 26 Apr 1813.
    Received from HM Sloop Demerary. Out of Custody the Vessel being liberated.

American Prisoners of War Held at Barbados During the War of 1812

Plant, Samuel   Prisoner 652. Rank: Seaman, from: Adelphia, Privateer.
    Cap: 24 Feb 1813 Surinam by Not Recorded Int: 20 May 1813 Escaped: 30 Jun 1813.
    Received from HM Sloop Crane. Part of Crew of Comet having charge of the Ship, which floundered at Sea. Surrendering themselves at Main's Point Surinam. Escaped Retaken Reentry 710.

Plant, Samuel   Prisoner 710. Rank: Seaman, from: Adelphia, Privateer.
    Cap: 24 Feb 1813 Surinam by Surinam Int: 02 Jul 1813 Dis: 11 Aug 1813.
    Ship Adelphia captured by the Comet and floundered at Sea. Retaken having escaped. Malmore American Cartel.

Platt, George   Prisoner 695. Rank: Seaman, from: HM Ship Bedford, Not Recorded.
    Cap: Not Recorded by Not Recorded Int: 12 Jun 1813 Dis: 11 Aug 1813.
    Received from HMS Vestal. Gave himself up as a Prisoner of War on Board HM Ship Bedford. Malmore American Cartel. (Date of capture not recorded.)

Plumb, Truman   Prisoner 225. Rank: Seaman, from: Blockade, Privateer.
    Cap: 31 Oct 1812 off Saba by HM Sloop Charybdis Int: 19 Nov 1812 Escaped: 22 Dec 1812.
    Received from HM Sloop Charybdis. Escaped Retaken 23 Dec 1812 (299).

Plumb, Truman   Prisoner 299. Rank: Seaman, from: Blockade, Privateer.
    Cap: 31 Oct 1812 off Saba by HM Sloop Charybdis Int: 19 Nov 1812 Dis: 10 Jul 1813.
    Received from HM Sloop Charybdis. Perseverance American Cartel.

Plummer, Ebenezer   Prisoner 380. Rank: Seaman, from: Decatur, Privateer.
    Cap: 16 Jan 1813 Lat 13.00 N, Long 41.00 N by HM Ship Surprise Int: 26 Jan 1813 Dis: 10 Jul 1813.
    Received from HM Ship Surprise. Perseverance American Cartel.

Pope, Abraham   Prisoner 98. Rank: Seaman, from: Dragon, Not Recorded.
    Cap: Not Recorded by Not Recorded Int: 13 Nov 1812 Dis: 10 Jul 1813.
    Part of the crew of the Ship Dragon. Received from HM Ship Mercury. Perseverance American Cartel. (Date of capture not recorded.)

Pope, Edward   Prisoner 272. Rank: Seaman, from: Rea, Privateer.
    Cap: 29 Nov 1812 off Barbados by HM Ship Lightning Int: 29 Nov 1812 Dis: 10 Jul 1813.
    Received from HM Ship Lightning. Ship having been captured by the Bona American. Perseverance American Cartel.

Pornette, Justin   Prisoner 1099. Rank: Seaman, from: Engineer, Letter of Marque.
    Cap: 21 Sep 1814 of Porto Rico by HM Ship Barossa Int: 29 Sep 1814 Dis: 08 Feb 1815.
    Received from HM Ship Barossa. Out of Custody being a Frenchman, Rear Adml Durham.

Post, Nelson   Prisoner 1203. Rank: Seaman, from: Fox, Privateer.
    Cap: 26 Dec 1814 off St Bartholomew by HM Brig Barbados Int: 14 Jan 1815 Dis: 31 Mar 1815.
    Received from HM Brig Barbados. Rear Adl Durham.

Potter, James   Prisoner 1076. Rank: Captain, from: Engineer, Letter of Marque.
    Cap: 21 Sep 1814 of Porto Rico by HM Ship Barossa Int: 29 Sep 1814 Escaped: 13 Jan 1815.
    Received from HM Ship Barossa. Escaped. Reentry 1266.

Potter, James   Prisoner 1266. Rank: Seaman, from: Fox, Privateer.
    Cap: 26 Dec 1814 off St Bartholomew by HM Brig Barbados Int: 15 Jan 1815 Dis: 14 Feb 1815.
    Received from HM Brig Barbados. Retaken former No 1076. HM Ship Piqua.

Poulson, Perry   Prisoner 279. Rank: Seaman, from: Rea, Privateer.
    Cap: 29 Nov 1812 off Barbados by HM Ship Lightning Int: 29 Nov 1812 Dis: 10 Jul 1813.
    Received from HM Ship Lightning. Ship having been captured by the Bona American. Perseverance American Cartel.

Pousland, Edward   Prisoner 751. Rank: Seaman, from: Frolic, Privateer.
    Cap: 25 Jan 1814 off St Thomas by HM Sloop Heron Int: 06 Feb 1814 Dis: 25 Apr 1814.
    Received from HM Sloop Heron. HM Ship Vestal Rear Admiral Durham.

Powers, James   Prisoner 1334. Rank: Seaman, from: Vidett, Letter of Marque.
    Cap: 14 Feb 1815 off St Bartholomew by HM Ship Dasher Int: 03 Mar 1815 Dis: 31 Mar 1815.
    Received from HM Ship Dasher. Out of Custody Rear Adl Durham.

Premiers, Joseph   Prisoner 639. Rank: Seaman, from: Active, Merchant Ship.
    Cap: 23 Feb 1813 off St Bartholomew by HM Ship Surprise Int: 11 Apr 1813 Dis: 11 Aug 1813.
    Received from HM Schooner Elizabeth. Malmore American Cartel.

Price, Constant W   Prisoner 90. Rank: Seaman, from: Providence, Privateer.
    Cap: 11 Sep 1812 off St. Barthlomew by HM Sloop Dominica Int: 13 Nov 1812 Dis: 10 Jul 1813.
    Received from HM Ship Mercury. Perseverance American Cartel.

Primus, Samuel   Prisoner 24. Rank: Seaman, from: Hope, Merchant Ship.
    Cap: 27 Sep 1812 Lat 22.30 N, Long 40.45 by HM Sloop Tribune Int: 22 Oct 1812 Dis: 24 Oct 1812.
    Received from HM Sloop Tribune. America on Parole per order of Captain Reynolds Tribune.

American Prisoners of War Held at Barbados During the War of 1812

Prince, Prince   Prisoner 438. Rank: Seaman, from: HM Sloop Arab, Not Recorded.
    Cap: Not Recorded by Not Recorded Int: 10 Apr 1813 Dis: 11 Aug 1813.
    Received from HM Sloop Arab. Part of Crew of HM Sloop Arab given up as Prisoner of War.
    Malmore American Cartel. (Date of capture not recorded.)

Prince, Silvesta   Prisoner 637. Rank: Seaman, from: Active, Merchant Ship.
    Cap: 23 Feb 1813 off St Bartholomew by HM Ship Surprise Int: 11 Apr 1813 Dis: 11 Aug 1813.
    Received from HM Schooner Elizabeth. Malmore American Cartel.

Prior, Christopher   Prisoner 49. Rank: Seaman, from: Providence, Privateer.
    Cap: 11 Sep 1812 off St. Barthlomew by HM Sloop Dominica Int: 13 Nov 1812 Dis: 10 Jul 1813.
    Received from HM Ship Mercury. Perseverance American Cartel.

Pulsifer, Ebenezer   Prisoner 349. Rank: Seaman, from: Decatur, Privateer.
    Cap: 16 Jan 1813 Lat 13.00 N, Long 41.00 N by HM Ship Surprise Int: 26 Jan 1813 Dis: 10 Jul 1813.
    Received from HM Ship Surprise. Perseverance American Cartel.

Purrington, Humphrey   Prisoner 442. Rank: Seaman, from: Isaac, Merchant Brig.
    Cap: 01 Jan 1813 off Porto Rico by HM Sloop Charybdis Int: 12 Feb 1813 Dis: 10 Apr 1813.
    Received from HM Brig Liberty. America on Parole Sir F. Laforey.

Quiel, Henry   Prisoner 1356. Rank: 2 Mate, from: Spencer, Merchant.
    Cap: 15 Feb 1815 off St Bartholomew by HMS Dasher Int: 03 Mar 1815 Dis: 31 Mar 1815.
    Received from HM Ship Dasher. Out of Custody Rear Adl Durham.

Quinar, Benjamin   Prisoner 513. Rank: Seaman, from: John, Privateer.
    Cap: 06 Feb 1813 Lat 10.0 N, Long 61.0 W by HM Sloop Peruvian Int: 20 Feb 1813 Dis: 11 Aug
    1813. Received from HM Ship Cumberland. Malmore American Cartel.

Quinar, Stephen   Prisoner 538. Rank: Seaman, from: John, Privateer.
    Cap: 06 Feb 1813 Lat 10.0 N, Long 61.0 W by HM Sloop Peruvian Int: 20 Feb 1813 Dis: 11 Aug
    1813. Received from HM Ship Cumberland. American Cartel Malmore.

Raco, Julias   Prisoner 34. Rank: Prize Master, from: Providence, Privateer.
    Cap: 11 Sep 1812 off St. Bartholomew by HM Sloop Dominica Int: 24 Oct 1812 Dis: 10 Jul 1813.
    Received from HM Sloop Vestal. Perseverance American Cartel.

Ragsxall, Alex   Prisoner 1321. Rank: Seaman, from: Whalebone, Merchant Schooner.
    Cap: 25 Jan 1815 off St Bartholomew by HMB Espringle Int: 09 Feb 1815 Dis: 31 Mar 1815.
    Received from HMB Satellite. Rear Adl Durham.

Ralph, William   Prisoner 1308. Rank: Seaman, from: Mary, Merchant Schooner.
    Cap: 15 Jan 1815 Lat 22.40, Long 66 by HM Ship Pique Int: 29 Jan 1815 Dis: 31 Mar 1815.
    Received from HMS Pique. Rear Adl Durham.

Ramsdall, Nathaniel   Prisoner 531. Rank: Seaman, from: John, Privateer.
    Cap: 06 Feb 1813 Lat 10.0 N, Long 61.0 W by HM Sloop Peruvian Int: 20 Feb 1813 Dis: 11 Aug
    1813. Received from HM Ship Cumberland. Malmore American Cartel.

Ramsden, Philip   Prisoner 398. Rank: Seaman, from: Decatur, Privateer.
    Cap: 16 Jan 1813 Lat 13.00 N, Long 41.00 N by HM Ship Surprise Int: 26 Jan 1813 Dis: 10 Jul 1813.
    Received from HM Ship Surprise. Perseverance American Cartel.

Ramsey, David C   Prisoner 707. Rank: Seaman, from: Saturn, Merchant Brig.
    Cap: 10 May 1813 off Martinique by HM Ship Mercury Int: 23 Jun 1813 Dis: 25 Jun 1813.
    Received from HM Ship Mercury. Into Merchant Ship for passage to Quebec.

Randall, Nathaniel   Prisoner 1128. Rank: Seaman, from: Nancy, Privateer.
    Cap: 06 Sep 1814 Lat 32 N, Long 47 W by HM Ship Piqua Int: 21 Oct 1814 Dis: 08 Feb 1815.
    Received from HMS Piqua. Taken by the Amelia Privateer. HM Ship Swiftsure.

Randelett, Thomas M   Prisoner 1172. Rank: Seaman, from: Dolphin, Letter of Marque.
    Cap: 04 Dec 1814 Lat 18.00 N, Long 60.00 W by HM Brig Columbia Int: 08 Dec 1814 Escaped: 01
    Jan 1815. Received from HM Brig Columbia. Escaped.

Randlet, John M   Prisoner 722. Rank: Master, from: Pocahontas, Merchant Schooner.
    Cap: 10 Aug 1812 Surinam by Surinam Int: 19 Jul 1813 Dis: 11 Aug 1813.
    Received from HM Ship Grampus. Malmore American Cartel.

Randolph, Henry   Prisoner 1304. Rank: Seaman, from: Mary, Merchant Schooner.
    Cap: 15 Jan 1815 Lat 22.40, Long 66 by HM Ship Pique Int: 29 Jan 1815 Dis: 14 Feb 1815.
    Received from HMS Pique. HM Ship Piqua.

Ranson, William John   Prisoner 701. Rank: Seaman, from: Saturn, Merchant Brig.
    Cap: 10 May 1813 off Martinique by HM Ship Mercury Int: 17 Jun 1813 Dis: 11 Aug 1813.
    Received from HM Ship Mercury. Malmore American Cartel.

Rawson, Charles   Prisoner 21. Rank: Seaman, from: Hope, Merchant Ship.
    Cap: 27 Sep 1812 Lat 22.30 N, Long 40.45 W by HM Ship Tribune Int: 22 Oct 1812 Dis: 24 Oct
    1812. Received from Ship Hope. America on Parole per order of Captain Reynolds Tribune.

American Prisoners of War Held at Barbados During the War of 1812

Ray, William   Prisoner 1019. Rank: Seaman, from: Not Recorded, Not Recorded.
    Cap: Not Recorded by Not Recorded Int: 01 Jul 1814 Dis: 22 Jul 1814.
    Received from HM Ship Orontes. (Not legible) from English Merchant Sloop. HM Ship Gloucester Rear Adml Durham. (Date of capture not recorded.)

Ray, William   Prisoner 1040. Rank: Seaman, from: Mary, Letter of Marque.
    Cap: 07 Jun 1814 La Quisa by HM Ship Heron Int: 31 Jul 1814 Dis: 31 Mar 1815.
    Received from HM Sloop Mosquito. Rear Adl Durham.

Rea, Benjamin   Prisoner 264. Rank: Prize Master, from: Rea, Privateer.
    Cap: 29 Nov 1812 off Barbados by HM Ship Lightning Int: 29 Nov 1812 Dis: 10 Jul 1813.
    Received from HM Ship Lightning. Ship having been captured by the Bona American. Perseverance American Cartel.

Read, Charles   Prisoner 859. Rank: Seaman, from: Chapman, Privateer.
    Cap: 28 Feb 1814 off St Bartholomew by Thistle Privateer Int: 26 Mar 1814 Dis: 25 Apr 1814.
    Received from HM Ship Palama. HM Ship Vestal.

Read, Richard   Prisoner 319. Rank: Master, from: James Murdock, Merchant Brig.
    Cap: 05 Jan 1813 Lat 21 N, Long 57 W by HM Sloop Nimrod Int: 11 Jan 1813 Dis: 04 Feb 1813.
    Received from HM Sloop Nimrod. Out of Custody the Vessel being liberated having a License.

Read, Richard   Prisoner 433. Rank: Master, from: James Murdock, Merchant Brig.
    Cap: 05 Jan 1812 Lat 21N, Long 57 W by HM Ship Nimrod Int: 05 Feb 1813 Dis: 10 Apr 1813.
    Received from Brig James Murdock. Out of Custody the Vessel being liberated.

Reamonsptras, ---   Prisoner 723. Rank: Seaman, from: Dart, Merchant Brig.
    Cap: Not Recorded by Not Recorded Int: 13 Sep 1813 Escaped: 22 Oct 1813.
    Received from Emma Army Ship. Part of Crew of Merchant Brig Dart. Escaped from the Naval Hospital. (First name not recorded. Date of capture not recorded.)

Reardon, Daniel   Prisoner 275. Rank: Seaman, from: Rea, Privateer.
    Cap: 29 Nov 1812 off Barbados by HM Ship Lightning Int: 29 Nov 1812 Dis: 10 Jul 1813.
    Received from HM Ship Lightning. Ship having been captured by the Bona American. Perseverance American Cartel.

Reed, John   Prisoner 297. Rank: Seaman, from: Benjamin Franklin, Privateer.
    Cap: Martinique by Not Recorded Int: 17 Dec 1812 Dis: 23 Apr 1813.
    Received from HM Schooner Elizabeth. Taken at Martinique having been attempting to cut out a Vessel. HM Ship Tribune. Not to be exchanged during the War having behaved in a wanton riotous (not legible). (Date of capture not recorded.)

Regair, Morgan   Prisoner 1260. Rank: Seaman, from: Fox, Privateer.
    Cap: 26 Dec 1814 off St Bartholomew by HM Brig Barbados Int: 14 Jan 1815 Dis: 08 Feb 1815.
    Received from HM Brig Barbados. HM Ship Swiftsure.

Reginald, Henry   Prisoner 1034. Rank: Seaman, from: North Star, Merchant Schooner.
    Cap: 10 Jun 1814 off St Bartholomew by HM Brig Crane Int: 20 Jul 1814 Escaped: 21 Jul 1814.
    Received from HM Ship Orntes. Escaped.

Reginald, Henry   Prisoner 1069. Rank: Seaman, from: Harmony, Merchant Brig.
    Cap: Not Recorded by Not Recorded Int: 22 Sep 1814 Escaped: 14 Dec 1814.
    Received from Merchant Brig Harmony. Part of Crew of Merchant Brig Harmony. Retaken former No 1034. Escaped. (Date of capture not recorded.)

Reid, Robert   Prisoner 1341. Rank: Seaman, from: Vidett, Letter of Marque.
    Cap: 14 Feb 1815 off St Bartholomew by HM Ship Dasher Int: 03 Mar 1815 Dis: 31 Mar 1815.
    Received from HM Ship Dasher. Out of Custody Rear Adl Durham.

Reid, Thomas   Prisoner 1018. Rank: Seaman, from: HM Sloop Port Mahon, Not Recorded.
    Cap: Not Recorded by Not Recorded Int: 27 Jun 1814 Dis: 22 Jul 1814.
    Received from HM Ship Heron. Part of Crew of HM Sloop Port Mahon. HM Ship Gloucester Rear Adml Durham. (Date of capture not recorded.)

Remble, Henry   Prisoner 200. Rank: Seaman, from: Blockade, Privateer.
    Cap: 31 Oct 1812 off Saba by HM Sloop Charybdis Int: 19 Nov 1812 Dis: 10 Jul 1813.
    Received from HM Sloop Charybdis. Perseverance American Cartel.

Rice, M   Prisoner 828. Rank: 1 Mate, from: Rattle Snake, Letter of Marque.
    Cap: 11 Mar 1814 Lat 24.07 N, Long 66.47 W by HM Ship Rhin Int: 25 Mar 1814 Dis: 22 Jul 1814.
    Received from HM Ship Rhin. HM Ship Gloucester Rear Admiral Durham.

Rice, Samuel   Prisoner 1065. Rank: Pilot, from: Mary, Letter of Marque.
    Cap: 07 Jun 1814 La Quisa by HM Ship Heron Int: 31 Jul 1814 Dis: 08 Feb 1815.
    Received from HM Sloop Mosquito. HM Ship Swiftsure.

Rich, John   Prisoner 1395. Rank: 3 Lieutenant, from: Avon, Privateer.
    Cap: 08 Mar 1815 off Nevis by HM Sloop Barbados Int: 13 Mar 1815 Dis: 15 Mar 1815.
    Received from HM Sloop Barbados. HMS Numen Rear Admiral Durham.

American Prisoners of War Held at Barbados During the War of 1812

Richards, James   Prisoner 158. Rank: Seaman, from: Yankee, Privateer.
  Cap: 25 Oct 1812 off Sombero by HM Sloop Peruvian Int: 13 Nov 1812 Dis: 10 Jul 1813.
  Received from HM Ship Mercury. Perseverance American Cartel.
Richards, John   Prisoner 1320. Rank: Seaman, from: Whalebone, Merchant Schooner.
  Cap: 25 Jan 1815 off St Bartholomew by HMB Espringle Int: 09 Feb 1815 Dis: 31 Mar 1815.
  Received from HMB Satellite. Rear Adl Durham.
Richards, Josiah   Prisoner 334. Rank: Surgeon, from: Decatur, Privateer.
  Cap: 16 Jan 1813 Lat 13.00 N, Long 41.00 N by HM Ship Surprise Int: 25 Jan 1813 Dis: 09 Feb 1813.
  Received from HM Ship Surprise. America being a non Combatant.
Richards, Rehobaham   Prisoner 169. Rank: Seaman, from: Yankee, Privateer.
  Cap: 25 Oct 1812 off Sombero by HM Sloop Peruvian Int: 13 Nov 1812 Dis: 10 Jul 1813.
  Received from HM Ship Mercury. Perseverance American Cartel.
Richardson, Addison   Prisoner 747. Rank: Captain, from: Frolic, Privateer.
  Cap: 25 Jan 1814 off St Thomas by HM Sloop Heron Int: 06 Feb 1814 Dis: 25 Apr 1814.
  Received from HM Sloop Heron. HM Ship Vestal Rear Admiral Durham.
Richardson, Edward   Prisoner 641. Rank: Seaman, from: Active, Merchant Ship.
  Cap: 23 Feb 1813 off St Bartholomew by HM Ship Surprise Int: 11 Apr 1813 Dis: 11 Aug 1813.
  Received from HM Schooner Elizabeth. Malmore American Cartel.
Richardson, James   Prisoner 31. Rank: Seaman, from: Hope, Merchant Ship.
  Cap: 27 Sep 1812 Lat 22.30 N, Long 40.45 by HM Sloop Tribune Int: 23 Oct 1812 Dis: 24 Oct 1812.
  Received from HM Sloop Tribune. Govn (not legible) having been taken (not legible).
Richardson, John   Prisoner 1351. Rank: Seaman, from: Vidett, Letter of Marque.
  Cap: 14 Feb 1815 off St Bartholomew by HMS Dasher Int: 03 Mar 1815 Dis: 31 Mar 1815.
  Received from HM Ship Dasher. Out of Custody Rear Adl Durham.
Richmond, Milton   Prisoner 131. Rank: Seaman, from: Providence, Privateer.
  Cap: 12 Sep 1812 off St. Bartholomew by HM Sloop Dominica Int: 13 Nov 1812 Dis: 10 Jul 1813.
  Received from HM Ship Mercury. Perseverance American Cartel.
Rickman, Richard   Prisoner 1063. Rank: Seaman, from: Mary, Letter of Marque.
  Cap: 07 Jun 1814 La Quisa by HM Ship Heron Int: 31 Jul 1814 Dis: 08 Feb 1815.
  Received from HM Sloop Mosquito. Riotous Character HM Ship Swiftsure Rear A Durham.
Ring, Joseph   Prisoner 1324. Rank: Seaman, from: Spencer, Merchant Schooner.
  Cap: 15 Feb 1815 off St Bartholomew by HM Ship Dasher Int: 25 Feb 1815 Dis: 31 Mar 1815.
  Received from Schooner Spencer. Out of Custody Rear Adl Durham.
Ringrose, William   Prisoner 886. Rank: Seaman, from: Hawk, Privateer.
  Cap: 26 Apr 1814 Near the Mona Passage by HM Ship Piqua Int: 20 Jun 1814 Dis: 22 Jul 1814.
  Received from HM Ship Vestal. HM Ship Gloucester Rear Admiral Durham.
Robbins, Henry   Prisoner 1379. Rank: Seaman, from: Laurence, Merchant.
  Cap: 14 Feb 1815 off Porto Rico by HMS Dasher Int: 04 Mar 1815 Dis: 31 Mar 1815.
  Received from HM Ship Dasher. Out of Custody Rear Adl Durham.
Roberts, John   Prisoner 955. Rank: Seaman, from: President, Privateer.
  Cap: 07 May 1814 off Porto Rico by HM Ship Piqua Int: 20 Jun 1814 Dis: 22 Jul 1814.
  Received from HM Ship Vestal. HM Ship Gloucester Rear Admiral Durham.
Roberts, Orias   Prisoner 194. Rank: Prize Master, from: Blockade, Privateer.
  Cap: 31 Oct 1812 off Saba by HM Sloop Charybdis Int: 19 Nov 1812 Escaped: 24 Apr 1813.
  Received from HM Sloop Charybdis. Escaped. Retaken Reentry (689).
Roberts, Orias   Prisoner 689. Rank: Prize Master, from: Blockade, Privateer.
  Cap: 31 Oct 1812 off Saba by HM Sloop Charybdis Int: 26 May 1813 Escaped: 08 Jun 1813.
  Received from HM Sloop Peruvian, having escaped & been retaken. Escaped.
Roberts, William   Prisoner 103. Rank: Seaman, from: Jane, Merchant Brig.
  Cap: 25 Sep 1812 at Sea by HM Sloop Spider Int: 13 Nov 1812 Dis: 17 Nov 1812.
  Received from HM Ship Mercury. Out of Custody per order of Sir F. Laforey being crew of a licensed vessel.
Robertson, Thomas   Prisoner 852. Rank: Seaman, from: Rattle Snake, Letter of Marque.
  Cap: 11 Mar 1814 Lat 24.07 N, Long 66.47 W by HM Ship Rhin Int: 25 Mar 1814 Dis: 25 Apr 1814.
  Received from HM Ship Rhin. HM Ship Vestal.
Robins, James   Prisoner 415. Rank: Seaman, from: Apollo, Merchant Ship.
  Cap: 22 Dec 1812 off Tenioff by HM Ship Grampus Int: 30 Jan 1813 Dis: 10 Jul 1813.
  Received from HM Sloop Demerary. Perseverance American Cartel.
Robins, Joshua   Prisoner 556. Rank: Seaman, from: Rebecca, Merchant Brig.
  Cap: 15 Jan 1813 off Demuary by Detained by Custom House Int: 02 Mar 1813 Dis: 27 May 1813.
  Received from Army Schooner Maria. America on Parole Sir Francis Laforey.

American Prisoners of War Held at Barbados During the War of 1812

Robins, William   Prisoner 136. Rank: Prize Master, from: Yankee, Privateer.
    Cap: 25 Oct 1812 off Sombero by HM Sloop Peruvian Int: 13 Nov 1812 Dis: 10 Jul 1813.
    Received from HM Ship Mercury. Perseverance American Cartel.

Robinson, James   Prisoner 1116. Rank: Seaman, from: Aquila, Privateer.
    Cap: 04 Sep 1814 Lat 22 N, Long 36 W by HM Ship Piqua Int: 21 Oct 1814 Dis: 31 Mar 1815.
    Received from HMS Piqua. Taken by the Whig Privateer. Rear Adl Durham.

Robinson, John   Prisoner 133. Rank: Lieutenant, from: Yankee, Privateer.
    Cap: 25 Oct 1812 off Sombero by HM Sloop Peruvian Int: 13 Nov 1812 Dis: 10 Jul 1813.
    Received from HM Ship Mercury. Perseverance American Cartel.

Robinson, Lemry   Prisoner 842. Rank: Seaman, from: Rattle Snake, Letter of Marque.
    Cap: 11 Mar 1814 Lat 24.07 N, Long 66.47 W by HM Ship Rhin Int: 25 Mar 1814 Dis: 25 Apr 1814.
    Received from HM Ship Rhin. HM Ship Vestal.

Robinson, William   Prisoner 1094. Rank: Seaman, from: Engineer, Letter of Marque.
    Cap: 21 Sep 1814 of Porto Rico by HM Ship Barossa Int: 29 Sep 1814 Dis: 08 Feb 1815.
    Received from HM Ship Barossa. HM Ship Swiftsure Concerned in a conspiracy to impair the guard.

Roche, Andrew   Prisoner 588. Rank: Seaman, from: Alexis, Privateer.
    Cap: 09 Mar 1813 Not Recorded by HM Ship Lightning Int: 22 Mar 1813 Dis: 11 Aug 1813.
    Received from HM Ship Lightning. English Retaken by Comet. Malmore American Cartel.

Roderick, Frank   Prisoner 366. Rank: Seaman, from: Decatur, Privateer.
    Cap: 16 Jan 1813 Lat 13.00 N, Long 41.00 N by HM Ship Surprise Int: 26 Jan 1813 Dis: 23 Apr 1813.
    Received from HM Ship Surprise. Escaped. Retaken shortly afterward HM Ship Tribune. Passage (not Legible).

Rodgers, Luke   Prisoner 974. Rank: Seaman, from: Fairy, Privateer.
    Cap: 20 Mar 1814 off Saba by HM Ship Ister Int: 20 Jun 1814 Dis: 22 Jul 1814.
    Received from HM Ship Vestal. HM Ship Gloucester Rear Admiral Durham. (Apparent duplicate of # 874. Luke Rogers.)

Roe, James   Prisoner 1113. Rank: Seaman, from: Mars, Privateer.
    Cap: 02 Sep 1814 Lat 41 N, Long 52 W by HM Ship Piqua Int: 21 Oct 1814 Dis: 31 Mar 1815.
    Received from HMS Piqua. Taken by the David Porter Privateer. Rear Adl Durham.

Rogers, Daniel   Prisoner 429. Rank: Seaman, from: Ocean, Merchant Schooner.
    Cap: 15 Aug 1812 Martinique by Detained at Martinique Int: 05 Feb 1813 Dis: 10 Jul 1813.
    Received from HM Ship Vestal. Perseverance American Cartel.

Rogers, Henry   Prisoner 305. Rank: Mate, from: Venus, Merchant Ship.
    Cap: 15 Dec 1812 Lat 32 N, Long 54 W by HM Ship Herald Int: 31 Dec 1812 Dis: 13 Mar 1813.
    Received from HM Ship Herald. America on Parole Sir F. Laforey.

Rogers, Henry   Prisoner 390. Rank: Seaman, from: Decatur, Privateer.
    Cap: 16 Jan 1813 Lat 13.00 N, Long 41.00 N by HM Ship Surprise Int: 26 Jan 1813 Dis: 10 Jul 1813.
    Received from HM Ship Surprise. Perseverance American Cartel.

Rogers, Luke   Prisoner 874. Rank: Seaman, from: Camilla, Not Recorded.
    Cap: 29 Mar 1814 Sombrero Passage by HM Ship Ister Int: 15 Apr 1814 Dis: 25 Apr 1814.
    Received from HM Ship Ister. Recaptured from Fairy Privateer. HM Ship Vestal.

Rogers, Robert   Prisoner 135. Rank: Prize Master, from: Yankee, Privateer.
    Cap: 25 Oct 1812 off Sombero by HM Sloop Peruvian Int: 13 Nov 1812 Dis: 10 Jul 1813.
    Received from HM Ship Mercury. Perseverance American Cartel.

Rogers, Smith   Prisoner 1082. Rank: Seaman, from: Engineer, Letter of Marque.
    Cap: 21 Sep 1814 of Porto Rico by HM Ship Barossa Int: 29 Sep 1814 Dis: 08 Feb 1815.
    Received from HM Ship Barossa. HM Ship Swiftsure Rear A Durham.

Roper, William   Prisoner 110. Rank: Prize Master, from: William Rathbone, Brig.
    Cap: 09 Oct 1812 at Sea by HM Sloop Charybdis Int: 13 Nov 1812 Dis: 10 Jul 1813.
    Received from HM Ship Mercury. Retaken Brig Part of Crew of Savory Jack Privateer. Perseverance American Cartel.

Rosenthon, John   Prisoner 918. Rank: Seaman, from: President, Privateer.
    Cap: 07 May 1814 off Porto Rico by HM Ship Piqua Int: 20 Jun 1814 Dis: 20 Jul 1814.
    Received from HM Ship Vestal. HM Sloop Hazard Rear Adml Durham.

Ross, Barney   Prisoner 446. Rank: Seaman, from: Isaac, Merchant Brig.
    Cap: 01 Jan 1813 off Porto Rico by HM Sloop Charybdis Int: 12 Feb 1813 Dis: 11 Aug 1813.
    Received from HM Brig Liberty. Malmore American Cartel.

Ross, David   Prisoner 502. Rank: Seaman, from: John, Privateer.
    Cap: 06 Feb 1813 Lat 10.0 N, Long 61.0 W by HM Sloop Peruvian Int: 20 Feb 1813 Dis: 11 Aug 1813. Received from HM Ship Cumberland. Malmore American Cartel.

American Prisoners of War Held at Barbados During the War of 1812

Ross, Thomas   Prisoner 111. Rank: Prize Master, from: William Rathbone, Brig.
    Cap: 09 Oct 1812 at Sea by HM Sloop Charybdis Int: 13 Nov 1812 Dis: 10 Jul 1813.
    Received from HM Ship Mercury. Retaken Brig Part of Crew of Savory Jack Privateer. Perseverance American Cartel.

Ross, Timothy   Prisoner 426. Rank: Master, from: Rising States, Merchant Schooner.
    Cap: 24 Jan 1813 Lat 27.30 N, Long 62.00 W by Ship Tiger Int: 05 Feb 1813 Dis: 13 Mar 1813.
    Received from the prize. America on Parole Sir Francis Laforey.

Ross, William   Prisoner 644. Rank: Seaman, from: (not legible) Hunter, Merchant Schooner.
    Cap: off Cayman by Not Recorded Int: 21 Apr 1813 Dis: 22 Jul 1813.
    Received from HM Sloop Surinam. Taken by a Letter of Marque. HM Ship Venus being a Pirate. (Date of capture not recorded.)

Ross, William   Prisoner 871. Rank: Seaman, from: Martin, Merchant.
    Cap: 13 Mar 1814 off St Thomas by HM Brig Swaggerer Int: 15 Apr 1814 Dis: 25 Apr 1814.
    Received from HM Ship Ister. HM Ship Vestal.

Ross, William   Prisoner 971. Rank: Seaman, from: Martin, Letter of Marque.
    Cap: 13 Mar 1814 off Saint Thomas by HM Brig Swaggerer Int: 20 Jun 1814 Escaped: 08 Jul 1814.
    Received from HM Ship Vestal. Escaped. (Apparent duplicate of # 871.)

Ross, William   Prisoner 1036. Rank: Seaman, from: North Star, Merchant Schooner.
    Cap: 10 Jun 1814 off St Bartholomew by HM Brig Crane Int: 22 Jul 1814 Dis: 22 Jul 1814.
    Retaken former No (971). HM Ship Gloucester Rear Adml Durham.

Roundy, Stephen C   Prisoner 517. Rank: Seaman, from: John, Privateer.
    Cap: 06 Feb 1813 Lat 10.0 N, Long 61.0 W by HM Sloop Peruvian Int: 20 Feb 1813 Dis: 11 Aug 1813. Received from HM Ship Cumberland. Malmore American Cartel.

Rowland, ---   Prisoner 45. Rank: Seaman, from: HM Ship Lightning, Not Recorded.
    Cap: Not Recorded by Not Recorded Int: 08 Nov 1812 Dis: 10 Jul 1813.
    Part of Crew of HM Ship Lightning; gave themselves up as Prisoners of War. Perseverance American Cartel. (First name not legible. Date of capture not recorded.)

Ruling, Arnold   Prisoner 854. Rank: Seaman, from: Rattle Snake, Letter of Marque.
    Cap: 11 Mar 1814 Lat 24.07 N, Long 66.47 W by HM Ship Rhin Int: 25 Mar 1814 Dis: 25 Apr 1814.
    Received from HM Ship Rhin. HM Ship Vestal.

Rum, John   Prisoner 1347. Rank: Seaman, from: Vidett, Letter of Marque.
    Cap: 14 Feb 1815 off St Bartholomew by HMS Dasher Int: 03 Mar 1815 Dis: 31 Mar 1815.
    Received from HM Ship Dasher. Out of Custody Rear Adl Durham.

Rupley, Luther   Prisoner 1184. Rank: Seaman, from: Not Recorded, Not Recorded.
    Cap: Granada by Not Recorded Int: 12 Jan 1815 Dis: 14 Feb 1815.
    Received from HM Brig Watsisin. (Not legible) at Granada. HM Ship Piqua. (Date of capture not recorded.)

Rutledge, James   Prisoner 1186. Rank: Seaman, from: Not Recorded, Not Recorded.
    Cap: Barbados by Not Recorded Int: 13 Jan 1815 Dis: 14 Feb 1815.
    Received from HM Brig Watsisin. (Not legible) at Barbados. HM Ship Piqua. (Date of capture not recorded.)

Sabine, John   Prisoner 193. Rank: Prize Master, from: Blockade, Privateer.
    Cap: 31 Oct 1812 off Saba by HM Sloop Charybdis Int: 19 Nov 1812 Dis: 10 Jul 1813.
    Received from HM Sloop Charybdis. Perseverance American Cartel.

Sage, William   Prisoner 501. Rank: Seaman, from: John, Privateer.
    Cap: 06 Feb 1813 Lat 10.0 N, Long 61.0 W by HM Sloop Peruvian Int: 20 Feb 1813 Dis: 11 Aug 1813. Received from HM Ship Cumberland. Malmore American Cartel.

Salisbury, Samuel   Prisoner 358. Rank: Seaman, from: Decatur, Privateer.
    Cap: 16 Jan 1813 Lat 13.00 N, Long 41.00 N by HM Ship Surprise Int: 26 Jan 1813 Dis: 10 Jul 1813.
    Received from HM Ship Surprise. Perseverance American Cartel.

Sanders, George   Prisoner 65. Rank: Seaman, from: Providence, Privateer.
    Cap: 11 Sep 1812 off St. Barthlomew by HM Sloop Dominica Int: 13 Nov 1812 Died: 07 Jan 1813.
    Received from HM Ship Mercury. Died at the Naval Hospital.

Sanderson, Daniel   Prisoner 618. Rank: Seaman, from: HM Ship Venus, Not Recorded.
    Cap: Not Recorded by Not Recorded Int: 02 Apr 1813 Dis: 11 Aug 1813.
    Received from HM Ship Venus. Part of Crew of HMS Venus. Malmore American Cartel. Malmore American Cartel. (Date of capture not recorded.)

Sands, John C   Prisoner 659. Rank: Seaman, from: Adelphia, Privateer.
    Cap: 24 Feb 1813 Surinam by Not Recorded Int: 20 May 1813 Dis: 11 Aug 1813.
    Received from HM Sloop Crane. Part of Crew of Comet having charge of the Ship, which floundered at Sea. Surrendering themselves at Main's Point Surinam. Malmore American Cartel.

American Prisoners of War Held at Barbados During the War of 1812

Saunders, Davis   Prisoner 91. Rank: Seaman, from: Providence, Privateer.
    Cap: 11 Sep 1812 off St. Barthlomew by HM Sloop Dominica Int: 13 Nov 1812 Dis: 10 Jul 1813.
    Received from HM Ship Mercury. Perseverance American Cartel.

Saunders, William   Prisoner 325. Rank: Seaman, from: James Murdock, Merchant Brig.
    Cap: 05 Jan 1813 Lat 21 N, Long 57 W by HM Sloop Nimrod Int: 11 Jan 1813 Dis: 04 Feb 1813.
    Received from HM Sloop Nimrod. Out of Custody the Vessel being liberated having a License.

Savage, P H   Prisoner 803. Rank: Seaman, from: Reassurance, Merchant Schooner.
    Cap: 25 Jan 1814 off Saint Bartholomew by HM Brig Barbados Int: 12 Feb 1814 Dis: 25 Apr 1814.
    Received from HM Schooner Ballahou. HM Ship Vestal.

Savage, Robert   Prisoner 891. Rank: Seaman, from: Hawk, Privateer.
    Cap: 26 Apr 1814 Near the Mona Passage by HM Ship Piqua Int: 20 Jun 1814 Dis: 20 Jul 1814.
    Received from HM Ship Vestal. HM Sloop Hazard Rear Adml Durham.

Savinia, Louis   Prisoner 1240. Rank: Seaman, from: Fox, Privateer.
    Cap: 26 Dec 1814 off St Bartholomew by HM Brig Barbados Int: 14 Jan 1815 Dis: 08 Feb 1815.
    Received from HM Brig Barbados. HM Ship Swiftsure.

Sawyer, John A   Prisoner 219. Rank: Seaman, from: Blockade, Privateer.
    Cap: 31 Oct 1812 off Saba by HM Sloop Charybdis Int: 19 Nov 1812 Dis: 10 Jul 1813.
    Received from HM Sloop Charybdis. Perseverance American Cartel.

Sawyer, John   Prisoner 1436. Rank: Seaman, from: Avon, Privateer.
    Cap: 08 Mar 1815 off Nevis by HM Sloop Barbados Int: 13 Mar 1815 Dis: 15 Mar 1815.
    Received from HM Sloop Barbados. HMS Numen Rear Admiral Durham.

Scan, Thomas   Prisoner 62. Rank: Seaman, from: Providence, Privateer.
    Cap: 11 Sep 1812 off St. Barthlomew by HM Sloop Dominica Int: 13 Nov 1812 Dis: 10 Jul 1813.
    Received from HM Ship Mercury. Broke into the Cabin (not legible) from the Martin Christy having freed the Lock. Perseverance American Cartel.

Scargle, William   Prisoner 1151. Rank: Seaman, from: High Flyer, Letter of Marque.
    Cap: 14 Nov 1814 off Anguilla by HM Ship Barossa Int: 18 Nov 1814 Escaped: 13 Jan 1815.
    Received from HM Ship Barossa. Escaped. Reentry 1270.

Scargle, William   Prisoner 1270. Rank: Seaman, from: Fox, Privateer.
    Cap: 26 Dec 1814 off St Bartholomew by HM Brig Barbados Int: 15 Jan 1815 Dis: 14 Feb 1815.
    Received from HM Brig Barbados. Retaken former No 1151. HM Ship Piqua.

Scott, Harry   Prisoner 1358. Rank: Seaman, from: Spencer, Merchant.
    Cap: 15 Feb 1815 off St Bartholomew by HMS Dasher Int: 03 Mar 1815 Dis: 31 Mar 1815.
    Received from HM Ship Dasher. Out of Custody Rear Adl Durham.

Scott, Thomas   Prisoner 1362. Rank: Seaman, from: Spencer, Merchant.
    Cap: 15 Feb 1815 off St Bartholomew by HMS Dasher Int: 03 Mar 1815 Dis: 31 Mar 1815.
    Received from HM Ship Dasher. Out of Custody Rear Adl Durham.

Scott, William   Prisoner 1367. Rank: Seaman, from: Spencer, Merchant.
    Cap: 15 Feb 1815 off St Bartholomew by HMS Dasher Int: 03 Mar 1815 Dis: 31 Mar 1815.
    Received from HM Ship Dasher. Out of Custody Rear Adl Durham.

Seapan, Donny   Prisoner 393. Rank: Seaman, from: Decatur, Privateer.
    Cap: 16 Jan 1813 Lat 13.00 N, Long 41.00 N by HM Ship Surprise Int: 26 Jan 1813 Dis: 10 Jul 1813.
    Received from HM Ship Surprise. Perseverance American Cartel.

Sergeant, William   Prisoner 1200. Rank: Seaman, from: Fox, Privateer.
    Cap: 26 Dec 1814 off St Bartholomew by HM Brig Barbados Int: 14 Jan 1815 Dis: 31 Mar 1815.
    Received from HM Brig Barbados. Rear Adl Durham.

Sessions, Pedro   Prisoner 938. Rank: Seaman, from: President, Privateer.
    Cap: 07 May 1814 off Porto Rico by HM Ship Piqua Int: 20 Jun 1814 Dis: 22 Jul 1814.
    Received from HM Ship Vestal. HM Ship Gloucester Rear Admiral Durham.

Seybest, George   Prisoner 1046. Rank: Seaman, from: Mary, Letter of Marque.
    Cap: 07 Jun 1814 La Quisa by HM Ship Heron Int: 31 Jul 1814 Dis: 31 Mar 1815.
    Received from HM Sloop Mosquito. Rear Adl Durham.

Shallus, William   Prisoner 600. Rank: Seaman, from: Thomas Penrose, Privateer.
    Cap: 23 Mar 1813 Lat 20.14 W, Long 61.20 W by HM Ship Tribune Int: 28 Mar 1813 Dis: 11 Aug 1813. Received from HM Ship Tribune. Malmore American Cartel.

Shanklen, Charles   Prisoner 324. Rank: Seaman, from: James Murdock, Merchant Brig.
    Cap: 05 Jan 1813 Lat 21 N, Long 57 W by HM Sloop Nimrod Int: 11 Jan 1813 Dis: 04 Feb 1813.
    Received from HM Sloop Nimrod. Out of Custody the Vessel being liberated having a License.

Shankley, Charles   Prisoner 1160. Rank: Seaman, from: High Flyer, Letter of Marque.
    Cap: 14 Nov 1814 off Anguilla by HM Ship Barossa Int: 18 Nov 1814 Escaped: 30 Dec 1814.
    Received from HM Ship Barossa. Escaped.

American Prisoners of War Held at Barbados During the War of 1812

Shanklin, Charles   Prisoner 436. Rank: Seaman, from: James Murdock, Merchant Brig.
    Cap: 05 Jan 1813 Lat 21N, Long 57 W by HM Ship Nimrod   Int: 05 Feb 1813   Dis: 13 Apr 1813.
    Received from Brig James Murdock. Out of Custody the Vessel being liberated.

Shearman, Peleg   Prisoner 267. Rank: Seaman, from: Rea, Privateer.
    Cap: 29 Nov 1812 off Barbados by HM Ship Lightning   Int: 29 Nov 1812   Dis: 25 Apr 1813.
    Received from HM Ship Lightning. Ship having been captured by the Bona American. Merchant Ship for England.

Sheffield, Acors   Prisoner 459. Rank: Seaman, from: Bowrey, Privateer.
    Cap: 02 Feb 1813 off Barbados by HM Sloop Opossum   Int: 18 Feb 1813   Dis: 11 Aug 1813.
    Received from HM Sloop Opossum. English Brig Captured by the Comet. Malmore American Cartel.

Shelah, Timothy   Prisoner 987. Rank: Seaman, from: Providence, Privateer.
    Cap: 11 Sep 1812 off Saint Bartholomew by HM Sloop Dominica   Int: 20 Jun 1814   Dis: 22 Jul 1814.
    Received from HM Ship Vestal. HM Ship Gloucester Rear Admiral Durham.

Sheldon, Charles J   Prisoner 1229. Rank: Seaman, from: Fox, Privateer.
    Cap: 26 Dec 1814 off St Bartholomew by HM Brig Barbados   Int: 14 Jan 1815   Dis: 08 Feb 1815.
    Received from HM Brig Barbados. HM Ship Swiftsure.

Sheldon, Nathanial   Prisoner 315. Rank: Seaman, from: Dolphin, Merchant Brig.
    Cap: 15 Dec 1812 near Bermuda by HM Sloop Nimrod   Int: 11 Jan 1813   Dis: 10 Jul 1813.
    Received from HM Sloop Nimrod. Perseverance American Cartel.

Shepherd, John   Prisoner 1410. Rank: Seaman, from: Avon, Privateer.
    Cap: 08 Mar 1815 off Nevis by HM Sloop Barbados   Int: 13 Mar 1815   Dis: 15 Mar 1815.
    Received from HM Sloop Barbados. HMS Numen Rear Admiral Durham.

Sherbourne, John   Prisoner 576. Rank: Seaman, from: St Bartholomew, Merchant Brig.
    Cap: 05 Mar 1813 Carlisle Bay by HM Ship Cumberland   Int: 10 Mar 1813   Dis: 06 Jun 1813.
    Received from HM Ship Cumberland. America on Parole Sir F. Laforey.

Sherry, Jonathan   Prisoner 241. Rank: Lieutenant, from: Yankee, Privateer.
    Cap: 25 Oct 1812 off Sombrero by HM Sloop Peruvian   Int: 19 Nov 1812   Dis: 10 Jul 1813.
    Received from HM Sloop Peruvian. Perseverance American Cartel.

Sherry, Joseph   Prisoner 702. Rank: Seaman, from: Saturn, Merchant Brig.
    Cap: 10 May 1813 off Martinique by HM Ship Mercury   Int: 17 Jun 1813   Dis: 11 Aug 1813.
    Received from HM Ship Mercury. Malmore American Cartel.

Shichlar, Henry   Prisoner 285. Rank: Seaman, from: Rea, Privateer.
    Cap: 29 Nov 1812 off Barbados by HM Ship Lightning   Int: 29 Nov 1812   Dis: 10 Jul 1813.
    Received from HM Ship Lightning. Ship having been captured by the Bona American. Perseverance American Cartel.

Shields, Francis D   Prisoner 420. Rank: Seaman, from: HM Ship Grampus, Not Recorded.
    Cap: Not Recorded by Not Recorded   Int: 30 Jan 1813   Dis: 10 Jul 1813.
    Received from HM Sloop Demerary. Part of Crew of HMS Grampus gave up as a Prisoner of War. Perseverance American Cartel. (Date of capture not recorded.)

Short, James   Prisoner 477. Rank: Mate, from: John, Privateer.
    Cap: 06 Feb 1813 Lat 10.0 N, Long 61.0 W by HM Sloop Peruvian   Int: 20 Feb 1813   Dis: 25 Apr 1813. Received from HM Ship Cumberland. Merchant Ship for England.

Shott, John   Prisoner 760. Rank: Seaman, from: Frolic, Privateer.
    Cap: 25 Jan 1814 off St Thomas by HM Sloop Heron   Int: 06 Feb 1814   Dis: 25 Apr 1814.
    Received from HM Sloop Heron. HM Ship Vestal.

Shusch, Adam   Prisoner 87. Rank: Seaman, from: Providence, Privateer.
    Cap: 11 Sep 1812 off St. Barthlomew by HM Sloop Dominica   Int: 13 Nov 1812   Dis: 10 Jul 1813.
    Received from HM Ship Mercury. Cut through the Ship (not legible) retaken immediately. Perseverance American Cartel.

Silsbee, John   Prisoner 831. Rank: Seaman, from: Rattle Snake, Letter of Marque.
    Cap: 11 Mar 1814 Lat 24.07 N, Long 66.47 W by HM Ship Rhin   Int: 25 Mar 1814   Dis: 25 Apr 1814.
    Received from HM Ship Rhin. HM Ship Vestal.

Simmonds, Andrew   Prisoner 1123. Rank: Seaman, from: Nancy, Privateer.
    Cap: 06 Sep 1814 Lat 32 N, Long 47 W by HM Ship Piqua   Int: 21 Oct 1814   Dis: 31 Mar 1815.
    Received from HMS Piqua. Taken by the Amelia Privateer. Rear Adl Durham.

Simmons, Joseph   Prisoner 816. Rank: Seaman, from: Fox, Privateer.
    Cap: Not Recorded by Not Recorded   Int: 22 Feb 1814   Dis: 25 Apr 1814.
    Received from HM Brig Liberty. Picked up in a Boat at Sea. Part of Crew of Fox Privateer. HM Ship Vestal. (Date of capture not recorded.)

Simmons, Mark   Prisoner 742. Rank: Prize Master, from: Frolic, Privateer.
    Cap: 25 Jan 1814 off St Thomas by HM Sloop Heron   Int: 06 Feb 1814   Dis: 22 Jul 1814.
    Received from HM Sloop Heron. HM Ship Gloucester Rear Adml Durham.

American Prisoners of War Held at Barbados During the War of 1812

Simmons, Thomas   Prisoner 171. Rank: Seaman, from: Yankee, Privateer.
    Cap: 25 Oct 1812 off Sombero by HM Sloop Peruvian Int: 13 Nov 1812 Dis: 10 Jul 1813.
    Received from HM Ship Mercury. Perseverance American Cartel.

Simon, James   Prisoner 29. Rank: Seaman, from: Hope, Merchant Ship.
    Cap: 27 Sep 1812 Lat 22.30 N, Long 40.45 by HM Sloop Tribune Int: 22 Oct 1812 Dis: 24 Oct 1812.
    Received from HM Sloop Tribune. America on Parole per order of Captain Reynolds Tribune.

Simons, Ebenezer   Prisoner 812. Rank: Seaman, from: Rebecca, Merchant Ship.
    Cap: Not Recorded by Not Recorded Int: 18 Feb 1814 Dis: 25 Apr 1814.
    Received from Ship Rebecca. Part of Crew of Merchant Ship Rebecca. HM Ship Vestal. (Date of capture not recorded.)

Simons, Ebenezer   Prisoner 980. Rank: Seaman, from: Polly, Merchant.
    Cap: 20 Mar 1814 off Saba by HM Ship Ister Int: 20 Jun 1814 Dis: 22 Jul 1814.
    Received from HM Ship Vestal. HM Ship Gloucester Rear Admiral Durham.

Simons, Richard   Prisoner 774. Rank: Seaman, from: HM Ship Venerable, Not Recorded.
    Cap: Not Recorded by Not Recorded Int: 04 Feb 1814 Dis: 25 Apr 1814.
    Received from HM Ship Venerable. Part of Crew of HM Ship Venerable. HM Ship Vestal. (Date of capture not recorded.)

Simpson, Daniel   Prisoner 1104. Rank: Seaman, from: Engineer, Letter of Marque.
    Cap: 21 Sep 1814 of Porto Rico by HM Ship Barossa Int: 29 Sep 1814 Dis: 31 Mar 1815.
    Received from HM Ship Barossa. Rear Adl Durham.

Simpson, Joseph   Prisoner 352. Rank: Seaman, from: Decatur, Privateer.
    Cap: 16 Jan 1813 Lat 13.00 N, Long 41.00 N by HM Ship Surprise Int: 26 Jan 1813 Dis: 10 Jul 1813.
    Received from HM Ship Surprise. Perseverance American Cartel.

Sinnett, Thomas   Prisoner 1050. Rank: Seaman, from: Mary, Letter of Marque.
    Cap: 07 Jun 1814 La Quisa by HM Ship Heron Int: 31 Jul 1814 Escaped: 13 Jan 1815.
    Received from HM Sloop Mosquito. Escaped. Reentry 1264.

Sinnett, Thomas   Prisoner 1264. Rank: Seaman, from: Fox, Privateer.
    Cap: 26 Dec 1814 off St Bartholomew by HM Brig Barbados Int: 15 Jan 1815 Dis: 31 Mar 1815.
    Received from HM Brig Barbados. Retaken former No 1050. Rear Adl Durham.

Smart, Samuel   Prisoner 879. Rank: Seaman, from: Not Recorded, Merchant.
    Cap: 31 Jan 1814 Lat 18.04 N, Long 59.00 W by HM Brig Barbados Int: 18 Apr 1814 Dis: 25 Apr 1814. Received from HM Ship Vestal. HM Ship Vestal.

Smart, Samuel   Prisoner 978. Rank: Seaman, from: Polly, Merchant.
    Cap: 20 Mar 1814 off Saba by HM Ship Ister Int: 20 Jun 1814 Dis: 22 Jul 1814.
    Received from HM Ship Vestal. HM Ship Gloucester Rear Admiral Durham. (Apparent duplicate of # 879.)

Smith, Bartholomew   Prisoner 1283. Rank: Seaman, from: Hero, Merchant Schooner.
    Cap: 14 Dec 1814 Lat 19.13, Long 64 by HMS Pique Int: 29 Jan 1815 Dis: 14 Feb 1815.
    Received from HMS Pique. HM Ship Piqua.

Smith, Charles   Prisoner 757. Rank: Seaman, from: Frolic, Privateer.
    Cap: 25 Jan 1814 off St Thomas by HM Sloop Heron Int: 06 Feb 1814 Dis: 25 Apr 1814.
    Received from HM Sloop Heron. HM Ship Vestal.

Smith, Daniel   Prisoner 1345. Rank: Seaman, from: Vidett, Letter of Marque.
    Cap: 14 Feb 1815 off St Bartholomew by HMS Dasher Int: 03 Mar 1815 Dis: 31 Mar 1815.
    Received from HM Ship Dasher. Out of Custody Rear Adl Durham.

Smith, George   Prisoner 30. Rank: Seaman, from: Hope, Merchant Ship.
    Cap: 27 Sep 1812 Lat 22.30 N, Long 40.45 by HM Sloop Tribune Int: 22 Oct 1812 Dis: 24 Oct 1812.
    Received from HM Sloop Tribune. America on Parole per order of Captain Reynolds Tribune.

Smith, George   Prisoner 301. Rank: Seaman, from: Carl Frederick, Privateer.
    Cap: 11 Oct 1812 at Sea by HM Sloop Ringdove Int: 29 Dec 1812 Dis: 10 Jul 1813.
    Received from HM Brig Liberty. Captured by the Odyssey in (not legible). Perseverance American Cartel.

Smith, George   Prisoner 785. Rank: Seaman, from: Fox, Privateer.
    Cap: Not Recorded by Not Recorded Int: 11 Feb 1814 Dis: 25 Apr 1814.
    Received from HM Brig Liberty. Picked up in a boat at Sea part of Crew of Fox. HM Ship Vestal. (Date of capture not recorded.)

Smith, Holsey   Prisoner 64. Rank: Seaman, from: Providence, Privateer.
    Cap: 11 Sep 1812 off St. Barthlomew by HM Sloop Dominica Int: 13 Nov 1812 Dis: 10 Jul 1813.
    Received from HM Ship Mercury. Perseverance American Cartel.

Smith, Jacob   Prisoner 320. Rank: Mate, from: James Murdock, Merchant Brig.
    Cap: 05 Jan 1813 Lat 21 N, Long 57 W by HM Sloop Nimrod Int: 11 Jan 1813 Dis: 04 Feb 1813.
    Received from HM Sloop Nimrod. Out of Custody the Vessel being liberated having a License.

American Prisoners of War Held at Barbados During the War of 1812

Smith, Jacob   Prisoner 434. Rank: Mate, from: James Murdock, Merchant Brig.
      Cap: 05 Jan 1813 Lat 21N, Long 57 W by HM Ship Nimrod Int: 05 Feb 1813 Dis: 10 Apr 1813.
      Received from Brig James Murdock. Out of Custody the Vessel being liberated.

Smith, John   Prisoner 296. Rank: Seaman, from: HM Store Ship Hyena, Not Recorded.
      Cap: Not Recorded by Not Recorded Int: 16 Dec 1812 Dis: 06 Jun 1813.
      Received from HM Store Ship Hyena. Part of Crew of HM Store Ship Hyena. America on Parole HM Ship Tribune. (Date of capture not recorded.)

Smith, John   Prisoner 890. Rank: Seaman, from: Hawk, Privateer.
      Cap: 26 Apr 1814 Near the Mona Passage by HM Ship Piqua Int: 20 Jun 1814 Dis: 20 Jul 1814.
      Received from HM Ship Vestal. HM Sloop Hazard Rear Adml Durham.

Smith, John   Prisoner 1117. Rank: Seaman, from: Aquila, Privateer.
      Cap: 04 Sep 1814 Lat 22 N, Long 36 W by HM Ship Piqua Int: 21 Oct 1814 Dis: 31 Mar 1815.
      Received from HMS Piqua. Taken by the Whig Privateer. Rear Adl Durham. John Smith (1st).

Smith, John   Prisoner 1127. Rank: Seaman, from: Nancy, Privateer.
      Cap: 06 Sep 1814 Lat 32 N, Long 47 W by HM Ship Piqua Int: 21 Oct 1814 Dis: 09 Nov 1814.
      Received from HMS Piqua. Taken by the Amelia Privateer. (Not legible) Riotous Character HM Ship Venerable having declared himself to be a British Subject.

Smith, John   Prisoner 1135. Rank: Seaman, from: Clio, Merchant Schooner.
      Cap: 13 Nov 1814 off Anguilla by HM Ship Barossa Int: 18 Nov 1814 Dis: 08 Feb 1815.
      Received from HM Ship Barossa. HM Ship Swiftsure. John Smith (3rd).

Smith, John   Prisoner 1224. Rank: Seaman, from: Fox, Privateer.
      Cap: 26 Dec 1814 off St Bartholomew by HM Brig Barbados Int: 14 Jan 1815 Dis: 08 Feb 1815.
      Received from HM Brig Barbados. HM Ship Swiftsure.

Smith, John   Prisoner 1280. Rank: Mate & Passenger, from: Hero, Merchant Schooner.
      Cap: 14 Dec 1814 Lat 19.13, Long 64 by HMS Pique Int: 29 Jan 1815 Dis: 31 Mar 1815.
      Received from HMS Pique. Rear Adl Durham.

Smith, John   Prisoner 1292. Rank: Seaman, from: Mary, Merchant Schooner.
      Cap: 15 Jan 1815 Lat 22.40, Long 66 by HM Ship Pique Int: 29 Jan 1815 Dis: 31 Mar 1815.
      Received from HMS Pique. Rear Adl Durham. John Smith (5th).

Smith, John   Prisoner 1423. Rank: Seaman, from: Avon, Privateer.
      Cap: 08 Mar 1815 off Nevis by HM Sloop Barbados Int: 13 Mar 1815 Dis: 15 Mar 1815.
      Received from HM Sloop Barbados. HMS Numen Rear Admiral Durham.

Smith, Jonathan W   Prisoner 929. Rank: Seaman, from: President, Privateer.
      Cap: 07 May 1814 off Porto Rico by HM Ship Piqua Int: 20 Jun 1814 Dis: 20 Jul 1814.
      Received from HM Ship Vestal. HM Sloop Hazard Rear Adml Durham.

Smith, Peter   Prisoner 1132. Rank: Supercargo, from: Clio, Merchant Schooner.
      Cap: 13 Nov 1814 off Anguilla by HM Ship Barossa Int: 18 Nov 1814 Dis: 21 Nov 1814.
      Received from HM Ship Barossa. Out of Custody noncombatant.

Smith, Robert B   Prisoner 423. Rank: Seaman, from: Anna, Not Recorded.
      Cap: 03 Jan 1813 off Maderia by HM Ship Cumberland Int: 30 Jan 1813 Dis: 10 Jul 1813.
      Received from HM Sloop Demerary. Recaptured from the Mars Privateer. Perseverance American Cartel.

Smith, Samuel   Prisoner 1404. Rank: Seaman, from: Avon, Privateer.
      Cap: 08 Mar 1815 off Nevis by HM Sloop Barbados Int: 13 Mar 1815 Dis: 15 Mar 1815.
      Received from HM Sloop Barbados. HMS Numen Rear Admiral Durham.

Smith, Thomas   Prisoner 1403. Rank: Seaman, from: Avon, Privateer.
      Cap: 08 Mar 1815 off Nevis by HM Sloop Barbados Int: 13 Mar 1815 Dis: 15 Mar 1815.
      Received from HM Sloop Barbados. HMS Numen Rear Admiral Durham.

Smith, William   Prisoner 129. Rank: Seaman, from: Providence, Privateer.
      Cap: 11 Sep 1812 off St. Bartholomew by HM Sloop Dominica Int: 13 Nov 1812 Dis: 10 Jul 1813.
      Received from HM Ship Mercury. Perseverance American Cartel.

Smith, William   Prisoner 675. Rank: Seaman, from: Sterling, Merchant Ship.
      Cap: 19 May 1813 Lat 22.00 N, Long 53.00 W by HM Ship Grampus Int: 26 May 1813 Dis: 11 Aug 1813. Received from HM Ship Grampus. Malmore American Cartel.

Smith, William   Prisoner 1016. Rank: Seaman, from: William, Merchant.
      Cap: 18 May 1814 off Charleston by HM Ship Ister Int: 21 Jun 1814 Dis: 22 Jul 1814.
      Received from HM Ship Ister. HM Ship Gloucester Rear Adml Durham.

Snow, Colier   Prisoner 847. Rank: Seaman, from: Rattle Snake, Letter of Marque.
      Cap: 11 Mar 1814 Lat 24.07 N, Long 66.47 W by HM Ship Rhin Int: 25 Mar 1814 Dis: 25 Apr 1814.
      Received from HM Ship Rhin. HM Ship Vestal.

American Prisoners of War Held at Barbados During the War of 1812

Snow, John   Prisoner 330. Rank: 1 Lieutenant, from: Apollo, Not Recorded.
>Cap: 22 Dec 1812 Lat 20.00 N, Long 17.00 W by HMS Ship Grampus Int: 21 Jan 1813 Dis: 12 Jun 1813. Received from HMS Grampus. Ship having been captured by the Rolla American Privateer. HM Sloop Indian for Passage to Bermuda Sir F Laforey.

Snow, John P   Prisoner 541. Rank: Seaman, from: John, Privateer.
>Cap: 06 Feb 1813 Lat 10.0 N, Long 61.0 W by HM Sloop Peruvian Int: 20 Feb 1813 Dis: 11 Aug 1813. Received from HM Ship Cumberland. American Cartel Malmore.

Souder, Concordi   Prisoner 1189. Rank: Seaman, from: Gallant Hull, Merchant.
>Cap: 26 Dec 1814 off St Bartholomew by HM Ship Barossa Int: 14 Jan 1815 Dis: 14 Feb 1815. Received from HMS Barossa. HM Ship Piqua.

Southwick, George   Prisoner 524. Rank: Seaman, from: John, Privateer.
>Cap: 06 Feb 1813 Lat 10.0 N, Long 61.0 W by HM Sloop Peruvian Int: 20 Feb 1813 Dis: 11 Aug 1813. Received from HM Ship Cumberland. Malmore American Cartel.

Southwick, George   Prisoner 750. Rank: Seaman, from: Frolic, Privateer.
>Cap: 25 Jan 1814 off St Thomas by HM Sloop Heron Int: 06 Feb 1814 Dis: 25 Apr 1814. Received from HM Sloop Heron. HM Ship Vestal Rear Admiral Durham.

Speed, Etmore   Prisoner 1416. Rank: Seaman, from: Avon, Privateer.
>Cap: 08 Mar 1815 off Nevis by HM Sloop Barbados Int: 13 Mar 1815 Dis: 15 Mar 1815. Received from HM Sloop Barbados. HMS Numen Rear Admiral Durham.

Spelsbury, Amos   Prisoner 572. Rank: Mate, from: St Bartholomew, Merchant Brig.
>Cap: 05 Mar 1813 Carlisle Bay by HM Ship Cumberland Int: 10 Mar 1813 Dis: 13 Mar 1813. Received from HM Ship Cumberland. America on Parole Sir Francis Laforey.

Spinney, Nathaniel   Prisoner 353. Rank: Seaman, from: Decatur, Privateer.
>Cap: 16 Jan 1813 Lat 13.00 N, Long 41.00 N by HM Ship Surprise Int: 26 Jan 1813 Dis: 10 Jul 1813. Received from HM Ship Surprise. Perseverance American Cartel.

Springer, Mark   Prisoner 577. Rank: Seaman, from: St Bartholomew, Merchant Brig.
>Cap: 05 Mar 1813 Carlisle Bay by HM Ship Cumberland Int: 10 Mar 1813 Dis: 06 Jun 1813. Received from HM Ship Cumberland. America on Parole Sir F. Laforey.

Stacey, Benjamin   Prisoner 736. Rank: Master, from: Jason, Merchant.
>Cap: 31 Dec 1813 Lat 12.00 N, Long 56.00 W by Venerable Int: 04 Feb 1814 Dis: 04 Feb 1814. Received from HM Ship Venerable. To America on Parole.

Stacey, John   Prisoner 368. Rank: Seaman, from: Decatur, Privateer.
>Cap: 16 Jan 1813 Lat 13.00 N, Long 41.00 N by HM Ship Surprise Int: 26 Jan 1813 Dis: 10 Jul 1813. Received from HM Ship Surprise. Perseverance American Cartel.

Stackney, Peter F   Prisoner 1106. Rank: Prize Master, from: Mars, Privateer.
>Cap: 01 Sep 1814 Lat 41 N, Long 52 W by HM Ship Piqua Int: 21 Oct 1814 Dis: 08 Feb 1815. Received from HMS Piqua. Taken by the David Porter Privateer. Returned to Custody not having taken the Oath of Allegiance agreeable to (not legible). HM Ship Swiftsure.

Stanley, Ralph   Prisoner 402. Rank: Seaman, from: Decatur, Privateer.
>Cap: 16 Jan 1813 Lat 13.00 N, Long 41.00 N by HM Ship Surprise Int: 26 Jan 1813 Dis: 10 Jul 1813. Received from HM Ship Surprise. Perseverance American Cartel.

Stanley, Samuel   Prisoner 1015. Rank: Seaman, from: William, Merchant.
>Cap: 18 May 1814 off Charleston by HM Ship Ister Int: 21 Jun 1814 Dis: 22 Jul 1814. Received from HM Ship Vestal. HM Ship Gloucester Rear Adml Durham.

Starks, Sands   Prisoner 1161. Rank: Seaman, from: High Flyer, Letter of Marque.
>Cap: 14 Nov 1814 off Anguilla by HM Ship Barossa Int: 18 Nov 1814 Dis: 08 Feb 1815. Received from HM Ship Barossa. HM Ship Swiftsure.

States, Leonard F   Prisoner 1043. Rank: Seaman, from: Mary, Letter of Marque.
>Cap: 07 Jun 1814 La Quisa by HM Ship Heron Int: 31 Jul 1814 Dis: 31 Mar 1815. Received from HM Sloop Mosquito. Rear Adl Durham.

Steel, Charles   Prisoner 596. Rank: Seaman, from: Thomas Penrose, Privateer.
>Cap: 23 Mar 1813 Lat 20.14 W, Long 61.20 W by HM Ship Tribune Int: 28 Mar 1813 Dis: 26 Apr 1813. Received from HM Ship Tribune. America on Parole Sir F. Laforey.

Steel, Thomas   Prisoner 850. Rank: Seaman, from: Rattle Snake, Letter of Marque.
>Cap: 11 Mar 1814 Lat 24.07 N, Long 66.47 W by HM Ship Rhin Int: 25 Mar 1814 Dis: 25 Apr 1814. Received from HM Ship Rhin. HM Ship Vestal.

Stephanus, Michael   Prisoner 1141. Rank: Passenger, from: High Flyer, Letter of Marque.
>Cap: 14 Nov 1814 off Anguilla by HM Ship Barossa Int: 18 Nov 1814 Dis: 18 Nov 1814. Received from HM Ship Barossa. Out of Custody being a passenger.

Stephens, John   Prisoner 341. Rank: Prize Master, from: Decatur, Privateer.
>Cap: 16 Jan 1813 Lat 13.00 N, Long 41.00 N by HM Ship Surprise Int: 26 Jan 1813 Dis: 10 Jul 1813. Received from HM Ship Surprise. Perseverance American Cartel.

American Prisoners of War Held at Barbados During the War of 1812

Stephens, William   Prisoner 931. Rank: Seaman, from: President, Privateer.
    Cap: 07 May 1814 off Porto Rico by HM Ship Piqua Int: 20 Jun 1814 Dis: 22 Jul 1814.
    Received from HM Ship Vestal. HM Ship Gloucester Rear Admiral Durham.

Stephenson, Stephen   Prisoner 157. Rank: Seaman, from: Yankee, Privateer.
    Cap: 25 Oct 1812 off Sombero by HM Sloop Peruvian Int: 13 Nov 1812 Dis: 10 Jul 1813.
    Received from HM Ship Mercury. Perseverance American Cartel.

Stevens, John   Prisoner 1414. Rank: Seaman, from: Avon, Privateer.
    Cap: 08 Mar 1815 off Nevis by HM Sloop Barbados Int: 13 Mar 1815 Dis: 15 Mar 1815.
    Received from HM Sloop Barbados. HMS Numen Rear Admiral Durham.

Stevens, Thomas   Prisoner 740. Rank: Master, from: Frolic, Privateer.
    Cap: 25 Jan 1814 off St Thomas by HM Sloop Heron Int: 06 Feb 1814 Dis: 22 Jul 1814.
    Received from HM Sloop Heron. HM Ship Gloucester Rear Admiral Durham.

Steward, John   Prisoner 578. Rank: Seaman, from: St Bartholomew, Merchant Brig.
    Cap: 05 Mar 1813 Carlisle Bay by HM Ship Cumberland Int: 10 Mar 1813 Dis: 06 Jun 1813.
    Received from HM Ship Cumberland. America on Parole Sir F. Laforey.

Stewart, John   Prisoner 109. Rank: Seaman, from: HM Brig Morne Fortunee, Not Recorded.
    Cap: Not Recorded by Not Recorded Int: 13 Nov 1812 Dis: 10 Jul 1813.
    Received from HM Ship Mercury. Part of Crew of HM Brig Morne Fortunee. Per Order Sir F. Laforey being part of crew of a Licensed Vessel. (Date of capture not recorded.)

Stocking, Seth   Prisoner 717. Rank: Seaman, from: Olive Branch, Merchant Brig.
    Cap: 12 Apr 1813 Lat 17.00 N, Long 59.30 W by HM Sloop Eclipse Int: 07 Jul 1813 Dis: 24 Jul 1813.
    Received from HM Sloop Eclipse. Out of Custody the Vessel being liberated.

Stockman, Christopher   Prisoner 1376. Rank: Seaman, from: Laurence, Merchant.
    Cap: 14 Feb 1815 off Porto Rico by HMS Dasher Int: 04 Mar 1815 Dis: 31 Mar 1815.
    Received from HM Ship Dasher. Out of Custody Rear Adl Durham.

Stole, John R   Prisoner 996. Rank: Seaman, from: Hawk, Privateer.
    Cap: 26 Apr 1814 Near the Mona Passage by HM Ship Piqua Int: 20 Jun 1814 Dis: 22 Jul 1814.
    Received from HM Ship Vestal. HM Ship Gloucester Rear Admiral Durham.

Stone, Benjamin   Prisoner 753. Rank: Seaman, from: Frolic, Privateer.
    Cap: 25 Jan 1814 off St Thomas by HM Sloop Heron Int: 06 Feb 1814 Dis: 25 Apr 1814.
    Received from HM Sloop Heron. HM Ship Vestal Rear Admiral Durham.

Stone, Samuel   Prisoner 499. Rank: Seaman, from: John, Privateer.
    Cap: 06 Feb 1813 Lat 10.0 N, Long 61.0 W by HM Sloop Peruvian Int: 20 Feb 1813 Dis: 11 Aug 1813. Received from HM Ship Cumberland. Malmore American Cartel. Samuel Stone (1st).

Stone, Samuel   Prisoner 525. Rank: Seaman, from: John, Privateer.
    Cap: 06 Feb 1813 Lat 10.0 N, Long 61.0 W by HM Sloop Peruvian Int: 20 Feb 1813 Dis: 11 Aug 1813. Received from HM Ship Cumberland. Malmore American Cartel. Samuel Stone (2nd).

Stone, Samuel   Prisoner 860. Rank: Seaman, from: Chapman, Privateer.
    Cap: 28 Feb 1814 off St Bartholomew by Thistle Privateer Int: 26 Mar 1814 Dis: 25 Apr 1814.
    Received from HM Ship Palama. HM Ship Vestal.

Stout, Thomas   Prisoner 198. Rank: Seaman, from: Blockade, Privateer.
    Cap: 31 Oct 1812 off Saba by HM Sloop Charybdis Int: 19 Nov 1812 Dis: 10 Jul 1813.
    Received from HM Sloop Charybdis. Perseverance American Cartel.

Stow, Thomas   Prisoner 1143. Rank: Passenger, from: High Flyer, Letter of Marque.
    Cap: 14 Nov 1814 off Anguilla by HM Ship Barossa Int: 18 Nov 1814 Dis: 21 Nov 1814.
    Received from HM Ship Barossa. Out of Custody being a noncombatant.

Strague, John   Prisoner 866. Rank: Seaman, from: Martha, Merchant Schooner.
    Cap: Not Recorded by Not Recorded Int: 01 Apr 1814 Dis: 25 Apr 1814.
    Received from Sloop Martha. Gave himself up as a Prisoner of War from Merchant Schooner Martha. HM Ship Vestal. (Date of capture not recorded.)

Strague, John   Prisoner 968. Rank: Seaman, from: Martha, Merchant Sloop.
    Cap: Not Recorded by Not Recorded Int: 20 Jun 1814 Dis: 22 Jul 1814.
    Received from HM Ship Vestal. Part of Crew of English Merchant Sloop Martha. HM Ship Gloucester Rear Admiral Durham. (Date of capture not recorded. Apparent duplicate of # 866.)

Strague, Stephen   Prisoner 865. Rank: Seaman, from: Martha, Merchant Schooner.
    Cap: Not Recorded by Not Recorded Int: 01 Apr 1814 Dis: 25 Apr 1814.
    Received from Sloop Martha. Gave himself up as a Prisoner of War from Merchant Schooner Martha. HM Ship Vestal. (Date of capture not recorded.)

Strague, Stephen   Prisoner 967. Rank: Seaman, from: Martha, Merchant Sloop.
    Cap: Not Recorded by Not Recorded Int: 20 Jun 1814 Dis: 22 Jul 1814.
    Received from HM Ship Vestal. Part of Crew of English Merchant Sloop Martha. HM Ship Gloucester Rear Admiral Durham. (Date of capture not recorded. Apparent duplicate of # 865.)

American Prisoners of War Held at Barbados During the War of 1812

Sturges, Bradley   Prisoner 99. Rank: Mate, from: Jane, Merchant Brig.
    Cap: 25 Sep 1812 at Sea by HM Sloop Spider Int: 13 Nov 1812 Dis: 17 Nov 1812.
    Received from HM Ship Mercury. Out of Custody per order of Sir F. Laforey being crew of a licensed vessel.

Sturges, William   Prisoner 1393. Rank: Seaman, from: Avon, Privateer.
    Cap: 08 Mar 1815 off Nevis by HM Sloop Barbados Int: 13 Mar 1815 Dis: 31 Mar 1815.
    Received from HM Sloop Barbados. Out of Custody Rear Adl Durham.

Sturtevant, Caleb   Prisoner 667. Rank: Seaman, from: William, Merchant Brig.
    Cap: 16 Apr 1813 Lat 35.00 N, Long 57.00 W by Heron Int: 22 May 1813 Dis: 11 Aug 1813.
    Received from HM Sloop Heron. Malmore American Cartel.

Summersville, George   Prisoner 432. Rank: Seaman, from: Ocean, Merchant Schooner.
    Cap: 15 Aug 1812 Martinique by Detained at Martinique Int: 05 Feb 1813 Dis: 10 Jul 1813.
    Received from HM Ship Vestal. Perseverance American Cartel.

Swain, Jonathan   Prisoner 671. Rank: Master, from: Sterling, Merchant Ship.
    Cap: 19 May 1813 Lat 22.00 N, Long 53.00 W by HM Ship Grampus Int: 25 May 1813 Dis: 05 Jun 1813. Received from HM Ship Grampus. America on Parole Sir F. Laforey.

Swain, Michael   Prisoner 1156. Rank: Seaman, from: High Flyer, Letter of Marque.
    Cap: 14 Nov 1814 off Anguilla by HM Ship Barossa Int: 18 Nov 1814 Dis: 31 Mar 1815.
    Received from HM Ship Barossa. Rear Adl Durham.

Swain, Rubin   Prisoner 673. Rank: Mate, from: Sterling, Merchant Ship.
    Cap: 19 May 1813 Lat 22.00 N, Long 53.00 W by HM Ship Grampus Int: 26 May 1813 Dis: 05 Jun 1813. Received from HM Ship Grampus. America on Parole Sir F. Laforey.

Swain, Thomas   Prisoner 738. Rank: 2 Lieutenant, from: Frolic, Privateer.
    Cap: 25 Jan 1814 off St Thomas by HM Sloop Heron Int: 06 Feb 1814 Dis: 22 Jul 1814.
    Received from HM Sloop Heron. HM Ship Gloucester Rear Admiral Durham.

Swaney, William   Prisoner 1428. Rank: Seaman, from: Avon, Privateer.
    Cap: 08 Mar 1815 off Nevis by HM Sloop Barbados Int: 13 Mar 1815 Dis: 15 Mar 1815.
    Received from HM Sloop Barbados. HMS Numen Rear Admiral Durham.

Swasey, Nathaniel   Prisoner 332. Rank: 1 Lieutenant, from: Decatur, Privateer.
    Cap: 16 Jan 1813 Lat 13.00 N, Long 41.00 N by HM Ship Surprise Int: 25 Jan 1813 Dis: 10 Jul 1813.
    Received from HM Ship Surprise. Perseverance American Cartel.

Swather, Jacob   Prisoner 121. Rank: Seaman, from: William Rathbone, Brig.
    Cap: 09 Oct 1812 at Sea by HM Sloop Charybdis Int: 13 Nov 1812 Dis: 10 Jul 1813.
    Received from HM Ship Mercury. Retaken Brig Part of Crew of Savory Jack Privateer. Perseverance American Cartel.

Sweatt, John P   Prisoner 242. Rank: Surgeon, from: Yankee, Privateer.
    Cap: 25 Oct 1812 off Sombrero by HM Sloop Peruvian Int: 19 Nov 1812 Dis: 02 Dec 1812.
    Received from HM Sloop Peruvian. Sir F. Laforey being a non Combatant.

Sweeny, Thomas   Prisoner 1294. Rank: Seaman, from: Mary, Merchant Schooner.
    Cap: 15 Jan 1815 Lat 22.40, Long 66 by HM Ship Pique Int: 29 Jan 1815 Dis: 31 Mar 1815.
    Received from HMS Pique. Rear Adl Durham.

Sweet, Daniel H   Prisoner 78. Rank: Seaman, from: Providence, Privateer.
    Cap: 11 Sep 1812 off St. Barthlomew by HM Sloop Dominica Int: 13 Nov 1812 Dis: 10 Jul 1813.
    Received from HM Ship Mercury. Perseverance American Cartel.

Swisey, Ames   Prisoner 1361. Rank: Seaman, from: Spencer, Merchant.
    Cap: 15 Feb 1815 off St Bartholomew by HMS Dasher Int: 03 Mar 1815 Dis: 31 Mar 1815.
    Received from HM Ship Dasher. Out of Custody Rear Adl Durham.

Sylva, Manuel   Prisoner 291. Rank: Seaman, from: HM Sloop Demerara, Not Recorded.
    Cap: Not Recorded by Not Recorded Int: 15 Dec 1812 Dis: 10 Jul 1813.
    Received from HM Sloop Demerara. Part of Crew of HM Sloop Demerara. Perseverance American Cartel. (Date of capture not recorded.)

Symonds, John   Prisoner 425. Rank: Seaman, from: Anna, Not Recorded.
    Cap: 03 Jan 1813 off Maderia by HM Ship Cumberland Int: 30 Jan 1813 Dis: 10 Jul 1813.
    Received from HM Sloop Demerary. Recaptured from the Mars Privateer. Perseverance American Cartel.

Tabor, Isaac   Prisoner 312. Rank: Seaman, from: Venus, Merchant Ship.
    Cap: 15 Dec 1812 Lat 32 N, Long 54 W by HM Ship Herald Int: 31 Dec 1812 Dis: 06 Jun 1813.
    Received from HM Ship Herald. America on Parole Sir F. Laforey.

Tafft, Nathan   Prisoner 255. Rank: Seaman, from: Brandy Wine, Merchant Brig.
    Cap: 17 Nov 1812 Lat 19.30, Long 57.00 W by HM Ship Lightning Int: 23 Nov 1812 Dis: 02 Dec 1812. Received from HM Ship Lightning. America on Parole Sir F. Laforey.

American Prisoners of War Held at Barbados During the War of 1812

Talbot, James   Prisoner 685. Rank: Seaman, from: Sterling, Merchant Ship.
    Cap: 19 May 1813 Lat 22.00 N, Long 53.00 W by HM Ship Grampus Int: 26 May 1813 Dis: 11 Aug 1813. Received from HM Ship Grampus. Malmore American Cartel.

Tarpish, Davis   Prisoner 1059. Rank: Seaman, from: Mary, Letter of Marque.
    Cap: 07 Jun 1814 La Quisa by HM Ship Heron Int: 31 Jul 1814 Dis: 31 Mar 1815.
    Received from HM Sloop Mosquito. Rear Adl Durham.

Tarr, John   Prisoner 759. Rank: Seaman, from: Frolic, Privateer.
    Cap: 25 Jan 1814 off St Thomas by HM Sloop Heron Int: 06 Feb 1814 Dis: 25 Apr 1814.
    Received from HM Sloop Heron. HM Ship Vestal.

Tateham, Daniel   Prisoner 1051. Rank: Seaman, from: Mary, Letter of Marque.
    Cap: 07 Jun 1814 La Quisa by HM Ship Heron Int: 31 Jul 1814 Dis: 08 Feb 1814.
    Received from HM Sloop Mosquito. Out of Custody being a Dane, Rear Adml Durham

Taylor, Edward   Prisoner 447. Rank: Seaman, from: Mary Caroline, Merchant Brig.
    Cap: 02 Jan 1813 off Porto Rico by HM Sloop Charybdis Int: 12 Feb 1813 Dis: 10 Apr 1813.
    Received from HM Brig Liberty. America on Parole Sir F. Laforey.

Taylor, George   Prisoner 1385. Rank: 1 Lieutenant, from: Avon, Privateer.
    Cap: 08 Mar 1815 off Nevis by HM Sloop Barbados Int: 05 Mar 1815 Dis: 31 Mar 1815.
    Received from HM Ship Dasher. Out of Custody Rear Adl Durham. (Date of Interment before Capture.)

Taylor, James   Prisoner 706. Rank: Seaman, from: Saturn, Merchant Brig.
    Cap: 10 May 1813 off Martinique by HM Ship Mercury Int: 17 Jun 1813 Dis: 11 Aug 1813.
    Received from HM Ship Mercury. Malmore American Cartel.

Taylor, John   Prisoner 900. Rank: Seaman, from: Hawk, Privateer.
    Cap: 26 Apr 1814 Near the Mona Passage by HM Ship Piqua Int: 20 Jun 1814 Dis: 20 Jul 1814.
    Received from HM Ship Vestal. HM Sloop Hazard Rear Adml Durham.

Taylor, Samuel   Prisoner 927. Rank: Seaman, from: President, Privateer.
    Cap: 07 May 1814 off Porto Rico by HM Ship Piqua Int: 20 Jun 1814 Dis: 20 Jul 1814.
    Received from HM Ship Vestal. HM Sloop Hazard Rear Adml Durham.

Thesen, Christopher   Prisoner 322. Rank: Seaman, from: James Murdock, Merchant Brig.
    Cap: 05 Jan 1813 Lat 21 N, Long 57 W by HM Sloop Nimrod Int: 11 Jan 1813 Dis: 20 Jan 1813.
    Received from HM Sloop Nimrod. Being Native of Sweden.

Thomas, David   Prisoner 604. Rank: Seaman, from: Thomas Penrose, Privateer.
    Cap: 23 Mar 1813 Lat 20.14 W, Long 61.20 W by HM Ship Tribune Int: 28 Mar 1813 Dis: 11 Aug 1813. Received from HM Ship Tribune. Malmore American Cartel.

Thomas, George   Prisoner 392. Rank: Seaman, from: Decatur, Privateer.
    Cap: 16 Jan 1813 Lat 13.00 N, Long 41.00 N by HM Ship Surprise Int: 26 Jan 1813 Dis: 10 Jul 1813.
    Received from HM Ship Surprise. Perseverance American Cartel.

Thomas, John   Prisoner 635. Rank: Seaman, from: Active, Merchant Ship.
    Cap: 23 Feb 1813 off St Bartholomew by HM Ship Surprise Int: 11 Apr 1813 Dis: 11 Aug 1813.
    Received from HM Schooner Elizabeth. Malmore American Cartel.

Thomas, John   Prisoner 845. Rank: Seaman, from: Rattle Snake, Letter of Marque.
    Cap: 11 Mar 1814 Lat 24.07 N, Long 66.47 W by HM Ship Rhin Int: 25 Mar 1814 Dis: 25 Apr 1814.
    Received from HM Ship Rhin. HM Ship Vestal.

Thomas, Thomas   Prisoner 1337. Rank: Seaman, from: Vidett, Letter of Marque.
    Cap: 14 Feb 1815 off St Bartholomew by HM Ship Dasher Int: 03 Mar 1815 Dis: 31 Mar 1815.
    Received from HM Ship Dasher. Out of Custody Rear Adl Durham. (First and last name the same.)

Thompson, Allen   Prisoner 1120. Rank: Seaman, from: Aquila, Privateer.
    Cap: 04 Sep 1814 Lat 22 N, Long 36 W by HM Ship Piqua Int: 21 Oct 1814 Dis: 09 Nov 1814.
    Received from HMS Piqua. Taken by the Whig Privateer. (Not legible) Riotous Character HM Ship Venerable having declared himself to be a British Subject.

Thompson, Henry   Prisoner 1301. Rank: Seaman, from: Mary, Merchant Schooner.
    Cap: 15 Jan 1815 Lat 22.40, Long 66 by HM Ship Pique Int: 29 Jan 1815 Dis: 31 Mar 1815.
    Received from HMS Pique. Rear Adl Durham.

Thompson, John   Prisoner 1047. Rank: Seaman, from: Mary, Letter of Marque.
    Cap: 07 Jun 1814 La Quisa by HM Ship Heron Int: 31 Jul 1814 Dis: 31 Mar 1815.
    Received from HM Sloop Mosquito. Rear Adl Durham.

Thompson, John   Prisoner 1206. Rank: Seaman, from: Fox, Privateer.
    Cap: 26 Dec 1814 off St Bartholomew by HM Brig Barbados Int: 14 Jan 1815 Dis: 08 Feb 1815.
    Received from HM Brig Barbados. HM Ship Swiftsure.

Thompson, Robert   Prisoner 26. Rank: Seaman, from: Hope, Merchant Ship.
    Cap: 27 Sep 1812 Lat 22.30 N, Long 40.45 by HM Sloop Tribune Int: 22 Oct 1812 Dis: 24 Oct 1812.
    Received from HM Sloop Tribune. America on Parole per order of Captain Reynolds Tribune.

American Prisoners of War Held at Barbados During the War of 1812

Thompson, William   Prisoner 177. Rank: Seaman, from: HM Ship Hyperion, Not Recorded.
    Cap: Not Recorded by Not Recorded Int: 14 Nov 1812 Dis: 29 Jan 1813.
    Received from HM Ship Hyperion. Gave up as Prisoners of War Part of the Crew of HM Ship Hyperion. Having decided to take the Oath of Allegiance to His Britannic Majesty. (Date of capture not recorded.)

Thompson, William   Prisoner 350. Rank: Seaman, from: Decatur, Privateer.
    Cap: 16 Jan 1813 Lat 13.00 N, Long 41.00 N by HM Ship Surprise Int: 26 Jan 1813 Dis: 10 Jul 1813.
    Received from HM Ship Surprise. Perseverance American Cartel.

Titcomb, John H   Prisoner 1166. Rank: Mate, from: Dolphin, Letter of Marque.
    Cap: 04 Dec 1814 Lat 18.00 N, Long 60.00 W by HM Brig Columbia Int: 08 Dec 1814 Dis: 31 Mar 1815. Received from HM Brig Columbia. Rear Adl Durham.

Titcomb, William   Prisoner 1170. Rank: Seaman, from: Dolphin, Letter of Marque.
    Cap: 04 Dec 1814 Lat 18.00 N, Long 60.00 W by HM Brig Columbia Int: 08 Dec 1814 Dis: 14 Feb 1815. Received from HM Brig Columbia. HM Ship Piqua.

Todd, William   Prisoner 1168. Rank: Seaman, from: Dolphin, Letter of Marque.
    Cap: 04 Dec 1814 Lat 18.00 N, Long 60.00 W by HM Brig Columbia Int: 08 Dec 1814 Dis: 14 Feb 1815. Received from HM Brig Columbia. HM Ship Piqua.

Tolly, George F   Prisoner 563. Rank: Seaman, from: Isabella, Merchant Brig.
    Cap: 08 Dec 1812 off Demuary by Detained by the Custom House Int: 02 Mar 1813 Dis: 11 Aug 1813. Received from Army Schooner Moushe. Malmore American Cartel.

Tompkins, Stockton   Prisoner 581. Rank: Seaman, from: HM Ship Vestal, Not Recorded.
    Cap: Not Recorded by Not Recorded Int: 16 Mar 1813 Dis: 11 Aug 1813.
    Received from HM Ship Vestal. Part of Crew of HM Ship Vestal. Malmore American Cartel. (Date of capture not recorded.)

Tool, Elijah   Prisoner 586. Rank: Seaman, from: Alexis, Privateer.
    Cap: 09 Mar 1813 Not Recorded by HM Ship Lightning Int: 22 Mar 1813 Dis: 11 Aug 1813.
    Received from HM Ship Lightning. English Retaken by Comet. Malmore American Cartel.

Tooley, William   Prisoner 902. Rank: Seaman, from: Hawk, Privateer.
    Cap: 26 Apr 1814 Near the Mona Passage by HM Ship Piqua Int: 20 Jun 1814 Dis: 20 Jul 1814.
    Received from HM Ship Vestal. HM Sloop Hazard Rear Adml Durham.

Tract, Horace   Prisoner 188. Rank: Prize Master, from: Blockade, Privateer.
    Cap: 31 Oct 1812 off Saba by HM Sloop Charybdis Int: 19 Nov 1812 Escaped: 24 Apr 1813.
    Received from HM Sloop Charybdis. Escaped. Retaken 645.

Tract, Horace   Prisoner 645. Rank: Prize Master, from: Not Recorded, Not Recorded.
    Cap: Not Recorded by Retaken Int: 27 Apr 1813 Dis: 10 Jul 1813.
    Received from The Constibles. Retaken former N 188. Perseverance American Cartel. (Date of capture not recorded.)

Traffick, Charles   Prisoner 1422. Rank: Seaman, from: Avon, Privateer.
    Cap: 08 Mar 1815 off Nevis by HM Sloop Barbados Int: 13 Mar 1815 Dis: 15 Mar 1815.
    Received from HM Sloop Barbados. HMS Numen Rear Admiral Durham.

Treat, Lathrop   Prisoner 719. Rank: Seaman, from: Olive Branch, Merchant Brig.
    Cap: 12 Apr 1813 Lat 17.00 N, Long 59.30 W by HM Sloop Eclipse Int: 07 Jul 1813 Dis: 24 Jul 1813.
    Received from HM Sloop Eclipse. Out of Custody the Vessel being liberated.

Treby, George   Prisoner 2. Rank: Mate, from: Hannibal, Merchant Brig.
    Cap: 14 Aug 1812 at sea by HM Sloop Ringdove Int: 24 Aug 1812 Dis: 08 Sep 1812.
    Received from HM Ship Vestal. By Application from Sir George Beckwith it being stated that they landed under a License. Confirmed by Sir F. Laforey.

Tribe, Morrell   Prisoner 1119. Rank: Seaman, from: Aquila, Privateer.
    Cap: 04 Sep 1814 Lat 22 N, Long 36 W by HM Ship Piqua Int: 21 Oct 1814 Dis: 31 Mar 1815.
    Received from HMS Piqua. Taken by the Whig Privateer. Rear Adl Durham.

Tripe, William H   Prisoner 882. Rank: Captain, from: Hawk, Privateer.
    Cap: 26 Apr 1814 Near the Mona Passage by HM Ship Piqua Int: 13 Jun 1814 Dis: 22 Jul 1814.
    Received from HM Ship Vestal. HM Ship Gloucester Rear Admiral Durham.

Tucker, William   Prisoner 329. Rank: Mate, from: Washington, Merchant Ship.
    Cap: 06 Nov 1812 Lat 36.00 N, Long 9.00 W by HM Ship Grampus Int: 21 Jan 1813 Dis: 17 Apr 1813. Received from HMS Grampus. Out of Custody the Vessel being liberated by Admiralty (not legible).

Tuckett, George   Prisoner 694. Rank: Seaman, from: HM Ship Bedford, Not Recorded.
    Cap: Not Recorded by Not Recorded Int: 12 Jun 1813 Dis: 11 Aug 1813.
    Received from HMS Vestal. Gave himself up as a Prisoner of War on Board HM Ship Bedford. Malmore American Cartel. (Date of capture not recorded.)

American Prisoners of War Held at Barbados During the War of 1812

Turner, Samuel   Prisoner 574. Rank: Seaman, from: St Bartholomew, Merchant Brig.
    Cap: 05 Mar 1813 Carlisle Bay by HM Ship Cumberland Int: 10 Mar 1813 Escaped: 01 Jun 1813.
    Received from HM Ship Cumberland. Escaped.

Turner, William   Prisoner 1299. Rank: Seaman, from: Mary, Merchant Schooner.
    Cap: 15 Jan 1815 Lat 22.40, Long 66 by HM Ship Pique Int: 29 Jan 1815 Dis: 14 Feb 1815.
    Received from HMS Pique. HM Ship Piqua.

Tusant, John   Prisoner 465. Rank: Seaman, from: John, Privateer.
    Cap: 06 Feb 1813 Lat 10.0 N, Long 61.0 W by HM Sloop Peruvian Int: 18 Feb 1813 Dis: 11 Aug 1813. Received from HM Ship Cumberland. Malmore American Cartel.

Twiddy, Stephen   Prisoner 1298. Rank: Seaman, from: Mary, Merchant Schooner.
    Cap: 15 Jan 1815 Lat 22.40, Long 66 by HM Ship Pique Int: 29 Jan 1815 Dis: 31 Mar 1815.
    Received from HMS Pique. Rear Adl Durham.

Twiddy, William   Prisoner 1307. Rank: Seaman, from: Mary, Merchant Schooner.
    Cap: 15 Jan 1815 Lat 22.40, Long 66 by HM Ship Pique Int: 29 Jan 1815 Dis: 31 Mar 1815.
    Received from HMS Pique. Rear Adl Durham.

Uluck, Thomas   Prisoner 597. Rank: Seaman, from: Thomas Penrose, Privateer.
    Cap: 23 Mar 1813 Lat 20.14 W, Long 61.20 W by HM Ship Tribune Int: 28 Mar 1813 Dis: 11 Aug 1813. Received from HM Ship Tribune. Malmore American Cartel.

Vickey, William   Prisoner 511. Rank: Seaman, from: John, Privateer.
    Cap: 06 Feb 1813 Lat 10.0 N, Long 61.0 W by HM Sloop Peruvian Int: 20 Feb 1813 Dis: 11 Aug 1813. Received from HM Ship Cumberland. Malmore American Cartel.

Vielo, Jean   Prisoner 1238. Rank: Seaman, from: Fox, Privateer.
    Cap: 26 Dec 1814 off St Bartholomew by HM Brig Barbados Int: 14 Jan 1815 Dis: 08 Feb 1815.
    Received from HM Brig Barbados. HM Ship Swiftsure.

Wacher, Martin   Prisoner 1407. Rank: Seaman, from: Avon, Privateer.
    Cap: 08 Mar 1815 off Nevis by HM Sloop Barbados Int: 13 Mar 1815 Dis: 15 Mar 1815.
    Received from HM Sloop Barbados. HMS Numen Rear Admiral Durham.

Wade, William   Prisoner 1381. Rank: Master, from: Vidett, Letter of Marque.
    Cap: 14 Feb 1815 off St Bartholomew by HMS Dasher Int: 05 Mar 1815 Dis: 31 Mar 1815.
    Received from HM Ship Dasher. Out of Custody Rear Adl Durham.

Wadley, Benjamin D   Prisoner 346. Rank: Seaman, from: Decatur, Privateer.
    Cap: 16 Jan 1813 Lat 13.00 N, Long 41.00 N by HM Ship Surprise Int: 26 Jan 1813 Dis: 10 Jul 1813.
    Received from HM Ship Surprise. Perseverance American Cartel.

Wagner, John   Prisoner 532. Rank: Seaman, from: John, Privateer.
    Cap: 06 Feb 1813 Lat 10.0 N, Long 61.0 W by HM Sloop Peruvian Int: 20 Feb 1813 Dis: 11 Aug 1813. Received from HM Ship Cumberland. Malmore American Cartel.

Wales, Daniel   Prisoner 1430. Rank: Seaman, from: Avon, Privateer.
    Cap: 08 Mar 1815 off Nevis by HM Sloop Barbados Int: 13 Mar 1815 Dis: 15 Mar 1815.
    Received from HM Sloop Barbados. HMS Numen Rear Admiral Durham.

Walker, George   Prisoner 83. Rank: Seaman, from: Providence, Privateer.
    Cap: 11 Sep 1812 off St. Barthlomew by HM Sloop Dominica Int: 13 Nov 1812 Dis: 10 Jul 1813.
    Received from HM Ship Mercury. Perseverance American Cartel.

Walker, George   Prisoner 1329. Rank: Seaman, from: Vidett, Letter of Marque.
    Cap: 14 Feb 1815 off St Bartholomew by HM Ship Dasher Int: 03 Mar 1815 Dis: 31 Mar 1815.
    Received from HM Ship Dasher. Out of Custody Rear Adl Durham.

Walker, James Scott   Prisoner 964. Rank: Clerk, from: President, Privateer.
    Cap: 07 May 1814 off Porto Rico by HM Ship Piqua Int: 20 Jun 1814 Dis: 22 Jul 1814.
    Received from HM Ship Piqua. HM Ship Gloucester Rear Admiral Durham.

Walsh, William   Prisoner 75. Rank: Seaman, from: Providence, Privateer.
    Cap: 11 Sep 1812 off St. Barthlomew by HM Sloop Dominica Int: 13 Nov 1812 Dis: 10 Jul 1813.
    Received from HM Ship Mercury. Perseverance American Cartel.

Walstrome, Samuel   Prisoner 1342. Rank: Seaman, from: Vidett, Letter of Marque.
    Cap: 14 Feb 1815 off St Bartholomew by HM Ship Dasher Int: 03 Mar 1815 Dis: 31 Mar 1815.
    Received from HM Ship Dasher. Out of Custody Rear Adl Durham.

Walters, John   Prisoner 700. Rank: Mate, from: Saturn, Merchant Brig.
    Cap: 10 May 1813 off Martinique by HM Ship Mercury Int: 17 Jun 1813 Dis: 10 Jul 1813.
    Received from HM Ship Mercury. Exchanged.

Walton, John   Prisoner 1169. Rank: Seaman, from: Dolphin, Letter of Marque.
    Cap: 04 Dec 1814 Lat 18.00 N, Long 60.00 W by HM Brig Columbia Int: 08 Dec 1814 Dis: 14 Feb 1815. Received from HM Brig Columbia. HM Ship Piqua.

Ward, James   Prisoner 166. Rank: Seaman, from: Yankee, Privateer.
    Cap: 25 Oct 1812 off Sombero by HM Sloop Peruvian Int: 13 Nov 1812 Dis: 10 Jul 1813.
    Received from HM Ship Mercury. Perseverance American Cartel.

American Prisoners of War Held at Barbados During the War of 1812

Ward, Samuel   Prisoner 397. Rank: Seaman, from: Decatur, Privateer.
    Cap: 16 Jan 1813 Lat 13.00 N, Long 41.00 N by HM Ship Surprise Int: 26 Jan 1813 Dis: 10 Jul 1813.
    Received from HM Ship Surprise. Perseverance American Cartel.

Warden, Charles   Prisoner 698. Rank: Seaman, from: HM Ship Bedford, Not Recorded.
    Cap: Not Recorded by Not Recorded Int: 15 Jun 1813 Dis: 11 Aug 1813.
    Received from HM Ship Lightning. Gave himself up as a Prisoner of War on Board HM Ship Bedford. Malmore American Cartel. (Date of capture not recorded.)

Ware, John   Prisoner 619. Rank: Seaman, from: HM Ship Venus, Not Recorded.
    Cap: Not Recorded by Not Recorded Int: 02 Apr 1813 Dis: 11 Aug 1813.
    Received from HM Ship Venus. Part of Crew of HMS Venus. Malmore American Cartel. Malmore American Cartel. (Date of capture not recorded.)

Warner, Benjamin   Prisoner 895. Rank: Seaman, from: Hawk, Privateer.
    Cap: 26 Apr 1814 Near the Mona Passage by HM Ship Piqua Int: 20 Jun 1814 Dis: 20 Jul 1814.
    Received from HM Ship Vestal. HM Sloop Hazard Rear Adml Durham.

Warren, David   Prisoner 666. Rank: Seaman, from: William, Merchant Brig.
    Cap: 16 Apr 1813 Lat 35.00 N, Long 57.00 W by Heron Int: 22 May 1813 Dis: 11 Aug 1813.
    Received from HM Sloop Heron. Malmore American Cartel.

Washington, George   Prisoner 25. Rank: Seaman, from: Hope, Merchant Ship.
    Cap: 27 Sep 1812 Lat 22.30 N, Long 40.45 by HM Sloop Tribune Int: 22 Oct 1812 Dis: 24 Oct 1812.
    Received from HM Sloop Tribune. America on Parole per order of Captain Reynolds Tribune.

Waterford, John H   Prisoner 999. Rank: Seaman, from: Hawk, Privateer.
    Cap: 26 Apr 1814 Near the Mona Passage by HM Ship Piqua Int: 20 Jun 1814 Dis: 22 Jul 1814.
    Received from HM Ship Vestal. HM Ship Gloucester Rear Admiral Durham.

Waterman, Cato   Prisoner 935. Rank: Seaman, from: President, Privateer.
    Cap: 07 May 1814 off Porto Rico by HM Ship Piqua Int: 20 Jun 1814 Dis: 22 Jul 1814.
    Received from HM Ship Vestal. HM Ship Gloucester Rear Admiral Durham.

Waters, Frank   Prisoner 614. Rank: Seaman, from: Thomas Penrose, Privateer.
    Cap: 23 Mar 1813 Lat 20.14 W, Long 61.20 W by HM Ship Tribune Int: 28 Mar 1813 Dis: 26 Apr 1813. Received from HM Ship Tribune. America on Parole Sir F. Laforey.

Watkins, Asa   Prisoner 734. Rank: Seaman, from: Santa Maria, Merchant Schooner.
    Cap: 04 Dec 1813 off St Thomas by HM Ship Cleopatra Int: 02 Feb 1814 Dis: 02 Feb 1814.
    Received from HM Brig Liberty. Rising States American Cartel. Rear Adml Sir F. Laforey.

Watson, James   Prisoner 1335. Rank: Seaman, from: Vidett, Letter of Marque.
    Cap: 14 Feb 1815 off St Bartholomew by HM Ship Dasher Int: 03 Mar 1815 Dis: 31 Mar 1815.
    Received from HM Ship Dasher. Out of Custody Rear Adl Durham.

Watson, Robert   Prisoner 192. Rank: Prize Master, from: Blockade, Privateer.
    Cap: 31 Oct 1812 off Saba by HM Sloop Charybdis Int: 19 Nov 1812 Dis: 10 Jul 1813.
    Received from HM Sloop Charybdis. Perseverance American Cartel.

Watson, Thomas   Prisoner 1109. Rank: Seaman, from: Mars, Privateer.
    Cap: 01 Sep 1814 Lat 41 N, Long 52 W by HM Ship Piqua Int: 21 Oct 1814 Dis: 08 Feb 1815.
    Received from HMS Piqua. Taken by the David Porter Privateer. HM Ship Swiftsure.

Weacom, Ebenezer   Prisoner 567. Rank: Lieutenant, from: John, Privateer.
    Cap: 06 Feb 1813 Lat 10 N, Long 61 W by HM Sloop Peruvian Int: 08 Mar 1813 Dis: 10 Jul 1813.
    Received from HM Sloop Arachne. Perseverance American Cartel.

Weanray, R   Prisoner 1003. Rank: Seaman, from: Hawk, Privateer.
    Cap: 26 Apr 1814 Near the Mona Passage by HM Ship Piqua Int: 20 Jun 1814 Dis: 22 Jul 1814.
    Received from HM Ship Vestal. HM Ship Gloucester Rear Admiral Durham.

Weaver, Benjamin   Prisoner 679. Rank: Seaman, from: Sterling, Merchant Ship.
    Cap: 19 May 1813 Lat 22.00 N, Long 53.00 W by HM Ship Grampus Int: 26 May 1813 Dis: 11 Aug 1813. Received from HM Ship Grampus. Malmore American Cartel.

Weaver, William   Prisoner 1359. Rank: Seaman, from: Spencer, Merchant.
    Cap: 15 Feb 1815 off St Bartholomew by HMS Dasher Int: 03 Mar 1815 Dis: 31 Mar 1815.
    Received from HM Ship Dasher. Out of Custody Rear Adl Durham.

Webb, Purnel   Prisoner 1134. Rank: Seaman, from: Clio, Merchant Schooner.
    Cap: 13 Nov 1814 off Anguilla by HM Ship Barossa Int: 18 Nov 1814 Dis: 31 Mar 1815.
    Received from HM Ship Barossa. Rear Adl Durham.

Webb, Thomas   Prisoner 321. Rank: Seaman, from: James Murdock, Merchant Brig.
    Cap: 05 Jan 1813 Lat 21 N, Long 57 W by HM Sloop Nimrod Int: 11 Jan 1813 Dis: 04 Feb 1813.
    Received from HM Sloop Nimrod. Out of Custody the Vessel being liberated having a License.

Webb, Thomas   Prisoner 435. Rank: Seaman, from: James Murdock, Merchant Brig.
    Cap: 05 Jan 1813 Lat 21N, Long 57 W by HM Ship Nimrod Int: 05 Feb 1813 Dis: 10 Apr 1813.
    Received from Brig James Murdock. Out of Custody the Vessel being liberated.

American Prisoners of War Held at Barbados During the War of 1812

Weeks, Rubin   Prisoner 9. Rank: Master, from: Hope, Merchant Ship.
    Cap: 27 Sep 1812 Lat 22.30 N, (Long) 40.45 W by HM Ship Tribune Int: 07 Oct 1812 Dis: 26 Oct 1812. Received from Ship Hope. America on Parole per order of Captain Reynolds Tribune.

Weeks, William   Prisoner 1262. Rank: Seaman, from: Fox, Privateer.
    Cap: 26 Dec 1814 off St Bartholomew by HM Brig Barbados Int: 14 Jan 1815 Dis: 08 Feb 1815. Received from HM Brig Barbados. HM Ship Swiftsure.

Weiden, Daniel   Prisoner 1228. Rank: Seaman, from: Fox, Privateer.
    Cap: 26 Dec 1814 off St Bartholomew by HM Brig Barbados Int: 14 Jan 1815 Dis: 08 Feb 1815. Received from HM Brig Barbados. HM Ship Swiftsure.

Weir, Robert   Prisoner 656. Rank: Seaman, from: Adelphia, Privateer.
    Cap: 24 Feb 1813 Surinam by Not Recorded Int: 20 May 1813 Dis: 11 Aug 1813. Received from HM Sloop Crane. Part of Crew of Comet having charge of the Ship, which floundered at Sea. Surrendering themselves at Main's Point Surinam. Malmore American Cartel.

Weld, Benjamin   Prisoner 629. Rank: Prize Master, from: Jane, Privateer.
    Cap: 06 Mar 1813 Lat 14.22 N, Long 65.35 W by HM Brig Swaggerer Int: 02 Apr 1813 Dis: 25 Apr 1813. Received from Army Schooner Maria. Recaptured from the Comet. Merchant Schooner for Newfoundland.

Weld, Thomas   Prisoner 1144. Rank: Passenger, from: High Flyer, Letter of Marque.
    Cap: 14 Nov 1814 off Anguilla by HM Ship Barossa Int: 18 Nov 1814 Dis: 21 Nov 1814. Received from HM Ship Barossa. Out of Custody being a noncombatant.

Wells, Francis   Prisoner 1406. Rank: Seaman, from: Avon, Privateer.
    Cap: 08 Mar 1815 off Nevis by HM Sloop Barbados Int: 13 Mar 1815 Dis: 15 Mar 1815. Received from HM Sloop Barbados. HMS Numen Rear Admiral Durham.

Wells, Henry Knox   Prisoner 212. Rank: Seaman, from: Blockade, Privateer.
    Cap: 31 Oct 1812 off Saba by HM Sloop Charybdis Int: 19 Nov 1812 Dis: 10 Jul 1813. Received from HM Sloop Charybdis. Perseverance American Cartel.

Wells, Horace   Prisoner 207. Rank: Seaman, from: Blockade, Privateer.
    Cap: 31 Oct 1812 off Saba by HM Sloop Charybdis Int: 19 Nov 1812 Dis: 10 Jul 1813. Received from HM Sloop Charybdis. Perseverance American Cartel. Cut through the hull Escaped Retaken Immediately,

Wells, Nathan   Prisoner 762. Rank: Seaman, from: Frolic, Privateer.
    Cap: 25 Jan 1814 off St Thomas by HM Sloop Heron Int: 06 Feb 1814 Dis: 25 Apr 1814. Received from HM Sloop Heron. HM Ship Vestal.

Wells, Oliver   Prisoner 236. Rank: Seaman, from: Blockade, Privateer.
    Cap: 31 Oct 1812 off Saba by HM Sloop Charybdis Int: 19 Nov 1812 Dis: 10 Jul 1813. Received from HM Sloop Charybdis. Perseverance American Cartel.

Wenwood, Godfrey   Prisoner 54. Rank: Seaman, from: Providence, Privateer.
    Cap: 11 Sep 1812 off St. Barthlomew by HM Sloop Dominica Int: 13 Nov 1812 Dis: 10 Jul 1813. Received from HM Ship Mercury. Perseverance American Cartel.

Wescott, Edward   Prisoner 802. Rank: Seaman, from: Reassurance, Merchant Schooner.
    Cap: 25 Jan 1814 off Saint Bartholomew by HM Brig Barbados Int: 12 Feb 1814 Dis: 25 Apr 1814. Received from HM Schooner Ballahou. HM Ship Vestal.

West, Henry   Prisoner 239. Rank: Seaman, from: Blockade, Privateer.
    Cap: 31 Oct 1812 off Saba by HM Sloop Charybdis Int: 19 Nov 1812 Dis: 23 Apr 1813. Received from HM Sloop Charybdis. HM Ship Tribune. Not to be exchanged during the War having behaved (not legible) in army.

West, John   Prisoner 809. Rank: Seaman, from: Goutlan, Merchant Schooner.
    Cap: 31 Jan 1814 off Saint Bartholomew by HM Brig Barbados Int: 12 Feb 1814 Dis: 25 Apr 1814. Received from HM Schooner Ballahou. HM Ship Vestal.

West, Stephen   Prisoner 1079. Rank: Seaman, from: Engineer, Letter of Marque.
    Cap: 21 Sep 1814 of Porto Rico by HM Ship Barossa Int: 29 Sep 1814 Dis: 08 Feb 1815. Received from HM Ship Barossa. HM Ship Swiftsure Rear A Durham.

Westcott, Samuel   Prisoner 52. Rank: Seaman, from: Providence, Privateer.
    Cap: 11 Sep 1812 off St. Barthlomew by HM Sloop Dominica Int: 13 Nov 1812 Dis: 10 Jul 1813. Received from HM Ship Mercury. Perseverance American Cartel.

Wharff, John   Prisoner 124. Rank: Seaman, from: William Rathbone, Brig.
    Cap: 09 Oct 1812 at Sea by HM Sloop Charybdis Int: 13 Nov 1812 Dis: 10 Jul 1813. Received from HM Ship Mercury. Retaken Brig Part of Crew of Savory Jack Privateer. Perseverance American Cartel.

Wheaton, Nathaniel   Prisoner 35. Rank: Prize Master, from: Providence, Privateer.
    Cap: 11 Sep 1812 off St. Bartholomew by HM Sloop Dominica Int: 24 Oct 1812 Dis: 10 Jul 1813. Received from HM Sloop Vestal. Perseverance American Cartel.

American Prisoners of War Held at Barbados During the War of 1812

Wheeler, David   Prisoner 139. Rank: Prize Master, from: Yankee, Privateer.
    Cap: 25 Oct 1812 off Sombero by HM Sloop Peruvian Int: 13 Nov 1812 Dis: 10 Jul 1813.
    Received from HM Ship Mercury. Perseverance American Cartel.

Wheeler, Job E   Prisoner 162. Rank: Seaman, from: Yankee, Privateer.
    Cap: 25 Oct 1812 off Sombero by HM Sloop Peruvian Int: 13 Nov 1812 Dis: 10 Jul 1813.
    Received from HM Ship Mercury. Perseverance American Cartel.

Wheelock, Nahor   Prisoner 167. Rank: Seaman, from: Yankee, Privateer.
    Cap: 25 Oct 1812 off Sombero by HM Sloop Peruvian Int: 13 Nov 1812 Dis: 10 Jul 1813.
    Received from HM Ship Mercury. Perseverance American Cartel.

Whippel, John   Prisoner 961. Rank: Seaman, from: President, Privateer.
    Cap: 07 May 1814 off Porto Rico by HM Ship Piqua Int: 20 Jun 1814 Dis: 22 Jul 1814.
    Received from HM Ship Vestal. HM Ship Gloucester Rear Admiral Durham.

White, George   Prisoner 290. Rank: Seaman, from: HM Sloop Demerara, Not Recorded.
    Cap: Not Recorded by Not Recorded Int: 15 Dec 1812 Dis: 20 Dec 1812.
    Received from HM Sloop Demerara. Part of Crew of HM Sloop Demerara. HM Sloop Demerara having given himself up as a British Subject. (Date of capture not recorded.)

White, Oliver   Prisoner 401. Rank: Seaman, from: Decatur, Privateer.
    Cap: 16 Jan 1813 Lat 13.00 N, Long 41.00 N by HM Ship Surprise Int: 26 Jan 1813 Dis: 10 Jul 1813.
    Received from HM Ship Surprise. Perseverance American Cartel.

Whitehead, Rubin   Prisoner 995. Rank: Seaman, from: Hawk, Privateer.
    Cap: 26 Apr 1814 Near the Mona Passage by HM Ship Piqua Int: 20 Jun 1814 Dis: 22 Jul 1814.
    Received from HM Ship Vestal. HM Ship Gloucester Rear Admiral Durham.

Whitmore, Joseph   Prisoner 381. Rank: Seaman, from: Decatur, Privateer.
    Cap: 16 Jan 1813 Lat 13.00 N, Long 41.00 N by HM Ship Surprise Int: 26 Jan 1813 Dis: 10 Jul 1813.
    Received from HM Ship Surprise. Perseverance American Cartel.

Whymn, Theodore   Prisoner 800. Rank: Seaman, from: Kirran, Merchant Brig.
    Cap: 25 Jan 1814 off Saint Bartholomew by HM Brig Barbados Int: 12 Feb 1814 Dis: 25 Apr 1814.
    Received from HM Schooner Ballahou. HM Ship Vestal.

Wilford, Charles   Prisoner 835. Rank: Seaman, from: Rattle Snake, Letter of Marque.
    Cap: 11 Mar 1814 Lat 24.07 N, Long 66.47 W by HM Ship Rhin Int: 25 Mar 1814 Dis: 25 Apr 1814.
    Received from HM Ship Rhin. HM Ship Vestal.

Wilkins, William   Prisoner 889. Rank: Seaman, from: Hawk, Privateer.
    Cap: 26 Apr 1814 Near the Mona Passage by HM Ship Piqua Int: 20 Jun 1814 Dis: 20 Jul 1814.
    Received from HM Ship Vestal. HM Sloop Hazard Rear Adml Durham.

Wilkinson, David   Prisoner 1044. Rank: Seaman, from: Mary, Letter of Marque.
    Cap: 07 Jun 1814 La Quisa by HM Ship Heron Int: 31 Jul 1814 Dis: 31 Mar 1815.
    Received from HM Sloop Mosquito. Rear Adl Durham.

William, George   Prisoner 908. Rank: Seaman, from: Hawk, Privateer.
    Cap: 26 Apr 1814 Near the Mona Passage by HM Ship Piqua Int: 20 Jun 1814 Dis: 20 Jul 1814.
    Received from HM Ship Vestal. HM Sloop Hazard Rear Adml Durham.

Williams, Charles   Prisoner 934. Rank: Seaman, from: President, Privateer.
    Cap: 07 May 1814 off Porto Rico by HM Ship Piqua Int: 20 Jun 1814 Dis: 22 Jul 1814.
    Received from HM Ship Vestal. HM Ship Gloucester Rear Admiral Durham.

Williams, George   Prisoner 1153. Rank: Seaman, from: High Flyer, Letter of Marque.
    Cap: 14 Nov 1814 off Anguilla by HM Ship Barossa Int: 18 Nov 1814 Dis: 31 Mar 1815.
    Received from HM Ship Barossa. Rear Adl Durham.

Williams, Henry   Prisoner 1202. Rank: Seaman, from: Fox, Privateer.
    Cap: 26 Dec 1814 off St Bartholomew by HM Brig Barbados Int: 14 Jan 1815 Dis: 08 Feb 1815.
    Received from HM Brig Barbados. HM Ship Swiftsure.

Williams, John   Prisoner 277. Rank: Seaman, from: Rea, Privateer.
    Cap: 29 Nov 1812 off Barbados by HM Ship Lightning Int: 29 Nov 1812 Dis: 10 Jul 1813.
    Received from HM Ship Lightning. Ship having been captured by the Bona American. Perseverance American Cartel.

Williams, John   Prisoner 407. Rank: Seaman, from: Decatur, Privateer.
    Cap: 16 Jan 1813 Lat 13.00 N, Long 41.00 N by HM Ship Surprise Int: 26 Jan 1813 Dis: 10 Jul 1813.
    Received from HM Ship Surprise. Perseverance American Cartel.

Williams, Lloyd   Prisoner 1289. Rank: Seaman, from: Mary, Merchant Schooner.
    Cap: 15 Jan 1815 Lat 22.40, Long 66 by HM Ship Pique Int: 29 Jan 1815 Dis: 14 Feb 1815.
    Received from HMS Pique. HM Ship Piqua.

Williams, Moses   Prisoner 440. Rank: Seaman, from: Blockade, Privateer.
    Cap: 31 Oct 1812 off Saba by HM Sloop Charybdis Int: 12 Feb 1813 Dis: 11 Aug 1813.
    Received from HM Brig Liberty. Malmore American Cartel.

American Prisoners of War Held at Barbados During the War of 1812

Williams, Peter   Prisoner 720. Rank: Seaman, from: Olive Branch, Merchant Brig.
    Cap: 12 Apr 1813 Lat 17.00 N, Long 59.30 W by HM Sloop Eclipse Int: 08 Jul 1813 Dis: 24 Jul 1813.
    Received from HM Sloop Eclipse. Out of Custody the Vessel being liberated.

Williams, Richard   Prisoner 684. Rank: Seaman, from: Sterling, Merchant Ship.
    Cap: 19 May 1813 Lat 22.00 N, Long 53.00 W by HM Ship Grampus Int: 26 May 1813 Dis: 11 Aug 1813. Received from HM Ship Grampus. Malmore American Cartel.

Williams, Robert   Prisoner 300. Rank: Seaman, from: Carl Frederick, Privateer.
    Cap: 11 Oct 1812 at Sea by HM Sloop Ringdove Int: 29 Dec 1812 Escaped: 24 Apr 1813.
    Received from HM Brig Liberty. Captured by the Odyssey in (not legible). Escaped.

Williams, Thomas   Prisoner 1055. Rank: Seaman, from: Mary, Letter of Marque.
    Cap: 07 Jun 1814 La Quisa by HM Ship Heron Int: 31 Jul 1814 Dis: 31 Mar 1815.
    Received from HM Sloop Mosquito. Rear Adl Durham.

Williams, William   Prisoner 461. Rank: Seaman, from: Bowrey, Privateer.
    Cap: 02 Feb 1813 off Barbados by HM Sloop Opossum Int: 18 Feb 1813 Dis: 11 Aug 1813.
    Received from HM Sloop Opossum. English Brig Captured by the Comet. Malmore American Cartel.

Williams, William   Prisoner 1162. Rank: Seaman, from: High Flyer, Letter of Marque.
    Cap: 14 Nov 1814 off Anguilla by HM Ship Barossa Int: 18 Nov 1814 Dis: 31 Mar 1815.
    Received from HM Ship Barossa. Rear Adl Durham.

Williams, William   Prisoner 1323. Rank: Seaman, from: Not Recorded, Not Recorded.
    Cap: Not Recorded by Not Recorded Int: 24 Feb 1815 Dis: 31 Mar 1815.
    Received from HMB Macos. (Not legible) on Shore. Out of Custody Rear Adl Durham. (Date of capture not recorded.)

Williamson, Peter   Prisoner 84. Rank: Seaman, from: Providence, Privateer.
    Cap: 11 Sep 1812 off St. Barthlomew by HM Sloop Dominica Int: 13 Nov 1812 Dis: 10 Jul 1813.
    Received from HM Ship Mercury. Perseverance American Cartel.

Willoughby, Charles   Prisoner 559. Rank: Seaman, from: Isabella, Merchant Brig.
    Cap: 08 Dec 1812 off Demuary by Detained by the Custom House Int: 02 Mar 1813 Dis: 11 Aug 1813. Received from Army Schooner Moushe. Malmore American Cartel.

Willoughby, Thomas   Prisoner 281. Rank: Seaman, from: Rea, Privateer.
    Cap: 29 Nov 1812 off Barbados by HM Ship Lightning Int: 29 Nov 1812 Dis: 10 Jul 1813.
    Received from HM Ship Lightning. Ship having been captured by the Bona American. Perseverance American Cartel.

Wilson, George   Prisoner 834. Rank: Seaman, from: Rattle Snake, Letter of Marque.
    Cap: 11 Mar 1814 Lat 24.07 N, Long 66.47 W by HM Ship Rhin Int: 25 Mar 1814 Dis: 25 Apr 1814.
    Received from HM Ship Rhin. HM Ship Vestal.

Wilson, Henry   Prisoner 611. Rank: Seaman, from: Thomas Penrose, Privateer.
    Cap: 23 Mar 1813 Lat 20.14 W, Long 61.20 W by HM Ship Tribune Int: 28 Mar 1813 Dis: 26 Apr 1813. Received from HM Ship Tribune. America on Parole Sir F. Laforey.

Wilson, Samuel   Prisoner 681. Rank: Seaman, from: Sterling, Merchant Ship.
    Cap: 19 May 1813 Lat 22.00 N, Long 53.00 W by HM Ship Grampus Int: 26 May 1813 Dis: 11 Aug 1813. Received from HM Ship Grampus. Malmore American Cartel.

Wilson, William   Prisoner 104. Rank: Seaman, from: Diana, Merchant Brig.
    Cap: 25 Sep 1812 at Sea by HM Sloop Spider Int: 13 Nov 1812 Dis: 02 Dec 1812.
    Received from HM Ship Mercury. Per Order Sir F. Laforey being part of crew of a Licensed Vessel.

Wilson, William   Prisoner 808. Rank: Seaman, from: Goutlan, Merchant Schooner.
    Cap: 31 Jan 1814 off Saint Bartholomew by HM Brig Barbados Int: 12 Feb 1814 Dis: 25 Apr 1814.
    Received from HM Schooner Ballahou. HM Ship Vestal.

Wilson, William   Prisoner 1374. Rank: Seaman, from: Vidett, Letter of Marque.
    Cap: 14 Feb 1815 off St Bartholomew by HMS Dasher Int: 04 Mar 1815 Dis: 31 Mar 1815.
    Received from HM Ship Dasher. Out of Custody Rear Adl Durham.

Wiltbeyer, Peter   Prisoner 594. Rank: 2 Mate, from: Thomas Penrose, Privateer.
    Cap: 23 Mar 1813 Lat 20.14 W, Long 61.20 W by HM Ship Tribune Int: 28 Mar 1813 Dis: 26 Apr 1813. Received from HM Ship Tribune. America on Parole Sir F. Laforey.

Wimblicour, David   Prisoner 396. Rank: Seaman, from: Decatur, Privateer.
    Cap: 16 Jan 1813 Lat 13.00 N, Long 41.00 N by HM Ship Surprise Int: 26 Jan 1813 Dis: 10 Jul 1813.
    Received from HM Ship Surprise. Perseverance American Cartel.

Wise, Alexis   Prisoner 589. Rank: Seaman, from: Alexis, Privateer.
    Cap: 09 Mar 1813 Not Recorded by HM Ship Lightning Int: 22 Mar 1813 Escaped: 30 Jun 1813.
    Received from HM Ship Lightning. English Retaken by Comet. Escaped. Retaken Reentry 712.

Wise, Alexis   Prisoner 712. Rank: Seaman, from: Not Recorded, Not Recorded.
    Cap: Not Recorded by Not Recorded Int: 05 Jul 1813 Dis: 11 Aug 1813.
    Received from HM Ship Grampus. Retaken former number (589). Malmore American Cartel. (Date of capture not recorded.)

American Prisoners of War Held at Barbados During the War of 1812

Woldridge, William   Prisoner 764. Rank: Seaman, from: Frolic, Privateer.
    Cap: 25 Jan 1814 off St Thomas by HM Sloop Heron Int: 06 Feb 1814 Dis: 25 Apr 1814.
    Received from HM Sloop Heron. HM Ship Vestal.

Wood, Bartholomew   Prisoner 1142. Rank: Passenger, from: High Flyer, Letter of Marque.
    Cap: 14 Nov 1814 off Anguilla by HM Ship Barossa Int: 18 Nov 1814 Dis: 21 Nov 1814.
    Received from HM Ship Barossa. Out of Custody being a noncombatant.

Wood, James   Prisoner 1348. Rank: Seaman, from: Vidett, Letter of Marque.
    Cap: 14 Feb 1815 off St Bartholomew by HMS Dasher Int: 03 Mar 1815 Dis: 31 Mar 1815.
    Received from HM Ship Dasher. Out of Custody Rear Adl Durham.

Wood, John F   Prisoner 485. Rank: Seaman, from: John, Privateer.
    Cap: 06 Feb 1813 Lat 10.0 N, Long 61.0 W by HM Sloop Peruvian Int: 20 Feb 1813 Dis: 11 Aug 1813. Received from HM Ship Cumberland. Malmore American Cartel.

Woodbury, Joseph   Prisoner 163. Rank: Seaman, from: Yankee, Privateer.
    Cap: 25 Oct 1812 off Sombero by HM Sloop Peruvian Int: 13 Nov 1812 Dis: 10 Jul 1813.
    Received from HM Ship Mercury. Perseverance American Cartel.

Woodis, Samuel   Prisoner 1167. Rank: Seaman, from: Dolphin, Letter of Marque.
    Cap: 04 Dec 1814 Lat 18.00 N, Long 60.00 W by HM Brig Columbia Int: 08 Dec 1814 Dis: 08 Feb 1815. Received from HM Brig Columbia. HM Ship Swiftsure.

Woodman, Thomas   Prisoner 1007. Rank: Seaman, from: Hawk, Privateer.
    Cap: 26 Apr 1814 Near the Mona Passage by HM Ship Piqua Int: 20 Jun 1814 Dis: 22 Jul 1814.
    Received from HM Ship Vestal. HM Ship Gloucester Rear Admiral Durham.

Woodward, Benjamin   Prisoner 858. Rank: Seaman, from: Chapman, Privateer.
    Cap: 28 Feb 1814 off St Bartholomew by Thistle Privateer Int: 26 Mar 1814 Dis: 25 Apr 1814.
    Received from HM Ship Palama. HM Ship Vestal.

Woodward, John   Prisoner 1421. Rank: Seaman, from: Avon, Privateer.
    Cap: 08 Mar 1815 off Nevis by HM Sloop Barbados Int: 13 Mar 1815 Dis: 15 Mar 1815.
    Received from HM Sloop Barbados. HMS Numen Rear Admiral Durham.

Wooldridge, Benjamin   Prisoner 520. Rank: Seaman, from: John, Privateer.
    Cap: 06 Feb 1813 Lat 10.0 N, Long 61.0 W by HM Sloop Peruvian Int: 20 Feb 1813 Dis: 11 Aug 1813. Received from HM Ship Cumberland. Malmore American Cartel.

Wooldridge, Robert   Prisoner 519. Rank: Seaman, from: John, Privateer.
    Cap: 06 Feb 1813 Lat 10.0 N, Long 61.0 W by HM Sloop Peruvian Int: 20 Feb 1813 Dis: 11 Aug 1813. Received from HM Ship Cumberland. Malmore American Cartel.

Woolford, Henry   Prisoner 46. Rank: Seaman, from: Tigre, Merchant Sloop.
    Cap: 09 Oct 1812 off St. Barthlomew by HM Ship Mercury Int: 13 Nov 1812 Dis: 02 Dec 1813.
    Received from HM Ship Mercury. Per Order Sir F. Laforey being part of crew of a Licensed Vessel.

Wormsley, Joseph   Prisoner 677. Rank: Seaman, from: Sterling, Merchant Ship.
    Cap: 19 May 1813 Lat 22.00 N, Long 53.00 W by HM Ship Grampus Int: 26 May 1813 Dis: 11 Aug 1813. Received from HM Ship Grampus. Malmore American Cartel.

Wright, Jonathan   Prisoner 227. Rank: Seaman, from: Blockade, Privateer.
    Cap: 31 Oct 1812 off Saba by HM Sloop Charybdis Int: 19 Nov 1812 Dis: 10 Jul 1813.
    Received from HM Sloop Charybdis. Perseverance American Cartel.

Wyatt, Daniel   Prisoner 56. Rank: Seaman, from: Providence, Privateer.
    Cap: 11 Sep 1812 off St. Barthlomew by HM Sloop Dominica Int: 13 Nov 1812 Dis: 10 Jul 1813.
    Received from HM Ship Mercury. Perseverance American Cartel.

Wyatt, William   Prisoner 413. Rank: Seaman, from: Apollo, Merchant Ship.
    Cap: 22 Dec 1812 off Tenioff by HM Ship Grampus Int: 30 Jan 1813 Dis: 10 Jul 1813.
    Received from HM Sloop Demerary. Perseverance American Cartel.

Wyncook, Ebenezer   Prisoner 148. Rank: Seaman, from: Yankee, Privateer.
    Cap: 25 Oct 1812 off Sombero by HM Sloop Peruvian Int: 13 Nov 1812 Dis: 10 Jul 1813.
    Received from HM Ship Mercury. Perseverance American Cartel.

Wynn, John   Prisoner 811. Rank: Seaman, from: HM Sloop Amaranthe, Not Recorded.
    Cap: Not Recorded by Not Recorded Int: 12 Feb 1814 Dis: 25 Apr 1814.
    Received from HM Schooner Ballahou. Part of the Crew of HM Sloop Amaranthe. HM Ship Vestal.
    (Date of capture not recorded.)

Yates, George   Prisoner 1382. Rank: Supercargo, from: Vidett, Letter of Marque.
    Cap: 14 Feb 1815 off St Bartholomew by HMS Dasher Int: 05 Mar 1815 Dis: 31 Mar 1815.
    Received from HM Ship Dasher. Out of Custody Rear Adl Durham.

Yeaton, Moses   Prisoner 1042. Rank: Seaman, from: Mary, Letter of Marque.
    Cap: 07 Jun 1814 La Quisa by HM Ship Heron Int: 31 Jul 1814 Escaped: 12 Sep 1814.
    Received from HM Sloop Mosquito. Escaped.

American Prisoners of War Held at Barbados During the War of 1812

Young, Benjamin   Prisoner 410. Rank: Seaman, from: Apollo, Merchant Ship.
    Cap: 22 Dec 1812 off Tenioff by HM Ship Grampus Int: 30 Jan 1813 Dis: 10 Jul 1813.
    Received from HM Sloop Demerary. Perseverance American Cartel.

Young, Samuel   Prisoner 1204. Rank: Seaman, from: Fox, Privateer.
    Cap: 26 Dec 1814 off St Bartholomew by HM Brig Barbados Int: 14 Jan 1815 Dis: 08 Feb 1815.
    Received from HM Brig Barbados. HM Ship Swiftsure.

American Prisoners of War Held at Barbados During the War of 1812

Numeric listing by prison number

1	Denison, Charles W	69	Hutchings, William
2	Treby, George	70	Little, William
3	Hussey, Samuel S	71	Mitchmore, John
4	Caswell, John R	72	Phippin, William
5	Haulbut, Nathanial	73	Bakagen, John
6	Hopkins, Nicholas	74	Burrell, Charles
7	King, Samuel W	75	Walsh, William
8	Bagman, Jacob	76	Bailoci, Thomas
9	Weeks, Rubin	77	Fenner, Charles
10	Paddock, Aaron	78	Sweet, Daniel H
11	Lefort, John	79	Jacobs, John
12	Deming, Henry	80	Cushing, Chance
13	Benner, Thomas	81	Parker, Thomas
14	Holden, Horace	82	Eainis, Ebenezer
15	Brown, Robert	83	Walker, George
16	Bogs, James	84	Williamson, Peter
17	Combs, William	85	Howard, Hyman
18	Joy, Robert M	86	Gardner, Willet C
19	Gordon, Sherwood H	87	Shusch, Adam
20	Bunker, Nathaniel	88	Bowdwish, John
21	Rawson, Charles	89	Marshall, Ellet
22	Forster, John	90	Price, Constant W
23	Johnson, John	91	Saunders, Davis
24	Primus, Samuel	92	Peterson, Peter
25	Washington, George	93	Brown, Ezekiah
26	Thompson, Robert	94	Myers, Charles
27	Bond, Oliver C	95	de la Statius, Levein
28	Coffin, Benjamin	96	Crowder, John
29	Simon, James	97	Eden, John
30	Smith, George	98	Pope, Abraham
31	Richardson, James	99	Sturges, Bradley
32	McFoy, Daniel	100	Farebrook, George
33	Arnold, Isaac	101	Picken, John
34	Raco, Julias	102	Curtis, John
35	Wheaton, Nathaniel	103	Roberts, William
36	Bevin, Thomas	104	Wilson, William
37	Gill, James	105	Condon, Joseph
38	Meadows, George	106	Butler, George
39	Pairse, John	107	Fielding, William
40	Greenwood, Maurice	108	Mackey, John
41	Bevin, John	109	Stewart, John
42	Meyer, John	110	Roper, William
43	Kent, Jacob Henry	111	Ross, Thomas
44	James, William	112	Babcock, William
45	Rowland, ---	113	Cole, Thomas
46	Woolford, Henry	114	Leaburn, Thomas
47	Hayford, Gardner	115	Cole, Stephen
48	Hawthorn, Stephen	116	Edwards, Thomas
49	Prior, Christopher	117	Craig, Alexander
50	Fisher, Lewis P	118	Parsons, Charles
51	Manson, Stephen	119	Green, James
52	Westcott, Samuel	120	Pique, Ville
53	Gibb, Thomas	121	Swather, Jacob
54	Wenwood, Godfrey	122	Egart, Jacob
55	Alleyn, John	123	Davis, John
56	Wyatt, Daniel	124	Wharff, John
57	Martin, William	125	Hansford, Stephen
58	James, Simon	126	Lawton, Thomas
59	Bruce, Jeremiah	127	Mason, May D
60	Harby, Levy	128	Biddle, John
61	McDaniel, John	129	Smith, William
62	Scan, Thomas	130	Martin, Silvenis P
63	Benson, William B	131	Richmond, Milton
64	Smith, Holsey	132	Barnard, Adonijah
65	Sanders, George	133	Robinson, John
66	Freeman, Joseph S	134	Cook, Benjamin
67	Crofton, Henry	135	Rogers, Robert
68	Martin, Isaac	136	Robins, William

American Prisoners of War Held at Barbados During the War of 1812

137	Clark, John	208	Moore, Robert
138	Kimball, Ezekiah	209	McDuff, Daniel
139	Wheeler, David	210	Beven, Lelah
140	Bartlett, Gibbon	211	Bigelow, Thomas C
141	Parker, Henry	212	Wells, Henry Knox
142	Batchelder, Jeremiah	213	Eldridge, Henry
143	Jones, Richard	214	Butler, Levi
144	Kimball, John	215	Hassard, Jason
145	Farnham, John	216	Hunt, Walter R
146	Adams, Theophilus B	217	Mansfield, Thomas
147	Kenniston, Daniel	218	Kingsberry, Sandford
148	Wyncook, Ebenezer	219	Sawyer, John A
149	Foot, Thomas	220	Belding, James
150	Francis, John	221	Higgins, William H
151	Maulton, Joseph	222	Monger, Bella
152	Flanders, Daniel	223	Bliss, Moses
153	Jacobs, Henry	224	Kelly, John
154	Coale, James	225	Plumb, Truman
155	Ives, William	226	Hosmer, George
156	Lukies, Thomas M	227	Wright, Jonathan
157	Stephenson, Stephen	228	Murray, Richard
158	Richards, James	229	McDuff, Phillp S
159	Maulton, Nathaniel	230	Griswald, Jerard
160	Copps, Darius	231	Palmer, Isaac
161	Evans, John	232	Merill, Charles
162	Wheeler, Job E	233	Cook, Aaron
163	Woodbury, Joseph	234	Deming, Maning
164	Jackson, Caleb	235	Clarke, James
165	Melbourne, William	236	Wells, Oliver
166	Ward, James	237	Griswald, Truman
167	Wheelock, Nahor	238	Flint, William
168	Patch, Joseph	239	West, Henry
169	Richards, Rehobaham	240	Pilsbury, Timothy
170	Perry, Onan	241	Sherry, Jonathan
171	Simmons, Thomas	242	Sweatt, John P
172	Noyes, Jeremiah	243	Julius, John
173	Lang, William	244	Kentfield, Eliza
174	McCeaver, Peter	245	Perkins, Michael
175	Houstaon, John	246	Deming, Isaac
176	Lowder, Samuel	247	Hardy, James
177	Thompson, William	248	Bowen, John
178	Luther, Alexander	249	Cegg, Phillip
179	Mie, Elisha	250	Davis, John
180	Dodd, Edward	251	Johnson, John
181	Fuller, Benjamin	252	Devins, Charles
182	Griswald, Josiah	253	Cleveland, David
183	Cooley, William	254	Gyles, William
184	Butler, Daniel	255	Tafft, Nathan
185	Olmstead, Jesse	256	Greene, Samuel
186	Belding, Clifford	257	James, Paul
187	Franklin, Moses	258	Bennett, Peter
188	Tract, Horace	259	Dugan, Able S
189	Edwards, Timothy R	260	Bouldin, Nathan L
190	Beadle, Maning	261	Maffet, John
191	Hushall, Stephen	262	McGill, James
192	Watson, Robert	263	Horace, Kemble
193	Sabine, John	264	Rea, Benjamin
194	Roberts, Orias	265	Mennedy, Bennet
195	Grimes, Richard	266	Fenderson, Nathaniel
196	Pardy, Daniel	267	Shearman, Peleg
197	Barne, Donny	268	Herbert, Peter
198	Stout, Thomas	269	Pate, James
199	Clark, George	270	Carroll, James
200	Remble, Henry	271	Harris, William
201	Hine, Henry	272	Pope, Edward
202	Delling, Lewis	273	Brown, William
203	Chaviens, Sidney	274	Hickey, William
204	Day, Grove	275	Reardon, Daniel
205	Holden, Arnold	276	Penyan, Antoine
206	Larcom, Robert	277	Williams, John
207	Wells, Horace	278	Kirby, Benjamin

American Prisoners of War Held at Barbados During the War of 1812

279	Poulson, Perry	350	Thompson, William
280	Godard, William	351	Fletcher, Samuel
281	Willoughby, Thomas	352	Simpson, Joseph
282	Jordon, Ralph	353	Spinney, Nathaniel
283	---, Philadelphia	354	Brian, Richard
284	Fortney, William	355	Ingless, John
285	Shichlar, Henry	356	Morrell, Richard
286	Anderson, Hugh	357	Mabread, Thomas
287	Hutchinson, Joseph	358	Salisbury, Samuel
288	Nay, John R	359	Hamilton, Benjamin
289	Fields, William	360	Knight, Solomon
290	White, George	361	Glover, Samuel
291	Sylva, Manuel	362	Henion, John
292	Mason, Simon	363	Cole, James
293	Patterson, David	364	Allman, Samuel
294	Hill, Daniel	365	Jarvis, Francis
295	Hawkins, Henry	366	Roderick, Frank
296	Smith, John	367	Fernado, Manuel
297	Reed, John	368	Stacey, John
298	Bayley, Joshua K	369	Lain, Samuel
299	Plumb, Truman	370	Flood, William
300	Williams, Robert	371	Coon, Caesar
301	Smith, George	372	Freeman, Peter
302	Merrit, Silvanus	373	Goodman, John
303	Murray, William	374	Foster, James
304	James, John	375	Gunney, Thomas
305	Rogers, Henry	376	Brockings, Samuel
306	Myers, Henry	377	Florintino, Andre
307	Phillips, John	378	Picket, John
308	Class, Peter	379	Goss, John
309	Cain, James	380	Plummer, Ebenezer
310	Lumtich, Laurance	381	Whitmore, Joseph
311	Allen, Richard	382	Buriman, Herman
312	Tabor, Isaac	383	Lloyd, John
313	Hussy, Abraham	384	Brown, Jesse
314	Jones, William	385	Corinth, Henry
315	Sheldon, Nathanial	386	Housan, Thomas
316	Johnson, Kelly	387	Mullin, John
317	Carter, John	388	Miller, Peter
318	English, John	389	Gerris, Jeremiah
319	Read, Richard	390	Rogers, Henry
320	Smith, Jacob	391	Pettingale, William
321	Webb, Thomas	392	Thomas, George
322	Thesen, Christopher	393	Seapan, Donny
323	Hamilton, Charles	394	Hodetron, John
324	Shanklen, Charles	395	Kimball, John W
325	Saunders, William	396	Wimblicour, David
326	Lynn, Herman	397	Ward, Samuel
327	Marshall, Phillip	398	Ramsden, Philip
328	Miller, Isaac	399	Hilton, Samuel
329	Tucker, William	400	Osborne, Ambrose
330	Snow, John	401	White, Oliver
331	Nichols, William	402	Stanley, Ralph
332	Swasey, Nathaniel	403	Bowden, Samuel
333	Bray, Isaac	404	Francis, Richard
334	Richards, Josiah	405	Doane, Henry
335	Giddings, Joseph	406	Clark, Benjamin
336	de Leon, Daniel	407	Williams, John
337	Brown, John	408	Place, John
338	Delile, Francis	409	Henry, David
339	Grush, Thomas	410	Young, Benjamin
340	Miller, Nicholas	411	Lewis, Daniel
341	Stephens, John	412	Cousins, John
342	Bickford, Paul	413	Wyatt, William
343	Coffin, Able	414	Butcher, Benjamin
344	Cushion, Nathaniel	415	Robins, James
345	Goodrich, Edward	416	Anderson, Jacob
346	Wadley, Benjamin D	417	Lewis, John
347	Jervett, Richard	418	Hall, Samuel
348	Pike, Jeremiah	419	Peters, John
349	Pulsifer, Ebenezer	420	Shields, Francis D

American Prisoners of War Held at Barbados During the War of 1812

421	Parker, John	492	Cruff, Tobias
422	Douglass, George	493	Millet, Joseph
423	Smith, Robert B	494	Griffen, Ebenezer
424	Henry, William	495	Doliver, William
425	Symonds, John	496	Baptist, John
426	Ross, Timothy	497	Hulon, Henry
427	Clinton, Ebenezer	498	Gale, Benjamin
428	Fort, Benjamin	499	Stone, Samuel
429	Rogers, Daniel	500	Humphreys, William
430	Fuller, Andrew	501	Sage, William
431	Howland, Robert	502	Ross, David
432	Summersville, George	503	Paine, Francis
433	Read, Richard	504	Caswell, Richard B
434	Smith, Jacob	505	Eldridge, Edmund
435	Webb, Thomas	506	Knight, John
436	Shanklin, Charles	507	Noah, Nathaniel
437	Michell, Phillip	508	Hobbeston, Thomas A
438	Prince, Prince	509	Lane, James
439	Norris, Samuel	510	Pierce, John
440	Williams, Moses	511	Vickey, William
441	Jackson, Harden	512	Brown, William
442	Purrington, Humphrey	513	Quinar, Benjamin
443	Page, George	514	Moore, Dennis
444	Estes, John	515	Humphreys, Edward
445	Doughty, Jacob	516	Baptist, John
446	Ross, Barney	517	Roundy, Stephen C
447	Taylor, Edward	518	Anderson, James
448	Loper, Lyon	519	Wooldridge, Robert
449	Elliott, Nathaniel	520	Wooldridge, Benjamin
450	Freeman, Pline	521	Brumbloom, Merit
451	Hewet, Robert	522	Harris, William
452	Marwich, Atwood	523	Bassett, Nathaniel
453	Le Foque, Gabriel	524	Southwick, George
454	Cathell, William	525	Stone, Samuel
455	Hossnogle, John	526	Pattee, John
456	Craps, James	527	Chapman, John
457	Baynard, Henry	528	McCarthy, James
458	Dipplac, Domike	529	Pease, James
459	Sheffield, Acors	530	Palfrey, Jonathan
460	Ausourd, John C	531	Ramsdall, Nathaniel
461	Williams, William	532	Wagner, John
462	Keyser, John	533	Hackleton, John
463	Labolt, Adam	534	Glover, John
464	Cheve, Daniel	535	Perry, John
465	Tusant, John	536	Francis, Oliver William
466	Brigam, Charles	537	Cliff, Thomas
467	Moody, David	538	Quinar, Stephen
468	Mason, Joseph J	539	Averell, Samuel
469	Babbit, Erasmus	540	Mason, James
470	Brown, John	541	Snow, John P
471	Bogman, James	542	Call, Henry P
472	Carnes, William	543	Grush, Thomas
473	Bacomon, Joseph	544	Doliver, William
474	Dean, W C	545	Dennis, James
475	Chase, Benjamin	546	Gribble, James
476	Clough, Samuel	547	Adams, William
477	Short, James	548	Blair, Robert
478	Hulen, Abraham	549	Clinton, Ebenezer
479	Chapman, Stephen	550	Flood, William
480	Buridge, Robert	551	Disney, George
481	Hawkins, Samuel	552	Freeman, Samuel
482	Holden, John	553	Blair, Hosea
483	Fisher, John	554	Latimore, Samuel
484	Hacker, Isaac	555	Morgan, Richard
485	Wood, John F	556	Robins, Joshua
486	Burgess, Francis	557	Hurbert, James
487	Hunt, Job	558	Blair, Harvey
488	Craft, Thomas	559	Willoughby, Charles
489	Brooks, Edward	560	Jeffery, Thomas
490	Dutch, Edward	561	Hercules, David
491	Burke, John C	562	Larkin, Lewis

American Prisoners of War Held at Barbados During the War of 1812

563	Tolly, George F	634	Cottle, John
564	Gardiner, Samuel	635	Thomas, John
565	Miller, Peter	636	Lewis, John
566	Fairfield, James M	637	Prince, Silvesta
567	Weacom, Ebenezer	638	Babut, Peter
568	Lemon, Niel C	639	Premiers, Joseph
569	Cleaves, Nathaniel	640	Lockwood, William
570	Gevine, William	641	Richardson, Edward
571	Cohoon, Isaiah	642	Latimore, Titus
572	Spelsbury, Amos	643	Foot, James
573	Kemble, Nathaniel	644	Ross, William
574	Turner, Samuel	645	Tract, Horace
575	Nye, Stephen	646	Benson, William B
576	Sherbourne, John	647	Ennick, William
577	Springer, Mark	648	Green, William
578	Steward, John	649	---, Antonio
579	Horner, James	650	Clarke, William
580	Garry, Alexander	651	Bartlett, William
581	Tompkins, Stockton	652	Plant, Samuel
582	Bird, Robert	653	Hooters, John
583	Horton, Henry	654	Davis, William
584	Hall, William	655	March, William
585	Labbi, Constant	656	Weir, Robert
586	Tool, Elijah	657	Green, John
587	Lookey, Joseph	658	Ouveire, Joseph
588	Roche, Andrew	659	Sands, John C
589	Wise, Alexis	660	Maria, Joseph
590	Ansley, John	661	Butheir, William
591	Dutilth, John A	662	Fetch, Elias
592	Moutrie, Henry W	663	Holbrook, Gideon
593	Burrows, William	664	Harlow, Lewis
594	Wiltbeyer, Peter	665	Bisbee, John
595	Peas, Joseph	666	Warren, David
596	Steel, Charles	667	Sturtevant, Caleb
597	Uluck, Thomas	668	Bisbee, Elijah
598	Garner, William	669	Keen, Tilden
599	Burton, William	670	Murrell, William
600	Shallus, William	671	Swain, Jonathan
601	Brown, James	672	Kelley, Joseph
602	Jones, William	673	Swain, Rubin
603	Fillerson, Thomas	674	Chadwick, Seth
604	Thomas, David	675	Smith, William
605	Bartlin, Thomas	676	Jackson, Frederick
606	Jackson, James	677	Wormsley, Joseph
607	Justice, John	678	Cook, John
608	Galley, Henry	679	Weaver, Benjamin
609	Lane, John	680	Laurence, Elisha
610	Andrew, Peter	681	Wilson, Samuel
611	Wilson, Henry	682	Coulfrey, Robert
612	Debot, Henry	683	Lipid, Caesar
613	Buck, Edward	684	Williams, Richard
614	Waters, Frank	685	Talbot, James
615	Knowls, Morton	686	Chanders, Dublin
616	Cinnan, Joseph	687	Fuller, Benjamin
617	Duncan, Charles	688	Griswald, Josiah
618	Sanderson, Daniel	689	Roberts, Orias
619	Ware, John	690	Lemon, Niel C
620	Clarke, Thomas	691	Mason, Joseph J
621	Lumsden, Stephen	692	Fullerton, Thomas
622	Milton, Thomas	693	Farris, James
623	Ballen, Elle	694	Tuckett, George
624	Jeppets, Benjamin	695	Platt, George
625	Landon, George	696	Boyle, George
626	Pemperton, Samuel	697	Blardile, Jacob
627	Lewis, John	698	Warden, Charles
628	Foxtrum, Samuel	699	Lines, William
629	Weld, Benjamin	700	Walters, John
630	Kelly, Jarret	701	Ranson, William John
631	Lee, Washington	702	Sherry, Joseph
632	Lewis, William	703	Hotchess, John
633	Morris, Peter	704	Hawse, Hance Thomas

American Prisoners of War Held at Barbados During the War of 1812

705	Coburne, Miles		776	Jones, John
706	Taylor, James		777	Duncan, William
707	Ramsey, David C		778	Helah, Timothy
708	Jackson, Gowan		779	Hall, John
709	Cowslip, Charles		780	Fortune, Thomas
710	Plant, Samuel		781	Fuller, William
711	Denny, John		782	Butler, Andrew
712	Wise, Alexis		783	James, John
713	Cartwright, Samuel		784	Foy, Daniel
714	Fenhorn, Morris		785	Smith, George
715	McCall, James		786	Page, Cato
716	Lathrop, Acahel		787	Headings, Isaac
717	Stocking, Seth		788	Davis, Joseph
718	Bates, Oran		789	Davis, John
719	Treat, Lathrop		790	Brown, John
720	Williams, Peter		791	Mann, Samuel
721	Macomber, Anson		792	Lange, James
722	Randlet, John M		793	Edwards, Jean
723	Reamonsptras, ---		794	Bell, Jacob
724	May, William		785	Parker, Charles
725	Griffen, William		796	Gildchrist, Simon
726	Lincon, Nathaniel		797	Boudy, William
727	Perry, Ebenezer		798	Fletcher, Benjamin
728	Harrison, John		799	Daniels, Nathaniel
729	Bailey, Ransfor		800	Whymn, Theodore
730	Burns, Peter		801	Harris, Benjamin
731	Burk, Henry		802	Wescott, Edward
732	Ames, Sears		803	Savage, P H
733	Green, Rathbourn		804	Mister, William
734	Watkins, Asa		805	Bailey, Thomas
735	Godfrey, John		806	Ashton, William
736	Stacey, Benjamin		807	Long, William
737	Odiorne, John		808	Wilson, William
738	Swain, Thomas		809	West, John
739	Brown, Joseph		810	Duncan, Jesse
740	Stevens, Thomas		811	Wynn, John
741	Berg, Daniel		812	Simons, Ebenezer
742	Simmons, Mark		813	Dennis, William
743	Perkins, Jonathan		814	Harris, James
744	Brown, Benjamin		815	Hastings, John
745	Jackson, George		816	Simmons, Joseph
746	Holden, Charles		817	Pelot, Samuel G
747	Richardson, Addison		818	Fitzgerald, John
748	Clemons, Samuuel		819	Johnson, James
749	Leach, George		820	Glover, Benjamin
750	Southwick, George		821	Jackson, George
751	Pousland, Edward		822	Ballentine, Samuel
752	Petengill, James		823	Collins, Stephen
753	Stone, Benjamin		824	Gardner, Francis
754	Newberry, John		825	Bangs, William
755	Johnson, Thomas		826	Pass, Benjamin
756	Buchannon, Robert		827	Myer, William F
757	Smith, Charles		828	Rice, M
758	Claxton, Robert		829	Adams, ---
759	Tarr, John		830	Halbrut, Henry
760	Shott, John		831	Silsbee, John
761	Andrews, Nathaniel		832	Cricall, South
762	Wells, Nathan		833	Burt, William
763	Murray, John		834	Wilson, George
764	Woldridge, William		835	Wilford, Charles
765	Harthorn, John		836	Looke, Jacob
766	Grey, Francis		837	Jerrett, Jasper
767	Madison, Alexander		838	Buckall, William
768	Backman, John		839	Groves, Thomas
769	Joseph, Nathaniel		840	Goss, John
770	Bangs, William		841	Grall, Charles
771	Joshua, John		842	Robinson, Lemry
772	Jackman, David		843	Fordick, Joseph
773	Patman, Samuel		844	Brown, Thomas
774	Simons, Richard		845	Thomas, John
775	Hughes, Thomas		846	Arnold, James

American Prisoners of War Held at Barbados During the War of 1812

No.	Name	No.	Name
847	Snow, Colier	917	Greer, John
848	Littlefield, Samuel	918	Rosenthon, John
849	Evarell, Samuel	919	Hidalgo, Balace
850	Steel, Thomas	920	Board, John P
851	Brush, Samuel	921	Johannes, Joseph
852	Robertson, Thomas	922	Hackett, John
853	Glading, Joseph	923	Melbourne, William
854	Ruling, Arnold	924	Harman, John
855	Ellis, Cornelius	925	George, John
856	Gair, Thomas	926	Davis, George
857	Hunter, John	927	Taylor, Samuel
858	Woodward, Benjamin	928	Fogg, John
859	Read, Charles	929	Smith, Jonathan W
860	Stone, Samuel	930	Knabbs, James
861	Hunter, Alexander	931	Stephens, William
862	Masters, Coons	932	Davis, John
863	Allan, Elisha	933	Barrett, Tobias
864	Chapman, James	934	Williams, Charles
865	Strague, Stephen	935	Waterman, Cato
866	Strague, John	936	Maria, John
867	Noble, D	937	Lorang, Monroe
868	Cook, Aaron	938	Sessions, Pedro
869	Backman, John	939	Fry, A Julius
870	Barron, John	940	Johnson, John
871	Ross, William	941	Adians, Jose
872	Lester, James	942	Ebein, Joseph
873	Dale, John	943	Joseph, Pedro
874	Rogers, Luke	944	Mendoza, Nicholas
875	Linch, William	945	Jones, Thomas
876	Nichols, William	946	Faleon, Jose B
877	Oakam, Archibald	947	Hidalgo, Vincent
878	Connor, Galen	948	Acomplado, August
879	Smart, Samuel	949	Acker, Jose
880	Jackson, James	950	Laes, Domingo
881	Knoulton, Asahal Joseph	951	De la Ench Parker, Jose
		952	Azunes, Jerune
882	Tripe, William H	953	Compeche, S Yaga
883	Anderson, John	954	Patens, Vincent
884	Ellwell, Samuel	955	Roberts, John
885	Antonio, John	956	De la Lantos Lepos, Jose
886	Ringrose, William		
887	Grace, John	957	Leman, Ambrose
888	Gilbert, Timothy	958	Albenans, Jose
889	Wilkins, William	959	Albery, Martine
890	Smith, John	960	Lacerf, Henry
891	Savage, Robert	961	Whippel, John
892	Lovely, Pasley	962	Montgomery, W P
893	Carter, John	963	Flinn, John F
894	Dame, John	964	Walker, James Scott
895	Warner, Benjamin	965	Craiss, John E
896	Marshall, Leway	966	Chapman, James
897	Coleman, William	967	Strague, Stephen
898	Bolding, Garrat	968	Strague, John
899	Bryant, Lewis	969	Noble, D
900	Taylor, John	970	Barron, John
901	Dodd, Joseph	971	Ross, William
902	Tooley, William	972	Lester, James
903	Oscott, Stephen	973	Dale, John
904	Blish, Samuel	974	Rodgers, Luke
905	Griest, William	975	Lynch, William
906	Brook, David	976	Nicholls, William
907	Paul, Daniel	977	Oakum, Archibald
908	William, George	978	Smart, Samuel
909	Jarvis, Isaac	979	Jackson, James
910	King, Joseph	980	Simons, Ebenezer
911	Percival, John	981	Backman, John
912	Jennings, John	982	Handcock, James
913	Jones, John	983	Bradie, Thomas
914	Adams, William	984	Peterson, Jacob
915	Mathey, James	985	Copper, William
916	Britade, E F	986	Berry, Owen

American Prisoners of War Held at Barbados During the War of 1812

987	Shelah, Timothy		1057	Hordoffer, John
988	Buckley, William		1058	Cameron, Archibald
989	Jordon, Simon		1059	Tarpish, Davis
990	Holmes, George		1060	Ellis, Joseph
991	Eldon, James S		1061	Jerome, John
992	Eblin, Aaron		1062	Mooring, Thomas
993	John, Davis		1063	Rickman, Richard
994	Bell, Zachariah		1064	Effords, John
995	Whitehead, Rubin		1065	Rice, Samuel
996	Stole, John R		1066	Larabee, Samuel
997	Caruthers, John		1067	Hathaway, William
998	Corwin, Thomas		1068	Briggs, William
999	Waterford, John H		1069	Reginald, Henry
1000	Parron, Henry		1070	Andrews, Amos
1001	Catlage, William		1071	Calder, William
1002	Frankland, William H		1072	Huntington, E
1003	Weanray, R		1073	Clossmann, P
1004	Harrison, Silus		1074	Dods, George
1005	Osborne, John		1075	Mincer, Joseph
1006	McQueen, Caleb		1076	Potter, James
1007	Woodman, Thomas		1077	Jackson, John
1008	Days, Thomas		1078	Baker, Daniel
1009	Jones, Paul		1079	West, Stephen
1010	Lorant, John		1080	Endley, James
1011	Johnstone, William		1081	Pendal, James
1012	Higgins, Freeman		1082	Rogers, Smith
1013	Clallow, William		1083	Harvey, Samuel
1014	Jones, David		1084	McDonald, John
1015	Stanley, Samuel		1085	Andrews, L
1016	Smith, William		1086	Cunie, Horace
1017	Lewis, Thomas		1087	Donald, Joseph
1018	Reid, Thomas		1088	Dickson, Henry
1019	Ray, William		1089	Johnson, George
1020	Berry, Owen		1090	Howes, Samuel
1021	Newell, Samuel Swift		1091	Davis, Wyatt B
1022	Dodd, Joseph		1092	Brodie, John
1023	Blish, Samuel		1093	Butman, Thomas
1024	Micons, John		1094	Robinson, William
1025	Card, James		1095	Brown, Robert
1026	Grove, George W		1096	Jones, John
1027	Hatchet, John		1097	Freeman, Philemon
1028	Bartridge, Henry		1098	Johnson, Frederick
1029	Johnson, Luke		1099	Pornette, Justin
1030	Adams, James		1100	Lyons, William
1031	Evans, Edward		1101	Kirby, Abel
1032	Newell, Charles		1102	Harvey, John
1033	Oscott, Stephen		1103	Douglass, James
1034	Frankland, William H		1104	Simpson, Daniel
1034	Reginald, Henry		1105	Newell, Samuel S
1035	Frankland, William H		1106	Stackney, Peter F
1036	Ross, William		1107	Lavis, Lewis
1037	Montgomery, W P		1108	Guanough, William
1038	Murray, James		1109	Watson, Thomas
1039	Backman, John		1110	Boggs, Francis
1040	Ray, William		1111	Hale, Christopher
1041	Hine, Isaiah		1112	Lahy, George
1042	Yeaton, Moses		1113	Roe, James
1043	States, Leonard F		1114	Davis, Francis
1044	Wilkinson, David		1115	Burk, Thomas
1045	Carpenter, William		1116	Robinson, James
1046	Seybest, George		1117	Smith, John
1047	Thompson, John		1118	Hanton, William
1048	Clarke, David		1119	Tribe, Morrell
1049	Guisar, Nicholas		1120	Thompson, Allen
1050	Sinnett, Thomas		1121	Hopkins, Richard L D
1051	Tateham, Daniel		1122	Frasier, John
1052	Cullin, Thomas		1123	Simmonds, Andrew
1053	Compstock, Stephen		1124	Furdge, Henry
1054	Coomais, Henry		1125	Dau, George
1055	Williams, Thomas		1126	Lee, Abraham
1056	Every, William		1127	Smith, John

American Prisoners of War Held at Barbados During the War of 1812

1128	Randall, Nathaniel	1199	Kinwright, John
1129	Brewer, Nathaniel	1200	Sergeant, William
1130	Hayward, Abraham	1201	Carli, William
1131	Baptist, Joseph S	1202	Williams, Henry
1132	Smith, Peter	1203	Post, Nelson
1133	Crowell, Prentiss	1204	Young, Samuel
1134	Webb, Purnel	1205	Croaker, Edward
1135	Smith, John	1206	Thompson, John
1136	Foster, Major	1207	Adams, John B
1137	Austin, Purnel	1208	Henry, John B
1138	Coleman, Christopher	1209	Fouche, Jean
1139	McHam, Daniel	1210	Paulin, Louis
1140	Blagze, John	1211	Edgar, Thomas
1141	Stephanus, Michael	1212	Clerge, Nicholas
1142	Wood, Bartholomew	1213	Hosse, Fourier
1143	Stow, Thomas	1214	Germon, Pierre
1144	Weld, Thomas	1215	Maxan, Darville
1145	Jouanin, John B	1216	Baptiste, Jean
1146	Brook, John E	1217	Farra, Vincent
1147	Connor, Peter	1218	Little, John
1148	Keasoner, Samuel	1219	Green, John
1149	Hallcock, Edward	1220	Pierre, John
1150	Kelley, James	1221	---, Celesbin
1151	Scargle, William	1222	Chabeau, Point
1152	Burns, John	1223	---, Fanhassie
1153	Williams, George	1224	Smith, John
1154	Downes, John	1225	Oackum, John
1155	Mathews, Edward	1226	Jerratt, Abraham
1156	Swain, Michael	1227	Carny, John
1157	Gregory, Cornelius	1228	Weiden, Daniel
1158	McCastin, James	1229	Sheldon, Charles J
1159	Bateman, Xenus	1230	Heislop, Matthew
1160	Shankley, Charles	1231	Hausford, Stephen
1161	Starks, Sands	1232	Brown, Benjamin
1162	Williams, William	1233	Boy, Jolly
1163	Grey, William	1234	Albantio, Augustin
1164	Hodgskins, Phillip	1235	La Crouse, Jean
1165	Johnson, Abel	1236	---, Alfonso
1166	Titcomb, John H	1237	De Loze, Jean
1167	Woodis, Samuel	1238	Vielo, Jean
1168	Todd, William	1239	De Forer, Victor
1169	Walton, John	1240	Savinia, Louis
1170	Titcomb, William	1241	---, Blondell
1171	Boddety, John	1242	Le Hoy, Jean B
1172	Randelett, Thomas M	1243	Dufroint, Julien
1173	Barbados, Joseph	1244	Hermines, Hoasa
1174	Coffin, Robert S	1245	---, Forsette
1175	Aldoe, William	1246	Alexander, Phillippe
1176	Hedrick, Samuel	1247	Boyd, James
1177	Bissell, Charles	1248	Banchi, Louis
1178	Bixby, James	1249	Lepierre, Francis
1179	Hester, Stephen	1250	McLean, Ferdin
1180	Bissit, John	1251	Mapano, Pedro
1181	Johnson, Joseph	1252	---, Cassimine
1182	Brown, James	1253	Blanchard, Louis
1183	Anderson, George	1254	Gravier, Gubviel
1184	Rupley, Luther	1255	Le Compte, Phillippe
1185	Brown, John	1256	Hazler, Henry
1186	Rutledge, James	1257	---, Alias
1187	Hoyt, Hapthtum	1258	Baker, Joseph
1188	Jenkins, Walter	1259	Gilbert, John
1189	Souder, Concordi	1260	Regair, Morgan
1190	Bonne, Jean Jack	1261	Crawford, John
1191	Hoyt, Charles	1262	Weeks, William
1192	Leany, Pierre L	1263	Cave, Matthew
1193	Hicks, John C	1264	Sinnett, Thomas
1194	De Brais, Henry	1265	Effords, John
1195	Dufrus, Simon	1266	Potter, James
1196	Harvey, Francis	1267	Donald, Joseph
1197	Mapaba, Pierre	1268	Brown, Robert
1198	Durive, Antoun	1269	Kirby, Able

American Prisoners of War Held at Barbados During the War of 1812

1270	Scargle, William	1341	Reid, Robert
1271	Davis, Wyatt B	1342	Walstrome, Samuel
1272	Blake, Daniel	1343	Parker, William
1273	Long, Joseph	1344	Dempson, John
1274	Briggs, William	1345	Smith, Daniel
1275	Lee, John	1346	Kingsbury, Joseph
1276	Midler, John	1347	Rum, John
1277	Pickering, William	1348	Wood, James
1278	Cross, John	1349	Denny, Thomas
1279	Brown, John	1350	Ingraham, Josiah
1280	Smith, John	1351	Richardson, John
1281	Birhau, Jacque	1352	Michael, Ed
1282	Kendall, David	1353	Dale, Arthur
1283	Smith, Bartholomew	1354	Hooram, William
1284	McDermott, Andrew	1355	Hayden, Uriah
1285	Kennedy, Henry	1356	Quiel, Henry
1286	Arnold, Charles	1357	Coleman, Charles
1287	Forbes, William	1358	Scott, Harry
1288	Brown, William	1359	Weaver, William
1289	Williams, Lloyd	1360	Miller, John
1290	---, Domingo	1361	Swisey, Ames
1291	Anden, Peter	1362	Scott, Thomas
1292	Smith, John	1363	Austin, David
1293	Allen, John	1364	Morris, Thomas
1294	Sweeny, Thomas	1365	Dennison, John
1295	Moss, Alfred	1366	Gardner, William
1296	Clarke, Rubin	1367	Scott, William
1297	Berham, John	1368	Everson, James
1298	Twiddy, Stephen	1369	Durham, Thomas
1299	Turner, William	1370	Blumore, Benjamin
1300	Forbes, Bracket	1371	Paget, Levi
1301	Thompson, Henry	1372	Manning, Joseph
1302	Clarke, James	1373	Metz, Joseph
1303	Jones, John	1374	Wilson, William
1304	Randolph, Henry	1375	Graner, Christopher
1305	Clarke, Barney	1376	Stockman, Christopher
1306	Cook, Francis	1377	Gifford, John
1307	Twiddy, William	1378	Michell, John
1308	Ralph, William	1379	Robbins, Henry
1309	Brown, Henry	1380	Carning, William
1310	Kennedy, Thomas D	1381	Wade, William
1311	Barer, Jacob	1382	Yates, George
1312	Hill, Shadrock	1383	Davis, John
1313	Cameron, Daniel	1384	Nye, David
1314	Bowman, John	1385	Taylor, George
1315	Crow, Robert	1386	Homes, Barblett
1316	Gilldon, John	1387	Hawkes, M
1317	Grambery, Samuel	1388	Bosson, John James
1318	May, William	1389	Hillman, Benjamin
1319	Deans, Penja	1390	Hidge, Josiah
1320	Richards, John	1391	Miller, James
1321	Ragsxall, Alex	1392	Bond, Thomas
1322	Mason, Charles	1393	Sturges, William
1323	Williams, William	1394	Ennis, John
1324	Ring, Joseph	1395	Rich, John
1325	Montgomery, John	1396	Gibbs, Moses
1326	Goldthwait, C	1397	Kemp, Nathaniel
1327	Hale, James	1398	Davis, Benjamin
1328	Hargood, Richard	1399	Newell, Thomas
1329	Walker, George	1400	Avis, John
1330	Harris, Benjamin	1401	Ferring, Isaiah
1331	Carthers, Richard	1402	Cook, C
1332	Norris, William	1403	Smith, Thomas
1333	Cassise, James	1404	Smith, Samuel
1334	Powers, James	1405	Knowles, Daniel
1335	Watson, James	1406	Wells, Francis
1336	Johnston, John	1407	Wacher, Martin
1337	Thomas, Thomas	1408	Lukin, ---
1338	Burchak, James	1409	Dill, David
1339	Barry, John	1410	Shepherd, John
1340	Cole, Nathaniel	1411	Cassiday, John

American Prisoners of War Held at Barbados During the War of 1812

1412	Caryle, Lawson		1433	Parker, Samuel
1413	Jack, John		1434	Merchant, James
1414	Stevens, John		1435	Carter, John
1415	Leon, Acy		1436	Sawyer, John
1416	Speed, Etmore		1437	Ebnoles, Wimlon
1417	Duett, Thomas		1438	Andrews, Eben
1418	Graves, Moses		1439	Baxter, Charles
1419	Lovell, William		1440	Abbot, Daniel
1420	Gallin, Samuel		1441	Courroix, Jean
1421	Woodward, John		1442	Forbes, William
1422	Traffick, Charles		1443	Gracey, Archibald
1423	Smith, John		1444	Archer, Nathaniel
1424	Howber, Serrin		1445	Crumbley, Benjamin
1425	Holmes, William		1446	Oakes, Jacob
1426	Goodwin, E		1447	Cony, Hudson
1427	Chase, A		1448	Peabody, George W
1428	Swaney, William		1449	Osburn, Able
1429	Curriel, Henry		1450	Felix, John
1430	Wales, Daniel		1451	Moasee, Abraham
1431	Hambert, William		1452	Johnson, Artemas
1432	Collins, John		1453	Humphreys, A Y

American Prisoners of War Held at Barbados During the War of 1812

Crew listing by ship

Active
- Babut, Peter
- Cottle, John
- Latimore, Titus
- Lewis, John
- Lockwood, William
- Premiers, Joseph
- Prince, Silvesta
- Richardson, Edward
- Thomas, John

Adelphia
- Bartlett, William
- Butheir, William
- Davis, William
- Green, John
- Hooters, John
- March, William
- Maria, Joseph
- Ouveire, Joseph
- Plant, Samuel
- Plant, Samuel
- Sands, John C
- Weir, Robert

Alexis
- Labbi, Constant
- Lookey, Joseph
- Roche, Andrew
- Tool, Elijah
- Wise, Alexis

Anna
- Douglass, George
- Henry, William
- Parker, John
- Smith, Robert B
- Symonds, John

Apollo
- Anderson, Jacob
- Butcher, Benjamin
- Cousins, John
- Hall, Samuel
- Lewis, Daniel
- Lewis, John
- Robins, James
- Snow, John
- Wyatt, William
- Young, Benjamin

Aquila
- Burk, Thomas
- Davis, Francis
- Hanton, William
- Robinson, James
- Smith, John
- Thompson, Allen
- Tribe, Morrell

Atalante
- Bell, Jacob
- Edwards, Jean
- Gildchrist, Simon
- Lange, James
- Mister, William
- Parker, Charles

Atlas
- Handcock, James

Avon
- Abbot, Daniel
- Andrews, Eben
- Avis, John
- Baxter, Charles
- Bond, Thomas
- Bosson, John James
- Carter, John
- Caryle, Lawson
- Cassiday, John
- Chase, A
- Collins, John
- Cook, C
- Courroix, Jean
- Curriel, Henry
- Davis, Benjamin
- Dill, David
- Duett, Thomas
- Ebnoles, Wimlon
- Ennis, John
- Ferring, Isaiah
- Forbes, William
- Gallin, Samuel
- Gibbs, Moses
- Goodwin, E
- Graves, Moses
- Hambert, William
- Hawkes, M
- Hidge, Josiah
- Hillman, Benjamin
- Holmes, William
- Homes, Barblett
- Howber, Serrin
- Jack, John
- Kemp, Nathaniel
- Knowles, Daniel
- Leon, Acy
- Lovell, William
- Lukin, ---
- Merchant, James
- Miller, James
- Newell, Thomas
- Nye, David
- Parker, Samuel
- Rich, John
- Sawyer, John
- Shepherd, John
- Smith, John
- Smith, Samuel
- Smith, Thomas
- Speed, Etmore
- Stevens, John
- Sturges, William
- Swaney, William
- Taylor, George
- Traffick, Charles
- Wacher, Martin
- Wales, Daniel
- Wells, Francis
- Woodward, John

Belfast
- Fenhorn, Morris

Benjamin Franklin
- Reed, John

Blanch
- Ashton, William
- Bailey, Thomas

Blockade
- Barne, Donny
- Beadle, Maning
- Belding, Clifford

American Prisoners of War Held at Barbados During the War of 1812

Belding, James
Beven, Lelah
Bigelow, Thomas C
Bliss, Moses
Butler, Daniel
Butler, Levi
Chaviens, Sidney
Clark, George
Clarke, James
Cook, Aaron
Cooley, William
Day, Grove
Delling, Lewis
Deming, Isaac
Deming, Maning
Dodd, Edward
Edwards, Timothy R
Eldridge, Henry
Flint, William
Franklin, Moses
Fuller, Benjamin
Fuller, Benjamin
Grimes, Richard
Griswald, Jerard
Griswald, Josiah
Griswald, Josiah
Griswald, Truman
Hassard, Jason
Higgins, William H
Hine, Henry
Holden, Arnold
Hosmer, George
Hunt, Walter R
Hushall, Stephen
Jackson, Harden
Kelly, John
Kingsberry, Sandford
Larcom, Robert
Mansfield, Thomas
McDuff, Daniel
McDuff, Phillp S
Merill, Charles
Mie, Elisha
Monger, Bella
Moore, Robert
Murray, Richard
Olmstead, Jesse
Palmer, Isaac
Pardy, Daniel
Perkins, Michael
Plumb, Truman
Plumb, Truman
Remble, Henry
Roberts, Orias
Roberts, Orias
Sabine, John
Sawyer, John A
Stout, Thomas
Tract, Horace
Watson, Robert
Wells, Henry Knox
Wells, Horace
Wells, Oliver
West, Henry
Williams, Moses
Wright, Jonathan

Bowrey

Ausourd, John C
Baynard, Henry
Cathell, William
Dipplac, Domike
Hossnogle, John
Keyser, John
Labolt, Adam
Sheffield, Acors
Williams, William

Brandy Wine

Bennett, Peter
Cleveland, David
Devins, Charles
Greene, Samuel
Gyles, William
James, Paul
Tafft, Nathan

Burnt

Bailey, Ransfor
Burns, Peter

Camilla

Dale, John
Lester, James
Linch, William
Nichols, William
Oakam, Archibald
Rogers, Luke

Carl Frederick

Merrit, Silvanus
Murray, William
Smith, George
Williams, Robert

Chapman

Hunter, Alexander
Masters, Coons
Read, Charles
Stone, Samuel
Woodward, Benjamin

Clio

Baptist, Joseph S
Crowell, Prentiss
Foster, Major
Smith, John
Smith, Peter
Webb, Purnel

Comet

---, Antonio
Newell, Samuel Swift

Decatur

Allman, Samuel
Bickford, Paul
Bowden, Samuel
Bray, Isaac
Brian, Richard
Brockings, Samuel
Brown, Jesse
Brown, John
Buriman, Herman
Clark, Benjamin
Coffin, Able
Cole, James
Coon, Caesar
Corinth, Henry
Cushion, Nathaniel
de Leon, Daniel
Delile, Francis
Doane, Henry
Fernado, Manuel
Fletcher, Samuel
Flood, William
Florintino, Andre
Foot, James
Foster, James
Francis, Richard
Freeman, Peter

American Prisoners of War Held at Barbados During the War of 1812

Gerris, Jeremiah
Giddings, Joseph
Glover, Samuel
Goodman, John
Goodrich, Edward
Goss, John
Grush, Thomas
Gunney, Thomas
Hamilton, Benjamin
Henion, John
Hilton, Samuel
Hodetron, John
Housan, Thomas
Ingless, John
Jarvis, Francis
Jervett, Richard
Kimball, John W
Knight, Solomon
Lain, Samuel
Lloyd, John
Mabread, Thomas
Miller, Nicholas
Miller, Peter
Miller, Peter
Morrell, Richard
Mullin, John
Nichols, William
Osborne, Ambrose
Pettingale, William
Picket, John
Pike, Jeremiah
Plummer, Ebenezer
Pulsifer, Ebenezer
Ramsden, Philip
Richards, Josiah
Roderick, Frank
Rogers, Henry
Salisbury, Samuel
Seapan, Donny
Simpson, Joseph
Spinney, Nathaniel
Stacey, John
Stanley, Ralph
Stephens, John
Swasey, Nathaniel
Thomas, George
Thompson, William
Wadley, Benjamin D
Ward, Samuel
White, Oliver
Whitmore, Joseph
Williams, John
Wimblicour, David

Delirious
Ennick, William

Diana
Butler, George
Condon, Joseph
Fielding, William
Wilson, William

Dolphin
Barbados, Joseph
Boddety, John
Carter, John
Coffin, Robert S
English, John
Johnson, Abel
Johnson, Kelly
Randelett, Thomas M
Sheldon, Nathanial
Titcomb, John H
Titcomb, William
Todd, William
Walton, John
Woodis, Samuel

Ellen
Griffen, William
Harrison, John
Lincon, Nathaniel
Perry, Ebenezer

Engineer
Andrews, Amos
Andrews, L
Baker, Daniel
Brodie, John
Brown, Robert
Butman, Thomas
Calder, William
Clossmann, P
Cunie, Horace
Davis, Wyatt B
Dickson, Henry
Dods, George
Donald, Joseph
Douglass, James
Endley, James
Freeman, Philemon
Harvey, John
Harvey, Samuel
Howes, Samuel
Huntington, E
Jackson, John
Johnson, Frederick
Johnson, George
Jones, John
Kirby, Abel
Lyons, William
McDonald, John
Mincer, Joseph
Newell, Samuel S
Pendal, James
Pornette, Justin
Potter, James
Robinson, William
Rogers, Smith
Simpson, Daniel
West, Stephen

Esperanza
Davis, Joseph

Fairy
Dale, John
Lester, James
Lynch, William
Nicholls, William
Oakum, Archibald
Rodgers, Luke

Fly
Ballen, Elle
Foxtrum, Samuel
Jeppets, Benjamin
Landon, George
Lewis, John
Milton, Thomas
Pemperton, Samuel

Fox
---, Alfonso
---, Alias
---, Blondell
---, Cassimine
---, Celesbin
---, Fanhassie
---, Forsette

American Prisoners of War Held at Barbados During the War of 1812

Adams, John B
Albantio, Augustin
Alexander, Phillippe
Baker, Joseph
Banchi, Louis
Baptiste, Jean
Blanchard, Louis
Bonne, Jean Jack
Boy, Jolly
Boyd, James
Brown, Benjamin
Brown, Robert
Carli, William
Carny, John
Cave, Matthew
Chabeau, Point
Clerge, Nicholas
Crawford, John
Croaker, Edward
Davis, Wyatt B
De Brais, Henry
De Forer, Victor
De Loze, Jean
Donald, Joseph
Dufroint, Julien
Dufrus, Simon
Durive, Antoun
Edgar, Thomas
Effords, John
Farra, Vincent
Fouche, Jean
Germon, Pierre
Gilbert, John
Gravier, Gubviel
Green, John
Harvey, Francis
Hausford, Stephen
Hazler, Henry
Headings, Isaac
Heislop, Matthew
Henry, John B
Hermines, Hoasa
Hicks, John C
Hosse, Fourier
Hoyt, Charles
Jerratt, Abraham
Kinwright, John
Kirby, Able
La Crouse, Jean
Le Compte, Phillippe
Le Hoy, Jean B
Leany, Pierre L
Lepierre, Francis
Little, John
Mapaba, Pierre
Mapano, Pedro
Maxan, Darville
McLean, Ferdin
Oackum, John
Page, Cato
Paulin, Louis
Pierre, John
Post, Nelson
Potter, James
Regair, Morgan
Savinia, Louis
Scargle, William
Sergeant, William
Sheldon, Charles J
Simmons, Joseph
Sinnett, Thomas
Smith, George
Smith, John
Thompson, John
Vielo, Jean
Weeks, William
Weiden, Daniel
Williams, Henry
Young, Samuel

Frolic

Andrews, Nathaniel
Backman, John
Backman, John
Backman, John
Bangs, William
Bangs, William
Berg, Daniel
Brown, Benjamin
Brown, Joseph
Buchannon, Robert
Claxton, Robert
Clemons, Samuuel
Dennis, William
Grey, Francis
Harris, James
Harthorn, John
Holden, Charles
Jackman, David
Jackson, George
Johnson, Thomas
Joseph, Nathaniel
Joshua, John
Leach, George
Madison, Alexander
Murray, John
Newberry, John
Odiorne, John
Patman, Samuel
Perkins, Jonathan
Petengill, James
Pousland, Edward
Richardson, Addison
Shott, John
Simmons, Mark
Smith, Charles
Southwick, George
Stevens, Thomas
Stone, Benjamin
Swain, Thomas
Tarr, John
Wells, Nathan
Woldridge, William

Gallant Hull

Bissit, John
Brown, James
Hester, Stephen
Jenkins, Walter
Johnson, Joseph
Souder, Concordi

Geneal Hamilton

Allan, Elisha

Georgianna

Helah, Timothy

Globe

Hastings, John

Goutlan

Duncan, Jesse
Long, William
West, John
Wilson, William

Greyhound

Adams, James

American Prisoners of War Held at Barbados During the War of 1812

Ames, Sears
Bartridge, Henry
Burk, Henry
Green, Rathbourn

Gustava

Freeman, Samuel

Hamilton

Le Foque, Gabriel
Marwich, Atwood

Hannibal

Denison, Charles W
Treby, George

Hart

Bradie, Thomas

Hawk

Adams, William
Anderson, John
Antonio, John
Bell, Zachariah
Blish, Samuel
Blish, Samuel
Bolding, Garrat
Brook, David
Bryant, Lewis
Buckley, William
Carter, John
Caruthers, John
Catlage, William
Coleman, William
Corwin, Thomas
Dame, John
Days, Thomas
Dodd, Joseph
Dodd, Joseph
Eblin, Aaron
Eldon, James S
Ellwell, Samuel
Frankland, William H
Gilbert, Timothy
Grace, John
Griest, William
Harrison, Silus
Holmes, George
Jarvis, Isaac
Jennings, John
John, Davis
Jones, John
Jones, Paul
Jordon, Simon
King, Joseph
Knoulton, Asahal Joseph
Lorant, John
Lovely, Pasley
Marshall, Leway
McQueen, Caleb
Osborne, John
Oscott, Stephen
Parron, Henry
Paul, Daniel
Percival, John
Ringrose, William
Savage, Robert
Smith, John
Stole, John R
Taylor, John
Tooley, William
Tripe, William H
Warner, Benjamin
Waterford, John H
Weanray, R
Whitehead, Rubin
Wilkins, William
William, George
Woodman, Thomas

Hero

Birhau, Jacque
Brown, John
Cross, John
Fitzgerald, John
Kendall, David
Kennedy, Henry
McDermott, Andrew
Midler, John
Pickering, William
Smith, Bartholomew
Smith, John

High Flyer

Austin, Purnel
Bateman, Xenus
Blagze, John
Brook, John E
Burns, John
Coleman, Christopher
Connor, Peter
Downes, John
Gregory, Cornelius
Grey, William
Hallcock, Edward
Jouanin, John B
Keasoner, Samuel
Kelley, James
Mathews, Edward
McCastin, James
McHam, Daniel
Scargle, William
Shankley, Charles
Starks, Sands
Stephanus, Michael
Stow, Thomas
Swain, Michael
Weld, Thomas
Williams, George
Williams, William
Wood, Bartholomew

HM Ship Levant

Humphreys, A Y
Johnson, Artemas

Hope

Anderson, George
Bond, Oliver C
Bunker, Nathaniel
Coffin, Benjamin
Gordon, Sherwood H
Joy, Robert M
Paddock, Aaron
Primus, Samuel
Rawson, Charles
Richardson, James
Simon, James
Smith, George
Thompson, Robert
Washington, George
Weeks, Rubin

Hunter

Ross, William

Isaac

Doughty, Jacob
Estes, John
Page, George
Purrington, Humphrey
Ross, Barney

Isabella

American Prisoners of War Held at Barbados During the War of 1812

    Blumore, Benjamin
    Gardiner, Samuel
    Hercules, David
    Jeffery, Thomas
    Larkin, Lewis
    Manning, Joseph
    Metz, Joseph
    Paget, Levi
    Tolly, George F
    Willoughby, Charles

Ivan Francisco
    Archer, Nathaniel
    Cony, Hudson
    Crumbley, Benjamin
    Felix, John
    Moasee, Abraham
    Oakes, Jacob
    Osburn, Able
    Peabody, George W

James Murdock
    Hamilton, Charles
    Lynn, Herman
    Marshall, Phillip
    Michell, Phillip
    Read, Richard
    Read, Richard
    Saunders, William
    Shanklen, Charles
    Shanklin, Charles
    Smith, Jacob
    Smith, Jacob
    Thesen, Christopher
    Webb, Thomas
    Webb, Thomas

Jane
    Curtis, John
    Farebrook, George
    Kelly, Jarret
    Lee, Washington
    Lewis, William
    Morris, Peter
    Picken, John
    Roberts, William
    Sturges, Bradley
    Weld, Benjamin

Jason
    Stacey, Benjamin

John
    Adams, William
    Anderson, James
    Averell, Samuel
    Babbit, Erasmus
    Bacomon, Joseph
    Baptist, John
    Baptist, John
    Bassett, Nathaniel
    Blair, Robert
    Bogman, James
    Brigam, Charles
    Brooks, Edward
    Brown, John
    Brown, William
    Brumbloom, Merit
    Burgess, Francis
    Buridge, Robert
    Burke, John C
    Call, Henry P
    Carnes, William
    Caswell, Richard B
    Chapman, John
    Chapman, Stephen
    Chase, Benjamin
    Cheve, Daniel
    Cleaves, Nathaniel
    Cliff, Thomas
    Clough, Samuel
    Craft, Thomas
    Cruff, Tobias
    Dean, W C
    Dennis, James
    Doliver, William
    Doliver, William
    Dutch, Edward
    Eldridge, Edmund
    Fairfield, James M
    Fisher, John
    Francis, Oliver William
    Gale, Benjamin
    Gevine, William
    Glover, John
    Gribble, James
    Griffen, Ebenezer
    Grush, Thomas
    Hacker, Isaac
    Hackleton, John
    Harris, William
    Hawkins, Samuel
    Hobbeston, Thomas A
    Holden, John
    Hulen, Abraham
    Hulon, Henry
    Humphreys, Edward
    Humphreys, William
    Hunt, Job
    Knight, John
    Lane, James
    Lemon, Niel C
    Lemon, Niel C
    Mason, James
    Mason, Joseph J
    Mason, Joseph J
    McCarthy, James
    Millet, Joseph
    Moody, David
    Moore, Dennis
    Noah, Nathaniel
    Paine, Francis
    Palfrey, Jonathan
    Pattee, John
    Pease, James
    Perry, John
    Pierce, John
    Quinar, Benjamin
    Quinar, Stephen
    Ramsdall, Nathaniel
    Ross, David
    Roundy, Stephen C
    Sage, William
    Short, James
    Snow, John P
    Southwick, George
    Stone, Samuel
    Stone, Samuel
    Tusant, John
    Vickey, William
    Wagner, John
    Weacom, Ebenezer
    Wood, John F
    Wooldridge, Benjamin
    Wooldridge, Robert

Josephus
    Arnold, Charles

American Prisoners of War Held at Barbados During the War of 1812

Kirran
- Boudy, William
- Daniels, Nathaniel
- Fletcher, Benjamin
- Whymn, Theodore

Laurence
- Carning, William
- Gifford, John
- Graner, Christopher
- Michell, John
- Robbins, Henry
- Stockman, Christopher

Lucretia
- May, William

Maria
- Chapman, James

Mars
- Boggs, Francis
- Guanough, William
- Hale, Christopher
- Lahy, George
- Lavis, Lewis
- Roe, James
- Stackney, Peter F
- Watson, Thomas

Martin
- Barron, John
- Barron, John
- Ross, William
- Ross, William

Mary
- ---, Domingo
- Allen, John
- Anden, Peter
- Barer, Jacob
- Berham, John
- Brown, Henry
- Brown, William
- Cameron, Archibald
- Carpenter, William
- Clarke, Barney
- Clarke, David
- Clarke, James
- Clarke, Rubin
- Compstock, Stephen
- Cook, Francis
- Coomais, Henry
- Cullin, Thomas
- Disney, George
- Effords, John
- Ellis, Joseph
- Every, William
- Flood, William
- Forbes, Bracket
- Forbes, William
- Guisar, Nicholas
- Hathaway, William
- Hine, Isaiah
- Hordoffer, John
- Jerome, John
- Jones, John
- Kennedy, Thomas D
- Larabee, Samuel
- Mooring, Thomas
- Moss, Alfred
- Ralph, William
- Randolph, Henry
- Ray, William
- Rice, Samuel
- Rickman, Richard
- Seybest, George
- Sinnett, Thomas
- Smith, John
- States, Leonard F
- Sweeny, Thomas
- Tarpish, Davis
- Tateham, Daniel
- Thompson, Henry
- Thompson, John
- Turner, William
- Twiddy, Stephen
- Twiddy, William
- Wilkinson, David
- Williams, Lloyd
- Williams, Thomas
- Yeaton, Moses

Mary Caroline
- Elliott, Nathaniel
- Freeman, Pline
- Loper, Lyon
- Taylor, Edward

Meatbone
- Lee, John

Mercator
- Miller, Isaac

Nancy
- Brewer, Nathaniel
- Dau, George
- Frasier, John
- Furdge, Henry
- Hayward, Abraham
- Hopkins, Richard L D
- James, John
- Lee, Abraham
- Randall, Nathaniel
- Simmonds, Andrew
- Smith, John

Neptune
- Bakagen, John
- Haulbut, Nathanial
- Hutchings, William
- Little, William
- Mitchmore, John
- Phippin, William

North Star
- Backman, John
- Card, James
- Evans, Edward
- Frankland, William H
- Frankland, William H
- Hatchet, John
- Johnson, Luke
- Montgomery, W P
- Murray, James
- Newell, Charles
- Oscott, Stephen
- Reginald, Henry
- Ross, William

Ocean
- Clinton, Ebenezer
- Clinton, Ebenezer
- Fort, Benjamin
- Fuller, Andrew
- Howland, Robert
- Rogers, Daniel
- Summersville, George

Old Friend
- Butler, Andrew
- Fortune, Thomas
- Foy, Daniel
- Fuller, William
- Godfrey, John

American Prisoners of War Held at Barbados During the War of 1812

    Hall, John
    James, John
    Mann, Samuel

Olive Branch
    Bates, Oran
    Lathrop, Acahel
    McCall, James
    Stocking, Seth
    Treat, Lathrop
    Williams, Peter

Orpha
    Caswell, John R
    Hussey, Samuel S

Perseverance
    Chapman, James

Phoenix
    Hawkins, Henry
    Hill, Daniel
    Mason, Simon
    Patterson, David

Pocahontas
    Fetch, Elias
    Randlet, John M

Polly
    Jackson, James
    Simons, Ebenezer
    Smart, Samuel

President
    Acker, Jose
    Acomplado, August
    Adians, Jose
    Albenans, Jose
    Albery, Martine
    Azunes, Jerune
    Barrett, Tobias
    Board, John P
    Britade, E F
    Compeche, S Yaga
    Craiss, John E
    Davis, George
    Davis, John
    De la Ench Parker, Jose
    De la Lantos Lepos, Jose
    Ebein, Joseph
    Faleon, Jose B
    Flinn, John F
    Fogg, John
    Fry, A Julius
    George, John
    Greer, John
    Hackett, John
    Harman, John
    Hidalgo, Balace
    Hidalgo, Vincent
    Johannes, Joseph
    Johnson, John
    Jones, Thomas
    Joseph, Pedro
    Knabbs, James
    Lacerf, Henry
    Laes, Domingo
    Leman, Ambrose
    Lorang, Monroe
    Maria, John
    Mathey, James
    Melbourne, William
    Mendoza, Nicholas
    Montgomery, W P
    Patens, Vincent
    Roberts, John
    Rosenthon, John
    Sessions, Pedro
    Smith, Jonathan W
    Stephens, William
    Taylor, Samuel
    Walker, James Scott
    Waterman, Cato
    Whippel, John
    Williams, Charles

Providence
    Alleyn, John
    Arnold, Isaac
    Bagman, Jacob
    Bailoci, Thomas
    Barnard, Adonijah
    Benson, William B
    Berry, Owen
    Biddle, John
    Bowdwish, John
    Brown, Ezekiah
    Bruce, Jeremiah
    Burrell, Charles
    Crofton, Henry
    Cushing, Chance
    de la Statius, Levein
    Eainis, Ebenezer
    Fenner, Charles
    Fisher, Lewis P
    Freeman, Joseph S
    Gardner, Willet C
    Gibb, Thomas
    Harby, Levy
    Hawthorn, Stephen
    Hayford, Gardner
    Hopkins, Nicholas
    Howard, Hyman
    Jacobs, John
    James, Simon
    King, Samuel W
    Lawton, Thomas
    Manson, Stephen
    Marshall, Ellet
    Martin, Isaac
    Martin, Silvenis P
    Martin, William
    Mason, May D
    McDaniel, John
    McFoy, Daniel
    Myers, Charles
    Parker, Thomas
    Peterson, Peter
    Price, Constant W
    Prior, Christopher
    Raco, Julias
    Richmond, Milton
    Sanders, George
    Saunders, Davis
    Scan, Thomas
    Shelah, Timothy
    Shusch, Adam
    Smith, Holsey
    Smith, William
    Sweet, Daniel H
    Walker, George
    Walsh, William
    Wenwood, Godfrey
    Westcott, Samuel
    Wheaton, Nathaniel
    Williamson, Peter
    Wyatt, Daniel

Rattle Snake
    Adams, ---

American Prisoners of War Held at Barbados During the War of 1812

Arnold, James
Brown, Thomas
Brush, Samuel
Buckall, William
Burt, William
Cricall, South
Ellis, Cornelius
Evarell, Samuel
Fordick, Joseph
Gair, Thomas
Glading, Joseph
Goss, John
Grall, Charles
Groves, Thomas
Halbrut, Henry
Hunter, John
Jerrett, Jasper
Littlefield, Samuel
Looke, Jacob
Myer, William F
Rice, M
Robertson, Thomas
Robinson, Lemry
Ruling, Arnold
Silsbee, John
Snow, Colier
Steel, Thomas
Thomas, John
Wilford, Charles
Wilson, George

Rea
   ---, Philadelphia
   Anderson, Hugh
   Bouldin, Nathan L
   Brown, William
   Carroll, James
   Dugan, Able S
   Fenderson, Nathaniel
   Fortney, William
   Godard, William
   Harris, William
   Herbert, Peter
   Hickey, William
   Horace, Kemble
   Jordon, Ralph
   Kirby, Benjamin
   Maffet, John
   McGill, James
   Mennedy, Bennet
   Pate, James
   Penyan, Antoine
   Pope, Edward
   Poulson, Perry
   Rea, Benjamin
   Reardon, Daniel
   Shearman, Peleg
   Shichlar, Henry
   Williams, John
   Willoughby, Thomas

Reassurance
   Harris, Benjamin
   Savage, P H
   Wescott, Edward

Rebecca
   Blair, Harvey
   Blair, Hosea
   Hurbert, James
   Latimore, Samuel
   Morgan, Richard
   Robins, Joshua

Rising States
   Ross, Timothy

Sally & Betsey
   Glover, Benjamin
   Jackson, George
   Johnson, James

San Francisco
   Bissell, Charles
   Bixby, James
   Hedrick, Samuel

Santa Maria
   Watkins, Asa

Saturn
   Coburne, Miles
   Hawse, Hance Thomas
   Hotchess, John
   Lines, William
   Ramsey, David C
   Ranson, William John
   Sherry, Joseph
   Taylor, James
   Walters, John

Shepherdess
   Benner, Thomas
   Bogs, James
   Brown, Robert
   Combs, William
   Deming, Henry
   Holden, Horace
   Lefort, John

Sophia
   Aldoe, William

Spencer
   Austin, David
   Coleman, Charles
   Davis, John
   Dennison, John
   Durham, Thomas
   Everson, James
   Gardner, William
   Hayden, Uriah
   Miller, John
   Montgomery, John
   Morris, Thomas
   Quiel, Henry
   Ring, Joseph
   Scott, Harry
   Scott, Thomas
   Scott, William
   Swisey, Ames
   Weaver, William

St Bartholomew
   Cohoon, Isaiah
   Kemble, Nathaniel
   Nye, Stephen
   Sherbourne, John
   Spelsbury, Amos
   Springer, Mark
   Steward, John
   Turner, Samuel

Sterling
   Chadwick, Seth
   Chanders, Dublin
   Cook, John
   Coulfrey, Robert
   Jackson, Frederick
   Kelley, Joseph
   Laurence, Elisha
   Lipid, Caesar
   Smith, William
   Swain, Jonathan
   Swain, Rubin

American Prisoners of War Held at Barbados During the War of 1812

Talbot, James
Weaver, Benjamin
Williams, Richard
Wilson, Samuel
Wormsley, Joseph

Susannah
- Macomber, Anson

Thomas Penrose
- Andrew, Peter
- Ansley, John
- Bartlin, Thomas
- Brown, James
- Buck, Edward
- Burrows, William
- Burton, William
- Debot, Henry
- Dutilth, John A
- Fillerson, Thomas
- Galley, Henry
- Garner, William
- Jackson, James
- Jones, William
- Justice, John
- Lane, John
- Moutrie, Henry W
- Peas, Joseph
- Shallus, William
- Steel, Charles
- Thomas, David
- Uluck, Thomas
- Waters, Frank
- Wilson, Henry
- Wiltbeyer, Peter

Tigre

Venus
- Woolford, Henry
- Allen, Richard
- Cain, James
- Class, Peter
- Hussy, Abraham
- Lumtich, Laurance
- Myers, Henry
- Phillips, John
- Rogers, Henry
- Tabor, Isaac

Vidett
- Barry, John
- Burchak, James
- Carthers, Richard
- Cassise, James
- Cole, Nathaniel
- Dale, Arthur
- Dempson, John
- Denny, Thomas
- Goldthwait, C
- Hale, James
- Hargood, Richard
- Harris, Benjamin
- Hooram, William
- Ingraham, Josiah
- Johnston, John
- Kingsbury, Joseph
- Michael, Ed
- Norris, William
- Parker, William
- Powers, James
- Reid, Robert
- Richardson, John
- Rum, John
- Smith, Daniel
- Thomas, Thomas

Wade, William
Walker, George
Walstrome, Samuel
Watson, James
Wilson, William
Wood, James
Yates, George

Washington
- Henry, David
- Place, John
- Tucker, William

Whalebone
- Bowman, John
- Cameron, Daniel
- Crow, Robert
- Deans, Penja
- Gilldon, John
- Grambery, Samuel
- Hill, Shadrock
- Mason, Charles
- May, William
- Ragsxall, Alex
- Richards, John

William
- Bisbee, Elijah
- Bisbee, John
- Clallow, William
- Harlow, Lewis
- Higgins, Freeman
- Holbrook, Gideon
- Johnstone, William
- Jones, David
- Keen, Tilden
- Murrell, William
- Smith, William
- Stanley, Samuel
- Sturtevant, Caleb
- Warren, David

William Rathbone
- Babcock, William
- Bevin, John
- Bevin, Thomas
- Cole, Stephen
- Cole, Thomas
- Craig, Alexander
- Davis, John
- Edwards, Thomas
- Egart, Jacob
- Gill, James
- Green, James
- Greenwood, Maurice
- Hansford, Stephen
- Kent, Jacob Henry
- Leaburn, Thomas
- Meadows, George
- Meyer, John
- Pairse, John
- Parsons, Charles
- Pique, Ville
- Roper, William
- Ross, Thomas
- Swather, Jacob
- Wharff, John

Yankee
- Adams, Theophilus B
- Bartlett, Gibbon
- Batchelder, Jeremiah
- Clark, John
- Coale, James
- Cook, Benjamin
- Copps, Darius

American Prisoners of War Held at Barbados During the War of 1812

Evans, John
Farnham, John
Flanders, Daniel
Foot, Thomas
Francis, John
Ives, William
Jackson, Caleb
Jacobs, Henry
Jones, Richard
Kenniston, Daniel
Kimball, Ezekiah
Kimball, John
Lang, William
Lukies, Thomas M
Maulton, Joseph
Maulton, Nathaniel
Melbourne, William
Noyes, Jeremiah
Parker, Henry
Patch, Joseph
Perry, Onan
Pilsbury, Timothy
Richards, James
Richards, Rehobaham
Robins, William
Robinson, John
Rogers, Robert
Sherry, Jonathan
Simmons, Thomas
Stephenson, Stephen
Sweatt, John P
Ward, James
Wheeler, David
Wheeler, Job E
Wheelock, Nahor
Woodbury, Joseph
Wyncook, Ebenezer

American Prisoners of War Held at Barbados During the War of 1812

Americans on British ships

Ballentine, Samuel
Bayley, Joshua K
Bird, Robert
Blake, Daniel
Blardile, Jacob
Bowen, John
Boyle, George
Briggs, William
Briggs, William
Brown, John
Cartwright, Samuel
Cegg, Phillip
Cinnan, Joseph
Clarke, Thomas
Clarke, William
Collins, Stephen
Copper, William
Cowslip, Charles
Craps, James
Crowder, John
Davis, John
Davis, John
Denny, John
Duncan, Charles
Duncan, William
Eden, John
Farris, James
Fields, William
Forster, John
Gardner, Francis
Garry, Alexander
Green, William
Grove, George W
Hall, William
Hardy, James
Hewet, Robert
Horner, James
Horton, Henry
Houstaon, John
Hutchinson, Joseph
Jackson, Gowan
James, William
Johnson, John
Johnson, John
Jones, John
Jones, William
Julius, John
Kentfield, Eliza
Knowls, Morton
Lewis, Thomas
Long, Joseph
Lowder, Samuel
Lumsden, Stephen
Luther, Alexander
Mackey, John
McCeaver, Peter
Micons, John
Nay, John R
Noble, D
Noble, D
Norris, Samuel
Pelot, Samuel G
Peters, John
Peterson, Jacob
Platt, George
Pope, Abraham
Prince, Prince
Ray, William
Reamonsptras, ---
Reginald, Henry
Reid, Thomas
Rowland, ---
Sanderson, Daniel
Shields, Francis D
Simons, Ebenezer
Simons, Richard
Smith, John
Stewart, John
Strague, John
Strague, John
Strague, Stephen
Strague, Stephen
Sylva, Manuel
Thompson, William
Tompkins, Stockton
Tuckett, George
Warden, Charles
Ware, John
White, George
Wynn, John

American Prisoners of War Held at Barbados During the War of 1812

Service affiliation not known

Benson, William B
Berry, Owen
Brown, John
Connor, Galen
Cook, Aaron
Fullerton, Thomas
Gracey, Archibald
Hodgskins, Phillip
Hoyt, Hapthtum
Hughes, Thomas
Jackson, James
Pass, Benjamin
Ray, William
Rupley, Luther
Rutledge, James
Smart, Samuel
Tract, Horace
Williams, William
Wise, Alexis

American Prisoners of War Held at New Providence During the War of 1812

---, Peter   Prisoner 108. Rank: Seaman, from: Romney, Merchant.
    Cap: Not Recorded by HMS Rattler Int: 22 Sep 1812 Dis: 24 Nov 1812.
    Received from HMS Rattler. Sent to Savannah in the American Cartel Delight. (Last name not recorded. Date and place of capture 'not 'not mentioned'.)

Abbott, Benjamin   Prisoner 687. Rank: 2 Master, from: Frolic, Man of War.
    Cap: 20 Apr 1814 Not Recorded by HMS Orpheus Int: 26 Apr 1814 Dis: 13 Jun 1814.
    United States Ship. Received from HMS Orpheus. Sent to Halifax in HMS Majestic order Aml Cochrane.

Abbott, Thomas   Prisoner 204. Rank: Passenger, from: Not Recorded, Merchant.
    Cap: Not Recorded by Privateer Unknown Int: 24 Oct 1812 Dis: 24 Oct 1812.
    Received from HMS Mosella. Sent to Charlestown in the British Cartel Nassau by order of the Governor. (Date, place, name of vessel and name of capturing ship 'not mentioned'.)

Accruma, Quashy   Prisoner 355. Rank: Seaman, from: George & Mary, Merchant.
    Cap: Not Recorded by Not Recorded Int: 14 Feb 1813 Dis: 14 Feb 1813.
    Wrecked among the islands and delivered themselves up. Sent to Norfolk in the British Cartel Eliza by order of the Governor. (Date of capture 'not mentioned'.)

Adams, John   Prisoner 38. Rank: Cook, from: Ceres, Merchant.
    Cap: 28 Jul 1812 Bahama Bank by Privateer Theodore Int: 01 Aug 1812 Dis: 06 Aug 1812.
    Received from Prize. Sent to Liverpool in the Ship Cora by order of the Governor.

Agreda, Joseph   Prisoner 272. Rank: Seaman, from: Viper, Man of War.
    Cap: Gulf of Mexico by HMS Narcissus Int: 30 Jan 1813 Dis: 14 Feb 1813.
    Brig. Received from HMS Moselle. Sent in the British Cartel Eliza to Norfolk by order of the Governor. (Date of capture 'not mentioned'.)

Airy, John   Prisoner 333. Rank: Seaman, from: Osprey, Merchant.
    Cap: Gulf of Mexico by HMS Moselle Int: 30 Jan 1813 Dis: 14 Feb 1813.
    Received from HMS Moselle. Sent in the British Cartel Eliza to Norfolk by order of the Governor. (Date of capture 'not mentioned'.)

Alexander, George   Prisoner 96. Rank: Seaman, from: Rapid, Privateer.
    Cap: Not Recorded by Not Recorded Int: 13 Sep 1812 Dis: 04 Feb 1813.
    Received from Government Schooner John Bull. Sent to Charlestown in the British Cartel Ann. (Date, place and name of capturing ship 'not mentioned'.)

Alexander, John   Prisoner 817. Rank: Seaman, from: Saturn, Letter of Marquis.
    Cap: Not Recorded by Venus Int: 29 Jan 1815 Dis:
    Schooner. Received from Venus. (Dates of capture and discharge not on roster.)

Algut, Adam   Prisoner 275. Rank: Seaman, from: Viper, Man of War.
    Cap: Gulf of Mexico by HMS Narcissus Int: 30 Jan 1813 Dis: 14 Feb 1813.
    Brig. Received from HMS Moselle. Sent in the British Cartel Eliza to Norfolk by order of the Governor. (Date of capture 'not mentioned'.)

Alice, John   Prisoner 468. Rank: Seaman, from: Caroline, Merchant.
    Cap: 12 Aug 1813 East out of Charleston by HMS Moselle & Privateer Brilliant Int: 25 Aug 1813 Dis: 13 Jun 1814.   Received from Privateer Brilliant. Sent to Halifax.

Allen, Ebenezer   Prisoner 34. Rank: Seaman, from: HM Schooner Decouverte, Not Recorded.
    Cap: 29 Jul 1812 Not Stated by HM Schooner Decouverte Int: 01 Aug 1812 Dis: 20 Aug 1812.
    Received from HM Schooner Decauverte. Gave themselves up as Prisoners of War. Being Part of the complement of the HMS Decouvete Lieut Richard Williams Commanding. Sent to Jamaica in HM Schooner Decouverte by order of Lieut Williams.

Allen, Prince   Prisoner 388. Rank: Seaman, from: Venus, Merchant.
    Cap: Not Recorded by Brilliant Privateer Int: 17 Mar 1813 Dis: 26 Apr 1814.
    Received from Prize. Sent to Rhode Island in the Cartel Liberty. (Date and place of capture 'not mentioned'.)

Allmond, Edmond   Prisoner 176. Rank: Seaman, from: Dash, Privateer.
    Cap: 12 Sep 1812 Coast of America by Rhodian & Variable Int: 23 Sep 1812 Dis: 24 Oct 1812.
    Received from Rhodian and Variable. Sent to Charlestown in the British Cartel Nassau by order of the Governor.

Almy, Eleazar   Prisoner 375. Rank: Seaman, from: Mary, Merchant.
    Cap: Not Recorded by Government Schooner Swift Int: 15 Mar 1813 Dis: 10 Apr 1813.
    Received from Government Schooner Swift. Sent to Charleston in the British Cartel Charlotte by order of the Governor. (Date and place of capture 'not mentioned'.)

Alsop, Mathew   Prisoner 82. Rank: Seaman, from: Hamer, Merchant.
    Cap: 01 Sep 1812 Off Abaco by Privateer Int: 02 Sep 1812 Dis: 24 Oct 1812.
    Received from Privateer. Sent to Charlestown in the British Cartel Nassau.

American Prisoners of War Held at New Providence During the War of 1812

Amderson, William   Prisoner 67. Rank: Seaman, from: Resolution, Merchant.
    Cap: 26 Jul 1812 Crooked Island Passage by HM Schooner Variable Int: 07 Aug 1812 Dis: 22 Sep 1812. Received from His Majesties Schooner Variable. Sent to new York United States of America.

Anderson, Edward   Prisoner 659. Rank: Seaman, from: Frolic, Man of War.
    Cap: 20 Apr 1814 Not Recorded by HMS Orpheus Int: 26 Apr 1814 Dis: 13 Jun 1814.
    United States Ship. Received from HMS Orpheus. Sent to Halifax in HMS Majestic per order of Commander in Chief Aml Cochrane.

Anderson, George   Prisoner 83. Rank: Seaman, from: Hamer, Merchant.
    Cap: 01 Sep 1812 Off Abaco by Privateer Int: 02 Sep 1812 Dis: 24 Oct 1812.
    Received from Privateer. Sent to Charlestown in the British Cartel Nassau.

Anderson, John   Prisoner 39. Rank: Steward, from: Ceres, Merchant.
    Cap: 28 Jul 1812 Bahama Bank by Privateer Theodore Int: 01 Aug 1812 Dis: 06 Aug 1812.
    Received from Prize. Sent to Liverpool in the Ship Cora by order of the Governor.

Anderson, Nathaniel   Prisoner 173. Rank: Seaman, from: Dash, Privateer.
    Cap: 12 Sep 1812 Coast of America by Rhodian & Variable Int: 23 Sep 1812 Dis: 24 Oct 1812.
    Received from Rhodian and Variable. Sent to Charlestown in the British Cartel Nassau by order of the Governor.

Anderson, Oliver   Prisoner 390. Rank: Seaman, from: Dominica Packet, Merchant.
    Cap: Not Recorded by HMS Variable Int: 30 Mar 1813 Dis: 27 Jun 1813.
    Recaptured from the American Privateer Comet. Received from Variable. Died. Fever. (Date and place of capture 'not mentioned'.)

Andrew, John   Prisoner 277. Rank: Seaman, from: Viper, Man of War.
    Cap: Gulf of Mexico by HMS Narcissus Int: 30 Jan 1813 Dis: 14 Feb 1813.
    Brig. Received from HMS Moselle. Sent in the British Cartel Eliza to Norfolk by order of the Governor. (Date of capture 'not mentioned'.)

Andrews, Asa   Prisoner 586. Rank: Seaman, from: Frolic, Man of War.
    Cap: 20 Apr 1814 Not Recorded by HMS Orpheus Int: 26 Apr 1814 Dis: 11 Jun 1814.
    United States Ship. Received from HMS Orpheus. Sent to Bermuda in HMS Orpheus per order Commander in Chief Aml Cochrane.

Anquin, Anthony   Prisoner 368. Rank: Prize Master, from: Hazard, Privateer.
    Cap: Not Recorded by Privateer Cutter Caledonia Int: 07 Mar 1813 Dis: 09 Mar 1813.
    Recaptured in the British Ship. Received from Caledonia. Sent to Jamaica in HMS Ship Moselle by the Governor. (Date and place of capture 'not mentioned'.)

Ansburgh, Martin   Prisoner 151. Rank: Seaman, from: Sarah Ann, Privateer.
    Cap: 13 Sep 1812 Coast of America by Rhodian & Variable Int: 23 Sep 1812 Dis: 24 Oct 1812.
    Received from Rhodian and Variable. Sent to Charlestown in the British Cartel Nassau.

Appleton, Daniel   Prisoner 614. Rank: Seaman, from: Frolic, Man of War.
    Cap: 20 Apr 1814 Not Recorded by HMS Orpheus Int: 26 Apr 1814 Dis: 13 Jun 1814.
    United States Ship. Received from HMS Orpheus. Sent to Halifax in HMS Majestic per order Aml Cochrane.

Argent, William   Prisoner 255. Rank: Seaman, from: Viper, Man of War.
    Cap: Gulf of Mexico by HMS Narcissus Int: 30 Jan 1813 Dis: 14 Feb 1813.
    United States Brig. Received from HMS Moselle. taken by the Police for Murder and as evidence. (Date of capture 'not mentioned'.)

Argent, William   Prisoner 415. Rank: Seaman, from: Viper, Man of War.
    Cap: Not Recorded by HM Ship Narcissus Int: 21 Apr 1813 Dis:
    Received from Police. (Date and place of capture 'not mentioned'. Date of discharge not on roster.)

Army, John   Prisoner 313. Rank: Seaman, from: Sheperd, Merchant.
    Cap: Gulf of Mexico by HMS Narcissus Int: 30 Jan 1813 Dis: 14 Feb 1813.
    Received from HMS Moselle. Sent to Norfolk in the British Cartel Eliza by order of the Governor. (Date of capture 'not mentioned'.)

Artary, Hose   Prisoner 780. Rank: Seaman, from: Ruby, Merchant Vessel.
    Cap: Not Recorded by Schooner Swift Int: 09 Jan 1815 Dis: .
    Received from Schooner Swift. (Date of capture and place of capture 'not mentioned'. Date of discharge not on roster.)

Ashby, Joseph   Prisoner 366. Rank: Seaman, from: Rose, Merchant.
    Cap: Not Recorded by HMS Rolus Int: 02 Mar 1813 Dis: 26 Apr 1814.
    Received from prize. Sent to Rhode Island in the Cartel Liberty. (Date and place of capture 'not mentioned'.)

American Prisoners of War Held at New Providence During the War of 1812

Ashton, David   Prisoner 213. Rank: Seaman, from: Venus, Merchant.
   Cap: Coast of America by HMS Moselle Int: 19 Nov 1812 Dis: 04 Feb 1813.
   Received from HMS Moselle. Sent to Charlestown in the British Cartel Ann by order of the Governor. (Date of capture 'not mentioned'.)

Atkins, William   Prisoner 628. Rank: Seaman, from: Frolic, Man of War.
   Cap: 20 Apr 1814 Not Recorded by HMS Orpheus Int: 26 Apr 1814 Dis: 13 Jun 1814.
   United States Ship. Received from HMS Orpheus. Sent to Halifax in HMS Majestic order Aml Cochrane.

Atkinson, Henry   Prisoner 457. Rank: Seaman, from: Gustavus, Not Recorded.
   Cap: 17 Jun 1813 Not Recorded by HMS Calibri Int: 24 Jul 1813 Dis: 26 Apr 1814.
   Detained from a Sweedish Schooner Gustavus. Received from HMS Calibri. Sent to Rhode Island in the Cartel Liberty.

Austin, James   Prisoner 640. Rank: Seaman, from: Frolic, Man of War.
   Cap: 20 Apr 1814 Not Recorded by HMS Orpheus Int: 26 Apr 1814 Dis: 13 Jun 1814.
   United States Ship. Received from HMS Orpheus. Sent to Halifax in HMS Majestic per order of Commander in Chief Aml Cochrane.

Ayas, John   Prisoner 535. Rank: Seaman, from: Sevant, Letter of Marquis.
   Cap: 04 Jan 1814 Not Recorded by HMS Forester Int: 12 Jan 1814 Dis: 13 Aug 1814.
   Brig. Received from HMS Forester. Sent to Bermuda HMS Surprise per order Commander in Chief.

Badson, Jacob   Prisoner 445. Rank: Seaman, from: Stanley, Merchant.
   Cap: Coast of America by Privateer Wellesley Int: 10 Jun 1813 Dis: 27 Jan 1814.
   Received from Government Schooner Swift. Embarked on board the Merchant Vessel to assist in navigating her to England. (Date of capture not recorded.)

Baker, Obadiah   Prisoner 394. Rank: Seaman, from: Dominica Packet, Merchant.
   Cap: Not Recorded by Privateer Baker Delight Int: 01 Apr 1813 Dis: 10 Apr 1813.
   Recaptured from the American Privateer Comet. Received from Privateer. Sent to Charleston in the British Cartel Charlotte by order of the Governor. (Date and place of capture 'not mentioned'.)

Baker, Oliver   Prisoner 488. Rank: Seaman, from: St. Polito, Merchant.
   Cap: 26 Nov 1813 At sea by Privateers Mars & Dash Int: 25 Dec 1813 Dis: 21 Apr 1814.
   Received from Privateer Mars. To assist in navigating to England.

Banks, John G   Prisoner 159. Rank: 1 Lieutenant, from: Dash, Privateer.
   Cap: 12 Sep 1812 Coast of America by Rhodian & Variable Int: 23 Sep 1812 Dis: 24 Oct 1812.
   Received from Rhodian and Variable. Sent to Charlestown in the British Cartel Nassau.

Baptiste, John   Prisoner 369. Rank: Seaman, from: Hazard, Privateer.
   Cap: Not Recorded by Privateer Cutter Caledonia Int: 07 Mar 1813 Dis: 13 Jun 1814.
   Recaptured in the British Ship. Received from Caledonia. Sent to Halifax HMS Majestic order of Adl Cochane. (Date and place of capture 'not mentioned'.)

Barke, N   Prisoner 196. Rank: Master, from: Not Recorded, Not Recorded.
   Cap: Not Recorded by Privateer Unknown Int: 24 Oct 1812 Dis: 24 Oct 1812.
   Received from HMS Mosella. Sent to Charlestown in the British Cartel Nassau by order of the Governor. (Date, place, name of vessel and name of capturing ship 'not mentioned'.)

Barnard, William   Prisoner 262. Rank: Seaman, from: Viper, Man of War.
   Cap: Gulf of Mexico by HMS Narcissus Int: 30 Jan 1813 Dis: 14 Feb 1813.
   United States Brig. Received from HMS Moselle. Sent in the British Cartel Eliza to Norfolk by order of the Governor. (Date of capture 'not mentioned'.)

Barnes, James   Prisoner 464. Rank: Seaman, from: Caroline, Merchant.
   Cap: 12 Aug 1813 East out of Charleston by HMS Moselle & Privateer Brilliant Int: 25 Aug 1813
   Dis: 26 Apr 1814. Received from Privateer Brilliant. Sent to Rhode Island in the Cartel Liberty.

Bass, Charles   Prisoner 604. Rank: Seaman, from: Frolic, Man of War.
   Cap: 20 Apr 1814 Not Recorded by HMS Orpheus Int: 26 Apr 1814 Dis: 13 Jun 1814.
   United States Ship. Received from HMS Orpheus. Sent to Halifax HMS Majestic order Aml Cochrane.

Batiss, John   Prisoner 736. Rank: Seaman, from: Gunboat 160, Man of War.
   Cap: Cumberland Sound by HMS Lacedaemonian Int: 19 Oct 1814 Dis: 18 Jan 1815.
   United States Gunboat. Received from HMS Lacedaemonian. Sent to Bermuda in HMS Childers. (Date of capture not on roster.)

Batteia, John   Prisoner 180. Rank: Seaman, from: Dash, Privateer.
   Cap: 12 Sep 1812 Coast of America by Rhodian & Variable Int: 23 Sep 1812 Dis: 24 Oct 1812.
   Received from Rhodian and Variable. Sent to Charlestown in the British Cartel Nassau by order of the Governor.

American Prisoners of War Held at New Providence During the War of 1812

Baxter, David   Prisoner 469. Rank: Seaman, from: Caroline, Merchant.
    Cap: 12 Aug 1813 East out of Charleston by HMS Moselle & Privateer Brilliant Int: 25 Aug 1813
    Dis: 04 Feb 1814. Received from Privateer Brilliant. Embarked on board the Providence to assist in navigating her to England.

Baydion, Peter   Prisoner 370. Rank: Seaman, from: Hazard, Privateer.
    Cap: Not Recorded by Privateer Cutter Caledonia Int: 07 Mar 1813 Dis: 13 Jun 1814.
    Recaptured in the British Ship. Received from Caledonia. Sent to Halifax HMS Majestic order of Adl Cochane. (Date and place of capture 'not mentioned'.)

Bayley, William   Prisoner 480. Rank: Seaman, from: Catalonia, Merchant.
    Cap: 23 Nov 1813 At sea by HMS Ringdove Int: 30 Nov 1813 Dis: 26 Apr 1814.
    Received from HMS Ringdove. Sent to Rhode Island in the Cartel Liberty.

Beason, James   Prisoner 593. Rank: Seaman, from: Frolic, Man of War.
    Cap: 20 Apr 1814 Not Recorded by HMS Orpheus Int: 26 Apr 1814 Dis: 13 Jun 1814.
    United States Ship. Received from HMS Orpheus. Sent to Halifax HMS Majestic order Aml Cochrane.

Beaudesire, Lewis   Prisoner 110. Rank: Mate, from: Alexander, Merchant.
    Cap: Not Recorded by HMS Sappho Int: 22 Sep 1812 Dis:
    Received from HMS Sappho. (Date and place of capture 'not mentioned'. Date of discharge not on roster.)

Beaver, Alan   Prisoner 235. Rank: Boatswain, from: Viper, Man of War.
    Cap: Gulf of Mexico by HMS Narcissus Int: 30 Jan 1813 Dis: 14 Feb 1813.
    United States Brig. Received from HMS Moselle. Sent in the British Cartel Eliza to Norfolk by order of the Governor. (Date of capture 'not mentioned'.)

Bell, George   Prisoner 576. Rank: Seaman, from: Frolic, Man of War.
    Cap: 20 Apr 1814 At sea by HMS Orpheus Int: 26 Apr 1814 Dis: 11 Jun 1814.
    United States Ship. Received from HMS Orpheus. Sent to Bermuda in HMS Orpheus order Aml Cochrane.

Bellewe, Louis   Prisoner 605. Rank: Seaman, from: Frolic, Man of War.
    Cap: 20 Apr 1814 Not Recorded by HMS Orpheus Int: 26 Apr 1814 Dis: 13 Jun 1814.
    United States Ship. Received from HMS Orpheus. Sent to Halifax HMS Majestic order Aml Cochrane.

Bellington, James   Prisoner 750. Rank: Seaman, from: Auroa, Letter of Marquis.
    Cap: Not Recorded by HM Shooner Cockchafer Int: 03 Dec 1814 Dis:
    Received from Cockchafer. (Date and place of capture 'not mentioned'. Date of discharge not on roster.)

Belson, Armand   Prisoner 44. Rank: Seaman, from: Ceres, Merchant.
    Cap: 28 Jul 1812 Bahama Bank by Privateer Theodore Int: 01 Aug 1812 Dis: 06 Aug 1812.
    Received from Prize. Sent to Liverpool in the Ship Cora by order of the Governor.

Benard, Lewis   Prisoner 171. Rank: Seaman, from: Dash, Privateer.
    Cap: 12 Sep 1812 Coast of America by Rhodian & Variable Int: 23 Sep 1812 Dis: 24 Oct 1812.
    Received from Rhodian and Variable. Sent to Charlestown in the British Cartel Nassau by order of the Governor.

Benjamin, Samuel   Prisoner 363. Rank: Seaman, from: Washington, Merchant.
    Cap: Not Recorded by Privateer Brilliant Int: 01 Mar 1813 Dis: 10 Apr 1813.
    Received from Prize. Sent to Charleston in the British Cartel Charlotte by order of the Governor. (Date and place of capture 'not mentioned'.)

Benson, Joline   Prisoner 349. Rank: Seaman, from: George & Mary, Merchant.
    Cap: Not Recorded by Not Recorded Int: 14 Feb 1813 Dis: 14 Feb 1813.
    Wrecked among the islands and delivered themselves up. Received from HMS Moselle. Sent to Norfolk in the British Cartel Eliza by order of the Governor. (Date of capture 'not mentioned'.)

Bentall, Ebenezer   Prisoner 43. Rank: Seaman, from: Ceres, Merchant.
    Cap: 28 Jul 1812 Bahama Bank by Privateer Theodore Int: 01 Aug 1812 Dis: 22 Sep 1812.
    Received from Prize. Sent to new York United States of America.

Bern, William   Prisoner 790. Rank: Seaman, from: Java, Letter of Marquis.
    Cap: Not Recorded by Cockchafer Int: 14 Jan 1815 Dis:
    Received from HM Schooner Cockchafer. (Dates of capture and discharge not on roster.)

Betty, Samuel   Prisoner 818. Rank: Seaman, from: Saturn, Letter of Marquis.
    Cap: Not Recorded by Venus Int: 29 Jan 1815 Dis: .
    Schooner. Received from Venus. (Dates of capture and discharge not on roster.)

Bigloss, Gagdon   Prisoner 97. Rank: Seaman, from: Rapid, Privateer.
    Cap: Not Recorded by Not Recorded Int: 13 Sep 1812 Dis: 04 Feb 1813.
    Received from Government Schooner John Bull. Sent to Charlestown in the British Cartel Ann. (Date, place and name of capturing ship 'not mentioned'.)

American Prisoners of War Held at New Providence During the War of 1812

Bileau, Julian   Prisoner 278. Rank: Seaman, from: Viper, Man of War.
    Cap: Gulf of Mexico by HMS Narcissus Int: 30 Jan 1813 Dis: 14 Feb 1813.
    Brig. Received from HMS Moselle. Sent in the British Cartel Eliza to Norfolk by order of the Governor. (Date of capture 'not mentioned'.)

Bill, John   Prisoner 25. Rank: Seaman, from: Non Parail, Privateer.
    Cap: 29 Jul 1812 Off Eleuthera by HM Schooner Decouverte Int: 01 Aug 1812 Dis: 22 Sep 1812.
    Received from HM Schooner Decauverte. Sent to New York United States of America.

Blackwell, Henry   Prisoner 175. Rank: Seaman, from: Dash, Privateer.
    Cap: 12 Sep 1812 Coast of America by Rhodian & Variable Int: 23 Sep 1812 Dis: 24 Oct 1812.
    Received from Rhodian and Variable. Sent to Charlestown in the British Cartel Nassau by order of the Governor.

Blair, John   Prisoner 683. Rank: Seaman, from: Frolic, Man of War.
    Cap: 20 Apr 1814 Not Recorded by HMS Orpheus Int: 26 Apr 1814 Dis: 13 Jun 1814.
    United States Ship. Received from HMS Orpheus. Sent to Halifax in HMS Majestic per order of Commander in Chief Aml Cochrane.

Bland, Richard   Prisoner 122. Rank: Boatswain, from: Sarah Ann, Privateer.
    Cap: 13 Sep 1812 Coast of America by Rhodian & Variable Int: 23 Sep 1812 Dis: 24 Oct 1812.
    Received from Rhodian & Variable. Sent to Charlestown in the British Cartel Nassau.

Blanking, Gerard   Prisoner 482. Rank: Seaman, from: Innocencia, Merchant.
    Cap: 26 Nov 1813 At sea by HMS Ringdove Int: 30 Nov 1813 Dis: 26 Apr 1814.
    Received from HMS Ringdove. Sent to Rhode Island in the Cartel Liberty.

Blasted, Jacob   Prisoner 564. Rank: Seaman, from: Frolic, Man of War.
    Cap: 20 Apr 1814 At sea by HMS Orpheus Int: 26 Apr 1814 Dis: 11 Jun 1814.
    United States Ship. Received from HMS Orpheus. Sent to Bermuda in HMS Orpheus order Aml Cochrane.

Bliss, Eli C   Prisoner 358. Rank: Seaman, from: Helen, Merchant.
    Cap: Not Recorded by Not Recorded Int: 14 Feb 1813 Dis: 14 Feb 1813.
    Wrecked among the islands and delivered themselves up. Sent to Norfolk in the British Cartel Eliza by order of the Governor. (Date of capture 'not mentioned'.)

Blunt, John   Prisoner 824. Rank: Seaman, from: William, Schooner.
    Cap: Not Recorded by Eleanor Int: 13 Feb 1815 Dis:
    Received from Privateer Eleanor. (Dates of capture and discharge not on roster.)

Bond, William   Prisoner 633. Rank: Seaman, from: Frolic, Man of War.
    Cap: 20 Apr 1814 Not Recorded by HMS Orpheus Int: 26 Apr 1814 Dis: 13 Jun 1814.
    United States Ship. Received from HMS Orpheus. Sent to Halifax in HMS Majestic order Aml Cochrane.

Booth, William   Prisoner 461. Rank: 2 Mate, from: Caroline, Merchant.
    Cap: 12 Aug 1813 East out of Charleston by HMS Moselle & Privateer Brilliant Int: 25 Aug 1813 Dis: . Received from Privateer Brilliant. (Date of discharge not on roster.)

Bowdlear, Thomas   Prisoner 521. Rank: Seaman, from: Lion, Merchant.
    Cap: Not Recorded by Privateer Mars Int: 30 Jan 1814 Dis: 08 Jul 1814.
    Received from Privateer Brilliant. Sent to Bermuda. (Date of capture not recorded.)

Bowen, William   Prisoner 785. Rank: Mate, from: No Name, Not Recorded.
    Cap: Not Recorded by Venus Int: 11 Jan 1815 Dis: .
    Received from Venus. (Dates capture and discharge not on roster.)

Bowling, J   Prisoner 404. Rank: Seaman, from: Wave, Merchant.
    Cap: Not Recorded by Privateer Wellesley Int: 05 Apr 1813 Dis: 19 Apr 1813.
    Received from Prize. Sent to England in the Ship Loyal Sam. (Date and place of capture 'not mentioned'.)

Bowshaw, Job   Prisoner 65. Rank: Seaman, from: Resolution, Merchant.
    Cap: 26 Jul 1812 Crooked Island Passage by HM Schooner Variable Int: 07 Aug 1812 Dis: 22 Sep 1812. Received from His Majesties Schooner Variable. Sent to new York United States of America.

Boyer, Richway   Prisoner 509. Rank: Seaman, from: Stephen Garard, Merchant.
    Cap: Not Recorded by Privateer Mars Int: 30 Jan 1814 Dis: 08 Jul 1814.
    Received from Prize. Sent to Bermuda. (Date of capture not recorded.)

Brackett, John   Prisoner 182. Rank: Seaman, from: Dash, Privateer.
    Cap: 12 Sep 1812 Coast of America by Rhodian & Variable Int: 23 Sep 1812 Dis: 24 Oct 1812.
    Received from Rhodian and Variable. Sent to Charlestown in the British Cartel Nassau by order of the Governor.

American Prisoners of War Held at New Providence During the War of 1812

Bradford, E   Prisoner 385. Rank: Seaman, from: Venus, Merchant.
    Cap: Not Recorded by Brilliant Privateer Int: 17 Mar 1813 Dis: 26 Apr 1814.
    Received from Prize. Sent to Rhode Island in the Cartel Liberty. (Date and place of capture 'not mentioned'.)

Bradshaw, John   Prisoner 49. Rank: Seaman, from: Augusta, Merchant.
    Cap: 02 Aug 1812 Island of Abaco by HM Schooner Decouverte Int: 05 Aug 1812 Dis: 22 Sep 1812.
    Received from Privateer. Sent to new York United States of America.

Bradshaw, John   Prisoner 530. Rank: Seaman, from: Lion, Merchant.
    Cap: 04 Jan 1814 Not Recorded by HMS Forester Int: 12 Jan 1814 Dis: 08 Jul 1814.
    Received from HMS Forester. Sent to Bermuda. (May be part of the crew of the Sevant.)

Bragan, Mathew   Prisoner 225. Rank: Seaman, from: Factor, Merchant.
    Cap: Coast of America by HMS Moselle Int: 19 Nov 1812 Dis: 04 Feb 1813.
    Received from HMS Moselle. Sent to Charlestown in the British Cartel Ann by order of the Governor. (Date of capture 'not mentioned'.)

Bray, A   Prisoner 495. Rank: Seaman, from: St. Polito, Merchant.
    Cap: 26 Nov 1813 At sea by Privateers Mars & Dash Int: 25 Dec 1813 Dis: 26 Apr 1814.
    Received from Privateer Mars. Sent to Rhode Island in the Cartel Liberty.

Brazier, William   Prisoner 519. Rank: Seaman, from: Lion, Merchant.
    Cap: Not Recorded by Privateer Mars Int: 30 Jan 1814 Dis: 08 Jul 1814.
    Received from Privateer Brilliant. Sent to Bermuda. (Date of capture not recorded.)

Breadhead, Richard   Prisoner 136. Rank: Seaman, from: Sarah Ann, Privateer.
    Cap: 13 Sep 1812 Coast of America by Rhodian & Variable Int: 23 Sep 1812 Dis: 24 Oct 1812.
    Received from Rhodian and Variable. Sent to Charlestown in the British Cartel Nassau.

Bredricke, William   Prisoner 297. Rank: Seaman, from: Viper, Man of War.
    Cap: Gulf of Mexico by HMS Narcissus Int: 30 Jan 1813 Dis: 14 Feb 1813.
    Brig. Received from HMS Moselle. Sent in the British Cartel Eliza to Norfolk by order of the Governor. (Date of capture 'not mentioned'.)

Brienies, John   Prisoner 645. Rank: Seaman, from: Frolic, Man of War.
    Cap: 20 Apr 1814 Not Recorded by HMS Orpheus Int: 26 Apr 1814 Dis: 13 Jun 1814.
    United States Ship. Received from HMS Orpheus. Sent to Halifax in HMS Majestic per order of Commander in Chief Aml Cochrane.

Brothers, James   Prisoner 325. Rank: Seaman, from: Osprey, Merchant.
    Cap: Gulf of Mexico by HMS Moselle Int: 30 Jan 1813 Dis: 14 Feb 1813.
    Received from HMS Moselle. Sent in the British Cartel Eliza to Norfolk by order of the Governor. (Date of capture 'not mentioned'.)

Brown, Daniel   Prisoner 378. Rank: Seaman, from: Apodaco, Merchant.
    Cap: Not Recorded by Government Schooner Swift Int: 15 Mar 1813 Dis: 13 Jun 1814.
    Received from Government Schooner Swift. Sent to Halifax HMS Majestic order of Adl Cochane. (Date and place of capture 'not mentioned'.)

Brown, Edward   Prisoner 612. Rank: Seaman, from: Frolic, Man of War.
    Cap: 20 Apr 1814 Not Recorded by HMS Orpheus Int: 26 Apr 1814 Dis: 13 Jun 1814.
    United States Ship. Received from HMS Orpheus. Sent to Halifax in HMS Majestic per order Aml Cochrane.

Brown, George   Prisoner 40. Rank: Seaman, from: Ceres, Merchant.
    Cap: 28 Jul 1812 Bahama Bank by Privateer Theodore Int: 01 Aug 1812 Dis: 22 Sep 1812.
    Received from Prize. Sent to new York United States of America.

Brown, John   Prisoner 289. Rank: Seaman, from: Viper, Man of War.
    Cap: Gulf of Mexico by HMS Narcissus Int: 30 Jan 1813 Dis: 14 Feb 1813.
    Brig. Received from HMS Moselle. Sent in the British Cartel Eliza to Norfolk by order of the Governor. (Date of capture 'not mentioned'.)

Brown, John   Prisoner 340. Rank: Mate, from: Dart, Merchant.
    Cap: Not Recorded by Not Recorded Int: 04 Feb 1813 Dis: 04 Feb 1813.
    Wrecked among the islands and delivered themselves up. Received from HMS Moselle. Sent to Charlestown in the British Cartel Ann by order of the Governor. (Date of capture 'not mentioned'.)

Brown, John   Prisoner 543. Rank: Seaman, from: Sevant, Letter of Marquis.
    Cap: 04 Jan 1814 Not Recorded by Not Legible Int: 12 Jan 1814 Dis: 16 Apr 1814.
    Brig. Received from HMS Forester. HMS Contest.

Brown, Joshua   Prisoner 80. Rank: Seaman, from: Hamer, Merchant.
    Cap: 01 Sep 1812 Off Abaco by Privateer Int: 02 Sep 1812 Dis: 24 Oct 1812.
    Received from Privateer. Sent to Charlestown in the British Cartel Nassau.

American Prisoners of War Held at New Providence During the War of 1812

Brown, N   Prisoner 285. Rank: Seaman, from: Viper, Man of War.
    Cap: Gulf of Mexico by HMS Narcissus   Int: 30 Jan 1813   Dis: 14 Feb 1813.
    Brig. Received from HMS Moselle. Sent in the British Cartel Eliza to Norfolk by order of the Governor. (Date of capture 'not mentioned'.)

Brown, Peter   Prisoner 177. Rank: Seaman, from: Dash, Privateer.
    Cap: 12 Sep 1812 Coast of America by Rhodian & Variable   Int: 23 Sep 1812   Dis: 24 Oct 1812.
    Received from Rhodian and Variable. Sent to Charlestown in the British Cartel Nassau by order of the Governor.

Brown, R   Prisoner 504. Rank: Seaman, from: St. Polito, Merchant.
    Cap: 26 Nov 1813 At sea by Privateers Mars & Dash   Int: 25 Dec 1813   Dis: 08 Jul 1814.
    Received from Privateer Mars. Sent to Bermuda per order Adml Cochrane.

Brown, William   Prisoner 100. Rank: Seaman, from: Endeavour, Merchant.
    Cap: 17 Sep 1812 Abaco Passage by Privateer Francis   Int: 17 Sep 1812   Dis: 24 Oct 1812.
    Received from Prize. Sent to Charlestown in the British Cartel Nassau.

Brown, William   Prisoner 549. Rank: Seaman, from: Not Recorded, Letter of Marquis.
    Cap: Not Recorded by Not Recorded   Int: 17 Feb 1814   Dis: 13 Aug 1814.
    Ship wrecked among the Bahama Keys. Sent to Bermuda per order of the Commander in Chief, HMS Surprise. (Date of capture and ship received from not recorded.)

Brown, William   Prisoner 630. Rank: Seaman, from: Frolic, Man of War.
    Cap: 20 Apr 1814 Not Recorded by HMS Orpheus   Int: 26 Apr 1814   Dis: 13 Jun 1814.
    United States Ship. Received from HMS Orpheus. Sent to Halifax in HMS Majestic order Aml Cochrane.

Brown, William   Prisoner 662. Rank: Seaman, from: Frolic, Man of War.
    Cap: 20 Apr 1814 Not Recorded by HMS Orpheus   Int: 26 Apr 1814   Dis: 13 Jun 1814.
    United States Ship. Received from HMS Orpheus. Sent to Halifax in HMS Majestic per order of Commander in Chief Aml Cochrane.

Brown, William   Prisoner 677. Rank: 2 Gunner, from: Frolic, Man of War.
    Cap: 20 Apr 1814 Not Recorded by HMS Orpheus   Int: 26 Apr 1814   Dis: 13 Jun 1814.
    United States Ship. Received from HMS Orpheus. Sent to Halifax in HMS Majestic per order of Commander in Chief Aml Cochrane.

Bruelle, Henry   Prisoner 798. Rank: Seaman, from: Java, Letter of Marquis.
    Cap: Not Recorded by Cockchafer   Int: 14 Jan 1815   Dis: 19 Jan 1815.
    Received from HM Schooner Cockchafer. To England. (Date of capture not on roster.)

Bruzel, James   Prisoner 688. Rank: Cook, from: Frolic, Man of War.
    Cap: 20 Apr 1814 Not Recorded by HMS Orpheus   Int: 26 Apr 1814   Dis: 13 Jun 1814.
    United States Ship. Received from HMS Orpheus. Sent to Halifax in HMS Majestic order Aml Cochrane.

Budick, Newton   Prisoner 830. Rank: Seaman, from: Hercules, Merchant Vessel.
    Cap: 09 Mar 1815 Not Recorded by HM Schooner Canso   Int: 13 Mar 1815   Dis:
    Recaptured Ship. Received from HM Schooner Canso. (Date of discharge not on roster.)

Buel, H   Prisoner 202. Rank: Seaman, from: Not Recorded, Merchant.
    Cap: Not Recorded by Privateer Unknown   Int: 24 Oct 1812   Dis: 24 Oct 1812.
    Received from HMS Mosella. Sent to Charlestown in the British Cartel Nassau by order of the Governor. (Date, place, name of vessel and name of capturing ship 'not mentioned'.)

Buggs, John   Prisoner 563. Rank: Seaman, from: Frolic, Man of War.
    Cap: 20 Apr 1814 At sea by HMS Orpheus   Int: 26 Apr 1814   Dis: 11 Jun 1814.
    United States Ship. Received from HMS Orpheus. Sent to Bermuda in HMS Orpheus order Aml Cochrane.

Buguest, Isaac   Prisoner 471. Rank: Seaman, from: Caroline, Merchant.
    Cap: 12 Aug 1813 East out of Charleston by HMS Moselle & Privateer Brilliant   Int: 25 Aug 1813   Dis: 27 Jan 1814. Received from Privateer Brilliant. Embarked on board the Nassau to assist in navigating her to England.

Bukefe, Bartholomew   Prisoner 726. Rank: Seaman, from: John, Merchant Vessel.
    Cap: Cumberland Sound by HMS Lacedaemonian   Int: 19 Oct 1814   Dis:
    Received from HMS Lacedaemonian. (Dates of capture and discharge not on roster.)

Bull, John   Prisoner 826. Rank: Seaman, from: William, Schooner.
    Cap: Not Recorded by Eleanor   Int: 13 Feb 1815   Dis:
    Received from Privateer Eleanor. (Dates of capture and discharge not on roster.)

Bundock, Benjamin   Prisoner 440. Rank: Seaman, from: Stanley, Merchant.
    Cap: Coast of America by Privateer Wellesley   Int: 08 Jun 1813   Dis: 26 Apr 1814.
    Received from Privateer Schooner Wellesley. Sent to Rhode Island in the Cartel Liberty. (Date of capture not recorded.)

American Prisoners of War Held at New Providence During the War of 1812

Bunker, B   Prisoner 500. Rank: Seaman, from: St. Polito, Merchant.
    Cap: 26 Nov 1813 At sea by Privateers Mars & Dash Int: 25 Dec 1813 Dis: 26 Apr 1814.
    Received from Privateer Mars. Sent to Rhode Island in the Cartel Liberty.

Bunker, John   Prisoner 833. Rank: Seaman, from: Hercules, Merchant Vessel.
    Cap: 09 Mar 1815 Not Recorded by HM Schooner Canso Int: 13 Mar 1815 Dis: .
    Recaptured Ship. Received from HM Schooner Canso. (Date of discharge not on roster.)

Burgess, John   Prisoner 621. Rank: Seaman, from: Frolic, Man of War.
    Cap: 20 Apr 1814 Not Recorded by HMS Orpheus Int: 26 Apr 1814 Dis: 13 Jun 1814.
    United States Ship. Received from HMS Orpheus. Sent to Halifax in HMS Majestic order Aml Cochrane.

Burke, Jacob   Prisoner 318. Rank: Seaman, from: Sheperd, Merchant.
    Cap: Gulf of Mexico by HMS Narcissus Int: 30 Jan 1813 Dis: 14 Feb 1813.
    Received from HMS Moselle. Sent to Norfolk in the British Cartel Eliza by order of the Governor. (Date of capture 'not mentioned'.)

Burke, Thomas   Prisoner 322. Rank: Seaman, from: Sheperd, Merchant.
    Cap: Gulf of Mexico by HMS Narcissus Int: 30 Jan 1813 Dis: 14 Feb 1813.
    Received from HMS Moselle. Sent to Norfolk in the British Cartel Eliza by order of the Governor. (Date of capture 'not mentioned'.)

Burns, John   Prisoner 198. Rank: Seaman, from: Not Recorded, Not Recorded.
    Cap: Not Recorded by Privateer Unknown Int: 24 Oct 1812 Dis: 24 Oct 1812.
    Received from HMS Mosella. Sent to Charlestown in the British Cartel Nassau by order of the Governor. (Date, place, name of vessel and name of capturing ship 'not mentioned'.)

Burredde, Mansfield   Prisoner 581. Rank: Seaman, from: Frolic, Man of War.
    Cap: 20 Apr 1814 Not Recorded by HMS Orpheus Int: 26 Apr 1814 Dis: 11 Jun 1814.
    United States Ship. Received from HMS Orpheus. Sent to Bermuda in HMS Orpheus per order Commander in Chief Aml Cochrane.

Butler, Benjamin   Prisoner 682. Rank: Seaman, from: Frolic, Man of War.
    Cap: 20 Apr 1814 Not Recorded by HMS Orpheus Int: 26 Apr 1814 Dis: 13 Jun 1814.
    United States Ship. Received from HMS Orpheus. Sent to Halifax in HMS Majestic per order of Commander in Chief Aml Cochrane.

Butler, John   Prisoner 517. Rank: Seaman, from: Lion, Merchant.
    Cap: Not Recorded by Privateer Mars Int: 30 Jan 1814 Dis:
    Received from Privateer Brilliant. (Dates of capture and discharge not on roster.)

Butler, John   Prisoner 541. Rank: Seaman, from: Sevant, Letter of Marquis.
    Cap: 04 Jan 1814 Not Recorded by HMS Forester Int: 12 Jan 1814 Dis: 07 Dec 1814.
    Brig. Received from HMS Forester. Order Commander in Chief.

Butler, Timothy   Prisoner 197. Rank: Seaman, from: Not Recorded, Not Recorded.
    Cap: Not Recorded by Privateer Unknown Int: 24 Oct 1812 Dis: 24 Oct 1812.
    Received from HMS Mosella. Sent to Charlestown in the British Cartel Nassau by order of the Governor. (Date, place, name of vessel and name of capturing ship 'not mentioned'.)

Cadet, John   Prisoner 229. Rank: Seaman, from: Ospray, Merchant.
    Cap: Not Recorded by Not Recorded Int: 02 Jan 1813 Dis: 04 Feb 1813.
    Reveived from HMS Variable. Sent to Charlestown in the British Cartel Ann by order of the Governor. (Date, place and name of capturing ship 'not mentioned'.)

Caivin, James   Prisoner 396. Rank: Seaman, from: Dominica Packet, Merchant.
    Cap: Not Recorded by Privateer Baker Delight Int: 01 Apr 1813 Dis: 10 Apr 1813.
    Recaptured from the American Privateer Comet. Received from Privateer. Sent to Charleston in the British Cartel Charlotte by order of the Governor. (Date and place of capture 'not mentioned'.)

Calem, Samuel   Prisoner 153. Rank: Seaman, from: Sarah Ann, Privateer.
    Cap: 13 Sep 1812 Coast of America by Rhodian & Variable Int: 23 Sep 1812 Dis: 24 Oct 1812.
    Received from Rhodian and Variable. Sent to Charlestown in the British Cartel Nassau.

Calhoon, Joseph   Prisoner 648. Rank: Seaman, from: Frolic, Man of War.
    Cap: 20 Apr 1814 Not Recorded by HMS Orpheus Int: 26 Apr 1814 Dis: 13 Jun 1814.
    United States Ship. Received from HMS Orpheus. Sent to Halifax in HMS Majestic per order of Commander in Chief Aml Cochrane.

Callett, John   Prisoner 373. Rank: Seaman, from: Hazard, Privateer.
    Cap: Not Recorded by Privateer Cutter Caledonia Int: 07 Mar 1813 Dis: 13 Jun 1814.
    Recaptured in the British Ship. Received from Caledonia. Sent to Halifax HMS Majestic order of Adl Cochane. (Date and place of capture 'not mentioned'.)

American Prisoners of War Held at New Providence During the War of 1812

Campbell, James   Prisoner 619. Rank: Seaman, from: Frolic, Man of War.
    Cap: 20 Apr 1814 Not Recorded by HMS Orpheus Int: 26 Apr 1814 Dis: 13 Jun 1814.
    United States Ship. Received from HMS Orpheus. Sent to Halifax in HMS Majestic order Aml Cochrane.

Campbell, John   Prisoner 391. Rank: Seaman, from: Dominica Packet, Merchant.
    Cap: Not Recorded by HMS Variable Int: 30 Mar 1813 Dis: 13 Jun 1814.
    Recaptured from the American Privateer Comet. Received from Variable. Sent to Halifax HMS Majestic. (Date and place of capture 'not mentioned'.)

Canagon, Daniel   Prisoner 167. Rank: Seaman, from: Dash, Privateer.
    Cap: 12 Sep 1812 Coast of America by Rhodian & Variable Int: 23 Sep 1812 Dis: 24 Oct 1812.
    Received from Rhodian and Variable. Sent to Charlestown in the British Cartel Nassau.

Cannon, Charles   Prisoner 321. Rank: Seaman, from: Sheperd, Merchant.
    Cap: Gulf of Mexico by HMS Narcissus Int: 30 Jan 1813 Dis: 14 Feb 1813.
    Received from HMS Moselle. Sent to Norfolk in the British Cartel Eliza by order of the Governor. (Date of capture 'not mentioned'.)

Canoll, Michael   Prisoner 596. Rank: Seaman, from: Frolic, Man of War.
    Cap: 20 Apr 1814 Not Recorded by HMS Orpheus Int: 26 Apr 1814 Dis: 13 Jun 1814.
    United States Ship. Received from HMS Orpheus. Sent to Halifax HMS Majestic order Aml Cochrane.

Card, Colonel   Prisoner 10. Rank: Boatswain, from: Non Parail, Privateer.
    Cap: 29 Jul 1812 Off Eleuthera (rest not legible) by HM Schooner Decouverte Int: 01 Aug 1812 Dis: 24 Oct 1812. Received from HM Schooner Decauverte. Sent to Charlestown in the British Cartel Nassau.

Carn, William   Prisoner 829. Rank: Seaman, from: Hercules, Merchant Vessel.
    Cap: 09 Mar 1815 Not Recorded by HM Schooner Canso Int: 13 Mar 1815 Dis:
    Recaptured Ship. Received from HM Schooner Canso. (Date of discharge not on roster.)

Carr, John   Prisoner 188. Rank: Seaman, from: Marquis de Casa Yayo, Merchant.
    Cap: 12 Sep 1812 Coast of America by Caledonia Privateer Int: 03 Oct 1812 Dis: 24 Nov 1812.
    Received from Prize. Sent to Savannah in the American Cartel Delight.

Carraway, John   Prisoner 158. Rank: Captain, from: Dash, Privateer.
    Cap: 12 Sep 1812 Coast of America by Rhodian & Variable Int: 23 Sep 1812 Dis: 24 Oct 1812.
    Received from Rhodian and Variable. Sent to Charlestown in the British Cartel Nassau.

Cavanagh, Peter   Prisoner 556. Rank: Seaman, from: Roberts, Merchant Vessel.
    Cap: 24 Feb 1814 At sea by HM Ship Rhin Int: 03 Mar 1814 Dis: 08 Jul 1814.
    His MS Rhin taken the recaptured Brig Roberts belonging to the American Privateer Schooner May, of 15 guns. Received from HMS Rhin. Sent to Bermuda.

Chamberlain, David   Prisoner 242. Rank: Seaman, from: Viper, Man of War.
    Cap: Gulf of Mexico by HMS Narcissus Int: 30 Jan 1813 Dis: 14 Feb 1813.
    United States Brig. Received from HMS Moselle. taken by the Police for Murder and as evidence. (Date of capture 'not mentioned'.)

Chamberlain, David   Prisoner 426. Rank: Seaman, from: Viper, Man of War.
    Cap: Not Recorded by HMS Narcissus Int: 13 May 1813 Dis: 26 Apr 1814.
    Received from Police. Sent to Rhode Island in the Cartel Liberty. (Date and place of capture 'not mentioned'.)

Chambers, William   Prisoner 627. Rank: Seaman, from: Frolic, Man of War.
    Cap: 20 Apr 1814 Not Recorded by HMS Orpheus Int: 26 Apr 1814 Dis: 13 Jun 1814.
    United States Ship. Received from HMS Orpheus. Sent to Halifax in HMS Majestic order Aml Cochrane.

Chandler, Samuel   Prisoner 511. Rank: Seaman, from: Stephen Garard, Merchant.
    Cap: Not Recorded by Privateer Mars Int: 30 Jan 1814 Dis: 13 Aug 1814.
    Received from Privateer Brilliant. Sent to Bermuda per order Commander in Chief, HMS Surprise. (Date of capture not recorded. May be part of the crew of the Lion.)

Chandler, Will   Prisoner 512. Rank: Seaman, from: Lion, Merchant.
    Cap: Not Recorded by Privateer Mars Int: 30 Jan 1814 Dis: 13 Aug 1814.
    Received from Privateer Brilliant. Sent to Bermuda per order Commander in Chief, HMS Surprise. (Date of capture not recorded.)

Chapple, John   Prisoner 660. Rank: Seaman, from: Frolic, Man of War.
    Cap: 20 Apr 1814 Not Recorded by HMS Orpheus Int: 26 Apr 1814 Dis: 13 Jun 1814.
    United States Ship. Received from HMS Orpheus. Sent to Halifax in HMS Majestic per order of Commander in Chief Aml Cochrane.

Chase, William   Prisoner 77. Rank: Seaman, from: Hamer, Merchant.
    Cap: 01 Sep 1812 Off Abaco by Privateer Int: 02 Sep 1812 Dis: 24 Oct 1812.
    Received from Privateer. Sent to Charlestown in the British Cartel Nassau.

American Prisoners of War Held at New Providence During the War of 1812

Chaves, M   Prisoner 719. Rank: Seaman, from: Not Recorded, Not Recorded.
>Cap: Not Recorded by Not Recorded Int: 13 Sep 1814 Dis: 18 Jan 1815.
>Received from Police. HMS Childers to Bermuda. (Date of capture not on roster.)

Cheesbourgh, Benjamin F   Prisoner 474. Rank: Seaman, from: Caroline, Merchant.
>Cap: 12 Aug 1813 East out of Charleston by HMS Moselle & Privateer Brilliant Int: 25 Aug 1813 Dis: 27 Jan 1814. Received from Privateer Brilliant. Embarked on board the Merchant Vessel New Providence to assist in navigating her to England. % Henry

Chester, John   Prisoner 194. Rank: Seaman, from: Marquis de Casa Yayo, Merchant.
>Cap: Not Recorded by Caledonia Privateer Int: 03 Oct 1812 Dis: 24 Oct 1812.
>Received from Prize. Sent to Charlestown in the British Cartel Nassau by order of the Governor. (Date and place of capture 'not mentioned'.)

Chester, Samuel   Prisoner 157. Rank: Seaman, from: Sarah Ann, Privateer.
>Cap: 13 Sep 1812 Coast of America by Rhodian & Variable Int: 23 Sep 1812 Dis: 25 Sep 1812.
>Received from Rhodian and Variable. Died. Fever.

Christie, Robert   Prisoner 636. Rank: Seaman, from: Frolic, Man of War.
>Cap: 20 Apr 1814 Not Recorded by HMS Orpheus Int: 26 Apr 1814 Dis: 13 Jun 1814.
>United States Ship. Received from HMS Orpheus. Sent to Halifax in HMS Majestic per order Aml Cochrane.

Church, William   Prisoner 384. Rank: Seaman, from: Venus, Merchant.
>Cap: Not Recorded by Brilliant Privateer Int: 17 Mar 1813 Dis: 10 Apr 1813.
>Received from Prize. Sent to Charleston in the British Cartel Charlotte by order of the Governor. (Date and place of capture 'not mentioned'.)

Clark, Charles   Prisoner 104. Rank: Seaman, from: Romney, Merchant.
>Cap: Not Recorded by HMS Rattler Int: 21 Sep 1812 Dis: 26 Nov 1812.
>Received from HMS Rattler. Sent to Charlestown in the British Cartel Nassau. (Date and place of capture 'not mentioned'.)

Clark, John   Prisoner 129. Rank: Seaman, from: Sarah Ann, Privateer.
>Cap: 13 Sep 1812 Coast of America by Rhodian & Variable Int: 23 Sep 1812 Dis: 24 Oct 1812.
>Received from Rhodian and Variable. Sent to Charlestown in the British Cartel Nassau.

Clarke, John   Prisoner 298. Rank: Seaman, from: Viper, Man of War.
>Cap: Gulf of Mexico by HMS Narcissus Int: 30 Jan 1813 Dis: 14 Feb 1813.
>Brig. Received from HMS Moselle. Sent to Norfolk in the British Cartel Eliza by order of the Governor. (Date of capture 'not mentioned'.)

Clarke, John   Prisoner 584. Rank: Seaman, from: Frolic, Man of War.
>Cap: 20 Apr 1814 Not Recorded by HMS Orpheus Int: 26 Apr 1814 Dis: 11 Jun 1814.
>United States Ship. Received from HMS Orpheus. Sent to Bermuda in HMS Orpheus per order Commander in Chief Aml Cochrane.

Clarke, John   Prisoner 815. Rank: Seaman, from: Saturn, Letter of Marquis.
>Cap: Not Recorded by Venus Int: 29 Jan 1815 Dis:
>Schooner. Received from Venus. (Dates of capture and discharge not on roster.)

Clarke, Joseph   Prisoner 723. Rank: Passenger, from: Fox, Merchant Vessel.
>Cap: Cumberland Sound by HMS Lacedaemonian Int: 19 Oct 1814 Dis:
>Received from HMS Lacedaemonian. (Dates of capture and discharge not on roster.)

Cleary, James   Prisoner 667. Rank: Seaman, from: Frolic, Man of War.
>Cap: 20 Apr 1814 Not Recorded by HMS Orpheus Int: 26 Apr 1814 Dis: 08 Jul 1814.
>United States Ship. Received from HMS Orpheus. Sent to Bermuda.

Climsted, Taber   Prisoner 793. Rank: Seaman, from: Java, Letter of Marquis.
>Cap: Not Recorded by Cockchafer Int: 14 Jan 1815 Dis: .
>Received from HM Schooner Cockchafer. (Dates of capture and discharge not on roster.)

Coal, John   Prisoner 365. Rank: Seaman, from: Washington, Merchant.
>Cap: Not Recorded by Privateer Brilliant Int: 01 Mar 1813 Dis: 10 Apr 1813.
>Received from Prize. Sent to Charleston in the British Cartel Charlotte by order of the Governor. (Date and place of capture 'not mentioned'.)

Cobb, ---   Prisoner 359. Rank: Seaman, from: Helen, Merchant.
>Cap: Not Recorded by Not Recorded Int: 14 Feb 1813 Dis: 14 Feb 1813.
>Wrecked among the islands and delivered themselves up. Sent to Norfolk in the British Cartel Eliza by order of the Governor. (First name not recorded. Date of capture 'not mentioned'.)

Coffin, George   Prisoner 611. Rank: Seaman, from: Frolic, Man of War.
>Cap: 20 Apr 1814 Not Recorded by HMS Orpheus Int: 26 Apr 1814 Dis: 13 Jun 1814.
>United States Ship. Received from HMS Orpheus. Sent to Halifax in HMS Majestic per order Aml Cochrane.

American Prisoners of War Held at New Providence During the War of 1812

Coggeeshall, Nathaniel   Prisoner 405. Rank: Seaman, from: Mary, Merchant.
    Cap: Not Recorded by Government Schooner Swift Int: 10 Apr 1813 Dis: 10 Apr 1813.
    Received from Government Schooner Swift. Sent to Charleston in the British Cartel Charlotte by order of the Governor. (Date and place of capture 'not mentioned'.)

Coglan, William   Prisoner 227. Rank: Seaman, from: Not Recorded, Not Recorded.
    Cap: Not Recorded by Not Recorded Int: 30 Nov 1812 Dis: 17 Dec 1812.
    Landed from the American Privateer at Watling Island. Died. Fever. (Date of capture not recorded.)

Collector, Jefferson   Prisoner 770. Rank: Seaman, from: Factor, Merchant Vessel.
    Cap: 07 Dec 1814 Sapello Sound by HM Ship Lacedaemonian Int: 16 Dec 1814 Dis:
    Received from HMS Lacedaemonian. (Date of discharge not on roster.)

Collins, Henry   Prisoner 91. Rank: Seaman, from: Phiebe V. Jane, Merchant.
    Cap: 25 Aug 1812 Coast of America by HMS Rhodian Int: 06 Sep 1812 Dis: 24 Oct 1812.
    Received from HM Brig Rhodian. Sent to Charlestown in the British Cartel Nassau.

Collins, William   Prisoner 816. Rank: Seaman, from: Saturn, Letter of Marquis.
    Cap: Not Recorded by Venus Int: 29 Jan 1815 Dis:
    Schooner. Received from Venus. (Dates of capture and discharge not on roster.)

Colman, William   Prisoner 515. Rank: Seaman, from: Lion, Merchant.
    Cap: Not Recorded by Privateer Mars Int: 30 Jan 1814 Dis: 27 Jan 1814.
    Received from Privateer Brilliant. Embarked on board Merchant Vessel to assist in navigating her to England. (Date of capture not recorded. Date of internment before date of discharge.)

Conklin, John   Prisoner 753. Rank: Seaman, from: Bossan, Merchant Vessel.
    Cap: 08 Aug 1814 St Helina Sound by HM Ship Lacedaemonian Int: 07 Dec 1814 Dis:
    Received from HMS Primrose. (Date of discharge not on roster.)

Connor, Samuel   Prisoner 267. Rank: Seaman, from: Viper, Man of War.
    Cap: Gulf of Mexico by HMS Narcissus Int: 30 Jan 1813 Dis: 14 Feb 1813.
    United States Brig. Received from HMS Moselle. Sent in the British Cartel Eliza to Norfolk by order of the Governor. (Date of capture 'not mentioned'.)

Cook, Anthony   Prisoner 165. Rank: Surgeon, from: Dash, Privateer.
    Cap: 12 Sep 1812 Coast of America by Rhodian & Variable Int: 23 Sep 1812 Dis: 24 Oct 1812.
    Received from Rhodian and Variable. Sent to Charlestown in the British Cartel Nassau.

Cook, J   Prisoner 557. Rank: Seaman, from: Roberts, Merchant Vessel.
    Cap: 24 Feb 1814 At sea by HM Ship Rhin Int: 03 Mar 1814 Dis: 15 Aug 1814.
    His MS Rhin taken the recaptured Brig Roberts belonging to the American Privateer Schooner May, of 15 guns. Received from HMS Rhin. Sent to Bermuda HMS Surprise order the Commander in Chief.

Cook, Robert   Prisoner 730. Rank: Seaman, from: Gunboat 160, Man of War.
    Cap: Cumberland Sound by HMS Lacedaemonian Int: 19 Oct 1814 Dis: .
    United States Gunboat. Received from HMS Lacedaemonian. (Dates of capture and discharge not on roster.)

Cooper, Benjamin   Prisoner 399. Rank: Seaman, from: Wave, Merchant.
    Cap: Not Recorded by Privateer Wellesley Int: 05 Apr 1813 Dis: 10 Apr 1813.
    Received from Prize. Sent to Charleston in the British Cartel Charlotte by order of the Governor. (Date and place of capture 'not mentioned'.)

Cooper, Richard   Prisoner 825. Rank: Seaman, from: William, Schooner.
    Cap: Not Recorded by Eleanor Int: 13 Feb 1815 Dis: .
    Received from Privateer Eleanor. (Dates of capture and discharge not on roster.)

Corbett, John   Prisoner 286. Rank: Seaman, from: Viper, Man of War.
    Cap: Gulf of Mexico by HMS Narcissus Int: 30 Jan 1813 Dis: 14 Feb 1813.
    Brig. Received from HMS Moselle. Sent in the British Cartel Eliza to Norfolk by order of the Governor. (Date of capture 'not mentioned'.)

Corey, Benjamin   Prisoner 777. Rank: Seaman, from: Ruby, Merchant Vessel.
    Cap: Not Recorded by Schooner Swift Int: 09 Jan 1815 Dis:
    Received from Schooner Swift. (Date of capture and place of capture 'not mentioned'. Date of discharge not on roster.)

Cotterill, Henry   Prisoner 473. Rank: Seaman, from: Caroline, Merchant.
    Cap: 12 Aug 1813 East out of Charleston by HMS Moselle & Privateer Brilliant Int: 25 Aug 1813 Dis: 27 Jan 1814. Received from Privateer Brilliant. Embarked on board the Merchant Vessel New Providence to assist in navigating her to England. % Dixon.

Cottineau, Huo   Prisoner 729. Rank: Masters Mate, from: Gunboat 160, Man of War.
    Cap: Cumberland Sound by HMS Lacedaemonian Int: 19 Oct 1814 Dis: .
    United States Gunboat. Received from HMS Lacedaemonian. (Dates of capture and discharge not on roster.)

American Prisoners of War Held at New Providence During the War of 1812

Coulken, William   Prisoner 293. Rank: Seaman, from: Viper, Man of War.
    Cap: Gulf of Mexico by HMS Narcissus Int: 30 Jan 1813 Dis: 14 Feb 1813.
    Brig. Received from HMS Moselle. Sent in the British Cartel Eliza to Norfolk by order of the Governor. (Date of capture 'not mentioned'.)

Cousins, John   Prisoner 617. Rank: Seaman, from: Frolic, Man of War.
    Cap: 20 Apr 1814 Not Recorded by HMS Orpheus Int: 26 Apr 1814 Dis: 08 Jul 1814.
    United States Ship. Received from HMS Orpheus. Sent to Bermuda.

Cousins, Samuel   Prisoner 607. Rank: Seaman, from: Frolic, Man of War.
    Cap: 20 Apr 1814 Not Recorded by HMS Orpheus Int: 26 Apr 1814 Dis: 13 Jun 1814.
    United States Ship. Received from HMS Orpheus. Sent to Halifax in HMS Majestic order Aml Cochrane.

Cox, Miles   Prisoner 56. Rank: Seaman, from: Olympus, Merchant.
    Cap: 05 Aug 1812 Island of Abaco by HM Schooner Decouverte Int: 07 Aug 1812 Dis: 22 Sep 1812.
    Received from HMS Decouverte. Sent to new York United States of America.

Crandall, William   Prisoner 352. Rank: Seaman, from: George & Mary, Merchant.
    Cap: Not Recorded by Not Recorded Int: 14 Feb 1813 Dis: 14 Feb 1813.
    Wrecked among the islands and delivered themselves up. Sent to Norfolk in the British Cartel Eliza by order of the Governor. (Date of capture 'not mentioned'.)

Crandle, Caleb   Prisoner 381. Rank: Seaman, from: Apodaco, Merchant.
    Cap: Not Recorded by Government Schooner Swift Int: 15 Mar 1813 Dis: 26 Apr 1814.
    Received from Government Schooner Swift. Sent to Rhode Island in the Cartel Liberty. (Date and place of capture 'not mentioned'.)

Crandwell, John   Prisoner 212. Rank: Seaman, from: Venus, Merchant.
    Cap: Coast of America by HMS Moselle Int: 19 Nov 1812 Dis: 04 Feb 1813.
    Received from HMS Moselle. Sent to Charlestown in the British Cartel Ann by order of the Governor. (Date of capture 'not mentioned'.)

Crane, James   Prisoner 299. Rank: Seaman, from: Viper, Man of War.
    Cap: Gulf of Mexico by HMS Narcissus Int: 30 Jan 1813 Dis: 14 Feb 1813.
    Brig. Received from HMS Moselle. Sent to Norfolk in the British Cartel Eliza by order of the Governor. (Date of capture 'not mentioned'.)

Crawell, Isaac   Prisoner 397. Rank: Seaman, from: Dominica Packet, Merchant.
    Cap: Not Recorded by Privateer Baker Delight Int: 01 Apr 1813 Dis: 10 Apr 1813.
    Recaptured from the American Privateer Comet. Received from Privateer. Sent to Charleston in the British Cartel Charlotte by order of the Governor. (Date and place of capture 'not mentioned'.)

Cross, William   Prisoner 315. Rank: Seaman, from: Sheperd, Merchant.
    Cap: Gulf of Mexico by HMS Narcissus Int: 30 Jan 1813 Dis: 14 Feb 1813.
    Received from HMS Moselle. Sent to Norfolk in the British Cartel Eliza by order of the Governor. (Date of capture 'not mentioned'.)

Crutch, George   Prisoner 300. Rank: Seaman, from: Viper, Man of War.
    Cap: Gulf of Mexico by HMS Narcissus Int: 30 Jan 1813 Dis: 14 Feb 1813.
    Brig. Received from HMS Moselle. Sent to Norfolk in the British Cartel Eliza by order of the Governor. (Date of capture 'not mentioned'.)

Cuffee, James   Prisoner 314. Rank: Seaman, from: Sheperd, Merchant.
    Cap: Gulf of Mexico by HMS Narcissus Int: 30 Jan 1813 Dis: 14 Feb 1813.
    Received from HMS Moselle. Sent to Norfolk in the British Cartel Eliza by order of the Governor. (Date of capture 'not mentioned'.)

Culverson, Noah   Prisoner 179. Rank: Seaman, from: Dash, Privateer.
    Cap: 12 Sep 1812 Coast of America by Rhodian & Variable Int: 23 Sep 1812 Dis: 24 Oct 1812.
    Received from Rhodian and Variable. Sent to Charlestown in the British Cartel Nassau by order of the Governor.

Cunningham, Alexander   Prisoner 256. Rank: Seaman, from: Viper, Man of War.
    Cap: Gulf of Mexico by HMS Narcissus Int: 30 Jan 1813 Dis: 14 Feb 1813.
    United States Brig. Received from HMS Moselle. Sent in the British Cartel Eliza to Norfolk by order of the Governor. (Date of capture 'not mentioned'.)

Cunningham, William   Prisoner 24. Rank: Seaman, from: Non Parail, Privateer.
    Cap: 29 Jul 1812 Off Eleuthera (rest not legible) by HM Schooner Decouverte Int: 01 Aug 1812 Dis: 24 Oct 1812. Received from HM Schooner Decauverte. Sent to Charlestown in the British Cartel Nassau by order of the Governor.

Curry, Joseph   Prisoner 244. Rank: Seaman, from: Viper, Man of War.
    Cap: Gulf of Mexico by HMS Narcissus Int: 30 Jan 1813 Dis: 14 Feb 1813.
    United States Brig. Received from HMS Moselle. Sent in the British Cartel Eliza to Norfolk by order of the Governor. (Date of capture 'not mentioned'.)

American Prisoners of War Held at New Providence During the War of 1812

Curtis, Stacy   Prisoner 713. Rank: Sail Maker, from: Frolic, Man of War.
    Cap: 20 Apr 1814 Not Recorded by HMS Orpheus   Int: 26 Apr 1814   Dis: .
    United States Ship. Received from HMS Orpheus. (Date of discharge not on roster.)

Curtis, Thomas R   Prisoner 429. Rank: Mate, from: Trimmer, Merchant.
    Cap: Bahama Island by Government Schooner John Bull   Int: 20 May 1813   Dis: 26 Apr 1814.
    Received from Government Schooner John Bull. Sent to Rhode Island in the Cartel Liberty. (Date of capture 'not mentioned'.)

Curtis, William L   Prisoner 433. Rank: Seaman, from: Trimmer, Merchant.
    Cap: Bahama Island by Government Schooner John Bull   Int: 20 May 1813   Dis: 26 Apr 1814.
    Received from Government Schooner John Bull. Sent to Rhode Island in the Cartel Liberty. (Date of capture 'not mentioned'.)

Damoulet, George   Prisoner 254. Rank: Seaman, from: Viper, Man of War.
    Cap: Gulf of Mexico by HMS Narcissus   Int: 30 Jan 1813   Dis: 14 Feb 1813.
    United States Brig. Received from HMS Moselle. Sent in the British Cartel Eliza to Norfolk by order of the Governor. (Date of capture 'not mentioned'.)

Daniel, John   Prisoner 185. Rank: Seaman, from: Dash, Privateer.
    Cap: 12 Sep 1812 Coast of America by Rhodian & Variable   Int: 23 Sep 1812   Dis: 24 Oct 1812.
    Received from Rhodian and Variable. Sent to Charlestown in the British Cartel Nassau by order of the Governor.

Daniels, John   Prisoner 751. Rank: Seaman, from: Auroa, Letter of Marquis.
    Cap: Not Recorded by HM Shooner Cockchafer   Int: 03 Dec 1814   Dis: .
    Received from Cockchafer. (Date and place of capture 'not mentioned'. Date of discharge not on roster.)

Darrell, N   Prisoner 195. Rank: Master, from: Not Recorded, Not Recorded.
    Cap: Not Recorded by Privateer Unknown   Int: 24 Oct 1812   Dis: 24 Oct 1812.
    Received from HMS Mosella. Sent to Charlestown in the British Cartel Nassau by order of the Governor. (Date, place, name of vessel and name of capturing ship 'not mentioned'.)

Daughty, Russell   Prisoner 524. Rank: Seaman, from: Lion, Merchant.
    Cap: 04 Jan 1814 Not Recorded by Privateer Mars   Int: 30 Jan 1814   Dis: 08 Jul 1814.
    Received from Privateer Brilliant. Sent to Bermuda. (Date of capture not recorded.)

Daur, Richard   Prisoner 131. Rank: Seaman, from: Sarah Ann, Privateer.
    Cap: 13 Sep 1812 Coast of America by Rhodian & Variable   Int: 23 Sep 1812   Dis: 24 Oct 1812.
    Received from Rhodian and Variable. Sent to Charlestown in the British Cartel Nassau.

Davis, George   Prisoner 90. Rank: Seaman, from: Phiebe V. Jane, Merchant.
    Cap: 25 Aug 1812 Coast of America by HMS Rhodian   Int: 06 Sep 1812   Dis: 24 Oct 1812.
    Received from HM Brig Rhodian. Sent to Charlestown in the British Cartel Nassau.

Davis, Hewlet   Prisoner 678. Rank: Seaman, from: Frolic, Man of War.
    Cap: 20 Apr 1814 Not Recorded by HMS Orpheus   Int: 26 Apr 1814   Dis: 13 Jun 1814.
    United States Ship. Received from HMS Orpheus. Sent to Halifax in HMS Majestic per order of Commander in Chief Aml Cochrane.

Davis, Samuel   Prisoner 400. Rank: Seaman, from: Wave, Merchant.
    Cap: Not Recorded by Privateer Wellesley   Int: 05 Apr 1813   Dis: 13 Jun 1814.
    Received from Prize. Sent to Halifax HMS Majestic. (Date and place of capture 'not mentioned'.)

Davis, William   Prisoner 444. Rank: Seaman, from: Stanley, Merchant.
    Cap: Coast of America by Privateer Wellesley   Int: 10 Jun 1813   Dis: 26 Apr 1814.
    Received from Government Schooner Swift. Sent to Rhode Island in the Cartel Liberty. (Date of capture not recorded.)

Day, Isaac   Prisoner 357. Rank: Mate, from: Helen, Merchant.
    Cap: Not Recorded by Not Recorded   Int: 14 Feb 1813   Dis: 14 Feb 1813.
    Wrecked among the islands and delivered themselves up. Sent to Norfolk in the British Cartel Eliza by order of the Governor. (Date of capture 'not mentioned'.)

Dean, Eanos   Prisoner 162. Rank: Gunner, from: Dash, Privateer.
    Cap: 12 Sep 1812 Coast of America by Rhodian & Variable   Int: 23 Sep 1812   Dis: 24 Oct 1812.
    Received from Rhodian and Variable. Sent to Charlestown in the British Cartel Nassau.

Deenn, High   Prisoner 625. Rank: Boatswains Mate, from: Frolic, Man of War.
    Cap: 20 Apr 1814 Not Recorded by HMS Orpheus   Int: 26 Apr 1814   Dis: 13 Jun 1814.
    United States Ship. Received from HMS Orpheus. Sent to Halifax in HMS Majestic order Aml Cochrane.

Delanghey, John   Prisoner 801. Rank: Seaman, from: Java, Letter of Marquis.
    Cap: Not Recorded by Cockchafer   Int: 14 Jan 1815   Dis: 04 Feb 1815.
    Received from HM Schooner Cockchafer. from Prison Ship. (Date of capture not on roster.)

American Prisoners of War Held at New Providence During the War of 1812

Delano, Laby   Prisoner 631. Rank: Seaman, from: Frolic, Man of War.
   Cap: 20 Apr 1814 Not Recorded by HMS Orpheus Int: 26 Apr 1814 Dis: 13 Jun 1814.
   United States Ship. Received from HMS Orpheus. Sent to Halifax in HMS Majestic order Aml Cochrane.

Delphia, John   Prisoner 134. Rank: Seaman, from: Sarah Ann, Privateer.
   Cap: 13 Sep 1812 Coast of America by Rhodian & Variable Int: 23 Sep 1812 Dis: 24 Oct 1812.
   Received from Rhodian and Variable. Sent to Charlestown in the British Cartel Nassau.

Dempson, Daniel   Prisoner 618. Rank: Seaman, from: Frolic, Man of War.
   Cap: 20 Apr 1814 Not Recorded by HMS Orpheus Int: 26 Apr 1814 Dis: 13 Jun 1814.
   United States Ship. Received from HMS Orpheus. Sent to Halifax in HMS Majestic order Aml Cochrane.

Dennis, James   Prisoner 528. Rank: Seaman, from: Lion, Merchant.
   Cap: 04 Jan 1814 Not Recorded by HMS Forester Int: 12 Jan 1814 Dis: 08 Jul 1814.
   Received from HMS Forester. Sent to Bermuda. (May be part of the crew of the Sevant.)

Denny, James   Prisoner 654. Rank: Seaman, from: Frolic, Man of War.
   Cap: 20 Apr 1814 Not Recorded by HMS Orpheus Int: 26 Apr 1814 Dis: 13 Jun 1814.
   United States Ship. Received from HMS Orpheus. Sent to Halifax in HMS Majestic per order of Commander in Chief Aml Cochrane.

Dents, John   Prisoner 371. Rank: Seaman, from: Hazard, Privateer.
   Cap: Not Recorded by Privateer Cutter Caledonia Int: 07 Mar 1813 Escaped: 25 Jun 1813.
   Recaptured in the British Ship. Received from Caledonia. Escaped. (Date and place of capture 'not mentioned'.)

Deole, Peter   Prisoner 765. Rank: Seaman, from: No Name, Not Recorded.
   Cap: Not Recorded by Not Recorded Int: 08 Dec 1814 Dis: 18 Jan 1815.
   Received from HM Sloop Childers. Sent to Bermuda in HMS Childers. (Date, place of capture and name of capturing ship 'not mentioned'.)

Depew, H. Y   Prisoner 700. Rank: Private, from: Frolic, Man of War.
   Cap: 20 Apr 1814 Not Recorded by HMS Orpheus Int: 26 Apr 1814 Dis: 13 Jun 1814.
   United States Ship. Received from HMS Orpheus. Sent to Halifax in HMS Majestic order Aml Cochrane.

Derrick, George   Prisoner 427. Rank: Seaman, from: Venus, Merchant.
   Cap: Not Recorded by Not Recorded Int: 05 May 1813 Dis: 26 Apr 1814.
   Received from Privateer Brillant. Sent to Rhode Island in the Cartel Liberty. (Date and place of capture 'not mentioned'.)

Dick, David   Prisoner 138. Rank: Seaman, from: Sarah Ann, Privateer.
   Cap: 13 Sep 1812 Coast of America by Rhodian & Variable Int: 23 Sep 1812 Dis: 14 Oct 1812.
   Received from Rhodian and Variable. Sent to Jamaica in HMS Sappho by order of the Governor.

Dickey, Robert   Prisoner 792. Rank: Seaman, from: Java, Letter of Marquis.
   Cap: Not Recorded by Cockchafer Int: 14 Jan 1815 Dis:
   Received from HM Schooner Cockchafer. (Dates of capture and discharge not on roster.)

Dickinson, H. Y   Prisoner 579. Rank: Seaman, from: Frolic, Man of War.
   Cap: 20 Apr 1814 At sea by HMS Orpheus Int: 26 Apr 1814 Dis: 11 Jun 1814.
   United States Ship. Received from HMS Orpheus. Sent to Bermuda in HMS Orpheus order Aml Cochrane.

Dobson, James   Prisoner 672. Rank: Seaman, from: Frolic, Man of War.
   Cap: 20 Apr 1814 Not Recorded by HMS Orpheus Int: 26 Apr 1814 Dis: 13 Jun 1814.
   United States Ship. Received from HMS Orpheus. Sent to Halifax in HMS Majestic per order of Commander in Chief Aml Cochrane.

Dodge, Lewis   Prisoner 35. Rank: Seaman, from: HM Schooner Decouverte, Not Recorded.
   Cap: 29 Jul 1812 Not Stated by HM Schooner Decouverte Int: 01 Aug 1812 Dis: 20 Aug 1812.
   Received from HM Schooner Decauverte. Gave themselves up as Prisoners of War. Being Part of the complement of the HMS Decouvete Lieut Richard Williams Commanding. Sent to Jamaica in HM Schooner Decouverte by order of Lieut Williams.

Dolson, Andrew   Prisoner 554. Rank: Prize Master, from: Roberts, Merchant Vessel.
   Cap: 24 Feb 1814 At sea by HM Ship Rhin Int: 03 Mar 1814 Dis: 04 Jun 1814.
   Received from HMS Rhin. Brig Roberts.

Dolton, Frederick W   Prisoner 587. Rank: --- Mate, from: Frolic, Man of War.
   Cap: 20 Apr 1814 Not Recorded by HMS Orpheus Int: 26 Apr 1814 Dis: 11 Jun 1814.
   United States Ship. Received from HMS Orpheus. Sent to Bermuda in HMS Orpheus per order Commander in Chief Aml Cochrane.

American Prisoners of War Held at New Providence During the War of 1812

Domina, M   Prisoner 412. Rank: Seaman, from: Portsmouth, Merchant.
   Cap: 16 Apr 1813 At sea by HM Ships Morgiana & Calibri Int: 20 Apr 1813 Dis: 26 Apr 1814.
   Received from HMS Morgiana. Sent to Rhode Island in the Cartel Liberty.

Dominique, John   Prisoner 588. Rank: Seaman, from: Frolic, Man of War.
   Cap: 20 Apr 1814 Not Recorded by HMS Orpheus Int: 26 Apr 1814 Dis: 11 Jun 1814.
   United States Ship. Received from HMS Orpheus. Sent to Bermuda in HMS Orpheus per order Commander in Chief Aml Cochrane.

Dorman, John   Prisoner 629. Rank: Boatswain, from: Frolic, Man of War.
   Cap: 20 Apr 1814 Not Recorded by HMS Orpheus Int: 26 Apr 1814 Dis: .
   United States Ship. Received from HMS Orpheus. (Date of discharge not on roster.)

Dosey, Dempsey   Prisoner 168. Rank: Seaman, from: Dash, Privateer.
   Cap: 12 Sep 1812 Coast of America by Rhodian & Variable Int: 23 Sep 1812 Dis: 24 Oct 1812.
   Received from Rhodian and Variable. Sent to Charlestown in the British Cartel Nassau.

Dowall, Robert M   Prisoner 324. Rank: Seaman, from: Osprey, Merchant.
   Cap: Gulf of Mexico by HMS Moselle Int: 30 Jan 1813 Dis: 14 Feb 1813.
   Received from HMS Moselle. Sent in the British Cartel Eliza to Norfolk by order of the Governor. (Date of capture 'not mentioned'.)

Downson, Charles   Prisoner 717. Rank: Seaman, from: Enterprise, Merchant Vessel.
   Cap: Not Recorded by Not Recorded Int: 22 Aug 1814 Dis: 18 Jan 1815.
   Received HMS Childers. HMS Childers to Bermuda. (Date of capture not on roster.)

Doyle, James   Prisoner 389. Rank: Seaman, from: Dominica Packet, Merchant.
   Cap: Not Recorded by HMS Variable Int: 30 Mar 1813 Dis: 15 Jul 1813.
   Recaptured from the American Privateer Comet. Received from Variable. Died Consumption. (Date and place of capture 'not mentioned'.)

Drown, John   Prisoner 354. Rank: Seaman, from: George & Mary, Merchant.
   Cap: Not Recorded by Not Recorded Int: 14 Feb 1813 Dis: 14 Feb 1813.
   Wrecked among the islands and delivered themselves up. Sent to Norfolk in the British Cartel Eliza by order of the Governor. (Date of capture 'not mentioned'.)

Dupua, Francis   Prisoner 9. Rank: Captain, from: Non Parail, Privateer.
   Cap: 29 Jul 1812 Off Eleuthera (rest not legible) by HM Schooner Decouverte Int: 01 Aug 1812 Dis: 24 Oct 1812. Received from HM Schooner Decauverte. Sent to Charlestown in the British Cartel Nassau.

Dyke, Sword   Prisoner 615. Rank: Seaman, from: Frolic, Man of War.
   Cap: 20 Apr 1814 Not Recorded by HMS Orpheus Int: 26 Apr 1814 Dis: 13 Jun 1814.
   United States Ship. Received from HMS Orpheus. Sent to Halifax in HMS Majestic per order Aml Cochrane.

Earl, William   Prisoner 137. Rank: Seaman, from: Sarah Ann, Privateer.
   Cap: 13 Sep 1812 Coast of America by Rhodian & Variable Int: 23 Sep 1812 Dis: 24 Oct 1812.
   Received from Rhodian and Variable. Sent to Charlestown in the British Cartel Nassau.

Eastman, Thomas   Prisoner 54. Rank: Mate, from: Olympus, Merchant.
   Cap: 05 Aug 1812 Island of Abaco by HM Schooner Decouverte Int: 07 Aug 1812 Dis: 20 Aug 1812.
   Received from HMS Decouverte. On parole by order of Government.

Edmunds, William   Prisoner 59. Rank: Seaman, from: Olympus, Merchant.
   Cap: 05 Aug 1812 Island of Abaco by HM Schooner Decouverte Int: 07 Aug 1812 Dis: 19 Sep 1812.
   Received from HMS Decouverte. Died. Fever.

Edwards, John   Prisoner 601. Rank: Seaman, from: Frolic, Man of War.
   Cap: 20 Apr 1814 Not Recorded by HMS Orpheus Int: 26 Apr 1814 Dis: 13 Jun 1814.
   United States Ship. Received from HMS Orpheus. Sent to Halifax HMS Majestic order Aml Cochrane.

Eldridge, David   Prisoner 545. Rank: Seaman, from: Not Recorded, Letter of Marquis.
   Cap: Not Recorded by Not Recorded Int: 17 Feb 1814 Dis: 07 Dec 1814.
   Ship wrecked among the Bahama Keys. Order Commander in Chief. (Date of capture and ship received from not recorded.)

Elelow, John   Prisoner 510. Rank: Seaman, from: Stephen Garard, Merchant.
   Cap: Not Recorded by Privateer Mars Int: 30 Jan 1814 Dis: 08 Jul 1814.
   Received from Prize. Sent to Bermuda. (Date of capture not recorded.)

Elger, Robert   Prisoner 570. Rank: Seaman, from: Frolic, Man of War.
   Cap: 20 Apr 1814 At sea by HMS Orpheus Int: 26 Apr 1814 Dis: 11 Jun 1814.
   United States Ship. Received from HMS Orpheus. Sent to Bermuda in HMS Orpheus order Aml Cochrane.

American Prisoners of War Held at New Providence During the War of 1812

Elget, William   Prisoner 434. Rank: Seaman, from: Elizabeth, Merchant.
    Cap: Not Recorded by Privateer Schooner Dash Int: 20 May 1813 Dis: 26 Apr 1814.
    Received from Privateer Schooner Dash. Sent to Rhode Island in the Cartel Liberty. (Date of capture 'not mentioned'.)

Ellingwood, Joseph   Prisoner 514. Rank: Seaman, from: Lion, Merchant.
    Cap: Not Recorded by Privateer Mars Int: 30 Jan 1814 Dis: 13 Aug 1814.
    Received from Privateer Brilliant. Sent to Bermuda HMS Surprise order Commander in Chief. (Date of capture not recorded.)

Ellis, William   Prisoner 768. Rank: Seaman, from: No Name, Not Recorded.
    Cap: Not Recorded by Not Recorded Int: 08 Dec 1814 Dis: 18 Jan 1815.
    Received from HM Sloop Childers. Sent to Bermuda in HMS Childers. (Date, place of capture and name of capturing ship 'not mentioned'.)

Ellsey, Thomas   Prisoner 312. Rank: Seaman, from: Sheperd, Merchant.
    Cap: Gulf of Mexico by HMS Narcissus Int: 30 Jan 1813 Dis: 14 Feb 1813.
    Received from HMS Moselle. Sent to Norfolk in the British Cartel Eliza by order of the Governor. (Date of capture 'not mentioned'.)

Elvin, John   Prisoner 652. Rank: Seaman, from: Frolic, Man of War.
    Cap: 20 Apr 1814 Not Recorded by HMS Orpheus Int: 26 Apr 1814 Dis: 13 Jun 1814.
    United States Ship. Received from HMS Orpheus. Sent to Halifax in HMS Majestic per order of Commander in Chief Aml Cochrane.

Emery, William   Prisoner 401. Rank: Seaman, from: Wave, Merchant.
    Cap: Not Recorded by Privateer Wellesley Int: 05 Apr 1813 Dis: 26 Apr 1814.
    Received from Prize. Sent to Rhode Island in the Cartel Liberty. (Date and place of capture 'not mentioned'.)

Emory, Samuel   Prisoner 472. Rank: Seaman, from: Caroline, Merchant.
    Cap: 12 Aug 1813 East out of Charleston by HMS Moselle & Privateer Brilliant Int: 25 Aug 1813 Dis: 26 Apr 1814. Received from Privateer Brilliant. Sent to Rhode Island in the Cartel Liberty.

Eowitt, John   Prisoner 551. Rank: Seaman, from: Not Recorded, Letter of Marquis.
    Cap: Not Recorded by Not Recorded Int: 17 Feb 1814 Dis:
    Ship wrecked among the Bahama Keys. (Dates of capture, discharge and ship received from not on roster.)

Eveleth, Francis   Prisoner 51. Rank: Mate, from: Augusta, Merchant.
    Cap: 02 Aug 1812 Island of Abaco by HM Schooner Decouverte Int: 07 Aug 1812 Dis: 20 Aug 1812.
    Received from HMS Decouverte. On parole by order of Government.

Every, George   Prisoner 438. Rank: Seaman, from: Balay, Merchant.
    Cap: Not Recorded by Privateer Schooner Dash Int: 20 May 1813 Dis: 26 Apr 1814.
    Received from Privateer Schooner Dash. Sent to Rhode Island in the Cartel Liberty. (Date of capture 'not mentioned'.)

Factor, George A   Prisoner 597. Rank: Cooper, from: Frolic, Man of War.
    Cap: 20 Apr 1814 Not Recorded by HMS Orpheus Int: 26 Apr 1814 Dis: 13 Jun 1814.
    United States Ship. Received from HMS Orpheus. Sent to Halifax HMS Majestic order Aml Cochrane.

Fairchild, Lewis   Prisoner 5. Rank: 4 Officer, from: Non Parail, Privateer.
    Cap: 29 Jul 1812 Off Eleuthera (rest not legible) by HM Schooner Decouverte Int: 01 Aug 1812 Dis: 24 Oct 1812. Received from HM Schooner Decauverte. Sent to Charlestown in the British Cartel Nassau.

Farrell, William   Prisoner 141. Rank: Seaman, from: Sarah Ann, Privateer.
    Cap: 13 Sep 1812 Coast of America by Rhodian & Variable Int: 23 Sep 1812 Dis: 24 Oct 1812.
    Received from Rhodian and Variable. Sent to Charlestown in the British Cartel Nassau.

Fauchild, Alexander   Prisoner 19. Rank: Seaman, from: Non Parail, Privateer.
    Cap: 29 Jul 1812 Off Eleuthera (rest not legible) by HM Schooner Decouverte Int: 01 Aug 1812 Dis: 24 Oct 1812. Received from HM Schooner Decauverte. Sent to Charlestown in the British Cartel Nassau by order of the Governor.

Feamon, Benjamin   Prisoner 796. Rank: Seaman, from: Java, Letter of Marquis.
    Cap: Not Recorded by Cockchafer Int: 14 Jan 1815 Dis: 04 Feb 1815.
    Received from HM Schooner Cockchafer. from Prison Ship. (Date of capture not on roster.)

Fennel, William   Prisoner 555. Rank: Seaman, from: Roberts, Merchant Vessel.
    Cap: 24 Feb 1814 At sea by HM Ship Rhin Int: 03 Mar 1814 Dis: 13 Aug 1814.
    Received from HMS Rhin. Sent to Bermuda order Commander in Chief.

Ferdinand, Abraham   Prisoner 50. Rank: Seaman, from: Augusta, Merchant.
    Cap: 02 Aug 1812 Island of Abaco by HM Schooner Decouverte Int: 05 Aug 1812 Dis: 22 Sep 1812.
    Received from HMS Decouverte. Sent to new York United States of America.

American Prisoners of War Held at New Providence During the War of 1812

Field, Samuel   Prisoner 613. Rank: Seaman, from: Frolic, Man of War.
    Cap: 20 Apr 1814 Not Recorded by HMS Orpheus Int: 26 Apr 1814 Dis: 13 Jun 1814.
    United States Ship. Received from HMS Orpheus. Sent to Halifax in HMS Majestic per order Aml Cochrane.

Fielder, J   Prisoner 498. Rank: Seaman, from: St. Polito, Merchant.
    Cap: 26 Nov 1813 At sea by Privateers Mars & Dash Int: 25 Dec 1813 Dis: 26 Apr 1814.
    Received from Privateer Mars. Sent to Rhode Island in the Cartel Liberty.

Fitcha, J S   Prisoner 456. Rank: Mate, from: Stanley, Merchant.
    Cap: Coast of America by Privateer Wellesley Int: 18 Jul 1813 Dis:
    Received from HMS Herald. (Dates of capture and discharge not on roster.)

Flanikin, John   Prisoner 835. Rank: Seaman, from: Hercules, Merchant Vessel.
    Cap: 09 Mar 1815 Not Recorded by HM Schooner Canso Int: 13 Mar 1815 Dis:
    Recaptured Ship. Received from HM Schooner Canso. (Date of discharge not on roster.)

Fleetstrom, Israel   Prisoner 757. Rank: Seaman, from: No Name, Not Recorded.
    Cap: 28 Nov 1814 St. Andrew Sound by HM Ship Primrose Int: 07 Dec 1814 Dis: 19 Jan 1815.
    Received from HMS Primrose. To England.

Flemming, Charles   Prisoner 791. Rank: Seaman, from: Java, Letter of Marquis.
    Cap: Not Recorded by Cockchafer Int: 14 Jan 1815 Dis:
    Received from HM Schooner Cockchafer. (Dates of capture and discharge not on roster.)

Flyn, Frederick   Prisoner 827. Rank: Seaman, from: Hercules, Merchant Vessel.
    Cap: 09 Mar 1815 Not Recorded by HM Schooner Canso Int: 13 Mar 1815 Dis: .
    Recaptured Ship. Received from HM Schooner Canso. (Date of discharge not on roster.)

Fogarty, G   Prisoner 232. Rank: Seaman, from: Factor, Merchant.
    Cap: Not Recorded by Not Recorded Int: 15 Jan 1813 Dis: 26 Apr 1814.
    Reveived from HMS Variable. Sent to Rhode Island in the Cartel Liberty. (Date, place and name of capturing ship 'not mentioned'.)

Fogarty, Robert   Prisoner 223. Rank: Seaman, from: Factor, Merchant.
    Cap: Coast of America by HMS Moselle Int: 19 Nov 1812 Dis: 24 Nov 1812.
    Received from HMS Moselle. Sent to Savannah in the American Cartel Delight. (Date of capture 'not mentioned'.)

Fogarty, Samuel   Prisoner 231. Rank: Seaman, from: Factor, Merchant.
    Cap: Not Recorded by Not Recorded Int: 15 Jan 1813 Dis: 26 Apr 1814.
    Reveived from HMS Variable. Sent to Rhode Island in the Cartel Liberty. (Date, place and name of capturing ship 'not mentioned'.)

Foreman, John   Prisoner 743. Rank: Seaman, from: Auroa, Letter of Marquis.
    Cap: Not Recorded by HM Shooner Cockchafer Int: 03 Dec 1814 Dis: .
    Received from Cockchafer. (Date and place of capture 'not mentioned'. Date of discharge not on roster.)

Forloney, James   Prisoner 379. Rank: Seaman, from: Apodaco, Merchant.
    Cap: Not Recorded by Government Schooner Swift Int: 15 Mar 1813 Dis:
    Received from Government Schooner Swift. (Date and place of capture 'not mentioned'. Date of discharge not on roster.)

Forster, Jonathan   Prisoner 52. Rank: Seaman, from: Augusta, Merchant.
    Cap: 02 Aug 1812 Island of Abaco by HM Schooner Decouverte Int: 07 Aug 1812 Dis: 22 Sep 1812.
    Received from HMS Decouverte. Sent to new York United States of America.

Foster, James   Prisoner 686. Rank: Gunner, from: Frolic, Man of War.
    Cap: 20 Apr 1814 Not Recorded by HMS Orpheus Int: 26 Apr 1814 Dis:
    United States Ship. Received from HMS Orpheus. (Date of discharge not on roster.)

Fotry, Duroc   Prisoner 779. Rank: Seaman, from: Ruby, Merchant Vessel.
    Cap: Not Recorded by Schooner Swift Int: 09 Jan 1815 Dis:
    Received from Schooner Swift. (Date of capture and place of capture 'not mentioned'. Date of discharge not on roster.)

Fowler, Isaac   Prisoner 693. Rank: Private, from: Frolic, Man of War.
    Cap: 20 Apr 1814 Not Recorded by HMS Orpheus Int: 26 Apr 1814 Dis: 13 Jun 1814.
    United States Ship. Received from HMS Orpheus. Sent to Halifax in HMS Majestic order Aml Cochrane.

Fowler, James   Prisoner 330. Rank: Seaman, from: Osprey, Merchant.
    Cap: Gulf of Mexico by HMS Moselle Int: 30 Jan 1813 Dis: 14 Feb 1813.
    Received from HMS Moselle. Sent in the British Cartel Eliza to Norfolk by order of the Governor. (Date of capture 'not mentioned'.)

American Prisoners of War Held at New Providence During the War of 1812

Fox, Edward   Prisoner 725. Rank: Master, from: Fox, Merchant Vessel.
  Cap: Cumberland Sound by HMS Lacedaemonian Int: 19 Oct 1814 Dis:
  Received from HMS Lacedaemonian. (Dates of capture and discharge not on roster.)

Foxwing, George   Prisoner 773. Rank: Mate, from: George & Joseph, Merchant Vessel.
  Cap: 07 Dec 1814 Daughboy Sound by HM Ship Lacedaemonian Int: 16 Dec 1814 Dis: 07 Dec 1814.
  Received from HMS Lacedaemonian. Order Commander in Chief. (Date of internment before date of discharge.)

Francis, John   Prisoner 11. Rank: Cook, from: Non Parail, Privateer.
  Cap: 29 Jul 1812 Off Eleuthera (rest not legible) by HM Schooner Decouverte Int: 01 Aug 1812 Dis: 22 Sep 1812. Received from HM Schooner Decauverte. Sent to new York United States of America.

Francis, John   Prisoner 60. Rank: Seaman, from: Olympus, Merchant.
  Cap: 05 Aug 1812 Island of Abaco by HM Schooner Decouverte Int: 07 Aug 1812 Dis: 22 Sep 1812.
  Received from HMS Decouverte. Sent to new York United States of America.

Francis, John   Prisoner 374. Rank: Seaman, from: Hazard, Privateer.
  Cap: Not Recorded by Privateer Cutter Caledonia Int: 07 Mar 1813 Dis: 27 May 1814.
  Recaptured in the British Ship. Received from Caledonia. HMS Cockchafer. (Date and place of capture 'not mentioned'.)

Fraser, Antoine   Prisoner 186. Rank: Seaman, from: Not Recorded, Not Recorded.
  Cap: Not Recorded by Police Int: 28 Sep 1812 Dis: 24 Oct 1812.
  Sent to Charlestown in the British Cartel Nassau by order of the Governor. (Date and place of capture 'not mentioned'.)

Fraser, Robert   Prisoner 85. Rank: Seaman, from: Nelly, Merchant.
  Cap: 25 Aug 1812 Coast of America by HMS Rhodian Int: 06 Sep 1812 Dis: 24 Oct 1812.
  Received from HM Brig Rhodian. Sent to Charlestown in the British Cartel Nassau.

Frasier, James   Prisoner 172. Rank: Seaman, from: Dash, Privateer.
  Cap: 12 Sep 1812 Coast of America by Rhodian & Variable Int: 23 Sep 1812 Dis: 24 Oct 1812.
  Received from Rhodian and Variable. Sent to Charlestown in the British Cartel Nassau by order of the Governor.

Frazer, Andrew   Prisoner 808. Rank: Seaman, from: Saturn, Letter of Marquis.
  Cap: Not Recorded by Venus Int: 29 Jan 1815 Dis:
  Schooner. Received from Venus. (Dates of capture and discharge not on roster.)

Freeman, Aaron   Prisoner 411. Rank: Seaman, from: Portsmouth, Merchant.
  Cap: 16 Apr 1813 At sea by HM Ships Morgiana & Calibri Int: 20 Apr 1813 Dis: 26 Apr 1814.
  Received from HMS Morgiana. Sent to Rhode Island in the Cartel Liberty.

Freeman, Charles   Prisoner 523. Rank: Seaman, from: Lion, Merchant.
  Cap: Not Recorded by Privateer Mars Int: 30 Jan 1814 Dis: 27 Jan 1814.
  Received from Privateer Brilliant. Embarked on board the Anna Merchant Vessel to assist in navigating her to England. (Date of capture not recorded. Date of internment before date of discharge.)

Freeman, Henry   Prisoner 320. Rank: Seaman, from: Sheperd, Merchant.
  Cap: Gulf of Mexico by HMS Narcissus Int: 30 Jan 1813 Dis: 14 Feb 1813.
  Received from HMS Moselle. Sent to Norfolk in the British Cartel Eliza by order of the Governor. (Date of capture 'not mentioned'.)

Freigar, Benjamin   Prisoner 115. Rank: Seaman, from: Alexander, Merchant.
  Cap: Not Recorded by HMS Sappho Int: 22 Sep 1812 Dis: 01 Oct 1812.
  Received from HMS Sappho. By order of the Governor being a Spaniard. (Date and place of capture 'not mentioned'.

French, John   Prisoner 361. Rank: Mate, from: Venus, Merchant.
  Cap: Not Recorded by Not Recorded Int: 14 Feb 1813 Dis: 14 Feb 1813.
  Wrecked among the islands and delivered themselves up. Sent to Norfolk in the British Cartel Eliza by order of the Governor. (Date of capture 'not mentioned'.)

Fresk, John   Prisoner 187. Rank: Seaman, from: Marquis de Casa Yayo, Merchant.
  Cap: 12 Sep 1812 Coast of America by Caledonia Privateer Int: 03 Oct 1812 Dis: 24 Nov 1812.
  Received from Prize. Sent to Savannah in the American Cartel Delight.

Frontence, John   Prisoner 27. Rank: Seaman, from: Non Parail, Privateer.
  Cap: 29 Jul 1812 Off Eleuthera by HM Schooner Decouverte Int: 01 Aug 1812 Dis: 29 Aug 1812.
  Received from HM Schooner Decauverte. A Boy.

Frourswell, Lewis   Prisoner 12. Rank: Seaman, from: Non Parail, Privateer.
  Cap: 29 Jul 1812 Off Eleuthera (rest not legible) by HM Schooner Decouverte Int: 01 Aug 1812 Dis: 22 Sep 1812. Received from HM Schooner Decauverte. Sent to new York United States of America.

Furance, George   Prisoner 532. Rank: Seaman, from: Sevant, Letter of Marquis.
  Cap: 04 Jan 1814 Not Recorded by HMS Forester Int: 12 Jan 1814 Dis: 08 Jul 1814.
  Brig. Received from HMS Forester. Sent to Bermuda.

American Prisoners of War Held at New Providence During the War of 1812

Gall, Thomas   Prisoner 821. Rank: Seaman, from: Saturn, Letter of Marquis.
    Cap: Not Recorded by Venus Int: 29 Jan 1815 Dis: 04 Feb 1815.
    Schooner. Received from Venus. from Prison Ship. (Date of capture not on roster.)

Gamache, John   Prisoner 215. Rank: Seaman, from: Venus, Merchant.
    Cap: Coast of America by HMS Moselle Int: 19 Nov 1812 Dis: 04 Feb 1813.
    Received from HMS Moselle. Sent to Charlestown in the British Cartel Ann by order of the Governor. (Date of capture 'not mentioned'.)

Garey, G   Prisoner 205. Rank: Passenger, from: Not Recorded, Merchant.
    Cap: Not Recorded by Privateer Unknown Int: 24 Oct 1812 Dis: 24 Oct 1812.
    Received from HMS Mosella. Sent to Charlestown in the British Cartel Nassau by order of the Governor. (Date, place, name of vessel and name of capturing ship 'not mentioned'.)

Gaul, John   Prisoner 146. Rank: Seaman, from: Sarah Ann, Privateer.
    Cap: 13 Sep 1812 Coast of America by Rhodian & Variable Int: 23 Sep 1812 Dis: 14 Oct 1812.
    Received from Rhodian and Variable. Sent to Jamaica in HMS Sappho by order of the Governor.

Germoirober, Martin   Prisoner 781. Rank: Seaman, from: Ruby, Merchant Vessel.
    Cap: Not Recorded by Schooner Swift Int: 09 Jan 1815 Dis:
    Received from Schooner Swift. (Date of capture and place of capture 'not mentioned'. Date of discharge not on roster.)

Gibbs, Daniel   Prisoner 170. Rank: Seaman, from: Dash, Privateer.
    Cap: 12 Sep 1812 Coast of America by Rhodian & Variable Int: 23 Sep 1812 Dis: 24 Oct 1812.
    Received from Rhodian and Variable. Sent to Charlestown in the British Cartel Nassau by order of the Governor.

Gilbert, George   Prisoner 181. Rank: Seaman, from: Dash, Privateer.
    Cap: 12 Sep 1812 Coast of America by Rhodian & Variable Int: 23 Sep 1812 Dis: 24 Oct 1812.
    Received from Rhodian and Variable. Sent to Charlestown in the British Cartel Nassau by order of the Governor.

Gile, Jacob   Prisoner 442. Rank: Seaman, from: Stanley, Merchant.
    Cap: Coast of America by Privateer Wellesley Int: 08 Jun 1813 Dis: 26 Apr 1814.
    Received from HMS Calibri. Sent to Rhode Island in the Cartel Liberty. (Date of capture not recorded.)

Givan, Francis   Prisoner 762. Rank: Seaman, from: No Name, Not Recorded.
    Cap: Not Recorded by Not Recorded Int: 08 Dec 1814 Dis: 18 Jan 1815.
    Received from HM Sloop Childers. Sent to Bermuda in HMS Childers. (Date, place of capture and name of capturing ship 'not mentioned'.)

Glass, James   Prisoner 142. Rank: Seaman, from: Sarah Ann, Privateer.
    Cap: 13 Sep 1812 Coast of America by Rhodian & Variable Int: 23 Sep 1812 Dis: 24 Oct 1812.
    Received from Rhodian and Variable. Sent to Charlestown in the British Cartel Nassau.

Glee, George   Prisoner 787. Rank: Seaman, from: No Name, Not Recorded.
    Cap: Not Recorded by Not Recorded Int: 14 Jan 1815 Dis:
    Received from Venus. (Dates capture and discharge not on roster.)

Goddard, John   Prisoner 685. Rank: Armorer, from: Frolic, Man of War.
    Cap: 20 Apr 1814 Not Recorded by HMS Orpheus Int: 26 Apr 1814 Dis: 13 Jun 1814.
    United States Ship. Received from HMS Orpheus. Sent to Halifax in HMS Majestic order Aml Cochrane.

Godfree, John   Prisoner 257. Rank: Seaman, from: Viper, Man of War.
    Cap: Gulf of Mexico by HMS Narcissus Int: 30 Jan 1813 Dis: 14 Feb 1813.
    United States Brig. Received from HMS Moselle. Sent in the British Cartel Eliza to Norfolk by order of the Governor. (Date of capture 'not mentioned'.)

Golin, Francis   Prisoner 764. Rank: Seaman, from: No Name, Not Recorded.
    Cap: Not Recorded by Not Recorded Int: 08 Dec 1814 Dis: 18 Jan 1815.
    Received from HM Sloop Childers. Sent to Bermuda in HMS Childers. (Date, place of capture and name of capturing ship 'not mentioned'.)

Goodwin, William   Prisoner 487. Rank: Seaman, from: St. Polito, Merchant.
    Cap: 26 Nov 1813 At sea by Privateers Mars & Dash Int: 23 Dec 1813 Dis: 26 Apr 1814.
    Received from Privateer Mars. Sent to Rhode Island in the Cartel Liberty.

Gordon, Francis   Prisoner 423. Rank: Seaman, from: Penobscot, Merchant Vessel.
    Cap: 10 Apr 1813 Not Recorded by HM Ship Variable Int: 27 Apr 1813 Dis:
    Received from HM Ship Variable.(Date of discharge not on roster.)

Gordon, Thomas   Prisoner 238. Rank: Seaman, from: Viper, Man of War.
    Cap: Gulf of Mexico by HMS Narcissus Int: 30 Jan 1813 Dis: 14 Feb 1813.
    United States Brig. Received from HMS Moselle. Sent in the British Cartel Eliza to Norfolk by order of the Governor. (Date of capture 'not mentioned'.)

American Prisoners of War Held at New Providence During the War of 1812

Gorham, John　Prisoner 360. Rank: Master, from: Venus, Merchant.
　　Cap: Not Recorded by Not Recorded　Int: 14 Feb 1813　Dis: 14 Feb 1813.
　　Wrecked among the islands and delivered themselves up. Sent to Norfolk in the British Cartel Eliza by order of the Governor. (Date of capture 'not mentioned'.)

Gosale, John　Prisoner 766. Rank: Seaman, from: No Name, Not Recorded.
　　Cap:　Not Recorded by Not Recorded　Int: 08 Dec 1814　Dis: 18 Jan 1815.
　　Received from HM Sloop Childers. Sent to Bermuda in HMS Childers. (Date, place of capture and name of capturing ship 'not mentioned'.)

Gouldin, William　Prisoner 552. Rank: Seaman, from: Not Recorded, Letter of Marquis.
　　Cap: Not Recorded by Not Recorded　Int: 17 Feb 1814　Dis: 13 Aug 1814.
　　Ship wrecked among the Bahama Keys. Sent to Bermuda order Commander in Chief. (Date of capture and ship received from not recorded.)

Grady, Annick　Prisoner 102. Rank: Seaman, from: Endeavour, Merchant.
　　Cap: 17 Sep 1812 Abaco Passage by Privateer Francis　Int: 17 Sep 1812　Dis: 26 Nov 1812.
　　Received from Prize. Sent to England by order of the Governor, M. S. Granger.

Gray, Aaron　Prisoner 81. Rank: Seaman, from: Hamer, Merchant.
　　Cap: 01 Sep 1812 Off Abaco by Privateer　Int: 02 Sep 1812　Dis: 24 Oct 1812.
　　Received from Privateer. Sent to Charlestown in the British Cartel Nassau.

Greemal, Louis　Prisoner 190. Rank: Seaman, from: Marquis de Casa Yayo, Merchant.
　　Cap: 12 Sep 1812 Coast of America by Caledonia Privateer　Int: 03 Oct 1812　Dis: 24 Nov 1812.
　　Received from Prize. Sent to Savannah in the American Cartel Delight.

Green, Vincent　Prisoner 820. Rank: Cook, from: Saturn, Letter of Marquis.
　　Cap: Not Recorded by Venus　Int: 29 Jan 1815　Dis: .
　　Schooner. Received from Venus. (Dates of capture and discharge not on roster.)

Greenway, Thomas　Prisoner 120. Rank: 1 Lieutenant, from: Sarah Ann, Privateer.
　　Cap: 13 Sep 1812 Coast of America by Rhodian & Variable　Int: 23 Sep 1812　Dis: 24 Oct 1812.
　　Received from Rhodian & Variable. Sent to Charlestown in the British Cartel Nassau.

Gregory, James　Prisoner 663. Rank: Seaman, from: Frolic, Man of War.
　　Cap: 20 Apr 1814 Not Recorded by HMS Orpheus　Int: 26 Apr 1814　Dis: 13 Jun 1814.
　　United States Ship. Received from HMS Orpheus. Sent to Halifax in HMS Majestic per order of Commander in Chief Aml Cochrane.

Griffy, John　Prisoner 788. Rank: Seaman, from: No Name, Not Recorded.
　　Cap:　Not Recorded by Not Recorded　Int: 14 Jan 1815　Dis: .
　　Received from Venus. (Dates capture and discharge not on roster.)

Grindall, James　Prisoner 711. Rank: Private, from: Frolic, Man of War.
　　Cap: 20 Apr 1814 Not Recorded by HMS Orpheus　Int: 26 Apr 1814　Dis: 13 Jun 1814.
　　United States Ship. Received from HMS Orpheus. Sent to Halifax.

Gross, John　Prisoner 419. Rank: Seaman, from: Penobscot, Merchant Vessel.
　　Cap: 10 Apr 1813 Not Recorded by HM Ship Variable　Int: 27 Apr 1813　Dis: 26 Apr 1814.
　　Received from HM Ship Variable. Sent to Rhode Island in the Cartel Liberty.

Gross, Samuel　Prisoner 424. Rank: Seaman, from: Penobscot, Merchant Vessel.
　　Cap: 10 Apr 1813 Not Recorded by HM Ship Variable　Int: 27 Apr 1813　Dis: 26 Apr 1814.
　　Received from HM Ship Variable. Sent to Rhode Island in the Cartel Liberty.

Guard, H. Y　Prisoner 573. Rank: Seaman, from: Frolic, Man of War.
　　Cap: 20 Apr 1814 At sea by HMS Orpheus　Int: 26 Apr 1814　Dis: 11 Jun 1814.
　　United States Ship. Received from HMS Orpheus. Sent to Bermuda in HMS Orpheus order Aml Cochrane.

Gutterage, William　Prisoner 812. Rank: Seaman, from: Saturn, Letter of Marquis.
　　Cap: Not Recorded by Venus　Int: 29 Jan 1815　Dis:
　　Schooner. Received from Venus. (Dates of capture and discharge not on roster.)

Hadley, James　Prisoner 701. Rank: Private, from: Frolic, Man of War.
　　Cap: 20 Apr 1814 Not Recorded by HMS Orpheus　Int: 26 Apr 1814　Dis: 13 Jun 1814.
　　United States Ship. Received from HMS Orpheus. Sent to Halifax in HMS Majestic order Aml Cochrane.

Hailey, John　Prisoner 544. Rank: Seaman, from: Not Recorded, Letter of Marquis.
　　Cap: Not Recorded by Not Recorded　Int: 17 Feb 1814　Dis: 04 Jun 1814.
　　Ship wrecked among the Bahama Keys. Brig Roberts. (Date of capture and ship received from not recorded.)

Hale, Benjamin　Prisoner 526. Rank: 2 Mate, from: Lion, Merchant.
　　Cap: 04 Jan 1814 Not Recorded by HMS Forester　Int: 12 Jan 1814　Dis:
　　Received from HMS Forester. (Date of discharge not on roster. May be part of the crew of the Sevant.)

American Prisoners of War Held at New Providence During the War of 1812

Halet, John   Prisoner 635. Rank: Seaman, from: Frolic, Man of War.
    Cap: 20 Apr 1814 Not Recorded by HMS Orpheus Int: 26 Apr 1814 Dis: 13 Jun 1814.
    United States Ship. Received from HMS Orpheus. Sent to Halifax in HMS Majestic per order Aml Cochrane.

Hall, Charles   Prisoner 673. Rank: Seaman, from: Frolic, Man of War.
    Cap: 20 Apr 1814 Not Recorded by HMS Orpheus Int: 26 Apr 1814 Dis: 13 Jun 1814.
    United States Ship. Received from HMS Orpheus. Sent to Halifax in HMS Majestic per order of Commander in Chief Aml Cochrane.

Hall, John   Prisoner 145. Rank: Seaman, from: Sarah Ann, Privateer.
    Cap: 13 Sep 1812 Coast of America by Rhodian & Variable Int: 23 Sep 1812 Dis: 24 Oct 1812.
    Received from Rhodian and Variable. Sent to Charlestown in the British Cartel Nassau.

Halladge, William   Prisoner 251. Rank: Seaman, from: Viper, Man of War.
    Cap: Gulf of Mexico by HMS Narcissus Int: 30 Jan 1813 Dis: 14 Feb 1813.
    United States Brig. Received from HMS Moselle. Sent in the British Cartel Eliza to Norfolk by order of the Governor. (Date of capture 'not mentioned'.)

Haller, Isaac   Prisoner 2. Rank: 1 Officer, from: Non Parail, Privateer.
    Cap: 29 Jul 1812 Off Eleuthera (rest not legible) by HM Schooner Decouverte Int: 01 Aug 1812 Dis: 22 Sep 1812. Received from HM Schooner Decauverte. Sent to new York United States of America.

Halm, John   Prisoner 203. Rank: Passenger, from: Not Recorded, Merchant.
    Cap: Not Recorded by Privateer Unknown Int: 24 Oct 1812 Dis: 24 Oct 1812.
    Received from HMS Mosella. Sent to Charlestown in the British Cartel Nassau by order of the Governor. (Date, place, name of vessel and name of capturing ship 'not mentioned'.)

Hammond, Benjamin   Prisoner 591. Rank: Seaman, from: Frolic, Man of War.
    Cap: 20 Apr 1814 Not Recorded by HMS Orpheus Int: 26 Apr 1814 Dis: 11 Jun 1814.
    United States Ship. Received from HMS Orpheus. Sent to Bermuda in HMS Orpheus per order Commander in Chief Aml Cochrane.

Handell, H. Y   Prisoner 666. Rank: Seaman, from: Frolic, Man of War.
    Cap: 20 Apr 1814 Not Recorded by HMS Orpheus Int: 26 Apr 1814 Dis: 13 Jun 1814.
    United States Ship. Received from HMS Orpheus. Sent to Halifax in HMS Majestic per order of Commander in Chief Aml Cochrane.

Hanis, David   Prisoner 610. Rank: Seaman, from: Frolic, Man of War.
    Cap: 20 Apr 1814 Not Recorded by HMS Orpheus Int: 26 Apr 1814 Dis: 13 Jun 1814.
    United States Ship. Received from HMS Orpheus. Sent to Halifax in HMS Majestic per order Aml Cochrane.

Hanson, John   Prisoner 463. Rank: Seaman, from: Caroline, Merchant.
    Cap: 12 Aug 1813 East out of Charleston by HMS Moselle & Privateer Brilliant Int: 25 Aug 1813 Dis: 27 Jan 1814. Received from Privateer Brilliant. Embarked on board the Wellington Merchant Vessel to assist in navigating her to England.

Hardy, William   Prisoner 334. Rank: Seaman, from: Osprey, Merchant.
    Cap: Gulf of Mexico by HMS Moselle Int: 30 Jan 1813 Dis: 14 Feb 1813.
    Received from HMS Moselle. Sent in the British Cartel Eliza to Norfolk by order of the Governor. (Date of capture 'not mentioned'.)

Harman, Henry   Prisoner 362. Rank: Seaman, from: Venus, Merchant.
    Cap: Not Recorded by Not Recorded Int: 14 Feb 1813 Dis: 14 Feb 1813.
    Wrecked among the islands and delivered themselves up. Sent to Norfolk in the British Cartel Eliza by order of the Governor. (Date of capture 'not mentioned'.)

Harred, James   Prisoner 127. Rank: Seaman, from: Sarah Ann, Privateer.
    Cap: 13 Sep 1812 Coast of America by Rhodian & Variable Int: 23 Sep 1812 Dis: 24 Oct 1812.
    Received from Rhodian and Variable. Sent to Charlestown in the British Cartel Nassau.

Harris, John   Prisoner 707. Rank: Private, from: Frolic, Man of War.
    Cap: 20 Apr 1814 Not Recorded by HMS Orpheus Int: 26 Apr 1814 Dis: 13 Jun 1814.
    United States Ship. Received from HMS Orpheus. Sent to Halifax in HMS Majestic order Aml Cochrane.

Harrison, Friak   Prisoner 14. Rank: Seaman, from: Non Parail, Privateer.
    Cap: 29 Jul 1812 Off Eleuthera (rest not legible) by HM Schooner Decouverte Int: 01 Aug 1812 Dis: 24 Oct 1812. Received from HM Schooner Decauverte. Sent to Charlestown in the British Cartel Nassau by order of the Governor.

Harrison, John   Prisoner 121. Rank: 2 Lieutenant, from: Sarah Ann, Privateer.
    Cap: 13 Sep 1812 Coast of America by Rhodian & Variable Int: 23 Sep 1812 Dis: 24 Oct 1812.
    Received from Rhodian & Variable. Sent to Charlestown in the British Cartel Nassau.

American Prisoners of War Held at New Providence During the War of 1812

Hart, George   Prisoner 669. Rank: Seaman, from: Frolic, Man of War.
    Cap: 20 Apr 1814 Not Recorded by HMS Orpheus Int: 26 Apr 1814 Dis: 13 Jun 1814.
    United States Ship. Received from HMS Orpheus. Sent to Halifax in HMS Majestic per order of Commander in Chief Aml Cochrane.

Hart, Prince   Prisoner 453. Rank: Seaman, from: Stanley, Merchant.
    Cap: Coast of America by Privateer Wellesley Int: 13 Jun 1813 Dis: 26 Apr 1814.
    Received from Privateer Rolla. Sent to Rhode Island in the Cartel Liberty. (Date of capture not recorded.)

Harvey, Edward   Prisoner 580. Rank: Seaman, from: Frolic, Man of War.
    Cap: 20 Apr 1814 At sea by HMS Orpheus Int: 26 Apr 1814 Dis: 11 Jun 1814.
    United States Ship. Received from HMS Orpheus. Sent to Bermuda in HMS Orpheus order Aml Cochrane.

Harvey, John   Prisoner 46. Rank: Seaman, from: Ceres, Merchant.
    Cap: 28 Jul 1812 Bahama Bank by Privateer Theodore Int: 02 Aug 1812 Dis: 22 Sep 1812.
    Received from Privateer. Sent to New York United States of America.

Hatch, Robert   Prisoner 448. Rank: Seaman, from: Stanley, Merchant.
    Cap: Coast of America by Privateer Wellesley Int: 13 Jun 1813 Dis: 26 Apr 1814.
    Received from Privateer Rolla. Sent to Rhode Island in the Cartel Liberty. (Date of capture not recorded.)

Hatch, Samuel   Prisoner 465. Rank: Seaman, from: Caroline, Merchant.
    Cap: 12 Aug 1813 East out of Charleston by HMS Moselle & Privateer Brilliant Int: 25 Aug 1813 Dis: 27 Jan 1814. Received from Privateer Brilliant. Embarked on board the Wellington Merchant Vessel to assist in navigating her to England.

Havey, Mack   Prisoner 489. Rank: Seaman, from: St. Polito, Merchant.
    Cap: 26 Nov 1813 At sea by Privateers Mars & Dash Int: 25 Dec 1813 Dis: 26 Apr 1814.
    Received from Privateer Mars. Sent to Rhode Island in the Cartel Liberty.

Hawkins, Joseph   Prisoner 351. Rank: Seaman, from: George & Mary, Merchant.
    Cap: Not Recorded by Not Recorded Int: 14 Feb 1813 Dis: 14 Feb 1813.
    Wrecked among the islands and delivered themselves up. Sent to Norfolk in the British Cartel Eliza by order of the Governor. (Date of capture 'not mentioned'.)

Hazard, Thomas   Prisoner 776. Rank: Seaman, from: George & Joseph, Merchant Vessel.
    Cap: 07 Dec 1814 Daughboy Sound by HM Ship Lacedaemonian Int: 16 Dec 1814 Dis:
    Received from HMS Lacedaemonian. (Date of discharge not on roster.)

Henley, Trim   Prisoner 237. Rank: Seaman, from: Viper, Man of War.
    Cap: Gulf of Mexico by HMS Narcissus Int: 30 Jan 1813 Dis: 14 Feb 1813.
    United States Brig. Received from HMS Moselle. Sent in the British Cartel Eliza to Norfolk by order of the Governor. (Date of capture 'not mentioned'.)

Henry, John   Prisoner 269. Rank: Seaman, from: Viper, Man of War.
    Cap: Gulf of Mexico by HMS Narcissus Int: 30 Jan 1813 Dis: 14 Feb 1813.
    United States Brig. Received from HMS Moselle. Sent in the British Cartel Eliza to Norfolk by order of the Governor. (Date of capture 'not mentioned'.)

Henthorn, William   Prisoner 738. Rank: Seaman, from: Gunboat 160, Man of War.
    Cap: Cumberland Sound by HMS Lacedaemonian Int: 19 Oct 1814 Dis: 18 Jan 1815.
    United States Gunboat. Received from HMS Lacedaemonian. Sent to Bermuda in HMS Childers. (Date of capture not on roster.)

Hetson, Matthew   Prisoner 641. Rank: Seaman, from: Frolic, Man of War.
    Cap: 20 Apr 1814 Not Recorded by HMS Orpheus Int: 26 Apr 1814 Dis: 13 Jun 1814.
    United States Ship. Received from HMS Orpheus. Sent to Halifax in HMS Majestic per order of Commander in Chief Aml Cochrane.

Hewitt, Michael   Prisoner 249. Rank: Seaman, from: Viper, Man of War.
    Cap: Gulf of Mexico by HMS Narcissus Int: 30 Jan 1813 Dis: 14 Feb 1813.
    United States Brig. Received from HMS Moselle. Sent in the British Cartel Eliza to Norfolk by order of the Governor. (Date of capture 'not mentioned'.)

Hill, George   Prisoner 342. Rank: Seaman, from: Dart, Merchant.
    Cap: Not Recorded by Not Recorded Int: 04 Feb 1813 Dis: 04 Feb 1813.
    Wrecked among the islands and delivered themselves up. Received from HMS Moselle. Sent to Charlestown in the British Cartel Ann by order of the Governor. (Date of capture 'not mentioned'.)

Hill, James A   Prisoner 566. Rank: Seaman, from: Frolic, Man of War.
    Cap: 20 Apr 1814 At sea by HMS Orpheus Int: 26 Apr 1814 Dis: 11 Jun 1814.
    United States Ship. Received from HMS Orpheus. Sent to Bermuda in HMS Orpheus order Aml Cochrane.

American Prisoners of War Held at New Providence During the War of 1812

Hoden, John   Prisoner 572. Rank: Seaman, from: Frolic, Man of War.
    Cap: 20 Apr 1814 At sea by HMS Orpheus Int: 26 Apr 1814 Dis: 11 Jun 1814.
    United States Ship. Received from HMS Orpheus. Sent to Bermuda in HMS Orpheus order Aml Cochrane.

Hog, Able   Prisoner 466. Rank: Seaman, from: Caroline, Merchant.
    Cap: 12 Aug 1813 East out of Charleston by HMS Moselle & Privateer Brilliant Int: 25 Aug 1813 Dis: 26 Apr 1814. Received from Privateer Brilliant. Sent to Rhode Island in the Cartel Liberty.

Hogan, Nath B   Prisoner 221. Rank: Seaman, from: Venus, Merchant.
    Cap: Coast of America by HMS Moselle Int: 19 Nov 1812 Dis: 24 Nov 1812.
    Received from HMS Moselle. Sent to Savannah in the American Cartel Delight. (Date of capture 'not mentioned'.)

Hoggins, Thomas   Prisoner 432. Rank: Seaman, from: Trimmer, Merchant.
    Cap: Bahama Island by Government Schooner John Bull Int: 20 May 1813 Dis: 26 Apr 1814.
    Received from Government Schooner John Bull. Sent to Rhode Island in the Cartel Liberty. (Date of capture 'not mentioned'.)

Holland, Stephen   Prisoner 55. Rank: Seaman, from: Olympus, Merchant.
    Cap: 05 Aug 1812 Island of Abaco by HM Schooner Decouverte Int: 07 Aug 1812 Dis: 22 Sep 1812.
    Received from HMS Decouverte. Sent to new York United States of America.

Holmes, Christian   Prisoner 661. Rank: Seaman, from: Frolic, Man of War.
    Cap: 20 Apr 1814 Not Recorded by HMS Orpheus Int: 26 Apr 1814 Dis: 13 Jun 1814.
    United States Ship. Received from HMS Orpheus. Sent to Halifax in HMS Majestic per order of Commander in Chief Aml Cochrane.

Holmes, John   Prisoner 338. Rank: Seaman, from: Osprey, Merchant.
    Cap: Gulf of Mexico by HMS Moselle Int: 30 Jan 1813 Dis: 14 Feb 1813.
    Received from HMS Moselle. Sent in the British Cartel Eliza to Norfolk by order of the Governor. (Date of capture 'not mentioned'.)

Holmes, Vincent   Prisoner 118. Rank: Seaman, from: Alexander, Merchant.
    Cap: Not Recorded by HMS Sappho Int: 22 Sep 1812 Dis: 23 Nov 1812.
    Received from HMS Sappho. Sent to Baltimore in the American Schooner George. (Date and place of capture 'not mentioned'.

Homet, Nathaniel   Prisoner 422. Rank: Seaman, from: Penobscot, Merchant Vessel.
    Cap: 10 Apr 1813 Not Recorded by HM Ship Variable Int: 27 Apr 1813 Dis: 26 Apr 1814.
    Received from HM Ship Variable. Sent to Rhode Island in the Cartel Liberty.

Hooper, Edward   Prisoner 79. Rank: Seaman, from: Hamer, Merchant.
    Cap: 01 Sep 1812 Off Abaco by Privateer Int: 02 Sep 1812 Dis: 24 Oct 1812.
    Received from Privateer. Sent to Charlestown in the British Cartel Nassau.

Hopkins, Steph   Prisoner 346. Rank: Master, from: George & Mary, Merchant.
    Cap: Not Recorded by Not Recorded Int: 14 Feb 1813 Dis: 14 Feb 1813.
    Wrecked among the islands and delivered themselves up. Received from HMS Moselle. Sent to Norfolk in the British Cartel Eliza by order of the Governor. (Date of capture 'not mentioned'.)

Horton, George A   Prisoner 592. Rank: Seaman, from: Frolic, Man of War.
    Cap: 20 Apr 1814 Not Recorded by HMS Orpheus Int: 26 Apr 1814 Dis: 11 Jun 1814.
    United States Ship. Received from HMS Orpheus. Sent to Bermuda in HMS Orpheus per order Commander in Chief Aml Cochrane.

Howard, Benjamin   Prisoner 383. Rank: Seaman, from: Venus, Merchant.
    Cap: Not Recorded by Brilliant Privateer Int: 17 Mar 1813 Dis:
    Received from Prize. (Date and place of capture 'not mentioned'. Date of discharge not on roster.)

Howard, John   Prisoner 804. Rank: Seaman, from: Java, Letter of Marquis.
    Cap: Not Recorded by Cockchafer Int: 14 Jan 1815 Dis:
    Received from HM Schooner Cockchafer. (Dates of capture and discharge not on roster.)

Howard, Wast   Prisoner 287. Rank: Seaman, from: Viper, Man of War.
    Cap: Gulf of Mexico by HMS Narcissus Int: 30 Jan 1813 Dis: 14 Feb 1813.
    Brig. Received from HMS Moselle. Sent in the British Cartel Eliza to Norfolk by order of the Governor. (Date of capture 'not mentioned'.)

Howler, Charles   Prisoner 191. Rank: Seaman, from: Marquis de Casa Yayo, Merchant.
    Cap: 12 Sep 1812 Coast of America by Caledonia Privateer Int: 03 Oct 1812 Dis: 24 Nov 1812.
    Received from Prize. Sent to Savannah in the American Cartel Delight.

Huckings, Israel   Prisoner 657. Rank: Seaman, from: Frolic, Man of War.
    Cap: 20 Apr 1814 Not Recorded by HMS Orpheus Int: 26 Apr 1814 Dis: 13 Jun 1814.
    United States Ship. Received from HMS Orpheus. Sent to Halifax in HMS Majestic per order of Commander in Chief Aml Cochrane.

American Prisoners of War Held at New Providence During the War of 1812

Huffs, Charles   Prisoner 609. Rank: Seaman, from: Frolic, Man of War.
    Cap: 20 Apr 1814 Not Recorded by HMS Orpheus Int: 26 Apr 1814 Dis: 13 Jun 1814.
    United States Ship. Received from HMS Orpheus. Sent to Halifax in HMS Majestic per order Aml Cochrane.

Humphreys, R. W   Prisoner 784. Rank: Master, from: No Name, Not Recorded.
    Cap: Not Recorded by Police Int: 10 Jan 1815 Dis: 16 Jan 1815.
    Received from Police. By order of the Governor. (Date of and place of capture 'not mentioned'.)

Hurst, William   Prisoner 123. Rank: Prize Master, from: Sarah Ann, Privateer.
    Cap: 13 Sep 1812 Coast of America by Rhodian & Variable Int: 23 Sep 1812 Dis: 24 Oct 1812.
    Received from Rhodian and Variable. Sent to Charlestown in the British Cartel Nassau.

Hushow, Newman   Prisoner 721. Rank: Master, from: Fox, Merchant Vessel.
    Cap: Cumberland Sound by HMS Lacedaemonian Int: 19 Oct 1814 Dis: 07 Dec 1814.
    Received from HMS Lacedaemonian. Order Commander in Chief. (Date of capture not on roster.)

Husill, John   Prisoner 8. Rank: Gunner, from: Non Parail, Privateer.
    Cap: 29 Jul 1812 Off Eleuthera (rest not legible) by HM Schooner Decouverte Int: 01 Aug 1812 Dis: 24 Oct 1812. Received from HM Schooner Decauverte. Sent to Charlestown in the British Cartel Nassau.

Hyman, Henry   Prisoner 795. Rank: Seaman, from: Java, Letter of Marquis.
    Cap: Not Recorded by Cockchafer Int: 14 Jan 1815 Dis:
    Received from HM Schooner Cockchafer. (Dates of capture and discharge not on roster.)

Hynes, John   Prisoner 211. Rank: Seaman, from: Venus, Merchant.
    Cap: Coast of America by HMS Moselle Int: 19 Nov 1812 Dis: 04 Feb 1813.
    Received from HMS Moselle. Sent to Charlestown in the British Cartel Ann by order of the Governor. (Date of capture 'not mentioned'.)

Inglefield, John   Prisoner 33. Rank: Seaman, from: HM Schooner Decouverte, Not Recorded.
    Cap: 29 Jul 1812 Not Stated by HM Schooner Decouverte Int: 01 Aug 1812 Dis: 20 Aug 1812.
    Received from HM Schooner Decauverte. Gave themselves up as Prisoners of War. Being Part of the complement of the HMS Decouvete Lieut Richard Williams Commanding. Sent to Jamaica in HM Schooner Decouverte by order of Lieut Williams.

Jackson, James   Prisoner 240. Rank: Seaman, from: Viper, Man of War.
    Cap: Gulf of Mexico by HMS Narcissus Int: 30 Jan 1813 Dis: 14 Feb 1813.
    United States Brig. Received from HMS Moselle. taken by the Police for Murder and as evidence. (Date of capture 'not mentioned'.)

Jackson, James   Prisoner 414. Rank: Seaman, from: Viper, Man of War.
    Cap: Not Recorded by HM Ship Narcissus Int: 21 Apr 1813 Dis: 26 Apr 1814.
    Received from Police. Sent to Rhode Island in the Cartel Liberty. (Date and place of capture 'not mentioned'.)

Jackson, James   Prisoner 513. Rank: Seaman, from: Lion, Merchant.
    Cap: Not Recorded by Privateer Mars Int: 30 Jan 1814 Dis: 27 Jan 1814.
    Received from Privateer Mars. Embarked on board Merchant Vessel Nassau to assist in navigating her to England. (Date of capture not recorded. Date of internment before date of discharge.)

Jackson, John   Prisoner 728. Rank: Masters Mate, from: Gunboat 160, Man of War.
    Cap: Cumberland Sound by HMS Lacedaemonian Int: 19 Oct 1814 Dis: 07 Dec 1814.
    United States Gunboat. Received from HMS Lacedaemonian. Order Commander in Chief. (Date of capture not on roster.)

Jackson, John   Prisoner 832. Rank: Seaman, from: Hercules, Merchant Vessel.
    Cap: 09 Mar 1815 Not Recorded by HM Schooner Canso Int: 13 Mar 1815 Dis:
    Recaptured Ship. Received from HM Schooner Canso. (Date of discharge not on roster.)

Jackson, Robert   Prisoner 749. Rank: Seaman, from: Auroa, Letter of Marquis.
    Cap: Not Recorded by HM Shooner Cockchafer Int: 03 Dec 1814 Dis: 20 Jan 1815.
    Received from Cockchafer. To England. (Date and place of capture 'not mentioned'.)

Jackson, Thomas   Prisoner 486. Rank: Seaman, from: St. Polito, Merchant.
    Cap: 26 Nov 1813 At sea by Privateers Mars & Dash Int: 23 Dec 1813 Dis: 26 Apr 1814.
    Received from Privateer Mars. Sent to Rhode Island in the Cartel Liberty.

Jackson, William   Prisoner 155. Rank: Seaman, from: Sarah Ann, Privateer.
    Cap: 13 Sep 1812 Coast of America by Rhodian & Variable Int: 23 Sep 1812 Dis: 24 Oct 1812.
    Received from Rhodian and Variable. Sent to Charlestown in the British Cartel Nassau.

Jackson, William   Prisoner 228. Rank: Seaman, from: Not Recorded, Not Recorded.
    Cap: Not Recorded by Police Int: 27 Dec 1812 Dis: 04 Feb 1813.
    Sent to Charlestown in the British Cartel Ann by order of the Governor. (Date and place of capture 'not mentioned'.)

American Prisoners of War Held at New Providence During the War of 1812

Jaibo, Joseph   Prisoner 124. Rank: Prize Master, from: Sarah Ann, Privateer.
    Cap: 13 Sep 1812 Coast of America by Rhodian & Variable Int: 23 Sep 1812 Dis: 24 Oct 1812.
    Received from Rhodian and Variable. Sent to Charlestown in the British Cartel Nassau.

James, Thomas   Prisoner 271. Rank: Seaman, from: Viper, Man of War.
    Cap: Gulf of Mexico by HMS Narcissus Int: 30 Jan 1813 Dis: 14 Feb 1813.
    United States Brig. Received from HMS Moselle. Sent in the British Cartel Eliza to Norfolk by order of the Governor. (Date of capture 'not mentioned'.)

Jameson, Daniel   Prisoner 574. Rank: Boatswains Mate, from: Frolic, Man of War.
    Cap: 20 Apr 1814 At sea by HMS Orpheus Int: 26 Apr 1814 Dis: 11 Jun 1814.
    United States Ship. Received from HMS Orpheus. Sent to Bermuda in HMS Orpheus order Aml Cochrane.

Jarvis, John   Prisoner 450. Rank: Seaman, from: Stanley, Merchant.
    Cap: Coast of America by Privateer Wellesley Int: 13 Jun 1813 Dis: 26 Apr 1814.
    Received from Privateer Rolla. Sent to Rhode Island in the Cartel Liberty. (Date of capture not recorded.)

Jefferies, Abraham   Prisoner 263. Rank: Seaman, from: Viper, Man of War.
    Cap: Gulf of Mexico by HMS Narcissus Int: 30 Jan 1813 Dis: 14 Feb 1813.
    United States Brig. Received from HMS Moselle. Sent in the British Cartel Eliza to Norfolk by order of the Governor. (Date of capture 'not mentioned'.)

Jefferies, Stephen   Prisoner 831. Rank: Seaman, from: Hercules, Merchant Vessel.
    Cap: 09 Mar 1815 Not Recorded by HM Schooner Canso Int: 13 Mar 1815 Dis:
    Recaptured Ship. Received from HM Schooner Canso. (Date of discharge not on roster.)

Jenkins, Anthony   Prisoner 452. Rank: Seaman, from: Stanley, Merchant.
    Cap: Coast of America by Privateer Wellesley Int: 13 Jun 1813 Dis: 26 Apr 1814.
    Received from Privateer Rolla. Sent to Rhode Island in the Cartel Liberty. (Date of capture not recorded.)

Jenkins, Dublin   Prisoner 449. Rank: Seaman, from: Stanley, Merchant.
    Cap: Coast of America by Privateer Wellesley Int: 13 Jun 1813 Dis: 26 Apr 1814.
    Received from Privateer Rolla. Sent to Rhode Island in the Cartel Liberty. (Date of capture not recorded.)

Jenkins, Zachrian   Prisoner 802. Rank: Seaman, from: Java, Letter of Marquis.
    Cap: Not Recorded by Cockchafer Int: 14 Jan 1815 Dis: 19 Jan 1815.
    Received from HM Schooner Cockchafer. To England. (Date of capture not on roster.)

Johnson, Hans P   Prisoner 740. Rank: Seaman, from: Gunboat 160, Man of War.
    Cap: Cumberland Sound by HMS Lacedaemonian Int: 19 Oct 1814 Dis: 18 Jan 1815.
    United States Gunboat. Received from HMS Lacedaemonian. Sent to Bermuda in HMS Childers. (Date of capture not on roster.)

Johnson, Henry   Prisoner 22. Rank: Seaman, from: Non Parail, Privateer.
    Cap: 29 Jul 1812 Off Eleuthera (rest not legible) by HM Schooner Decouverte Int: 01 Aug 1812 Dis: 24 Oct 1812. Received from HM Schooner Decauverte. Sent to Charlestown in the British Cartel Nassau by order of the Governor.

Johnson, Henry   Prisoner 417. Rank: Seaman, from: Penobscot, Merchant Vessel.
    Cap: 10 Apr 1813 Not Recorded by HM Ship Variable Int: 27 Apr 1813 Dis: 26 Apr 1814.
    Received from HM Ship Variable. Sent to Rhode Island in the Cartel Liberty.

Johnson, Henry   Prisoner 759. Rank: Seaman, from: No Name, Not Recorded.
    Cap: Not Recorded by Not Recorded Int: 08 Dec 1814 Dis: 18 Jan 1815.
    Received from HM Sloop Childers. Sent to Bermuda in HMS Childers. (Date, place of capture and name of capturing ship 'not mentioned'.)

Johnson, Jacob   Prisoner 105. Rank: Seaman, from: Romney, Merchant.
    Cap: Not Recorded by HMS Rattler Int: 21 Sep 1812 Dis: 26 Nov 1812.
    Received from HMS Rattler. Sent to Charlestown in the British Cartel Nassau. (Date and place of capture 'not mentioned'.)

Johnson, James   Prisoner 575. Rank: Seaman, from: Frolic, Man of War.
    Cap: 20 Apr 1814 At sea by HMS Orpheus Int: 26 Apr 1814 Dis: 11 Jun 1814.
    United States Ship. Received from HMS Orpheus. Sent to Bermuda in HMS Orpheus order Aml Cochrane.

Johnson, John   Prisoner 567. Rank: 2 Gunner, from: Frolic, Man of War.
    Cap: 20 Apr 1814 At sea by HMS Orpheus Int: 26 Apr 1814 Dis: 11 Jun 1814.
    United States Ship. Received from HMS Orpheus. Sent to Bermuda in HMS Orpheus order Aml Cochrane.

American Prisoners of War Held at New Providence During the War of 1812

Johnson, John   Prisoner 632. Rank: Seaman, from: Frolic, Man of War.
    Cap: 20 Apr 1814 Not Recorded by HMS Orpheus Int: 26 Apr 1814 Dis: 13 Jun 1814.
    United States Ship. Received from HMS Orpheus. Sent to Halifax in HMS Majestic order Aml Cochrane.

Johnson, John   Prisoner 656. Rank: Seaman, from: Frolic, Man of War.
    Cap: 20 Apr 1814 Not Recorded by HMS Orpheus Int: 26 Apr 1814 Dis: 13 Jun 1814.
    United States Ship. Received from HMS Orpheus. Sent to Halifax in HMS Majestic per order of Commander in Chief Aml Cochrane.

Johnson, Nathaniel   Prisoner 720. Rank: Carpenter, from: Not Recorded, Not Recorded.
    Cap: Not Recorded by Not Recorded Int: 18 Oct 1814 Dis: 26 Jan 1815.
    Received from Police. By order of the Governor. (Date of capture not on roster.)

Johnson, Thomas   Prisoner 109. Rank: Seaman, from: Romney, Merchant.
    Cap: Not Recorded by HMS Rattler Int: 22 Sep 1812 Dis: 24 Nov 1812.
    Received from HMS Rattler. Sent to Savannah in the American Cartel Delight. (Date and place of capture 'not mentioned'.)

Johnson, William   Prisoner 69. Rank: Seaman, from: HMS Variable, Not Recorded.
    Cap: 26 Jul 1812 Not Stated by HM Schooner Variable Int: 14 Aug 1812 Dis: 22 Sep 1812.
    Received from His Majesties Schooner Variable. Part of the crew of the Variable being an American. Sent to new York United States of America.

Johnson, William   Prisoner 747. Rank: Seaman, from: Auroa, Letter of Marquis.
    Cap: Not Recorded by HM Shooner Cockchafer Int: 03 Dec 1814 Dis:
    Received from Cockchafer. (Date and place of capture 'not mentioned'. Date of discharge not on roster.)

Johnston, Joseph   Prisoner 409. Rank: Seaman, from: Portsmouth, Merchant.
    Cap: 16 Apr 1813 At sea by HM Ships Morgiana & Calibri Int: 20 Apr 1813 Dis: 13 Jun 1814.
    Received from HMS Morgiana. Sent to Halifax HMS Majestic.

Jones, Benjamin   Prisoner 288. Rank: Seaman, from: Viper, Man of War.
    Cap: Gulf of Mexico by HMS Narcissus Int: 30 Jan 1813 Dis: 14 Feb 1813.
    Brig. Received from HMS Moselle. Sent in the British Cartel Eliza to Norfolk by order of the Governor. (Date of capture 'not mentioned'.)

Jones, Charles   Prisoner 193. Rank: Seaman, from: Molly, Merchant.
    Cap: 12 Sep 1812 Coast of America by Caledonia Privateer Int: 03 Oct 1812 Dis: 24 Nov 1812.
    Received from Prize. Sent to Savannah in the American Cartel Delight.

Jones, Henry   Prisoner 799. Rank: Seaman, from: Java, Letter of Marquis.
    Cap: Not Recorded by Cockchafer Int: 14 Jan 1815 Dis: .
    Received from HM Schooner Cockchafer. (Dates of capture and discharge not on roster.)

Jones, John   Prisoner 261. Rank: Seaman, from: Viper, Man of War.
    Cap: Gulf of Mexico by HMS Narcissus Int: 30 Jan 1813 Dis: 14 Feb 1813.
    United States Brig. Received from HMS Moselle. Sent in the British Cartel Eliza to Norfolk by order of the Governor. (Date of capture 'not mentioned'.)

Jones, Lewis   Prisoner 462. Rank: Seaman, from: Caroline, Merchant.
    Cap: 12 Aug 1813 East out of Charleston by HMS Moselle & Privateer Brilliant Int: 25 Aug 1813 Dis: 04 Feb 1814. Received from Privateer Brilliant. Embarked on board the Providence to assist in navigating her to England.

Jones, Rowland   Prisoner 84. Rank: Mate, from: Nelly, Merchant.
    Cap: 25 Aug 1812 Coast of America by HMS Rhodian Int: 06 Sep 1812 Dis:
    Received from HM Brig Rhodian. (Date of discharge not on roster.)

Jordon, Christian   Prisoner 712. Rank: Carpenter, from: Frolic, Man of War.
    Cap: 20 Apr 1814 Not Recorded by HMS Orpheus Int: 26 Apr 1814 Dis: .
    United States Ship. Received from HMS Orpheus. (Date of discharge not on roster.)

Joseph, James   Prisoner 709. Rank: Private, from: Frolic, Man of War.
    Cap: 20 Apr 1814 Not Recorded by HMS Orpheus Int: 26 Apr 1814 Dis: 13 Jun 1814.
    United States Ship. Received from HMS Orpheus. Sent to Halifax.

Joseph, James   Prisoner 710. Rank: Private, from: Frolic, Man of War.
    Cap: 20 Apr 1814 Not Recorded by HMS Orpheus Int: 26 Apr 1814 Dis: 30 Dec 1814.
    United States Ship. Received from HMS Orpheus. Died. Consumption.

Joseph, John   Prisoner 316. Rank: Seaman, from: Sheperd, Merchant.
    Cap: Gulf of Mexico by HMS Narcissus Int: 30 Jan 1813 Dis: 14 Feb 1813.
    Received from HMS Moselle. Sent to Norfolk in the British Cartel Eliza by order of the Governor. (Date of capture 'not mentioned'.)

American Prisoners of War Held at New Providence During the War of 1812

Joseph, John   Prisoner 326. Rank: Seaman, from: Osprey, Merchant.
    Cap: Gulf of Mexico by HMS Moselle Int: 30 Jan 1813 Dis: 14 Feb 1813.
    Received from HMS Moselle. Sent in the British Cartel Eliza to Norfolk by order of the Governor. (Date of capture 'not mentioned'.)

Justice, John   Prisoner 616. Rank: Seaman, from: Frolic, Man of War.
    Cap: 20 Apr 1814 Not Recorded by HMS Orpheus Int: 26 Apr 1814 Dis: 13 Jun 1814.
    United States Ship. Received from HMS Orpheus. Sent to Halifax in HMS Majestic per order Aml Cochrane.

Keating, John   Prisoner 595. Rank: 2 Mate, from: Frolic, Man of War.
    Cap: 20 Apr 1814 Not Recorded by HMS Orpheus Int: 26 Apr 1814 Dis: 13 Jun 1814.
    United States Ship. Received from HMS Orpheus. Sent to Halifax HMS Majestic order Aml Cochrane.

Keinsburgh, Henry   Prisoner 140. Rank: Seaman, from: Sarah Ann, Privateer.
    Cap: 13 Sep 1812 Coast of America by Rhodian & Variable Int: 23 Sep 1812 Dis: 24 Oct 1812.
    Received from Rhodian and Variable. Sent to Charlestown in the British Cartel Nassau.

Kelly, T   Prisoner 496. Rank: Seaman, from: St. Polito, Merchant.
    Cap: 26 Nov 1813 At sea by Privateers Mars & Dash Int: 25 Dec 1813 Dis: 26 Apr 1814.
    Received from Privateer Mars. Sent to Rhode Island in the Cartel Liberty.

Kelly, William   Prisoner 819. Rank: Seaman, from: Saturn, Letter of Marquis.
    Cap: Not Recorded by Venus Int: 29 Jan 1815 Dis: .
    Schooner. Received from Venus. (Dates of capture and discharge not on roster.)

Kemmens, John   Prisoner 113. Rank: Seaman, from: Alexander, Merchant.
    Cap: Not Recorded by HMS Sappho Int: 22 Sep 1812 Dis: 23 Nov 1812.
    Received from HMS Sappho. Sent to Baltimore in the American Schooner George. (Date and place of capture 'not mentioned'.

Kennedy, Michael   Prisoner 294. Rank: Seaman, from: Viper, Man of War.
    Cap: Gulf of Mexico by HMS Narcissus Int: 30 Jan 1813 Dis: 14 Feb 1813.
    Brig. Received from HMS Moselle. Sent in the British Cartel Eliza to Norfolk by order of the Governor. (Date of capture 'not mentioned'.)

Kindred, James   Prisoner 284. Rank: Seaman, from: Viper, Man of War.
    Cap: Gulf of Mexico by HMS Narcissus Int: 30 Jan 1813 Dis: 14 Feb 1813.
    Brig. Received from HMS Moselle. Sent in the British Cartel Eliza to Norfolk by order of the Governor. (Date of capture 'not mentioned'.)

King, Thivdore   Prisoner 335. Rank: Seaman, from: Osprey, Merchant.
    Cap: Gulf of Mexico by HMS Moselle Int: 30 Jan 1813 Dis: 14 Feb 1813.
    Received from HMS Moselle. Sent in the British Cartel Eliza to Norfolk by order of the Governor. (Date of capture 'not mentioned'.)

Kinley, H   Prisoner 295. Rank: Seaman, from: Viper, Man of War.
    Cap: Gulf of Mexico by HMS Narcissus Int: 30 Jan 1813 Dis: 14 Feb 1813.
    Brig. Received from HMS Moselle. Sent in the British Cartel Eliza to Norfolk by order of the Governor. (Date of capture 'not mentioned'.)

Kitterlas, Samuel   Prisoner 57. Rank: Seaman, from: Olympus, Merchant.
    Cap: 05 Aug 1812 Island of Abaco by HM Schooner Decouverte Int: 07 Aug 1812 Dis: 22 Sep 1812.
    Received from HMS Decouverte. Sent to new York United States of America.

Labelle, Prince   Prisoner 94. Rank: Seaman, from: Rapid, Privateer.
    Cap: Not Recorded by Not Recorded Int: 13 Sep 1812 Dis: 04 Feb 1813.
    Received from Government Schooner John Bull. Sent to Charlestown in the British Cartel Ann. (Date, place and name of capturing ship 'not mentioned'.)

Lambert, A   Prisoner 210. Rank: Seaman, from: Venus, Merchant.
    Cap: Coast of America by HMS Moselle Int: 19 Nov 1812 Dis: 04 Feb 1813.
    Received from HMS Moselle. Sent to Charlestown in the British Cartel Ann by order of the Governor. (Date of capture 'not mentioned'.)

Lameson, Pierre   Prisoner 92. Rank: Captain, from: Rapid, Privateer.
    Cap: Not Recorded by Not Recorded Int: 13 Sep 1812 Dis: 09 Mar 1813.
    Received from Government Schooner John Bull. Sent to Jamaica in HM Sloop Moselle by the Governor. (Date, place and name of capturing ship 'not mentioned'.)

Landerkin, Richard   Prisoner 30. Rank: Yeoman Skeets, from: HM Schooner Decouverte, Not Recorded.
    Cap: 29 Jul 1812 Not Stated by HM Schooner Decouverte Int: 01 Aug 1812 Dis: 20 Aug 1812.
    Received from HM Schooner Decauverte. Gave themselves up as Prisoners of War. Being Part of the complement of the HMS Decouvete Lieut Richard Williams Commanding. Sent to Jamaica in HM Schooner Decouverte by order of Lieut Williams.

American Prisoners of War Held at New Providence During the War of 1812

Lane, Alexander   Prisoner 769. Rank: Owner, from: Factor, Merchant Vessel.
    Cap: 07 Dec 1814 Sapello Sound by HM Ship Lacedaemonian Int: 16 Dec 1814 Dis: 07 Dec 1814.
    Received from HMS Lacedaemonian. Order Commander in Chief. (Date of internment before date of discharge.)

Lane, Eben   Prisoner 154. Rank: Seaman, from: Sarah Ann, Privateer.
    Cap: 13 Sep 1812 Coast of America by Rhodian & Variable Int: 23 Sep 1812 Dis: 24 Oct 1812.
    Received from Rhodian and Variable. Sent to Charlestown in the British Cartel Nassau.

Lane, Joseph   Prisoner 160. Rank: 2 Lieutenant, from: Dash, Privateer.
    Cap: 12 Sep 1812 Coast of America by Rhodian & Variable Int: 23 Sep 1812 Dis: 24 Oct 1812.
    Received from Rhodian and Variable. Sent to Charlestown in the British Cartel Nassau.

Latham, Thomas   Prisoner 164. Rank: Prize Master, from: Dash, Privateer.
    Cap: 12 Sep 1812 Coast of America by Rhodian & Variable Int: 23 Sep 1812 Dis: 24 Oct 1812.
    Received from Rhodian and Variable. Sent to Charlestown in the British Cartel Nassau.

Law, Nicholas   Prisoner 283. Rank: Seaman, from: Viper, Man of War.
    Cap: Gulf of Mexico by HMS Narcissus Int: 30 Jan 1813 Dis: 14 Feb 1813.
    Brig. Received from HMS Moselle. Sent in the British Cartel Eliza to Norfolk by order of the Governor. (Date of capture 'not mentioned'.)

Lawton, Henry   Prisoner 446. Rank: Seaman, from: Stanley, Merchant.
    Cap: Coast of America by Privateer Wellesley Int: 10 Jun 1813 Dis: 10 Jul 1813.
    Received from Government Schooner Swift. By order of the Governor. (Date of capture not recorded.)

Lear, Alexander   Prisoner 603. Rank: Seaman, from: Frolic, Man of War.
    Cap: 20 Apr 1814 Not Recorded by HMS Orpheus Int: 26 Apr 1814 Dis: 13 Jun 1814.
    United States Ship. Received from HMS Orpheus. Sent to Halifax HMS Majestic order Aml Cochrane.

Lear, George   Prisoner 117. Rank: Seaman, from: Alexander, Merchant.
    Cap: Not Recorded by HMS Sappho Int: 22 Sep 1812 Dis: 23 Nov 1812.
    Received from HMS Sappho. Sent to Baltimore in the American Schooner George. (Date and place of capture 'not mentioned'.

Lemon, James   Prisoner 594. Rank: 2 Mate, from: Frolic, Man of War.
    Cap: 20 Apr 1814 Not Recorded by HMS Orpheus Int: 26 Apr 1814 Dis: 13 Jun 1814.
    United States Ship. Received from HMS Orpheus. Sent to Halifax HMS Majestic order Aml Cochrane.

Lennell, J   Prisoner 395. Rank: Seaman, from: Dominica Packet, Merchant.
    Cap: Not Recorded by Privateer Baker Delight Int: 01 Apr 1813 Dis: 10 Apr 1813.
    Recaptured from the American Privateer Comet. Received from Privateer. Sent to Charleston in the British Cartel Charlotte by order of the Governor. (Date and place of capture 'not mentioned'.)

Lewi, John   Prisoner 239. Rank: Seaman, from: Viper, Man of War.
    Cap: Gulf of Mexico by HMS Narcissus Int: 30 Jan 1813 Dis: 14 Feb 1813.
    United States Brig. Received from HMS Moselle. Sent in the British Cartel Eliza to Norfolk by order of the Governor. (Date of capture 'not mentioned'.)

Lewis, Ebenezer   Prisoner 247. Rank: Seaman, from: Viper, Man of War.
    Cap: Gulf of Mexico by HMS Narcissus Int: 30 Jan 1813 Dis: 14 Feb 1813.
    United States Brig. Received from HMS Moselle. Sent in the British Cartel Eliza to Norfolk by order of the Governor. (Date of capture 'not mentioned'.)

Light, William   Prisoner 828. Rank: Seaman, from: Hercules, Merchant Vessel.
    Cap: 09 Mar 1815 Not Recorded by HM Schooner Canso Int: 13 Mar 1815 Dis: .
    Recaptured Ship. Received from HM Schooner Canso. (Date of discharge not on roster.)

Lindstroon, Gustaus   Prisoner 133. Rank: Seaman, from: Sarah Ann, Privateer.
    Cap: 13 Sep 1812 Coast of America by Rhodian & Variable Int: 23 Sep 1812 Dis: 24 Oct 1812.
    Received from Rhodian and Variable. Sent to Charlestown in the British Cartel Nassau.

Lingo, Woodman   Prisoner 148. Rank: Seaman, from: Sarah Ann, Privateer.
    Cap: 13 Sep 1812 Coast of America by Rhodian & Variable Int: 23 Sep 1812 Dis: 24 Oct 1812.
    Received from Rhodian and Variable. Sent to Charlestown in the British Cartel Nassau.

Linguire, Abraham   Prisoner 290. Rank: Seaman, from: Viper, Man of War.
    Cap: Gulf of Mexico by HMS Narcissus Int: 30 Jan 1813 Dis: 14 Feb 1813.
    Brig. Received from HMS Moselle. Sent in the British Cartel Eliza to Norfolk by order of the Governor. (Date of capture 'not mentioned'.)

Lion, James S   Prisoner 731. Rank: Seaman, from: Gunboat 160, Man of War.
    Cap: Cumberland Sound by HMS Lacedaemonian Int: 19 Oct 1814 Dis: .
    United States Gunboat. Received from HMS Lacedaemonian. (Dates of capture and discharge not on roster.)

American Prisoners of War Held at New Providence During the War of 1812

Livingston, William   Prisoner 6. Rank: 5 Officer, from: Non Parail, Privateer.
    Cap: 29 Jul 1812 Off Eleuthera (rest not legible) by HM Schooner Decouverte Int: 01 Aug 1812 Dis: 24 Oct 1812. Received from HM Schooner Decauverte. Sent to Charlestown in the British Cartel Nassau.

Lombard, Ephrim   Prisoner 36. Rank: Seaman, from: HM Schooner Decauverte, Not Recorded.
    Cap: 29 Jul 1812 Not Stated by HM Schooner Decauverte Int: 01 Aug 1812 Dis: 20 Aug 1812. Received from HM Schooner Decauverte. Gave themselves up as Prisoners of War. Being Part of the complement of the HMS Decouvete Lieut Richard Williams Commanding. Sent to Jamaica in HM Schooner Decouverte by order of Lieut Williams.

Lyman, Paul   Prisoner 647. Rank: Seaman, from: Frolic, Man of War.
    Cap: 20 Apr 1814 Not Recorded by HMS Orpheus Int: 26 Apr 1814 Dis: 13 Jun 1814. United States Ship. Received from HMS Orpheus. Sent to Halifax in HMS Majestic per order of Commander in Chief Aml Cochrane.

Lynn, William   Prisoner 166. Rank: Steward, from: Dash, Privateer.
    Cap: 12 Sep 1812 Coast of America by Rhodian & Variable Int: 23 Sep 1812 Dis: 24 Oct 1812. Received from Rhodian and Variable. Sent to Charlestown in the British Cartel Nassau.

Madden, Frederick   Prisoner 112. Rank: Seaman, from: Alexander, Merchant.
    Cap: Not Recorded by HMS Sappho Int: 22 Sep 1812 Dis: . Received from HMS Sappho. (Date and place of capture 'not mentioned'. Date of discharge not on roster.)

Magrath, F   Prisoner 304. Rank: Seaman, from: Viper, Man of War.
    Cap: Gulf of Mexico by HMS Narcissus Int: 30 Jan 1813 Dis: 14 Feb 1813. Brig. Received from HMS Moselle. Sent to Norfolk in the British Cartel Eliza by order of the Governor. (Date of capture 'not mentioned'.)

Mamer, Michael   Prisoner 689. Rank: Sergeant Marines, from: Frolic, Man of War.
    Cap: 20 Apr 1814 Not Recorded by HMS Orpheus Int: 26 Apr 1814 Dis: 13 Jun 1814. United States Ship. Received from HMS Orpheus. Sent to Halifax in HMS Majestic order Aml Cochrane.

Mangine, John B   Prisoner 703. Rank: Private, from: Frolic, Man of War.
    Cap: 20 Apr 1814 Not Recorded by HMS Orpheus Int: 26 Apr 1814 Dis: 13 Jun 1814. United States Ship. Received from HMS Orpheus. Sent to Halifax in HMS Majestic order Aml Cochrane.

Mariner, Joseph   Prisoner 571. Rank: Seaman, from: Frolic, Man of War.
    Cap: 20 Apr 1814 At sea by HMS Orpheus Int: 26 Apr 1814 Dis: 11 Jun 1814. United States Ship. Received from HMS Orpheus. Sent to Bermuda in HMS Orpheus order Aml Cochrane.

Marshal, L   Prisoner 107. Rank: Seaman, from: Romney, Merchant.
    Cap: Not Recorded by HMS Rattler Int: 21 Sep 1812 Dis: 23 Nov 1812. Received from HMS Rattler. Sent to Baltimore in the American Schooner George. (Date and place of capture 'not mentioned'.)

Marshall, Elias J   Prisoner 310. Rank: Seaman, from: Sheperd, Merchant.
    Cap: Gulf of Mexico by HMS Narcissus Int: 30 Jan 1813 Dis: 14 Feb 1813. Received from HMS Moselle. Sent to Norfolk in the British Cartel Eliza by order of the Governor. (Date of capture 'not mentioned'.)

Marshall, George   Prisoner 234. Rank: Gunner, from: Viper, Man of War.
    Cap: Gulf of Mexico by HMS Narcissus Int: 30 Jan 1813 Dis: 14 Feb 1813. United States Brig. Received from HMS Moselle. Sent in the British Cartel Eliza to Norfolk by order of the Governor. (Date of capture 'not mentioned'.)

Marshall, John   Prisoner 803. Rank: Seaman, from: Java, Letter of Marquis.
    Cap: Not Recorded by Cockchafer Int: 14 Jan 1815 Dis: 04 Feb 1815. Received from HM Schooner Cockchafer. from Prison Ship. (Date of capture not on roster.)

Martin, Francis   Prisoner 98. Rank: Seaman, from: Rapid, Privateer.
    Cap: Not Recorded by Not Recorded Int: 13 Sep 1812 Dis: 04 Feb 1813. Received from Government Schooner John Bull. Sent to Charlestown in the British Cartel Ann. (Date, place and name of capturing ship 'not mentioned'.)

Martin, Henry B   Prisoner 1. Rank: Captain, from: Non Parail, Privateer.
    Cap: 29 Jul 1812 Off Eleuthera (rest not legible) by HM Schooner Decouverte Int: 01 Aug 1812 Dis: 24 Oct 1812. Received from HM Schooner Decauverte. Sent to Charlestown in the British Cartel Nassau.

Martin, John   Prisoner 149. Rank: Seaman, from: Sarah Ann, Privateer.
    Cap: 13 Sep 1812 Coast of America by Rhodian & Variable Int: 23 Sep 1812 Dis: 24 Oct 1812. Received from Rhodian and Variable. Sent to Charlestown in the British Cartel Nassau.

American Prisoners of War Held at New Providence During the War of 1812

Martin, John D   Prisoner 345. Rank: Supercargo, from: George & Mary, Merchant.
> Cap: Not Recorded by Not Recorded Int: 14 Feb 1813 Dis: 14 Feb 1813.
> Wrecked among the islands and delivered themselves up. Received from HMS Moselle. Sent to Norfolk in the British Cartel Eliza by order of the Governor. (Date of capture 'not mentioned'.)

Martin, Richard   Prisoner 319. Rank: Seaman, from: Sheperd, Merchant.
> Cap: Gulf of Mexico by HMS Narcissus Int: 30 Jan 1813 Dis: 14 Feb 1813.
> Received from HMS Moselle. Sent to Norfolk in the British Cartel Eliza by order of the Governor. (Date of capture 'not mentioned'.)

Martin, Thomas   Prisoner 20. Rank: Seaman, from: Non Parail, Privateer.
> Cap: 29 Jul 1812 Off Eleuthera (rest not legible) by HM Schooner Decouverte Int: 01 Aug 1812 Dis: 24 Oct 1812. Received from HM Schooner Decauverte. Sent to Charlestown in the British Cartel Nassau by order of the Governor.

Martin, William   Prisoner 789. Rank: 2 Mate, from: Java, Letter of Marquis.
> Cap: Not Recorded by Cockchafer Int: 14 Jan 1815 Dis:
> Received from HM Schooner Cockchafer. (Dates of capture and discharge not on roster.)

Martin, Zebard   Prisoner 152. Rank: Seaman, from: Sarah Ann, Privateer.
> Cap: 13 Sep 1812 Coast of America by Rhodian & Variable Int: 23 Sep 1812 Dis: 24 Oct 1812.
> Received from Rhodian and Variable. Sent to Charlestown in the British Cartel Nassau.

Mary, Ezekiel   Prisoner 608. Rank: Seaman, from: Frolic, Man of War.
> Cap: 20 Apr 1814 Not Recorded by HMS Orpheus Int: 26 Apr 1814 Dis: 13 Jun 1814.
> United States Ship. Received from HMS Orpheus. Sent to Halifax in HMS Majestic order Aml Cochrane.

Maryfield, George   Prisoner 537. Rank: Seaman, from: Sevant, Letter of Marquis.
> Cap: 04 Jan 1814 Not Recorded by HMS Forester Int: 12 Jan 1814 Dis: 13 Aug 1814.
> Brig. Received from HMS Forester. Sent to Bermuda HMS Surprise per order the Commander in Chief.

Mason, George   Prisoner 745. Rank: Seaman, from: Auroa, Letter of Marquis.
> Cap: Not Recorded by HM Shooner Cockchafer Int: 03 Dec 1814 Dis:
> Received from Cockchafer. (Date and place of capture 'not mentioned'. Date of discharge not on roster.)

Mason, Richard   Prisoner 624. Rank: Seaman, from: Frolic, Man of War.
> Cap: 20 Apr 1814 Not Recorded by HMS Orpheus Int: 26 Apr 1814 Dis: 13 Jun 1814.
> United States Ship. Received from HMS Orpheus. Sent to Halifax in HMS Majestic order Aml Cochrane.

Matthews, Edward   Prisoner 189. Rank: Seaman, from: Marquis de Casa Yayo, Merchant.
> Cap: 12 Sep 1812 Coast of America by Caledonia Privateer Int: 03 Oct 1812 Dis: 24 Nov 1812.
> Received from Prize. Sent to Savannah in the American Cartel Delight.

Maxwell, George   Prisoner 439. Rank: Seaman, from: Stanley, Merchant.
> Cap: Coast of America by Privateer Wellesley Int: 08 Jun 1813 Dis: 26 Apr 1814.
> Received from Privateer Schooner Wellesley. Sent to Rhode Island in the Cartel Liberty. (Date of capture not recorded.)

McCate, F   Prisoner 150. Rank: Seaman, from: Sarah Ann, Privateer.
> Cap: 13 Sep 1812 Coast of America by Rhodian & Variable Int: 23 Sep 1812 Dis: 24 Oct 1812.
> Received from Rhodian and Variable. Sent to Charlestown in the British Cartel Nassau.

McFaith, John   Prisoner 266. Rank: Seaman, from: Viper, Man of War.
> Cap: Gulf of Mexico by HMS Narcissus Int: 30 Jan 1813 Dis: 14 Feb 1813.
> United States Brig. Received from HMS Moselle. Sent in the British Cartel Eliza to Norfolk by order of the Governor. (Date of capture 'not mentioned'.)

McKenzie, John   Prisoner 217. Rank: Seaman, from: Venus, Merchant.
> Cap: Coast of America by HMS Moselle Int: 19 Nov 1812 Dis: 04 Feb 1813.
> Received from HMS Moselle. Sent to Charlestown in the British Cartel Ann by order of the Governor. (Date of capture 'not mentioned'.)

McLeod, Donald   Prisoner 233. Rank: Seaman, from: Eleanor, Merchant.
> Cap: Not Recorded by HMS Southampton Int: 24 Jan 1813 Dis: 04 Feb 1813.
> Received from HMS Variable. Sent to Charlestown in the British Cartel Ann. (Date and place capture 'not mentioned'.)

McLevy, Henry   Prisoner 809. Rank: Seaman, from: Saturn, Letter of Marquis.
> Cap: Not Recorded by Venus Int: 29 Jan 1815 Dis: 04 Feb 1815.
> Schooner. Received from Venus. from Prison Ship. (Date of capture not on roster.)

McNeill, Edmund   Prisoner 13. Rank: Seaman, from: Non Parail, Privateer.
> Cap: 29 Jul 1812 Off Eleuthera (rest not legible) by HM Schooner Decouverte Int: 01 Aug 1812 Dis: 22 Sep 1812. Received from HM Schooner Decauverte. Sent to new York United States of America.

American Prisoners of War Held at New Providence During the War of 1812

Meek, Thomas   Prisoner 620. Rank: Seaman, from: Frolic, Man of War.
    Cap: 20 Apr 1814 Not Recorded by HMS Orpheus Int: 26 Apr 1814 Dis: 13 Jun 1814.
    United States Ship. Received from HMS Orpheus. Sent to Halifax in HMS Majestic order Aml Cochrane.

Metzgar, John   Prisoner 758. Rank: Passenger, from: No Name, Not Recorded.
    Cap: 28 Nov 1814 St. Andrew Sound by HM Ship Primrose Int: 07 Dec 1814 Dis: 07 Dec 1814.
    Received from HMS Primrose. Order Commander in Chief.

Meyers, Thomas   Prisoner 245. Rank: Seaman, from: Viper, Man of War.
    Cap: Gulf of Mexico by HMS Narcissus Int: 30 Jan 1813 Dis: 14 Feb 1813.
    United States Brig. Received from HMS Moselle. Sent in the British Cartel Eliza to Norfolk by order of the Governor. (Date of capture 'not mentioned'.)

Miade, John   Prisoner 811. Rank: Seaman, from: Saturn, Letter of Marquis.
    Cap: Not Recorded by Venus Int: 29 Jan 1815 Dis:
    Schooner. Received from Venus. (Dates of capture and discharge not on roster.)

Micanger, Michael   Prisoner 718. Rank: Prize Master, from: Enterprise, Merchant Vessel.
    Cap: Not Recorded by Not Recorded Int: 27 Aug 1814 Dis: 26 Oct 1814.
    Received from HMS Cockchafer. Sent to Bermuda in HMS Wolverine. (Date of capture not on roster.)

Michael, ---   Prisoner 755. Rank: Seaman, from: Harriet & Ann, Merchant Vessel.
    Cap: 26 Nov 1814 Doughby Sound by HM Ship Primrose Int: 07 Dec 1814 Dis: .
    Received from HMS Primrose. (First name not recorded. Date of discharge not on roster.)

Michael, John   Prisoner 739. Rank: Seaman, from: Gunboat 160, Man of War.
    Cap: Cumberland Sound by HMS Lacedaemonian Int: 19 Oct 1814 Dis: 18 Jan 1815.
    United States Gunboat. Received from HMS Lacedaemonian. Sent to Bermuda in HMS Childers. (Date of capture not on roster.)

Miller, Charles   Prisoner 41. Rank: Seaman, from: Ceres, Merchant.
    Cap: 28 Jul 1812 Bahama Bank by Privateer Theodore Int: 01 Aug 1812 Dis: 06 Aug 1812.
    Received from Prize. Sent to Liverpool in the Ship Cora by order of the Governor.

Miller, Henry   Prisoner 671. Rank: Seaman, from: Frolic, Man of War.
    Cap: 20 Apr 1814 Not Recorded by HMS Orpheus Int: 26 Apr 1814 Dis: 13 Jun 1814.
    United States Ship. Received from HMS Orpheus. Sent to Halifax in HMS Majestic per order of Commander in Chief Aml Cochrane.

Miller, James J   Prisoner 93. Rank: Prize Master, from: Rapid, Privateer.
    Cap: Not Recorded by Not Recorded Int: 13 Sep 1812 Dis: 04 Feb 1813.
    Received from Government Schooner John Bull. Sent to Charlestown in the British Cartel Ann. (Date, place and name of capturing ship 'not mentioned'.)

Mills, James   Prisoner 392. Rank: Seaman, from: Dominica Packet, Merchant.
    Cap: Not Recorded by HMS Variable Int: 30 Mar 1813 Dis: 19 Apr 1813.
    Recaptured from the American Privateer Comet. Received from Variable. Sent to Europe in the Ship Loyal Sam. (Date and place of capture 'not mentioned'.)

Mills, William A   Prisoner 810. Rank: Seaman, from: Saturn, Letter of Marquis.
    Cap: Not Recorded by Venus Int: 29 Jan 1815 Dis: 04 Feb 1815.
    Schooner. Received from Venus. from Prison Ship. (Date of capture not on roster.)

Milne, Alexander   Prisoner 250. Rank: Seaman, from: Viper, Man of War.
    Cap: Gulf of Mexico by HMS Narcissus Int: 30 Jan 1813 Dis: 14 Feb 1813.
    United States Brig. Received from HMS Moselle. Sent in the British Cartel Eliza to Norfolk by order of the Governor. (Date of capture 'not mentioned'.)

Mitchell, Edward   Prisoner 806. Rank: Seaman, from: Saturn, Letter of Marquis.
    Cap: Not Recorded by Venus Int: 29 Jan 1815 Dis: .
    Schooner. Received from Venus. (Dates of capture and discharge not on roster.)

Momell, Thomas   Prisoner 111. Rank: Seaman, from: Alexander, Merchant.
    Cap: Not Recorded by HMS Sappho Int: 22 Sep 1812 Dis: 23 Nov 1812.
    Received from HMS Sappho. Sent to Baltimore in the American Schooner George. (Date and place of capture 'not mentioned'.)

Momus, Anthony   Prisoner 402. Rank: Seaman, from: Wave, Merchant.
    Cap: Not Recorded by Privateer Wellesley Int: 05 Apr 1813 Dis: 10 Apr 1813.
    Received from Prize. Sent to Charleston by order of the Governor. (Date and place of capture 'not mentioned'.)

Monneys, R   Prisoner 89. Rank: Seaman, from: Phiebe V. Jane, Merchant.
    Cap: 25 Aug 1812 Coast of America by HMS Rhodian Int: 06 Sep 1812 Dis: 17 Oct 1812.
    Received from HM Brig Rhodian. Sent to England by order of the Governor.

American Prisoners of War Held at New Providence During the War of 1812

Moodie, John   Prisoner 507. Rank: Seaman, from: Stephen Garard, Merchant.
    Cap: Not Recorded by Privateer Mars Int: 30 Jan 1814 Dis: 08 Jul 1814.
    Received from Prize. Sent to Bermuda. (Date of capture not recorded.)

Moon, Richard   Prisoner 119. Rank: Captain, from: Sarah Ann, Privateer.
    Cap: 13 Sep 1812 Coast of America by Rhodian & Variable Int: 23 Sep 1812 Dis: 24 Oct 1812.
    Received from Rhodian & Variable. Sent to Charlestown in the British Cartel Nassau.

Mooran, Thomas   Prisoner 273. Rank: Seaman, from: Viper, Man of War.
    Cap: Gulf of Mexico by HMS Narcissus Int: 30 Jan 1813 Dis: 14 Feb 1813.
    Brig. Received from HMS Moselle. Sent in the British Cartel Eliza to Norfolk by order of the Governor. (Date of capture 'not mentioned'.)

Morgan, T   Prisoner 481. Rank: Seaman, from: Catalonia, Merchant.
    Cap: 23 Nov 1813 At sea by HMS Ringdove Int: 30 Nov 1813 Dis:
    Received from HMS Ringdove. (Date of discharge not on roster.)

Morris, Manuel   Prisoner 642. Rank: Seaman, from: Frolic, Man of War.
    Cap: 20 Apr 1814 Not Recorded by HMS Orpheus Int: 26 Apr 1814 Dis: 13 Jun 1814.
    United States Ship. Received from HMS Orpheus. Sent to Halifax in HMS Majestic per order of Commander in Chief Aml Cochrane.

Moulden, Isaac   Prisoner 343. Rank: Seaman, from: Dart, Merchant.
    Cap: Not Recorded by Not Recorded Int: 04 Feb 1813 Dis: 04 Feb 1813.
    Wrecked among the islands and delivered themselves up. Received from HMS Moselle. Sent to Charlestown in the British Cartel Ann by order of the Governor. (Date of capture 'not mentioned'.)

Munrow, William   Prisoner 410. Rank: Seaman, from: Portsmouth, Merchant.
    Cap: 16 Apr 1813 At sea by HM Ships Morgiana & Calibri Int: 20 Apr 1813 Dis: 26 Apr 1814.
    Received from HMS Morgiana. Sent to Rhode Island in the Cartel Liberty.

Murray, Alexander   Prisoner 585. Rank: Seaman, from: Frolic, Man of War.
    Cap: 20 Apr 1814 Not Recorded by HMS Orpheus Int: 26 Apr 1814 Dis: 11 Jun 1814.
    United States Ship. Received from HMS Orpheus. Sent to Bermuda in HMS Orpheus per order Commander in Chief Aml Cochrane.

Musure, Caleb   Prisoner 222. Rank: Seaman, from: Factor, Merchant.
    Cap: Coast of America by HMS Moselle Int: 19 Nov 1812 Dis: 24 Nov 1812.
    Received from HMS Moselle. Sent to Savannah in the American Cartel Delight. (Date of capture 'not mentioned'.)

Neelby, James   Prisoner 305. Rank: Seaman, from: Viper, Man of War.
    Cap: Gulf of Mexico by HMS Narcissus Int: 30 Jan 1813 Dis: 14 Feb 1813.
    Brig. Received from HMS Moselle. Sent to Norfolk in the British Cartel Eliza by order of the Governor. (Date of capture 'not mentioned'.)

Neeres, James   Prisoner 680. Rank: Seaman, from: Frolic, Man of War.
    Cap: 20 Apr 1814 Not Recorded by HMS Orpheus Int: 26 Apr 1814 Dis: 13 Jun 1814.
    United States Ship. Received from HMS Orpheus. Sent to Halifax in HMS Majestic per order of Commander in Chief Aml Cochrane.

Neill, D M   Prisoner 4. Rank: 3 Officer, from: Non Parail, Privateer.
    Cap: 29 Jul 1812 Off Eleuthera (rest not legible) by HM Schooner Decouverte Int: 01 Aug 1812 Dis: 24 Oct 1812. Received from HM Schooner Decauverte. Sent to Charlestown in the British Cartel Nassau.

Nicola, John   Prisoner 763. Rank: Seaman, from: No Name, Not Recorded.
    Cap: Not Recorded by Not Recorded Int: 08 Dec 1814 Dis: 18 Jan 1815.
    Received from HM Sloop Childers. Sent to Bermuda in HMS Childers. (Date, place of capture and name of capturing ship 'not mentioned'.)

Norbao, Peter   Prisoner 756. Rank: Master, from: No Name, Not Recorded.
    Cap: 28 Nov 1814 St. Andrew Sound by HM Ship Primrose Int: 07 Dec 1814 Dis: 20 Jan 1815.
    Received from HMS Primrose. Died. Fever.

Northam, Stephen   Prisoner 376. Rank: Seaman, from: Mary, Merchant.
    Cap: Not Recorded by Government Schooner Swift Int: 15 Mar 1813 Dis: 10 Apr 1813.
    Received from Government Schooner Swift. Sent to Charleston in the British Cartel Charlotte by order of the Governor. (Date and place of capture 'not mentioned'.)

Northorp, John   Prisoner 653. Rank: Seaman, from: Frolic, Man of War.
    Cap: 20 Apr 1814 Not Recorded by HMS Orpheus Int: 26 Apr 1814 Dis: 13 Jun 1814.
    United States Ship. Received from HMS Orpheus. Sent to Halifax in HMS Majestic per order of Commander in Chief Aml Cochrane.

American Prisoners of War Held at New Providence During the War of 1812

Norton, Edward   Prisoner 697. Rank: Private, from: Frolic, Man of War.
    Cap: 20 Apr 1814 Not Recorded by HMS Orpheus Int: 26 Apr 1814 Dis: 13 Jun 1814.
    United States Ship. Received from HMS Orpheus. Sent to Halifax in HMS Majestic order Aml Cochrane.

Nye, Stephen   Prisoner 578. Rank: Seaman, from: Frolic, Man of War.
    Cap: 20 Apr 1814 At sea by HMS Orpheus Int: 26 Apr 1814 Dis: 11 Jun 1814.
    United States Ship. Received from HMS Orpheus. Sent to Bermuda in HMS Orpheus order Aml Cochrane.

Odell, Samuel   Prisoner 522. Rank: Seaman, from: Lion, Merchant.
    Cap: Not Recorded by Privateer Mars Int: 30 Jan 1814 Dis: 08 Jul 1814.
    Received from Privateer Brilliant. Sent to Bermuda. (Date of capture not recorded.)

O'Hara, James   Prisoner 241. Rank: Seaman, from: Viper, Man of War.
    Cap: Gulf of Mexico by HMS Narcissus Int: 30 Jan 1813 Dis: 14 Feb 1813.
    United States Brig. Received from HMS Moselle. Sent in the British Cartel Eliza to Norfolk by order of the Governor. (Date of capture 'not mentioned'.)

Oldham, Thomas   Prisoner 813. Rank: Seaman, from: Saturn, Letter of Marquis.
    Cap: Not Recorded by Venus Int: 29 Jan 1815 Dis:
    Schooner. Received from Venus. (Dates of capture and discharge not on roster.)

Oliver, Samuel   Prisoner 28. Rank: Boatswains Mate, from: HM Schooner Decouverte, Not Recorded.
    Cap: 29 Jul 1812 Not Stated by HM Schooner Decouverte Int: 01 Aug 1812 Dis: 20 Aug 1812.
    Received from HM Schooner Decauverte. Gave themselves up as Prisoners of War. Being Part of the complement of the HMS Decouvete Lieut Richard Williams Commanding. Sent to Jamaica in HM Schooner Decouverte by order of Lieut Williams.

Ondicot, N. F   Prisoner 525. Rank: 1 Mate, from: Lion, Merchant.
    Cap: 04 Jan 1814 Not Recorded by HMS Forester Int: 12 Jan 1814 Dis: .
    Received from HMS Forester. (Date of discharge not on roster. May be part of the crew of the Sevant.)

Onion, Stephen P   Prisoner 805. Rank: 2 Mate, from: Saturn, Letter of Marquis.
    Cap: Not Recorded by Venus Int: 29 Jan 1815 Dis: .
    Schooner. Received from Venus. (Dates of capture and discharge not on roster.)

Orimsley, John   Prisoner 253. Rank: Seaman, from: Viper, Man of War.
    Cap: Gulf of Mexico by HMS Narcissus Int: 30 Jan 1813 Dis: 14 Feb 1813.
    United States Brig. Received from HMS Moselle. Sent in the British Cartel Eliza to Norfolk by order of the Governor. (Date of capture 'not mentioned'.)

Osmond, Henry   Prisoner 606. Rank: 2 Gunner, from: Frolic, Man of War.
    Cap: 20 Apr 1814 Not Recorded by HMS Orpheus Int: 26 Apr 1814 Dis: 13 Jun 1814.
    United States Ship. Received from HMS Orpheus. Sent to Halifax in HMS Majestic order Aml Cochrane.

Ostend, Robert   Prisoner 407. Rank: Seaman, from: Portsmouth, Merchant.
    Cap: 16 Apr 1813 At sea by HM Ships Morgiana & Calibri Int: 20 Apr 1813 Dis: 26 Apr 1814.
    Received from HMS Morgiana. Sent to Rhode Island in the Cartel Liberty.

Ournan, John F   Prisoner 114. Rank: Seaman, from: Alexander, Merchant.
    Cap: Not Recorded by HMS Sappho Int: 22 Sep 1812 Dis: 24 Nov 1812.
    Received from HMS Sappho. Sent to Savannah in the American Cartel Delight. (Date and place of capture 'not mentioned'.

Paine, Thomas   Prisoner 727. Rank: Commander, from: Gunboat 160, Man of War.
    Cap: Cumberland Sound by HMS Lacedaemonian Int: 19 Oct 1814 Dis:
    United States Gunboat. Received from HMS Lacedaemonian. (Dates of capture and discharge not on roster.)

Paislaw, William   Prisoner 291. Rank: Seaman, from: Viper, Man of War.
    Cap: Gulf of Mexico by HMS Narcissus Int: 30 Jan 1813 Dis: 14 Feb 1813.
    Brig. Received from HMS Moselle. Sent in the British Cartel Eliza to Norfolk by order of the Governor. (Date of capture 'not mentioned'.)

Panner, James   Prisoner 147. Rank: Seaman, from: Sarah Ann, Privateer.
    Cap: 13 Sep 1812 Coast of America by Rhodian & Variable Int: 23 Sep 1812 Dis: 24 Oct 1812.
    Received from Rhodian and Variable. Sent to Charlestown in the British Cartel Nassau.

Paradu, Mathew   Prisoner 329. Rank: Seaman, from: Osprey, Merchant.
    Cap: Gulf of Mexico by HMS Moselle Int: 30 Jan 1813 Dis: 14 Feb 1813.
    Received from HMS Moselle. Sent in the British Cartel Eliza to Norfolk by order of the Governor. (Date of capture 'not mentioned'.)

American Prisoners of War Held at New Providence During the War of 1812

Parish, John   Prisoner 31. Rank: Captain Master, from: HM Schooner Decouverte, Not Recorded.
    Cap: 29 Jul 1812 Not Stated by HM Schooner Decouverte Int: 01 Aug 1812 Dis: 20 Aug 1812.
    Received from HM Schooner Decauverte. Gave themselves up as Prisoners of War. Being Part of the complement of the HMS Decouvete Lieut Richard Williams Commanding. Sent to Jamaica in HM Schooner Decouverte by order of Lieut Williams.

Parker, John D   Prisoner 665. Rank: Seaman, from: Frolic, Man of War.
    Cap: 20 Apr 1814 Not Recorded by HMS Orpheus Int: 26 Apr 1814 Dis: 13 Jun 1814.
    United States Ship. Received from HMS Orpheus. Sent to Halifax in HMS Majestic per order of Commander in Chief Aml Cochrane.

Parrell, John   Prisoner 130. Rank: Seaman, from: Sarah Ann, Privateer.
    Cap: 13 Sep 1812 Coast of America by Rhodian & Variable Int: 23 Sep 1812 Dis: 24 Oct 1812.
    Received from Rhodian and Variable. Sent to Charlestown in the British Cartel Nassau.

Parrott, Robert   Prisoner 735. Rank: Seaman, from: Gunboat 160, Man of War.
    Cap: Cumberland Sound by HMS Lacedaemonian Int: 19 Oct 1814 Dis:
    United States Gunboat. Received from HMS Lacedaemonian. (Dates of capture and discharge not on roster.)

Parsons, Absolum   Prisoner 771. Rank: Seaman, from: Factor, Merchant Vessel.
    Cap: 07 Dec 1814 Sapello Sound by HM Ship Lacedaemonian Int: 16 Dec 1814 Dis: .
    Received from HMS Lacedaemonian. (Date of discharge not on roster.)

Parsons, Andrew   Prisoner 602. Rank: Seaman, from: Frolic, Man of War.
    Cap: 20 Apr 1814 Not Recorded by HMS Orpheus Int: 26 Apr 1814 Dis: 13 Jun 1814.
    United States Ship. Received from HMS Orpheus. Sent to Halifax HMS Majestic order Aml Cochrane.

Pease, Nathaniel   Prisoner 248. Rank: Seaman, from: Viper, Man of War.
    Cap: Gulf of Mexico by HMS Narcissus Int: 30 Jan 1813 Dis: 14 Feb 1813.
    United States Brig. Received from HMS Moselle. Sent in the British Cartel Eliza to Norfolk by order of the Governor. (Date of capture 'not mentioned'.)

Pedrick, George   Prisoner 590. Rank: Seaman, from: Frolic, Man of War.
    Cap: 20 Apr 1814 Not Recorded by HMS Orpheus Int: 26 Apr 1814 Dis: 11 Jun 1814.
    United States Ship. Received from HMS Orpheus. Sent to Bermuda in HMS Orpheus per order Commander in Chief Aml Cochrane.

Peter, Manuel   Prisoner 16. Rank: Seaman, from: Non Parail, Privateer.
    Cap: 29 Jul 1812 Off Eleuthera (rest not legible) by HM Schooner Decouverte Int: 01 Aug 1812 Dis: 24 Oct 1812. Received from HM Schooner Decauverte. Sent to Charlestown in the British Cartel Nassau by order of the Governor.

Peterson, James   Prisoner 650. Rank: Seaman, from: Frolic, Man of War.
    Cap: 20 Apr 1814 Not Recorded by HMS Orpheus Int: 26 Apr 1814 Dis: 13 Jun 1814.
    United States Ship. Received from HMS Orpheus. Sent to Halifax in HMS Majestic per order of Commander in Chief Aml Cochrane.

Peterson, John   Prisoner 47. Rank: Seaman, from: Ceres, Merchant.
    Cap: 28 Jul 1812 Bahama Bank by Privateer Theodore Int: 02 Aug 1812 Dis: 06 Aug 1812.
    Received from Privateer. Sent to Liverpool in the Ship Cora by order of the Governor.

Philips, Joseph   Prisoner 455. Rank: Seaman, from: Stanley, Merchant.
    Cap: Coast of America by Privateer Wellesley Int: 16 Jul 1813 Dis: 26 Apr 1814.
    Received from Privateer Wellesley. Sent to Rhode Island in the Cartel Liberty. (Date of capture not recorded.)

Philips, Samuel   Prisoner 236. Rank: Carpenter, from: Viper, Man of War.
    Cap: Gulf of Mexico by HMS Narcissus Int: 30 Jan 1813 Dis: 14 Feb 1813.
    United States Brig. Received from HMS Moselle. Sent in the British Cartel Eliza to Norfolk by order of the Governor. (Date of capture 'not mentioned'.)

Philips, Thomas   Prisoner 317. Rank: Seaman, from: Sheperd, Merchant.
    Cap: Gulf of Mexico by HMS Narcissus Int: 30 Jan 1813 Dis: 14 Feb 1813.
    Received from HMS Moselle. Sent to Norfolk in the British Cartel Eliza by order of the Governor. (Date of capture 'not mentioned'.)

Philips, William   Prisoner 265. Rank: Seaman, from: Viper, Man of War.
    Cap: Gulf of Mexico by HMS Narcissus Int: 30 Jan 1813 Dis: 14 Feb 1813.
    United States Brig. Received from HMS Moselle. taken by the Police for Murder and as evidence. (Date of capture 'not mentioned'.)

Philips, William   Prisoner 416. Rank: Seaman, from: Viper, Man of War.
    Cap: Not Recorded by HM Ship Narcissus Int: 21 Apr 1813 Dis: 26 Apr 1814.
    Received from Police. Sent to Rhode Island in the Cartel Liberty. (Date and place of capture 'not mentioned'.)

American Prisoners of War Held at New Providence During the War of 1812

Pick, Ralph   Prisoner 99. Rank: Seaman, from: Endeavour, Merchant.
    Cap: 17 Sep 1812 Abaco Passage by Privateer Francis Int: 17 Sep 1812 Dis: 24 Oct 1812.
    Received from Prize. Sent to Charlestown in the British Cartel Nassau.

Pictom, Peleg   Prisoner 778. Rank: Seaman, from: Ruby, Merchant Vessel.
    Cap: Not Recorded by Schooner Swift Int: 09 Jan 1815 Dis:
    Received from Schooner Swift. (Date of capture and place of capture 'not mentioned'. Date of discharge not on roster.)

Pierce, John   Prisoner 484. Rank: Seaman, from: Innocencia, Merchant.
    Cap: 26 Nov 1813 At sea by HMS Ringdove Int: 30 Nov 1813 Dis: 26 Apr 1814.
    Received from HMS Ringdove. Sent to Rhode Island in the Cartel Liberty.

Pinnard, John   Prisoner 132. Rank: Seaman, from: Sarah Ann, Privateer.
    Cap: 13 Sep 1812 Coast of America by Rhodian & Variable Int: 23 Sep 1812 Dis: 24 Oct 1812.
    Received from Rhodian and Variable. Sent to Charlestown in the British Cartel Nassau.

Pitcher, Peleg Sprague   Prisoner 772. Rank: Master, from: George & Joseph, Merchant Vessel.
    Cap: 07 Dec 1814 Daughboy Sound by HM Ship Lacedaemonian Int: 16 Dec 1814 Dis: 04 Feb 1815.
    Received from HMS Lacedaemonian. from Prison Ship.

Pitman, John   Prisoner 598. Rank: --- Mate, from: Frolic, Man of War.
    Cap: 20 Apr 1814 Not Recorded by HMS Orpheus Int: 26 Apr 1814 Dis: 13 Jun 1814.
    United States Ship. Received from HMS Orpheus. Sent to Halifax HMS Majestic order Aml Cochrane.

Pitt, Ceazar   Prisoner 822. Rank: Pilot, from: Saturn, Letter of Marquis.
    Cap: Not Recorded by Venus Int: 29 Jan 1815 Dis:
    Schooner. Received from Venus. (Dates of capture and discharge not on roster.)

Pittsford, Francis   Prisoner 508. Rank: Seaman, from: Stephen Garard, Merchant.
    Cap: Not Recorded by Privateers Mars Int: 30 Jan 1814 Dis: 04 Jun 1814.
    Received from Prize. Brig Roberts. Or Francis Potter. (Date of capture not recorded.)

Pluck, Michael   Prisoner 139. Rank: Seaman, from: Sarah Ann, Privateer.
    Cap: 13 Sep 1812 Coast of America by Rhodian & Variable Int: 23 Sep 1812 Dis: 14 Oct 1812.
    Received from Rhodian and Variable. Sent to Jamaica in HMS Sappho by order of the Governor.

Portell, James   Prisoner 675. Rank: Seaman, from: Frolic, Man of War.
    Cap: 20 Apr 1814 Not Recorded by HMS Orpheus Int: 26 Apr 1814 Dis: 13 Jun 1814.
    United States Ship. Received from HMS Orpheus. Sent to Halifax in HMS Majestic per order of Commander in Chief Aml Cochrane.

Porter, G   Prisoner 493. Rank: Seaman, from: St. Polito, Merchant.
    Cap: 26 Nov 1813 At sea by Privateers Mars & Dash Int: 25 Dec 1813 Dis: 26 Apr 1814.
    Received from Privateer Mars. Sent to Rhode Island in the Cartel Liberty.

Porter, Samuel   Prisoner 708. Rank: Private, from: Frolic, Man of War.
    Cap: 20 Apr 1814 Not Recorded by HMS Orpheus Int: 26 Apr 1814 Dis: 13 Jun 1814.
    United States Ship. Received from HMS Orpheus. Sent to Halifax in HMS Majestic order Aml Cochrane.

Potter, Patrick   Prisoner 490. Rank: Seaman, from: St. Polito, Merchant.
    Cap: 26 Nov 1813 At sea by Privateers Mars & Dash Int: 25 Dec 1813 Dis: 26 Apr 1814.
    Received from Privateer Mars. Sent to Rhode Island in the Cartel Liberty.

Powell, Hew   Prisoner 421. Rank: Seaman, from: Penobscot, Merchant Vessel.
    Cap: 10 Apr 1813 Not Recorded by HM Ship Variable Int: 27 Apr 1813 Dis: 26 Apr 1814.
    Received from HM Ship Variable. Sent to Rhode Island in the Cartel Liberty.

Powell, Michael   Prisoner 280. Rank: Seaman, from: Viper, Man of War.
    Cap: Gulf of Mexico by HMS Narcissus Int: 30 Jan 1813 Dis: 14 Feb 1813.
    Brig. Received from HMS Moselle. Sent in the British Cartel Eliza to Norfolk by order of the Governor. (Date of capture 'not mentioned'.)

Prado, Joseph   Prisoner 42. Rank: Seaman, from: Ceres, Merchant.
    Cap: 28 Jul 1812 Bahama Bank by Privateer Theodore Int: 01 Aug 1812 Dis: 06 Aug 1812.
    Received from Prize. Sent to Liverpool in the Ship Cora by order of the Governor.

Price, Charles   Prisoner 301. Rank: Seaman, from: Viper, Man of War.
    Cap: Gulf of Mexico by HMS Narcissus Int: 30 Jan 1813 Dis: 14 Feb 1813.
    Brig. Received from HMS Moselle. Sent to Norfolk in the British Cartel Eliza by order of the Governor. (Date of capture 'not mentioned'.)

Price, Jacob   Prisoner 66. Rank: Seaman, from: Resolution, Merchant.
    Cap: 26 Jul 1812 Crooked Island Passage by HM Schooner Variable Int: 07 Aug 1812 Dis: 22 Sep 1812. Received from His Majesties Schooner Variable. Sent to new York United States of America.

American Prisoners of War Held at New Providence During the War of 1812

Price, John   Prisoner 582. Rank: Seaman, from: Frolic, Man of War.
    Cap: 20 Apr 1814 Not Recorded by HMS Orpheus Int: 26 Apr 1814 Dis: 11 Jun 1814.
    United States Ship. Received from HMS Orpheus. Sent to Bermuda in HMS Orpheus per order Commander in Chief Aml Cochrane.

Price, Thomas   Prisoner 814. Rank: Seaman, from: Saturn, Letter of Marquis.
    Cap: Not Recorded by Venus Int: 29 Jan 1815 Dis:
    Schooner. Received from Venus. (Dates of capture and discharge not on roster.)

Purslaw, John   Prisoner 760. Rank: Seaman, from: No Name, Not Recorded.
    Cap: Not Recorded by Not Recorded Int: 08 Dec 1814 Dis: 18 Jan 1815.
    Received from HM Sloop Childers. Sent to Bermuda in HMS Childers. (Date, place of capture and name of capturing ship 'not mentioned'.)

Quail, Thomas   Prisoner 430. Rank: Seaman, from: Trimmer, Merchant.
    Cap: Bahama Island by Government Schooner John Bull Int: 20 May 1813 Dis: 26 Apr 1814.
    Received from Government Schooner John Bull. Sent to Rhode Island in the Cartel Liberty. (Date of capture 'not mentioned'.)

Qumo, Harto   Prisoner 783. Rank: Seaman, from: Ruby, Merchant Vessel.
    Cap: Not Recorded by Schooner Swift Int: 09 Jan 1815 Dis:
    Received from Schooner Swift. (Date of capture and place of capture 'not mentioned'. Date of discharge not on roster.)

Ragon, Laurence   Prisoner 382. Rank: Seaman, from: Apodaco, Merchant.
    Cap: Not Recorded by Government Schooner Swift Int: 15 Mar 1813 Dis: 25 Jul 1813.
    Received from Government Schooner Swift. To HMS Moselle. (Date and place of capture 'not mentioned'.)

Raines, Charles   Prisoner 264. Rank: Seaman, from: Viper, Man of War.
    Cap: Gulf of Mexico by HMS Narcissus Int: 30 Jan 1813 Dis: 14 Feb 1813.
    United States Brig. Received from HMS Moselle. Sent in the British Cartel Eliza to Norfolk by order of the Governor. (Date of capture 'not mentioned'.)

Ramsey, Samuel   Prisoner 644. Rank: Seaman, from: Frolic, Man of War.
    Cap: 20 Apr 1814 Not Recorded by HMS Orpheus Int: 26 Apr 1814 Dis: 13 Jun 1814.
    United States Ship. Received from HMS Orpheus. Sent to Halifax in HMS Majestic per order of Commander in Chief Aml Cochrane.

Randolph, George   Prisoner 694. Rank: Private, from: Frolic, Man of War.
    Cap: 20 Apr 1814 Not Recorded by HMS Orpheus Int: 26 Apr 1814 Dis: 13 Jun 1814.
    United States Ship. Received from HMS Orpheus. Sent to Halifax in HMS Majestic order Aml Cochrane.

Rea, Ebenezer   Prisoner 48. Rank: Seaman, from: Augusta, Merchant.
    Cap: 02 Aug 1812 Island of Abaco by HM Schooner Decouverte Int: 05 Aug 1812 Dis: 22 Sep 1812.
    Received from Privateer. Sent to new York United States of America.

Read, Thomas   Prisoner 70. Rank: Seaman, from: Not Recorded, Not Recorded.
    Cap: Not Recorded by Police Int: 29 Aug 1812 Dis: 22 Sep 1812.
    Sent to new York United States of America. (Date of capture not on roster.)

Redfield, Eben   Prisoner 199. Rank: Master, from: Not Recorded, Not Recorded.
    Cap: Not Recorded by Privateer Unknown Int: 24 Oct 1812 Dis: 24 Oct 1812.
    Received from HMS Mosella. Sent to Charlestown in the British Cartel Nassau by order of the Governor. (Date, place, name of vessel and name of capturing ship 'not mentioned'.)

Reges, ---   Prisoner 437. Rank: Seaman, from: Recovery, Merchant.
    Cap: Not Recorded by Privateer Schooner Dash Int: 20 May 1813 Dis: 26 Apr 1814.
    Received from Privateer Schooner Dash. Sent to Rhode Island in the Cartel Liberty. (First name not recorded. Date of capture 'not mentioned'.)

Reid, Henry   Prisoner 71. Rank: Seaman, from: Not Recorded, Not Recorded.
    Cap: Not Recorded by Not Recorded Int: 01 Sep 1812 Dis: 22 Sep 1812.
    Received from Privateer. Sent to New York United States of America. (Entry may be in error, appears internment date and ship received from should be part of next line. May have been apprehended by Police as was prisoner number 70 Thomas Read. (Date of capture not on roster.)

Reife, John   Prisoner 637. Rank: Seaman, from: Frolic, Man of War.
    Cap: 20 Apr 1814 Not Recorded by HMS Orpheus Int: 26 Apr 1814 Dis: 13 Jun 1814.
    United States Ship. Received from HMS Orpheus. Sent to Halifax in HMS Majestic per order Aml Cochrane.

Reio, Peter   Prisoner 372. Rank: Seaman, from: Hazard, Privateer.
    Cap: Not Recorded by Privateer Cutter Caledonia Int: 07 Mar 1813 Dis: 13 Jun 1814.
    Recaptured in the British Ship. Received from Caledonia. Sent to Halifax HMS Majestic order of Adl Cochane. (Date and place of capture 'not mentioned'.)

American Prisoners of War Held at New Providence During the War of 1812

Remo, Joseph Prisoner 406. Rank: Seaman, from: Brothers, Merchant.
    Cap: Not Recorded by Privateer Eleanor Int: 15 Apr 1813 Dis: 13 Jun 1814.
    Received from Privateer. Sent to Halifax HMS Majestic. (Date and place of capture 'not mentioned'.)

Renimond, J Prisoner 501. Rank: Seaman, from: St. Polito, Merchant.
    Cap: 26 Nov 1813 At sea by Privateers Mars & Dash Int: 25 Dec 1813 Dis: 26 Apr 1814.
    Received from Privateer Mars. Sent to Rhode Island in the Cartel Liberty.

Reynolds, W B Prisoner 577. Rank: Seaman, from: Frolic, Man of War.
    Cap: 20 Apr 1814 At sea by HMS Orpheus Int: 26 Apr 1814 Dis: 11 Jun 1814.
    United States Ship. Received from HMS Orpheus. Sent to Bermuda in HMS Orpheus order Aml Cochrane.

Rhodes, James Prisoner 447. Rank: Seaman, from: Stanley, Merchant.
    Cap: Coast of America by Privateer Wellesley Int: 13 Jun 1813 Dis: 26 Apr 1814.
    Received from Privateer Rolla. Sent to Rhode Island in the Cartel Liberty. (Date of capture not recorded.)

Rhodes, Zachariah Prisoner 823. Rank: Seaman, from: William, Schooner.
    Cap: Not Recorded by Eleanor Int: 13 Feb 1815 Dis:
    Received from Privateer Eleanor. (Dates of capture and discharge not on roster.)

Richardson, James Prisoner 386. Rank: Seaman, from: Venus, Merchant.
    Cap: Not Recorded by Brilliant Privateer Int: 17 Mar 1813 Dis: 26 Apr 1814.
    Received from Prize. Sent to Rhode Island in the Cartel Liberty. (Date and place of capture 'not mentioned'.)

Richardson, James Prisoner 470. Rank: Seaman, from: Caroline, Merchant.
    Cap: 12 Aug 1813 East out of Charleston by HMS Moselle & Privateer Brilliant Int: 25 Aug 1813 Dis: 26 Apr 1814. Received from Privateer Brilliant. Sent to Rhode Island in the Cartel Liberty.

Richardson, John Prisoner 698. Rank: Private, from: Frolic, Man of War.
    Cap: 20 Apr 1814 Not Recorded by HMS Orpheus Int: 26 Apr 1814 Dis: 13 Jun 1814.
    United States Ship. Received from HMS Orpheus. Sent to Halifax in HMS Majestic order Aml Cochrane.

Richardson, William Prisoner 296. Rank: Seaman, from: Viper, Man of War.
    Cap: Gulf of Mexico by HMS Narcissus Int: 30 Jan 1813 Dis: 14 Feb 1813.
    Brig. Received from HMS Moselle. Sent in the British Cartel Eliza to Norfolk by order of the Governor. (Date of capture 'not mentioned'.)

Richardson, William Prisoner 742. Rank: Seaman, from: Auroa, Letter of Marquis.
    Cap: Not Recorded by HM Shooner Cockchafer Int: 03 Dec 1814 Dis:
    Received from Cockchafer. (Date and place of capture 'not mentioned'. Date of discharge not on roster.)

Richer, Stephen Prisoner 76. Rank: Seaman, from: Hamer, Merchant.
    Cap: 01 Sep 1812 Off Abaco by Privateer Int: 02 Sep 1812 Dis: 24 Oct 1812.
    Received from Privateer. Sent to Charlestown in the British Cartel Nassau.

Ricker, Edward G Prisoner 599. Rank: Seaman, from: Frolic, Man of War.
    Cap: 20 Apr 1814 Not Recorded by HMS Orpheus Int: 26 Apr 1814 Dis: 13 Jun 1814.
    United States Ship. Received from HMS Orpheus. Sent to Halifax HMS Majestic order Aml Cochrane.

Rickets, John Prisoner 169. Rank: Seaman, from: Dash, Privateer.
    Cap: 12 Sep 1812 Coast of America by Rhodian & Variable Int: 23 Sep 1812 Dis: 24 Oct 1812.
    Received from Rhodian and Variable. Sent to Charlestown in the British Cartel Nassau.

Ringold, Henry Prisoner 282. Rank: Seaman, from: Viper, Man of War.
    Cap: Gulf of Mexico by HMS Narcissus Int: 30 Jan 1813 Dis: 13 Feb 1813.
    Brig. Received from HMS Moselle. Died. Killed by another prisoner. (Date of capture 'not mentioned'.)

Roache, Thomas Prisoner 260. Rank: Seaman, from: Viper, Man of War.
    Cap: Gulf of Mexico by HMS Narcissus Int: 30 Jan 1813 Dis: 14 Feb 1813.
    United States Brig. Received from HMS Moselle. Sent in the British Cartel Eliza to Norfolk by order of the Governor. (Date of capture 'not mentioned'.)

Roberts, George Prisoner 125. Rank: Gunner, from: Sarah Ann, Privateer.
    Cap: 13 Sep 1812 Coast of America by Rhodian & Variable Int: 23 Sep 1812 Dis: 14 Oct 1812.
    Received from Rhodian and Variable. Sent to Jamaica in HMS Sappho by order of the Governor.

Roberts, Henry Prisoner 230. Rank: Seaman, from: Ospray, Merchant.
    Cap: Not Recorded by Not Recorded Int: 02 Jan 1813 Dis: 04 Feb 1813.
    Reveived from HMS Variable. Sent to Charlestown in the British Cartel Ann by order of the Governor. (Date, place and name of capturing ship 'not mentioned'.)

Roberts, James Prisoner 192. Rank: Seaman, from: Molly, Merchant.
    Cap: 12 Sep 1812 Coast of America by Caledonia Privateer Int: 03 Oct 1812 Dis: 24 Nov 1812.
    Received from Prize. Sent to Savannah in the American Cartel Delight.

American Prisoners of War Held at New Providence During the War of 1812

Roberts, James   Prisoner 303. Rank: Seaman, from: Viper, Man of War.
    Cap: Gulf of Mexico by HMS Narcissus   Int: 30 Jan 1813   Dis: 14 Feb 1813.
    Brig. Received from HMS Moselle. Sent to Norfolk in the British Cartel Eliza by order of the Governor. (Date of capture 'not mentioned'.)

Roberts, John   Prisoner 292. Rank: Seaman, from: Viper, Man of War.
    Cap: Gulf of Mexico by HMS Narcissus   Int: 30 Jan 1813   Dis: 14 Feb 1813.
    Brig. Received from HMS Moselle. Sent in the British Cartel Eliza to Norfolk by order of the Governor. (Date of capture 'not mentioned'.)

Roberts, John   Prisoner 478. Rank: Seaman, from: Catalonia, Merchant.
    Cap: 23 Nov 1813 At sea by HMS Ringdove   Int: 30 Nov 1813   Dis: 26 Apr 1814.
    Received from HMS Ringdove. Sent to Rhode Island in the Cartel Liberty.

Roberts, William   Prisoner 207. Rank: Seaman, from: William Dart, Merchant.
    Cap: Coast of America by Caledonia Privateer   Int: 17 Nov 1812   Dis: 23 Nov 1812.
    Received from Prize. Sent to Baltimore in the American Schooner George. (Date of capture 'not mentioned'.)

Robertson, James   Prisoner 144. Rank: Seaman, from: Sarah Ann, Privateer.
    Cap: 13 Sep 1812 Coast of America by Rhodian & Variable   Int: 23 Sep 1812   Dis: 24 Oct 1812.
    Received from Rhodian and Variable. Sent to Charlestown in the British Cartel Nassau.

Robertson, John   Prisoner 101. Rank: Seaman, from: Endeavour, Merchant.
    Cap: 17 Sep 1812 Abaco Passage by Privateer Francis   Int: 17 Sep 1812   Dis: 24 Oct 1812.
    Received from Prize. Sent to Charlestown in the British Cartel Nassau.

Robertson, William   Prisoner 103. Rank: Seaman, from: Romney, Merchant.
    Cap: Not Recorded by HMS Rattler   Int: 17 Sep 1812   Dis: 26 Nov 1812.
    Received from HMS Rattler. Sent to Charlestown in the British Cartel Nassau. (Date and place of capture 'not mentioned'.)

Robeson, William S   Prisoner 209. Rank: Seaman, from: Venus, Merchant.
    Cap: Coast of America by HMS Moselle   Int: 19 Nov 1812   Dis: 04 Feb 1813.
    Received from HMS Moselle. Sent to Charlestown in the British Cartel Ann by order of the Governor. (Date of capture 'not mentioned'.)

Robins, Hiland   Prisoner 702. Rank: Private, from: Frolic, Man of War.
    Cap: 20 Apr 1814 Not Recorded by HMS Orpheus   Int: 26 Apr 1814   Dis: 13 Jun 1814.
    United States Ship. Received from HMS Orpheus. Sent to Halifax in HMS Majestic order Aml Cochrane.

Robinson, Charles   Prisoner 459. Rank: Seaman, from: Not Recorded, Not Recorded.
    Cap: Not Recorded by Not Recorded   Int: 31 Jul 1813   Dis: 26 Apr 1814.
    Received from HMS Calibri. Sent to Rhode Island in the Cartel Liberty.

Robinson, David   Prisoner 336. Rank: Seaman, from: Osprey, Merchant.
    Cap: Gulf of Mexico by HMS Moselle   Int: 30 Jan 1813   Dis: 14 Feb 1813.
    Received from HMS Moselle. Sent in the British Cartel Eliza to Norfolk by order of the Governor. (Date of capture 'not mentioned'.)

Robinson, John   Prisoner 178. Rank: Seaman, from: Dash, Privateer.
    Cap: 12 Sep 1812 Coast of America by Rhodian & Variable   Int: 23 Sep 1812   Dis: 24 Oct 1812.
    Received from Rhodian and Variable. Sent to Charlestown in the British Cartel Nassau by order of the Governor.

Robinson, John   Prisoner 546. Rank: Seaman, from: Not Recorded, Letter of Marquis.
    Cap: Not Recorded by Not Recorded   Int: 17 Feb 1814   Dis: 13 Aug 1814.
    Ship wrecked among the Bahama Keys. Sent to Bermuda per order of the Commander in Chief, HMS Surprise. (Date of capture and ship received from not recorded.)

Robinson, Shadrick   Prisoner 431. Rank: Seaman, from: Trimmer, Merchant.
    Cap: Bahama Island by Government Schooner John Bull   Int: 20 May 1813   Dis: 26 Apr 1813.
    Received from Government Schooner John Bull. Sent to Rhode Island in the Cartel Liberty. (Date of capture 'not mentioned'.)

Rogers, Asa   Prisoner 681. Rank: Seaman, from: Frolic, Man of War.
    Cap: 20 Apr 1814 Not Recorded by HMS Orpheus   Int: 26 Apr 1814   Dis: 13 Jun 1814.
    United States Ship. Received from HMS Orpheus. Sent to Halifax in HMS Majestic per order of Commander in Chief Aml Cochrane.

Rogers, Francis   Prisoner 583. Rank: Seaman, from: Frolic, Man of War.
    Cap: 20 Apr 1814 Not Recorded by HMS Orpheus   Int: 26 Apr 1814   Dis: 11 Jun 1814.
    United States Ship. Received from HMS Orpheus. Sent to Bermuda in HMS Orpheus per order Commander in Chief Aml Cochrane.

American Prisoners of War Held at New Providence During the War of 1812

Rogers, Nathaniel   Prisoner 639. Rank: Seaman, from: Frolic, Man of War.
    Cap: 20 Apr 1814 Not Recorded by HMS Orpheus Int: 26 Apr 1814 Dis: 11 Jun 1814.
    United States Ship. Received from HMS Orpheus. Sent to Bermuda in HMS Orpheus per order Aml Cochrane.

Rogers, Thomas   Prisoner 143. Rank: Seaman, from: Sarah Ann, Privateer.
    Cap: 13 Sep 1812 Coast of America by Rhodian & Variable Int: 23 Sep 1812 Dis: 14 Oct 1812.
    Received from Rhodian and Variable. Sent to Jamaica in HMS Sappho by order of the Governor.

Rolston, Andrew   Prisoner 418. Rank: Seaman, from: Penobscot, Merchant Vessel.
    Cap: 10 Apr 1813 Not Recorded by HM Ship Variable Int: 27 Apr 1813 Dis: 10 Jul 1813.
    Received from HM Ship Variable. By order of the Governor.

Roper, John   Prisoner 73. Rank: Seaman, from: Harmony, Merchant.
    Cap: 28 Aug 1812 Off Abaco by Privateer Int: 01 Sep 1812 Dis: 22 Sep 1812.
    Received from Privateer. Sent to new York United States of America.

Ross, Robert   Prisoner 477. Rank: Master, from: Catalonia, Merchant.
    Cap: 23 Nov 1813 At sea by HMS Ringdove Int: 30 Nov 1813 Dis: 01 Jan 1814.
    Received from HMS Ringdove. Died. Consumption.

Ross, William   Prisoner 774. Rank: Seaman, from: George & Joseph, Merchant Vessel.
    Cap: 07 Dec 1814 Daughboy Sound by HM Ship Lacedaemonian Int: 16 Dec 1814 Dis: 19 Jan 1815.
    Received from HMS Lacedaemonian. To England.

Rosseter, D F   Prisoner 344. Rank: Master, from: Dart, Merchant.
    Cap: Not Recorded by Not Recorded Int: 04 Feb 1813 Dis: 04 Feb 1813.
    Wrecked among the islands and delivered themselves up. Received from HMS Moselle. Sent to Charlestown in the British Cartel Ann by order of the Governor. (Date of capture 'not mentioned'.)

Routh, James   Prisoner 491. Rank: Seaman, from: St. Polito, Merchant.
    Cap: 26 Apr 1813 At sea by Privateers Mars & Dash Int: 25 Dec 1813 Dis: 04 Feb 1814.
    Received from Privateer Mars. Embarked on board the Providence Merchant Vessel to assist in navigating her to England.

Rowe, Elias B   Prisoner 695. Rank: Private, from: Frolic, Man of War.
    Cap: 20 Apr 1814 Not Recorded by HMS Orpheus Int: 26 Apr 1814 Dis: 13 Jun 1814.
    United States Ship. Received from HMS Orpheus. Sent to Halifax in HMS Majestic order Aml Cochrane.

Rowe, James   Prisoner 670. Rank: Seaman, from: Frolic, Man of War.
    Cap: 20 Apr 1814 Not Recorded by HMS Orpheus Int: 26 Apr 1814 Dis: 13 Jun 1814.
    United States Ship. Received from HMS Orpheus. Sent to Halifax in HMS Majestic per order of Commander in Chief Aml Cochrane.

Rumbsy, William   Prisoner 547. Rank: Seaman, from: Not Recorded, Letter of Marquis.
    Cap: Not Recorded by Not Recorded Int: 17 Feb 1814 Dis: 13 Aug 1814.
    Ship wrecked among the Bahama Keys. Sent to Bermuda per order of the Commander in Chief, HMS Surprise. (Date of capture and ship received from not recorded.)

Sallisbury, James   Prisoner 454. Rank: Seaman, from: Stanley, Merchant.
    Cap: Coast of America by Privateer Wellesley Int: 16 Jul 1813 Dis: 26 Apr 1814.
    Received from Privateer Wellesley. Sent to Rhode Island in the Cartel Liberty. (Date of capture not recorded.)

Samoe, D   Prisoner 714. Rank: Seaman, from: Amelia, Letter of Marquis.
    Cap: 22 Jun 1813 Not Recorded by HMS Sophie Int: 29 May 1814 Dis: 07 Dec 1814.
    Received from HMS Sophie. Order Commander in Chief.

Sanborn, Daniel   Prisoner 398. Rank: Seaman, from: Dominica Packet, Merchant.
    Cap: Not Recorded by Privateer Baker Delight Int: 01 Apr 1813 Dis: 10 Apr 1813.
    Recaptured from the American Privateer Comet. Received from Privateer. Sent to Charleston in the British Cartel Charlotte by order of the Governor. (Date and place of capture 'not mentioned'.)

Sanderson, Jacob   Prisoner 534. Rank: Seaman, from: Sevant, Letter of Marquis.
    Cap: 04 Jan 1814 Not Recorded by HMS Forester Int: 12 Jan 1814 Dis: 13 Aug 1814.
    Brig. Received from HMS Forester. Sent to Bermuda HMS Surprise per order Commander in Chief.

Sandford, Samuel   Prisoner 281. Rank: Seaman, from: Viper, Man of War.
    Cap: Gulf of Mexico by HMS Narcissus Int: 30 Jan 1813 Dis: 14 Feb 1813.
    Brig. Received from HMS Moselle. Sent in the British Cartel Eliza to Norfolk by order of the Governor. (Date of capture 'not mentioned'.)

Saunders, Anthony   Prisoner 782. Rank: Seaman, from: Ruby, Merchant Vessel.
    Cap: Not Recorded by Schooner Swift Int: 09 Jan 1815 Dis: 04 Feb 1815.
    Received from Schooner Swift. from Prison Ship. (Date of capture and place of capture 'not mentioned'.)

American Prisoners of War Held at New Providence During the War of 1812

Saunders, William   Prisoner 428. Rank: Master, from: Trimmer, Merchant.
    Cap: Bahama Island by Government Schooner John Bull Int: 20 May 1813 Dis:
    Received from Government Schooner John Bull. (Date of capture 'not mentioned'. Date of discharge not on roster.)

Savage, F   Prisoner 88. Rank: Seaman, from: Phiebe V. Jane, Merchant.
    Cap: 25 Aug 1812 Coast of America by HMS Rhodian Int: 06 Sep 1812 Dis: 08 Oct 1812.
    Received from HM Brig Rhodian. By order of the Governor being a Spaniard.

Sayer, Joseph   Prisoner 775. Rank: Seaman, from: George & Joseph, Merchant Vessel.
    Cap: 07 Dec 1814 Daughboy Sound by HM Ship Lacedaemonian Int: 16 Dec 1814 Dis:
    Received from HMS Lacedaemonian. (Date of discharge not on roster.)

Scaurahon, Samuel   Prisoner 64. Rank: Seaman, from: Resolution, Merchant.
    Cap: 26 Jul 1812 Crooked Island Passage by HM Schooner Variable Int: 07 Aug 1812 Dis: 22 Sep 1812. Received from His Majesties Schooner Variable. Sent to new York United States of America.

Schaafer, C   Prisoner 206. Rank: Passenger, from: Not Recorded, Merchant.
    Cap: Not Recorded by Privateer Unknown Int: 24 Oct 1812 Dis: 24 Oct 1812.
    Received from HMS Mosella. Sent to Charlestown in the British Cartel Nassau by order of the Governor. (Date, place, name of vessel and name of capturing ship 'not mentioned'.)

Schuyler, Philip   Prisoner 748. Rank: Seaman, from: Auroa, Letter of Marquis.
    Cap: Not Recorded by HM Shooner Cockchafer Int: 03 Dec 1814 Dis:
    Received from Cockchafer. (Date and place of capture 'not mentioned'. Date of discharge not on roster.)

Scriggin, Charles   Prisoner 380. Rank: Seaman, from: Apodaco, Merchant.
    Cap: Not Recorded by Government Schooner Swift Int: 15 Mar 1813 Dis: 26 Apr 1814.
    Received from Government Schooner Swift. Sent to Rhode Island in the Cartel Liberty. (Date and place of capture 'not mentioned'.)

Serett, T   Prisoner 494. Rank: Seaman, from: St. Polito, Merchant.
    Cap: 26 Nov 1813 At sea by Privateers Mars & Dash Int: 25 Dec 1813 Dis: 26 Apr 1814.
    Received from Privateer Mars. Sent to Rhode Island in the Cartel Liberty.

Sergeant, Charles   Prisoner 649. Rank: Seaman, from: Frolic, Man of War.
    Cap: 20 Apr 1814 Not Recorded by HMS Orpheus Int: 26 Apr 1814 Dis: 13 Jun 1814.
    United States Ship. Received from HMS Orpheus. Sent to Halifax in HMS Majestic per order of Commander in Chief Aml Cochrane.

Seribble, H. Y   Prisoner 622. Rank: Seaman, from: Frolic, Man of War.
    Cap: 20 Apr 1814 Not Recorded by HMS Orpheus Int: 26 Apr 1814 Dis: 13 Jun 1814.
    United States Ship. Received from HMS Orpheus. Sent to Halifax in HMS Majestic order Aml Cochrane.

Seward, N   Prisoner 499. Rank: Seaman, from: St. Polito, Merchant.
    Cap: 26 Nov 1813 At sea by Privateers Mars & Dash Int: 25 Dec 1813 Dis: 26 Apr 1814.
    Received from Privateer Mars. Sent to Rhode Island in the Cartel Liberty.

Shacklay, J   Prisoner 559. Rank: Seaman, from: Roberts, Merchant Vessel.
    Cap: 24 Feb 1814 At sea by HM Ship Rhin Int: 03 Mar 1814 Dis: 15 Aug 1814.
    His MS Rhin taken the recaptured Brig Roberts belonging to the American Privateer Schooner May, of 15 guns. Received from HMS Rhin. Sent to Bermuda HMS Surprise order the Commander in Chief.

Shafer, ---   Prisoner 690. Rank: Sergeant Marines, from: Frolic, Man of War.
    Cap: 20 Apr 1814 Not Recorded by HMS Orpheus Int: 26 Apr 1814 Dis: 13 Jun 1814.
    United States Ship. Received from HMS Orpheus. Sent to Halifax in HMS Majestic order Aml Cochrane. (First name not recorded.)

Shaffer, James   Prisoner 807. Rank: Seaman, from: Saturn, Letter of Marquis.
    Cap: Not Recorded by Venus Int: 29 Jan 1815 Dis:
    Schooner. Received from Venus. (Dates of capture and discharge not on roster.)

Shearon, John   Prisoner 309. Rank: Seaman, from: Viper, Man of War.
    Cap: Gulf of Mexico by HMS Narcissus Int: 30 Jan 1813 Dis: 14 Feb 1813.
    Brig. Received from HMS Moselle. Sent to Norfolk in the British Cartel Eliza by order of the Governor. (Date of capture 'not mentioned'.)

Shekman, Sol   Prisoner 220. Rank: Seaman, from: Venus, Merchant.
    Cap: Coast of America by HMS Moselle Int: 19 Nov 1812 Dis: 23 Nov 1812.
    Received from HMS Moselle. Sent to Baltimore in the American Schooner George. (Date of capture 'not mentioned'.)

Shellock, James   Prisoner 337. Rank: Seaman, from: Osprey, Merchant.
    Cap: Gulf of Mexico by HMS Moselle Int: 30 Jan 1813 Dis: 14 Feb 1813.
    Received from HMS Moselle. Sent in the British Cartel Eliza to Norfolk by order of the Governor. (Date of capture 'not mentioned'.)

American Prisoners of War Held at New Providence During the War of 1812

Shephard, John   Prisoner 45. Rank: Seaman, from: Ceres, Merchant.
    Cap: 28 Jul 1812 Bahama Bank by Privateer Theodore Int: 02 Aug 1812 Dis: 22 Sep 1812.
    Received from Privateer. Sent to New York United States of America.

Sherlock, Charles   Prisoner 655. Rank: Seaman, from: Frolic, Man of War.
    Cap: 20 Apr 1814 Not Recorded by HMS Orpheus Int: 26 Apr 1814 Dis: 13 Jun 1814.
    United States Ship. Received from HMS Orpheus. Sent to Halifax in HMS Majestic per order of Commander in Chief Aml Cochrane.

Shilley, John   Prisoner 279. Rank: Seaman, from: Viper, Man of War.
    Cap: Gulf of Mexico by HMS Narcissus Int: 30 Jan 1813 Dis: 14 Feb 1813.
    Brig. Received from HMS Moselle. Sent in the British Cartel Eliza to Norfolk by order of the Governor. (Date of capture 'not mentioned'.)

Shumo, Samuel   Prisoner 106. Rank: Seaman, from: Romney, Merchant.
    Cap: Not Recorded by HMS Rattler Int: 21 Sep 1812 Dis: 23 Nov 1812.
    Received from HMS Rattler. Sent to Baltimore in the American Schooner George. (Date and place of capture 'not mentioned'.)

Sibley, Ill   Prisoner 21. Rank: Seaman, from: Non Parail, Privateer.
    Cap: 29 Jul 1812 Off Eleuthera (rest not legible) by HM Schooner Decouverte Int: 01 Aug 1812 Dis: 24 Oct 1812. Received from HM Schooner Decauverte. Sent to Charlestown in the British Cartel Nassau by order of the Governor.

Silvee, H   Prisoner 23. Rank: Seaman, from: Non Parail, Privateer.
    Cap: 29 Jul 1812 Off Eleuthera (rest not legible) by HM Schooner Decouverte Int: 01 Aug 1812 Dis: 24 Oct 1812. Received from HM Schooner Decauverte. Sent to Charlestown in the British Cartel Nassau by order of the Governor.

Simon, John   Prisoner 328. Rank: Seaman, from: Osprey, Merchant.
    Cap: Gulf of Mexico by HMS Moselle Int: 30 Jan 1813 Dis: 14 Feb 1813.
    Received from HMS Moselle. Sent in the British Cartel Eliza to Norfolk by order of the Governor. (Date of capture 'not mentioned'.)

Slattou, John   Prisoner 26. Rank: Seaman, from: Non Parail, Privateer.
    Cap: 29 Jul 1812 Off Eleuthera by HM Schooner Decouverte Int: 01 Aug 1812 Dis: 17 Oct 1812.
    Received from HM Schooner Decauverte. Sent to England order of the Governor.

Small, William   Prisoner 658. Rank: Seaman, from: Frolic, Man of War.
    Cap: 20 Apr 1814 Not Recorded by HMS Orpheus Int: 26 Apr 1814 Dis: 13 Jun 1814.
    United States Ship. Received from HMS Orpheus. Sent to Halifax in HMS Majestic per order of Commander in Chief Aml Cochrane.

Smith, E   Prisoner 505. Rank: Seaman, from: St. Polito, Merchant.
    Cap: 26 Nov 1813 At sea by Privateers Mars & Dash Int: 25 Dec 1813 Dis: 08 Jul 1814.
    Received from Privateer Mars. Sent to Bermuda per order Adml Cochrane.

Smith, George   Prisoner 542. Rank: Seaman, from: Sevant, Letter of Marquis.
    Cap: 04 Jan 1814 Not Recorded by HMS Forester Int: 12 Jan 1814 Dis: 13 Aug 1814.
    Brig. Received from HMS Forester. Sent to Bermuda.

Smith, Isaac   Prisoner 651. Rank: Seaman, from: Frolic, Man of War.
    Cap: 20 Apr 1814 Not Recorded by HMS Orpheus Int: 26 Apr 1814 Dis: 13 Jun 1814.
    United States Ship. Received from HMS Orpheus. Sent to Halifax in HMS Majestic per order of Commander in Chief Aml Cochrane.

Smith, Jacob   Prisoner 61. Rank: Seaman, from: Resolution, Merchant.
    Cap: 26 Jul 1812 Crooked Island Passage by HM Schooner Variable Int: 07 Aug 1812 Dis: 22 Sep 1812. Received from His Majesties Schooner Variable. Sent to new York United States of America.

Smith, John   Prisoner 219. Rank: Seaman, from: Venus, Merchant.
    Cap: Coast of America by HMS Moselle Int: 19 Nov 1812 Dis: 24 Nov 1812.
    Received from HMS Moselle. Sent to Savannah in the American Cartel Delight. (Date of capture 'not mentioned'.)

Smith, John   Prisoner 569. Rank: 2 Mate, from: Frolic, Man of War.
    Cap: 20 Apr 1814 At sea by HMS Orpheus Int: 26 Apr 1814 Dis: 11 Jun 1814.
    United States Ship. Received from HMS Orpheus. Sent to Bermuda in HMS Orpheus order Aml Cochrane.

Smith, John   Prisoner 767. Rank: Seaman, from: No Name, Not Recorded.
    Cap: Not Recorded by Not Recorded Int: 08 Dec 1814 Dis: 18 Jan 1815.
    Received from HM Sloop Childers. Sent to Bermuda in HMS Childers. (Date, place of capture and name of capturing ship 'not mentioned'.)

Smith, Peter   Prisoner 676. Rank: Seaman, from: Frolic, Man of War.
    Cap: 20 Apr 1814 Not Recorded by HMS Orpheus Int: 26 Apr 1814 Dis: 27 Apr 1814.
    United States Ship. Received from HMS Orpheus. HMS Orpheus

American Prisoners of War Held at New Providence During the War of 1812

Smith, Samuel   Prisoner 623. Rank: Seaman, from: Frolic, Man of War.
  Cap: 20 Apr 1814 Not Recorded by HMS Orpheus Int: 26 Apr 1814 Dis: 13 Jun 1814.
  United States Ship. Received from HMS Orpheus. Sent to Halifax in HMS Majestic order Aml Cochrane.

Smith, Solomon   Prisoner 341. Rank: Seaman, from: Dart, Merchant.
  Cap: Not Recorded by Not Recorded Int: 04 Feb 1813 Dis: 04 Feb 1813.
  Wrecked among the islands and delivered themselves up. Received from HMS Moselle. Sent to Charlestown in the British Cartel Ann by order of the Governor. (Date of capture 'not mentioned'.)

Smith, William   Prisoner 786. Rank: Seaman, from: No Name, Not Recorded.
  Cap: Not Recorded by Not Recorded Int: 14 Jan 1815 Dis: 19 Jan 1815.
  Received from Venus. To England. (Date of and place of capture 'not mentioned'.)

Snell, Charles   Prisoner 733. Rank: Seaman, from: Gunboat 160, Man of War.
  Cap: Cumberland Sound by HMS Lacedaemonian Int: 19 Oct 1814 Dis:
  United States Gunboat. Received from HMS Lacedaemonian. (Dates of capture and discharge not on roster.)

Sneston, Thomas   Prisoner 441. Rank: Seaman, from: Stanley, Merchant.
  Cap: Coast of America by Privateer Wellesley Int: 08 Jun 1813 Dis: 26 Apr 1814.
  Received from HMS Calibri. Sent to Rhode Island in the Cartel Liberty. (Date of capture not recorded.)

Snowdon, John   Prisoner 668. Rank: Seaman, from: Frolic, Man of War.
  Cap: 20 Apr 1814 Not Recorded by HMS Orpheus Int: 26 Apr 1814 Dis: 13 Jun 1814.
  United States Ship. Received from HMS Orpheus. Sent to Halifax in HMS Majestic per order of Commander in Chief Aml Cochrane.

Snver, H. C   Prisoner 497. Rank: Seaman, from: St. Polito, Merchant.
  Cap: 26 Nov 1813 At sea by Privateers Mars & Dash Int: 25 Dec 1813 Dis: 26 Apr 1814.
  Received from Privateer Mars. Sent to Rhode Island in the Cartel Liberty.

Softon, James   Prisoner 302. Rank: Seaman, from: Viper, Man of War.
  Cap: Gulf of Mexico by HMS Narcissus Int: 30 Jan 1813 Dis: 14 Feb 1813.
  Brig. Received from HMS Moselle. Sent to Norfolk in the British Cartel Eliza by order of the Governor. (Date of capture 'not mentioned'.)

Soule, Asa   Prisoner 72. Rank: Seaman, from: Harmony, Merchant.
  Cap: 28 Aug 1812 Off Abaco by Privateer Int: 01 Sep 1812 Dis: 22 Sep 1812.
  Received from Privateer. Sent to new York United States of America.

Sovein, John   Prisoner 15. Rank: Seaman, from: Non Parail, Privateer.
  Cap: 29 Jul 1812 Off Eleuthera (rest not legible) by HM Schooner Decouverte Int: 01 Aug 1812 Dis: 24 Oct 1812. Received from HM Schooner Decauverte. Sent to Charlestown in the British Cartel Nassau by order of the Governor.

Spence, Robert   Prisoner 568. Rank: Gunners Mate, from: Frolic, Man of War.
  Cap: 20 Apr 1814 At sea by HMS Orpheus Int: 26 Apr 1814 Dis: 11 Jun 1814.
  United States Ship. Received from HMS Orpheus. Sent to Bermuda in HMS Orpheus order Aml Cochrane.

Spillard, Robert   Prisoner 705. Rank: Private, from: Frolic, Man of War.
  Cap: 20 Apr 1814 Not Recorded by HMS Orpheus Int: 26 Apr 1814 Dis: 13 Jun 1814.
  United States Ship. Received from HMS Orpheus. Sent to Halifax in HMS Majestic order Aml Cochrane.

Sroan, Dermias   Prisoner 216. Rank: Seaman, from: Venus, Merchant.
  Cap: Coast of America by HMS Moselle Int: 19 Nov 1812 Dis: 04 Feb 1813.
  Received from HMS Moselle. Sent to Charlestown in the British Cartel Ann by order of the Governor. (Date of capture 'not mentioned'.)

Stack, Samuel   Prisoner 540. Rank: Seaman, from: Sevant, Letter of Marquis.
  Cap: 04 Jan 1814 Not Recorded by HMS Forester Int: 12 Jan 1814 Dis: 13 Aug 1814.
  Brig. Received from HMS Forester. Sent to Bermuda HMS Surprise per order the Commander in Chief.

Stage, Abraham   Prisoner 737. Rank: Seaman, from: Gunboat 160, Man of War.
  Cap: Cumberland Sound by HMS Lacedaemonian Int: 19 Oct 1814 Dis: 18 Jan 1815.
  United States Gunboat. Received from HMS Lacedaemonian. Sent to Bermuda in HMS Childers. (Date of capture not on roster.)

Stanley, Timothy   Prisoner 529. Rank: Seaman, from: Lion, Merchant.
  Cap: 04 Jan 1814 Not Recorded by HMS Forester Int: 12 Jan 1814 Dis: 08 Jul 1814.
  Received from HMS Forester. Sent to Bermuda. (May be part of the crew of the Sevant.)

American Prisoners of War Held at New Providence During the War of 1812

Sterling, Elizah   Prisoner 32. Rank: Seaman, from: HM Schooner Decouverte, Not Recorded.
    Cap: 29 Jul 1812 Not Stated by HM Schooner Decouverte Int: 01 Aug 1812 Dis: 20 Aug 1812.
    Received from HM Schooner Decauverte. Gave themselves up as Prisoners of War. Being Part of the complement of the HMS Decouvete Lieut Richard Williams Commanding. Sent to Jamaica in HM Schooner Decouverte by order of Lieut Williams.

Stevens, Daniel   Prisoner 553. Rank: Seaman, from: Not Recorded, Letter of Marquis.
    Cap: Not Recorded by Not Recorded Int: 17 Feb 1814 Dis: 21 Apr 1814.
    Ship wrecked among the Bahama Keys. Brig James for England. (Date of capture and ship received from not recorded.)

Stevens, Luen   Prisoner 638. Rank: Seaman, from: Frolic, Man of War.
    Cap: 20 Apr 1814 Not Recorded by HMS Orpheus Int: 26 Apr 1814 Dis: 13 Jun 1814.
    United States Ship. Received from HMS Orpheus. Sent to Halifax in HMS Majestic per order Aml Cochrane.

Steward, Hosea   Prisoner 62. Rank: Seaman, from: Resolution, Merchant.
    Cap: 26 Jul 1812 Crooked Island Passage by HM Schooner Variable Int: 07 Aug 1812 Dis: 22 Sep 1812. Received from His Majesties Schooner Variable. Sent to new York United States of America.

Stewart, Robert   Prisoner 797. Rank: Seaman, from: Java, Letter of Marquis.
    Cap: Not Recorded by Cockchafer Int: 14 Jan 1815 Dis:
    Received from HM Schooner Cockchafer. (Dates of capture and discharge not on roster.)

Stewart, Stephen C   Prisoner 794. Rank: Seaman, from: Java, Letter of Marquis.
    Cap: Not Recorded by Cockchafer Int: 14 Jan 1815 Dis:
    Received from HM Schooner Cockchafer. (Dates of capture and discharge not on roster.)

Stewart, Thomas   Prisoner 243. Rank: Seaman, from: Viper, Man of War.
    Cap: Gulf of Mexico by HMS Narcissus Int: 30 Jan 1813 Dis: 14 Feb 1813.
    United States Brig. Received from HMS Moselle. Sent in the British Cartel Eliza to Norfolk by order of the Governor. (Date of capture 'not mentioned'.)

Stickney, Emey   Prisoner 539. Rank: Seaman, from: Sevant, Letter of Marquis.
    Cap: 04 Jan 1814 Not Recorded by HMS Forester Int: 12 Jan 1814 Dis: 13 Aug 1814.
    Brig. Received from HMS Forester. Sent to Bermuda HMS Surprise per order the Commander in Chief.

Stole, Robert   Prisoner 208. Rank: Seaman, from: William Dart, Merchant.
    Cap: Coast of America by Caledonia Privateer Int: 17 Nov 1812 Dis: 24 Nov 1812.
    Received from Prize. Sent to Savannah in the American Cartel Delight. (Date of capture 'not mentioned'.)

Stone, James   Prisoner 531. Rank: Seaman, from: Sevant, Letter of Marquis.
    Cap: 04 Jan 1814 Not Recorded by HMS Forester Int: 12 Jan 1814 Dis: 08 Jul 1814.
    Brig. Received from HMS Forester. Sent to Bermuda.

Studdle, Surimeau   Prisoner 538. Rank: Seaman, from: Sevant, Letter of Marquis.
    Cap: 04 Jan 1814 Not Recorded by HMS Forester Int: 12 Jan 1814 Dis: 13 Aug 1814.
    Brig. Received from HMS Forester. Sent to Bermuda HMS Surprise per order the Commander in Chief.

Studly, Simeon   Prisoner 467. Rank: Seaman, from: Caroline, Merchant.
    Cap: 12 Aug 1813 East out of Charleston by HMS Moselle & Privateer Brilliant Int: 25 Aug 1813 Dis: . Received from Privateer Brilliant. (Date of discharge not on roster.)

Suitter, William   Prisoner 135. Rank: Seaman, from: Sarah Ann, Privateer.
    Cap: 13 Sep 1812 Coast of America by Rhodian & Variable Int: 23 Sep 1812 Dis: 24 Oct 1812.
    Received from Rhodian and Variable. Sent to Charlestown in the British Cartel Nassau.

Sulliff, William   Prisoner 724. Rank: Seaman, from: Fox, Merchant Vessel.
    Cap: Cumberland Sound by HMS Lacedaemonian Int: 19 Oct 1819 Dis: 07 Dec 1814.
    Received from HMS Lacedaemonian. Order Commander in Chief. (Date of capture not on roster.)

Sweeney, John   Prisoner 834. Rank: Seaman, from: Hercules, Merchant Vessel.
    Cap: 09 Mar 1815 Not Recorded by HM Schooner Canso Int: 13 Mar 1815 Dis:
    Recaptured Ship. Received from HM Schooner Canso. (Date of discharge not on roster.)

Swift, James   Prisoner 331. Rank: Seaman, from: Osprey, Merchant.
    Cap: Gulf of Mexico by HMS Moselle Int: 30 Jan 1813 Dis: 14 Feb 1813.
    Received from HMS Moselle. Sent in the British Cartel Eliza to Norfolk by order of the Governor. (Date of capture 'not mentioned'.)

Tabor, Joseph   Prisoner 350. Rank: Seaman, from: George & Mary, Merchant.
    Cap: Not Recorded by Not Recorded Int: 14 Feb 1813 Dis: 14 Feb 1813.
    Wrecked among the islands and delivered themselves up. Sent to Norfolk in the British Cartel Eliza by order of the Governor. (Date of capture 'not mentioned'.)

American Prisoners of War Held at New Providence During the War of 1812

Tall, John   Prisoner 589. Rank: Seaman, from: Frolic, Man of War.
    Cap: 20 Apr 1814 Not Recorded by HMS Orpheus Int: 26 Apr 1814 Dis: 11 Jun 1814.
    United States Ship. Received from HMS Orpheus. Sent to Bermuda in HMS Orpheus per order Commander in Chief Aml Cochrane.

Tallman, John   Prisoner 201. Rank: Seaman, from: Not Recorded, Merchant.
    Cap: Not Recorded by Privateer Unknown Int: 24 Oct 1812 Dis: 24 Oct 1812.
    Received from HMS Mosella. Sent to Charlestown in the British Cartel Nassau by order of the Governor. (Date, place, name of vessel and name of capturing ship 'not mentioned'.)

Tallman, William   Prisoner 353. Rank: Seaman, from: George & Mary, Merchant.
    Cap: Not Recorded by Not Recorded Int: 14 Feb 1813 Dis: 14 Feb 1813.
    Wrecked among the islands and delivered themselves up. Sent to Norfolk in the British Cartel Eliza by order of the Governor. (Date of capture 'not mentioned'.)

Tandy, John   Prisoner 761. Rank: Seaman, from: No Name, Not Recorded.
    Cap: Not Recorded by Not Recorded Int: 08 Dec 1814 Dis: 18 Jan 1815.
    Received from HM Sloop Childers. Sent to Bermuda in HMS Childers. (Date, place of capture and name of capturing ship 'not mentioned'.)

Tausk, Samuel   Prisoner 664. Rank: Seaman, from: Frolic, Man of War.
    Cap: 20 Apr 1814 Not Recorded by HMS Orpheus Int: 26 Apr 1814 Dis: 13 Jun 1814.
    United States Ship. Received from HMS Orpheus. Sent to Halifax in HMS Majestic per order of Commander in Chief Aml Cochrane.

Taylor, Alexander   Prisoner 156. Rank: Seaman, from: Sarah Ann, Privateer.
    Cap: 13 Sep 1812 Coast of America by Rhodian & Variable Int: 23 Sep 1812 Dis: 14 Oct 1812.
    Received from Rhodian and Variable. Sent to Jamaica in HMS Sappho by order of the Governor.

Taylor, Charles   Prisoner 732. Rank: Seaman, from: Gunboat 160, Man of War.
    Cap: Cumberland Sound by HMS Lacedaemonian Int: 19 Oct 1814 Dis: 18 Jan 1815.
    United States Gunboat. Received from HMS Lacedaemonian. Sent to Bermuda in HMS Childers. (Date of capture not on roster.)

Taylor, George   Prisoner 626. Rank: Master at Arms, from: Frolic, Man of War.
    Cap: 20 Apr 1814 Not Recorded by HMS Orpheus Int: 26 Apr 1814 Dis: 13 Jun 1814.
    United States Ship. Received from HMS Orpheus. Sent to Halifax in HMS Majestic order Aml Cochrane.

Taylor, Joseph   Prisoner 393. Rank: Seaman, from: Dominica Packet, Merchant.
    Cap: Not Recorded by HMS Variable Int: 30 Mar 1813 Dis:
    Recaptured from the American Privateer Comet. Received from Variable. (Date and place of capture 'not mentioned'. Date of discharge not on roster.)

Taylor, Thomas   Prisoner 323. Rank: Seaman, from: Sheperd, Merchant.
    Cap: Gulf of Mexico by HMS Narcissus Int: 30 Jan 1813 Dis: 14 Feb 1813.
    Received from HMS Moselle. Sent to Norfolk in the British Cartel Eliza by order of the Governor. (Date of capture 'not mentioned'.)

Templeman, M   Prisoner 218. Rank: Seaman, from: Venus, Merchant.
    Cap: Coast of America by HMS Moselle Int: 19 Nov 1812 Dis: 24 Nov 1812.
    Received from HMS Moselle. Sent to Savannah in the American Cartel Delight. (Date of capture 'not mentioned'.)

Teufton, James   Prisoner 692. Rank: Corporal, from: Frolic, Man of War.
    Cap: 20 Apr 1814 Not Recorded by HMS Orpheus Int: 26 Apr 1814 Dis: 13 Jun 1814.
    United States Ship. Received from HMS Orpheus. Sent to Halifax in HMS Majestic order Aml Cochrane.

Thomas, George   Prisoner 252. Rank: Seaman, from: Viper, Man of War.
    Cap: Gulf of Mexico by HMS Narcissus Int: 30 Jan 1813 Dis: 14 Feb 1813.
    United States Brig. Received from HMS Moselle. Sent in the British Cartel Eliza to Norfolk by order of the Governor. (Date of capture 'not mentioned'.)

Thomas, William   Prisoner 214. Rank: Seaman, from: Venus, Merchant.
    Cap: Coast of America by HMS Moselle Int: 19 Nov 1812 Dis: 04 Feb 1813.
    Received from HMS Moselle. Sent to Charlestown in the British Cartel Ann by order of the Governor. (Date of capture 'not mentioned'.)

Thompson, James   Prisoner 600. Rank: Seaman, from: Frolic, Man of War.
    Cap: 20 Apr 1814 Not Recorded by HMS Orpheus Int: 26 Apr 1814 Dis: 13 Jun 1814.
    United States Ship. Received from HMS Orpheus. Sent to Halifax HMS Majestic order Aml Cochrane.

Thompson, John   Prisoner 18. Rank: Seaman, from: Non Parail, Privateer.
    Cap: 29 Jul 1812 Off Eleuthera (rest not legible) by HM Schooner Decouverte Int: 01 Aug 1812 Dis: 24 Oct 1812. Received from HM Schooner Decauverte. Sent to Charlestown in the British Cartel Nassau by order of the Governor.

American Prisoners of War Held at New Providence During the War of 1812

Thompson, William   Prisoner 479. Rank: Seaman, from: Catalonia, Merchant.
    Cap: 23 Nov 1813 At sea by HMS Ringdove Int: 30 Nov 1813 Dis: 26 Apr 1814.
    Received from HMS Ringdove. Sent to Rhode Island in the Cartel Liberty.

Thomson, John   Prisoner 408. Rank: Seaman, from: Portsmouth, Merchant.
    Cap: 16 Apr 1813 At sea by HM Ships Morgiana & Calibri Int: 20 Apr 1813 Dis: 26 Apr 1814.
    Received from HMS Morgiana. Sent to Rhode Island in the Cartel Liberty.

Thorton, James   Prisoner 307. Rank: Seaman, from: Viper, Man of War.
    Cap: Gulf of Mexico by HMS Narcissus Int: 30 Jan 1813 Dis: 14 Feb 1813.
    Brig. Received from HMS Moselle. Sent to Norfolk in the British Cartel Eliza by order of the Governor. (Date of capture 'not mentioned'.)

Tillow, George   Prisoner 308. Rank: Seaman, from: Viper, Man of War.
    Cap: Gulf of Mexico by HMS Narcissus Int: 30 Jan 1813 Dis: 14 Feb 1813.
    Brig. Received from HMS Moselle. Sent to Norfolk in the British Cartel Eliza by order of the Governor. (Date of capture 'not mentioned'.)

Tilton, Peter   Prisoner 483. Rank: Seaman, from: Innocencia, Merchant.
    Cap: 26 Nov 1813 At sea by HMS Ringdove Int: 30 Nov 1813 Dis: 26 Apr 1814.
    Received from HMS Ringdove. Sent to Rhode Island in the Cartel Liberty.

Tisdale, Ster. J   Prisoner 485. Rank: Seaman, from: Innocencia, Merchant.
    Cap: 26 Nov 1813 At sea by HMS Ringdove Int: 30 Nov 1813 Dis: 26 Oct 1814.
    Received from HMS Ringdove. Sent to Bermuda HMS Wolverine.

Todd, Daniel   Prisoner 691. Rank: Corporal, from: Frolic, Man of War.
    Cap: 20 Apr 1814 Not Recorded by HMS Orpheus Int: 26 Apr 1814 Dis: 13 Jun 1814.
    United States Ship. Received from HMS Orpheus. Sent to Halifax in HMS Majestic order Aml Cochrane.

Todd, James   Prisoner 274. Rank: Seaman, from: Viper, Man of War.
    Cap: Gulf of Mexico by HMS Narcissus Int: 30 Jan 1813 Dis: 14 Feb 1813.
    Brig. Received from HMS Moselle. Sent in the British Cartel Eliza to Norfolk by order of the Governor. (Date of capture 'not mentioned'.)

Todd, Robert   Prisoner 699. Rank: Private, from: Frolic, Man of War.
    Cap: 20 Apr 1814 Not Recorded by HMS Orpheus Int: 26 Apr 1814 Dis: 13 Jun 1814.
    United States Ship. Received from HMS Orpheus. Sent to Halifax in HMS Majestic order Aml Cochrane.

Toria, ---   Prisoner 435. Rank: Seaman, from: Elizabeth, Merchant.
    Cap: Not Recorded by Privateer Schooner Dash Int: 20 May 1813 Dis: 26 Apr 1814.
    Received from Privateer Schooner Dash. Sent to Rhode Island in the Cartel Liberty. (First name not recorded. Date of capture 'not mentioned.')

Tower, James   Prisoner 704. Rank: Private, from: Frolic, Man of War.
    Cap: 20 Apr 1814 Not Recorded by HMS Orpheus Int: 26 Apr 1814 Dis: 13 Jun 1814.
    United States Ship. Received from HMS Orpheus. Sent to Halifax in HMS Majestic order Aml Cochrane.

Traston, Daniel T   Prisoner 706. Rank: Private, from: Frolic, Man of War.
    Cap: 20 Apr 1814 Not Recorded by HMS Orpheus Int: 26 Apr 1814 Dis: 13 Jun 1814.
    United States Ship. Received from HMS Orpheus. Sent to Halifax in HMS Majestic order Aml Cochrane.

Travers, Frederick   Prisoner 128. Rank: Seaman, from: Sarah Ann, Privateer.
    Cap: 13 Sep 1812 Coast of America by Rhodian & Variable Int: 23 Sep 1812 Dis: 24 Oct 1812.
    Received from Rhodian and Variable. Sent to Charlestown in the British Cartel Nassau.

Travis, George   Prisoner 403. Rank: Seaman, from: Wave, Merchant.
    Cap: Not Recorded by Privateer Wellesley Int: 05 Apr 1813 Dis: 06 Apr 1813.
    Received from Prize. Sent to England in the Ship Loyal Sam. (Date and place of capture 'not mentioned'.)

Tredway, Henry   Prisoner 744. Rank: Seaman, from: Auroa, Letter of Marquis.
    Cap: Not Recorded by HM Shooner Cockchafer Int: 03 Dec 1814 Dis: 10 Jan 1815.
    Received from Cockchafer. Writ of Habeas Corpus. (Date and place of capture 'not mentioned'.)

Tucker, D. F   Prisoner 527. Rank: 3 Mate, from: Lion, Merchant.
    Cap: 04 Jan 1814 Not Recorded by HMS Forester Int: 12 Jan 1814 Dis: 08 Jul 1814.
    Received from HMS Forester. Sent to Bermuda. (May be part of the crew of the Sevant.)

Tucker, John B   Prisoner 679. Rank: Seaman, from: Frolic, Man of War.
    Cap: 20 Apr 1814 Not Recorded by HMS Orpheus Int: 26 Apr 1814 Dis: 07 Dec 1814.
    United States Ship. Received from HMS Orpheus. Order Commander in Chief.

American Prisoners of War Held at New Providence During the War of 1812

Tuman, Philip   Prisoner 752. Rank: Seaman, from: Auroa, Letter of Marquis.
> Cap: Not Recorded by HM Shooner Cockchafer   Int: 03 Dec 1814   Dis: 20 Jan 1815.
> Received from Cockchafer. To England. (Date and place of capture 'not mentioned'.)

Tumanic, James   Prisoner 558. Rank: Seaman, from: Roberts, Merchant Vessel.
> Cap: 24 Feb 1814 At sea by HM Ship Rhin   Int: 03 Mar 1814   Dis: 15 Aug 1814.
> His MS Rhin taken the recaptured Brig Roberts belonging to the American Privateer Schooner May, of 15 guns. Received from HMS Rhin. Sent to Bermuda HMS Surprise order the Commander in Chief.

Tunis, John   Prisoner 116. Rank: Seaman, from: Alexander, Merchant.
> Cap: Not Recorded by HMS Sappho   Int: 22 Sep 1812   Dis: 24 Nov 1812.
> Received from HMS Sappho. Sent to Savannah in the American Cartel Delight. (Date and place of capture 'not mentioned'.

Tutle, Noah   Prisoner 436. Rank: Seaman, from: Recovery, Merchant.
> Cap: Not Recorded by Privateer Schooner Dash   Int: 20 May 1813   Dis: 26 Apr 1814.
> Received from Privateer Schooner Dash. Sent to Rhode Island in the Cartel Liberty. (Date of capture 'not mentioned'.)

Vance, John   Prisoner 306. Rank: Seaman, from: Viper, Man of War.
> Cap: Gulf of Mexico by HMS Narcissus   Int: 30 Jan 1813   Dis: 14 Feb 1813.
> Brig. Received from HMS Moselle. Sent to Norfolk in the British Cartel Eliza by order of the Governor. (Date of capture 'not mentioned'.)

Vauding, Howard   Prisoner 86. Rank: Seaman, from: Nelly, Merchant.
> Cap: 25 Aug 1812 Coast of America by HMS Rhodian   Int: 06 Sep 1812   Dis: 24 Oct 1812.
> Received from HM Brig Rhodian. Sent to Charlestown in the British Cartel Nassau.

Vickery, C   Prisoner 503. Rank: Seaman, from: St. Polito, Merchant.
> Cap: 26 Nov 1813 At sea by Privateers Mars & Dash   Int: 25 Dec 1813   Dis: 08 Jul 1814.
> Received from Privateer Mars. Sent to Bermuda per order Adml Cochrane.

Vosso, Mathew   Prisoner 29. Rank: 2 Master, from: HM Schooner Decouverte, Not Recorded.
> Cap: 29 Jul 1812 Not Stated by HM Schooner Decouverte   Int: 01 Aug 1812   Dis: 20 Aug 1812.
> Received from HM Schooner Decauverte. Gave themselves up as Prisoners of War. Being Part of the complement of the HMS Decouvete Lieut Richard Williams Commanding. Sent to Jamaica in HM Schooner Decouverte by order of Lieut Williams.

Waggoner, Henry   Prisoner 161. Rank: Boatswain, from: Dash, Privateer.
> Cap: 12 Sep 1812 Coast of America by Rhodian & Variable   Int: 23 Sep 1812   Dis: 24 Oct 1812.
> Received from Rhodian and Variable. Sent to Charlestown in the British Cartel Nassau.

Waiter, James A   Prisoner 311. Rank: Seaman, from: Sheperd, Merchant.
> Cap: Gulf of Mexico by HMS Narcissus   Int: 30 Jan 1813   Dis: 14 Feb 1813.
> Received from HMS Moselle. Sent to Norfolk in the British Cartel Eliza by order of the Governor. (Date of capture 'not mentioned'.)

Waldrown, Trom   Prisoner 836. Rank: Seaman, from: Hercules, Merchant Vessel.
> Cap: 09 Mar 1815 Not Recorded by HM Schooner Canso   Int: 13 Mar 1815   Dis:
> Recaptured Ship. Received from HM Schooner Canso. (Date of discharge not on roster.)

Walker, Peter   Prisoner 643. Rank: Seaman, from: Frolic, Man of War.
> Cap: 20 Apr 1814 Not Recorded by HMS Orpheus   Int: 26 Apr 1814   Dis: 13 Jun 1814.
> United States Ship. Received from HMS Orpheus. Sent to Halifax in HMS Majestic per order of Commander in Chief Aml Cochrane.

Walker, Samuel   Prisoner 425. Rank: Seaman, from: John, Merchant.
> Cap: Not Recorded by Privateer Dash   Int: 29 Apr 1813   Dis: 26 Apr 1814.
> Received from Prize. Sent to Rhode Island in the Cartel Liberty. (Date and place of capture 'not mentioned'.)

Wallace, Newport   Prisoner 356. Rank: Seaman, from: George & Mary, Merchant.
> Cap: Not Recorded by Not Recorded   Int: 14 Feb 1813   Dis: 14 Feb 1813.
> Wrecked among the islands and delivered themselves up. Sent to Norfolk in the British Cartel Eliza by order of the Governor. (Date of capture 'not mentioned'.)

Wallis, John   Prisoner 634. Rank: Seaman, from: Frolic, Man of War.
> Cap: 20 Apr 1814 Not Recorded by HMS Orpheus   Int: 26 Apr 1814   Dis: 13 Jun 1814.
> United States Ship. Received from HMS Orpheus. Sent to Halifax in HMS Majestic per order Aml Cochrane.

Ward, Cuffee   Prisoner 476. Rank: Not Recorded, from: Not Recorded, Not Recorded.
> Cap: Not Recorded by Not Recorded   Int: Dis: 26 Apr 1814.
> (Dates of capture and internment not recorded). Sent to Rhode Island in the Cartel Liberty.

Wardwell, Soloman   Prisoner 518. Rank: Seaman, from: Lion, Merchant.
> Cap: Not Recorded by Privateer Mars   Int: 30 Jan 1814   Dis: 08 Jul 1814.
> Received from Privateer Brilliant. Sent to Bermuda. (Date of capture not recorded.)

American Prisoners of War Held at New Providence During the War of 1812

Warkery, Peter   Prisoner 492. Rank: Seaman, from: St. Polito, Merchant.
  Cap: 26 Nov 1813 At sea by Privateers Mars & Dash Int: 25 Dec 1813 Dis: 26 Apr 1814.
  Received from Privateer Mars. Sent to Rhode Island in the Cartel Liberty.

Wasam, Charles   Prisoner 200. Rank: Seaman, from: Not Recorded, Not Recorded.
  Cap: Not Recorded by Privateer Unknown Int: 24 Oct 1812 Dis: 24 Oct 1812.
  Received from HMS Mosella. Sent to Charlestown in the British Cartel Nassau by order of the Governor. (Date, place, name of vessel and name of capturing ship 'not mentioned'.)

Wasson, Daniel   Prisoner 562. Rank: Seaman, from: Roberts, Merchant Vessel.
  Cap: 24 Feb 1814 At sea by HM Ship Rhin Int: 03 Mar 1814 Dis: 08 Jul 1814.
  His MS Rhin taken the recaptured Brig Roberts belonging to the American Privateer Schooner May, of 15 guns. Received from HMS Rhin. Sent to Bermuda.

Watson, George   Prisoner 387. Rank: Seaman, from: Venus, Merchant.
  Cap: Not Recorded by Brilliant Privateer Int: 17 Mar 1813 Dis: 26 Apr 1814.
  Received from Prize. Sent to Rhode Island in the Cartel Liberty. (Date and place of capture 'not mentioned'.)

Way, Samuel   Prisoner 74. Rank: Seaman, from: Harmony, Merchant.
  Cap: 28 Aug 1812 Off Abaco by Privateer Int: 01 Sep 1812 Dis: 24 Oct 1812.
  Received from Privateer. Sent to Charlestown in the British Cartel Nassau.

Way, William   Prisoner 58. Rank: Seaman, from: Olympus, Merchant.
  Cap: 05 Aug 1812 Island of Abaco by HM Schooner Decouverte Int: 07 Aug 1812 Dis: 22 Sep 1812.
  Received from HMS Decouverte. Sent to new York United States of America.

Weagg, Erasmas R   Prisoner 722. Rank: Passanger, from: Fox, Merchant Vessel.
  Cap: Cumberland Sound by HMS Lacedaemonian Int: 19 Oct 1814 Dis: 07 Dec 1814.
  Received from HMS Lacedaemonian. Order Commander in Chief. (Date of capture not on roster.)

Weaton, E P   Prisoner 413. Rank: Seaman, from: Portsmouth, Merchant.
  Cap: 16 Apr 1813 At sea by HM Ships Morgiana & Calibri Int: 20 Apr 1813 Dis: 26 Apr 1814.
  Received from HMS Morgiana. Sent to Rhode Island in the Cartel Liberty.

Weaver, William   Prisoner 246. Rank: Seaman, from: Viper, Man of War.
  Cap: Gulf of Mexico by HMS Narcissus Int: 30 Jan 1813 Dis: 14 Feb 1813.
  United States Brig. Received from HMS Moselle. Sent in the British Cartel Eliza to Norfolk by order of the Governor. (Date of capture 'not mentioned'.)

Webb, Henry   Prisoner 367. Rank: Seaman, from: Eliza, Merchant.
  Cap: Not Recorded by HMS Rolus Int: 02 Mar 1813 Dis: 19 Apr 1813.
  Received from prize. Sent to Europe in the Ship Loyal Sam. (Date and place of capture 'not mentioned'.)

Webster, W. H   Prisoner 716. Rank: Actor, from: Not Recorded, Not Recorded.
  Cap: Not Recorded by Not Recorded Int: 16 Aug 1814 Dis: 26 Oct 1814.
  Received from Police. Sent to Bermuda in HMS Wolverine. (Date of capture not on roster.)

Weeks, Joseph   Prisoner 550. Rank: Seaman, from: Not Recorded, Letter of Marquis.
  Cap: Not Recorded by Not Recorded Int: 17 Feb 1814 Dis: 07 Dec 1814.
  Ship wrecked among the Bahama Keys. Order Commander in Chief. (Date of capture and ship received from not recorded.)

Weeks, William   Prisoner 75. Rank: Seaman, from: Hamer, Merchant.
  Cap: 01 Sep 1812 Off Abaco by Privateer Int: 02 Sep 1812 Dis: 24 Oct 1812.
  Received from Privateer. Sent to Charlestown in the British Cartel Nassau.

Weidman, John   Prisoner 276. Rank: Seaman, from: Viper, Man of War.
  Cap: Gulf of Mexico by HMS Narcissus Int: 30 Jan 1813 Dis: 14 Feb 1813.
  Brig. Received from HMS Moselle. Sent in the British Cartel Eliza to Norfolk by order of the Governor. (Date of capture 'not mentioned'.)

Welman, Timothy   Prisoner 533. Rank: Seaman, from: Sevant, Letter of Marquis.
  Cap: 04 Jan 1814 Not Recorded by HMS Forester Int: 12 Jan 1814 Dis: 08 Jul 1814.
  Brig. Received from HMS Forester. Sent to Bermuda.

Welton, William   Prisoner 443. Rank: Seaman, from: Stanley, Merchant.
  Cap: Coast of America by Privateer Wellesley Int: 09 Jun 1813 Dis: 26 Apr 1814.
  Received from HMS Calibri. Sent to Rhode Island in the Cartel Liberty. (Date of capture not recorded.)

West, Edward   Prisoner 17. Rank: Seaman, from: Non Parail, Privateer.
  Cap: 29 Jul 1812 Off Eleuthera (rest not legible) by HM Schooner Decouverte Int: 01 Aug 1812 Dis: 24 Oct 1812. Received from HM Schooner Decauverte. Sent to Charlestown in the British Cartel Nassau by order of the Governor.

American Prisoners of War Held at New Providence During the War of 1812

West, Simon   Prisoner 224. Rank: Seaman, from: Factor, Merchant.
    Cap: Coast of America by HMS Moselle Int: 19 Nov 1812 Dis: 04 Feb 1813.
    Received from HMS Moselle. Sent to Charlestown in the British Cartel Ann by order of the Governor. (Date of capture 'not mentioned'.)

Westun, ---   Prisoner 226. Rank: Seaman, from: Not Recorded, Not Recorded.
    Cap: Not Recorded by Not Recorded Int: 30 Nov 1812 Dis: 04 Feb 1813.
    Landed from the American Privateer at Watling Island. Sent to Charlestown in the British Cartel Ann by order of the Governor. (First name not recorded. Date of capture not recorded.)

Wheaton, Benjamin   Prisoner 347. Rank: Mate, from: George & Mary, Merchant.
    Cap: Not Recorded by Not Recorded Int: 14 Feb 1813 Dis: 14 Feb 1813.
    Wrecked among the islands and delivered themselves up. Received from HMS Moselle. Sent to Norfolk in the British Cartel Eliza by order of the Governor. (Date of capture 'not mentioned'.)

Wheeler, James   Prisoner 327. Rank: Seaman, from: Osprey, Merchant.
    Cap: Gulf of Mexico by HMS Moselle Int: 30 Jan 1813 Dis: 14 Feb 1813.
    Received from HMS Moselle. Sent in the British Cartel Eliza to Norfolk by order of the Governor. (Date of capture 'not mentioned'.)

Whik, Joseph   Prisoner 377. Rank: Seaman, from: Apodaco, Merchant.
    Cap: Not Recorded by Government Schooner Swift Int: 15 Mar 1813 Dis:
    Received from Government Schooner Swift. (Date and place of capture 'not mentioned'. (Dates of capture and discharge not on roster.)

Whilehurst, Jos   Prisoner 174. Rank: Seaman, from: Dash, Privateer.
    Cap: 12 Sep 1812 Coast of America by Rhodian & Variable Int: 23 Sep 1812 Dis: 24 Oct 1812.
    Received from Rhodian and Variable. Sent to Charlestown in the British Cartel Nassau by order of the Governor.

Whilehurst, Will   Prisoner 183. Rank: Seaman, from: Dash, Privateer.
    Cap: 12 Sep 1812 Coast of America by Rhodian & Variable Int: 23 Sep 1812 Dis: 24 Oct 1812.
    Received from Rhodian and Variable. Sent to Charlestown in the British Cartel Nassau by order of the Governor.

Whipby, Israel   Prisoner 548. Rank: Seaman, from: Not Recorded, Letter of Marquis.
    Cap: Not Recorded by Not Recorded Int: 17 Feb 1814 Dis: 13 Aug 1814.
    Ship wrecked among the Bahama Keys. Sent to Bermuda per order of the Commander in Chief, HMS Surprise. (Date of capture and ship received from not recorded.)

Whitney, John   Prisoner 734. Rank: Seaman, from: Gunboat 160, Man of War.
    Cap: Cumberland Sound by HMS Lacedaemonian Int: 19 Oct 1814 Dis:
    United States Gunboat. Received from HMS Lacedaemonian. (Dates of capture and discharge not on roster.)

Wicks, Thomas   Prisoner 332. Rank: Seaman, from: Osprey, Merchant.
    Cap: Gulf of Mexico by HMS Moselle Int: 30 Jan 1813 Dis: 14 Feb 1813.
    Received from HMS Moselle. Sent in the British Cartel Eliza to Norfolk by order of the Governor. (Date of capture 'not mentioned'.)

Wilcox, James   Prisoner 715. Rank: Supercargo, from: Not Recorded, Not Recorded.
    Cap: Not Recorded by Not Recorded Int: 16 Aug 1814 Dis:
    Received from Police. (Dates of capture and discharge not on roster.)

Wilford, John   Prisoner 800. Rank: Seaman, from: Java, Letter of Marquis.
    Cap: Not Recorded by Cockchafer Int: 14 Jan 1815 Dis:
    Received from HM Schooner Cockchafer. (Dates of capture and discharge not on roster.)

Wilkey, Frederick   Prisoner 364. Rank: Seaman, from: Washington, Merchant.
    Cap: Not Recorded by Privateer Brilliant Int: 01 Mar 1813 Dis: 10 Apr 1813.
    Received from Prize. Sent to Charleston in the British Cartel Charlotte by order of the Governor. (Date and place of capture 'not mentioned'.)

Willett, George   Prisoner 420. Rank: Seaman, from: Penobscot, Merchant Vessel.
    Cap: 10 Apr 1813 Not Recorded by HM Ship Variable Int: 27 Apr 1813 Dis: 26 Apr 1814.
    Received from HM Ship Variable. Sent to Rhode Island in the Cartel Liberty.

Williams, Jacob   Prisoner 37. Rank: 2 Mate, from: Ceres, Merchant.
    Cap: 28 Jul 1812 Bahama Bank by Privateer Theodore Int: 01 Aug 1812 Dis: 22 Sep 1812.
    Received from Prize. Sent to new York United States of America.

Williams, James   Prisoner 339. Rank: Seaman, from: Osprey, Merchant.
    Cap: Gulf of Mexico by HMS Moselle Int: 30 Jan 1813 Dis: 14 Feb 1813.
    Received from HMS Moselle. Sent in the British Cartel Eliza to Norfolk by order of the Governor. (Date of capture 'not mentioned'.)

American Prisoners of War Held at New Providence During the War of 1812

Williams, John   Prisoner 68. Rank: Seaman, from: Resolution, Merchant.
    Cap: 26 Jul 1812 Crooked Island Passage by HM Schooner Variable Int: 07 Aug 1812 Dis: 22 Sep 1812. Received from His Majesties Schooner Variable. Sent to new York United States of America.

Williams, John   Prisoner 674. Rank: Seaman, from: Frolic, Man of War.
    Cap: 20 Apr 1814 Not Recorded by HMS Orpheus Int: 26 Apr 1814 Dis: 13 Jun 1814. United States Ship. Received from HMS Orpheus. Sent to Halifax in HMS Majestic per order of Commander in Chief Aml Cochrane.

Williams, Thomas   Prisoner 270. Rank: Seaman, from: Viper, Man of War.
    Cap: Gulf of Mexico by HMS Narcissus Int: 30 Jan 1813 Dis: 14 Feb 1813. United States Brig. Received from HMS Moselle. Sent in the British Cartel Eliza to Norfolk by order of the Governor. (Date of capture 'not mentioned'.)

Williams, Thomas   Prisoner 684. Rank: Seaman, from: Frolic, Man of War.
    Cap: 20 Apr 1814 Not Recorded by HMS Orpheus Int: 26 Apr 1814 Dis: 13 Jun 1814. United States Ship. Received from HMS Orpheus. Sent to Halifax in HMS Majestic order Aml Cochrane.

Williamson, Charles   Prisoner 565. Rank: Seaman, from: Frolic, Man of War.
    Cap: 20 Apr 1814 At sea by HMS Orpheus Int: 26 Apr 1814 Dis: 11 Jun 1814. United States Ship. Received from HMS Orpheus. Sent to Bermuda in HMS Orpheus order Aml Cochrane.

Wilson, Anthony   Prisoner 163. Rank: Prize Master, from: Dash, Privateer.
    Cap: 12 Sep 1812 Coast of America by Rhodian & Variable Int: 23 Sep 1812 Dis: 24 Oct 1812. Received from Rhodian and Variable. Sent to Charlestown in the British Cartel Nassau.

Wilson, Cornelius   Prisoner 741. Rank: Seaman, from: Gunboat 160, Man of War.
    Cap: Cumberland Sound by HMS Lacedaemonian Int: 19 Oct 1814 Dis: United States Gunboat. Received from HMS Lacedaemonian. (Dates of capture and discharge not on roster.)

Wilson, James   Prisoner 259. Rank: Seaman, from: Viper, Man of War.
    Cap: Gulf of Mexico by HMS Narcissus Int: 30 Jan 1813 Dis: 14 Feb 1813. United States Brig. Received from HMS Moselle. Sent in the British Cartel Eliza to Norfolk by order of the Governor. (Date of capture 'not mentioned'.)

Wilson, James   Prisoner 268. Rank: Seaman, from: Viper, Man of War.
    Cap: Gulf of Mexico by HMS Narcissus Int: 30 Jan 1813 Dis: 14 Feb 1813. United States Brig. Received from HMS Moselle. Sent in the British Cartel Eliza to Norfolk by order of the Governor. (Date of capture 'not mentioned'.)

Wilson, James   Prisoner 696. Rank: Private, from: Frolic, Man of War.
    Cap: 20 Apr 1814 Not Recorded by HMS Orpheus Int: 26 Apr 1814 Dis: 13 Jun 1814. United States Ship. Received from HMS Orpheus. Sent to Halifax in HMS Majestic order Aml Cochrane.

Wilson, Thomas   Prisoner 63. Rank: Seaman, from: Resolution, Merchant.
    Cap: 26 Jul 1812 Crooked Island Passage by HM Schooner Variable Int: 07 Aug 1812 Dis: 22 Sep 1812. Received from His Majesties Schooner Variable. Sent to new York United States of America.

Windall, Jr., Abraham   Prisoner 520. Rank: Seaman, from: Lion, Merchant.
    Cap: Not Recorded by Privateer Mars Int: 30 Jan 1814 Dis: 08 Jul 1814. Received from Privateer Brilliant. Sent to Bermuda. (Date of capture not recorded.)

Wing, Judah   Prisoner 646. Rank: Seaman, from: Frolic, Man of War.
    Cap: 20 Apr 1814 Not Recorded by HMS Orpheus Int: 26 Apr 1814 Dis: 13 Jun 1814. United States Ship. Received from HMS Orpheus. Sent to Halifax in HMS Majestic per order of Commander in Chief Aml Cochrane.

Winslow, Henry   Prisoner 348. Rank: Mate, from: George & Mary, Merchant.
    Cap: Not Recorded by Not Recorded Int: 14 Feb 1813 Dis: 14 Feb 1813. Wrecked among the islands and delivered themselves up. Received from HMS Moselle. Sent to Norfolk in the British Cartel Eliza by order of the Governor. (Date of capture 'not mentioned'.)

Wirton, Henry   Prisoner 458. Rank: 2 Mate, from: Not Recorded, Not Recorded.
    Cap: Not Recorded by Not Recorded Int: 29 Jul 1813 Dis: Received from HMS Calibri. (Dates capture and discharge not on roster.)

Wise, Will   Prisoner 3. Rank: 2 Officer, from: Non Parail, Privateer.
    Cap: 29 Jul 1812 Off Eleuthera (rest not legible) by HM Schooner Decouverte Int: 01 Aug 1812 Dis: 22 Sep 1812. Received from HM Schooner Decauverte. Sent to new York United States of America.

Witter, Robert   Prisoner 451. Rank: Seaman, from: Stanley, Merchant.
    Cap: Coast of America by Privateer Wellesley Int: 13 Jun 1813 Dis: 26 Apr 1814. Received from Privateer Rolla. Sent to Rhode Island in the Cartel Liberty. (Date of capture not recorded.)

American Prisoners of War Held at New Providence During the War of 1812

Woodan, William   Prisoner 7. Rank: Pilot, from: Non Parail, Privateer.
    Cap: 29 Jul 1812 Off Eleuthera (rest not legible) by HM Schooner Decouverte Int: 01 Aug 1812 Dis: 24 Oct 1812. Received from HM Schooner Decauverte. Sent to Charlestown in the British Cartel Nassau.

Woodburn, John   Prisoner 95. Rank: Seaman, from: Rapid, Privateer.
    Cap: Not Recorded by Not Recorded Int: 13 Sep 1812 Dis: 04 Feb 1813.
    Received from Government Schooner John Bull. Sent to Charlestown in the British Cartel Ann. (Date, place and name of capturing ship 'not mentioned'.)

Woodbury, F   Prisoner 502. Rank: Seaman, from: St. Polito, Merchant.
    Cap: 26 Nov 1813 At sea by Privateers Mars & Dash Int: 25 Dec 1813 Dis: 26 Apr 1814.
    Received from Privateer Mars. Sent to Rhode Island in the Cartel Liberty.

Woodbury, Nathaniel   Prisoner 53. Rank: Seaman, from: Augusta, Merchant.
    Cap: 02 Aug 1812 Island of Abaco by HM Schooner Decouverte Int: 07 Aug 1812 Dis: 22 Sep 1812.
    Received from HMS Decouverte. Sent to new York United States of America.

Woodfield, Thomas   Prisoner 561. Rank: Seaman, from: Roberts, Merchant Vessel.
    Cap: 24 Feb 1814 At sea by HM Ship Rhin Int: 03 Mar 1814 Dis: 15 Aug 1814.
    His MS Rhin taken the recaptured Brig Roberts belonging to the American Privateer Schooner May, of 15 guns. Received from HMS Rhin. Sent to Bermuda HMS Surprise by order Commander in Chief.

Woodwith, George   Prisoner 754. Rank: Seaman, from: Catherine Eliza, Merchant Vessel.
    Cap: 25 Nov 1814 Doughby Sound by HM Ship Primrose Int: 07 Dec 1814 Dis:
    Received from HMS Primrose. (Date of discharge not on roster.)

Wright, James   Prisoner 560. Rank: Seaman, from: Roberts, Merchant Vessel.
    Cap: 24 Feb 1814 At sea by HM Ship Rhin Int: 03 Mar 1814 Dis: 08 Jul 1814.
    His MS Rhin taken the recaptured Brig Roberts belonging to the American Privateer Schooner May, of 15 guns. Received from HMS Rhin. Sent to Bermuda.

Wright, William   Prisoner 516. Rank: Seaman, from: Lion, Merchant.
    Cap: Not Recorded by Privateer Mars Int: 30 Jan 1814 Dis: 27 Jan 1814.
    Received from Privateer Brilliant. Embarked on board Merchant Vessel Anna to assist in navigating her to England. (Date of capture not recorded. Date of internment before date of discharge.)

Yard, Jethew   Prisoner 746. Rank: Seaman, from: Auroa, Letter of Marquis.
    Cap: Not Recorded by HM Shooner Cockchafer Int: 03 Dec 1814 Dis:
    Received from Cockchafer. (Date and place of capture 'not mentioned'. Date of discharge not on roster.)

Young, Isaac   Prisoner 126. Rank: Captain, from: Sarah Ann, Privateer.
    Cap: 13 Sep 1812 Coast of America by Rhodian & Variable Int: 23 Sep 1812 Dis: 24 Oct 1812.
    Received from Rhodian and Variable. Sent to Charlestown in the British Cartel Nassau.

Young, Joseph   Prisoner 87. Rank: Mate, from: Phiebe V. Jane, Merchant.
    Cap: 25 Aug 1812 Coast of America by HMS Rhodian Int: 06 Sep 1812 Dis:
    Received from HM Brig Rhodian. (Date of discharge not on roster.)

Young, Luke   Prisoner 184. Rank: Seaman, from: Dash, Privateer.
    Cap: 12 Sep 1812 Coast of America by Rhodian & Variable Int: 23 Sep 1812 Dis: 24 Oct 1812.
    Received from Rhodian and Variable. Sent to Charlestown in the British Cartel Nassau by order of the Governor.

Young, William   Prisoner 78. Rank: Seaman, from: Hamer, Merchant.
    Cap: 01 Sep 1812 Off Abaco by Privateer Int: 02 Sep 1812 Dis: 24 Oct 1812.
    Received from Privateer. Sent to Charlestown in the British Cartel Nassau.

Young, William   Prisoner 536. Rank: Seaman, from: Sevant, Letter of Marquis.
    Cap: 04 Jan 1814 Not Recorded by HMS Forester Int: 12 Jan 1814 Dis: 13 Aug 1814.
    Brig. Received from HMS Forester. Sent to Bermuda HMS Surprise per order Commander in Chief.

Zirick, Mata   Prisoner 258. Rank: Seaman, from: Viper, Man of War.
    Cap: Gulf of Mexico by HMS Narcissus Int: 30 Jan 1813 Dis: 14 Feb 1813.
    United States Brig. Received from HMS Moselle. Sent in the British Cartel Eliza to Norfolk by order of the Governor. (Date of capture 'not mentioned'.)

American Prisoners of War Held at New Providence During the War of 1812

Numeric listing by prison number

1	Martin, Henry B	68	Williams, John
2	Haller, Isaac	69	Johnson, William
3	Wise, Will	70	Read, Thomas
4	Neill, D M	71	Reid, Henry
5	Fairchild, Lewis	72	Soule, Asa
6	Livingston, William	73	Roper, John
7	Woodan, William	74	Way, Samuel
8	Husill, John	75	Weeks, William
9	Dupua, Francis	76	Richer, Stephen
10	Card, Colonel	77	Chase, William
11	Francis, John	78	Young, William
12	Frourswell, Lewis	79	Hooper, Edward
13	McNeill, Edmund	80	Brown, Joshua
14	Harrison, Friak	81	Gray, Aaron
15	Sovein, John	82	Alsop, Mathew
16	Peter, Manuel	83	Anderson, George
17	West, Edward	84	Jones, Rowland
18	Thompson, John	85	Fraser, Robert
19	Fauchild, Alexander	86	Vauding, Howard
20	Martin, Thomas	87	Young, Joseph
21	Sibley, Ill	88	Savage, F
22	Johnson, Henry	89	Monneys, R
23	Silvee, H	90	Davis, George
24	Cunningham, William	91	Collins, Henry
25	Bill, John	92	Lameson, Pierre
26	Slattou, John	93	Miller, James J
27	Frontence, John	94	Labelle, Prince
28	Oliver, Samuel	95	Woodburn, John
29	Vosso, Mathew	96	Alexander, George
30	Landerkin, Richard	97	Bigloss, Gagdon
31	Parish, John	98	Martin, Francis
32	Sterling, Elizah	99	Pick, Ralph
33	Inglefield, John	100	Brown, William
34	Allen, Ebenezer	101	Robertson, John
35	Dodge, Lewis	102	Grady, Annick
36	Lombard, Ephrim	103	Robertson, William
37	Williams, Jacob	104	Clark, Charles
38	Adams, John	105	Johnson, Jacob
39	Anderson, John	106	Shumo, Samuel
40	Brown, George	107	Marshal, L
41	Miller, Charles	108	---, Peter
42	Prado, Joseph	109	Johnson, Thomas
43	Bentall, Ebenezer	110	Beaudesire, Lewis
44	Belson, Armand	111	Momell, Thomas
45	Shephard, John	112	Madden, Frederick
46	Harvey, John	113	Kemmens, John
47	Peterson, John	114	Ournan, John F
48	Rea, Ebenezer	115	Freigar, Benjamin
49	Bradshaw, John	116	Tunis, John
50	Ferdinand, Abraham	117	Lear, George
51	Eveleth, Francis	118	Holmes, Vincent
52	Forster, Jonathan	119	Moon, Richard
53	Woodbury, Nathaniel	120	Greenway, Thomas
54	Eastman, Thomas	121	Harrison, John
55	Holland, Stephen	122	Bland, Richard
56	Cox, Miles	123	Hurst, William
57	Kitterlas, Samuel	124	Jaibo, Joseph
58	Way, William	125	Roberts, George
59	Edmunds, William	126	Young, Isaac
60	Francis, John	127	Harred, James
61	Smith, Jacob	128	Travers, Frederick
62	Steward, Hosea	129	Clark, John
63	Wilson, Thomas	130	Parrell, John
64	Scaurahon, Samuel	131	Daur, Richard
65	Bowshaw, Job	132	Pinnard, John
66	Price, Jacob	133	Lindstroon, Gustaus
67	Amderson, William	134	Delphia, John

American Prisoners of War Held at New Providence During the War of 1812

135	Suitter, William		205	Garey, G
136	Breadhead, Richard		206	Schaafer, C
137	Earl, William		207	Roberts, William
138	Dick, David		208	Stole, Robert
139	Pluck, Michael		209	Robeson, William S
140	Keinsburgh, Henry		210	Lambert, A
141	Farrell, William		211	Hynes, John
142	Glass, James		212	Crandwell, John
143	Rogers, Thomas		213	Ashton, David
144	Robertson, James		214	Thomas, William
145	Hall, John		215	Gamache, John
146	Gaul, John		216	Sroan, Dermias
147	Panner, James		217	McKenzie, John
148	Lingo, Woodman		218	Templeman, M
149	Martin, John		219	Smith, John
150	McCate, F		220	Shekman, Sol
151	Ansburgh, Martin		221	Hogan, Nath B
152	Martin, Zebard		222	Musure, Caleb
153	Calem, Samuel		223	Fogarty, Robert
154	Lane, Eben		224	West, Simon
155	Jackson, William		225	Bragan, Mathew
156	Taylor, Alexander		226	Westun, ---
157	Chester, Samuel		227	Coglan, William
158	Carraway, John		228	Jackson, William
159	Banks, John G		229	Cadet, John
160	Lane, Joseph		230	Roberts, Henry
161	Waggoner, Henry		231	Fogarty, Samuel
162	Dean, Eanos		232	Fogarty, G
163	Wilson, Anthony		233	McLeod, Donald
164	Latham, Thomas		234	Marshall, George
165	Cook, Anthony		235	Beaver, Alan
166	Lynn, William		236	Philips, Samuel
167	Canagon, Daniel		237	Henley, Trim
168	Dosey, Dempsey		238	Gordon, Thomas
169	Rickets, John		239	Lewi, John
170	Gibbs, Daniel		240	Jackson, James
171	Benard, Lewis		241	O'Hara, James
172	Frasier, James		242	Chamberlain, David
173	Anderson, Nathaniel		243	Stewart, Thomas
174	Whilehurst, Jos		244	Curry, Joseph
175	Blackwell, Henry		245	Meyers, Thomas
176	Allmond, Edmond		246	Weaver, William
177	Brown, Peter		247	Lewis, Ebenezer
178	Robinson, John		248	Pease, Nathaniel
179	Culverson, Noah		249	Hewitt, Michael
180	Batteia, John		250	Milne, Alexander
181	Gilbert, George		251	Halladge, William
182	Brackett, John		252	Thomas, George
183	Whilehurst, Will		253	Orimsley, John
184	Young, Luke		254	Damoulet, George
185	Daniel, John		255	Argent, William
186	Fraser, Antoine		256	Cunningham, Alexander
187	Fresk, John		257	Godfree, John
188	Carr, John		258	Zirick, Mata
189	Matthews, Edward		259	Wilson, James
190	Greemal, Louis		260	Roache, Thomas
191	Howler, Charles		261	Jones, John
192	Roberts, James		262	Barnard, William
193	Jones, Charles		263	Jefferies, Abraham
194	Chester, John		264	Raines, Charles
195	Darrell, N		265	Philips, William
196	Barke, N		266	McFaith, John
197	Butler, Timothy		267	Connor, Samuel
198	Burns, John		268	Wilson, James
199	Redfield, Eben		269	Henry, John
200	Wasam, Charles		270	Williams, Thomas
201	Tallman, John		271	James, Thomas
202	Buel, H		272	Agreda, Joseph
203	Halm, John		273	Mooran, Thomas
204	Abbott, Thomas		274	Todd, James

American Prisoners of War Held at New Providence During the War of 1812

275	Algut, Adam	345	Martin, John D
276	Weidman, John	346	Hopkins, Steph
277	Andrew, John	347	Wheaton, Benjamin
278	Bileau, Julian	348	Winslow, Henry
279	Shilley, John	349	Benson, Joline
280	Powell, Michael	350	Tabor, Joseph
281	Sandford, Samuel	351	Hawkins, Joseph
282	Ringold, Henry	352	Crandall, William
283	Law, Nicholas	353	Tallman, William
284	Kindred, James	354	Drown, John
285	Brown, N	355	Accruma, Quashy
286	Corbett, John	356	Wallace, Newport
287	Howard, Wast	357	Day, Isaac
288	Jones, Benjamin	358	Bliss, Eli C
289	Brown, John	359	Cobb, ---
290	Linguire, Abraham	360	Gorham, John
291	Paislaw, William	361	French, John
292	Roberts, John	362	Harman, Henry
293	Coulken, William	363	Benjamin, Samuel
294	Kennedy, Michael	364	Wilkey, Frederick
295	Kinley, H	365	Coal, John
296	Richardson, William	366	Ashby, Joseph
297	Bredricke, William	367	Webb, Henry
298	Clarke, John	368	Anquin, Anthony
299	Crane, James	369	Baptiste, John
300	Crutch, George	370	Baydion, Peter
301	Price, Charles	371	Dents, John
302	Softon, James	372	Reio, Peter
303	Roberts, James	373	Callett, John
304	Magrath, F	374	Francis, John
305	Neelby, James	375	Almy, Eleazar
306	Vance, John	376	Northam, Stephen
307	Thorton, James	377	Whik, Joseph
308	Tillow, George	378	Brown, Daniel
309	Shearon, John	379	Forloney, James
310	Marshall, Elias J	380	Scriggin, Charles
311	Waiter, James A	381	Crandle, Caleb
312	Ellsey, Thomas	382	Ragon, Laurence
313	Army, John	383	Howard, Benjamin
314	Cuffee, James	384	Church, William
315	Cross, William	385	Bradford, E
316	Joseph, John	386	Richardson, James
317	Philips, Thomas	387	Watson, George
318	Burke, Jacob	388	Allen, Prince
319	Martin, Richard	389	Doyle, James
320	Freeman, Henry	390	Anderson, Oliver
321	Cannon, Charles	391	Campbell, John
322	Burke, Thomas	392	Mills, James
323	Taylor, Thomas	393	Taylor, Joseph
324	Dowall, Robert M	394	Baker, Obadiah
325	Brothers, James	395	Lennell, J
326	Joseph, John	396	Caivin, James
327	Wheeler, James	397	Crawell, Isaac
328	Simon, John	398	Sanborn, Daniel
329	Paradu, Mathew	399	Cooper, Benjamin
330	Fowler, James	400	Davis, Samuel
331	Swift, James	401	Emery, William
332	Wicks, Thomas	402	Momus, Anthony
333	Airy, John	403	Travis, George
334	Hardy, William	404	Bowling, J
335	King, Thivdore	405	Coggeeshall, Nathaniel
336	Robinson, David	406	Remo, Joseph
337	Shellock, James	407	Ostend, Robert
338	Holmes, John	408	Thomson, John
339	Williams, James	409	Johnston, Joseph
340	Brown, John	410	Munrow, William
341	Smith, Solomon	411	Freeman, Aaron
342	Hill, George	412	Domina, M
343	Moulden, Isaac	413	Weaton, E P
344	Rosseter, D F	414	Jackson, James

American Prisoners of War Held at New Providence During the War of 1812

415	Argent, William	485	Tisdale, Ster. J
416	Philips, William	486	Jackson, Thomas
417	Johnson, Henry	487	Goodwin, William
418	Rolston, Andrew	488	Baker, Oliver
419	Gross, John	489	Havey, Mack
420	Willett, George	490	Potter, Patrick
421	Powell, Hew	491	Routh, James
422	Homet, Nathaniel	492	Warkery, Peter
423	Gordon, Francis	493	Porter, G
424	Gross, Samuel	494	Serett, T
425	Walker, Samuel	495	Bray, A
426	Chamberlain, David	496	Kelly, T
427	Derrick, George	497	Snver, H. C
428	Saunders, William	498	Fielder, J
429	Curtis, Thomas R	499	Seward, N
430	Quail, Thomas	500	Bunker, B
431	Robinson, Shadrick	501	Renimond, J
432	Hoggins, Thomas	502	Woodbury, F
433	Curtis, William L	503	Vickery, C
434	Elget, William	504	Brown, R
435	Toria, ---	505	Smith, E
436	Tutle, Noah	506	
437	Reges, ---	507	Moodie, John
438	Every, George	508	Pittsford, Francis
439	Maxwell, George	509	Boyer, Richway
440	Bundock, Benjamin	510	Elelow, John
441	Sneston, Thomas	511	Chandler, Samuel
442	Gile, Jacob	512	Chandler, Will
443	Welton, William	513	Jackson, James
444	Davis, William	514	Ellingwood, Joseph
445	Badson, Jacob	515	Colman, William
446	Lawton, Henry	516	Wright, William
447	Rhodes, James	517	Butler, John
448	Hatch, Robert	518	Wardwell, Soloman
449	Jenkins, Dublin	519	Brazier, William
450	Jarvis, John	520	Windall, Jr., Abraham
451	Witter, Robert	521	Bowdlear, Thomas
452	Jenkins, Anthony	522	Odell, Samuel
453	Hart, Prince	523	Freeman, Charles
454	Sallisbury, James	524	Daughty, Russell
455	Philips, Joseph	525	Ondicot, N. F
456	Fitcha, J S	526	Hale, Benjamin
457	Atkinson, Henry	527	Tucker, D. F
458	Wirton, Henry	528	Dennis, James
459	Robinson, Charles	529	Stanley, Timothy
460		530	Bradshaw, John
461	Booth, William	531	Stone, James
462	Jones, Lewis	532	Furance, George
463	Hanson, John	533	Welman, Timothy
464	Barnes, James	534	Sanderson, Jacob
465	Hatch, Samuel	535	Ayas, John
466	Hog, Able	536	Young, William
467	Studly, Simeon	537	Maryfield, George
468	Alice, John	538	Studdle, Surimeau
469	Baxter, David	539	Stickney, Emey
470	Richardson, James	540	Stack, Samuel
471	Buguest, Isaac	541	Butler, John
472	Emory, Samuel	542	Smith, George
473	Cotterill, Henry	543	Brown, John
474	Cheesbourgh, Benjamin F	544	Hailey, John
475		545	Eldridge, David
476	Ward, Cuffee	546	Robinson, John
477	Ross, Robert	547	Rumbsy, William
478	Roberts, John	548	Whipby, Israel
479	Thompson, William	549	Brown, William
480	Bayley, William	550	Weeks, Joseph
481	Morgan, T	551	Eowitt, John
482	Blanking, Gerard	552	Gouldin, William
483	Tilton, Peter	553	Stevens, Daniel
484	Pierce, John	554	Dolson, Andrew

American Prisoners of War Held at New Providence During the War of 1812

555	Fennel, William		625	Deenn, High
556	Cavanagh, Peter		626	Taylor, George
557	Cook, J		627	Chambers, William
558	Tumanic, James		628	Atkins, William
559	Shacklay, J		629	Dorman, John
560	Wright, James		630	Brown, William
561	Woodfield, Thomas		631	Delano, Laby
562	Wasson, Daniel		632	Johnson, John
563	Buggs, John		633	Bond, William
564	Blasted, Jacob		634	Wallis, John
565	Williamson, Charles		635	Halet, John
566	Hill, James A		636	Christie, Robert
567	Johnson, John		637	Reife, John
568	Spence, Robert		638	Stevens, Luen
569	Smith, John		639	Rogers, Nathaniel
570	Elger, Robert		640	Austin, James
571	Mariner, Joseph		641	Hetson, Matthew
572	Hoden, John		642	Morris, Manuel
573	Guard, H. Y		643	Walker, Peter
574	Jameson, Daniel		644	Ramsey, Samuel
575	Johnson, James		645	Brienies, John
576	Bell, George		646	Wing, Judah
577	Reynolds, W B		647	Lyman, Paul
578	Nye, Stephen		648	Calhoon, Joseph
579	Dickinson, H. Y		649	Sergeant, Charles
580	Harvey, Edward		650	Peterson, James
581	Burredde, Mansfield		651	Smith, Isaac
582	Price, John		652	Elvin, John
583	Rogers, Francis		653	Northorp, John
584	Clarke, John		654	Denny, James
585	Murray, Alexander		655	Sherlock, Charles
586	Andrews, Asa		656	Johnson, John
587	Dolton, Frederick W		657	Huckings, Israel
588	Dominique, John		658	Small, William
589	Tall, John		659	Anderson, Edward
590	Pedrick, George		660	Chapple, John
591	Hammond, Benjamin		661	Holmes, Christian
592	Horton, George A		662	Brown, William
593	Beason, James		663	Gregory, James
594	Lemon, James		664	Tausk, Samuel
595	Keating, John		665	Parker, John D
596	Canoll, Michael		666	Handell, H. Y
597	Factor, George A		667	Cleary, James
598	Pitman, John		668	Snowdon, John
599	Ricker, Edward G		669	Hart, George
600	Thompson, James		670	Rowe, James
601	Edwards, John		671	Miller, Henry
602	Parsons, Andrew		672	Dobson, James
603	Lear, Alexander		673	Hall, Charles
604	Bass, Charles		674	Williams, John
605	Bellewe, Louis		675	Portell, James
606	Osmond, Henry		676	Smith, Peter
607	Cousins, Samuel		677	Brown, William
608	Mary, Ezekiel		678	Davis, Hewlet
609	Huffs, Charles		679	Tucker, John B
610	Hanis, David		680	Neeres, James
611	Coffin, George		681	Rogers, Asa
612	Brown, Edward		682	Butler, Benjamin
613	Field, Samuel		683	Blair, John
614	Appleton, Daniel		684	Williams, Thomas
615	Dyke, Sword		685	Goddard, John
616	Justice, John		686	Foster, James
617	Cousins, John		687	Abbott, Benjamin
618	Dempson, Daniel		688	Bruzel, James
619	Campbell, James		689	Mamer, Michael
620	Meek, Thomas		690	Shafer, ---
621	Burgess, John		691	Todd, Daniel
622	Seribble, H. Y		692	Teufton, James
623	Smith, Samuel		693	Fowler, Isaac
624	Mason, Richard		694	Randolph, George

American Prisoners of War Held at New Providence During the War of 1812

695	Rowe, Elias B		765	Deole, Peter
696	Wilson, James		766	Gosale, John
697	Norton, Edward		767	Smith, John
698	Richardson, John		768	Ellis, William
699	Todd, Robert		769	Lane, Alexander
700	Depew, H. Y		770	Collector, Jefferson
701	Hadley, James		771	Parsons, Absolum
702	Robins, Hiland		772	Pitcher, Peleg Sprague
703	Mangine, John B		773	Foxwing, George
704	Tower, James		774	Ross, William
705	Spillard, Robert		775	Sayer, Joseph
706	Traston, Daniel T		776	Hazard, Thomas
707	Harris, John		777	Corey, Benjamin
708	Porter, Samuel		778	Pictom, Peleg
709	Joseph, James		779	Fotry, Duroc
710	Joseph, James		780	Artary, Hose
711	Grindall, James		781	Germoirober, Martin
712	Jordon, Christian		782	Saunders, Anthony
713	Curtis, Stacy		783	Qumo, Harto
714	Samoe, D		784	Humphreys, R. W
715	Wilcox, James		785	Bowen, William
716	Webster, W. H		786	Smith, William
717	Downson, Charles		787	Glee, George
718	Micanger, Michael		788	Griffy, John
719	Chaves, M		789	Martin, William
720	Johnson, Nathaniel		790	Bern, William
721	Hushow, Newman		791	Flemming, Charles
722	Weagg, Erasmas R		792	Dickey, Robert
723	Clarke, Joseph		793	Climsted, Taber
724	Sulliff, William		794	Stewart, Stephen C
725	Fox, Edward		795	Hyman, Henry
726	Bukefe, Bartholomew		796	Feamon, Benjamin
727	Paine, Thomas		797	Stewart, Robert
728	Jackson, John		798	Bruelle, Henry
729	Cottineau, Huo		799	Jones, Henry
730	Cook, Robert		800	Wilford, John
731	Lion, James S		801	Delanghey, John
732	Taylor, Charles		802	Jenkins, Zachrian
733	Snell, Charles		803	Marshall, John
734	Whitney, John		804	Howard, John
735	Parrott, Robert		805	Onion, Stephen P
736	Batiss, John		806	Mitchell, Edward
737	Stage, Abraham		807	Shaffer, James
738	Henthorn, William		808	Frazer, Andrew
739	Michael, John		809	McLevy, Henry
740	Johnson, Hans P		810	Mills, William A
741	Wilson, Cornelius		811	Miade, John
742	Richardson, William		812	Gutterage, William
743	Foreman, John		813	Oldham, Thomas
744	Tredway, Henry		814	Price, Thomas
745	Mason, George		815	Clarke, John
746	Yard, Jethew		816	Collins, William
747	Johnson, William		817	Alexander, John
748	Schuyler, Philip		818	Betty, Samuel
749	Jackson, Robert		819	Kelly, William
750	Bellington, James		820	Green, Vincent
751	Daniels, John		821	Gall, Thomas
752	Tuman, Philip		822	Pitt, Ceazar
753	Conklin, John		823	Rhodes, Zachariah
754	Woodwith, George		824	Blunt, John
755	Michael, ---		825	Cooper, Richard
756	Norbao, Peter		826	Bull, John
757	Fleetstrom, Israel		827	Flyn, Frederick
758	Metzgar, John		828	Light, William
759	Johnson, Henry		829	Carn, William
760	Purslaw, John		830	Budick, Newton
761	Tandy, John		831	Jefferies, Stephen
762	Givan, Francis		832	Jackson, John
763	Nicola, John		833	Bunker, John
764	Golin, Francis		834	Sweeney, John

American Prisoners of War Held at New Providence During the War of 1812

835	Flanikin, John
836	Waldrown, Trom

American Prisoners of War Held at New Providence During the War of 1812

Crew Listing by Ship

Alexander
- Beaudesire, Lewis
- Freigar, Benjamin
- Holmes, Vincent
- Kemmens, John
- Lear, George
- Madden, Frederick
- Momell, Thomas
- Ournan, John F
- Tunis, John

Amelia
- Samoe, D

Apodaco
- Brown, Daniel
- Crandle, Caleb
- Forloney, James
- Ragon, Laurence
- Scriggin, Charles
- Whik, Joseph

Augusta
- Bradshaw, John
- Eveleth, Francis
- Ferdinand, Abraham
- Forster, Jonathan
- Rea, Ebenezer
- Woodbury, Nathaniel

Auroa
- Bellington, James
- Daniels, John
- Foreman, John
- Jackson, Robert
- Johnson, William
- Mason, George
- Richardson, William
- Schuyler, Philip
- Tredway, Henry
- Tuman, Philip
- Yard, Jethew

Balay
- Every, George

Bossan
- Conklin, John

Brothers
- Remo, Joseph

Caroline
- Alice, John
- Barnes, James
- Baxter, David
- Booth, William
- Buguest, Isaac
- Cheesbourgh, Benjamin F
- Cotterill, Henry
- Emory, Samuel
- Hanson, John
- Hatch, Samuel
- Hog, Able
- Jones, Lewis
- Richardson, James
- Studly, Simeon

Catalonia
- Bayley, William
- Morgan, T
- Roberts, John
- Ross, Robert
- Thompson, William

Catherine Eliza
- Woodwith, George

Ceres
- Adams, John
- Anderson, John
- Belson, Armand
- Bentall, Ebenezer
- Brown, George
- Harvey, John
- Miller, Charles
- Peterson, John
- Prado, Joseph
- Shephard, John
- Williams, Jacob

Dart
- Brown, John
- Hill, George
- Moulden, Isaac
- Rosseter, D F
- Smith, Solomon

Dash
- Allmond, Edmond
- Anderson, Nathaniel
- Banks, John G
- Batteia, John
- Benard, Lewis
- Blackwell, Henry
- Brackett, John
- Brown, Peter
- Canagon, Daniel
- Carraway, John
- Cook, Anthony
- Culverson, Noah
- Daniel, John
- Dean, Eanos
- Dosey, Dempsey
- Frasier, James
- Gibbs, Daniel
- Gilbert, George
- Lane, Joseph
- Latham, Thomas
- Lynn, William
- Rickets, John
- Robinson, John
- Waggoner, Henry
- Whilehurst, Jos
- Whilehurst, Will
- Wilson, Anthony
- Young, Luke

Dominica Packet
- Anderson, Oliver
- Baker, Obadiah
- Caivin, James
- Campbell, John
- Crawell, Isaac
- Doyle, James
- Lennell, J
- Mills, James

Dominica Packet
- Sanborn, Daniel
- Taylor, Joseph

Eleanor
- McLeod, Donald

Eliza
- Webb, Henry

Elizabeth
- Elget, William
- Toria, ---

Endeavour
- Brown, William
- Grady, Annick

American Prisoners of War Held at New Providence During the War of 1812

          Pick, Ralph
          Robertson, John

Enterprise
          Downson, Charles
          Micanger, Michael

Factor
          Bragan, Mathew
          Collector, Jefferson
          Fogarty, G
          Fogarty, Robert
          Fogarty, Samuel
          Lane, Alexander
          Musure, Caleb
          Parsons, Absolum
          West, Simon

Fox
          Clarke, Joseph
          Fox, Edward
          Hushow, Newman
          Sulliff, William
          Weagg, Erasmas R

Frolic
          Abbott, Benjamin
          Anderson, Edward
          Andrews, Asa
          Appleton, Daniel
          Atkins, William
          Austin, James
          Bass, Charles
          Beason, James
          Bell, George
          Bellewe, Louis
          Blair, John
          Blasted, Jacob
          Bond, William
          Brienies, John
          Brown, Edward
          Brown, William
          Brown, William
          Brown, William
          Bruzel, James
          Buggs, John
          Burgess, John
          Burredde, Mansfield
          Butler, Benjamin
          Calhoon, Joseph
          Campbell, James
          Canoll, Michael
          Chambers, William
          Chapple, John
          Christie, Robert
          Clarke, John
          Cleary, James
          Coffin, George
          Cousins, John
          Cousins, Samuel
          Curtis, Stacy
          Davis, Hewlet
          Deenn, High
          Delano, Laby
          Dempson, Daniel
          Denny, James
          Depew, H. Y
          Dickinson, H. Y
          Dobson, James
          Dolton, Frederick W
          Dominique, John
          Dorman, John
          Dyke, Sword
          Edwards, John

Elger, Robert
Elvin, John
Factor, George A
Field, Samuel
Foster, James
Fowler, Isaac
Goddard, John
Gregory, James
Grindall, James
Guard, H. Y
Hadley, James
Halet, John
Hall, Charles
Hammond, Benjamin
Handell, H. Y
Hanis, David
Harris, John
Hart, George
Harvey, Edward
Hetson, Matthew
Hill, James A
Hoden, John
Holmes, Christian
Horton, George A
Huckings, Israel
Huffs, Charles
Jameson, Daniel
Johnson, James
Johnson, John
Johnson, John
Johnson, John
Jordon, Christian
Joseph, James
Joseph, James
Justice, John
Keating, John
Lear, Alexander
Lemon, James
Lyman, Paul
Mamer, Michael
Mangine, John B
Mariner, Joseph
Mary, Ezekiel
Mason, Richard
Meek, Thomas
Miller, Henry
Morris, Manuel
Murray, Alexander
Neeres, James
Northorp, John
Norton, Edward
Nye, Stephen
Osmond, Henry
Parker, John D
Parsons, Andrew
Pedrick, George
Peterson, James
Pitman, John
Portell, James
Porter, Samuel
Price, John
Ramsey, Samuel
Randolph, George
Reife, John
Reynolds, W B
Richardson, John
Ricker, Edward G
Robins, Hiland
Rogers, Asa
Rogers, Francis

American Prisoners of War Held at New Providence During the War of 1812

Rogers, Nathaniel
Rowe, Elias B
Rowe, James
Sergeant, Charles
Seribble, H. Y
Shafer, ---
Sherlock, Charles
Small, William
Smith, Isaac
Smith, John
Smith, Peter
Smith, Samuel
Snowdon, John
Spence, Robert
Spillard, Robert
Stevens, Luen
Tall, John
Tausk, Samuel
Taylor, George
Teufton, James
Thompson, James
Todd, Daniel
Todd, Robert
Tower, James
Traston, Daniel T
Tucker, John B
Walker, Peter
Wallis, John
Williams, John
Williams, Thomas
Williamson, Charles
Wilson, James
Wing, Judah

George & Joseph
    Foxwing, George
    Hazard, Thomas
    Pitcher, Peleg Sprague
    Ross, William
    Sayer, Joseph

George & Mary
    Accruma, Quashy
    Benson, Joline
    Crandall, William
    Drown, John
    Hawkins, Joseph
    Hopkins, Steph
    Martin, John D
    Tabor, Joseph
    Tallman, William
    Wallace, Newport
    Wheaton, Benjamin
    Winslow, Henry

Gunboat 160
    Batiss, John
    Cook, Robert
    Cottineau, Huo
    Henthorn, William
    Jackson, John
    Johnson, Hans P
    Lion, James S
    Michael, John
    Paine, Thomas
    Parrott, Robert
    Snell, Charles
    Stage, Abraham
    Taylor, Charles
    Whitney, John
    Wilson, Cornelius

Gustavus
    Atkinson, Henry

Hamer
    Alsop, Mathew
    Anderson, George
    Brown, Joshua
    Chase, William
    Gray, Aaron
    Hooper, Edward

Hamer
    Richer, Stephen
    Weeks, William
    Young, William

Harmony
    Roper, John
    Soule, Asa
    Way, Samuel

Harriet & Ann
    Michael, ---

Hazard
    Anquin, Anthony
    Baptiste, John
    Baydion, Peter
    Callett, John
    Dents, John
    Francis, John
    Reio, Peter

Helen
    Bliss, Eli C
    Cobb, ---
    Day, Isaac

Hercules
    Budick, Newton
    Bunker, John
    Carn, William
    Flanikin, John
    Flyn, Frederick
    Jackson, John
    Jefferies, Stephen
    Light, William
    Sweeney, John
    Waldrown, Trom

Innocencia
    Blanking, Gerard
    Pierce, John
    Tilton, Peter
    Tisdale, Ster. J

Java
    Bern, William
    Bruelle, Henry
    Climsted, Taber
    Delanghey, John
    Dickey, Robert
    Feamon, Benjamin
    Flemming, Charles
    Howard, John
    Hyman, Henry
    Jenkins, Zachrian
    Jones, Henry
    Marshall, John
    Martin, William
    Stewart, Robert
    Stewart, Stephen C
    Wilford, John

John
    Bukefe, Bartholomew
    Walker, Samuel

Lion
    Bowdlear, Thomas
    Bradshaw, John
    Brazier, William
    Butler, John

American Prisoners of War Held at New Providence During the War of 1812

Chandler, Will
Colman, William
Daughty, Russell
Dennis, James
Ellingwood, Joseph
Freeman, Charles
Hale, Benjamin
Jackson, James
Odell, Samuel
Ondicot, N. F
Stanley, Timothy
Tucker, D. F
Wardwell, Soloman
Windall, Jr., Abraham
Wright, William

Marquis de Casa Yayo
Carr, John
Chester, John
Fresk, John
Greemal, Louis
Howler, Charles
Matthews, Edward

Mary
Almy, Eleazar
Coggeeshall, Nathaniel
Northam, Stephen

Molly
Jones, Charles
Roberts, James

Nelly
Fraser, Robert
Jones, Rowland
Vauding, Howard

No Name
Bowen, William
Deole, Peter
Ellis, William
Fleetstrom, Israel
Givan, Francis
Glee, George
Golin, Francis
Gosale, John
Griffy, John
Humphreys, R. W
Johnson, Henry
Metzgar, John
Nicola, John
Norbao, Peter
Purslaw, John
Smith, John
Smith, William
Tandy, John

Non Parail
Bill, John
Card, Colonel
Cunningham, William
Dupua, Francis
Fairchild, Lewis
Fauchild, Alexander
Francis, John
Frontence, John
Frourswell, Lewis
Haller, Isaac
Harrison, Friak
Husill, John
Johnson, Henry
Livingston, William
Martin, Henry B
Martin, Thomas
McNeill, Edmund

Neill, D M
Peter, Manuel
Sibley, Ill
Silvee, H
Slattou, John
Sovein, John
Thompson, John
West, Edward
Wise, Will
Woodan, William

Olympus
Cox, Miles
Eastman, Thomas
Edmunds, William
Francis, John
Holland, Stephen
Kitterlas, Samuel
Way, William

Ospray
Cadet, John
Roberts, Henry

Osprey
Airy, John
Brothers, James
Dowall, Robert M
Fowler, James
Hardy, William
Holmes, John
Joseph, John
King, Thivdore
Paradu, Mathew
Robinson, David
Shellock, James
Simon, John
Swift, James
Wheeler, James
Wicks, Thomas
Williams, James

Penobscot
Gordon, Francis
Gross, John
Gross, Samuel
Homet, Nathaniel
Johnson, Henry
Powell, Hew
Rolston, Andrew
Willett, George

Phiebe V. Jane
Collins, Henry
Davis, George
Monneys, R
Savage, F
Young, Joseph

Portsmouth
Domina, M
Freeman, Aaron
Johnston, Joseph
Munrow, William
Ostend, Robert
Thomson, John
Weaton, E P

Rapid
Alexander, George
Bigloss, Gagdon
Labelle, Prince
Lameson, Pierre
Martin, Francis
Miller, James J
Woodburn, John

American Prisoners of War Held at New Providence During the War of 1812

Recovery
- Reges, ---
- Tutle, Noah

Resolution
- Amderson, William
- Bowshaw, Job
- Price, Jacob
- Scaurahon, Samuel
- Smith, Jacob
- Steward, Hosea
- Williams, John
- Wilson, Thomas

Roberts
- Cavanagh, Peter
- Cook, J
- Dolson, Andrew
- Fennel, William
- Shacklay, J
- Tumanic, James
- Wasson, Daniel
- Woodfield, Thomas
- Wright, James

Romney
- ---, Peter
- Clark, Charles
- Johnson, Jacob
- Johnson, Thomas
- Marshal, L
- Robertson, William
- Shumo, Samuel

Rose
- Ashby, Joseph

Ruby
- Artary, Hose
- Corey, Benjamin
- Fotry, Duroc
- Germoirober, Martin
- Pictom, Peleg
- Qumo, Harto
- Saunders, Anthony

Sarah Ann
- Ansburgh, Martin
- Bland, Richard
- Breadhead, Richard
- Calem, Samuel
- Chester, Samuel
- Clark, John
- Daur, Richard
- Delphia, John
- Dick, David
- Earl, William
- Farrell, William
- Gaul, John
- Glass, James
- Greenway, Thomas
- Hall, John
- Harred, James
- Harrison, John
- Hurst, William
- Jackson, William
- Jaibo, Joseph
- Keinsburgh, Henry
- Lane, Eben
- Lindstroon, Gustaus
- Lingo, Woodman
- Martin, John
- Martin, Zebard
- McCate, F
- Moon, Richard
- Panner, James
- Parrell, John
- Pinnard, John
- Pluck, Michael
- Roberts, George
- Robertson, James
- Rogers, Thomas
- Suitter, William
- Taylor, Alexander
- Travers, Frederick
- Young, Isaac

Saturn
- Alexander, John
- Betty, Samuel
- Clarke, John
- Collins, William
- Frazer, Andrew
- Gall, Thomas
- Green, Vincent
- Gutterage, William
- Kelly, William
- McLevy, Henry
- Miade, John
- Mills, William A
- Mitchell, Edward
- Oldham, Thomas
- Onion, Stephen P
- Pitt, Ceazar
- Price, Thomas
- Shaffer, James

Sevant
- Ayas, John
- Brown, John
- Butler, John
- Furance, George
- Maryfield, George
- Sanderson, Jacob
- Smith, George
- Stack, Samuel
- Stickney, Emey
- Stone, James
- Studdle, Surimeau
- Welman, Timothy
- Young, William

Sheperd
- Army, John
- Burke, Jacob
- Burke, Thomas
- Cannon, Charles
- Cross, William
- Cuffee, James
- Ellsey, Thomas
- Freeman, Henry
- Joseph, John
- Marshall, Elias J
- Martin, Richard
- Philips, Thomas
- Taylor, Thomas
- Waiter, James A

St. Polito
- Baker, Oliver
- Bray, A
- Brown, R
- Bunker, B
- Fielder, J
- Goodwin, William
- Havey, Mack
- Jackson, Thomas
- Kelly, T
- Porter, G
- Potter, Patrick

American Prisoners of War Held at New Providence During the War of 1812

        Renimond, J
        Routh, James
        Serett, T
        Seward, N
        Smith, E
        Snver, H. C
        Vickery, C
        Warkery, Peter
        Woodbury, F

Stanley
        Badson, Jacob
        Bundock, Benjamin
        Davis, William
        Fitcha, J S
        Gile, Jacob
        Hart, Prince
        Hatch, Robert
        Jarvis, John
        Jenkins, Anthony
        Jenkins, Dublin
        Lawton, Henry
        Maxwell, George
        Philips, Joseph
        Rhodes, James
        Sallisbury, James
        Sneston, Thomas
        Welton, William
        Witter, Robert

Stephen Garard
        Boyer, Richway
        Chandler, Samuel
        Elelow, John
        Moodie, John
        Pittsford, Francis

Trimmer
        Curtis, Thomas R
        Curtis, William L
        Hoggins, Thomas
        Quail, Thomas
        Robinson, Shadrick
        Saunders, William

Venus
        Allen, Prince
        Ashton, David
        Bradford, E
        Church, William
        Crandwell, John
        Derrick, George
        French, John
        Gamache, John
        Gorham, John
        Harman, Henry
        Hogan, Nath B
        Howard, Benjamin
        Hynes, John
        Lambert, A
        McKenzie, John
        Richardson, James
        Robeson, William S
        Shekman, Sol
        Smith, John
        Sroan, Dermias
        Templeman, M
        Thomas, William
        Watson, George

Viper
        Agreda, Joseph
        Algut, Adam
        Andrew, John
        Argent, William
        Argent, William
        Barnard, William
        Beaver, Alan
        Bileau, Julian
        Bredricke, William
        Brown, John
        Brown, N
        Chamberlain, David
        Chamberlain, David
        Clarke, John
        Connor, Samuel
        Corbett, John
        Coulken, William
        Crane, James
        Crutch, George
        Cunningham, Alexander
        Curry, Joseph
        Damoulet, George
        Godfree, John
        Gordon, Thomas
        Halladge, William
        Henley, Trim
        Henry, John
        Hewitt, Michael
        Howard, Wast
        Jackson, James
        Jackson, James
        James, Thomas
        Jefferies, Abraham
        Jones, Benjamin
        Jones, John
        Kennedy, Michael
        Kindred, James
        Kinley, H
        Law, Nicholas
        Lewi, John
        Lewis, Ebenezer
        Linguire, Abraham
        Magrath, F
        Marshall, George
        McFaith, John
        Meyers, Thomas
        Milne, Alexander
        Mooran, Thomas
        Neelby, James
        O'Hara, James
        Orimsley, John
        Paislaw, William
        Pease, Nathaniel
        Philips, Samuel
        Philips, William
        Philips, William
        Powell, Michael
        Price, Charles
        Raines, Charles
        Richardson, William
        Ringold, Henry
        Roache, Thomas
        Roberts, James
        Roberts, John
        Sandford, Samuel
        Shearon, John
        Shilley, John
        Softon, James
        Stewart, Thomas
        Thomas, George
        Thorton, James
        Tillow, George
        Todd, James
        Vance, John

American Prisoners of War Held at New Providence During the War of 1812

    Weaver, William
    Weidman, John
    Williams, Thomas
    Wilson, James
    Wilson, James
    Zirick, Mata

<u>Washington</u>
    Benjamin, Samuel
    Coal, John
    Wilkey, Frederick

<u>Wave</u>
    Bowling, J
    Cooper, Benjamin
    Davis, Samuel

    Emery, William
    Momus, Anthony
    Travis, George

<u>William</u>
    Blunt, John
    Bull, John
    Cooper, Richard
    Rhodes, Zachariah

<u>William Dart</u>
    Roberts, William
    Stole, Robert

American Prisoners of War Held at New Providence During the War of 1812

Americans on British Ships

Allen, Ebenezer
Dodge, Lewis
Inglefield, John
Johnson, William
Landerkin, Richard
Lombard, Ephrim
Oliver, Samuel
Parish, John
Sterling, Elizah
Vosso, Mathew

American Prisoners of War Held at New Providence During the War of 1812

Service affiliation not known

Abbott, Thomas
Barke, N
Brown, William
Buel, H
Burns, John
Butler, Timothy
Chaves, M
Coglan, William
Darrell, N
Eldridge, David
Eowitt, John
Fraser, Antoine
Garey, G
Gouldin, William
Hailey, John
Halm, John
Jackson, William
Johnson, Nathaniel
Read, Thomas
Redfield, Eben
Reid, Henry
Robinson, Charles
Robinson, John
Rumbsy, William
Schaafer, C
Stevens, Daniel
Tallman, John
Ward, Cuffee
Wasam, Charles
Webster, W. H
Weeks, Joseph
Westun, ---
Whipby, Israel
Wilcox, James
Wirton, Henry

American Prisoners of War Held at New Providence During the War of 1812

United States Marines

Depew, H.
Fowler, Isaac
Grindall, James
Hadley, James
Harris, John
Joseph, James
Joseph, James
Mamer, Michael
Mangine, John
Norton, Edward
Porter, Samuel
Randolph, George
Richardson, John
Robins, Hiland
Rowe, Elias
Shafer, ---
Spillard, Robert
Teufton, James
Todd, Daniel
Todd, Robert
Tower, James
Traston, Daniel
Wilson, James

American Prisoners of War Held at New Providence During the War of 1812

Americans on British Ships

Allen, Ebenezer
Dodge, Lewis
Inglefield, John
Johnson, William
Landerkin, Richard
Lombard, Ephrim
Oliver, Samuel
Parish, John
Sterling, Elizah
Vosso, Mathew

American Prisoners of War Held at Newfoundland During the War of 1812

Addeson, Littleton   Prisoner 207. Rank: Passenger, from: Castor, Not Recorded.
    Cap: 28 Aug 1812 Not Recorded by HMS Antelope Int: 28 Aug 1812 Dis: 31 Aug 1812.
    Ship. Received from HMS Antelope. To the Alert for a passage to the United States per order Sir Thomas Duckworth.

Afhont, Benjamin   Prisoner 255. Rank: Seaman, from: Rockland of New York, Not Recorded.
    Cap: 31 Aug 1812 Not Recorded by Henry Privateer Int: 31 Aug 1812 Dis: 31 Aug 1812.
    Brig. Received from Henry Privateer. To the Alert for a passage to the United States per order Sir Thomas Duckworth.

Aikien, Job   Prisoner 16. Rank: Mate, from: Arab of Marblehead, Merchant Vessel.
    Cap: 22 Jul 1812 New York by Not Recorded Int: 22 Jul 1812 Dis: 31 Aug 1812.
    Ship. Received from HMS Avenger. To the Alert for a passage to the United States per order Sir Thomas Duckworth.

Allden, Benjamin   Prisoner 351. Rank: Mate, from: Teasor, Not Recorded.
    Cap: 14 Oct 1812 Not Recorded by HMS Hazard Int: 14 Oct 1812 Dis: 03 Nov 1812.
    Received from HMS Avenger. To the United States of America.

Allen, George   Prisoner 355. Rank: Seaman, from: HMS Hazard, Not Recorded.
    Cap: 26 Oct 1812 Not Recorded by HMS Hazard Int: 26 Oct 1812 Dis: 03 Nov 1812.
    Citizen of America. Received from HMS Avenger. To the United States of America.

Allen, John   Prisoner 5. Rank: Seaman, from: Lydia of New York, Merchant Vessel.
    Cap: 08 Jul 1812 New York by HMS Jason Int: 08 Jul 1812 Dis: 31 Aug 1812.
    Ship. Received from HMS Jason. To the Alert for a passage to the United States per order Sir Thomas Duckworth.

Amey, Prince   Prisoner 46. Rank: Seaman, from: Nancy of New York, Not Recorded.
    Cap: 01 Aug 1812 Not Recorded by Not Recorded Int: 01 Aug 1812 Dis: 31 Aug 1812.
    Brig. Received from HMS Hazard. To the United States per order Sir Thomas Duckworth on Board the Alert.

Andrews, Benjamin   Prisoner 27. Rank: Master, from: Orient of Marblehead, Not Recorded.
    Cap: 28 Jul 1812 Not Recorded by Not Recorded Int: 28 Jul 1812 Dis: 31 Aug 1812.
    Ship. Received from Hazard. To the United States per order Sir Thomas Duckworth on Board the Alert.

Andrews, John   Prisoner 82. Rank: Seaman, from: Adriatic, Not Recorded.
    Cap: 01 Aug 1812 Not Recorded by Not Recorded Int: 01 Aug 1812 Dis: 31 Aug 1812.
    Ship. Received from HMS Avenger. To the Alert for a passage to the United States per order Sir Thomas Duckworth.

Ashbridge, Joseph H   Prisoner 335. Rank: Master, from: Susannah, Not Recorded.
    Cap: 24 Sep 1812 Not Recorded by Not Recorded Int: 24 Sep 1812 Dis: 18 Oct 1812.
    Brig. Received from HMS Hazard. On parole.

Atkins, Joseph   Prisoner 137. Rank: Master, from: Swallow, Not Recorded.
    Cap: 18 Aug 1812 Not Recorded by Not Recorded Int: 18 Aug 1812 Dis:
    Schooner. Received from Electra. (Date of discharge not on roster.)

Atwell, Zacharius   Prisoner 116. Rank: Master, from: Pocahunter of Boston, Not Recorded.
    Cap: 03 Aug 1812 Not Recorded by Not Recorded Int: 03 Aug 1812 Dis: 31 Aug 1812.
    Ship. Received from HMS Avenger. To the Alert for a passage to the United States per order Sir Thomas Duckworth.

Bailey, Robert   Prisoner 187. Rank: Passenger, from: Castor, Not Recorded.
    Cap: 28 Aug 1812 Not Recorded by HMS Antelope Int: 28 Aug 1812 Dis: 31 Aug 1812.
    Ship. Received from HMS Antelope. To the Alert for a passage to the United States per order Sir Thomas Duckworth.

Baker, James   Prisoner 349. Rank: Seaman, from: Adaline, Not Recorded.
    Cap: 14 Oct 1812 Not Recorded by HMS Avenger Int: 14 Oct 1812 Dis:
    Brig. Received from HMS Avenger. (Date of discharge not on roster.)

Bampton, William   Prisoner 182. Rank: Passenger, from: Castor, Not Recorded.
    Cap: 28 Aug 1812 Not Recorded by HMS Antelope Int: 28 Aug 1812 Dis: 31 Aug 1812.
    Ship. Received from HMS Antelope. To the Alert for a passage to the United States per order Sir Thomas Duckworth.

Banners, George   Prisoner 112. Rank: Passenger, from: Adriatic of New York, Not Recorded.
    Cap: 03 Aug 1812 Not Recorded by Not Recorded Int: 03 Aug 1812 Dis:
    Ship. Received from HMS Avenger. (Date of discharge not on roster.)

Banter, James   Prisoner 199. Rank: Passenger, from: Castor, Not Recorded.
    Cap: 28 Aug 1812 Not Recorded by HMS Antelope Int: 28 Aug 1812 Dis: 31 Aug 1812.
    Ship. Received from HMS Antelope. To the Alert for a passage to the United States per order Sir Thomas Duckworth.

American Prisoners of War Held at Newfoundland During the War of 1812

Baptiste, --- Prisoner 212. Rank: Passenger, from: Castor, Not Recorded.
 Cap: 28 Aug 1812 Not Recorded by HMS Antelope Int: 28 Aug 1812 Dis: 31 Aug 1812.
 Ship. Received from HMS Antelope. To the Alert for a passage to the United States per order Sir Thomas Duckworth. (First name not recorded.)

Baptiste, John Prisoner 178. Rank: Passenger, from: Castor, Not Recorded.
 Cap: 28 Aug 1812 Not Recorded by HMS Antelope Int: 28 Aug 1812 Dis: 31 Aug 1812.
 Ship. Received from HMS Antelope. To the Alert for a passage to the United States per order Sir Thomas Duckworth.

Barbarow, Joseph Prisoner 150. Rank: Passenger, from: Castor, Not Recorded.
 Cap: 19 Aug 1812 Not Recorded by HMS Antelope Int: 19 Aug 1812 Dis:
 Ship. Received from HMS Antelope. (Date of discharge not on roster.)

Barrows, Thomas Prisoner 123. Rank: Passenger, from: Union of Philadelphia, Not Recorded.
 Cap: 06 Aug 1812 Not Recorded by HMS Jason Int: 06 Aug 1812 Dis:
 Brig. Received from HMS Jason. (Date of discharge not on roster.)

Barto, Daniel Prisoner 96. Rank: Seaman, from: Gleaner, Not Recorded.
 Cap: 01 Aug 1812 Not Recorded by Not Recorded Int: 01 Aug 1812 Dis: 31 Aug 1812.
 Brig. Received from HMS Avenger. To the Alert for a passage to the United States per order Sir Thomas Duckworth.

Batcheldor, Cotton Prisoner 258. Rank: Seaman, from: Rockland of New York, Not Recorded.
 Cap: 31 Aug 1812 Not Recorded by Henry Privateer Int: 31 Aug 1812 Dis: 31 Aug 1812.
 Brig. Received from Henry Privateer. To the Alert for a passage to the United States per order Sir Thomas Duckworth.

Baylard, Jean Prisoner 151. Rank: Passenger, from: Castor, Not Recorded.
 Cap: 19 Aug 1812 Not Recorded by HMS Antelope Int: 19 Aug 1812 Dis:
 Ship. Received from HMS Antelope. (Date of discharge not on roster.)

Bellan, John Prisoner 85. Rank: Seaman, from: Adriatic, Not Recorded.
 Cap: 01 Aug 1812 Not Recorded by Not Recorded Int: 01 Aug 1812 Dis: 31 Aug 1812.
 Ship. Received from HMS Avenger. To the Alert for a passage to the United States per order Sir Thomas Duckworth.

Bennett, John Prisoner 78. Rank: Seaman, from: Adriatic, Not Recorded.
 Cap: 01 Aug 1812 Not Recorded by Not Recorded Int: 01 Aug 1812 Dis: 31 Aug 1812.
 Ship. Received from HMS Avenger. To the Alert for a passage to the United States per order Sir Thomas Duckworth.

Benson, Benjamin Prisoner 77. Rank: Seaman, from: Adriatic, Not Recorded.
 Cap: 01 Aug 1812 Not Recorded by Not Recorded Int: 01 Aug 1812 Dis: 31 Aug 1812.
 Ship. Received from HMS Avenger. To the Alert for a passage to the United States per order Sir Thomas Duckworth.

Benthall, William Prisoner 24. Rank: Master, from: Aracreon of Newburry Port, Not Recorded.
 Cap: 28 Jul 1812 Not Recorded by Not Recorded Int: 28 Jul 1812 Dis: 31 Aug 1812.
 Schooner. Received from HMS Avenger. To the Alert for a passage to the United States per order Sir Thomas Duckworth.

Berry, Isaac Prisoner 235. Rank: Mate, from: William Tell, Not Recorded.
 Cap: 31 Aug 1812 Not Recorded by Not Recorded Int: 31 Aug 1812 Dis: 31 Aug 1812.
 Ship. Received from HMS Jason. To the Alert for a passage to the United States per order Sir Thomas Duckworth.

Blake, Robert Prisoner 347. Rank: Seaman, from: Adaline, Not Recorded.
 Cap: 14 Oct 1812 Not Recorded by HMS Avenger Int: 14 Oct 1812 Dis:
 Brig. Received from HMS Avenger. (Date of discharge not on roster.)

Blake, William Prisoner 352. Rank: Seaman, from: HMS Hazard, Not Recorded.
 Cap: 26 Oct 1812 Not Recorded by HMS Hazard Int: 26 Oct 1812 Dis: 03 Nov 1812.
 Citizen of America. Received from HMS Avenger. To the United States of America.

Bolden, Edward Prisoner 67. Rank: Seaman, from: Arab of Marblehead, Not Recorded.
 Cap: 01 Aug 1812 Not Recorded by Not Recorded Int: 01 Aug 1812 Dis: 31 Aug 1812.
 Ship. Received from HMS Hazard. To the Alert for a passage to the United States per order Sir Thomas Duckworth.

Boldoon, Garrett Prisoner 257. Rank: Seaman, from: Rockland of New York, Not Recorded.
 Cap: 31 Aug 1812 Not Recorded by Henry Privateer Int: 31 Aug 1812 Dis: 31 Aug 1812.
 Brig. Received from Henry Privateer. To the Alert for a passage to the United States per order Sir Thomas Duckworth.

American Prisoners of War Held at Newfoundland During the War of 1812

Bound, Isaac   Prisoner 9. Rank: Seaman, from: Lydia of New York, Merchant Vessel.
    Cap: 08 Jul 1812 New York by HMS Jason Int: 08 Jul 1812 Dis: 31 Aug 1812.
    Ship. Received from HMS Jason. To the Alert for a passage to the United States per order Sir Thomas Duckworth.

Boyd, James   Prisoner 161. Rank: Seaman, from: Castor, Not Recorded.
    Cap: 28 Aug 1812 Not Recorded by HMS Antelope Int: 28 Aug 1812 Dis: 31 Aug 1812.
    Ship. Received from HMS Antelope. To the Alert for a passage to the United States per order Sir Thomas Duckworth.

Brady, Jesson   Prisoner 190. Rank: Passenger, from: Castor, Not Recorded.
    Cap: 28 Aug 1812 Not Recorded by HMS Antelope Int: 28 Aug 1812 Escaped: 30 Aug 1812.
    Ship. Received from HMS Antelope. Escaped.

Brady, Jesson   Prisoner 272. Rank: Seaman, from: Castor, Not Recorded.
    Cap: 01 Sep 1812 Not Recorded by St. Johns Int: 01 Sep 1812 Dis:
    Ship. Received from Antelope. Received from prison ship. 190 (Old prisoner number, recaptured. Date of discharge not on roster.)

Brady, Jesson   Prisoner 358. Rank: Seaman, from: HMS Hazard, Not Recorded.
    Cap: 04 Nov 1812 Not Recorded by HMS Hazard Int: 26 Oct 1812 Dis:
    Citizen of America. Received from HMS Avenger. (Date of discharge not on roster. Date of interment before date of capture.)

Briggs, Nathan   Prisoner 29. Rank: Master, from: Nancy of New York, Not Recorded.
    Cap: 28 Jul 1812 Not Recorded by Not Recorded Int: 28 Jul 1812 Dis: 31 Aug 1812.
    Brig. Received from Hazard. To the United States per order Sir Thomas Duckworth on Board the Alert.

Briggs, Shaddok   Prisoner 356. Rank: Seaman, from: HMS Hazard, Not Recorded.
    Cap: 26 Oct 1812 Not Recorded by HMS Hazard Int: 26 Oct 1812 Dis: 03 Nov 1812.
    Citizen of America. Received from HMS Avenger. To the United States of America.

Brooks, Thomas   Prisoner 240. Rank: Seaman, from: William Tell, Not Recorded.
    Cap: 31 Aug 1812 Not Recorded by Not Recorded Int: 31 Aug 1812 Dis: 31 Aug 1812.
    Ship. Received from HMS Jason. To the Alert for a passage to the United States per order Sir Thomas Duckworth.

Broomley, Philip   Prisoner 222. Rank: Seaman, from: Dolphin, Not Recorded.
    Cap: 28 Aug 1812 Not Recorded by HMS Antelope Int: 28 Aug 1812 Dis: 31 Aug 1812.
    Brig. Received from HMS Antelope. To the Alert for a passage to the United States per order Sir Thomas Duckworth.

Broughton, Glover   Prisoner 53. Rank: Seaman, from: Orient, Not Recorded.
    Cap: 01 Aug 1812 Not Recorded by Not Recorded Int: 01 Aug 1812 Dis: 31 Aug 1812.
    Ship. Received from HMS Hazard. To the Alert for a passage to the United States per order Sir Thomas Duckworth.

Broughton, Nicholas   Prisoner 47. Rank: Mate, from: Orient, Not Recorded.
    Cap: 01 Aug 1812 Not Recorded by Not Recorded Int: 01 Aug 1812 Dis: 31 Aug 1812.
    Ship. Received from HMS Hazard. To the United States per order Sir Thomas Duckworth on Board the Alert.

Brown, Ambrose James   Prisoner 155. Rank: Master, from: Castor, Not Recorded.
    Cap: 19 Aug 1812 Not Recorded by HMS Antelope Int: 19 Aug 1812 Dis: 31 Aug 1812.
    Ship. Received from HMS Antelope. To the Alert for a passage to the United States per order Sir Thomas Duckworth.

Brown, John   Prisoner 246. Rank: Mate, from: Fairplay of Alexandia, Not Recorded.
    Cap: 31 Aug 1812 Not Recorded by Henry Privateer Int: 31 Aug 1812 Dis: 31 Aug 1812.
    Schooner. Received from Henry Privateer. To the Alert for a passage to the United States per order Sir Thomas Duckworth.

Brown, John   Prisoner 275. Rank: Seaman, from: Fame, Not Recorded.
    Cap: 04 Sep 1812 Not Recorded by HMS Electra Int: 04 Sep 1812 Dis: 03 Nov 1812.
    Sloop. Received from HMS Electra. To the United States of America.

Brown, John   Prisoner 62. Rank: Seaman, from: Dolphin, Not Recorded.
    Cap: 01 Aug 1812 Not Recorded by Not Recorded Int: 01 Aug 1812 Dis: 31 Aug 1812.
    Brig. Received from HMS Hazard. (Captured by Hornet, recaptured by the Hazard.) To the Alert for a passage to the United States per order Sir Thomas Duckworth.

Brown, Peter   Prisoner 229. Rank: Seaman, from: W. P. Johnston, Not Recorded.
    Cap: 31 Aug 1812 Not Recorded by Not Recorded Int: 31 Aug 1812 Dis: 31 Aug 1812.
    Ship. Received from HMS Jason. To the Alert for a passage to the United States per order Sir Thomas Duckworth.

American Prisoners of War Held at Newfoundland During the War of 1812

Bunker, Daniel   Prisoner 325. Rank: Seaman, from: Enterprise of New York, Not Recorded.
    Cap: 24 Sep 1812 Not Recorded by HMS Hazard Int: 24 Sep 1812 Dis: 03 Nov 1812.
    Ship. Received from HMS Hazard. To the United States of America.

Burch, Thomas   Prisoner 317. Rank: Seaman, from: Enterprise of New York, Not Recorded.
    Cap: 24 Sep 1812 Not Recorded by Not Recorded Int: 24 Sep 1812 Dis: 03 Nov 1812.
    Ship. Received from HMS Hazard. To the United States of America.

Burke, Richard   Prisoner 231. Rank: Seaman, from: W. P. Johnston, Not Recorded.
    Cap: 31 Aug 1812 Not Recorded by Not Recorded Int: 31 Aug 1812 Dis: 31 Aug 1812.
    Ship. Received from HMS Jason. To the Alert for a passage to the United States per order Sir Thomas Duckworth.

Burnham, Richard S   Prisoner 315. Rank: Mate, from: Enterprise of New York, Not Recorded.
    Cap: 24 Sep 1812 Not Recorded by Not Recorded Int: 24 Sep 1812 Dis: 03 Nov 1812.
    Ship. Received from HMS Hazard. To the United States of America.

Bush, George   Prisoner 88. Rank: Seaman, from: Pocahunter of Boston, Not Recorded.
    Cap: 01 Aug 1812 Not Recorded by Not Recorded Int: 01 Aug 1812 Dis: 31 Aug 1812.
    Ship. Received from HMS Avenger. To the Alert for a passage to the United States per order Sir Thomas Duckworth.

Cantfield, John   Prisoner 58. Rank: Seaman, from: Dolphin, Not Recorded.
    Cap: 01 Aug 1812 Not Recorded by Not Recorded Int: 01 Aug 1812 Dis: 31 Aug 1812.
    Brig. Received from HMS Hazard. (Captured by Hornet, recaptured by the Hazard.) To the Alert for a passage to the United States per order Sir Thomas Duckworth.

Card, Henry   Prisoner 165. Rank: Seaman, from: Castor, Not Recorded.
    Cap: 28 Aug 1812 Not Recorded by HMS Antelope Int: 28 Aug 1812 Dis: 31 Aug 1812.
    Ship. Received from HMS Antelope. To the Alert for a passage to the United States per order Sir Thomas Duckworth.

Carlow, James   Prisoner 8. Rank: Seaman, from: Lydia of New York, Merchant Vessel.
    Cap: 08 Jul 1812 New York by HMS Jason Int: 08 Jul 1812 Dis: 31 Aug 1812.
    Ship. Received from HMS Jason. To the Alert for a passage to the United States per order Sir Thomas Duckworth.

Carpenter, James   Prisoner 146. Rank: Seaman, from: Rockland, Not Recorded.
    Cap: 18 Aug 1812 Not Recorded by Not Recorded Int: 18 Aug 1812 Dis: 31 Aug 1812.
    Brig. Received from Fly Privateer. To the Alert for a passage to the United States per order Sir Thomas Duckworth.

Cartwright, Alexander   Prisoner 314. Rank: Master, from: Enterprise of New York, Not Recorded.
    Cap: 21 Sep 1812 Not Recorded by Not Recorded Int: 21 Sep 1812 Dis: 18 Oct 1812.
    Ship. Received from HMS Hazard. On parole.

Chairman, Elezis   Prisoner 54. Rank: Seaman, from: Orient, Not Recorded.
    Cap: 01 Aug 1812 Not Recorded by Not Recorded Int: 01 Aug 1812 Dis: 31 Aug 1812.
    Ship. Received from HMS Hazard. To the Alert for a passage to the United States per order Sir Thomas Duckworth.

Chambers, William   Prisoner 49. Rank: Seaman, from: Orient, Not Recorded.
    Cap: 01 Aug 1812 Not Recorded by Not Recorded Int: 01 Aug 1812 Dis: 31 Aug 1812.
    Ship. Received from HMS Hazard. To the United States per order Sir Thomas Duckworth on Board the Alert.

Chapman, Israel   Prisoner 2. Rank: Mate, from: Lydia of New York, Merchant Vessel.
    Cap: 08 Jul 1812 New York by HMS Jason Int: 08 Jul 1812 Dis: 31 Aug 1812.
    Ship. Received from HMS Jason. To the Alert for a passage to the United States per order Sir Thomas Duckworth.

Chase, Franklin   Prisoner 71. Rank: Seaman, from: Arab of Marblehead, Not Recorded.
    Cap: 01 Aug 1812 Not Recorded by Not Recorded Int: 01 Aug 1812 Dis: 31 Aug 1812.
    Ship. Received from HMS Hazard. To the Alert for a passage to the United States per order Sir Thomas Duckworth.

Clarke, Hubert   Prisoner 346. Rank: Seaman, from: Adaline, Not Recorded.
    Cap: 14 Oct 1812 Not Recorded by HMS Avenger Int: 14 Oct 1812 Dis:
    Brig. Received from HMS Avenger. (Date of discharge not on roster.)

Claw, Jacob   Prisoner 245. Rank: Seaman, from: William Tell, Not Recorded.
    Cap: 31 Aug 1812 Not Recorded by Not Recorded Int: 31 Aug 1812 Dis: 31 Aug 1812.
    Ship. Received from HMS Jason. To the Alert for a passage to the United States per order Sir Thomas Duckworth.

American Prisoners of War Held at Newfoundland During the War of 1812

Clerk, Samuel   Prisoner 179. Rank: Passenger, from: Castor, Not Recorded.
    Cap: 28 Aug 1812 Not Recorded by HMS Antelope Int: 28 Aug 1812 Dis: 31 Aug 1812.
    Ship. Received from HMS Antelope. To the Alert for a passage to the United States per order Sir Thomas Duckworth.

Cleveland, Ezekiel   Prisoner 334. Rank: Seaman, from: Susannah, Not Recorded.
    Cap: 24 Sep 1812 Not Recorded by HMS Hazard Int: 24 Sep 1812 Dis: 03 Nov 1812.
    Brig. Received from HMS Hazard. To the United States of America.

Clewley, William   Prisoner 193. Rank: Passenger, from: Castor, Not Recorded.
    Cap: 28 Aug 1812 Not Recorded by HMS Antelope Int: 28 Aug 1812 Dis: 31 Aug 1812.
    Ship. Received from HMS Antelope. To the Alert for a passage to the United States per order Sir Thomas Duckworth.

Cobb, Elijah   Prisoner 154. Rank: Master, from: Castor, Not Recorded.
    Cap: 19 Aug 1812 Not Recorded by HMS Antelope Int: 19 Aug 1812 Dis: 31 Aug 1812.
    Ship. Received from HMS Antelope. To the Alert for a passage to the United States per order Sir Thomas Duckworth.

Cobby, Joseph   Prisoner 316. Rank: Seaman, from: Enterprise of New York, Not Recorded.
    Cap: 24 Sep 1812 Not Recorded by Not Recorded Int: 24 Sep 1812 Dis: 03 Nov 1812.
    Ship. Received from HMS Hazard. To the United States of America.

Cole, Elisha   Prisoner 289. Rank: Seaman, from: Pilgrim, Not Recorded.
    Cap: 04 Sep 1812 Not Recorded by HMS Electra Int: 04 Sep 1812 Dis: 03 Nov 1812.
    Schooner. Received from HMS Electra. To the United States of America.

Colee, Jacob   Prisoner 169. Rank: Passenger, from: Castor, Not Recorded.
    Cap: 28 Aug 1812 Not Recorded by HMS Antelope Int: 28 Aug 1812 Escaped: 30 Aug 1812.
    Ship. Received from HMS Antelope. Escaped.

Colee, Jacob   Prisoner 267. Rank: Seaman, from: Castor, Not Recorded.
    Cap: 01 Sep 1812 Not Recorded by St. Johns Int: 01 Sep 1812 Dis: 03 Nov 1812.
    Ship. Received from Antelope. Received from prison ship. 169 (Old prisoner number, recaptured.) To the United States of America.

Coleman, William   Prisoner 14. Rank: Seaman, from: Lydia of New York, Merchant Vessel.
    Cap: 08 Jul 1812 New York by HMS Jason Int: 08 Jul 1812 Dis: 31 Aug 1812.
    Ship. Received from HMS Jason. To the Alert for a passage to the United States per order Sir Thomas Duckworth.

Conner, David   Prisoner 111. Rank: Sailing Master, from: Dolphin, Not Recorded.
    Cap: 02 Aug 1812 Not Recorded by HMS Hazard Int: 02 Aug 1812 Dis: 31 Aug 1812.
    Brig. Recaputered by Hazard. United States Sloop of War Hornet. Received from HMS Hazard. To the Alert for a passage to the United States per order Sir Thomas Duckworth.

Conner, Samiel   Prisoner 327. Rank: Mate, from: Susannah, Not Recorded.
    Cap: 24 Sep 1812 Not Recorded by HMS Hazard Int: 24 Sep 1812 Dis: 03 Nov 1812.
    Brig. Received from HMS Hazard. To the United States of America.

Cooke, Earl   Prisoner 185. Rank: Passenger, from: Castor, Not Recorded.
    Cap: 28 Aug 1812 Not Recorded by HMS Antelope Int: 28 Aug 1812 Dis: 31 Aug 1812.
    Ship. Received from HMS Antelope. To the Alert for a passage to the United States per order Sir Thomas Duckworth.

Corbett, Samuel   Prisoner 43. Rank: Seaman, from: Nancy of New York, Not Recorded.
    Cap: 01 Aug 1812 Not Recorded by Not Recorded Int: 01 Aug 1812 Dis: 31 Aug 1812.
    Brig. Received from HMS Hazard. To the United States per order Sir Thomas Duckworth on Board the Alert.

Crandall, Amos   Prisoner 184. Rank: Passenger, from: Castor, Not Recorded.
    Cap: 28 Aug 1812 Not Recorded by HMS Antelope Int: 28 Aug 1812 Dis: 31 Aug 1812.
    Ship. Received from HMS Antelope. To the Alert for a passage to the United States per order Sir Thomas Duckworth.

Crosby, Elijah Cobb   Prisoner 157. Rank: Boy, from: William Tell, Not Recorded.
    Cap: 27 Aug 1812 Not Recorded by William P. Johnston Int: 27 Aug 1812 Dis:
    Ship. Received from HMS Jason. (Date of discharge not on roster.)

Crosby, Josiah   Prisoner 239. Rank: Seaman, from: William Tell, Not Recorded.
    Cap: 31 Aug 1812 Not Recorded by Not Recorded Int: 31 Aug 1812 Dis: 31 Aug 1812.
    Ship. Received from HMS Jason. To the Alert for a passage to the United States per order Sir Thomas Duckworth.

Crowell, Anthony   Prisoner 36. Rank: Seaman, from: Elizabeth of Yarmouth, Not Recorded.
    Cap: 01 Aug 1812 Not Recorded by Not Recorded Int: 01 Aug 1812 Dis: 31 Aug 1812.
    Schooner. Received from HMS Hazard. To the United States per order Sir Thomas Duckworth on Board the Alert.

American Prisoners of War Held at Newfoundland During the War of 1812

Crowell, Isaac   Prisoner 37. Rank: Seaman, from: Elizabeth of Yarmouth, Not Recorded.
    Cap: 01 Aug 1812 Not Recorded by Not Recorded Int: 01 Aug 1812 Dis: 31 Aug 1812.
    Schooner. Received from HMS Hazard. To the United States per order Sir Thomas Duckworth on Board the Alert.

Crowell, Isaiah   Prisoner 28. Rank: Master, from: Elizabeth of Yarmouth, Not Recorded.
    Cap: 28 Jul 1812 Not Recorded by Not Recorded Int: 28 Jul 1812 Dis: 31 Aug 1812.
    Schooner. Received from Hazard. To the United States per order Sir Thomas Duckworth on Board the Alert.

Damoor, Thomas   Prisoner 189. Rank: Passenger, from: Castor, Not Recorded.
    Cap: 28 Aug 1812 Not Recorded by HMS Antelope Int: 28 Aug 1812 Dis: 31 Aug 1812.
    Ship. Received from HMS Antelope. To the Alert for a passage to the United States per order Sir Thomas Duckworth.

Davis, John   Prisoner 357. Rank: Seaman, from: HMS Hazard, Not Recorded.
    Cap: 26 Oct 1812 Not Recorded by HMS Hazard Int: 26 Oct 1812 Dis: 03 Nov 1812.
    Citizen of America. Received from HMS Avenger. To the United States of America.

Davis, Moses   Prisoner 230. Rank: Seaman, from: W. P. Johnston, Not Recorded.
    Cap: 31 Aug 1812 Not Recorded by Not Recorded Int: 31 Aug 1812 Dis: 31 Aug 1812.
    Ship. Received from HMS Jason. To the Alert for a passage to the United States per order Sir Thomas Duckworth.

Davis, Peter   Prisoner 180. Rank: Passenger, from: Castor, Not Recorded.
    Cap: 28 Aug 1812 Not Recorded by HMS Antelope Int: 28 Aug 1812 Dis: 31 Aug 1812.
    Ship. Received from HMS Antelope. To the Alert for a passage to the United States per order Sir Thomas Duckworth.

Day, William   Prisoner 350. Rank: Seaman, from: Adaline, Not Recorded.
    Cap: 14 Oct 1812 Not Recorded by HMS Avenger Int: 14 Oct 1812 Dis:
    Brig. Received from HMS Avenger. (Date of discharge not on roster.)

Dent, William   Prisoner 89. Rank: Seaman, from: Pocahunter of Boston, Not Recorded.
    Cap: 01 Aug 1812 Not Recorded by Not Recorded Int: 01 Aug 1812 Dis: 31 Aug 1812.
    Ship. Received from HMS Avenger. To the Alert for a passage to the United States per order Sir Thomas Duckworth.

Deval, William   Prisoner 102. Rank: Mate, from: Triton of New Bedford, Not Recorded.
    Cap: 02 Aug 1812 Not Recorded by Not Recorded Int: 02 Aug 1812 Dis: 31 Aug 1812.
    Ship. Received from HMS Avenger. To the Alert for a passage to the United States per order Sir Thomas Duckworth.

Dibladen, John   Prisoner 250. Rank: Seaman, from: Fairplay of Alexandia, Not Recorded.
    Cap: 31 Aug 1812 Not Recorded by Henry Privateer Int: 31 Aug 1812 Dis: 31 Aug 1812.
    Schooner. Received from Henry Privateer. To the Alert for a passage to the United States per order Sir Thomas Duckworth.

Dilno, Joseph   Prisoner 120. Rank: Boy, from: Arab of Marblehead, Not Recorded.
    Cap: 03 Aug 1812 Not Recorded by Not Recorded Int: 03 Aug 1812 Dis:
    Ship. Received from HMS Avenger. (Date of discharge not on roster.)

Dilno, Warren   Prisoner 118. Rank: Master, from: Arab of Marblehead, Not Recorded.
    Cap: 03 Aug 1812 Not Recorded by Not Recorded Int: 03 Aug 1812 Dis: 31 Aug 1812.
    Ship. Received from HMS Avenger. To the Alert for a passage to the United States per order Sir Thomas Duckworth.

Donogh, Joseph W   Prisoner 360. Rank: Seaman, from: HMS Hazard, Not Recorded.
    Cap: 10 Nov 1812 Not Recorded by Comet Int: 10 Nov 1812 Dis:
    Citizen of America. Received from HMS Avenger. (Date of discharge not on roster.)

Dornbar, James   Prisoner 205. Rank: Passenger, from: Castor, Not Recorded.
    Cap: 28 Aug 1812 Not Recorded by HMS Antelope Int: 28 Aug 1812 Dis: 31 Aug 1812.
    Ship. Received from HMS Antelope. To the Alert for a passage to the United States per order Sir Thomas Duckworth.

Douglass, Hatley   Prisoner 248. Rank: Mate, from: Fairplay of Alexandia, Not Recorded.
    Cap: 31 Aug 1812 Not Recorded by Henry Privateer Int: 31 Aug 1812 Dis: 31 Aug 1812.
    Schooner. Received from Henry Privateer. To the Alert for a passage to the United States per order Sir Thomas Duckworth.

Dow, John   Prisoner 12. Rank: Seaman, from: Lydia of New York, Merchant Vessel.
    Cap: 08 Jul 1812 New York by HMS Jason Int: 08 Jul 1812 Dis: 31 Aug 1812.
    Ship. Received from HMS Jason. To the Alert for a passage to the United States per order Sir Thomas Duckworth.

American Prisoners of War Held at Newfoundland During the War of 1812

Drew, James   Prisoner 238. Rank: Seaman, from: William Tell, Not Recorded.
    Cap: 31 Aug 1812 Not Recorded by Not Recorded Int: 31 Aug 1812 Dis: 31 Aug 1812.
    Ship. Received from HMS Jason. To the Alert for a passage to the United States per order Sir Thomas Duckworth.

Dublin, Thomas   Prisoner 109. Rank: Seaman, from: Adriatic of New York, Not Recorded.
    Cap: 02 Aug 1812 Not Recorded by Not Recorded Int: 02 Aug 1812 Dis: 31 Aug 1812.
    Ship. Received from HMS Avenger. To the Alert for a passage to the United States per order Sir Thomas Duckworth.

Dufour, Aime   Prisoner 152. Rank: Passenger, from: Castor, Not Recorded.
    Cap: 19 Aug 1812 Not Recorded by HMS Antelope Int: 19 Aug 1812 Dis:
    Ship. Received from HMS Antelope. (Date of discharge not on roster.)

Dunn, James   Prisoner 114. Rank: Master, from: Gleaner of Boston, Not Recorded.
    Cap: 03 Aug 1812 Not Recorded by Not Recorded Int: 03 Aug 1812 Dis: 31 Aug 1812.
    Brig. Received from HMS Avenger. To the Alert for a passage to the United States per order Sir Thomas Duckworth.

Eaton, Henry   Prisoner 278. Rank: Seaman, from: Fame, Not Recorded.
    Cap: 04 Sep 1812 Not Recorded by HMS Electra Int: 04 Sep 1812 Dis: 03 Nov 1812.
    Sloop. Received from HMS Electra. To the United States of America.

Edmonston, Elisha   Prisoner 203. Rank: Passenger, from: Castor, Not Recorded.
    Cap: 28 Aug 1812 Not Recorded by HMS Antelope Int: 28 Aug 1812 Dis: 31 Aug 1812.
    Ship. Received from HMS Antelope. To the Alert for a passage to the United States per order Sir Thomas Duckworth.

Edwards, William   Prisoner 41. Rank: Seaman, from: Nancy of New York, Not Recorded.
    Cap: 01 Aug 1812 Not Recorded by Not Recorded Int: 01 Aug 1812 Dis: 31 Aug 1812.
    Brig. Received from HMS Hazard. To the United States per order Sir Thomas Duckworth on Board the Alert.

Ennick, William   Prisoner 274. Rank: Seaman, from: Eagle, Not Recorded.
    Cap: 01 Sep 1812 Not Recorded by Civil Powers Int: 01 Sep 1812 Dis: 03 Nov 1812.
    Belonging to the Brig Eagle of Bristol. Received from England. To the United States of America.

Everleigh, William   Prisoner 208. Rank: Passenger, from: Castor, Not Recorded.
    Cap: 28 Aug 1812 Not Recorded by HMS Antelope Int: 28 Aug 1812 Escaped: 31 Aug 1812.
    Ship. Received from HMS Antelope. Escaped.

Everleigh, William   Prisoner 273. Rank: Seaman, from: Castor, Not Recorded.
    Cap: 01 Sep 1812 Not Recorded by St. Johns Int: 01 Sep 1812 Dis: 03 Nov 1812.
    Ship. Received from Antelope. Received from prison ship. 208 (Old prisoner number, recaptured.) To the United States of America.

Farmer, Prince   Prisoner 10. Rank: Seaman, from: Lydia of New York, Merchant Vessel.
    Cap: 08 Jul 1812 New York by HMS Jason Int: 08 Jul 1812 Dis: 31 Aug 1812.
    Ship. Received from HMS Jason. To the Alert for a passage to the United States per order Sir Thomas Duckworth.

Fearson, Benjamin   Prisoner 131. Rank: Seaman, from: Perseverance, Not Recorded.
    Cap: 10 Aug 1812 Not Recorded by Not Recorded Int: 10 Aug 1812 Dis: 31 Aug 1812.
    Brig. Received from HMS Atalante. To the Alert for a passage to the United States per order Sir Thomas Duckworth.

Fenton, Charles   Prisoner 339. Rank: Seaman, from: Sprightly, Not Recorded.
    Cap: 29 Sep 1812 Not Recorded by Not Recorded Int: 24 Sep 1812 Dis: 03 Nov 1812.
    Brig. Recaptured by Hazard. Received from HMS Hazard. To the United States of America. (Date of interment before date of capture.)

Finch, Stephen   Prisoner 254. Rank: Seaman, from: Rockland of New York, Not Recorded.
    Cap: 31 Aug 1812 Not Recorded by Henry Privateer Int: 31 Aug 1812 Dis: 31 Aug 1812.
    Brig. Received from Henry Privateer. To the Alert for a passage to the United States per order Sir Thomas Duckworth.

Fisher, Henry   Prisoner 220. Rank: Seaman, from: Dolphin, Not Recorded.
    Cap: 28 Aug 1812 Not Recorded by HMS Antelope Int: 28 Aug 1812 Dis: 31 Aug 1812.
    Brig. Received from HMS Antelope. To the Alert for a passage to the United States per order Sir Thomas Duckworth.

Florance, Charles   Prisoner 261. Rank: Seaman, from: Rockland of New York, Not Recorded.
    Cap: 31 Aug 1812 Not Recorded by Henry Privateer Int: 31 Aug 1812 Dis: 31 Aug 1812.
    Brig. Received from Henry Privateer. To the Alert for a passage to the United States per order Sir Thomas Duckworth.

American Prisoners of War Held at Newfoundland During the War of 1812

Florance, David   Prisoner 264. Rank: Seaman, from: Rockland of New York, Not Recorded.
    Cap: 31 Aug 1812 Not Recorded by Henry Privateer Int: 31 Aug 1812 Dis: 31 Aug 1812.
    Brig. Received from Henry Privateer. To the Alert for a passage to the United States per order Sir Thomas Duckworth.

Folger, Robert   Prisoner 39. Rank: Mate, from: Nancy of New York, Not Recorded.
    Cap: 01 Aug 1812 Not Recorded by Not Recorded Int: 01 Aug 1812 Dis: 31 Aug 1812.
    Brig. Received from HMS Hazard. To the United States per order Sir Thomas Duckworth on Board the Alert.

Forrester, Peter   Prisoner 51. Rank: Seaman, from: Orient, Not Recorded.
    Cap: 01 Aug 1812 Not Recorded by Not Recorded Int: 01 Aug 1812 Dis: 31 Aug 1812.
    Ship. Received from HMS Hazard. To the Alert for a passage to the United States per order Sir Thomas Duckworth.

Foster, Esaw   Prisoner 277. Rank: Seaman, from: Fame, Not Recorded.
    Cap: 04 Sep 1812 Not Recorded by HMS Electra Int: 04 Sep 1812 Dis: 03 Nov 1812.
    Sloop. Received from HMS Electra. To the United States of America.

Fowler, Ceasar   Prisoner 126. Rank: Seaman, from: Castor of New Bedford, Not Recorded.
    Cap: 06 Aug 1812 Not Recorded by Not Recorded Int: 06 Aug 1812 Dis: 31 Aug 1812.
    Ship. Received from HMS Antelope. To the Alert for a passage to the United States per order Sir Thomas Duckworth.

Frederick, John   Prisoner 128. Rank: Seaman, from: Castor of New Bedford, Not Recorded.
    Cap: 06 Aug 1812 Not Recorded by Not Recorded Int: 06 Aug 1812 Dis: 31 Aug 1812.
    Ship. Received from HMS Antelope. To the Alert for a passage to the United States per order Sir Thomas Duckworth.

Gall, John   Prisoner 68. Rank: Seaman, from: Arab of Marblehead, Not Recorded.
    Cap: 01 Aug 1812 Not Recorded by Not Recorded Int: 01 Aug 1812 Dis: 31 Aug 1812.
    Ship. Received from HMS Hazard. To the Alert for a passage to the United States per order Sir Thomas Duckworth.

Gardener, James   Prisoner 22. Rank: Master, from: Union of Philadelphia, Not Recorded.
    Cap: 28 Jul 1812 Not Recorded by Not Recorded Int: 28 Jul 1812 Dis: 31 Aug 1812.
    Brig. Received from HMS Jason. To the Alert for a passage to the United States per order Sir Thomas Duckworth.

Gardener, Josiah   Prisoner 94. Rank: Seaman, from: Gleaner, Not Recorded.
    Cap: 01 Aug 1812 Not Recorded by Not Recorded Int: 01 Aug 1812 Dis: 31 Aug 1812.
    Brig. Received from HMS Avenger. To the Alert for a passage to the United States per order Sir Thomas Duckworth.

Gardener, Thomas H   Prisoner 127. Rank: Seaman, from: Castor of New Bedford, Not Recorded.
    Cap: 06 Aug 1812 Not Recorded by Not Recorded Int: 06 Aug 1812 Dis: 03 Nov 1812.
    Ship. Received from HMS Antelope. To the Alert for a passage to the United States per order Sir Thomas Duckworth.

Garriques, Elmslie   Prisoner 113. Rank: Passenger, from: Adriatic of New York, Not Recorded.
    Cap: 03 Aug 1812 Not Recorded by Not Recorded Int: 03 Aug 1812 Dis:
    Ship. Received from HMS Avenger. (Date of discharge not on roster.)

Gillies, John   Prisoner 156. Rank: Passenger, from: Castor, Not Recorded.
    Cap: 19 Aug 1812 Not Recorded by HMS Antelope Int: 19 Aug 1812 Dis:
    Ship. Received from HMS Antelope. (Date of discharge not on roster.)

Gilpen, George   Prisoner 99. Rank: Mate, from: Gleaner, Not Recorded.
    Cap: 01 Aug 1812 Not Recorded by Not Recorded Int: 01 Aug 1812 Dis: 31 Aug 1812.
    Brig. Received from HMS Avenger. To the Alert for a passage to the United States per order Sir Thomas Duckworth.

Goldbrite, Jonathan   Prisoner 280. Rank: Seaman, from: Fame, Not Recorded.
    Cap: 04 Sep 1812 Not Recorded by HMS Electra Int: 04 Sep 1812 Dis: 03 Nov 1812.
    Sloop. Received from HMS Electra. To the United States of America.

Gomlay, James   Prisoner 243. Rank: Seaman, from: William Tell, Not Recorded.
    Cap: 31 Aug 1812 Not Recorded by Not Recorded Int: 31 Aug 1812 Dis: 31 Aug 1812.
    Ship. Received from HMS Jason. To the Alert for a passage to the United States per order Sir Thomas Duckworth.

Gonnes, Morser   Prisoner 66. Rank: Seaman, from: Arab of Marblehead, Not Recorded.
    Cap: 01 Aug 1812 Not Recorded by Not Recorded Int: 01 Aug 1812 Dis: 31 Aug 1812.
    Ship. Received from HMS Hazard. To the Alert for a passage to the United States per order Sir Thomas Duckworth.

American Prisoners of War Held at Newfoundland During the War of 1812

Goodbartlett, William   Prisoner 76. Rank: Seaman, from: Adriatic, Not Recorded.
    Cap: 01 Aug 1812 Not Recorded by Not Recorded Int: 01 Aug 1812 Dis: 31 Aug 1812.
    Ship. Received from HMS Avenger. To the Alert for a passage to the United States per order Sir Thomas Duckworth.

Gould, Nathaniel   Prisoner 303. Rank: Seaman, from: William Davis, Not Recorded.
    Cap: 04 Sep 1812 Not Recorded by HMS Electra Int: 04 Sep 1812 Dis: 03 Nov 1812.
    Schooner. Received from HMS Electra. To the United States of America.

Graves, Alexander   Prisoner 173. Rank: Passenger, from: Castor, Not Recorded.
    Cap: 28 Aug 1812 Not Recorded by HMS Antelope Int: 28 Aug 1812 Dis: 31 Aug 1812.
    Ship. Received from HMS Antelope. To the Alert for a passage to the United States per order Sir Thomas Duckworth.

Gray, John   Prisoner 236. Rank: 2 Mate, from: William Tell, Not Recorded.
    Cap: 31 Aug 1812 Not Recorded by Not Recorded Int: 31 Aug 1812 Dis: 31 Aug 1812.
    Ship. Received from HMS Jason. To the Alert for a passage to the United States per order Sir Thomas Duckworth.

Greelief, Matthews   Prisoner 219. Rank: Seaman, from: Dolphin, Not Recorded.
    Cap: 28 Aug 1812 Not Recorded by HMS Antelope Int: 28 Aug 1812 Dis: 31 Aug 1812.
    Brig. Received from HMS Antelope. To the Alert for a passage to the United States per order Sir Thomas Duckworth.

Gridler, John   Prisoner 48. Rank: Mate, from: Orient, Not Recorded.
    Cap: 01 Aug 1812 Not Recorded by Not Recorded Int: 01 Aug 1812 Dis: 31 Aug 1812.
    Ship. Received from HMS Hazard. To the United States per order Sir Thomas Duckworth on Board the Alert.

Haldon, Lewis   Prisoner 363. Rank: Seaman, from: HMS Hazard, Not Recorded.
    Cap: 26 Nov 1812 Not Recorded by Comet Int: 26 Nov 1812 Dis:
    Citizen of America. Received from HMS Avenger. (Date of discharge not on roster.)

Hale, James   Prisoner 13. Rank: Supercargo, from: Lydia of New York, Merchant Vessel.
    Cap: 08 Jul 1812 New York by HMS Jason Int: 08 Jul 1812 Dis:
    Ship. Received from HMS Jason. (Date of discharge not on roster.)

Hamilton, George W   Prisoner 6. Rank: Seaman, from: Lydia of New York, Merchant Vessel.
    Cap: 08 Jul 1812 New York by HMS Jason Int: 08 Jul 1812 Dis: 31 Aug 1812.
    Ship. Received from HMS Jason. To the Alert for a passage to the United States per order Sir Thomas Duckworth.

Hammond, Samuel   Prisoner 31. Rank: Master, from: Caroline New Bedford, Not Recorded.
    Cap: 28 Jul 1812 Not Recorded by Not Recorded Int: 28 Jul 1812 Dis: 31 Aug 1812.
    Schooner. Received from Jason. To the United States per order Sir Thomas Duckworth on Board the Alert.

Harding, Nehemiah   Prisoner 342. Rank: Master, from: Adaline, Not Recorded.
    Cap: 14 Oct 1812 Not Recorded by HMS Avenger Int: 14 Oct 1812 Dis: 18 Oct 1812.
    Brig. Received from HMS Avenger. On parole.

Hardy, Risdam   Prisoner 176. Rank: Passenger, from: Castor, Not Recorded.
    Cap: 28 Aug 1812 Not Recorded by HMS Antelope Int: 28 Aug 1812 Dis: 31 Aug 1812.
    Ship. Received from HMS Antelope. To the Alert for a passage to the United States per order Sir Thomas Duckworth.

Harmerchant, Peter   Prisoner 69. Rank: Seaman, from: Arab of Marblehead, Not Recorded.
    Cap: 01 Aug 1812 Not Recorded by Not Recorded Int: 01 Aug 1812 Dis: 31 Aug 1812.
    Ship. Received from HMS Hazard. To the Alert for a passage to the United States per order Sir Thomas Duckworth.

Harris, David   Prisoner 215. Rank: Seaman, from: Eliza, Not Recorded.
    Cap: 28 Aug 1812 Not Recorded by HMS Antelope Int: 28 Aug 1812 Dis: 31 Aug 1812.
    Brig. Received from HMS Antelope. To the Alert for a passage to the United States per order Sir Thomas Duckworth.

Hastings, Rufus   Prisoner 64. Rank: Seaman, from: Dolphin, Not Recorded.
    Cap: 01 Aug 1812 Not Recorded by Not Recorded Int: 01 Aug 1812 Dis: 31 Aug 1812.
    Brig. Received from HMS Hazard. (Captured by Hornet, recaptured by the Hazard.) To the Alert for a passage to the United States per order Sir Thomas Duckworth.

Heason, James   Prisoner 143. Rank: Boy, from: William Davis, Not Recorded.
    Cap: 18 Aug 1812 Not Recorded by Not Recorded Int: 18 Aug 1812 Dis: 31 Aug 1812.
    Schooner. Received from Electra. To the Alert for a passage to the United States per order Sir Thomas Duckworth.

American Prisoners of War Held at Newfoundland During the War of 1812

Heath, James   Prisoner 343. Rank: Seaman, from: Adaline, Not Recorded.
    Cap: 14 Oct 1812 Not Recorded by HMS Avenger Int: 14 Oct 1812 Dis:
    Brig. Received from HMS Avenger. (Date of discharge not on roster.)

Hemby, Leith   Prisoner 344. Rank: Seaman, from: Adaline, Not Recorded.
    Cap: 14 Oct 1812 Not Recorded by HMS Avenger Int: 14 Oct 1812 Dis:
    Brig. Received from HMS Avenger. (Date of discharge not on roster.)

Henderson, Israel   Prisoner 341. Rank: Seaman, from: Sprightly, Not Recorded.
    Cap: 29 Sep 1812 Not Recorded by Not Recorded Int: 24 Sep 1812 Dis: 03 Nov 1812.
    Brig. Recaptured by Hazard. Received from HMS Hazard. To the United States of America. (Date of interment before date of capture.)

Herman, John   Prisoner 209. Rank: Passenger, from: Castor, Not Recorded.
    Cap: 28 Aug 1812 Not Recorded by HMS Antelope Int: 28 Aug 1812 Dis: 31 Aug 1812.
    Ship. Received from HMS Antelope. To the Alert for a passage to the United States per order Sir Thomas Duckworth.

Hewland, Rous   Prisoner 164. Rank: Seaman, from: Castor, Not Recorded.
    Cap: 28 Aug 1812 Not Recorded by HMS Antelope Int: 28 Aug 1812 Dis: 31 Aug 1812.
    Ship. Received from HMS Antelope. To the Alert for a passage to the United States per order Sir Thomas Duckworth.

Higgins, Aquilla   Prisoner 281. Rank: Seaman, from: Pilgrim, Not Recorded.
    Cap: 04 Sep 1812 Not Recorded by HMS Electra Int: 04 Sep 1812 Dis: 03 Nov 1812.
    Schooner. Received from HMS Electra. To the United States of America.

Higgins, Hutcel   Prisoner 290. Rank: Seaman, from: Swallow, Not Recorded.
    Cap: 04 Sep 1812 Not Recorded by HMS Electra Int: 04 Sep 1812 Dis: 03 Nov 1812.
    Schooner. Received from HMS Electra. To the United States of America.

Higgins, Jesse   Prisoner 122. Rank: Midshipman, from: Essex, Not Recorded.
    Cap: 06 Aug 1812 Not Recorded by HMS Atalante & HMS Pomone Int: 06 Aug 1812 Dis:
    Frigate. Taken in Brig Leander. Recaptured by Atalante. Received from HMS Avenger. (Date of discharge not on roster.)

Higgins, John   Prisoner 44. Rank: Seaman, from: Nancy of New York, Not Recorded.
    Cap: 01 Aug 1812 Not Recorded by Not Recorded Int: 01 Aug 1812 Dis: 31 Aug 1812.
    Brig. Received from HMS Hazard. To the United States per order Sir Thomas Duckworth on Board the Alert.

Higgins, Joshua   Prisoner 295. Rank: Seaman, from: Swallow, Not Recorded.
    Cap: 04 Sep 1812 Not Recorded by HMS Electra Int: 04 Sep 1812 Dis: 03 Nov 1812.
    Schooner. Received from HMS Electra. To the United States of America.

Higgins, Moses   Prisoner 138. Rank: Master, from: Pilgrim, Not Recorded.
    Cap: 18 Aug 1812 Not Recorded by Not Recorded Int: 18 Aug 1812 Dis:
    Schooner. Received from Electra. (Date of discharge not on roster.)

Higgins, Moses   Prisoner 142. Rank: Boy, from: Pilgrim, Not Recorded.
    Cap: 18 Aug 1812 Not Recorded by Not Recorded Int: 18 Aug 1812 Dis:
    Schooner. Received from Electra. (Date of discharge not on roster.)

Hillman, Benjamin   Prisoner 158. Rank: Mate, from: Castor, Not Recorded.
    Cap: 28 Aug 1812 Not Recorded by HMS Antelope Int: 28 Aug 1812 Dis: 31 Aug 1812.
    Ship. Received from HMS Antelope. To the Alert for a passage to the United States per order Sir Thomas Duckworth.

Hitchings, Benjamin   Prisoner 25. Rank: Master, from: Polafox of Boston, Not Recorded.
    Cap: 28 Jul 1812 Not Recorded by Not Recorded Int: 28 Jul 1812 Dis: 31 Aug 1812.
    Brig. Received from HMS Jason. To the Alert for a passage to the United States per order.

Hodman, John   Prisoner 32. Rank: Boy, from: Orient of Marblehead, Not Recorded.
    Cap: 31 Jul 1812 Not Recorded by Not Recorded Int: 31 Jul 1812 Dis: 31 Aug 1812.
    Ship. Received from HMS Jason. To the United States per order Sir Thomas Duckworth on Board the Alert.

Hoffman, John   Prisoner 59. Rank: Seaman, from: Dolphin, Not Recorded.
    Cap: 01 Aug 1812 Not Recorded by Not Recorded Int: 01 Aug 1812 Dis: 31 Aug 1812.
    Brig. Received from HMS Hazard. (Captured by Hornet, recaptured by the Hazard.) To the Alert for a passage to the United States per order Sir Thomas Duckworth.

Holden, Henry   Prisoner 100. Rank: Seaman, from: Triton of New Bedford, Not Recorded.
    Cap: 01 Aug 1812 Not Recorded by Not Recorded Int: 01 Aug 1812 Dis: 31 Aug 1812.
    Ship. Received from HMS Avenger. To the Alert for a passage to the United States per order Sir Thomas Duckworth.

American Prisoners of War Held at Newfoundland During the War of 1812

Homan, James   Prisoner 313. Rank: Seaman, from: Essex, Not Recorded.
    Cap: 04 Sep 1812 Not Recorded by HMS Electra Int: 04 Sep 1812 Dis: 03 Nov 1812.
    Schooner. Received from HMS Electra. To the United States of America.

Homer, John   Prisoner 38. Rank: Seaman, from: Elizabeth of Yarmouth, Not Recorded.
    Cap: 01 Aug 1812 Not Recorded by Not Recorded Int: 01 Aug 1812 Dis: 31 Aug 1812.
    Schooner. Received from HMS Hazard. To the United States per order Sir Thomas Duckworth on Board the Alert.

Hopkins, Elkenah   Prisoner 291. Rank: Seaman, from: Swallow, Not Recorded.
    Cap: 04 Sep 1812 Not Recorded by HMS Electra Int: 04 Sep 1812 Dis: 03 Nov 1812.
    Schooner. Received from HMS Electra. To the United States of America.

Houghton, Timothy   Prisoner 18. Rank: Seaman, from: Arab of Marblehead, Merchant Vessel.
    Cap: 22 Jul 1812 New York by Not Recorded Int: 22 Jul 1812 Dis: 31 Aug 1812.
    Ship. Received from HMS Avenger. To the Alert for a passage to the United States per order Sir Thomas Duckworth.

Howard, Thomas   Prisoner 11. Rank: Seaman, from: Lydia of New York, Merchant Vessel.
    Cap: 08 Jul 1812 New York by HMS Jason Int: 08 Jul 1812 Dis: 31 Aug 1812.
    Ship. Received from HMS Jason. To the Alert for a passage to the United States per order Sir Thomas Duckworth.

Howes, Isaac   Prisoner 33. Rank: Mate, from: Elizabeth of Yarmouth, Not Recorded.
    Cap: 01 Aug 1812 Not Recorded by Not Recorded Int: 01 Aug 1812 Dis: 31 Aug 1812.
    Schooner. Received from HMS Hazard. To the United States per order Sir Thomas Duckworth on Board the Alert.

Huntly, Augustus   Prisoner 19. Rank: Seaman, from: Arab of Marblehead, Merchant Vessel.
    Cap: 22 Jul 1812 New York by Not Recorded Int: 22 Jul 1812 Dis: 31 Aug 1812.
    Ship. Received from HMS Avenger. To the Alert for a passage to the United States per order Sir Thomas Duckworth.

Hurd, Seth   Prisoner 305. Rank: Seaman, from: William Davis, Not Recorded.
    Cap: 04 Sep 1812 Not Recorded by HMS Electra Int: 04 Sep 1812 Dis: 03 Nov 1812.
    Schooner. Received from HMS Electra. To the United States of America.

Hurl, Joseph   Prisoner 323. Rank: Seaman, from: Enterprise of New York, Not Recorded.
    Cap: 24 Sep 1812 Not Recorded by Not Recorded Int: 24 Sep 1812 Dis: 03 Nov 1812.
    Ship. Received from HMS Hazard. To the United States of America.

Hyde, Richard   Prisoner 20. Rank: Seaman, from: Arab of Marblehead, Merchant Vessel.
    Cap: 22 Jul 1812 New York by Not Recorded Int: 22 Jul 1812 Dis: 31 Aug 1812.
    Ship. Received from HMS Avenger. To the Alert for a passage to the United States per order Sir Thomas Duckworth.

Ingles, John   Prisoner 260. Rank: Seaman, from: Rockland of New York, Not Recorded.
    Cap: 31 Aug 1812 Not Recorded by Henry Privateer Int: 31 Aug 1812 Dis: 31 Aug 1812.
    Brig. Received from Henry Privateer. To the Alert for a passage to the United States per order Sir Thomas Duckworth.

Jackson, Daniel   Prisoner 211. Rank: Passenger, from: Castor, Not Recorded.
    Cap: 28 Aug 1812 Not Recorded by HMS Antelope Int: 28 Aug 1812 Dis: 31 Aug 1812.
    Ship. Received from HMS Antelope. To the Alert for a passage to the United States per order Sir Thomas Duckworth.

Jackson, Elisha   Prisoner 177. Rank: Passenger, from: Castor, Not Recorded.
    Cap: 28 Aug 1812 Not Recorded by HMS Antelope Int: 28 Aug 1812 Escaped: 30 Aug 1812.
    Ship. Received from HMS Antelope. Escaped.

Jackson, Elisha   Prisoner 271. Rank: Seaman, from: Castor, Not Recorded.
    Cap: 01 Sep 1812 Not Recorded by St. Johns Int: 01 Sep 1812 Dis: 03 Nov 1812.
    Ship. Received from Antelope. Received from prison ship. 177 (Old prisoner number, recaptured.) To the United States of America.

Jacobs, John Christopher   Prisoner 79. Rank: Seaman, from: Adriatic, Not Recorded.
    Cap: 01 Aug 1812 Not Recorded by Not Recorded Int: 01 Aug 1812 Dis: 31 Aug 1812.
    Ship. Received from HMS Avenger. To the Alert for a passage to the United States per order Sir Thomas Duckworth.

James, William   Prisoner 3. Rank: Seaman, from: Lydia of New York, Merchant Vessel.
    Cap: 08 Jul 1812 New York by HMS Jason Int: 08 Jul 1812 Dis: 31 Aug 1812.
    Ship. Received from HMS Jason. To the Alert for a passage to the United States per order Sir Thomas Duckworth.

Jarvis, John   Prisoner 288. Rank: Seaman, from: Pilgrim, Not Recorded.
    Cap: 04 Sep 1812 Not Recorded by HMS Electra Int: 04 Sep 1812 Dis: 03 Nov 1812.
    Schooner. Received from HMS Electra. To the United States of America.

American Prisoners of War Held at Newfoundland During the War of 1812

Jenkins, John   Prisoner 228. Rank: Seaman, from: W. P. Johnston, Not Recorded.
    Cap: 31 Aug 1812 Not Recorded by Not Recorded Int: 31 Aug 1812 Dis: 31 Aug 1812.
    Ship. Received from HMS Jason. To the Alert for a passage to the United States per order Sir Thomas Duckworth.

Jenkins, Thomas   Prisoner 340. Rank: Seaman, from: Sprightly, Not Recorded.
    Cap: 29 Sep 1812 Not Recorded by Not Recorded Int: 24 Sep 1812 Dis: 03 Nov 1812.
    Brig. Recaptured by Hazard. Received from HMS Hazard. To the United States of America. (Date of interment before date of capture.)

Jenny, Joseph L   Prisoner 159. Rank: Mate, from: Castor, Not Recorded.
    Cap: 28 Aug 1812 Not Recorded by HMS Antelope Int: 28 Aug 1812 Dis: 31 Aug 1812.
    Ship. Received from HMS Antelope. To the Alert for a passage to the United States per order Sir Thomas Duckworth.

Johnson, John   Prisoner 87. Rank: Seaman, from: Pocahunter of Boston, Not Recorded.
    Cap: 01 Aug 1812 Not Recorded by Not Recorded Int: 01 Aug 1812 Dis: 31 Aug 1812.
    Ship. Received from HMS Avenger. To the Alert for a passage to the United States per order Sir Thomas Duckworth.

Johnston, Charles   Prisoner 192. Rank: Passenger, from: Castor, Not Recorded.
    Cap: 28 Aug 1812 Not Recorded by HMS Antelope Int: 28 Aug 1812 Dis: 31 Aug 1812.
    Ship. Received from HMS Antelope. To the Alert for a passage to the United States per order Sir Thomas Duckworth.

Johnston, Ebar   Prisoner 81. Rank: Seaman, from: Adriatic, Not Recorded.
    Cap: 01 Aug 1812 Not Recorded by Not Recorded Int: 01 Aug 1812 Dis: 31 Aug 1812.
    Ship. Received from HMS Avenger. To the Alert for a passage to the United States per order Sir Thomas Duckworth.

Johnston, James   Prisoner 45. Rank: Seaman, from: Nancy of New York, Not Recorded.
    Cap: 01 Aug 1812 Not Recorded by Not Recorded Int: 01 Aug 1812 Dis: 31 Aug 1812.
    Brig. Received from HMS Hazard. To the United States per order Sir Thomas Duckworth on Board the Alert. James Johnston (1).

Johnston, James   Prisoner 72. Rank: Seaman, from: Triton of New Bedford, Not Recorded.
    Cap: 01 Aug 1812 Not Recorded by Not Recorded Int: 01 Aug 1812 Dis: 31 Aug 1812.
    Ship. Received from HMS Avenger. To the Alert for a passage to the United States per order Sir Thomas Duckworth. James Johnston (2).

Jones, Benjamin   Prisoner 331. Rank: Seaman, from: Susannah, Not Recorded.
    Cap: 24 Sep 1812 Not Recorded by HMS Hazard Int: 24 Sep 1812 Dis: 03 Nov 1812.
    Brig. Received from HMS Hazard. To the United States of America.

Jones, James   Prisoner 200. Rank: Passenger, from: Castor, Not Recorded.
    Cap: 28 Aug 1812 Not Recorded by HMS Antelope Int: 28 Aug 1812 Dis: 31 Aug 1812.
    Ship. Received from HMS Antelope. To the Alert for a passage to the United States per order Sir Thomas Duckworth. James Jones (1).

Jones, John   Prisoner 206. Rank: Passenger, from: Castor, Not Recorded.
    Cap: 28 Aug 1812 Not Recorded by HMS Antelope Int: 28 Aug 1812 Dis: 31 Aug 1812.
    Ship. Received from HMS Antelope. To the Alert for a passage to the United States per order Sir Thomas Duckworth. John Jones (2).

Jones, William   Prisoner 60. Rank: Seaman, from: Dolphin, Not Recorded.
    Cap: 01 Aug 1812 Not Recorded by Not Recorded Int: 01 Aug 1812 Dis: 31 Aug 1812.
    Brig. Received from HMS Hazard. (Captured by Hornet, recaptured by the Hazard.) To the Alert for a passage to the United States per order Sir Thomas Duckworth.

Kelly, Acy   Prisoner 34. Rank: Seaman, from: Elizabeth of Yarmouth, Not Recorded.
    Cap: 01 Aug 1812 Not Recorded by Not Recorded Int: 01 Aug 1812 Dis: 31 Aug 1812.
    Schooner. Received from HMS Hazard. To the United States per order Sir Thomas Duckworth on Board the Alert.

Kelly, Isaac   Prisoner 204. Rank: Passenger, from: Castor, Not Recorded.
    Cap: 28 Aug 1812 Not Recorded by HMS Antelope Int: 28 Aug 1812 Dis: 31 Aug 1812.
    Ship. Received from HMS Antelope. To the Alert for a passage to the United States per order Sir Thomas Duckworth.

Keys, Benjamin   Prisoner 353. Rank: Seaman, from: HMS Hazard, Not Recorded.
    Cap: 26 Oct 1812 Not Recorded by HMS Hazard Int: 26 Oct 1812 Dis: 03 Nov 1812.
    Citizen of America. Received from HMS Avenger. To the United States of America.

Lahy, Peter   Prisoner 326. Rank: Seaman, from: Enterprise of New York, Not Recorded.
    Cap: 24 Sep 1812 Not Recorded by HMS Hazard Int: 24 Sep 1812 Dis: 03 Nov 1812.
    Ship. Received from HMS Hazard. To the United States of America.

American Prisoners of War Held at Newfoundland During the War of 1812

Lambert, William   Prisoner 202. Rank: Passenger, from: Castor, Not Recorded.
    Cap: 28 Aug 1812 Not Recorded by HMS Antelope Int: 28 Aug 1812 Dis: 31 Aug 1812.
    Ship. Received from HMS Antelope. To the Alert for a passage to the United States per order Sir Thomas Duckworth.

Lamson, Joshua G   Prisoner 139. Rank: Passenger, from: Castor, Not Recorded.
    Cap: 18 Aug 1812 Not Recorded by HMS Antelope Int: 18 Aug 1812 Dis:
    Ship. Received from HMS Antelope. (Date of discharge not on roster.)

Larraley, William   Prisoner 201. Rank: Passenger, from: Castor, Not Recorded.
    Cap: 28 Aug 1812 Not Recorded by HMS Antelope Int: 28 Aug 1812 Dis: 31 Aug 1812.
    Ship. Received from HMS Antelope. To the Alert for a passage to the United States per order Sir Thomas Duckworth.

Las, Charles   Prisoner 83. Rank: Seaman, from: Adriatic, Not Recorded.
    Cap: 01 Aug 1812 Not Recorded by Not Recorded Int: 01 Aug 1812 Dis: 31 Aug 1812.
    Ship. Received from HMS Avenger. To the Alert for a passage to the United States per order Sir Thomas Duckworth.

Lathey, John   Prisoner 223. Rank: Seaman, from: Dolphin, Not Recorded.
    Cap: 28 Aug 1812 Not Recorded by HMS Antelope Int: 28 Aug 1812 Dis: 31 Aug 1812.
    Brig. Received from HMS Antelope. To the Alert for a passage to the United States per order Sir Thomas Duckworth.

Lawly, James   Prisoner 345. Rank: Seaman, from: Adaline, Not Recorded.
    Cap: 14 Oct 1812 Not Recorded by HMS Avenger Int: 14 Oct 1812 Dis:
    Brig. Received from HMS Avenger. (Date of discharge not on roster.)

Lawson, Henry   Prisoner 232. Rank: Seaman, from: W. P. Johnston, Not Recorded.
    Cap: 31 Aug 1812 Not Recorded by Not Recorded Int: 31 Aug 1812 Dis: 31 Aug 1812.
    Ship. Received from HMS Jason. To the Alert for a passage to the United States per order Sir Thomas Duckworth.

Lee, William   Prisoner 256. Rank: Seaman, from: Rockland of New York, Not Recorded.
    Cap: 31 Aug 1812 Not Recorded by Henry Privateer Int: 31 Aug 1812 Dis: 31 Aug 1812.
    Brig. Received from Henry Privateer. To the Alert for a passage to the United States per order Sir Thomas Duckworth.

Letham, Henry   Prisoner 153. Rank: Master, from: Castor, Not Recorded.
    Cap: 19 Aug 1812 Not Recorded by HMS Antelope Int: 19 Aug 1812 Dis:
    Ship. Received from HMS Antelope. (Date of discharge not on roster.)

Lewis, John   Prisoner 214. Rank: Seaman, from: Eliza, Not Recorded.
    Cap: 28 Aug 1812 Not Recorded by HMS Antelope Int: 28 Aug 1812 Dis: 31 Aug 1812.
    Brig. Received from HMS Antelope. To the Alert for a passage to the United States per order Sir Thomas Duckworth.

Lewis, Robenson   Prisoner 129. Rank: Master, from: Castor of New Bedford, Not Recorded.
    Cap: 08 Aug 1812 Not Recorded by Not Recorded Int: 06 Aug 1812 Dis: 31 Aug 1812.
    Ship. Received from HMS Antelope. To the Alert for a passage to the United States per order Sir Thomas Duckworth. (Date of interment before date of capture.)

Lewis, Thomas   Prisoner 163. Rank: Seaman, from: Castor, Not Recorded.
    Cap: 28 Aug 1812 Not Recorded by HMS Antelope Int: 28 Aug 1812 Dis: 31 Aug 1812.
    Ship. Received from HMS Antelope. To the Alert for a passage to the United States per order Sir Thomas Duckworth.

Lewis, William   Prisoner 92. Rank: Seaman, from: Gleaner, Not Recorded.
    Cap: 01 Aug 1812 Not Recorded by Not Recorded Int: 01 Aug 1812 Dis: 31 Aug 1812.
    Brig. Received from HMS Avenger. To the Alert for a passage to the United States per order Sir Thomas Duckworth.

Linnel, Uriah   Prisoner 297. Rank: Seaman, from: William Davis, Not Recorded.
    Cap: 04 Sep 1812 Not Recorded by HMS Electra Int: 04 Sep 1812 Dis: 03 Nov 1812.
    Schooner. Received from HMS Electra. To the United States of America.

Little, John   Prisoner 338. Rank: Seaman, from: Sprightly, Not Recorded.
    Cap: 29 Sep 1812 Not Recorded by Not Recorded Int: 24 Sep 1812 Dis: 03 Nov 1812.
    Brig. Recaptured by Hazard. Received from HMS Hazard. To the United States of America. (Date of interment before date of capture.)

Lovett, Pyam   Prisoner 117. Rank: Passenger, from: Pocahunter of Boston, Not Recorded.
    Cap: 03 Aug 1812 Not Recorded by Not Recorded Int: 03 Aug 1812 Dis:
    Ship. (Date of discharge not on roster.)

American Prisoners of War Held at Newfoundland During the War of 1812

Low, Frederick   Prisoner 105. Rank: Mate, from: Pocahunter of Boston, Not Recorded.
    Cap: 02 Aug 1812 Not Recorded by Not Recorded Int: 02 Aug 1812 Dis: 31 Aug 1812.
    Received from HMS Avenger. To the Alert for a passage to the United States per order Sir Thomas Duckworth.

Lowe, James   Prisoner 181. Rank: Passenger, from: Castor, Not Recorded.
    Cap: 28 Aug 1812 Not Recorded by HMS Antelope Int: 28 Aug 1812 Dis: 31 Aug 1812.
    Ship. Received from HMS Antelope. To the Alert for a passage to the United States per order Sir Thomas Duckworth.

Malson, Thomas   Prisoner 15. Rank: Seaman, from: Polafox of Boston, Merchant Vessel.
    Cap: 21 Jul 1812 New York by Not Recorded Int: 21 Jul 1812 Dis: 31 Aug 1812.
    Brig. Received from HMS Jason. To the Alert for a passage to the United States per order Sir Thomas Duckworth.

Marshall, James   Prisoner 90. Rank: Seaman, from: Pocahunter of Boston, Not Recorded.
    Cap: 01 Aug 1812 Not Recorded by Not Recorded Int: 01 Aug 1812 Dis: 31 Aug 1812.
    Ship. Received from HMS Avenger. To the Alert for a passage to the United States per order Sir Thomas Duckworth.

Martin, Alexander   Prisoner 191. Rank: Passenger, from: Castor, Not Recorded.
    Cap: 28 Aug 1812 Not Recorded by HMS Antelope Int: 28 Aug 1812 Dis: 31 Aug 1812.
    Ship. Received from HMS Antelope. To the Alert for a passage to the United States per order Sir Thomas Duckworth.

Mason, George   Prisoner 174. Rank: Passenger, from: Castor, Not Recorded.
    Cap: 28 Aug 1812 Not Recorded by HMS Antelope Int: 28 Aug 1812 Escaped: 30 Aug 1812.
    Ship. Received from HMS Antelope. Escaped.

Mason, George   Prisoner 270. Rank: Seaman, from: Castor, Not Recorded.
    Cap: 01 Sep 1812 Not Recorded by St. Johns Int: 01 Sep 1812 Dis: 03 Nov 1812.
    Ship. Received from Antelope. Received from prison ship. 174 (Old prisoner number, recaptured.) To the United States of America.

Massey, William   Prisoner 42. Rank: Seaman, from: Nancy of New York, Not Recorded.
    Cap: 01 Aug 1812 Not Recorded by Not Recorded Int: 01 Aug 1812 Dis: 31 Aug 1812.
    Brig. Received from HMS Hazard. To the United States per order Sir Thomas Duckworth on Board the Alert.

Mathews, George   Prisoner 21. Rank: Seaman, from: Polafox of Philadelphia, Not Recorded.
    Cap: 22 Jul 1812 Not Recorded by Not Recorded Int: 22 Jul 1812 Dis: 31 Aug 1812.
    Brig. Received from HMS Jason. To the Alert for a passage to the United States per order Sir Thomas Duckworth.

Matthews, Daniel   Prisoner 224. Rank: Acting Mate, from: Dolphin, Not Recorded.
    Cap: 28 Aug 1812 Not Recorded by HMS Antelope Int: 28 Aug 1812 Dis: 31 Aug 1812.
    Brig. Received from HMS Antelope. To the Alert for a passage to the United States per order Sir Thomas Duckworth.

Matthews, Henry   Prisoner 188. Rank: Passenger, from: Castor, Not Recorded.
    Cap: 28 Aug 1812 Not Recorded by HMS Antelope Int: 28 Aug 1812 Dis: 31 Aug 1812.
    Ship. Received from HMS Antelope. To the Alert for a passage to the United States per order Sir Thomas Duckworth.

Mawrey, Lewis Alexis   Prisoner 149. Rank: Passenger, from: Castor, Not Recorded.
    Cap: 19 Aug 1812 Not Recorded by HMS Antelope Int: 19 Aug 1812 Dis:
    Ship. Received from HMS Antelope. (Date of discharge not on roster.)

Mayo, Henan   Prisoner 302. Rank: Seaman, from: William Davis, Not Recorded.
    Cap: 04 Sep 1812 Not Recorded by HMS Electra Int: 04 Sep 1812 Dis: 03 Nov 1812.
    Schooner. Received from HMS Electra. To the United States of America.

Mayo, Samuel   Prisoner 301. Rank: Seaman, from: William Davis, Not Recorded.
    Cap: 04 Sep 1812 Not Recorded by HMS Electra Int: 04 Sep 1812 Dis: 03 Nov 1812.
    Schooner. Received from HMS Electra. To the United States of America.

Mayo, Theodore   Prisoner 284. Rank: Seaman, from: Pilgrim, Not Recorded.
    Cap: 04 Sep 1812 Not Recorded by HMS Electra Int: 04 Sep 1812 Dis: 03 Nov 1812.
    Schooner. Received from HMS Electra. To the United States of America.

McColl, Charles   Prisoner 101. Rank: Passenger, from: Arab of Marblehead, Not Recorded.
    Cap: 02 Aug 1812 Not Recorded by Not Recorded Int: 02 Aug 1812 Dis:
    Received from HMS Avenger. (Date of discharge not on roster.)

American Prisoners of War Held at Newfoundland During the War of 1812

McConnel, Joseph   Prisoner 210. Rank: Passenger, from: Castor, Not Recorded.
    Cap: 28 Aug 1812 Not Recorded by HMS Antelope Int: 28 Aug 1812 Dis: 31 Aug 1812.
    Ship. Received from HMS Antelope. To the Alert for a passage to the United States per order Sir Thomas Duckworth.

McKie, Richard   Prisoner 251. Rank: Seaman, from: Fairplay of Alexandia, Not Recorded.
    Cap: 31 Aug 1812 Not Recorded by Henry Privateer Int: 31 Aug 1812 Dis: 31 Aug 1812.
    Schooner. Received from Henry Privateer. To the Alert for a passage to the United States per order Sir Thomas Duckworth.

McLennan, John   Prisoner 213. Rank: Mate, from: Eliza, Not Recorded.
    Cap: 28 Aug 1812 Not Recorded by HMS Antelope Int: 28 Aug 1812 Dis: 31 Aug 1812.
    Brig. Received from HMS Antelope. To the Alert for a passage to the United States per order Sir Thomas Duckworth.

Middleton, Charles   Prisoner 244. Rank: Seaman, from: William Tell, Not Recorded.
    Cap: 31 Aug 1812 Not Recorded by Not Recorded Int: 31 Aug 1812 Dis: 31 Aug 1812.
    Ship. Received from HMS Jason. To the Alert for a passage to the United States per order Sir Thomas Duckworth.

Millet, John   Prisoner 262. Rank: Seaman, from: Rockland of New York, Not Recorded.
    Cap: 31 Aug 1812 Not Recorded by Henry Privateer Int: 31 Aug 1812 Dis: 31 Aug 1812.
    Brig. Received from Henry Privateer. To the Alert for a passage to the United States per order Sir Thomas Duckworth.

Mitchell, James   Prisoner 241. Rank: Seaman, from: William Tell, Not Recorded.
    Cap: 31 Aug 1812 Not Recorded by Not Recorded Int: 31 Aug 1812 Dis: 31 Aug 1812.
    Ship. Received from HMS Jason. To the Alert for a passage to the United States per order Sir Thomas Duckworth.

Moore, John   Prisoner 84. Rank: Seaman, from: Adriatic, Not Recorded.
    Cap: 01 Aug 1812 Not Recorded by Not Recorded Int: 01 Aug 1812 Dis: 31 Aug 1812.
    Ship. Received from HMS Avenger. To the Alert for a passage to the United States per order Sir Thomas Duckworth.

Moore, Thomas   Prisoner 333. Rank: Seaman, from: Susannah, Not Recorded.
    Cap: 24 Sep 1812 Not Recorded by HMS Hazard Int: 24 Sep 1812 Dis:
    Brig. Received from HMS Hazard. (Date of discharge not on roster.)

Morgan, Alexander   Prisoner 1. Rank: Master, from: Lydia of New York, Merchant Vessel.
    Cap: 08 Jul 1812 New York by HMS Jason Int: 08 Jul 1812 Dis: 31 Aug 1912.
    Ship. Received from HMS Jason. To the Alert for a passage to the United States per order Sir Thomas Duckworth.

Morse, Abraham   Prisoner 311. Rank: Seaman, from: William Davis, Not Recorded.
    Cap: 04 Sep 1812 Not Recorded by HMS Electra Int: 04 Sep 1812 Dis: 03 Nov 1812.
    Schooner. Received from HMS Electra. To the United States of America.

Morse, George C   Prisoner 312. Rank: Seaman, from: Essex, Not Recorded.
    Cap: 04 Sep 1812 Not Recorded by HMS Electra Int: 04 Sep 1812 Dis: 03 Nov 1812.
    Schooner. Received from HMS Electra. To the United States of America.

Murrel, Benjamin   Prisoner 322. Rank: Seaman, from: Enterprise of New York, Not Recorded.
    Cap: 24 Sep 1812 Not Recorded by Not Recorded Int: 24 Sep 1812 Dis: 03 Nov 1812.
    Ship. Received from HMS Hazard. To the United States of America.

Murry, George   Prisoner 354. Rank: Seaman, from: HMS Hazard, Not Recorded.
    Cap: 26 Oct 1812 Not Recorded by HMS Hazard Int: 26 Oct 1812 Dis: 03 Nov 1812.
    Citizen of America. Received from HMS Avenger. To the United States of America.

Myder, Thomas   Prisoner 172. Rank: Passenger, from: Castor, Not Recorded.
    Cap: 28 Aug 1812 Not Recorded by HMS Antelope Int: 28 Aug 1812 Dis: 31 Aug 1812.
    Ship. Received from HMS Antelope. To the Alert for a passage to the United States per order Sir Thomas Duckworth.

Myers, David   Prisoner 218. Rank: Seaman, from: Dolphin, Not Recorded.
    Cap: 28 Aug 1812 Not Recorded by HMS Antelope Int: 28 Aug 1812 Dis: 31 Aug 1812.
    Brig. Received from HMS Antelope. To the Alert for a passage to the United States per order Sir Thomas Duckworth.

Nail, Robert   Prisoner 328. Rank: Seaman, from: Susannah, Not Recorded.
    Cap: 24 Sep 1812 Not Recorded by HMS Hazard Int: 24 Sep 1812 Dis: 03 Nov 1812.
    Brig. Received from HMS Hazard. To the United States of America.

Newcomb, John   Prisoner 35. Rank: Seaman, from: Elizabeth of Yarmouth, Not Recorded.
    Cap: 01 Aug 1812 Not Recorded by Not Recorded Int: 01 Aug 1812 Dis: 31 Aug 1812.
    Schooner. Received from HMS Hazard. To the United States per order Sir Thomas Duckworth on Board the Alert.

American Prisoners of War Held at Newfoundland During the War of 1812

Nicholson, Julby   Prisoner 133. Rank: Seaman, from: Polly of Chatham, Not Recorded.
    Cap: 15 Aug 1812 Not Recorded by Not Recorded Int: 15 Aug 1812 Dis: 31 Aug 1812.
    Schooner. Received from HMS Electra. To the Alert for a passage to the United States per order Sir Thomas Duckworth.

Nicholson, Silas   Prisoner 136. Rank: Master, from: Polly, Not Recorded.
    Cap: 18 Aug 1812 Not Recorded by Not Recorded Int: 18 Aug 1812 Dis:
    Schooner. Received from Electra. (Date of discharge not on roster.)

Norton, James   Prisoner 197. Rank: Passenger, from: Castor, Not Recorded.
    Cap: 28 Aug 1812 Not Recorded by HMS Antelope Int: 28 Aug 1812 Dis: 31 Aug 1812.
    Ship. Received from HMS Antelope. To the Alert for a passage to the United States per order Sir Thomas Duckworth.

Oxley, John   Prisoner 40. Rank: Seaman, from: Nancy of New York, Not Recorded.
    Cap: 01 Aug 1812 Not Recorded by Not Recorded Int: 01 Aug 1812 Dis: 31 Aug 1812.
    Brig. Received from HMS Hazard. To the United States per order Sir Thomas Duckworth on Board the Alert.

Palmer, Frances   Prisoner 319. Rank: Seaman, from: Enterprise of New York, Not Recorded.
    Cap: 24 Sep 1812 Not Recorded by Not Recorded Int: 24 Sep 1812 Dis: 03 Nov 1812.
    Ship. Received from HMS Hazard. To the United States of America.

Palmer, Robert   Prisoner 318. Rank: Seaman, from: Enterprise of New York, Not Recorded.
    Cap: 24 Sep 1812 Not Recorded by Not Recorded Int: 24 Sep 1812 Dis: 03 Nov 1812.
    Ship. Received from HMS Hazard. To the United States of America.

Palyery, John   Prisoner 324. Rank: Seaman, from: Enterprise of New York, Not Recorded.
    Cap: 24 Sep 1812 Not Recorded by Not Recorded Int: 24 Sep 1812 Dis: 03 Nov 1812.
    Ship. Received from HMS Hazard. To the United States of America.

Parks, Guy   Prisoner 198. Rank: Passenger, from: Castor, Not Recorded.
    Cap: 28 Aug 1812 Not Recorded by HMS Antelope Int: 28 Aug 1812 Dis: 31 Aug 1812.
    Ship. Received from HMS Antelope. To the Alert for a passage to the United States per order Sir Thomas Duckworth.

Parnell, Benjamin   Prisoner 130. Rank: Seaman, from: Perseverance, Not Recorded.
    Cap: 10 Aug 1812 Not Recorded by Not Recorded Int: 10 Aug 1812 Dis: 31 Aug 1812.
    Brig. Received from HMS Atalante. To the Alert for a passage to the United States per order Sir Thomas Duckworth.

Pass, Thomas   Prisoner 61. Rank: Seaman, from: Dolphin, Not Recorded.
    Cap: 01 Aug 1812 Not Recorded by Not Recorded Int: 01 Aug 1812 Dis: 01 Aug 1812.
    Brig. Received from HMS Hazard. (Captured by Hornet, recaptured by the Hazard.) To the Alert for a passage to the United States per order Sir Thomas Duckworth.

Pattengale, Daniel   Prisoner 279. Rank: Seaman, from: Fame, Not Recorded.
    Cap: 04 Sep 1812 Not Recorded by HMS Electra Int: 04 Sep 1812 Dis: 03 Nov 1812.
    Sloop. Received from HMS Electra. To the United States of America.

Pearce, George   Prisoner 121. Rank: Masters Mate, from: Essex, Not Recorded.
    Cap: 06 Aug 1812 Not Recorded by HMS Atalante & HMS Pomone Int: 06 Aug 1812 Dis: 31 Aug 1812. Frigate. Taken in Brig Leander. Recaptured by Atalante. Received from HMS Avenger. To the Alert for a passage to the United States.

Peckham, William   Prisoner 23. Rank: Master, from: 3 Friends New Bedford, Not Recorded.
    Cap: 28 Jul 1812 Not Recorded by Not Recorded Int: 28 Jul 1812 Dis: 31 Aug 1812.
    Schooner. Received from HMS Jason. To the Alert for a passage to the United States per order Sir Thomas Duckworth.

Peerce, John   Prisoner 221. Rank: Seaman, from: Dolphin, Not Recorded.
    Cap: 28 Aug 1812 Not Recorded by HMS Antelope Int: 28 Aug 1812 Dis: 31 Aug 1812.
    Brig. Received from HMS Antelope. To the Alert for a passage to the United States per order Sir Thomas Duckworth.

Pepper, Daniel   Prisoner 294. Rank: Seaman, from: Swallow, Not Recorded.
    Cap: 04 Sep 1812 Not Recorded by HMS Electra Int: 04 Sep 1812 Dis: 03 Nov 1812.
    Schooner. Received from HMS Electra. To the United States of America.

Perry, Joseph   Prisoner 336. Rank: Seaman, from: Not Recorded, Not Recorded.
    Cap: 24 Sep 1812 St. Johns, Newfoundland by Not Recorded Int: 24 Sep 1812 Dis: 03 Nov 1812.
    Gave himself up as an American. Received from HMS Hazard. To the United States of America.

Peters, John   Prisoner 106. Rank: Seaman, from: Pocahunter of Boston, Not Recorded.
    Cap: 02 Aug 1812 Not Recorded by Not Recorded Int: 02 Aug 1812 Dis: 31 Aug 1812.
    Received from HMS Avenger. To the Alert for a passage to the United States per order Sir Thomas Duckworth.

American Prisoners of War Held at Newfoundland During the War of 1812

Phillips, William   Prisoner 56. Rank: Seaman, from: Orient, Not Recorded.
    Cap: 01 Aug 1812 Not Recorded by Not Recorded Int: 01 Aug 1812 Dis: 31 Aug 1812.
    Ship. Received from HMS Hazard. To the Alert for a passage to the United States per order Sir Thomas Duckworth.

Pinder, William   Prisoner 329. Rank: Seaman, from: Susannah, Not Recorded.
    Cap: 24 Sep 1812 Not Recorded by HMS Hazard Int: 24 Sep 1812 Dis: 03 Nov 1812.
    Brig. Received from HMS Hazard. To the United States of America.

Potenger, Richard   Prisoner 63. Rank: Seaman, from: Dolphin, Not Recorded.
    Cap: 01 Aug 1812 Not Recorded by Not Recorded Int: 01 Aug 1812 Dis: 31 Aug 1812.
    Brig. Received from HMS Hazard. (Captured by Hornet, recaptured by the Hazard.) To the Alert for a passage to the United States per order Sir Thomas Duckworth.

Powell, Thomas   Prisoner 330. Rank: Seaman, from: Susannah, Not Recorded.
    Cap: 24 Sep 1812 Not Recorded by HMS Hazard Int: 24 Sep 1812 Dis: 03 Nov 1812.
    Brig. Received from HMS Hazard. To the United States of America.

Pray, Joshua N   Prisoner 140. Rank: Master, from: Rockland, Not Recorded.
    Cap: 18 Aug 1812 Not Recorded by Not Recorded Int: 18 Aug 1812 Dis: 31 Aug 1812.
    Brig. Received from Fly Privateer. To the Alert for a passage to the United States.

Pritchard, Paul   Prisoner 141. Rank: Passenger, from: Castor, Not Recorded.
    Cap: 18 Aug 1812 Not Recorded by Antelope Int: 18 Aug 1812 Dis: .
    Ship. Received from HMS Antelope. (Date of discharge not on roster.)

Pullen, William F   Prisoner 75. Rank: Seaman, from: Triton of New Bedford, Not Recorded.
    Cap: 01 Aug 1812 Not Recorded by Not Recorded Int: 01 Aug 1812 Dis: 31 Aug 1812.
    Ship. Received from HMS Avenger. To the Alert for a passage to the United States per order Sir Thomas Duckworth. (Middle name not legible.)

Purse, John   Prisoner 125. Rank: Seaman, from: Cyrus, Not Recorded.
    Cap: 06 Aug 1812 Not Recorded by Not Recorded Int: 06 Aug 1812 Dis: 31 Aug 1812.
    Received from Jason. To the Alert for a passage to the United States per order Sir Thomas Duckworth.

Rando, Francis   Prisoner 93. Rank: Seaman, from: Gleaner, Not Recorded.
    Cap: 01 Aug 1812 Not Recorded by Not Recorded Int: 01 Aug 1812 Dis: 31 Aug 1812.
    Brig. Received from HMS Avenger. To the Alert for a passage to the United States per order Sir Thomas Duckworth.

Reder, Arnold   Prisoner 247. Rank: Mate, from: Fairplay of Alexandia, Not Recorded.
    Cap: 31 Aug 1812 Not Recorded by Henry Privateer Int: 31 Aug 1812 Dis: 31 Aug 1812.
    Schooner. Received from Henry Privateer. To the Alert for a passage to the United States per order Sir Thomas Duckworth.

Refiner, Henry   Prisoner 195. Rank: Passenger, from: Castor, Not Recorded.
    Cap: 28 Aug 1812 Not Recorded by HMS Antelope Int: 28 Aug 1812 Dis: 31 Aug 1812.
    Ship. Received from HMS Antelope. To the Alert for a passage to the United States per order Sir Thomas Duckworth.

Richardson, John   Prisoner 226. Rank: Seaman, from: W. P. Johnston, Not Recorded.
    Cap: 31 Aug 1812 Not Recorded by Not Recorded Int: 31 Aug 1812 Dis: 31 Aug 1812.
    Ship. Received from HMS Jason. To the Alert for a passage to the United States per order Sir Thomas Duckworth.

Richardson, William   Prisoner 55. Rank: Seaman, from: Orient, Not Recorded.
    Cap: 01 Aug 1812 Not Recorded by Not Recorded Int: 01 Aug 1812 Dis: 31 Aug 1812.
    Ship. Received from HMS Hazard. To the Alert for a passage to the United States per order Sir Thomas Duckworth.

Ring, Bartholomew   Prisoner 30. Rank: Master, from: Cyrus of Gloucester, Not Recorded.
    Cap: 28 Jul 1812 Not Recorded by Not Recorded Int: 28 Jul 1812 Dis: 31 Aug 1812.
    Brig. Received from Jason. To the United States per order Sir Thomas Duckworth on Board the Alert.

Roberts, Joseph   Prisoner 86. Rank: Seaman, from: Pocahunter of Boston, Not Recorded.
    Cap: 01 Aug 1812 Not Recorded by Not Recorded Int: 01 Aug 1812 Dis: 31 Aug 1812.
    Ship. Received from HMS Avenger. To the Alert for a passage to the United States per order Sir Thomas Duckworth.

Robertson, John   Prisoner 168. Rank: Boy, from: Castor, Not Recorded.
    Cap: 28 Aug 1812 Not Recorded by HMS Antelope Int: 28 Aug 1812 Dis: 31 Aug 1812.
    Ship. Received from HMS Antelope. To the Alert for a passage to the United States per order Sir Thomas Duckworth.

Robinson, Antonia   Prisoner 160. Rank: Seaman, from: Castor, Not Recorded.
    Cap: 28 Aug 1812 Not Recorded by HMS Antelope Int: 28 Aug 1812 Dis: 31 Aug 1812.
    Ship. Received from HMS Antelope. To the Alert for a passage to the United States per order Sir Thomas Duckworth.

American Prisoners of War Held at Newfoundland During the War of 1812

Robinson, Ecy   Prisoner 95. Rank: Seaman, from: Gleaner, Not Recorded.
    Cap: 01 Aug 1812 Not Recorded by Not Recorded Int: 01 Aug 1812 Dis: 31 Aug 1812.
    Brig. Received from HMS Avenger. To the Alert for a passage to the United States per order Sir Thomas Duckworth.

Rogers, Asa   Prisoner 135. Rank: Master, from: William Davis, Not Recorded.
    Cap: 18 Aug 1812 Not Recorded by Not Recorded Int: 18 Aug 1812 Dis:
    Schooner. Received from Electra. (Date of discharge not on roster.)

Rogers, Elesa   Prisoner 309. Rank: Seaman, from: William Davis, Not Recorded.
    Cap: 04 Sep 1812 Not Recorded by HMS Electra Int: 04 Sep 1812 Dis: 03 Nov 1812.
    Schooner. Received from HMS Electra. To the United States of America.

Rogers, Ezekiel   Prisoner 310. Rank: Seaman, from: William Davis, Not Recorded.
    Cap: 04 Sep 1812 Not Recorded by HMS Electra Int: 04 Sep 1812 Dis: 03 Nov 1812.
    Schooner. Received from HMS Electra. To the United States of America.

Rogers, Moores   Prisoner 115. Rank: Master, from: Triton of New Bedford, Not Recorded.
    Cap: 03 Aug 1812 Not Recorded by Not Recorded Int: 03 Aug 1812 Dis: 31 Aug 1812.
    Ship. Received from HMS Avenger. To the Alert for a passage to the United States per order Sir Thomas Duckworth.

Rogers, Nathaniel   Prisoner 52. Rank: Seaman, from: Orient, Not Recorded.
    Cap: 01 Aug 1812 Not Recorded by Not Recorded Int: 01 Aug 1812 Dis: 31 Aug 1812.
    Ship. Received from HMS Hazard. To the Alert for a passage to the United States per order Sir Thomas Duckworth.

Rogers, Richard   Prisoner 304. Rank: Seaman, from: William Davis, Not Recorded.
    Cap: 04 Sep 1812 Not Recorded by HMS Electra Int: 04 Sep 1812 Dis: 03 Nov 1812.
    Schooner. Received from HMS Electra. To the United States of America.

Rogers, Uriah   Prisoner 308. Rank: Seaman, from: William Davis, Not Recorded.
    Cap: 04 Sep 1812 Not Recorded by HMS Electra Int: 04 Sep 1812 Dis: 03 Nov 1812.
    Schooner. Received from HMS Electra. To the United States of America.

Roper, William   Prisoner 108. Rank: Mate, from: Adriatic of New York, Not Recorded.
    Cap: 02 Aug 1812 Not Recorded by Not Recorded Int: 02 Aug 1812 Dis: 31 Aug 1812.
    Ship. Received from HMS Avenger. To the Alert for a passage to the United States per order Sir Thomas Duckworth.

Rosseau, Pievie   Prisoner 147. Rank: Passenger, from: Castor, Not Recorded.
    Cap: 19 Aug 1812 Not Recorded by HMS Antelope Int: 19 Aug 1812 Dis:
    Ship. Received from HMS Antelope. (Date of discharge not on roster.)

Row, Abraham   Prisoner 17. Rank: Seaman, from: Arab of Marblehead, Merchant Vessel.
    Cap: 22 Jul 1812 New York by Not Recorded Int: 22 Jul 1812 Dis: 31 Aug 1812.
    Ship. Received from HMS Avenger. To the Alert for a passage to the United States per order Sir Thomas Duckworth.

Russel, William   Prisoner 171. Rank: Passenger, from: Castor, Not Recorded.
    Cap: 28 Aug 1812 Not Recorded by HMS Antelope Int: 28 Aug 1812 Escaped: 30 Aug 1812.
    Ship. Received from HMS Antelope. Escaped.

Russel, William   Prisoner 359. Rank: Seaman, from: HMS Hazard, Not Recorded.
    Cap: 09 Nov 1812 Not Recorded by Avenger Int: 09 Nov 1812 Dis:
    Citizen of America. Received from HMS Avenger. (Date of discharge not on roster.)

Russell, William   Prisoner 269. Rank: Seaman, from: Castor, Not Recorded.
    Cap: 01 Sep 1812 Not Recorded by St. Johns Int: 01 Sep 1812 Dis:
    Ship. Received from Antelope. Received from prison ship. 171 (Old prisoner number, recaptured. Date of discharge not on roster.)

Shepard, James   Prisoner 103. Rank: Seaman, from: Triton of New Bedford, Not Recorded.
    Cap: 02 Aug 1812 Not Recorded by Not Recorded Int: 02 Aug 1812 Dis: 31 Aug 1812.
    Ship. Received from HMS Avenger. To the Alert for a passage to the United States per order Sir Thomas Duckworth.

Slakenn, William   Prisoner 252. Rank: Seaman, from: Rockland of New York, Not Recorded.
    Cap: 31 Aug 1812 Not Recorded by Henry Privateer Int: 31 Aug 1812 Dis: 31 Aug 1812.
    Brig. Received from Henry Privateer. To the Alert for a passage to the United States per order Sir Thomas Duckworth.

Smith, Jacob   Prisoner 332. Rank: Seaman, from: Susannah, Not Recorded.
    Cap: 24 Sep 1812 Not Recorded by HMS Hazard Int: 24 Sep 1812 Dis: 03 Nov 1812.
    Brig. Received from HMS Hazard. To the United States of America.

American Prisoners of War Held at Newfoundland During the War of 1812

Smith, John   Prisoner 249. Rank: Mate, from: Fairplay of Alexandia, Not Recorded.
    Cap: 31 Aug 1812 Not Recorded by Henry Privateer Int: 31 Aug 1812 Dis: 31 Aug 1812.
    Schooner. Received from Henry Privateer. To the Alert for a passage to the United States per order Sir Thomas Duckworth.

Smith, John   Prisoner 307. Rank: Seaman, from: William Davis, Not Recorded.
    Cap: 04 Sep 1812 Not Recorded by HMS Electra Int: 04 Sep 1812 Dis: 03 Nov 1812.
    Schooner. Received from HMS Electra. To the United States of America.

Smith, John   Prisoner 50. Rank: Seaman, from: Orient, Not Recorded.
    Cap: 01 Aug 1812 Not Recorded by Not Recorded Int: 01 Aug 1812 Dis: 31 Aug 1812.
    Ship. Received from HMS Hazard. To the Alert for a passage to the United States per order Sir Thomas Duckworth.

Smith, Reuben   Prisoner 306. Rank: Seaman, from: William Davis, Not Recorded.
    Cap: 04 Sep 1812 Not Recorded by HMS Electra Int: 04 Sep 1812 Dis: 03 Nov 1812.
    Schooner. Received from HMS Electra. To the United States of America.

Smith, William   Prisoner 107. Rank: Seaman, from: Pocahunter of Boston, Not Recorded.
    Cap: 02 Aug 1812 Not Recorded by Not Recorded Int: 02 Aug 1812 Dis: 31 Aug 1812.
    Received from HMS Avenger. To the Alert for a passage to the United States per order Sir Thomas Duckworth.

Smith, Junior, Daniel   Prisoner 26. Rank: Supercargo, from: Union of Philadelphia, Not Recorded.
    Cap: 28 Jul 1812 Not Recorded by Not Recorded Int: 28 Jul 1812 Dis: 31 Aug 1812.
    Brig. Received from HMS Jason. To the Alert for a passage to the United States per order.

Snow, Herman   Prisoner 293. Rank: Seaman, from: Swallow, Not Recorded.
    Cap: 04 Sep 1812 Not Recorded by HMS Electra Int: 04 Sep 1812 Dis: 03 Nov 1812.
    Schooner. Received from HMS Electra. To the United States of America.

Snow, Josiah H   Prisoner 292. Rank: Seaman, from: Swallow, Not Recorded.
    Cap: 04 Sep 1812 Not Recorded by HMS Electra Int: 04 Sep 1812 Dis: 03 Nov 1812.
    Schooner. Received from HMS Electra. To the United States of America.

Sparks, Robert   Prisoner 73. Rank: Seaman, from: Triton of New Bedford, Not Recorded.
    Cap: 01 Aug 1812 Not Recorded by Not Recorded Int: 01 Aug 1812 Dis: 31 Aug 1812.
    Ship. Received from HMS Avenger. To the Alert for a passage to the United States per order Sir Thomas Duckworth.

Sparrow, Abner H   Prisoner 287. Rank: Seaman, from: Pilgrim, Not Recorded.
    Cap: 04 Sep 1812 Not Recorded by HMS Electra Int: 04 Sep 1812 Dis: 03 Nov 1812.
    Schooner. Received from HMS Electra. To the United States of America.

Sparrow, Jesse   Prisoner 144. Rank: Seaman, from: Swallow, Not Recorded.
    Cap: 18 Aug 1812 Not Recorded by Not Recorded Int: 18 Aug 1812 Dis: 31 Aug 1812.
    Schooner. Received from Electra. To the Alert for a passage to the United States per order Sir Thomas Duckworth.

Sparrow, John   Prisoner 282. Rank: Seaman, from: Pilgrim, Not Recorded.
    Cap: 04 Sep 1812 Not Recorded by HMS Electra Int: 04 Sep 1812 Dis: 03 Nov 1812.
    Schooner. Received from HMS Electra. To the United States of America.

Sparrow, Samuel   Prisoner 283. Rank: Seaman, from: Pilgrim, Not Recorded.
    Cap: 04 Sep 1812 Not Recorded by HMS Electra Int: 04 Sep 1812 Dis: 03 Nov 1812.
    Schooner. Received from HMS Electra. To the United States of America.

Sparrow, Thomas   Prisoner 286. Rank: Seaman, from: Pilgrim, Not Recorded.
    Cap: 04 Sep 1812 Not Recorded by HMS Electra Int: 04 Sep 1812 Dis: 03 Nov 1812.
    Schooner. Received from HMS Electra. To the United States of America.

Spraggs, Samuel S   Prisoner 216. Rank: Seaman, from: Eliza, Not Recorded.
    Cap: 28 Aug 1812 Not Recorded by HMS Antelope Int: 28 Aug 1812 Dis: 31 Aug 1812.
    Brig. Received from HMS Antelope. To the Alert for a passage to the United States per order Sir Thomas Duckworth.

Stephens, John   Prisoner 263. Rank: Seaman, from: Rockland of New York, Not Recorded.
    Cap: 31 Aug 1812 Not Recorded by Henry Privateer Int: 31 Aug 1812 Dis: 31 Aug 1812.
    Brig. Received from Henry Privateer. To the Alert for a passage to the United States per order Sir Thomas Duckworth.

Sullevan, Josia   Prisoner 98. Rank: Seaman, from: Gleaner, Not Recorded.
    Cap: 01 Aug 1812 Not Recorded by Not Recorded Int: 01 Aug 1812 Dis: 31 Aug 1812.
    Brig. Received from HMS Avenger. To the Alert for a passage to the United States per order Sir Thomas Duckworth.

American Prisoners of War Held at Newfoundland During the War of 1812

Swan, Richard   Prisoner 57. Rank: Seaman, from: Dolphin, Not Recorded.
    Cap: 01 Aug 1812 Not Recorded by Not Recorded Int: 01 Aug 1812 Dis: 31 Aug 1812.
    Brig. Received from HMS Hazard. (Captured by Hornet, recaptured by the Hazard.) To the Alert for a passage to the United States per order Sir Thomas Duckworth.

Sweitman, Samuel   Prisoner 4. Rank: Seaman, from: Lydia of New York, Merchant Vessel.
    Cap: 08 Jul 1812 New York by HMS Jason Int: 08 Jul 1812 Dis: 31 Aug 1812.
    Ship. Received from HMS Jason. To the Alert for a passage to the United States per order Sir Thomas Duckworth.

Swinton, Thomas   Prisoner 253. Rank: Seaman, from: Rockland of New York, Not Recorded.
    Cap: 31 Aug 1812 Not Recorded by Henry Privateer Int: 31 Aug 1812 Dis: 31 Aug 1812.
    Brig. Received from Henry Privateer. To the Alert for a passage to the United States per order Sir Thomas Duckworth.

Taylor, John   Prisoner 265. Rank: Seaman, from: Rockland of New York, Not Recorded.
    Cap: 31 Aug 1812 Not Recorded by Henry Privateer Int: 31 Aug 1812 Dis: 31 Aug 1812.
    Brig. Received from Henry Privateer. To the Alert for a passage to the United States per order Sir Thomas Duckworth.

Taylor, John   Prisoner 285. Rank: Seaman, from: Pilgrim, Not Recorded.
    Cap: 04 Sep 1812 Not Recorded by HMS Electra Int: 04 Sep 1812 Dis: 03 Nov 1812.
    Schooner. Received from HMS Electra. To the United States of America.

Thacter, Loavette   Prisoner 91. Rank: Mate, from: Pocahunter of Boston, Not Recorded.
    Cap: 01 Aug 1812 Not Recorded by Not Recorded Int: 01 Aug 1812 Dis: 31 Aug 1812.
    Ship. Received from HMS Avenger. To the Alert for a passage to the United States per order Sir Thomas Duckworth.

Thompson, John   Prisoner 321. Rank: Seaman, from: Enterprise of New York, Not Recorded.
    Cap: 24 Sep 1812 Not Recorded by Not Recorded Int: 24 Sep 1812 Dis:
    Ship. Received from HMS Hazard. (Date of discharge not on roster.)

Thompson, John   Prisoner 361. Rank: Seaman, from: HMS Hazard, Not Recorded.
    Cap: 21 Nov 1812 Not Recorded by Comet Int: 21 Nov 1812 Dis:
    Citizen of America. Received from HMS Avenger. (Date of discharge not on roster.)

Titus, Henry   Prisoner 65. Rank: Seanan, from: Dolphin, Not Recorded.
    Cap: 01 Aug 1812 Not Recorded by Not Recorded Int: 01 Aug 1812 Dis: 31 Aug 1812.
    Brig. Received from HMS Hazard. (Captured by Hornet, recaptured by the Hazard.) To the Alert for a passage to the United States per order Sir Thomas Duckworth.

Tollinsby, William   Prisoner 266. Rank: Master, from: W. P. Johnston, Not Recorded.
    Cap: 31 Aug 1812 Not Recorded by Not Recorded Int: 31 Aug 1812 Dis: 31 Aug 1812.
    Ship. Received from HMS Jason. To the Alert for a passage to the United States per order Sir Thomas Duckworth.

Treacy, James   Prisoner 145. Rank: Mate, from: Rockland, Not Recorded.
    Cap: 18 Aug 1812 Not Recorded by Not Recorded Int: 18 Aug 1812 Dis: 31 Aug 1812.
    Brig. Received from Fly Privateer. To the Alert for a passage to the United States per order Sir Thomas Duckworth.

Tredwell, Benjamin   Prisoner 119. Rank: Master, from: Adriatic of New York, Not Recorded.
    Cap: 03 Aug 1812 Not Recorded by Not Recorded Int: 03 Aug 1812 Dis: 31 Aug 1812.
    Ship. Received from HMS Avenger. To the Alert for a passage to the United States per order Sir Thomas Duckworth.

Trip, Odis   Prisoner 74. Rank: Seaman, from: Triton of New Bedford, Not Recorded.
    Cap: 01 Aug 1812 Not Recorded by Not Recorded Int: 01 Aug 1812 Dis: 31 Aug 1812.
    Ship. Received from HMS Avenger. To the Alert for a passage to the United States per order Sir Thomas Duckworth.

Turel, James   Prisoner 299. Rank: Seaman, from: William Davis, Not Recorded.
    Cap: 04 Sep 1812 Not Recorded by HMS Electra Int: 04 Sep 1812 Dis: 03 Nov 1812.
    Schooner. Received from HMS Electra. To the United States of America.

Turk, Samuel   Prisoner 124. Rank: Seaman, from: Polafox of Boston, Not Recorded.
    Cap: 06 Aug 1812 Not Recorded by Not Recorded Int: 06 Aug 1812 Dis: 31 Aug 1812.
    Brig. Received from HMS Jason. To the Alert for a passage to the United States.

Turner, James   Prisoner 70. Rank: Seaman, from: Arab of Marblehead, Not Recorded.
    Cap: 01 Aug 1812 Not Recorded by Not Recorded Int: 01 Aug 1812 Dis: 31 Aug 1812.
    Ship. Received from HMS Hazard. To the Alert for a passage to the United States per order Sir Thomas Duckworth.

Turner, Stephen   Prisoner 296. Rank: Seaman, from: William Davis, Not Recorded.
    Cap: 04 Sep 1812 Not Recorded by HMS Electra Int: 04 Sep 1812 Dis: 03 Nov 1812.
    Schooner. Received from HMS Electra. To the United States of America. Stephen Turner (1).

American Prisoners of War Held at Newfoundland During the War of 1812

Turner, Stephen   Prisoner 300. Rank: Seaman, from: William Davis, Not Recorded.
    Cap: 04 Sep 1812 Not Recorded by HMS Electra Int: 04 Sep 1812 Dis: 03 Nov 1812.
    Schooner. Received from HMS Electra. To the United States of America. Stephen Turner (2).

Twipen, Peter   Prisoner 97. Rank: Seaman, from: Gleaner, Not Recorded.
    Cap: 01 Aug 1812 Not Recorded by Not Recorded Int: 01 Aug 1812 Dis: 31 Aug 1812.
    Brig. Received from HMS Avenger. To the Alert for a passage to the United States per order Sir Thomas Duckworth.

Vaissiaire, Jean Victor   Prisoner 148. Rank: Passenger, from: Castor, Not Recorded.
    Cap: 19 Aug 1812 Not Recorded by HMS Antelope Int: 19 Aug 1812 Dis:
    Ship. Received from HMS Antelope. (Date of discharge not on roster.)

Valley, James   Prisoner 242. Rank: Seaman, from: William Tell, Not Recorded.
    Cap: 31 Aug 1812 Not Recorded by Not Recorded Int: 31 Aug 1812 Dis: 31 Aug 1812.
    Ship. Received from HMS Jason. To the Alert for a passage to the United States per order Sir Thomas Duckworth.

Veadier, John   Prisoner 7. Rank: Seaman, from: Lydia of New York, Merchant Vessel.
    Cap: 08 Jul 1812 New York by HMS Jason Int: 08 Jul 1812 Dis: 31 Aug 1812.
    Ship. Received from HMS Jason. To the Alert for a passage to the United States per order Sir Thomas Duckworth.

Vendrick, Solomon   Prisoner 298. Rank: Seaman, from: William Davis, Not Recorded.
    Cap: 04 Sep 1812 Not Recorded by HMS Electra Int: 04 Sep 1812 Dis: 03 Nov 1812.
    Schooner. Received from HMS Electra. To the United States of America.

Waine, Benjamin   Prisoner 134. Rank: Master, from: Eliza, Not Recorded.
    Cap: 18 Aug 1812 Not Recorded by Not Recorded Int: 18 Aug 1812 Dis: 31 Aug 1812.
    Brig. Received from HMS Antelope. To the Alert for a passage to the United States per order Sir Thomas Duckworth.

Waine, George   Prisoner 320. Rank: Seaman, from: Enterprise of New York, Not Recorded.
    Cap: 24 Sep 1812 Not Recorded by Not Recorded Int: 24 Sep 1812 Dis: 03 Nov 1812.
    Ship. Received from HMS Hazard. To the United States of America.

Wallis, John   Prisoner 183. Rank: Passenger, from: Castor, Not Recorded.
    Cap: 28 Aug 1812 Not Recorded by HMS Antelope Int: 28 Aug 1812 Dis: 31 Aug 1812.
    Ship. Received from HMS Antelope. To the Alert for a passage to the United States per order Sir Thomas Duckworth.

Walton, Daniel   Prisoner 276. Rank: Seaman, from: Fame, Not Recorded.
    Cap: 04 Sep 1812 Not Recorded by HMS Electra Int: 04 Sep 1812 Dis: 03 Nov 1812.
    Sloop. Received from HMS Electra. To the United States of America.

Whales, John   Prisoner 259. Rank: Mate, from: Rockland of New York, Not Recorded.
    Cap: 31 Aug 1812 Not Recorded by Henry Privateer Int: 31 Aug 1812 Dis: 31 Aug 1812.
    Brig. Received from Henry Privateer. To the Alert for a passage to the United States per order Sir Thomas Duckworth.

Whales, Luke   Prisoner 217. Rank: Seaman, from: Dolphin, Not Recorded.
    Cap: 28 Aug 1812 Not Recorded by HMS Antelope Int: 28 Aug 1812 Dis: 31 Aug 1812.
    Brig. Received from HMS Antelope. To the Alert for a passage to the United States per order Sir Thomas Duckworth.

Wheeler, James   Prisoner 175. Rank: Passenger, from: Castor, Not Recorded.
    Cap: 28 Aug 1812 Not Recorded by HMS Antelope Int: 28 Aug 1812 Dis: 31 Aug 1812.
    Ship. Received from HMS Antelope. To the Alert for a passage to the United States per order Sir Thomas Duckworth.

Wheet, John   Prisoner 80. Rank: Seaman, from: Adriatic, Not Recorded.
    Cap: 01 Aug 1812 Not Recorded by Not Recorded Int: 01 Aug 1812 Dis: 31 Aug 1812.
    Ship. Received from HMS Avenger. To the Alert for a passage to the United States per order Sir Thomas Duckworth.

White, Henry   Prisoner 186. Rank: Passenger, from: Castor, Not Recorded.
    Cap: 28 Aug 1812 Not Recorded by HMS Antelope Int: 28 Aug 1812 Dis: 31 Aug 1812.
    Ship. Received from HMS Antelope. To the Alert for a passage to the United States per order Sir Thomas Duckworth.

White, Joseph   Prisoner 196. Rank: Passenger, from: Castor, Not Recorded.
    Cap: 28 Aug 1812 Not Recorded by HMS Antelope Int: 28 Aug 1812 Dis: 31 Aug 1812.
    Ship. Received from HMS Antelope. To the Alert for a passage to the United States per order Sir Thomas Duckworth.

White, Joseph   Prisoner 348. Rank: Seaman, from: Adaline, Not Recorded.
    Cap: 14 Oct 1812 Not Recorded by HMS Avenger Int: 14 Oct 1812 Dis:
    Brig. Received from HMS Avenger. (Date of discharge not on roster.)

American Prisoners of War Held at Newfoundland During the War of 1812

Whitty, John   Prisoner 337. Rank: Seaman, from: Sprightly, Not Recorded.
  Cap: 29 Sep 1812 Not Recorded by Not Recorded Int: 24 Sep 1812 Dis: 03 Nov 1812.
  Brig. Recaptured by Hazard. Received from HMS Hazard. To the United States of America. (Date of interment before date of capture.)

Wight, Samuel   Prisoner 364. Rank: Seaman, from: HMS Hazard, Not Recorded.
  Cap: 26 Nov 1812 Not Recorded by Comet Int: 26 Nov 1812 Dis:
  Citizen of America. Received from HMS Avenger. (Date of discharge not on roster.)

William, Charles   Prisoner 104. Rank: Seaman, from: Triton of New Bedford, Not Recorded.
  Cap: 02 Aug 1812 Not Recorded by Not Recorded Int: 02 Aug 1812 Dis: 31 Aug 1812.
  Ship. Received from HMS Avenger. To the Alert for a passage to the United States per order Sir Thomas Duckworth.

William, David   Prisoner 170. Rank: Passenger, from: Castor, Not Recorded.
  Cap: 28 Aug 1812 Not Recorded by HMS Antelope Int: 28 Aug 1812 Escaped: 30 Aug 1812.
  Ship. Received from HMS Antelope. Escaped.

Williams, David   Prisoner 268. Rank: Seaman, from: Castor, Not Recorded.
  Cap: 01 Sep 1812 Not Recorded by St. Johns Int: 01 Sep 1812 Dis:
  Ship. Received from Antelope. Received from prison ship. 170 (Old prisoner number, recaptured. Date of discharge not on roster.)

Williams, John   Prisoner 110. Rank: Seaman, from: Adriatic of New York, Not Recorded.
  Cap: 02 Aug 1812 Not Recorded by Not Recorded Int: 02 Aug 1812 Dis: 31 Aug 1812.
  Ship. Received from HMS Avenger. To the Alert for a passage to the United States per order Sir Thomas Duckworth.

Williams, John   Prisoner 233. Rank: Seaman, from: W. P. Johnston, Not Recorded.
  Cap: 31 Aug 1812 Not Recorded by Not Recorded Int: 31 Aug 1812 Dis: 31 Aug 1812.
  Ship. Received from HMS Jason. To the Alert for a passage to the United States per order Sir Thomas Duckworth. John Williams (1).

Williams, John   Prisoner 237. Rank: Seaman, from: William Tell, Not Recorded.
  Cap: 31 Aug 1812 Not Recorded by Not Recorded Int: 31 Aug 1812 Dis: 31 Aug 1812.
  Ship. Received from HMS Jason. To the Alert for a passage to the United States per order Sir Thomas Duckworth. John Williams (2).

Williams, Joseph   Prisoner 194. Rank: Passenger, from: Castor, Not Recorded.
  Cap: 28 Aug 1812 Not Recorded by HMS Antelope Int: 28 Aug 1812 Dis: 31 Aug 1812.
  Ship. Received from HMS Antelope. To the Alert for a passage to the United States per order Sir Thomas Duckworth.

Williams, Joseph   Prisoner 362. Rank: Seaman, from: HMS Hazard, Not Recorded.
  Cap: 26 Nov 1812 Not Recorded by Comet Int: 26 Nov 1812 Dis:
  Citizen of America. Received from HMS Avenger. (Date of discharge not on roster.)

Williams, Rock   Prisoner 225. Rank: Mate, from: W. P. Johnston, Not Recorded.
  Cap: 31 Aug 1812 Not Recorded by Not Recorded Int: 31 Aug 1812 Dis: 31 Aug 1812.
  Ship. Received from HMS Jason. To the Alert for a passage to the United States per order Sir Thomas Duckworth.

Willson, David   Prisoner 227. Rank: Seaman, from: W. P. Johnston, Not Recorded.
  Cap: 31 Aug 1812 Not Recorded by Not Recorded Int: 31 Aug 1812 Dis: 31 Aug 1812.
  Ship. Received from HMS Jason. To the Alert for a passage to the United States per order Sir Thomas Duckworth.

Willyard, William   Prisoner 234. Rank: Seaman, from: W. P. Johnston, Not Recorded.
  Cap: 31 Aug 1812 Not Recorded by Not Recorded Int: 31 Aug 1812 Dis: 31 Aug 1812.
  Ship. Received from HMS Jason. To the Alert for a passage to the United States per order Sir Thomas Duckworth.

Wing, Nathaniel   Prisoner 167. Rank: Seaman, from: Castor, Not Recorded.
  Cap: 28 Aug 1812 Not Recorded by HMS Antelope Int: 28 Aug 1812 Dis: 31 Aug 1812.
  Ship. Received from HMS Antelope. To the Alert for a passage to the United States per order Sir Thomas Duckworth.

Woodward, John   Prisoner 132. Rank: Seaman, from: Perseverance, Not Recorded.
  Cap: 10 Aug 1812 Not Recorded by Not Recorded Int: 10 Aug 1812 Dis: 31 Aug 1812.
  Brig. Received from HMS Atalante. To the Alert for a passage to the United States per order Sir Thomas Duckworth.

Yates, George   Prisoner 162. Rank: Seaman, from: Castor, Not Recorded.
  Cap: 28 Aug 1812 Not Recorded by HMS Antelope Int: 28 Aug 1812 Dis: 31 Aug 1812.
  Ship. Received from HMS Antelope. To the Alert for a passage to the United States per order Sir Thomas Duckworth.

American Prisoners of War Held at Newfoundland During the War of 1812

Young, Oliver   Prisoner 166. Rank: Seaman, from: Castor, Not Recorded.
    Cap: 28 Aug 1812 Not Recorded by HMS Antelope Int: 28 Aug 1812 Dis: 31 Aug 1812.
    Ship. Received from HMS Antelope. To the Alert for a passage to the United States per order Sir Thomas Duckworth.

American Prisoners of War Held at Newfoundland During the War of 1812

Numeric listing by prison number

1	Morgan, Alexander	68	Gall, John
2	Chapman, Israel	69	Harmerchant, Peter
3	James, William	70	Turner, James
4	Sweitman, Samuel	71	Chase, Franklin
5	Allen, John	72	Johnston, James
6	Hamilton, George W	73	Sparks, Robert
7	Veadier, John	74	Trip, Odis
8	Carlow, James	75	Pullen, William F
9	Bound, Isaac	76	Goodbartlett, William
10	Farmer, Prince	77	Benson, Benjamin
11	Howard, Thomas	78	Bennett, John
12	Dow, John	79	Jacobs, John Christopher
13	Hale, James	80	Wheet, John
14	Coleman, William	81	Johnston, Ebar
15	Malson, Thomas	82	Andrews, John
16	Aikien, Job	83	Las, Charles
17	Row, Abraham	84	Moore, John
18	Houghton, Timothy	85	Bellan, John
19	Huntly, Augustus	86	Roberts, Joseph
20	Hyde, Richard	87	Johnson, John
21	Mathews, George	88	Bush, George
22	Gardener, James	89	Dent, William
23	Peckham, William	90	Marshall, James
24	Benthall, William	91	Thacter, Loavette
25	Hitchings, Benjamin	92	Lewis, William
26	Smith, Junior, Daniel	93	Rando, Francis
27	Andrews, Benjamin	94	Gardener, Josiah
28	Crowell, Isaiah	95	Robinson, Ecy
29	Briggs, Nathan	96	Barto, Daniel
30	Ring, Bartholomew	97	Twipen, Peter
31	Hammond, Samuel	98	Sullevan, Josia
32	Hodman, John	99	Gilpen, George
33	Howes, Isaac	100	Holden, Henry
34	Kelly, Acy	101	McColl, Charles
35	Newcomb, John	102	Deval, William
36	Crowell, Anthony	103	Shepard, James
37	Crowell, Isaac	104	William, Charles
38	Homer, John	105	Low, Frederick
39	Folger, Robert	106	Peters, John
40	Oxley, John	107	Smith, William
41	Edwards, William	108	Roper, William
42	Massey, William	109	Dublin, Thomas
43	Corbett, Samuel	110	Williams, John
44	Higgins, John	111	Conner, David
45	Johnston, James	112	Banners, George
46	Amey, Prince	113	Garriques, Elmslie
47	Broughton, Nicholas	114	Dunn, James
48	Gridler, John	115	Rogers, Moores
49	Chambers, William	116	Atwell, Zacharius
50	Smith, John	117	Lovett, Pyam
51	Forrester, Peter	118	Dilno, Warren
52	Rogers, Nathaniel	119	Tredwell, Benjamin
53	Broughton, Glover	120	Dilno, Joseph
54	Chairman, Elezis	121	Pearce, George
55	Richardson, William	122	Higgins, Jesse
56	Phillips, William	123	Barrows, Thomas
57	Swan, Richard	124	Turk, Samuel
58	Cantfield, John	125	Purse, John
59	Hoffman, John	126	Fowler, Ceasar
60	Jones, William	127	Gardener, Thomas H
61	Pass, Thomas	128	Frederick, John
62	Brown, John	129	Lewis, Robenson
63	Potenger, Richard	130	Parnell, Benjamin
64	Hastings, Rufus	131	Fearson, Benjamin
65	Titus, Henry	132	Woodward, John
66	Gonnes, Morser	133	Nicholson, Julby
67	Bolden, Edward	134	Waine, Benjamin

American Prisoners of War Held at Newfoundland During the War of 1812

135	Rogers, Asa	205	Dornbar, James
136	Nicholson, Silas	206	Jones, John
137	Atkins, Joseph	207	Addeson, Littleton
138	Higgins, Moses	208	Everleigh, William
139	Lamson, Joshua G	209	Herman, John
140	Pray, Joshua N	210	McConnel, Joseph
141	Pritchard, Paul	211	Jackson, Daniel
142	Higgins, Moses	212	Baptiste, ---
143	Heason, James	213	McLennan, John
144	Sparrow, Jesse	214	Lewis, John
145	Treacy, James	215	Harris, David
146	Carpenter, James	216	Spraggs, Samuel S
147	Rosseau, Pievie	217	Whales, Luke
148	Vaissiaire, Jean Victor	218	Myers, David
149	Mawrey, Lewis Alexis	219	Greelief, Matthews
150	Barbarow, Joseph	220	Fisher, Henry
151	Baylard, Jean	221	Peerce, John
152	Dufour, Aime	222	Broomley, Philip
153	Letham, Henry	223	Lathey, John
154	Cobb, Elijah	224	Matthews, Daniel
155	Brown, Ambrose James	225	Williams, Rock
156	Gillies, John	226	Richardson, John
157	Crosby, Elijah Cobb	227	Willson, David
158	Hillman, Benjamin	228	Jenkins, John
159	Jenny, Joseph L	229	Brown, Peter
160	Robinson, Antonia	230	Davis, Moses
161	Boyd, James	231	Burke, Richard
162	Yates, George	232	Lawson, Henry
163	Lewis, Thomas	233	Williams, John
164	Hewland, Rous	234	Willyard, William
165	Card, Henry	235	Berry, Isaac
166	Young, OLiver	236	Gray, John
167	Wing, Nathaniel	237	Williams, John
168	Robertson, John	238	Drew, James
169	Colee, Jacob	239	Crosby, Josiah
170	William, David	240	Brooks, Thomas
171	Russel, William	241	Mitchell, James
172	Myder, Thomas	242	Valley, James
173	Graves, Alexander	243	Gomlay, James
174	Mason, George	244	Middleton, Charles
175	Wheeler, James	245	Claw, Jacob
176	Hardy, Risdam	246	Brown, John
177	Jackson, Elisha	247	Reder, Arnold
178	Baptiste, John	248	Douglass, Hatley
179	Clerk, Samuel	249	Smith, John
180	Davis, Peter	250	Dibladen, John
181	Lowe, James	251	McKie, Richard
182	Bampton, William	252	Slakenn, William
183	Wallis, John	253	Swinton, Thomas
184	Crandall, Amos	254	Finch, Stephen
185	Cooke, Earl	255	Afhont, Benjamin
186	White, Henry	256	Lee, William
187	Bailey, Robert	257	Boldoon, Garrett
188	Matthews, Henry	258	Batcheldor, Cotton
189	Damoor, Thomas	259	Whales, John
190	Brady, Jesson	260	Ingles, John
191	Martin, Alexander	261	Florance, Charles
192	Johnston, Charles	262	Millet, John
193	Clewley, William	263	Stephens, John
194	Williams, Joseph	264	Florance, David
195	Refiner, Henry	265	Taylor, John
196	White, Joseph	266	Tollinsby, William
197	Norton, James	267	Colee, Jacob
198	Parks, Guy	268	Williams, David
199	Banter, James	269	Russell, William
200	Jones, James	270	Mason, George
201	Larraley, William	271	Jackson, Elisha
202	Lambert, William	272	Brady, Jesson
203	Edmonston, Elisha	273	Everleigh, William
204	Kelly, Isaac	274	Ennick, William

American Prisoners of War Held at Newfoundland During the War of 1812

275	Brown, John		321	Thompson, John
276	Walton, Daniel		322	Murrel, Benjamin
277	Foster, Esaw		323	Hurl, Joseph
278	Eaton, Henry		324	Palyery, John
279	Pattengale, Daniel		325	Bunker, Daniel
280	Goldbrite, Jonathan		326	Lahy, Peter
281	Higgins, Aquilla		327	Conner, Samiel
282	Sparrow, John		328	Nail, Robert
283	Sparrow, Samuel		329	Pinder, William
284	Mayo, Theodore		330	Powell, Thomas
285	Taylor, John		331	Jones, Benjamin
286	Sparrow, Thomas		332	Smith, Jacob
287	Sparrow, Abner H		333	Moore, Thomas
288	Jarvis, John		334	Cleveland, Ezekiel
289	Cole, Elisha		335	Ashbridge, Joseph H
290	Higgins, Hutcel		336	Perry, Joseph
291	Hopkins, Elkenah		337	Whitty, John
292	Snow, Josiah H		338	Little, John
293	Snow, Herman		339	Fenton, Charles
294	Pepper, Daniel		340	Jenkins, Thomas
295	Higgins, Joshua		341	Henderson, Israel
296	Turner, Stephen		342	Harding, Nehemiah
297	Linnel, Uriah		343	Heath, James
298	Vendrick, Solomon		344	Hemby, Leith
299	Turel, James		345	Lawly, James
300	Turner, Stephen		346	Clarke, Hubert
301	Mayo, Samuel		347	Blake, Robert
302	Mayo, Henan		348	White, Joseph
303	Gould, Nathaniel		349	Baker, James
304	Rogers, Richard		350	Day, William
305	Hurd, Seth		351	Allden, Benjamin
306	Smith, Reuben		352	Blake, William
307	Smith, John		353	Keys, Benjamin
308	Rogers, Uriah		354	Murry, George
309	Rogers, Elesa		355	Allen, George
310	Rogers, Ezekiel		356	Briggs, Shaddok
311	Morse, Abraham		357	Davis, John
312	Morse, George C		358	Brady, Jesson
313	Homan, James		359	Russel, William
314	Cartwright, Alexander		360	Donogh, Joseph W
315	Burnham, Richard S		361	Thompson, John
316	Cobby, Joseph		362	Williams, Joseph
317	Burch, Thomas		363	Haldon, Lewis
318	Palmer, Robert		364	Wight, Samuel
319	Palmer, Frances			
320	Waine, George			

American Prisoners of War Held at Newfoundland During the War of 1812

Crew Listing by Ship

<u>3 Friends New Bedford</u>
    Peckham, William
<u>Adaline</u>
    Baker, James
    Blake, Robert
    Clarke, Hubert
    Day, William
    Harding, Nehemiah
    Heath, James
    Hemby, Leith
    Lawly, James
    White, Joseph
<u>Adriatic</u>
    Andrews, John
    Bellan, John
    Bennett, John
    Benson, Benjamin
    Goodbartlett, William
    Jacobs, John Christopher
    Johnston, Ebar
    Las, Charles
    Moore, John
    Wheet, John
<u>Adriatic of New York</u>
    Banners, George
    Dublin, Thomas
    Garriques, Elmslie
    Roper, William
    Tredwell, Benjamin
    Williams, John
<u>Arab of Marblehead</u>
    Aikien, Job
    Bolden, Edward
    Chase, Franklin
    Dilno, Joseph
    Dilno, Warren
    Gall, John
    Gonnes, Morser
    Harmerchant, Peter
    Houghton, Timothy
    Huntly, Augustus
    Hyde, Richard
    McColl, Charles
    Row, Abraham
    Turner, James
<u>Aracreon of Newburry Port</u>
    Benthall, William
<u>Caroline New Bedford</u>
    Hammond, Samuel
<u>Castor</u>
    Addeson, Littleton
    Bailey, Robert
    Bampton, William
    Banter, James
    Baptiste, ---
    Baptiste, John
    Barbarow, Joseph
    Baylard, Jean
    Boyd, James
    Brady, Jesson
    Brady, Jesson
    Brown, Ambrose James
    Card, Henry
    Clerk, Samuel
    Clewley, William
    Cobb, Elijah
    Colee, Jacob
    Colee, Jacob
    Cooke, Earl
    Crandall, Amos
    Damoor, Thomas
    Davis, Peter
    Dornbar, James
    Dufour, Aime
    Edmonston, Elisha
    Everleigh, William
    Everleigh, William
    Gillies, John
    Graves, Alexander
    Hardy, Risdam
    Herman, John
    Hewland, Rous
    Hillman, Benjamin
    Jackson, Daniel
    Jackson, Elisha
    Jackson, Elisha
    Jenny, Joseph L
    Johnston, Charles
    Jones, James
    Jones, John
    Kelly, Isaac
    Lambert, William
    Lamson, Joshua G
    Larraley, William
    Letham, Henry
    Lewis, Thomas
    Lowe, James
    Martin, Alexander
    Mason, George
    Mason, George
    Matthews, Henry
    Mawrey, Lewis Alexis
    McConnel, Joseph
    Myder, Thomas
    Norton, James
    Parks, Guy
    Pritchard, Paul
    Refiner, Henry
    Robertson, John
    Robinson, Antonia
    Rosseau, Pievie
    Russel, William
    Russell, William
    Vaissiaire, Jean Victor
    Wallis, John
    Wheeler, James
    White, Henry
    White, Joseph
    William, David
    Williams, David
    Williams, Joseph
    Wing, Nathaniel
    Yates, George
    Young, OLiver
<u>Castor of New Bedford</u>
    Fowler, Ceasar
    Frederick, John
    Gardener, Thomas H
    Lewis, Robenson
<u>Cyrus</u>
    Purse, John
<u>Cyrus of Gloucester</u>
    Ring, Bartholomew

American Prisoners of War Held at Newfoundland During the War of 1812

Dolphin
- Broomley, Philip
- Brown, John
- Cantfield, John
- Conner, David
- Fisher, Henry
- Greelief, Matthews
- Hastings, Rufus
- Hoffman, John
- Jones, William
- Lathey, John
- Matthews, Daniel
- Myers, David
- Pass, Thomas
- Peerce, John
- Potenger, Richard
- Swan, Richard
- Titus, Henry
- Whales, Luke

Eagle
- Ennick, William

Eliza
- Harris, David
- Lewis, John
- McLennan, John
- Spraggs, Samuel S
- Waine, Benjamin

Elizabeth of Yarmouth
- Crowell, Anthony
- Crowell, Isaac
- Crowell, Isaiah
- Homer, John
- Howes, Isaac
- Kelly, Acy
- Newcomb, John

Enterprise of New York
- Bunker, Daniel
- Burch, Thomas
- Burnham, Richard S
- Cartwright, Alexander
- Cobby, Joseph
- Hurl, Joseph
- Lahy, Peter
- Murrel, Benjamin
- Palmer, Frances
- Palmer, Robert
- Palyery, John
- Thompson, John
- Waine, George

Essex
- Higgins, Jesse
- Homan, James
- Morse, George C
- Pearce, George

Fairplay of Alexandia
- Brown, John
- Dibladen, John
- Douglass, Hatley
- McKie, Richard
- Reder, Arnold
- Smith, John

Fame
- Brown, John
- Eaton, Henry
- Foster, Esaw
- Goldbrite, Jonathan
- Pattengale, Daniel
- Walton, Daniel

Gleaner
- Barto, Daniel
- Gardener, Josiah
- Gilpen, George
- Lewis, William
- Rando, Francis
- Robinson, Ecy
- Sullevan, Josia
- Twipen, Peter

Gleaner of Boston
- Dunn, James

Lydia of New York
- Allen, John
- Bound, Isaac
- Carlow, James
- Chapman, Israel
- Coleman, William
- Dow, John
- Farmer, Prince
- Hale, James
- Hamilton, George W
- Howard, Thomas
- James, William
- Morgan, Alexander
- Sweitman, Samuel
- Veadier, John

Nancy of New York
- Amey, Prince
- Briggs, Nathan
- Corbett, Samuel
- Edwards, William
- Folger, Robert
- Higgins, John
- Johnston, James
- Massey, William
- Oxley, John

Orient
- Broughton, Glover
- Broughton, Nicholas
- Chairman, Elezis
- Chambers, William
- Forrester, Peter
- Gridler, John
- Phillips, William
- Richardson, William
- Rogers, Nathaniel
- Smith, John

Orient of Marblehead
- Andrews, Benjamin
- Hodman, John

Perseverance
- Fearson, Benjamin
- Parnell, Benjamin
- Woodward, John

Pilgrim
- Cole, Elisha
- Higgins, Aquilla
- Higgins, Moses
- Higgins, Moses
- Jarvis, John
- Mayo, Theodore
- Sparrow, Abner H
- Sparrow, John
- Sparrow, Samuel
- Sparrow, Thomas
- Taylor, John

Pocahunter of Boston
- Atwell, Zacharius
- Bush, George
- Dent, William
- Johnson, John
- Lovett, Pyam

American Prisoners of War Held at Newfoundland During the War of 1812

Low, Frederick
Marshall, James
Peters, John
Roberts, Joseph
Smith, William
Thacter, Loavette

Polafox of Boston
   Hitchings, Benjamin
   Malson, Thomas
   Turk, Samuel

Polafox of Philadelphia
   Mathews, George

Polly
   Nicholson, Silas

Polly of Chatham
   Nicholson, Julby

Rockland
   Carpenter, James
   Pray, Joshua N
   Treacy, James

Rockland of New York
   Afhont, Benjamin
   Batcheldor, Cotton
   Boldoon, Garrett
   Finch, Stephen
   Florance, Charles
   Florance, David
   Ingles, John
   Lee, William
   Millet, John
   Slakenn, William
   Stephens, John
   Swinton, Thomas
   Taylor, John
   Whales, John

Sprightly
   Fenton, Charles
   Henderson, Israel
   Jenkins, Thomas
   Little, John
   Whitty, John

Susannah
   Ashbridge, Joseph H
   Cleveland, Ezekiel
   Conner, Samiel
   Jones, Benjamin
   Moore, Thomas
   Nail, Robert
   Pinder, William
   Powell, Thomas
   Smith, Jacob

Swallow
   Atkins, Joseph
   Higgins, Hutcel
   Higgins, Joshua
   Hopkins, Elkenah
   Pepper, Daniel
   Snow, Herman
   Snow, Josiah H
   Sparrow, Jesse

Teasor
   Allden, Benjamin

Triton of New Bedford
   Deval, William
   Holden, Henry
   Johnston, James
   Pullen, William F
   Rogers, Moores
   Shepard, James
   Sparks, Robert
   Trip, Odis
   William, Charles

Union of Philadelphia
   Barrows, Thomas
   Gardener, James
   Smith, Junior, Daniel

W. P. Johnston
   Brown, Peter
   Burke, Richard
   Davis, Moses
   Jenkins, John
   Lawson, Henry
   Richardson, John
   Tollinsby, William
   Williams, John
   Williams, Rock
   Willson, David
   Willyard, William

William Davis
   Gould, Nathaniel
   Heason, James
   Hurd, Seth
   Linnel, Uriah
   Mayo, Henan
   Mayo, Samuel
   Morse, Abraham
   Rogers, Asa
   Rogers, Elesa
   Rogers, Ezekiel
   Rogers, Richard
   Rogers, Uriah
   Smith, John
   Smith, Reuben
   Turel, James
   Turner, Stephen
   Turner, Stephen
   Vendrick, Solomon

William Tell
   Berry, Isaac
   Brooks, Thomas
   Claw, Jacob
   Crosby, Elijah Cobb
   Crosby, Josiah
   Drew, James
   Gomlay, James
   Gray, John
   Middleton, Charles
   Mitchell, James
   Valley, James
   Williams, John

Service affiliation not known

Perry, Joseph

American Prisoners of War Held at Newfoundland During the War of 1812

Americans on British Ships

Allen, George
Blake, William
Brady, Jesson
Briggs, Shaddok
Davis, John
Donogh, Joseph
Haldon, Lewis
Keys, Benjamin
Murry, George
Russel, William
Thompson, John
Wight, Samuel
Williams, Joseph